▶ Software Engineering

Methods and Management

Software Engineering

Methods and Management

Anneliese von Mayrhauser

Department of Computer Science
Illinois Institute of Technology
Chicago, Illinois

ACADEMIC PRESS, INC.

Harcourt Brace Jovanovich, Publishers

Boston   San Diego   New York
London   Sydney   Tokyo   Toronto

ACADEMIC PRESS, INC.
1250 Sixth Avenue, San Diego, CA 92101

United Kingdom Edition published by
ACADEMIC PRESS LIMITED
24-28 Oval Road, London NW1 7DX

"DBASE" is a trademark owned by Ashton-Tate Corporation.
"Lotus 1-2-3" is a trademark owned by Lotus Corporation.
"MSDOS" is a trademark owned by Microsoft Corporation.
"SUPERCALC" is a trademark owned by Computer Associates International, Inc.
"UNIX" is a trademark owned by American Telephone and Telegraph Company.
"VM operating system" and "OS360" are trademarks owned by IBM Corporation.

Library of Congress Cataloging-in-Publication Data

Von Mayrhauser, Anneliese.
    Software engineering : methods and management / Anneliese von
Mayrhauser.
        p.   cm.
    Bibliography: p.
    Includes index.
    ISBN 0-12-727320-4 (alk. paper)
    1. Software engineering.   I.   Title.
QA76.758.V66   1990   89-15162
005.1--dc20   CIP

Printed in the United States of America
90 91 92 93   9 8 7 6 5 4 3 2 1

To my mother, Notburga Amschler, who taught me the love of learning and the stamina to keep learning.

To my brother, Dr. Hubert Leonhard Amschler, the best brother anyone could ask for.

To my husband, Richard Strafford Andrews, and to my son, Thomas Hubert Llewellyn Andrews, who provided the loving and nurturing environment I needed to write this book.

◢ Contents

vii

► Acknowledgement

Many people helped me in various stages of writing this book: colleagues, students, and friends. Their names are too numerous to list. Prominent among them are Dr. Victor Basili and Dr. Ted Lewis, both of whom provided important guidance and encouragement in organizing the material, Karna Thulin, Amy Kasmar, Patrick Schroeder, and three student editors in IIT's technical writing program: Judith Carr, Don Dressel, and Deborah Walsh, as well as their instructor John Cleland. I am also grateful to Lucy Shyu and David Han who helped with the editorial changes, and to Compositors Corporation, the typesetter. Joni Hopkins McDonald from Academic Press has been a wonderful production editor. My thanks to all.

► Foreword

It has been my belief that people often take too narrow a view of software engineering. I believe a software methodology to be a set of techniques organized into methods that can be managed and integrated into a process model. The implication is that there are many process models, methods, and techniques. Engineering refers to the selection, refinement, and integration of these techniques and methods into a process model that is appropriate for the problem, application, and environment to which the methodology is applied. That is, project characteristics help us decide how to engineer the process to achieve the appropriate product characteristics.

Most text books offer either a canned software methodology in the form of a process model or a set of non-integrated methods. This book takes a major step forward in capturing the above definition of software engineering.

Software Engineering: Methods and Management is a full-year text on software engineering that has many strengths. It provides a very broad, and yet thorough, treatment of all phases of the software life cycle, from planning through maintenance and operation. It treats areas such as management and measurement within the life cycle organization.

This text recognizes that there are multiple software life cycle models and provides justification and guidelines for where each is appropriate. It offers many techniques and methods within each phase, allowing the user to choose the appropriate one for the given environment. It covers design techniques ranging from functional decomposition to object-oriented design, and notations from a Process Design Language to dataflow diagrams. It offers a mix of formal and pragmatic approaches, recognizing the importance of formalism but also the necessity of pragmatism.

A consistent set of examples is carried throughout the text. When covering a set of methods, the text illustrates them by using these examples, allowing the reader to understand the applications of the methods and to compare them. Thus, the reader does not see a method only applied to the "perfect" example for that method. This approach provides the reader with more insight into the method.

This book was intended primarily as a classroom textbook but it also makes an excellent reference guide for practitioners.

—Victor R. Basili

▶ Preface

Intended Audience

This book is intended as a primary textbook for a two-semester course sequence on software engineering in a computer science curriculum. The first part (course) teaches methods and techniques for developing software, and the second part (course) builds on the knowledge of the first and introduces the student to the management of software engineering projects.

This book is not intended for the beginner in the field of computer science or programming. Such a reader may miss or fail to understand some examples and concepts. For example, the section on monitors requires knowledge about parallel processes and interprocess communication and can only be fully appreciated with knowledge of parallel processing. As a result, this book is intended for courses at the mezzanine/first year graduate level. This is not unusual for a software engineering course, and the university where I teach is no exception, where the software engineering course is commonly taken by seniors and graduate students. At this point, they have been exposed to data structures and algorithms, systems programming and assemblers, a first course in operating systems, computer architecture, and some theory. Common mathematics background includes calculus and some statistics (e.g., covariance, statistical significance, normal density function, means, and variances).

Part I assumes some undergraduate education in computer science. Students who lack this preparation need to do some background reading, or the material may be somewhat difficult to comprehend. An effort was made, however, to provide the graduate student who has little previous computer science background with references to material that might be helpful in closing the gap. Many institutions have nontraditional graduate students, such as career changers, and professionals from other fields, who will need this. When the material in this book was taught in software engineering courses at Illinois Institute of Technology, we sometimes had class participants from other departments and with varying backgrounds. While they did some extra work to make up for deficiencies, none of them had problems understanding the material.

Beyond a Textbook

This book is intended to serve not only as a textbook but also as a reliable source for software engineering. While an instructor may only cover a subset of the techniques described in this book, he or she has choices and can select from the techniques that are the most appropriate for the class project and the audience. It is possible to select a series of topics that are mostly applied and practical in nature, but it is also possible to present some more research-oriented, experimental, or theoretical material. The choice depends on the objectives of the particular course and the interests of the students. This book tries to present a balanced mix of both. Thus, it is neither fully theoretical nor entirely applied.

The book has easy and hard parts, and the instructor may select those that fit the background of the students. For example, one may skip formal methods and algorithms for formal methods for an undergraduate class, yet still get the students interested in pursuing this area in the future. This book facilitates this through inclusion of more advanced material and references for further study. Another course may want to emphasize formal or more advanced material and thus spend more time on those. The point is that material is included that can fit a variety of backgrounds and course emphases as well as provide information that is useful for reference after a software engineering course is over. Even when only some sections in a chapter are selected for teaching, the chapter as a whole provides a context that will help the students extend their knowledge easily in any given area.

Balance Formalism and Pragmatism

The book aims for a good mix of formalism and pragmatism without overburdening the reader. Mathematical notation is introduced where appropriate. When an axiomatic (mathematical) approach is taken, the examples are either simple, short, or relate to knowledge the reader is likely to have (e.g., first order logic in formal descriptions of specifications instead of other techniques that require more groundwork). The reader is directed to pertinent literature for more in–depth coverage of other techniques. A similar approach was taken for formal verification methods. Hoare's Axioms could have been presented, but instead a simple, straightforward technique that had two other advantages was presented:

▶ it is related to another notation that had been explained before (pseudocode, a less formal design language) and

▶ it provided a basis for discussing parallel programs and synchronization problems for software.

The choice does not mean that the other methods are inferior, only that, for teaching purposes, the one chosen gives the best "return," since it serves more than one purpose.

To bring these "two worlds" together is indeed a challenge. One danger is to emphasize one area too much. The other is to fail to do justice to either area. It is hoped that this text will interest the applied student or professional to look into more theoretical or experimental aspects of software engineering and that the research-minded individual will find a sound grounding in practical application.

Two Example Projects Throughout

In order to avoid too many examples, it was decided to illustrate the use of all software engineering concepts and techniques in the book with two major examples. These examples are significant enough to provide the readers with a working knowledge of the methods presented and enable them to appreciate the need for some of the techniques. With the double objective of application and research for this book, two projects were selected that would illustrate both of these aspects of software engineering.

One is a business application problem that processes data and fills in forms for tax preparation. The second project is more experimental and has more of a computer science flavor. Software is to be built that can analyze programs structurally and extract metrics measurements that are then used to determine similarities between programs statistically. The project is introduced as a plagiarism detector. Subsequent analysis quickly shows that this objective is not at all easy to achieve, and that this project is experimental in nature with a set of unresolved issues.

These two examples are used throughout the book to illustrate methods and techniques. Since the projects are very dissimilar, both are not always used for every method—some methods work better with one or the other type of problem. Originally, it was planned to guide the readers through the entire example in every development phase and every method but, looking at the amount of documentation that was produced for these projects, this idea was quickly abandoned as too voluminous and impractical. Rather, an aspect or part of the example projects is used to illustrate a point, method, technique, notation, etc. This provides the reader with a partial deliverable and an illustration as to how this partial deliverable was developed. Completing the remaining work is often specified in the "problems and questions" section at the end. Any such exercise contains guidance as to how the remaining work is to be done. Thus working through the problems and questions at the end of sections is an important part of the book.

Emphasis on Early Development Phases

Special emphasis is given to the early phases in the software development lifecycle, especially requirements collection and requirements analysis. It is an area that is often neglected and rarely taught thoroughly in the software engineering curriculum. Most students are given rather precise specifications in their programming classes but balk at having to develop requirements. Without some extra coaching, they tend to feel that somehow the user or the instructor did not describe the problem adequately—and from experience in other courses when the problem description was a specification document, this is not surprising. This indicates a need for thorough, step-by-step coverage of this material, and the text tries to do just that. Besides discussing all relevant activities during the requirements stage, it works through examples to illustrate how requirements are collected and analyzed in a specific situation.

Part II emphasizes project selection and the development and upkeep of a viable project portfolio that is aligned with the goals of the company or the department that develops software. A significant amount of managerial effort is spent assessing a product's viability and potential success, yet many textbooks do not spend much time on this; neither do they teach formal techniques of decision making. Yet the problems that a software manager often faces could be helped tremendously if he or she knew about decision-making methods. A whole section (12.5.) is devoted to evaluation and decision making.

The managerial aspects of a feasibility study are also discussed at length. This section complements Chapters 3 and 4 of Part I, where the product aspects of collecting and analyzing requirements were explained. Part II helps in planning a feasibility study, setting the framework for the requirements analysis and feasibility study, and deals with how to refine possible alternatives (as well as with making decisions). Assessing risk and uncertainty are also important managerial activities. While many project management texts cover some of the task or product related (technical) material, few provide any detail on how to deal with politics, resistance to projects and game playing, much less on how to negotiate commitment.

These issues are as important for the success of a software project as a good set of plans for various project activities. Like a good plan, they must be considered early. Since not all projects are the same, not all plans can be, either. This is why it is important to provide a standard plan that can be modified to suit the need. Also discussed is a checklist of planning activities and plans for single and multiple releases. Proper models for managerial planning are crucial to success. This includes scheduling, effort, cost, and productivity estimation as well as sizing. Part of Chapter 12 and Chapters 13 and 14 cover management tasks that are important early in the development life cycle.

New Approach

Part II takes a new approach to software project management: *management by metrics*. This simply means that special emphasis is placed on quantifying effects or likely effects of planning and plan execution. This starts with project selection, proceeds through feasibility analysis and high level project planning, continues through methodology definition and quantification of estimation and quality models, and culminates in a set of measurable guidelines for software development. By describing how metrics and predictive models (e.g., cost and effort estimation) can be developed, the foundation is built for the readers to develop their own customized set of product and process metrics as well as evaluate the efficacy of existing metrics and models.

The reader will find topics commonly associated with project management: project selection based on company objectives; methods of feasibility study; decision making with and without uncertainty; cost-benefit evaluation; risk analysis; definitions of planning activities and variations due to using different process models, impact of schedule compression and increased parallelism; a standard plan, with variations due to different degrees of phase overlap or incremental development; cost and effort estimation; sizing; scheduling; personnel selection; task design and group work; planning and achieving high group productivity coupled with effective communication between groups; leadership; solution of personnel problems and prevention of unwanted turnover; and development guidelines.

What makes this book different is that it provides state-of-the-art models and metrics with all of these topics. Some are more developed and detailed than others. Existing models and metrics are given with their range of applicability, their advantages, and their disadvantages, so that informed choices can be made. Since a textbook should not only recite existing metrics and models that may or may not stay usable, the development of metrics and models is discussed at some length. While some managers may never need nor want to develop their own, at least they will know what is involved. They will be able to see the importance of validation and continued upgrade, so that they can keep models viable over time.

Emphasis on People

Techniques do not make a project productive. People do. One aspect of management leadership is to provide an effective environment for the software development effort. Part II explains how to do this. It involves dealing with issues such as job satisfaction and turnover and designing tasks for software developers that build on their strengths and interests while maintaining high productivity for the project. It includes leadership strategies, structuring development teams, the role of rewards and corrective feedback, dealing with team conflict, communication between teams, and building on the strengths of various organizational structures while avoiding their pitfalls.

Chapter 15 is devoted to people issues in software development. It does not stop at giving "cooking recipes" for various situations, but, more importantly, explains why they work by providing the reader with foundations of organizational psychology upon which the guidelines are based. Thus, when concepts such as the various team structures are explained, the knowledge is present to adapt them successfully to most any development situation.

Most new techniques or methodologies are introduced with the idea that they will increase productivity or result in higher quality software. This is not necessarily realistic, even though technically many new techniques should work. Often the reason why they don't is that nobody considered how a new technique will affect people. Work can become too specialized or too all-encompassing. A new technique may deprive developers of necessary feedback about their work. It is therefore important for a manager to be able to look beyond the technical implications of methodology, techniques, and standard; he or she must be able to assess their impact on the development group. This book tries to give some usable answers to this issue.

Contents and Organization

Part I explains methods and techniques commonly used throughout the software development life cycle. Chapter 1 starts with a series of definitions that have been used for the term "software engineering." Then the concept of development phases and phase activities is introduced. These form the basis for sequential software development life-cycle models. Maintenance and operation of software and the activities associated with these are explained next. Since many slightly different definitions of sequential or waterfall life cycles exist for software development, some alternatives are presented and compared to the standard definition used in this text. Activities and phases are associated with milestones and quality control. Not all software development projects can or should be done using a sequential life-cycle model. Nonsequential life-cycle models are explained. Guidelines help to select the best approach for various development situations. Lastly, the impact these development activities have on the requirements for a good software engineer are outlined.

Chapter 1 sets the stage for all other chapters in both parts.

Chapter 2 introduces problem statements and how to evaluate them. Then the two major projects are introduced: a personal tax preparation system and a plagiarism detector or program analyzer.

Since these two projects are used as basis for examples throughout the text, it is important that they be read or taught at this time. An instructor may decide to shorten the presentation of one or the other of the projects, to substitute his or her own, or to describe both projects as they are presented in the book. Those who wish to give their students a short introduction into metrics have an opportunity to use Section 2.4.2. in this regard. It lends itself to talk about other metrics.

Chapters 3 and 4 deal with developing and analyzing requirements for a solution. Chapter 3 emphasizes the development and analysis of functional requirements diagrams. Functional requirements are derived for the tax preparation system and the plagiarism detector. To round out the picture, some alternate methods to derive functional requirements are discussed.

Depending on the objectives for a course, the instructor may decide to discuss only one of the projects (3.3. or 3.5.), or to reduce coverage on alternate methods (3.6.) and leave these topics as further reading.

Chapter 4 deals with developing a statement of qualitative requirements such as performance, human factors, security, adaptability, maintenance, and the like. It provides a checklist of qualitative requirements and discusses product capabilities, development constraints, and desired product benefits. Since much of modern, successful software development is user driven, developing requirements is approached from this perspective. In Section 4.5. the situation that occurs when requirements are not derived through the user is addressed. Requirements need to be analyzed for consistency and technical feasibility and whether the product will be able to realize expected benefits. Section 4.6. discusses techniques for this. Examples using the two major projects are interspersed throughout the chapter.

In a software engineering course one would probably discuss the material up to 4.4. When time does not allow a thorough treatment of the remainder of the chapter, or when issues such as benefits analysis and feasibility study are topics for a project management course, Sections 4.6.1. and 4.6.2. may be skimmed or skipped altogether.

Chapter 5 describes specifications. The objectives of specifications and the content of a specification document are explained first. Then languages and notations for writing specifications are introduced. These include formal and informal notations that can be used for a variety of problems. As an example of an English narrative specification, a partial specification for the program analyzer is given and evaluated. Other methods that describe aspects of specifications include decision tables, cause-effect graphs, and state transition diagrams. One whole section is devoted to developing specifications for qualitative requirements from the preceding chapter. The chapter closes with guidelines for verification and validation of specifications.

In a first course, one would probably discuss 5.1.–5.5., then select those specification languages from 5.6. that the instructor considers the most important. This may vary from instructor to instructor. Some would consider a formal notation like the one described by Meyer as most important, while others would prefer EBNF or even restrict discussion to the English narrative of Section 5.6.2. When conditions and associated actions are described, the instructor has an option to select either the presentation of decision tables or cause-effect diagrams. It is best to cover the section on describing system states (5.6.4.), at least part of the section on specifying qualitative requirements (5.7.), and Sections 5.8–5.11.

Chapters 6, 7, and 8 deal with various aspects of design. Chapter 6 serves as an introduction to the topic of software design. It covers general strategies and describes notations that are used in the two later chapters to describe system structure and program structure design.

When there is no time to present all of Chapter 6, Sections 6.2.3.2. and 6.2.3.3. could be skipped—they present examples of abstract data types. Likewise, when parallel programming is not considered a topic that needs to be covered in a software engineering course, Section 6.3.3. can be omitted. Note, however, that this also precludes discussing design verification (8.6.4.), since this later section needs knowledge about path expressions.

Chapter 7 discusses software system structure design and presents five different approaches: abstract machine and levels of abstraction, message-based structure, phases, data-flow method and organization diagrams, and object-oriented design. It also discusses how to evaluate the quality of system interfaces and connections and compares the advantages and disadvantages of the five techniques. Examples are given throughout the chapter.

An instructor may decide to limit presentation on design methods to one or two and skip the others. This is facilitated through the general introduction that provides a short explanation of these methods. If not all design methods are presented, care must be taken in the summary section that the comparison of methods is still understandable to the student.

Chapter 8 deals with detailed design. Methods for program structure and detailed design include source-transform-sink analysis and stepwise refinement. Measures for structural quality are given. This chapter also deals with the issue of designing for quality requirements (such as performance, portability, adaptability, etc.). Three methods for verification and validation of designs are introduced: design walk-throughs, design rationalization, and a verification method for parallel program designs. Examples are interspersed throughout the chapter.

In a software engineering course that is oriented mainly towards pragmatism, Sections 8.6.3. and 8.6.4. may be omitted. An instructor may decide to discuss only one of the two methods and skip either 8.2.1. or 8.2.2.

Chapter 9 explains coding. Since this is not a text for beginners, it is assumed that the readers already have coding skills. The chapter explains how to translate a design into code. Then a short overview of what makes good coding style is presented. This section can serve as a reminder or refresher or as background material for a discussion about which coding standards a student project group should define for itself. Next, two important quality aspects of code are discussed: reliability and performance. Sometimes existing code needs to be improved, which may involve improving clarity and structure or improving performance. Methods for either are presented. Section 9.6. explains how to do code walk-throughs. Examples are interspersed throughout this chapter to illustrate the concepts and methods.

When only part of the chapter can be presented in a class, the section on programming style (9.3.) can be assigned as homework and be complemented by a short classroom discussion. Not all software engineering classes discuss performance issues (9.4.2.) or code improvements (9.5.). This can shorten the material significantly. However, it is recommended that at least some aspects of performance improvements (9.5.2.) be discussed.

Chapter 10 deals with testing the code. It explains elements of the testing process as an introduction. Then it proceeds to explain three types of program and unit testing: code-based testing, functional and specification-based testing, and fault injection as a method to measure testing progress and estimate product quality. The methods are compared. The remainder of the chapter deals with methods for system and integration testing, acceptance and field testing, debugging, and what goes into a testplan.

Chapter 11 provides a pragmatic treatment of issues during operation and maintenance of software. Besides explaining the elements of the maintenance process, it discusses the need for documentation and training to keep software alive. It also addresses how to institute user feedback and maintenance procedures, how to perform maintenance, and how to recognize when software is obsolete or "dead."

Part II starts with a definition of management by metrics, a rationale for this approach, and the types of metrics commonly found throughout the software development life cycle (12.2.–12.4.). Great emphasis is placed on how to measure software quality (12.5.2.). Management by metrics is based on quality metrics and (where estimation comes into play) on models that are based on metrics. Section 12.3. explains the development of quality metrics and models and includes details on all steps of their development. For those who are not interested in this level of detail, some of the material can be skipped (e.g., 12.3.1.–12.3.3.). It is, however, important to be familiar with model validation, since this is a necessary aspect for using off-the-shelf metrics and models. Example metrics illustrate process and product metrics (12.4.). Since a major portion of management tasks involves making decisions, some of which have far-reaching consequences or involve consideration of many criteria and factors, the chapter ends with a section on evaluation and decision making (12.5.). A formal framework is introduced

(12.5.1.) and illustrated with a major example (12.5.2.). A formal approach is based on gathering information about relevant aspects of a situation (12.5.3.), what they mean (12.5.4.), which aspects are preferable (12.5.5.), and how to make a decision (12.5.6.). Sometimes it is useful to illustrate graphically the value of alternatives. Section 12.5.7. discusses one such method. Section 12.5.8. summarizes the approach and explains the advantages and disadvantages of a formal approach together with guidelines as to when and how to use it.

Chapter 13 discusses techniques that are useful for the early phases of the project life cycle. They range from project selection to the top-level project plan. Projects should be aligned with the long-term and short-term objectives of an organization. Section 13.2. explains how to select projects for inclusion into the project portfolio and how to weed out those that would not further such goals properly. The approach is quantitative and amenable to metrics. Several examples and case studies illustrate the use of the method (13.2.2., 13.2.4., and 13.2.5.). After a project has been selected, a feasibility study is commissioned (13.3.). Material in Section 13.3. includes how to set the evaluation framework, how to plan a feasibility study, how to manage a requirements analysis, and how to refine alternatives. This section is the complement to Chapters 3 and 4. Often, choices carry risk of failure. Software projects are no exception. Section 13.4. explores various methods for assessing and reducing project risk. A detailed method with examples follows the framework set in Chapter 12. Projects sometimes fail because of resistance within an organization. Section 13.5. explains how to assess the degree of resistance to projects, how to negotiate commitment, and how to determine whether a project is worthwhile undertaking based on the degree of resistance that is likely. This completes the feasibility study and risk assessment procedures. When a project has received the go-ahead, a top-level project plan needs to be made. Section 13.6. discusses the development of such a plan—including degrees of phase overlap and necessary planning activities—and provides a top-level plan for single and multiple releases.

Chapter 14 introduces models that are useful for managerial planning. These include network models to support scheduling (14.2.), particularly CPM and PERT. Section 14.3. discusses various models for cost and effort estimation. First, general principles and assumptions of cost estimation are introduced (14.3.1.). These include guidelines on how to plan a cost and effort estimation "miniproject," how to set goals, how cost and effort estimation are related, and what types of models exist. The next three sections discuss three types of effort and cost estimation models: algorithmic models that are based on analytic reasoning about project behavior (14.3.2.); experiential, statistical models that use an historic database of project data and statistical techniques, such as regression, to develop estimation models (14.3.3.); and subjective experience, where the experience and knowledge of experts determines the value of estimates (14.3.4.). Section 14.3.5. explains how to use estimation models for maximum accuracy, how to update models, and how to evaluate estimation quality. Most effort and cost models rely on size as their major independent variable. A section on sizing (14.4.) explains how to use various size measures for estimation purposes. Chapter 14 explains both top-down and bottom-up estimation and identifies advantages and disadvantages of all estimation models. Emphasis is placed on clarifying that no single estimation method always works and that methods should be selected *together* to ensure proper estimation quality. In addition, a formal approach is described for developing quality estimation models. This is in line with the approach taken throughout the book, i.e., to go beyond summarizing how to use various techniques and results and to provide the readers with a framework for their own techniques and results.

Chapter 15 is devoted to personnel issues. It combines discussion of concepts with many case studies to illustrate situations that may occur during a software project. The chapter begins with a discussion of relevant concepts from organizational psychology (15.2.) that are important and useful for the software project manager. This starts with a categorization of how organizations may view people (15.2.1.) and hence tend to deal with them. Section 15.2.2. describes the importance of (unwanted) turnover as a prime hindrance to productivity and the role of job satisfaction in project success. Guidelines point out how these insights can be applied to software development. Section 15.2.3. describes communication networks. This helps the project manager plan for necessary communication between people and groups. A highly motivated person is more likely to be a highly productive person. Sections 15.2.5. and 15.2.6. explore what motivates software developers and how rewards can be effective in strengthening such motivation. The role of corrective feedback is also explored.

The next four sections are devoted to analyzing several well-known software team concepts with regard to their strengths and weaknesses: the chief programmer team (15.3.), the egoless programming team (15.4.), the surgical team (15.5.), and the revised chief programmer team (15.6.). The material from Section 15.2. (particularly task design) is used to advocate changes to the team concepts that will allow all team members to be most productive, motivated, and effective. Each section also addresses how to facilitate professional growth. This goes beyond merely citing definitions for these team concepts. It provides a framework for putting them to use. Merely assigning role responsibilities to team members has rarely worked. Sections 15.3.–15.6. provide the additional knowledge necessary to adapt team concepts to practically relevant project organizations combining theory and examples.

Effective leadership is a key ingredient to project success. Section 15.8. explores various leadership strategies that are useful for a software development effort. In spite of all planning and consideration when teams are formed, sooner or later teams will experience conflict. Section 15.9. explains various types of conflict that can arise in a team and suggests ways how to deal with it.

Teams and their leadership have to fit into the structure of an organization. Section 15.10. discusses various organizational forms and how they accommodate a software development life cycle and possible team concepts. Small scale efforts are distinguished from bigger projects.

Chapter 16 finally integrates all methods into a cohesive set of software development guidelines. These guidelines span technical issues (the techniques one ought to use (16.2.1.)), product issues (16.2.2.), and management issues (project control guidelines (16.2.3.)). Guidelines alone are only one step toward successful projects. Figuring out which ought to be followed (16.3.) in various situations and how to tell whether they are being followed (16.4.) are just as important, as is finding out whether following them had a positive impact (i.e., whether they are useful). In accordance with the emphasis of this book, metrics are proposed in the form of a scoring system that can be used to track use and usefulness of guidelines throughout a project's lifetime. When scores are low, indicating that guidelines are not followed enough, corrective action is indicated (16.5.). In this way, the material presented in this book culminates in a set of quantifiable software development guidelines that can drive software projects.

▶ Part I ◀

Methods

▶ 1

Introduction

1.1. Overview

This chapter provides an understanding of the software development process and its activities. It informally introduces many technical terms through examples or short definitions. The term "software engineering" has evolved over the past 25 years to mean the collection of methods and techniques used to develop and maintain software. Perhaps one of the best ways to understand software engineering as a process is to divide it into phases of a life cycle, beginning with the start of a software development project and ending with discarding obsolete or dysfunctional software products.

The concept of a software life cycle is central to software engineering methods. The purpose of a life-cycle definition is to provide an understanding of the software engineering process so that it can be monitored and controlled. The classical approach is the sequential software development life cycle or "Waterfall Model." Phases of this model are discussed in terms of their activities, inputs, and outputs.

While a sequentially phased software development life cycle has many advantages, it is not a panacea. Limitations of the Waterfall Model are apparent when investigating the assumptions underlying this classic life-cycle concept. This chapter explains several alternate approaches to software development that overcome the shortcomings of this paradigm. Guidelines for the selection of sequential and nonsequential life-cycle approaches are also given.

3

1.2.   What Is Software Engineering?

Software engineering is a subdiscipline of computer science that offers methods and techniques to develop and maintain quality software to solve problems. "Software" is the term used for computer programs and all documents associated with them, such as user manuals.

Software engineering deals with areas of computer science, such as compiler construction and operating systems; it applies to applications in such areas as business, scientific research, recreation, medicine, production, banking, traffic control, meteorology, and law. Software solutions range from simple record keeping to sophisticated decision making. We will show with three definitions how different emphases can be given to various aspects of software engineering.

Definition 1: Software Engineering is the study of the *principles* and *methodologies* for developing and maintaining software systems. [Zelk78]

This definition of software engineering emphasizes principles and methodologies. Principles generally refer to accepted laws and rules according to which nature, machines, or systems work or operate. Methodologies deal with how to construct a machine or a system to operate according to plan. Principles deal with understanding, while methodologies focus on doing. For example, a software engineering principle says that every program ought to provide error messages when something goes wrong. The corresponding methodology is to check each input to see if it is valid and echo it back to the user when it isn't.

Definition 1 stresses the dynamic nature of the software engineering discipline. Software engineering *studies* these principles and methodologies. This study means understanding the laws governing the life of software systems by learning about existing laws and striving to discover new ones. The latter case often happens when new application areas evolve.

Software engineering reaches beyond software development. Most software, once developed, is not "frozen;" errors are detected, and the original application changes or expands. Accordingly, software is modified to accommodate new objectives. This part of the life of a software system is called *maintenance*. Methodologies have been developed to maintain software.

Definition 1 essentially states two concerns:

▶   the need to understand how software systems work from the time they are first thought about to the time they are phased out and thrown away and

▶ ways to use this understanding (i.e., methodologies) for the development and maintenance of software.

Definition 2: Software engineering is the *practical* application of scientific knowledge in the design and construction of computer programs and the associated *documentation* required to develop, operate, and maintain them. It is also known as *software development* or *software production*. [Boeh76]

This definition emphasizes the use of existing knowledge about software development, not the development of new techniques and methodologies. It stresses that a software engineer is interested in practical solutions to problems.

This definition explicitly states what software is, namely computer programs *and* associated documentation. Software is not just code, and documentation is more than comments in the code. Anything necessary to develop, operate, and maintain the program is part of the software system.

Documentation includes development information (the "blueprints" of the software). It may also include operator manuals, which explain how to install and run the software, how to back up files, etc. User manuals are also part of the documentation. They serve as reference material to the user and explain all features of the software and how to use it.

Definition 3: Software engineering deals with the establishment of sound engineering principles and methods in order to *economically* obtain software that is *reliable* and *works on real machines*. [Baue72]

This definition emphasizes three practical aspects surrounding software and its development, which fall into the category of *software quality*. We want software that works where we need it to work (i.e., on real machines in its actual working environment). Software should operate dependably as specified, and it should be affordable and cost effective.

As we will see later, there are many quality characteristics associated with software quality and various ways to measure or estimate it. One reason is that quality software, at a reasonable price, places a cost-effectiveness constraint on the range of methods and techniques that are useful and applicable in any given development or maintenance situation.

These three definitions of software engineering are useful for several reasons:

▶ They all contain useful information on the meaning of software engineering and its activities, products, and philosophy.

▶ None of them are wrong. Some are more useful in certain situations than others; e.g., sometimes a short definition is sufficient, while at other times one with more detailed information is more helpful.

▶ They emphasize various aspects of the software development process and its objectives.

▶ Software engineering is an evolving discipline. When new terms that describe concepts, principles, or methodologies are coined, there are multiple definitions for the same term (An example of this appears in the next section: the software development life cycle). Sometimes we end up with different schools of thought (and definitions) for similar techniques and concepts. After a while, standard definitions may evolve, but not always.

▶ The definitions give some historical perspective.

New problems in new application areas stimulate the development of new techniques to solve them. As a result, software engineering is a rapidly growing field that profits from advances in computer technology as well as from insights in application areas. For example, researchers in the Artificial Intelligence (AI) field have started to explore new methods and techniques to engineer their software.

Problems and Questions

1. State your own definition of "Software Engineering" and justify it.

1.3.   Sequential Software Life-Cycle Models

1.3.1.   Phase Definition and Quality Control

Software product life cycles are characterized by different *stages* or *phases*. There is more than one way to structure the software life cycle into phases. A well-defined phase is characterized by *activities*, a set of *deliverables* that result from the activities in that particular phase, and the set of applicable *quality control measures* for that phase. In addition, a set of inputs of information (written and otherwise) is necessary to perform the activities for a given phase. The outputs (deliverables) produced by a phase may be inputs to a later phase.

The end of a phase is called a *milestone*. Milestones make the phases more visible, which improves the control and measurement of progress. They clarify the progress to the development team and the customer, and they usually involve a set of deliverables.

If a milestone entails the delivery of a report, document, or product, it is easy to measure whether or not the end of a phase has been reached. If the quality of the deliverable can be measured, then the achievement of the goals of a phase can be evaluated. This evaluation makes it possible to determine whether development can go on to the next phase, whether improvements are necessary, or whether the results are so discouraging that the entire project should be discontinued. This evaluation is called *phase testing.*

At least, the life cycle can be divided between development and maintenance. *Development* encompasses the activities until the software becomes operational. *Maintenance* covers the life of a software system from the time it is installed until it is phased out. These definitions are too broad to be useful in practice. The development phase is usually broken up into many other activities.

The most commonly used stages in the software development life cycle are (cf. [Zelk79], [Gilb83], [Royc70]) problem definition, requirements analysis, specifications, design, coding, testing, and operation and maintenance.

There are other software life cycle phases in addition to those listed above. They are all in the category of waterfall models. Software development cascades from the highest phase down to more detail and implementation (cf. Figure 1.1).

The goal is never to return to a previous phase once it is completed (however, there are various reasons why cycling backwards may be advantageous). Through the quality assurance steps built into this pattern, the waterfall model offers good control over the development process.

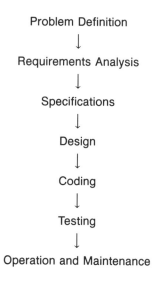

Problem Definition
↓
Requirements Analysis
↓
Specifications
↓
Design
↓
Coding
↓
Testing
↓
Operation and Maintenance

Figure 1.1 Software Life Cycle.

1.3.1.1. *Problem Definition*

The goal of the problem definition phase is to define the problem in user terms as precisely as possible. Precision is important because we cannot develop a solution to the problem if we do not understand what the problem is. We must also remember that it is the *user's* problem and that the user is the ultimate arbiter of what the problem is and isn't.

The software engineer must determine how to best solve the problem abstractly, translate the solution back into its real life equivalent, and provide the user with a solution to the original problem. Problem definition also helps the *user* to better understand the problem.

The result of this phase is a document that defines the problem in terms of the user's objectives and major constraints.

1.3.1.2. *Requirements Analysis*

Once a problem is thoroughly understood, the requirements and general feasibility of the solution must be determined. *Requirements analysis* seeks to determine the characteristics of an acceptable solution and the tools, facilities, and people available for developing a solution. Requirements often conflict with one another, or they are not economically feasible given the techniques and tools available. Trade-offs may be possible and need to be negotiated.

Requirements analysis has three major objectives:

▶ A clear understanding should exist between the user and the developer of what a solution should provide.

▶ There should be an agreement on the range of acceptability and possible trade-offs, resulting in a set of acceptance criteria based on objectives and constraints. In case there are questions about feasibility, a formal feasibility study may be necessary to analyze the requirements with regard to constraints.

▶ A project plan should be made to implement the software with a schedule, budget, and requirements as to what will be delivered at the end of each phase. If there will be several versions, a version plan is also needed. This plan indicates how and when versions will be developed and it defines their successive functionality and capabilities.

Often this information is included in a requirements document and attached to a contract or a formal letter of understanding, so both parties know what to expect.

1.3.1.3. Specifications

The objectives of the specification phase are to describe what the solution looks like:

▶ what inputs the system is going to process,

▶ what functions it will perform for each input,

▶ what the corresponding outputs will be, and

▶ whether the specified system meets the requirements and whether its further development conforms to the project plan or whether the project plan must be altered.

The degree of detail and formality of the specifications depends on the complexity of the system, the size of the development group, and other economic and quality constraints. In general, specifications describe *what* the solution looks like—what the envisioned software system will do, the way it will accept and process data and provide corresponding output—but *not how* it will do all that.

This specification document often serves as a preliminary user manual. Its phase test uses test cases that test the functions described in the specifications. These can show inconsistencies and errors in how the specifications describe functions, inputs, and outputs. They can also be used later to test the finished product against the specifications. Then they are called functional test cases. The specifications provide additional information that helps to monitor and, if necessary, to update the development plan.

1.3.1.4. Design

While specifications concentrate on *what* the solution (the software system to be implemented) will do, the *design* describes *how* the solution will be implemented. Design structures the system into its logically and functionally cohesive parts or modules. It also selects proper data structures and algorithms for the implementation of the input and output data and the system functions.

When we have a large software system, design often has substages (such as system architecture design [Myer76] or baseline design [Metz81]) that identify major subsystems and how they interrelate and which modules perform which functions within one or more subsystems. Module design or detailed design follows.

Design documents are the deliverables. As before, there is a quality control step. The design is checked to see if it is correct with design test cases. This quality control can have different degrees of formality.

1.3.1.5. Coding

The objective of the *coding* phase is to translate the solution into actual code. Ideally, no code should be written until design for that part of the software system has been successfully completed. (We cannot be sure that we are coding the correct solution, if we cannot describe it.) Exceptions to this rule will be discussed in Section 1.3.2.

The coding phase is complete when all code is written and documented, compiles error-free, and follows any coding rules and standards of the project. Phase test for the coding phase involves code reading alone and in groups. Test cases are manually traced through the code (e.g., code inspections, walk-throughs). The test plan must be finished at the end of the coding phase, and it describes how and when to test what part of the code.

1.3.1.6. Testing

The written code should be tested rigorously based on the required quality characteristics. This is the objective of the *testing phase*. Testing usually proceeds in several steps. As soon as code has been written, it should be tested. First pieces (modules) are tested in isolation. This is called a *unit test*.

Later, modules are tested in groups to see whether they interact properly. This is called an *integration test*.

In most instances, we must test the newly developed software system in its actual running environment. If there are several environments, then each must be tested in what is called a *system test*.

It may be desirable to bring up a software system with different configurations or operating system options of the same system. Then we must perform an *installation test* after the system is installed at the site where it will operate.

Ultimately, the software must meet the user's requirements. An *acceptance test* determines whether the user is convinced that his requirements are met.

All users may not be involved in an acceptance test. Rather, the software is tested in a controlled environment by some users with the developers present. This is called an *alpha test*. A *beta test* involves releasing a software product to some "friendly" users to find problems in a live environment. Both prevent serious problems from going into the field.

Some applications cannot tolerate errors. Examples of such applications include software for nuclear reactor control, flight control support in aircraft, patient monitoring in intensive care units in hospitals, and many military applications. Such software development projects have to use *formal verification* methods for their critical modules or components to ensure correctness. These methods use first order logic and mathematical reasoning to prove correctness.

Testing requires a test plan that describes what is to be tested and when and how it is to be tested. In its most detailed form, the test plan includes a specification of the test cases and the expected outputs.

1.3.1.7. Operation and Maintenance

After software has been successfully installed, it must be kept operational. This is the objective of the maintenance phase. Maintenance fixes bugs (*corrective maintenance*), adapts software to new environments and new and modified uses (*adaptive maintenance*), and improves software (*perfective maintenance*).

Maintenance includes all activities that are necessary to keep production software operational. Maintenance handles problems and tracks them (through a problem log or trouble report). User trouble reports are formal or informal reports that describe failures and the resulting user problems. Often they are the primary driver for maintenance activities.

Maintenance also ensures that multiple versions of a software product will not cause confusion and that changes are properly incorporated into software and associated documentation. This requires retesting all parts of the software that are affected by a change. This testing is called *regression testing*.

Because of changes in the code and user needs, software ages over time. To determine whether it is worthwhile to keep the product alive, we need to keep track of the costs of maintaining a product. Problem and cost-effectiveness logs are important sources of information to determine the quality and viability of software. Maintenance determines when software has become obsolete or nonmaintainable because the costs of further changes are prohibitive when compared to the benefits gained from it. It may be better to start over and develop a totally new product with new development techniques, new approaches to the solution, new features, and new hardware. For example, the operating system OS 360 not only incorporated new OS algorithms and a new design approach but also reflected a totally new philosophy as well: upward compatibility. Users could run programs developed on small machines on bigger machines of the same family.

Maintenance consumes a significant part of a software product's life-cycle efforts. (e.g., [Zelk78] states 67%, others report 60% to 76% [Myer76], [Gilb83], [Boeh77].) These figures indicate that maintenance is the most costly phase.

1.3.2. Analysis

1.3.2.1. Deliverables

Every phase of the software development life cycle has its own objectives and deliverables. Table 1.1 shows the deliverables for each phase of the software development life cycle.

Table 1.1 The software development life cycle.

Phase		Deliverables
Problem Definition	(WHY)	Problem definition document, proposal, objectives, major constraints.
Requirements Analysis	(WHAT)	Requirements document, preliminary budget, schedule (plan), objectives, constraints, acceptance test criteria, version plan (start of test plan), feasibility study reports.
Specifications	(WHAT)	Specification documents (preliminary user manual), functional test cases, (revised) development plan.
Design	(HOW)	Design document (architecture, detailed design), design test cases.
Coding	(HOW)	Code documented, compiled error-free according to coding standards, test cases used for code reading, final test plan.
Testing	(HOW WELL)	Tested code, finalized documents, including training, user, and system manuals in all required versions, signed acceptance agreement, maintenance charter, post-project evaluation.
Maintenance	(ALL ABOVE)	Problem log, version control document, (results of) 6 month quality evaluation, cost-effectiveness log to determine age of software, all other documents in their current form.

1.3.2.2. Model Characteristics

The software development life cycle presented in this chapter falls into the classical category of the waterfall model. This model has three important characteristics:

▶ Previous phases must be successfully completed before the next phases are begun.

▶ Every deliverable undergoes a rigorous quality assurance step called a phase test.

▶ After a successful phase test, the deliverable is "frozen" and can only be changed through a formal change request. This rule prevents wild changes and the resulting problems.

1.3.2.3. Model Variations

There are many alternate ways to structure the software life cycle into phases. They reflect different views of development stages and how activities are related.

McClure's variation of the software development life cycle [Mccl81] adds two additional phases, documentation and turnover, between testing and operation and maintenance. Previously, documentation was part of the activities in all phases.

This modified life-cycle definition, which contains a separate documentation phase, does not imply that there is no documentation activity until testing is complete. Rather, after testing is complete, the final versions of all documentation are prepared and evaluated for consistency and correctness. The set of documents includes training manuals, systems manuals, maintenance manuals, and reference manuals. The code is checked a final time for up-to-date comments, but documentation started much earlier. Now the final versions of all pertinent documents are either verified and cross-checked (with documentation of earlier development stages) or written (i.e., the final versions of the manuals just mentioned). The documentation cannot be turned over to the user unless it is complete. The turnover phase includes installation, acceptance test, and training.

Some activities can overlap and, with enough manpower, can decrease total development time. Overlapping activities is possible only if all the related activities of the previous phase have been completed. For instance, if design of a part of the system and its interface has been successfully completed and frozen, the design can be coded while other design activities for different systems or subsystem parts are still going on. Design changes in those other parts must not affect the completed design.

Metzger's ([Metz81]) life-cycle definition combines some of the early phases and separates some testing activities into different phases. The *definition* phase combines Problem Definition and Requirements Analysis of the earlier life-cycle definition. His *design* phase incorporates the Specification and the Design phase of Figure 1.1. *Programming* includes coding, module test, integration test, and documentation.

Only the *system test*, which has become a phase of its own for organizational reasons, is left out of the programming phase. An independent group performs a new set of tests in an environment that is as lifelike as possible. The *acceptance* phase includes demonstrations to the customer, and the formal approval process is based on criteria in the contract or in another document (such as a letter of understanding). The fact that the system test and the acceptance test have become separate phases underscores their importance.

The last phase, *installation and operation*, includes installation, the installation test, and the activities of the operational life of the product as seen in the previous definitions of the maintenance phase.

1.3.2.4. Exceptions

Reasons may exist to move to a later phase before all work on the previous phase is complete; e.g., a feasibility study may necessitate implementation before design is complete. Experimental coding can evaluate the crucial points of a candidate design.

Schedule compression is another reason to allow phase overlap. To compress the schedule, we start coding some parts before the design of the entire system is complete. We should make sure that the design of the part to be coded has been successfully completed. These parts are usually self-contained, logical, or functional units. They may be subsystems, subprograms, or modules and will be defined later. We want them to be self-contained to avoid the consideration of how they might interact with each other, because some of the parts have not been designed yet. Before coding for a unit can be started, its interactions with the environment, called interfaces, must be precisely defined. Systems, subsystems, and modules all have interfaces.

In some projects it is impossible to determine what the system should look like or how to go about implementing it. In such a situation, a pilot implementation is useful. A *pilot system* determines if the main objective is feasible and shows by implementation that it is. While it is a full software system, the pilot system is often a little "rough around the edges," because its main objective is exploratory, not production-oriented. The goal of a pilot system is to provide us with feedback and guidance in defining a better and more useful final product.

A related technique is *rapid prototyping*. This technique might define a core or a subset of functions first, fully implement them, learn from the effort, and cycle back to earlier phases to use the feedback of the implementation. There are two kinds of rapid prototyping [Bott85]. *Mock-ups* show the full user interface (how user and software can and will interact with each other), so that the user can determine as early as the specification stage whether the developed specifications are useful and enhance productivity. The other kind may be called *breadboards*. They have a subset of critical functions for the software product but no user interface. This kind of prototyping shows the developers whether their principal ideas about implementation are sound. If developers expect to improve their knowledge through implementing the solution to an important subproblem, they will use experience with the prototype to guide them in further development efforts. Mock-ups are used to test what the system should look like to the user, while breadboards examine how to implement functions.

Developers cycle through development phases more than once, using the experience from the previous implementation to improve the current one. A software product may evolve in several such cycles.

1.3.2.5. Limitations

Software life-cycle models of the waterfall variety are among the first important attempts to structure the software life cycle. However, the waterfall model has limitations.

Like a waterfall, progress flows in one direction only, towards completion of the project (from one phase to the next). Schedule compression relaxes this requirement but introduces new complexities.

Well-defined phases, frozen deliverables, and formal change control make the waterfall model a tightly controlled approach to software development. The waterfall model's success hinges, however, on the ability

▶ to set objectives,

▶ to state requirements explicitly,

▶ to freeze deliverables at the end of each phase, and

▶ to gather all the knowledge necessary for planning the entire project in the beginning.

The waterfall model's original objectives were to make small, manageable, individual development steps (the phases) and to provide enough control to prevent runaway projects. There are a few problems that have caused dissatisfaction with this phased life-cycle approach.

▶ The new software system becomes useful only when it is totally finished, which may create problems for cash flow and conflict with organizational (financial) objectives or constraints. Too much money may be tied up during the time the software is developed.

▶ Neither user nor management can see how good or bad the system is until it comes in. The users may not have a chance to get used to the system gradually.

▶ Changes that "aren't supposed to happen," are not viewed kindly, neither for requirements nor during the operational life of the system. This can shorten the software's useful life.

Because of these shortcomings, other process models have appeared. They are based on the concept of iteration and evolution.

Problems and Questions

1. What is the difference between a Pilot and a Prototype? When does a pilot system make sense?

2. What types of maintenance are there?

3. Why can maintenance be so difficult?

1.4. Nonsequential Software Development Life-Cycle Models

1.4.1. Evolution Through Feedback

In this section we will discuss four nonsequential life-cycle models that do not require full knowledge of all requirements. They allow iterative cycles in the software development process, and they emphasize feedback to improve development steps. Their iterative nature limits the amount of money an organization has to commit for a development cycle, provides useful systems with increasing functionality, and uses feedback during development and operation to improve software quality and user acceptance. Thus, these nonsequential life-cycle models overcome the major problems of the waterfall model.

The evolutionary process models differ about when and how often feedback is allowed in an iterative cycle, reflecting varying needs for feedback in different development situations.

1.4.2. The Evolutionary Life Cycle

Like the traditional waterfall model, *evolutionary development* [Gilb85] starts out with a set of objectives that specify quality and cost associated with reaching goals. The big phases of the linear life-cycle model, which include all activities of a phase for the entire system and all its features, are cut into smaller chunks. The way we select chunks follows a philosophy: What is the cheapest (easiest) way to develop something that is useful and gets me onto the road to reach my ultimate objectives? "Critical success features" are selected, because without them the system will not be useful. In subsequent iterations we add others that have become the most useful. Then the partial system is built. We start with a basic design that is easy to change and adapt. In later cycles we will change the system, but the idea is that the changes never become too big. The advantage of this incremental approach is that the users see something they can use much earlier than if the entire system had been built in one full sweep. Before new features are added, an evaluation step affords the user repeated input into development. The danger of developing a product past the user is minimized. The developers receive frequent feedback (which is important for some people to feel satisfied with their work). Figure 1.2. shows the Evolutionary Life Cycle [Gilb85].

In evolutionary development the four steps per iteration through the smaller loop are closely related to specification, design, coding, testing, and continuous performance monitoring, which resembles the waterfall model. The difference is in their size and the frequent user feedback that is built into this model. We can expect similar deliverables in kind, if not in size, which are updated at each iteration to reflect the changes that have taken place.

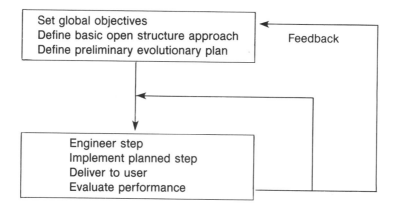

Figure 1.2 Evolutionary Life Cycle.

A related technique for structuring the development process is *iterative enhancement*. Developed by Basili and Turner [Basi75] it recommends structuring the problem to allow the design and implementation of successively larger subsets of the problem solution. Iterative enhancement is a repeat process that starts with a minimal or core solution and implements successively larger solutions. Thus, the software product evolves in successively enhanced versions.

Iterative enhancement, like evolutionary development, orients itself according to global product objectives. The identification of successive enhancements requires a preliminary evolutionary plan and a basic open structure approach (like the evolutionary life cycle). Chapters 4 and 6 present applications on how to sequence versions and design decisions.

1.4.3. The Eternal Development Cycle

The *eternal development cycle* [Demi85] closes the loop between the first and the last phase of development and considers continuous reevaluation and change (cf. Figure 1.3). Unlike the evolutionary life cycle, feedback happens at the end and always leads to modified objectives; it cannot merely apply to the implementation of the current objectives.

We go through the entire life cycle (to the point of turning the product over to the user), evaluate its quality, and analyze what went right and wrong. Based on that, new objectives are defined, and we go through the cycle again. In this way a software product evolves and changes with its environment. Depending on the size of each change and the magnitude of the associated development effort, we can have short or long cycles and faster or slower feedback.

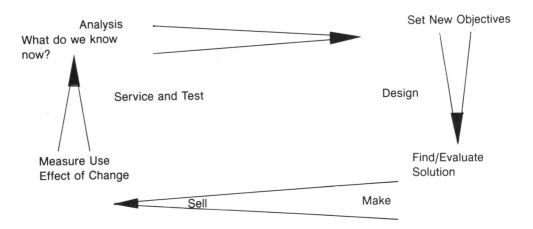

Figure 1.3 Eternal Development Cycle [DEMI85].

1.4.4.   The Expert System Life Cycle

This life-cycle concept [Haye83] deals with the problem of not knowing exactly before-hand what will go into designing and implementing a new system in a specific area, i.e., expert systems. Solving this problem requires frequent feedback between all development steps. The steps cannot be separated as in the previous two evolutionary process models.

Expert systems evolve gradually, need a lot of experimentation, and are usually developed in an evolutionary or incremental manner. Incremental means that over time more features or solutions are added to a set of minimal or core features. The first step is problem *identification* (previously called problem definition). The expert (whose knowledge is crucial to building an expert system) and the knowledge engineer (who tries to build a system having the knowledge and reasoning power of an expert) identify the problem area and scope. They must also determine whether and which other participants (other experts or developers) are necessary. Resource needs and development goals are identified. Because solving the entire problem may be too large a task, a small, representative subproblem is identified. The knowledge acquisition process for this subproblem begins. This process is related to the previously named requirements analysis.

Next, we must put the knowledge into a *conceptual framework*. The expert and the knowledge engineer try to find concepts that represent the expert's knowledge and how information flows during the problem-solving process. Think, for example, of how a medical doctor uses information about symptoms in the process of diagnosing an illness. Usually the doctor defines subtasks and identifies strategies to deal with these subtasks. The expert and knowledge engineer do the same. Concepts may be exploratory; often it is not clear how well they will work.

After specifying concepts, we must develop a *formal representation* into which we can map these concepts. This representation can include language and tools. The objective of this step is to design formal structures to organize the knowledge. Conceptualization and formalization are somewhat related to the specification phase.

The fourth step is *implementation*. The knowledge engineer formulates rules and control structure as well as information structure, which represents the concepts and formalized knowledge. The result is a prototype program that tests how well we conceptualized and formalized the knowledge of the expert on the subproblem. This step encompasses design, coding, and testing.

Next, the expert *evaluates the performance* of the prototype and gives the knowledge engineer feedback for the revision. This feedback corresponds to a well-defined objective for the exploratory system's operational life (which may be very short). We gather information for improvement.

The stages in this process model are not well-defined or independent. For example, if the knowledge engineer cannot find good rules during the implementation, then he may go back and reformulate the knowledge. Using the prototype may require correcting or revising results of earlier stages. We can and do go back from one stage to any earlier stage in this development model; iterative cycles are an integral part of it. When we go back for another full iterative cycle, we specify additional capabilities (i.e., another interesting subproblem or refinement of a problem). We then figure out which capabilities are more important than others, and we implement and evaluate as before. Sometimes, all we need to do in an iteration step is to refine previously implemented knowledge. However, a new feature may also require new knowledge about a subproblem not included earlier.

As the system grows, the knowledge base as implemented can become unmanageable in size or organization. Sometimes this requires the knowledge engineer and the expert to find a new way to conceptualize expertise. Knowledge must be reorganized so that it is suitably structured for the required reasoning process. Then we go a full cycle and end up with a new system, not a modification and extension of the previous one. More than one such rebirth is rare, however. To summarize, expert system development proceeds from simple to increasingly hard tasks. Organization and representation of expert knowledge is incrementally improved.

The expert system process does not fit the waterfall model. Consequently some people developing AI software complain that "the world of AI does not fit easily into the gray, faceless environment of the software engineer." [Morr85] The waterfall model does not favor the feedback and transfer of later knowledge into previous phases. Occasionally, these same problems may apply to other applications.

Figure 1.4. shows the feedback loops of the expert system life cycle. It is called a completely connected communication network, reflecting how communication and feedback flows between phases. This kind of work set-up is much harder to control and manage than the traditional waterfall approach. The number of iterations through phases is unknown, and objectives may shift. It may be hard to assess progress.

1.4.5. Embedded Phased Approach

The last process model combines the idea of evolution (iteration) with well-defined sequential development steps similar to the waterfall model. What makes it different from the evolutionary life cycle and the eternal development cycle is more frequent feedback specifically geared toward all development phases of the waterfall model.

The embedded phased approach is useful for projects that are complex enough to force partitioning of development into smaller, manageable steps. We divide the project into small, definable chunks, similar to the products by evolutionary cycles in Gilb's model or a version produced by iterative enhancement. We close the loop from maintenance to problem (re)definition which is similar to the eternal development cycle.

We still have a "small life cycle" inside that loop. The current set of objectives drives the definition of the (sub)problem to be solved in the next development cycle. For these, requirements are written, adapted, or expanded. The same holds true for specifications, design, coding, and test. Feedback from the existing versions of the deliverables for these phases will also be considered when those for the next development cycle are prepared. Figure 1.5 indicates this feedback with arrows to all phases.

Maintenance now evaluates. What used to be called adaptive and perfective maintenance became a new incremental development cycle. Figure 1.5 shows the embedded phased approach with the evaluation arrow on the left, indicating feedback for the vari-

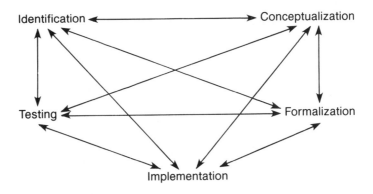

Figure 1.4 Expert System Life Cycle.

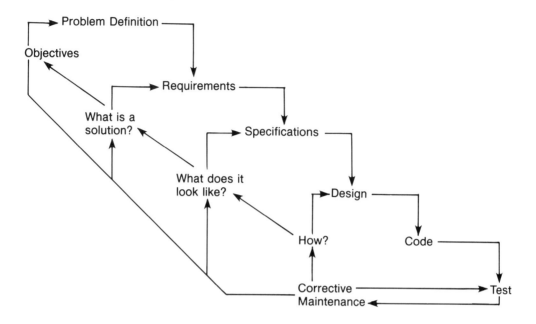

Figure 1.5 Embedded Phased Approach.

ous conceptual phases. This approach includes the advantages of the waterfall model with the advantages of the evolutionary approach. Every iteration will have a new schedule and budget.

Whether or not we should develop the software in one full sweep depends on the size, complexity, objectives (organizational, financial, technical), and the degree of vagueness of the project. The reason for embedding the traditional approach and merging it with the evolutionary one is not to create another definition but to emphasize that the techniques of the waterfall model can be used in an evolutionary context.

1.4.6. Analysis

Nonsequential life-cycle models are appropriate in the following situations:

1. We do not know exactly what we need to solve the problem, because the problem is vague. The waterfall model would freeze decisions on requirements before the user is ready. If we allow the user and the developer to learn from a prototype and then proceed to build the production system, we will have to allow feedback in the development cycle. There may be more than one such cycle, because learning doesn't necessarily happen in one step. An evolutionary approach is more appropriate.

2.   We don't know exactly how to design and implement the solution. Many research projects (artificial intelligence applications such as expert system development) fall into this category. The picture becomes clear when implementation and feedback increase our knowledge of how to design it.

3.   Uncertainties and risks prevent us from making complete plans more than a year in advance (necessary for large projects, if we are to develop them with the phased approach of the waterfall model). We may have to develop a smaller system at first and improve it in a subsequent development cycle. This does not mean that we will not use the phases of the waterfall model during a given cycle, but it means we will have more than one cycle. The problem of planning for an extended time frame is related to the size and complexity of the project as well as its vagueness.

4.   The needs of the users are known, but how to put them into a technical framework is not apparent. This problem calls for experimentation, making the expert system life cycle more appropriate.

5.   We are not sure that the basic concepts work. We must perform a feasibility study for the concepts, e.g., build a pilot or throw-away system. Then code is written as part of an earlier phase, which is a classic exception to the waterfall model's rule, "no code until design complete."

6.   Massive changes are expected, which can result from users using the system and exploring their needs. It can also happen in research or exploratory projects. We should either use an evolutionary approach or prepare to do several cycles through the traditional software development life cycle.

These six situations point to a nonsequential life-cycle model; however, they are not without risks. An iterative life-cycle model requires an open-ended, flexible approach to software development. Designers must choose extendable and adaptable design approaches. Such designs will also simplify maintenance. Maintenance, strictly speaking, no longer exists in incremental and evolutionary process models. It has become a series of evolutionary steps.

1.5. Summary

This chapter explained several definitions of software engineering based on various philosophies about software production, research, and development. The definitions reflect differing goals and objectives for creating software.

In their refinement, the definitions of software engineering lead to definitions of activities and stages of software development; they lead to process definitions. This chapter discussed various process models, beginning with the classic waterfall model and its deliverables. Variations of the waterfall model include McClure's and Metzger's phase definitions, which reflect different views on activities and their overlap. Development activities are emphasized by separating them into a phase of their own (e.g., system testing), or they are deemphasized by grouping them together with other activities (e.g., detailed design and coding becomes implementation). In this way, deliverables and milestones for activities become more or less visible, depending on how activities are grouped into phases. Other variations of the waterfall model relax the strict phase sequence. We discussed phase overlap as a means for schedule compression, pilots, prototyping, mock-ups, and breadboards.

Software life-cycle models of the waterfall variety are among the first attempts to structure the software life cycle. Well-defined phases, frozen deliverables, and formal change control make the waterfall model a tightly controlled approach to software development. Its limitations stem from the fact that it requires complete knowledge of all requirements, commitment of all financial resources during the development time (without "having anything to show" until the system is ready), and no mechanism for feedback and product evolution. For development situations in which these limitations would pose problems, a sequential process model is inappropriate.

We discussed nonsequential process models that support product evolution and incremental development: the evolutionary life cycle, the eternal development cycle, the expert system life cycle, and the embedded phased approach. Another evolutionary model, similar to those discussed, is the spiral model [Boeh88].

The nonsequential life-cycle models do not require either full knowledge of requirements or the up-front commitment of funds for full scale development. Feedback between phases is a natural part of these process models. They vary in how often, at which points, and for which activity in the software development process feedback is given and integrated into the product. An incremental approach requires an open-ended, flexible approach to software development. Designers must choose extendable and adaptable design approaches.

Nonsequential life-cycle models grew out of the insight that software lives and evolves and that a process model should reflect such software evolution through the integration of feedback and iteration of development activities. Current process models will not be the last word on life-cycle definitions. As our understanding of software development and evolution grows, there will be new, improved models to describe the process.

Problems and Questions

1.   A major computer manufacturer decides to completely redevelop its virtual machine operating system. Do you suggest an evolutionary approach? Why or why not? Should the users first try a small increment of it? Why is or is it not useful?

2. You want to build a compiler for a new language. What are the advantages of fast prototyping? (How) does your argument change, if it is to be developed for several machine architectures? While PASCAL is hardly new, you may answer your question with this language in mind. Can you suggest subsets for incremental development?

3. Someone says to you: "I do not build systems incrementally, because it is impossible to manage their development. All the changes kill any budget estimates that I could possibly make. The only thing that I can say for sure is that my estimate for the first budget will be correct. The rest I cannot guarantee, and my boss needs something better than that." What do you answer?

4. In an evolutionary development approach, the users see the system early and frequently. What does that mean for a situation where the "users" are a market identified and targeted by the marketing department? Would you use the waterfall model instead? What else could you do? What are the advantages and disadvantages?

5. Part of the specification phase should be the implementation of a mock-up so that the users can see whether the user interface meets their needs before further development goes underway. What is your opinion on this?

6. List the advantages and disadvantages of the waterfall model and the evolutionary development model.

7. What are the objectives of structuring software development into phases?

8. Are any of the definitions for the software development life cycle "best"? Why or why not? What are their strengths and weaknesses? Define your own and explain why and when you think it is the one that should be used.

9. Why do builders of expert systems use an evolutionary approach to software development?

10. Can an evolutionary software development approach do away with maintenance? Why or why not?

▶ 2
Problem Definition

2.1. Overview

This chapter explains how to define a problem through interaction with the user, how to formulate a problem statement, and how to evaluate a problem statement. Two examples are used: a personal tax preparation system and a plagiarism detector for programs. They have different characteristics and represent both ends of a spectrum of possible problem statements.

The first example problem is the type that is short and somewhat vague. The developers must spend time gathering information about the user and the specifics of the user's problem. This type of problem is common with business and nonscientific applications. A great deal of effort is spent determining the exact nature of the problem (and its solution).

The second example, on the other hand, is a "method" in full detail. It resembles a specification of the function more than a problem, because it includes the precise method necessary to solve the problem. Does this mean that an analysis of such a problem statement is superfluous? After all, more detailed information seems to be available. No. The plagiarism detector example shows how important it is to investigate whether implementing the given method would even solve the problem. Detailed information on a problem is common in technical, scientific, or mathematical areas. It is also more common with a user who thinks "close to the computer," has computer or software development experience, or has thought about the specifics of a problem on a detailed level. In general, when the available problem statement is very detailed and prescribes what method is to be implemented in software to solve a problem, we should ask whether that method, indeed, would solve the problem. This gives the problem statement evaluation a different emphasis than that of the first problem type.

Drafting a problem statement and analyzing it is vital to successful software development. It precludes software that solves a different problem than the one that the user has. Software that does not solve the user's problem can be virtually useless, which is why defining the problem properly is important. It sets the direction for all future efforts. It also formalizes and tests the level of understanding between developers and users. A problem definition forms the basis for determining whether software would solve the problem at all and, if so, to what degree.

A problem statement is the first deliverable in the software development life cycle. Usually it is done via user interviews, marketing studies, or user initiative (request for proposal). This activity is highly problem- and user-oriented. Consequently, the software engineer needs communication skills and user application experience. Helping to define a problem is often part of a system analyst's job description.

The approaches for problem statement evaluation will be different for the business and nonscientific problems versus those of a scientific or mathematical nature. They also vary with the degree of detail initially provided. This chapter emphasizes this by providing two fundamentally different problem statements and analyzing them. In practice, problems may fall in between these two categories, and then a combination of the two approaches may be used.

After working through this chapter, you should know what a problem statement is, how to analyze it, and what techniques may be used to develop a viable problem definition.

2.2.   What Is a Problem Statement?

Before we can find a computer solution to a problem, we must determine what the problem is. It is important to keep in mind that the problem is a *user* problem, and the users are the ones who need a solution for it. These users may come directly to the developers, or a marketing representative may approach a development group. The software is needed to solve a real problem, and therefore the software engineer is a problem solver, just like other engineers.

Often the problem is described in vague terms. "I need to automate my accounting system" or "I want my computer to do my tax return for me" or "I want to automate the school library" or "I want a program which optimizes functions" or "I just started my own dentist (lawyer's, general practitioner's, consulting, etc.) practice. Couldn't I have the computer keep my client records, bill my clients, etc.? Why don't you develop a system for me." The list of possible problem descriptions is endless, and their presentation is unavoidably vague.

For example, in the case of the accounting system, we don't know what needs to be accounted for, why, how much, and why a solution involving a computer is being sought. To make matters even more complicated, maybe we will need to learn accounting and what tasks and activities are involved.

The second case specifies taxes, but does not specify how easy or complicated they are, why a computer is to be employed, or the state or country. Again, we may have to learn something about taxes first, before we can understand the scope of the problem.

The third example, an automated system for the school library, is also vague. "Automating what?" is a possible first question. What aspect of the library? Checking out books? Returning books? Sending renewal notices? Computing fines? Ordering new books? Ordering books from other libraries? Cataloging? Library Search? Topic Search? Author Search? All or which part of the above? What type of library is it? Does it do any of this now? How would they like to run the library in the future? These questions have a significant impact on the scope of the problem and its constraints.

In the fourth example, the user needs help with function optimization. But there are many types of optimizations: constrained and unconstrained ones, linear and nonlinear functions or constraints, one-dimensional or multidimensional problems. Not only do the optimization problems differ, but so do the solution methods. No single method could solve all conceivable optimization problems. Are we talking about maximization or minimization? In other words, it is not clear just what the problem is or why it is a problem and what the intent of optimizing is. In fact, maybe a computer solution is really not necessary. The one-sentence problem definition did not specify whether there are constraints on a solution (e.g., I need it tomorrow.) or whether the constraints are appropriate.

The last case has general and specific attributes. Generally, the problem involves automating the office of a practicing professional; specifically, it is the office of a lawyer, dentist, medical doctor, etc. However, unless we know what type of work is involved in keeping records in any of these cases, (often several methods are conceivable and commonly used) and which particular one the professional employs or prefers, we won't understand the problem. There is no indication of the scope or degree of sophistication of the desired system.

The questions that were asked for each of the "problem definitions" were aimed at *understanding the problem*. They asked for more information about the problem to find answers for the unknowns in the problem statement. The mechanism of asking questions usually involves a set of *what, why,* and *scope* questions. These questions are geared toward defining the problem in all its aspects and dimensions and describing what is required. Most problems are not totally general but are restricted in scope.

   After asking questions in these categories, it is important to write down and analyze the current understanding of the question. Do you know everything there is to know about the problem? Are there any contradictions in how the problem presents itself? If so, they need to be resolved. At this point we focus on the problem, not on solutions.

2.3. Problem Statement Evaluation

After the problem has been specified, a solution should be considered. This step is called *making a plan,* and the solution does not always involve the use of a computer. There is a range of questions to be asked:

▶ What is to be achieved?

▶ What are the characteristics of a viable solution?

▶ Does the solution have parts?

▶ How do they interact with each other to provide the problem solution?

▶ Why do they interact in the ways described?

▶ Can we do better than that?

▶ When does the solution have to be in place in order to be useful?

▶ Who has the problem, and who must be provided with a solution?

▶ Are there several classes of people involved or just one?

▶ How do people do their work now?

▶ In what sort of environment do they work?

▶ What are the areas for improvement?

It is important to know everything about the problem and the environment in which the solution is to be used. It also helps to ask the following questions:

▶ How is this problem similar to others I have seen?

▶ What related problems are there?

▶ Are there solutions for them that might be used?

▶ Is there any software for it on the market? If so, is it any good?

If a full-scale solution of the problem looks impossible, the following questions may be helpful:

▶ Would it be possible to solve a special case or a part of the problem?

▶ Can I translate the problem into one I know how to solve?

The intent of these questions is to establish measurable hard criteria for a solution.

Next, the solution and solution criteria must be evaluated. The following questions should be used:

▶ Why will this solve the problem? For instance, will a tax preparation system solve the problem if it doesn't assist the user in the preparation of the data on an on-going basis? Is it going to solve the problem if it doesn't help to organize other money matters as well, such as balancing bank accounts, credit card statements, phone bills, and all other categories of income and expense that might be tax relevant?

▶ What is the worth of a solution that does all of that, part of it, only tax forms?

▶ Are there priorities?

Questions like these not only explore the boundaries of the problem and the environment in which the problem occurs, but they also help to develop priorities for parts of the problem and its solution.

Questions for the optimization problem might include the following:

▶ Is implementing an optimization package that handles 1,000 variables by approximation a solution?

▶ Is it be possible to reduce the number of variables *before* optimization so that an exact method could be used?

It may be necessary to investigate the theory, mathematical or otherwise, that forms the basis of the solution. It may not cover the particular application, or it may not always assure correct results. Convergence of algorithms is a good example of that. If that is the case, it is important to understand what, if anything, could go wrong with the solution.

Avoid starting the next phase too early, even though defining the problem may seem slow and tedious. It may be difficult to communicate with the user, and it would be nicer to plunge right in and "get something done," but it is extremely important to correctly define the problem and figure out what the solution would look like. Otherwise, we may be preparing to solve an existing but inappropriate problem. This can be frustrating for the developers when they realize it later and must "do it all over again." Sometimes it is necessary to build a prototype to learn more about the problem and user needs.

This first phase provides an understanding of the direction into which the development team must go to solve the user's problem. It is also important to be able to recognize when that goal has been accomplished. Solution criteria must be established that is precise enough to measure the quality of any solution, so that the most cost-effective one can be selected.

2.4. Examples

2.4.1. Personal Tax Preparation System

There are three types of questions to ask about a personal tax preparation system: what, why, and what is the scope? The following is a draft of a problem statement for a personal tax preparation system.

Draft

A personal Tax Preparation (TAP) system for a professional with wages and consulting income is sought. This system should keep relevant tax information during the year, calculate taxes, and help to organize both the data collection process during the year and the completion of tax forms at the year's end. It should also make sure that all the pertinent information has been entered and prevent inconsistent returns. Data that are carried over or must be kept for the next year will be handled also. Relevant tax information includes all types of income, such as wages from various employers, interest and dividend income, royalties, and consulting income. In addition, there are tax deductible expenses, such as business-related travel expenses, and expenses related to the consulting activities, (telephone costs, materials and supplies, and office rental). The actual expense categories may vary from year to year. Finally, there is a wide variety of personal deductions ranging from medical expenses to interest payments on a home mortgage. The third category to be handled includes taxes that have been paid during the year or have been refunded from last year's return. Income and expenses are accounted for through the cash accounting system (i.e., income is recorded in the year received and expenses are recorded in the year paid).

If taxes are prepared in Illinois, for example, the following schedules and forms are often involved: forms 1040, or for simpler returns 1040A or 1040EZ; 1040-ES; 1040-SE;

IL 1040; IL 1040-ES; and schedules A, B, C. The system should be able to prepare those forms and schedules on an ongoing basis. Because some information can go on more than one schedule, the system should allow "what-if" questions to determine the most favorable choice. For tax-planning purposes, other temporary data may be added to determine if and when estimated taxes have to be paid or what the tax impact of an investment decision would be.

Currently, these tasks are done manually with something resembling a "shoebox" method (where receipts are collected during the year and entered into lists at irregular intervals). The chance of losing information or misfiling is great; the interfaces of tax record preparation with its other related systems are complex in the sense that various manual lists must be kept. An example might involve a particular check that paid for a deductible expense. In this case, the financial record keeping with the bank and the category of expense have this check in common. Where should it be filed? An automated system could simplify and streamline tax record keeping with a positive impact on the related financial systems, such as bank accounts, charge accounts, and general accounting. Manual computation of all the items of information for tax forms is a tedious error-prone process, especially when it must be done repeatedly for tax-planning purposes.

Because of audits and estimated taxes, it is necessary to keep multiyear information. An organized system for that information would simplify record keeping, especially if it was easy to determine which individual items made up a particular figure; e.g., what were the individual medical expenses totalling $2,398.31 on last year's return and where can the physical receipts be found? Because tax forms tend to change every year, it should be possible to rename or add lines in schedules and forms.

The client prefers to have the tax preparation system on a personal computer.

Commentary

Which questions does this problem statement answer? Which other questions need to be asked? It is clear what must be achieved: tax preparation as an ongoing activity. It is for an individual only and is not meant for a professional tax preparation service, because a professional service need not worry about where all the receipts are but faces a high volume of returns for many different types of customers. This problem will make a difference in priorities for the various aspects of the system: ours must have an elaborate record-keeping facility but does not need the generality of a system developed for a professional tax service.

We have the names for schedules that are currently used, but do the developers understand what tax preparation with these schedules means? If not, they will have to learn. Often, this learning process has to be a quick one, and sometimes it overlaps early phases of development. If it is not done, the chances of providing the user with something useful are slim. In this example, developers may obtain information from the IRS (which provides publications) or colleges and other institutions that offer courses in tax preparation. Finally, a consultant can answer the relevant questions. The problem statement above hints at what might happen if the developers do not know enough about tax preparation. They may overlook the first incompleteness in the problem statement: no schedule or form is given for royalty income. The misunderstanding that could occur is to assume that only the forms mentioned are to be implemented, although the text implies otherwise. It is necessary to check the English terms against schedules and forms used. Is this all the data that needs to be handled, or is there more data that wasn't mentioned?

After the developer's representatives have studied the basic rules of the IRS for filling out the various tax forms, they probably would want a second interview with the client to clarify some of the remaining open questions: Although you may have more than one employer, are they all from the same state? Does the entire tax table have to be implemented, or is manual entry of taxes owed OK? If not, which tax table is applicable? How smart does the system have to be? The system may range from a mere record keeping and tax form filing program to an expert system that can give advice and point out aspects of the return that are likely to cause an audit and that suggest alternative strategies. How much may be manual and how much must be automated? The answer depends on several factors, such as

▶ Are taxes looked up in the tax booklet and then entered manually, and can any information carried over from last year's return be done manually?

▶ How many different consulting jobs does the client usually have?

▶ How many sources of interest, dividend income, royalties, and business expense items are there? Is there a maximum and a minimum for these items?

▶ For form 2106, is the standard mileage rate or the full cost method used?

▶ Which of the professional expense categories are applicable, or will they all be implemented?

▶ Are there any personal deductions that never occur?

▶ Will the system have to compute estimated tax payments?

▶ What is the filing status?

▶ Is it likely to change?

▶ Should more than one filing status be implemented?

▶ What sources of receipts are there, e.g., how many bank accounts, credit card accounts, etc.?

▶ Since the set of schedules may vary over time, should the system be able to handle new schedules? If so, how? How about changes in the tax forms?

These questions relate to the flexibility of the system with respect to changes. The answers to these questions will point the way to different implementation approaches. Some of the questions did not imply an automated system at all; they only provided more specific information on the nature of the customer's problem. It may happen that a revised, better organized "shoebox" system will be the easier solution. It depends on the complexity of the return. Because the tax record keeping also interfaces with accounting and keeping of bank accounts, it is wise to find out what additional information they keep.

Some of the information gathered so far may be the result of requirements analysis rather than problem analysis; indeed, we have reached the border between the two. When and where the line between the two is drawn depends on the level of detail and the developers' familiarity with the problem in general and the client's problem in particular.

Once a problem is formulated well, more technical ideas may surface as to the generic nature of the client's problem and a solution for it. The terms will be very general; no specific implementations are envisioned, unless they were prescribed by the client. However, as soon as the problem is successfully described, a process of abstraction that relates the user's problem to the generic problem type should take place. Consider the following example.

A viable solution consists of a data entry system with a database for tax relevant data in a variety of categories, cross referencing capabilities, some mathematical functions (e.g., category), temporary ("what if" questions) and permanent data categories, editing facilities, and consistency checks). Such a solution must interface with the other "sister systems," i.e., balancing bank accounts, credit card accounts, utility bills, and whatever other accounts there are. Record keeping alone is not likely to be valuable, because one of the problems (i.e., efficient handling of "what-if" questions) would not be covered. As described, the system has two major parts: (1) the database and data editing functions that are important for record keeping on an ongoing basis and (2) the tax preparation per se, which takes the information from the database and, after computing totals, puts it on the proper lines of the tax forms. These two parts interact with each other through the database of tax relevant information. The tax computation uses the database as the basis for its work and flags incomplete information. A viable solution also has a back-referencing system, which reconstructs the detail information for any line of a tax form or schedule that is a sum of composites.

There are several "generic" problems (and their solutions) that help to solve the overall problem. For example, there are data records in multiple categories. Every data record can have several classes of attributes associated with it. Attributes of like types are added in their dollar field. These types can be user-defined or predefined. Data records are retrieved according to various attribute patterns (e.g., all medical expenses, all consulting income, etc). Summary items, such as total medical deductions, total schedule A deductions, etc., exist in several hierarchies.

We also have detail items, such as the receipt for payment of an appendicitis operation. Because information will be printed in specific layout, we have a forms problem. This problem is complicated by the fact that the information must be assembled into the particular form dictated by the layout of the tax forms.

For personal computers, many software packages are available for database work and for spreadsheet analysis (which is what the tax preparation is all about). Examples of such software include DBASEIII, SUPERCALC, Multiplan, and Lotus-1-2-3. They can all handle at least part of the work, but at times they may need to interface with another program, or simple BASIC routines may have to be written to enable a smooth interface. On the other hand, there are actual tax preparation systems that are sold for various personal computers. The problem statement analysis at this point must gather information about the various choices and compile their advantages and disadvantages.

Publications, like *Consumer Report* and special issues of magazines geared towards software for the personal computer, are good sources of information. In order to make a decision we also need more information from the user. What is available, and can additional software be bought, if needed? In our example, buying off-the-shelf software is out of the question; the user already has a database program and a spreadsheet program and wants something specialized and custom-made.

Now we are ready to investigate the requirements of a solution in more detail, describing the types of data and activities and the layout of the human machine interface as well as other constraints and qualitative requirements.

2.4.2. A Plagiarism Detector

2.4.2.1. *The Problem*

Draft

The next problem concerns an instructor for a high-volume undergraduate programming course who, with his teaching assistants, must grade up to 400 programs at a time. The programs are written in PASCAL, with approximately 500–600 executable lines of code. They run on the main school computer. Through the grapevine, the instructor learned that some students have plagiarized other students' programs, and he wants to put a stop to it. Unfortunately, because of the work load finding the culprits is not easy; approximately 80 to 90 percent of the plagiarized programs are not detected. To speed up the work, an automated tool that detects unusually similar pieces of code must be developed. This tool will be used by all graders to compare target programs to other programs that have been analyzed by the system so far.

Obviously, something more sophisticated than a file comparison program is necessary. Editing of comments or variable names would already circumvent that. Sometimes parts of the program are copied (such as crucial subroutines) and other parts are rewritten. In addition, the language currently used in the course is unlikely to change. More likely is that this and other classes may want to adopt the plagiarism detector. The automated solution will be based on a technique developed by Ottenstein [Otte76], which uses program descriptors derived by applying software metrics methods [Hals77].

Commentary

This problem, has a clear statement and even prescribes the method to use. Because of the volume, a computerized solution is obviously preferrable to a manual one, if it will work. This fact requires a close look at the suggested method. Besides that, it is important to know the graders' qualifications and whether there is any information that should be put into the grade file or other student records. How class files and programs are arranged is a question for requirements analysis; however, the decision to have a batch and/or interactive system and to compare student program printouts must be made now. First, let us look at the technique that will be employed for program analysis and see whether it gives rise to more questions.

2.4.2.2. *Software Metrics and Plagiarism Detection*

Software metrics is a discipline that involves the measurement and quantitative analysis of software and the software development process. In this example, we are concerned only with quantitative descriptors that help to compare programs for similarity. For other aspects of software metrics, see Chapter 12. The method described here is based on an article by Ottenstein [Otte76] and a book by Halstead [Hals77]. For measurement purposes, we can describe a program in terms of the operators and operands it uses (i.e., how many different ones there are, how often they are used), its length, its volume and how much it could be increased or decreased, the density of the information, and program purity.

Several basic quantities must be measured.

n_1 := number of unique or distinct operators in the program

n_2 := number of unique or distinct operands in the program

N_1 := total use of operators

N_2 := total use of operands

$f_{1,j}$:= number of times the jth most frequent operator occurs ($j = 1, \ldots, n_1$)

$f_{2,j}$:= number of times the jth most frequent operand occurs ($j = 1, \ldots, n_2$)

We will order and number all operators and operands in order of frequency.

The *vocabulary* n of a program is defined as the sum of the distinct operators and operands:

$$n := n_1 + n_2.$$

The *Implementation Length* N is the sum of the total use of operators and operands:

$$N := N_1 + N_2.$$

We can also express N, N_1, and N_2 in terms of operator and operand frequencies, because N_1 is the sum of all operator frequencies $f_{1,j}$ ($j = 1, \ldots n_1$) and N_2 is the sum of all operand frequencies $f_{2,j}$ ($j = 1, \ldots, n_2$). Adding both of these sums gives the implementation length N.

These quantities are a concise way of describing the use of operands and operators in a program. None of these quantities would change if a second program was generated from the first by renaming variables and rearranging statements where order is not important, which is a relatively simple way of plagiarizing a program. It is very effective when combined with rearranging the program format and rewriting comments. However, the original and the plagiarized version would retain the same values for n_1, n_2, N_1, N_2, N, and all the $f_{i,j}$.

Programs with identical values for all these quantities would be looked at more closely. Identical counts may not mean that programs are identical. Two programs may use the same number of operands and operators, but the actual operators may be very dissimilar. For practical purposes, however, when comparing programs that are supposed to have equal functionality, two programs that come so close in these metrics should raise a warning flag. Besides this simple way of changing a program, there are various easy modifications that change the total usage counts of operators and operands but not always the number of distinct operators and operands. These changes are called *impurities* of the code. For example, an impurity can be created by subtracting and adding the same quantity several times. This will change N_1 and N_2 but not n_1 or n_2. The final result of the computation is also the same. There are six major types of impurities. Some of them change n_1 and N_1, others change only the totals.

1. **Complementary operations.** They are sometimes called self-cancelling operations and are introduced when two operations cancel each other out:

```
TERM := P + Q – S;
PROD := TERM * TERM – TERM + TERM;
```

The last two operations could have been left out without any change in the effect of the computation:

$$TERM : = P + Q + S;$$
$$PROD := TERM * TERM;$$

The values for the program metrics for both versions are given below:

	n_1	n_2	N_1	N_2
version 1	4	5	7	9
version 2	4	5	5	7

Both versions have the same operator and operand count. They differ by two in their usage counts for the operators and the operands. Note that if an operator was used that had not been introduced, the operator count would be different between the two versions.

2. **Synonymous operands.** Operands that use two different names for the same thing can also disturb the actual values for the program metrics, as illustrated by the following example:

Version 1:   *Version 2:*
T1 := P+Q;   T1 := P+Q;
T2 := P;+Q;
R   := T1 * T2;   R   := T1 * T1;

Their metric values are

	n_1	n_2	N_1	N_2
version 1	3	5	6	9
version 2	3	4	4	6

3. **Ambiguous operands.** This situation occurs when the same operand name is used to refer to different things at different places in the program, as in the following example:

$$R:= P + Q;$$
.
.
.
.
$$R:= S - T;$$

What we have here is a reuse of the variable for a different purpose.

4. **Unwarranted assignment.** This is actually the opposite of type 3. In this case, a combination of terms is assigned a unique name but used only once; the new name serves no useful purpose.

Version 1:	Version 2:
T1 := P+Q;	
R := T1^2;	R := (P+Q)^2;

5. **Unfactored Expressions.** This is a relatively rare impurity. No easy, straightforward, general mechanical method for removal exists.

Version 1:	Version 2:
R := P*P + 2*P*Q + Q*Q;	R := (P+Q)^2;

The second version is the factored equivalent of the first. In order to detect such unfactored expressions, each expression must be factored, provided that a factored version of it exists.

Some of those impurities can be removed by a program that detects these. For example, wherever a complementary operation is found the usage counts for operands and operators are not increased for the self-cancelling parts of the expression. This results in an identical quadruple of counts for both candidate programs. It should be emphasized that impurities do not necessarily constitute a bad programming practice. In fact, some impurities can increase the readability of the code and thus improve its quality.

The major premise underlying the use of the quadruple of operator and operand counts is that programs with identical values for their program descriptor quadruples (n_1, n_2, N_1, N_2) are very unusual. Thus, if we find such a pair of programs, they are candidates for possible plagiarism. Because of the perturbations caused by impurities, it would be wise to also check programs with nearly identical quadruples. But how much is "nearly identical," and where does the characteristic of "nearly identical" stop? Statistically speaking, the programs under scrutiny can be processes to yield such quantities as mean, median, standard deviation, and minimum and maximum values for n_1, n_2, N_1, N_2. If two programs have similar counts close to the mean, it is less significant as an indicator for possible plagiarism. On the other hand, two programs with close counts away from the mean are statistically more likely to be plagiarized.

Because of this, a measure should be defined that accounts for this probability. This measure is based on the means vector $m = (m_1, m_2, m_3, m_4)$, where m_1 is the mean of all n_1 values of all programs, m_2 is the average of n_2, m_3 is the average of N_1, and m_4 is the mean of all N_2 values. Because unique operators and operands and total use of operators and operands are statistically related in a program, we must define and use a covariance matrix CM together with the means vector m to define the multivariate normal density function $f(x)$ that measures the probability of a quadruple x occuring for a program.

With this function we can define a measure for how far away from the mean we are as the fraction $f(x)/f(m)$. This function is 1 when x is the mean m and continually decreases as the program descriptor x moves away from the mean, approaching zero towards the tail of the distribution. When combined with similar program descriptor quadruples, low values of this similarity function indicate that there is a high probability of plagiarism.

Some software developers may not be familiar with statistical concepts, such as significance, covariance, or normal density function. For them, the technical side of the problem will involve determining statistical significance, how a covariance matrix is computed, or what a normal density function looks like. These concepts are discussed in the chapters on specifications and design. All we need to know now is that implementing these concepts is part of the problem posed to the software developers.

With the above analysis method, we can write a program to automatically compute descriptor quadruples for all programs that will be compared and to determine the possibility of plagiarism by statistical means, (i.e., computing the fraction $f(x)/f(m)$ for close programs). There are two major problems with this approach as described: one is how to deal with impurity classes and the other relates to partially plagiarized programs where only certain parts (like the major processing algorithms) have been plagiarized, but I/O modules are different. Ideally, the method should deal with the most frequently occurring impurities and with program parts and individual modules.

2.4.2.3. Problem Discussion

This problem seems to have a ready-made solution, (i.e., implementing a program that counts operators and operands in a PASCAL program and computes statistical quantities that measure the probability of plagiarism). The problem is so well specified, that we can use the problem statement as a start for the specifications. But can we really? Since the method has advantages and disadvantages, and some of the functionality will require significantly more effort than others, it is important to clarify how the method is linked to grading programs for a particular course.

To recapitulate, the problem is plagiarism detection for programs and their parts. It is a problem for the following reasons:

▶   There is a high volume of programs;

▶   Grading work is distributed among several people;

▶   There is a lack of reliable communication paths for program analysis results;

▶   Plagiarism of program parts adds additional complexity;

▶   Simple modifications veil plagiarism; and

▶   Comparison of programs is a nontrivial task.

The scope of the problem includes the following:

▶ Potential candidates should be targetted.

▶ Programs and program parts and their I/O layout must be analyzed. The volume is 400 programs, about 10–15 per semester. The program size is approximately 400–600 executable lines of code. The instructor volunteered to consider both interactive and batch evaluation. If in batch, then evaluation should happen automatically when programs are submitted by students (they do that at the present time with a **To-Professor** command from their student account). The instructor also forsees that there may be detail questions about analysis results afterwards. Comparison of printed output, although done visually by the graders, is not feasible and is dropped from the problem scope.

▶ The users include at least five graders and an instructor with overriding rights (grades).

▶ Communication and correlation of analyses is a must (interactively).

▶ Record keeping (program characteristics and grades, "past similarity" index for repeaters) should be extensive. It is not clear what should go into it or how it may relate to other student records.

▶ Prescribed method for analysis.

▶ Frequency of analysis is approximately one to three weeks (when programming assignments are due).

Applicability analysis of method includes the following:

Simple: method without impurity detection, whole programs, program parts as indicated by grader.

Medium: simple impurities (1,2,4), possibly not all.

Hard: impurities of class 3, 5. Automatic detection of different functional parts (I/O versus computation).

This list of issues and reasons for the problem shows two emerging aspects of the problem: the analysis itself and the comparison and interpretation of the results. The user has trouble with both aspects at the moment. To answer questions about which implementation alternative would be the most cost effective, we need to know more about how the analysis works and how it is embedded within the grading process for a course.

This calls for requirements analysis to understand the present system and how it would work manually.

The instructor (the user in charge) wants the basic comparison procedure implemented without knowing the quality of the result. Is it necessary to know? The instructor hopes to find the answer by using the basic system.

The future user gave us information on the problem, requirements for a solution, and what the solution would have to look like. In fact, the current information is "specification heavy." Sometimes a problem stated in this way seems so well defined that it is easy to rush ahead and implement. But we should remember to look at what the implementation is for and what the problem is. This example is a case in point. We almost have functional specifications for what the program analyzer will do with operators and operands; however, we must clear vague areas first. For instance, the environment of the program analyzer is not well defined, so the scope is unclear. Also, the usefulness of program analysis for plagiarism detection is unknown, and that is the original problem. Lastly, the ultimate purpose of the whole analysis system seems to be shifting from a plagiarism detector to an exploratory system (which analysis might work in practice and how well). That is a totally different problem focus.

The acronym for this Program Analysis System is PAS for the remainder of the book.

2.5. Summary

This chapter discussed how to develop a problem statement and analyze it. The major emphasis in this phase is on understanding the problem through asking what, why, and scope questions. Problem statement evaluation connects the problem to high-level characteristics of a solution, which may happen through rephrasing the problem until all vagueness and misunderstandings between user and system analyst are cleared up.

The examples showed two ends of a spectrum of possible problems (from vague to detailed). In the first example, the problem needed to be clarified and defined precisely. In the second, precision and detail were abundant. But did they describe the problem and its solution properly? These two types of examples illustrate two different approaches and two different types of questions that must be asked. The first type of problem definition activity requires time for collecting information on the problem. The second example requires asking questions about the problem and solution information that is present. Usually a combination of these two approaches is useful.

The benefits of a good problem statement are obvious: the problem and its scope are well-defined, and further development activities are focused. Sometimes the real problem will evolve with the building of software for its solution. Thus, the precision of a problem statement may depend on the type of problem. Risks arise when unclear problem statements become misleading to the developers and the users do not know how or have no opportunity to recognize that early.

Some process models consider problem definition as a part of requirements analysis, not as a separate phase.

Problems and Questions

1. a) Write down a set of questions to define the problem of automating the handling of all departmental student files in the computer science department.

   b) Interview the users (departmental secretary, adviser, faculty).

   c) Write a problem definition and evaluation.

2. Do a problem definition for a medical doctor who wants to automate all accounting, client files, and other business aspects in his office.

3. A software consultant asks you to automate her project and appointment book, including day-today, weekly, monthly, semi-annual, annual, and project-directed, long-range planning. The tool should include measurement and evaluation for estimates of time required to perform tasks and to finish projects.

   a) Is this a valid problem? What is the problem?

   b) Do you know why this is a problem?

   c) What is the possible scope of the problem?

   d) What are the questions that you would ask her to find out more about her problem?

▶ 3

Functional
Requirements
Collection

3.1. Overview

This chapter explains the process of collecting functional requirements and developing a functional requirements description. Functional requirements describe in detail how the implemented system will function: what it can do, what information is transformed, and how to achieve the desired outcomes.

Requirements collection provides a precise picture of what a viable solution requires. Without precise requirements, it is impossible to evaluate the finished product objectively (e.g., does it have all features and functions required?). Without requirements this can be only a gut-level decision. This lack of objectivity is dangerous when fulfillment of a contract is at stake or when significant amounts of effort and money are invested in a project.

The input for the requirements phase is the problem statement and further information from the user or a user representative. This additional information is collected during the requirements phase and analyzed. This analysis forms the basis for the requirements document, the deliverable of the requirements phase. The requirements document is input to the specification phase. Functional requirements, discussed in this chapter, form part of the requirements document.

Systems analysts, in cooperation with a user or user representative, collect and analyze functional requirements. Observation of users in their current environment (physical system) may provide this information. The systems analyst understands functional requirements techniques, possesses some application knowledge, and can assess the combined impact and feasibility of functional requirements. Communication skills are essential, while ergonomic skills are desirable.

A variety of methods exists to develop functional requirements, ranging from prose to formal methods. This chapter emphasizes a particular method, namely *functional requirements diagrams* [Gilb83], [Gane79], [Dema79], [Dema82]. In the technique presented here, this method will be augmented by additional English descriptions to enhance understanding.

The chapter explains the processes involved in developing diagrams from an existing system or from manual procedures and analyzing them to develop an abstract system description that includes its functions and data. This process provides a description of what the proposed system will be able to do, i.e., its functionality. Two additional methods to express functional requirements are explained in Section 3.6. One of them is PSL [Teic77], (a formal language that supports an automated tool, PSA). The other technique that helps to express functional requirements is the diagramming technique of Warnier-Orr [Orr77].

This chapter uses the two examples (tax preparation and plagiarism detection) that were introduced in the previous chapter. They illustrate how to use the techniques and concepts of collecting functional requirements. Thus, the reader will see how to proceed from a problem statement to collecting requirements. In the process, the different characteristics of the two examples become evident; therefore, requirements collection proceeds differently. The tax preparation problem is essentially a data and forms problem, and its activities are driven by the layout of the forms and the data they require. The plagiarism detector is an algorithmic problem, where the crucial nature of the activities is reflected in the size, complexity, and type of information that is collected as functional requirements.

At the end of this chapter you will know how to develop and analyze functional requirements diagrams. You will also know how to use PSL and Warnier-Orr diagrams, two alternate techniques to describe functional requirements.

3.2. Developing Functional Requirements Diagrams

Requirements analysis further explains and refines the initial picture of the problem with an emphasis on requirements and goals. The focus is on the interface between the user or user classes and the computer, keeping in mind that the best solution may not be *software*. Sometimes a manual system will be adequate.

Requirements collection takes a detailed look at how the current or manual system system works. It defines how the system is embedded in its environment in more detail than during problem definition. Problem definition is concerned with how the problem manifests itself. Now we establish the functional principles of the solution to the problem by using the details of the system as the user may have it now. We will probably do this manually, perhaps as the user needs it to become integrated into the overall environment. This collection does not involve suggesting or defining layout or formats for the computer solution, which is a task of the specification phase. Rather, it is concerned with the workings and interactions of all the activities of the user system. Requirements collection determines in detail all flows of information between the activities.

The user must be interviewed conscientiously, which may require considerable patience and the ability to communicate on both sides. The systems analyst needs to speak and, more importantly, to understand the user's terminology and the essential aspects of the application area. Frequently, more than one interview is necessary, especially for multiple user classes. Most expensive errors are caused by not understanding the user. Consequently, the programmers don't know what to program. Requirements analysis further clarifies the understanding between all user types and the software engineer.

The case of the "automated doctor's office" has several user types:

▶ the *secretary*, who types the bills, letters to pharmaceutical companies, and other assorted correspondence;

▶ the *nurse*, who records data about the patient;

▶ the *lab technician*, who writes down the results of tests and updates the inventory list and materials used;

▶ the *doctor*, who states the symptoms, possible diagnoses, current treatment plan, the patient's response to the treatment, current medication, etc.

There are other permanent patient characteristics, e.g., known allergies, which insurance company (if any) will pay the medical expenses. The listed user types have different goals and activities within the system "doctor's office," and they generate different kinds of information.

All information from these interviews is compiled, categorized, and analyzed for consistency, completeness, and sufficient detail. Feasibility of the project must be established; wherever requirements conflict, they must be reconciled and trade-offs must be made. These trade-offs are usually based on priorities which should be discussed with the customer. When the customer is the organization itself, (i.e., in-house development of software) priorities are given through refinement and interpretation of goals. There are goals for the users and goals for the developers.

User interviews provide information that may apply to more than one phase of development. For instance, the user may have already explained some requirements while he was explaining the problem. Also, during requirements collection he may indicate how he would like the solution implemented which is a design statement. When information that applies to later development phases becomes available, we do not ignore it. Rather, we write it down under the appropriate category (to avoid confusion). During requirements analysis, there are various categories of requirements to analyze, although the information is not necessarily provided according to those categories. The analysts may have to separate information by category to clarify the picture. Much of an analyst's work is organizing, sifting, and categorizing information until a structure emerges that is clear and can be analyzed.

The result of this phase is a requirements document. It serves as an agreement between the user and the developing organization.

Functional requirements collection determines *who* does *what* with *which information* (data objects). In the doctor's office example, we have defined

▶ some of the people who handle records (who),

▶ what information they need for their job, and

▶ which information they provide for which other people's work.

In the beginning, we should focus on people who are doing the job now or who would do it. We can make a list of the people and their roles, needs, and responsibilities. Then we must ask them to explain in more detail what they are doing. This information should be included on the list. Next, we must describe the type of data objects they are using or generating while performing their activities. The activity descriptions must be detailed enough to determine which activity modifies or generates which data object; but they should not be so fine that no data seems to have changed or been created for the other people who are working within the system.

Besides activities and the data objects, we must describe their interrelationships. The people in the system work together and provide each other with data. Without understanding the interdependencies of all system parts, it is impossible to build an abstract model of the system and its underlying principles. This model is then translated into a software system. A full, detailed description of the actual or physical system is the first step towards specifying the requirements for the software system.

Functional requirements diagrams provide an understanding of the principles of the system that is to be automated. If it is currently a manual system, we must study the system as it is right now. This includes the organization within which it works (if the system is embedded within an organization), which people perform the work and what they do, which paperwork is exchanged between them and prepared in the current mode of operation (it is important to be specific about the documents involved), and what exactly is everybody doing down to the lowest level activities. A requirements diagram like this is called a *physical requirements diagram*, because it describes the characteristics and principles of the current mode of dealing with the problem. It is the result of asking certain questions. How do you do the work now? What does the current system do? What types of data are processed and in which way? Who does what? What kinds of information do they need? What is the outcome of their work?

Later, these physical requirements diagrams are analyzed, and the activities are transformed into their abstractions, resulting in an *abstract requirements diagram*. Let us first see what requirements diagrams look like. They are developed to describe a system (physical or abstract) in terms of its *activities* and the *flow of data* through it. Every system processes data that flows from one processing station to the next. Sometimes the data is transformed at a station, and at other times it is used to produce a modified data item together with other information.

There are three types of processing stations (activities). First, there are *activities* that take data, transform them, and pass them on to other stations. In the diagram they are drawn as boxes with an activity name inside. Incoming and outgoing arcs, which are annotated with the name of the data, indicate that data are received and sent and what particular data are involved. Second, there are *sources* that originate but do not process data. They have outgoing arcs for the data objects they generate. Lastly, there are *sinks*, which receive data but do not process it. Such data are characterized by incoming arcs. Sources and sinks are drawn as boxes with two extra horizontal lines annotated by the source or destination name. Sources and sinks are the system's interfaces to the environment; they are not part of the processing. They may be an activity (internal) to a sister system, but they are outside the system for which we are drawing a requirements diagram. Finally, some systems store data (e.g., in file folders). Data is stored if it is kept somewhere until needed and if it is not changed or transformed in any way. In the requirements diagram, this is indicated by a box, that is open to the right and annotated with the *filename*. Figure 3.1 shows these components of a requirements diagram.

During problem analysis, we started by asking global questions and then refining them. Similarly, we will start out drawing high-level requirements diagrams and subse-

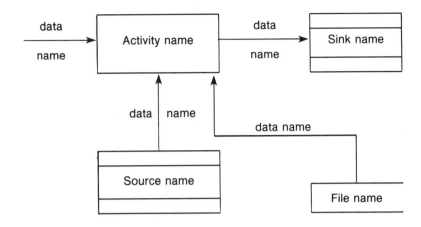

Figure 3.1. Data directionary for diagram in Figure 3.3.

quently refining them into more detail. A top-down requirements analysis starts with global names for activities and data. The activities and data are subsequently refined in detail so that we understand the working of the system well enough to do it ourselves manually (if that is what is done right now). The questions we have to ask include the following:

1.   What are the categories of data? Sometimes the user will give a mound of detail information that must be put into categories to be conceptualized. This provides major data classes or categories. Sometimes the user will specify those major data categories.

2.   What are the subcategories? When users specify global information, such as "billing data," not all the data in the class may be the same. Besides the fact that the data may have varying parts, there may be data subcategories that will have to be processed differently. For these reasons, we need to ask about subcategories.

3.   How are the data in the different subcategories processed? Subcategories of data may have different processing needs; therefore, it is important to know what they are. This is a question about activities (as opposed to data) of the system.

4.   Are there subactivities to an activity? An activity may entail a range of little tasks, which make up the activity when taken together. Such major activities are candidates for refinement.

5.   What information is needed by which part of the subactivities? Not every subactivity needs all parts of the input data objects of the higher level activity. We can use this question to find out which information is needed for which subactivity and

which is not. Characteristics of filed data are the following: they are written down, they are put into a file folder, and several people look at them in order to do their work.

6.   From which file could some of the data come? Some data does not result from processing; rather, it has been stored for referencing and is used but not modified. This data is best kept in files. We should try to isolate those data objects, because they are conceptually different and will be handled differently. All data that are kept over long periods of time and are referenced somewhere along the line are candidates for files. Characteristics of filed data include: data is written down, put into file folders, or shared among several people or distinct activities.

7.   To define sinks and sources, questions about users and user classes are asked: How many people are involved in or would use the system? What data do they provide for it, and what data do they obtain? What do they do with it? Is any data sensitive (needs to be secured) and what levels of security? Some of these questions are scope questions geared toward defining the boundaries of the system and how it interacts with possible sister systems. These questions can have significant impact on describing the new system, its data, organization, and activities.

8.   Further scope questions are helpful in drawing up abstract requirements diagrams (e.g., where are the shortcomings of the system?). Answers may result in the creation of new features and activities. Because the abstract requirements diagram focuses on the features and functionality of the proposed system, the analyst asks questions about how the users feel about the current system and its features, whether there should be any additional ones, why, their importance (ranking) or unimportance. Ranking of features includes two aspects:

▶   their importance to automate and

▶   their general importance to the operation.

To come up with a ranking, it is necessary to have a clear understanding of the degree of automation that would best benefit the user(s).

These last questions, while they provide more data than what the requirements diagram reflects, is important for the following reasons:

▶   They help to clarify activities and data flows as well as data descriptions.

▶   They provide information to define system boundaries and interfaces to other sister systems.

▶   Answers to them can be obtained during user interviews at the same time as the information needed to develop the functional requirements diagrams.

▶ They provide information on how to interpret the diagrams, and they point out possible alternatives for implementation.

Note that functional requirements diagrams describe only one aspect of the requirements, the system. This description needs to be annotated with user goals, so that the development organization can assess the feasibility and consistency of user objectives within resource and other feasibility constraints. This information provides the basis for a qualitative requirements definition (see Chapter 4).

The primary objective of these questions is to

▶ define major data objects and activities,

▶ subsequently refine data objects into their constituent parts, and

▶ partition activities into smaller pieces called subsystems.

Additional questions can be found in [King84]. All these individual requirements diagrams are part of the physical system description. A requirements diagram therefore consists of the top-level diagram (which is what we started out with), the second, third, etc. to the bottom level diagrams, activity descriptions for each basic activity, and data descriptions for the major data objects and their subparts. Thus, a full requirements diagram has three dimensions: the description of the data, the description of the activities, and the interconnection of activities through the data that are produced or transformed during the activities. To illustrate this concept, we will look at the tax preparation system of the previous chapter.

3.3. Requirements Diagrams for a Tax Preparation System

The previous chapter introduced individual tax return preparation as a problem. Before embarking on a solution, we should find out how the problem is currently handled. The current situation will show what kinds of data are necessary and will be processed, and which activities are involved, where data are generated and kept or sent. We should consider sources and sinks first. A logical source is the individual who prepares taxes (the user), because she generates data for the preparation activity but is not a part of it. Sinks of the system are the IRS and the Department of Internal Revenue of the respective state(s) that gets the final tax return forms. These are sinks, because they are the destination of the final return but are not a part of the preparation activity. The top-level activity is tax preparation. For this activity we need data such as employment, self-employment and interest income information, amount of taxes paid, and deductions. These categories of information are necessary to fill out the tax forms and compute taxes due (or the tax refund) and to compute totals in all relevant income and expense categories. Figure 3.2 shows the top-level diagram for tax preparation.

This is not all the processing or detail information that may be necessary for the task. We do not know which subactivities make up the major activity "tax preparation," nor do we have information on the types of income, taxes, deductions, etc. These items are provided by the next refinement steps.

To refine the tax preparation activity, we must ask questions about the different data objects generated by the user box:

1. How are income types handled? It turns out that different types of income are put on different schedules. Interest income goes on Schedule B, consulting income is reported on Schedule C and needed on Form SE, and wage income affects Form 1040 and the state form, (e.g., IL-1040). Preparing any of these forms is part of the overall activity. As a result, we can refine the top-level activity to filling out the individual forms, and we can refine the data category income to wages, interest, and consulting income.

2. How are tax types handled? Essentially there are two types of taxes: federal taxes and state taxes. Federal taxes are used to fill in Form 1040, while state taxes are put on the respective state forms and possibly other state forms if an out-of-state tax credit is claimed (this handles the situation where a user has worked and received income in more than one state).

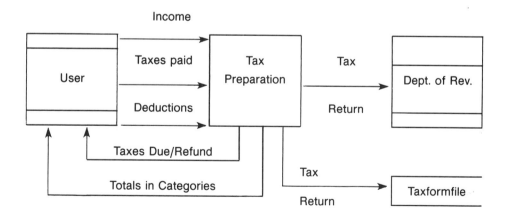

Figure 3.2 Top-Level View of Tax Preparation.

3. How are deduction types handled? Our user has two types of deductions: those that belong on Schedule A (personal deductions) and those that belong on Schedule C (business expenses).

These three question areas provide a lot of structural information; the types of income, taxes, and deductions were defined in detail, and the top-level activity was subdivided into three subactivities: handling income, handling taxes, and handling deductions.

This is a possible refinement, but is it a good one? Which data objects are the outcome of these actions, and how do they relate to the data object "tax return," which will be passed to the tax authorities (i.e., the sinks of the diagram) and will be stored in the file of tax returns? This is not clear, and there is no obvious answer. Because our structuring efforts should lead us to the data object "tax return," partitioning of data objects that does not facilitate building tax returns is not necessarily desirable. Therefore, this last refinement may be a dead end. However, that does not mean that we have wasted our time. Although handling the types of income, tax, and deductions turned out to be a less desirable partitioning, the three questions we asked helped to describe the data objects in our system in detail, and we ended up defining subcategories of the three major data classes (i.e., income, taxes, and deductions).

A further look at processing reveals that the activities center on filling in parts of various forms and schedules. Partitioning the problem into handling individual forms is a natural refinement. This definition of subactivities also shows well-defined data objects as outcomes (i.e., the completed form or schedule).

Often we must ask questions about the system boundary which means analyzing the sources and sinks of the current diagram so that we can determine whether there are some activities hidden or pushed outside of the system (which really should belong inside). In our example, we should examine the source, "user," to help us to understand how data are generated.

Q: "From where do you get your data?"

A: "From my shoeboxes (files) where I keep all the receipts and tax information during the year. When I get a receipt, I put it there."

Q: "What information do you file?"

A: "W2-forms, cancelled checks to substantiate deductions and expenses, credit card statements, and income receipts."

Q: "Which file or files do they go into?"

A: "I have one box for deduction receipts and one for W2 forms and other income statements from banks. When I get them, I file them, and at the end of the year, I consolidate the information. Then I also go through my cancelled checks one by one for each bank account (to see whether any of them qualify for a deduction) and put them into piles, according to each type of deduction."

This information changes the diagram. Three files (**TAXES, INCOME**, and **DEDUCTIONS**) are introduced, into which the user deposits all the information. The **TAXES** file contains how much tax was paid to which government agency. At this time state taxes, federal taxes, and FICA taxes may have been paid. The **INCOME** file has records of all income received, including income from employment (on one or more W2 Forms), interest statements from banks, and all receipts for consulting and other professional income. The **DEDUCTIONS** file contains receipts for deductible expenses that were paid by cash or through credit cards. They show date, purpose, amount, and payee information. The tax preparation takes the data out of these three files and consolidates it. Our requirements diagram now looks like the one in Figure 3.3. The diagram shows explicitly the interface to the sister system, which balances bank accounts and keeps banking information on all of the accounts. Because this sister system generates information for the tax system but is outside of the tax system, it is considered to be a source in the diagram. We do not make assumptions about the internal working of this system; we assume only that it provides information to the tax system through its **CHECKS** file. This **CHECKS** file is important, because it holds information on deductible expenses that were paid by check.

Furthermore, the new diagram shows an explicit data entry/update activity in addition to the tax preparation activity. This resulted from investigating the system boundary at the "user" interface. The user enters information as it becomes available. Because data entry errors are possible, updates are necessary so that errors can be corrected.

We also have more detailed information on data objects. The names of all data objects, what they consist of, and, if necessary, an explanatory remark, are listed in the *data dictionary* in Table 3.1. It shows several levels of data. For example, the data object "Income" can be one of two types: wages or nonwages. Nonwages consists of consulting income or interest income. The data dictionary tries to keep the refinements of a data object together to simplify understanding. All data objects used in Figure 3.3 are listed in the data dictionary in Table 3.1. The example illustrates that there can be different types of data objects, e.g., sorted deductions that range from personal deductions such as medical expenses on schedule A through all types of business expenses for Schedule C. Also, they can have different parts, such as the W2 Form, which has personal information, wages, and taxes paid as constituent parts.

Table 3.1   Data directionary for diagram in Figure 3.3.

Data object	Parts(p)[1]/Options(o)[2]	Explanation
Income	o:wages	Taxable wage income from W2 Form.
	nonwages	Income other than wages.
Nonwages	o:intrst	Interest income from savings accts.
	consulting	Income from professional activities.
W2	p:wages	
	personal info	All personal information on W2 Form.
	taxes paid	State, federal, and FICA tax payments.
	FICA wages	Social security wages as shown on W2.
Taxes paid	p:State taxes paid	Amount and state for which taxes were paid.
	Fed taxes paid	Amount of federal tax paid for given W2 Form.
	FICA taxes paid	Withholdings for social security.
Deductions	o:noncheck deds	Deductions with cash or credit card receipts.
	check deds	Deductions where receipt is cancelled check.
Sorted deds	o:pers ded	Deductions for Schedule A.
	bus exps	Deductions for Schedule C.
Checks	o:check deds	See above.
	nondeds	Cancelled checks which do not represent receipts for deductions.
Federal forms	p:1040	Entire data object consists of all forms necessary to file federal tax return for client.
	A	
	B	Names of schedules and forms are the parts of the data object.
	C	
	SE	
State j forms	p:state1040j	State version of 1040 for state j. ($j = 1, \ldots, k$).
	CRj	Form to claim tax credit for out of state taxes.
	state j A	State versions of federal forms and schedules. Varies between states.
	state j B	
	state j C	
	state i forms	When out of state tax credit is claimed, state j often requires copies of the other states' returns (all i not equal to j).

[1]parts (p) specifies parts of a data object (i.e., W2 consists of wages and personal information and taxes paid).
[2]options (o) indicates that there are variations in a data object (e.g., income may consist of wages alone, nonwages alone, or both wages and nonwages. Wages and nonwages are the two types of income).

Table 3.2 shows all the file names in alphabetical order with explanations for what type of data object the file contains. Currently, the descriptions are in informal English, but as refinement proceeds, we will see increasing formality. The files in the diagram di-

Table 3.2 File explanations for diagram in Figure 3.3.

Filename	Content description
Checks File	This file contains all cancelled checks ordered by account from all banks. Each check carries bank ID, check number, date, amount, purpose, and payee information. Checks are arranged in order of increasing check numbers within a bank's account.
Deductions File	This file contains all receipts for deductions that do not involve cancelled checks. The receipts show date, purpose, amount, and payee information. They may be cash receipts or credit card receipts. They are ordered according to minor deduction category (e.g., medical expenses).
Income File	This file contains all receipts for income received, i.e., all W2 forms, all interest statements from banks with an indication whether it is taxable, and all receipts for consulting and other professional income. All income shows its source and the extent to which it is tax deferable, nontaxable, or fully taxable by federal or state law. The receipts are ordered by income category, i.e., wages, interest, consulting.
Taxes File	This file contains information on how much tax was paid to which government agency (state taxes, federal taxes, FICA). It is ordered by tax category and shows which employer deducted how much by what date. Since no estimated tax is paid, no records for that purpose are kept.

rectly represent the actual files (or shoeboxes) that the user manipulates. Their contents are explained in user terms.

Like the data objects and files, we should also explain the activities of Figure 3.3 (when they are not self-evident) in a list. We use descriptions from the problem statement and augment them with the new information. Table 3.3 provides a list of activity explanations. Tax data-entry/update, for example, is an activity that includes putting the data objects into files, editing the files and extracting information from data objects. The "sort" activity sorts all types of income, tax, and deduction information. When sorting deductions, the activity uses records from the deduction receipts file and the check entries (which represent deductions) from the check file. Sorting is done according to the deduction categories for personal deductions and business expenses.

This is an example of an abstraction and a refinement: sorting can be refined into sorting for deduction, sorting for income, and sorting for taxes. Sorting is an activity that is common to all three activities, varying only in the data objects that are sorted. Thus, sorting is an abstraction. To improve the diagram, we must show similar action principles as units of activity together. We can do this by incorporating activity 3 (one type of sorting) within activity 4, which includes the rest of the sorting. We will call it "activity 4'." The sorted results are used as inputs for preparing the forms.

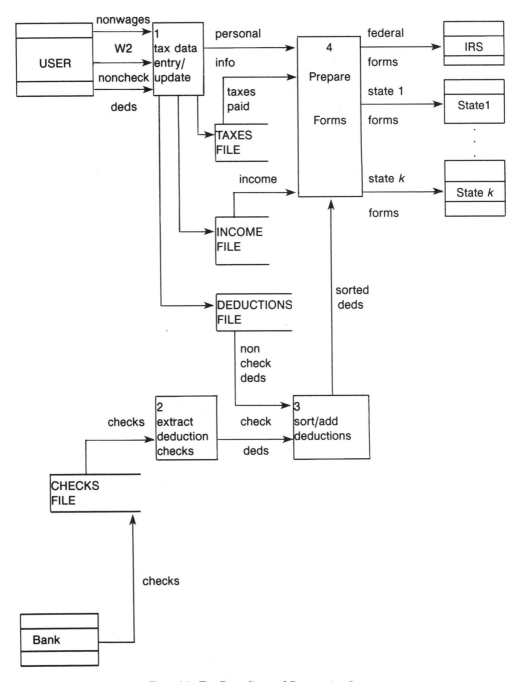

Figure 3.3 Tax Recording and Preparation System.

Table 3.3 Activity descriptions for diagram in Figure 3.3.

#	Activity	Description
1	Tax data entry/update	The "shoebox" is taken and all information that is tax relevant is ordered and put into files for income, deductions, and taxes. Because some of the physical receipts have information that needs to be put in more than one filing category, separate sheets of paper with duplicate information must be made out. This is the case when tax information is taken from the W2 Form and put into the tax file or when income information from the W2 Form is filed in the income file. Personal information that is needed to initialize the tax forms is passed on. Cross-checks and correction of errors is done.
2	Extract deduction checks	This activity goes through the cancelled checks, bank by bank, and passes along every cancelled check that represents a deductible expense.
3	Sort and add deductions	Cancelled checks and other receipts for deductible expenses are sorted into minor categories and put into little piles. Totals are computed.
4	Prepare forms	This activity uses the ordered and sorted information, tallies up totals in all categories, and puts the information on the proper line(s) of the tax form(s). Consistency checks are performed, and when information is missing, it is requested. Tallies and detail information on them are produced for record-keeping purposes.

Preparing the various forms is another possible refinement. Before we do that, however, we should determine whether any of the forms have information and subactivities in common. Some of them do, because the first part of most forms involves filling in personal information such as name and social security number. This is a separate activity, common to all forms that require personal information. We will call these subactivities, "Heading 1040," "Heading Schedule A," etc. In summary, "activity 4" is refined into three sections:

4.1. Sorting activities (includes module 3),

4.2. Heading preparation, and

4.3. Forms compilation.

Figure 3.4 shows the refinement of the sorting activity (4.1). The refinement activities for sorting are as follows:

4.1.1.   Sort and/add taxes paid,

4.1.2.   Sort and/add incomes, and

4.1.3.   Sort and/add deduction types.

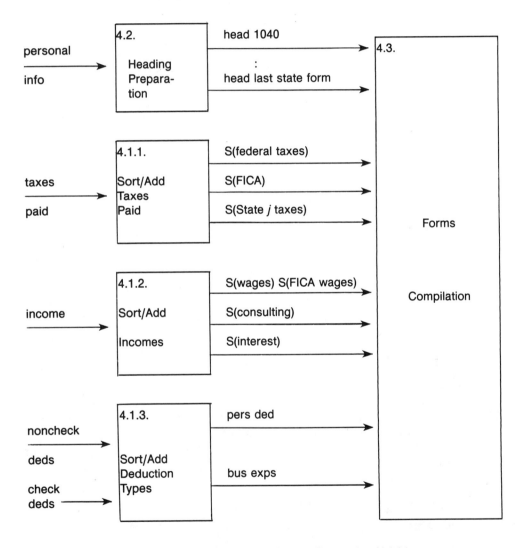

Figure 3.4 Refinement of Sort and Forms Preparation Activities.

The forms compilation module also files the information, summary, and detail in the forms and detail files for the various forms in question. The refinement of the activity also resulted in intermediate data objects, which are the result of performing these activities. Table 3.4 lists those newly generated data objects and refinements of previous ones not contained in Table 3.1. We included details on the heading information for

Table 3.4 Data object refinement for Figure 3.4.

Data Object	parts(p)/options(o)	
personal ded	(o) medical	Medical, dental, drugs.
	(o) taxes A	Deductable taxes like state, local, real estate etc. taxes paid.
	(o) interest exp	Interest paid on mortgages, etc.
	(o) contributions	Contributions to tax deductible causes.
	(o) casualty/theft	Loss through theft.
	(o) misc. ded	Union dues, tax return prep and other allowable deductions.
head 1040	(p) name	Name of user.
	(p) ssn	Social security number.
	(p) address	Address of user.
	(p) marital status	Single, divorced, widowed, etc.
	(p) exceptions	Number of exceptions to be claimed.
	(o) spouse	Name of spouse.
	(o) ssn-spouse	Social security number of spouse.
head last state		State version of the 1040 Form for last state for which a return has to be filed.
S(federal taxes)		Sum of federal taxes paid. This is the sum of income tax and FICA tax paid from all W2 Forms.
S(FICA)		Sum of FICA taxes paid from all W2 Forms.
S(FICA wages)		Total social security wages from W2 Forms.
S(state j taxes)		Sum of all taxes which have been paid to state j
S(wages)		Sum of wages from all W2 Forms.
S(consulting)		Sum of all consulting and self-employment income.
S(interest)		Sum of all interest income.
noncheck deds	(p) ded type	Determines which form the deduction will go on.
	(p) amount	$ amount
	(p) explanation	Accounting information.
check deds	(p) ded type	Same as above.
	(p) amount	Same as above.
	(p) explanation	Same as above.
	(p) bank info	Bank ID, check no., etc.
ded type	(o) bus ded	Ded is for business (Schedule C).
	(o) pers ded	Ded is personal (Schedule A).

Form 1040 only. Details for the headings of the other forms are similar and can be derived by looking at the forms to see what personal information they require. Usually only name and social security number are required. The new information in Table 3.4 is also part of the data dictionary.

Some of the new data objects result from rearranging information (parts of other data objects); e.g., part of the heading information comes from W2 Forms: *sorted deds* results from rearranging deductions according to their *ded type* (a part of the data objects, *non-check deds*, and *check deds*). The *ded type* data object determines the type of *sorted deds: pers ded* or *bus exps*. We disassembled one data object into its parts and reassembled a new data object that is necessary for another activity.

Figure 3.4 does not show any files into which detail information is put. This is done to keep the figure simpler and to concentrate on the decomposition aspect of requirements analysis. The reader is invited to augment the diagram to show which files would hold detail and summary information.

Figure 3.5 shows the next step, refinement of forms compilation (4.3.) into one activity per form to be filled out, i.e.,

4.3.1.   1040 compilation

4.3.2.   (Schedule) A

4.3.3.   (Schedule) B

4.3.4.   (Schedule) C

4.3.5.   (Schedule) SE

4.3.6.   state 1040 (e.g., IL1040)

:

:

4.3.*   last state form to be filled out

4.3.20.   Print returns/detail

Some data objects that were newly created through refined activities are given in Table 3.5 and represent intermediate data objects. In this example, they are part of the *federal form* or *state j form* data object.

The information is generated by one activity and is necessary as input to another. The tax forms are data objects, too, and therefore, must be described also. For brevity, we will define only Schedule A (Table 3.6). The items in the middle column still reflect subcategories and may be refined until they become a line-by-line description of the form or schedule. Table 3.7 explains the files used in Figure 3.5.

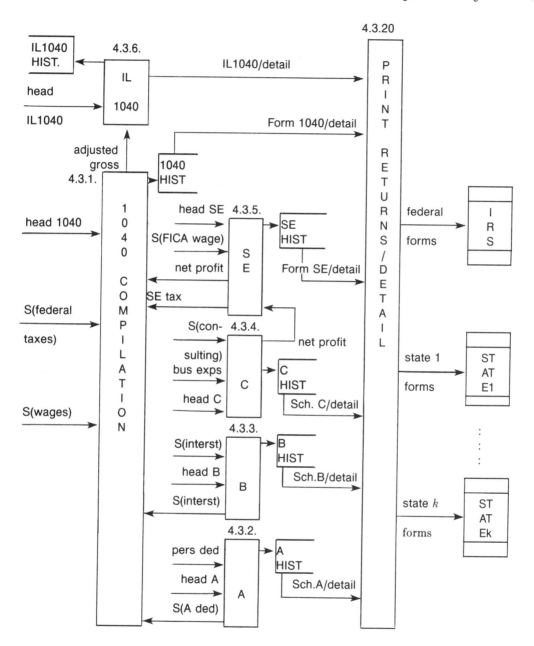

Figure 3.5 Refinement of Forms Compilation.

Table 3.5 Newly created data objects.

Data Object	Explanation
adjusted gross	Adjusted gross income. Sum of all income types minus all deductions.
net profit	Consulting income after business deductions.
SE tax	Self-employment tax from Form SE.
S(A ded)	Sum of deduction from Schedule A, last line.
IL1040/detail	All necessary information in proper order to fill in IL1040 and/or all detail information on summary lines of IL1040.
Form 1040/detail	All information necessary in proper order to fill in 1040, and/or all detail information on summary information on 1040.
Form SE/detail	All necessary information necessary in proper order to fill in SE, and/or all detail information on summary information on SE.
Sch. C/detail	All necessary information necessary in proper order to fill in C and/or all detail information on summary information on C.
Sch. B/detail	All necessary information necessary in proper order to fill in B and/or all detail information on summary information on B.
Sch. A/detail	All necessary information necessary in proper order to fill in A and/or all detail information on summary information on A.

Table 3.6 Schedule A data object (Sch. A/detail).

Data object	Parts(p)/Options(o)	Explanations
Sch. A/detail	(o) Sched. A	All necessary information to fill in Schedule A.
	(o) A detail	Detailed information on how summary information on any given line of A is composed (e.g., a list of medical expenses that make up the total medical expenses).
Sched. A	(p) Head A	Name, ssn.
	(p) medical	Medical, dental, drugs.
	(p) taxes A	State, local, real estate, etc., paid.
	(p) interest exp	Mortgage, etc.
	(p) contributions	to eligible causes.
	(p) casualty/theft	Summary and Form 4684.
	(p) misc ded	Union dues, etc..
	(p) summary	Total deductions, standard ded, Total Schedule A ded.

None of the activities have a data object flowing to more than one other activity. Likewise, data are consolidated through activities; they do not merge on their own account. For example, the heading for a particular schedule and the rest of the information that goes on that schedule are outputs from two different activities and cannot be joined into one data object. Joining is an activity in its own right and must be drawn as an activity

Table 3.7 File explanations for diagram in Figure 3.5.

File Name	Content Description
IL1040 HIST	Contains all information needed to print IL1040 form and any detail list of items for it.
1040 HIST	Contains all information needed to print 1040 form and any detail list of items for it.
SE HIST	Contains all information needed to print SE form and any detail list of items for it.
C HIST	Contains all information needed to print C form and any detail list of items for it.
B HIST	Contains all information needed to print B form and any detail list of items for it.
A HIST	Contains all information needed to print A form and any detail list of items for it.

box for which both data objects are inputs. However, we can have more than one data object flow between two units of activity, and data in a file can be shared by more than one activity.

The data objects defined in the data dictionary may be elements (taxes paid on W2 Form) or collections of information (the tax return). Data objects can have parts that are present more than once (e.g., medical deductions) or are optional (there might not be any medical deductions). When we named the data objects, we used names that appear on the tax forms. Descriptive names make the data dictionary more understandable. Names should describe the data object or what facts are known about it. The explanatory section of the data dictionary describes the object in more detail.

The example analysis started with defining and naming the data objects and then asked what to do with them. A name for a data object may be unavailable or very vague, which usually indicates that the analyst does not know enough about it yet and must find out more before proceeding.

The finished set of requirements diagrams shows how data flows between activities. As mentioned earlier, the diagram does *not* show flow of control and does not describe conditions that cause actions to be performed (or not to be performed, as the case may be).

Problems and Questions

1.   Develop a functional requirements diagram, data dictionary, and file definitions for the sister system that balances and manages bank accounts.

2.   Develop a functional requirements diagram, data dictionary, and file definitions for a system that keeps track of a professional's investments during the year. It should interface with the tax preparation system.

3.   Develop a functional requirements diagram, data dictionary, and file definitions for the doctor's office of Chapter 2.

4.   As further extensions and refinement levels to the tax preparation system, add diagrams and data objects that describe how Schedules B and C are handled.

3.4. Analyzing Requirements Diagrams

There are six reasons for a requirements diagram to show how the user prepares a tax return.

First, and most importantly, it helps us to understand how the tax preparation process works.

Secondly, uncovering the underlying structure of the system aids further requirements analysis. We decomposed the system through a combination of refinement and abstraction steps into smaller subsystems, which are more easily understood.

Third, we can now examine the physical requirements diagram to see if it processes data effectively and efficiently and decide on possible improvements. In the tax preparation system, a statement said that deduction receipts come in several flavors: cash, credit card, and checks. But, the user's description noted that only the cancelled checks are related to an accounting system (for bank accounts). Conceptually, the credit card accounts can be managed the same way, with their own file or set of files. Even cash receipts can be entered into a file of their own. Processing the cash receipts in the sister system "cash box" is simply a subset of the tasks of the sister systems bank and credit cards. Looking at the related systems this way results in conceptual integrity and uniformity and in a simpler overall system. For instance we can get rid of the (artificial) distinction of check versus noncheck deductions. This distinction arose because checks are physically different from other receipts for deductions. The physical requirements diagram describes the system as is. Therefore, physically different data objects are different data objects in the diagram.

The physical requirements diagram, which describes the people, documents, and surrounding organization with their physical characteristics, is a useful stepping stone towards deriving the abstract requirements diagram. The latter tends to be more parsimonious: it will only keep the information and the indispensable parts of the data objects, regardless of what is currently being exchanged between people (and their activities). It strips the personal aspects from the procedural ones and concentrates on what is done, not on who does it. It proceeds from actual data files and objects to abstract ones, by analyzing usage patterns (e.g., all deduction types have the same processing in common, i.e., sorting into deduction categories). Superfluous data parts are stripped so that the minimal necessary data are exchanged between activities. Only those parts of the physical data objects that are eventually read by some other activity are kept in files.

For example, the information on a check (and consequently in the checking account file), includes the bank, check number, payee, amount, date, and whether it is relevant for tax purposes and, if so, for what type of deduction. The tax preparation needs only the deduction type and amount. Should we therefore keep only that information inside the tax system? Is there ever a situation when more is useful or required?

Yes. When a state or federal IRS asks for clarification or orders an audit, then it helps to have a list of individual items that together compose the total deduction amount in a particular category. We need information on where to find the receipt, which tells us three things. First, the physical requirements diagram was incomplete, because the sinks that are given as system boundaries have not been examined properly. Second, we have successfully used the abstraction process for quality control. Finally, we need all that information to locate the physical receipt. The reader may want to augment the requirements diagrams to include the necessary changes.

The fourth reason for a requirement diagram is that it allows us to check for consistency. Checking for completeness was already done as a side effect in the third example. To check for consistency, we will focus on the data flow and ensure the following:

(a)   All refinements are consistent with their immediately superordinate level. The inputs to refined activities should be (parts of the) inputs to the next higher level. There should be no unexplained data objects.

(b)   There are no data flows between activities of different subsystems that are not existent on the higher level. If two activities did not have data flows between them, neither can their refinements. Otherwise they are inconsistent with their higher level. Conversely, data flows cannot disappear in a refinement.

(c)   There are no "instantaneous" data generations for nonsources. To verify this we must look at the activity description and see whether the "new" data object is a result of processing the input data objects.

(d)   Data must not disappear without good cause. Good cause means that data were modified or used for modification of a data object. Again, we must study the activity description. If the data "disappeared," and the activity is not a sink, we must ask whether that particular data object was superfluous to begin with; the activity did not need it.

The fifth reason is that the requirements diagram can be used to examine the boundaries of the system and its interfaces with sister systems. Will these interfaces pose constraints that we have not yet integrated into the requirements diagram? Will they pose constraints based on the data objects that constitute the data interface? Will it affect the processing of information?

In the requirements diagram for the tax system, the file of cancelled checks is such an entity. Because it has to fulfill needs (constraints) of both the banking system and the tax system, a check entry has parts that are needed for tax preparation but not checkbook balancing and vice versa. This requires separating the tax-relevant checks from the others and constitutes an "interface activity" that would not be necessary if there was no interface with the bank sister system. Why must it interface with that system? The answer is that balancing accounts is another automation objective (so far unrealized). The answer to this question clarifies another objective by using the requirements diagram as a starting point. The answer to "Do we have to implement that, too?" when applied to sister systems and interfaces to them, will provide information on the scope of the problem and on requirements for its solution.

Finally, we can also use the requirements diagram and its structure to assess the cost-effectiveness of subsystems, which gives us an opportunity for budgeting and scheduling between activities, at least on a comparative basis. Also it may be used to assess how much benefit, if any, the automation of a given subsystem will provide. Knowing this fact we can establish priorities and absolute requirements for the functionality of the system.

The tax record keeping and tax preparation system are an example of this. There are two parts: tax record keeping and actual tax preparation. Without records, we cannot prepare taxes. However, record keeping will only marginally improve tax preparation. When tax preparation is a feature of the system, the following tedious and error-prone tasks are supported:

▶ sort and merge all the information,

▶ compute the correct totals,

▶ cross reference items automatically (who has never copied entries from one form to another incorrectly?), and

▶ back reference when we must know the constituent parts of the totals in their various categories.

The last two are especially helpful, if we want understandable (and auditable) records.

From the five categories outlined above, we can ask questions about the subsystems, about their activities, and about interfaces between the system and its sister systems. In this way, we can establish priorities and constraints and use them to rank the effectiveness of the various system parts and their importance.

3.5. Requirements Diagrams for the Plagiarism Detector

Let us take the second example from the previous chapter and list all information currently known about the "user." There is more than one user, namely the graders, the instructor, and the students. The students provide programs (with student ID and assignment number), and the graders and the instructor provide grades. Information about the students and the assignment is entered into files. Programs are analyzed and compared with other programs for the same assignment. These results are kept in files. Records, including the grade for the assignment, are kept in a student file. Figure 3.6 shows the top level of the requirements diagram. Note that the grader box is neither a

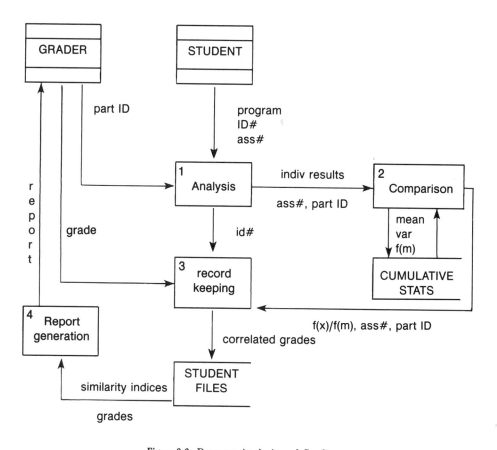

Figure 3.6 Program Analysis and Grading.

sink nor a destination, because it sends and receives data. However, because it is not an activity within the system, it is drawn as a double-banded box.

There are four major activities:

1. analysis (of individual programs or parts),

2. comparison (of individual analysis results with other students' work with an update of cumulative results),

3. record keeping (where grades are associated with student ID, assignment number, and similarity indices to keep a record of suspicious behavior and to indicate which other students' work the assignment resembles), and

4. report preparation.

Data include:

1. programs;

2. identifying keys for student, program, and the program part that was or is to be analyzed;

3. analysis results $(n_1, n_2, N_1, N_2, f(x))$ for the individual program or program part;

4. cumulative results $(CM, f(m))$;

5. correlation sets, i.e., those objects to which the analyzed object is most similar. (This will probably be a sequence of the form {ID , prog, part ID, f(x)}, where the first part indicates the student work that is currently being analyzed. This data is needed in order to keep a record of suspicious behavior and to assess the predictive quality of the method for the graders. For example, there may be several students who have close similarity indices, even though further analysis of the program shows that their assignments are rather dissimilar. It is useful to keep this information around.);

6. grades; and

7. student records, which now may include data 5 and 6. Depending on the set-up for the course, other information about the student may be included, such as exam grades, homework grades, etc.

At this point several fuzzy areas at the boundaries have emerged:

▶ the organization and the information in the student file, which contains more information than analysis results and grades and

▶ the role of the grader (user). Just how much will they interact with the system? With each other?

Because the method for analysis has its shortcomings, the expert must provide an additional interpretation of analysis results in order to guide the analysis. Indicating the parts of the program and sets of programs to be analyzed is one area that needs further exploring. How much must the grader do, how much will the system do? The answers depend on the sophistication of the analysis and how the results will be used. Several possible alternatives exist (see Chapter 2). They should all be explored to provide an understanding of the possible benefits inherent in the alternatives and to clarify the system boundaries.

One additional feature would probably be most welcome, namely an interface with student records so, for further reference, pertinent summaries of analysis results can be kept with a student's grades. Another feature results from the limitations of the analysis method: keeping and managing a similarity index history with grader evaluation. This would help to see, over time, which problems the system runs into as it is used and what certain similarity indices mean at the semantic level. This can be a very valuable source of information for further system improvement. Note that this goes beyond grading and addresses the meta level of the analysis of the method itself. It could not easily be done manually.

So far, we have given answers to questions about inputs to and outputs from the system, who provides or receives them, what the activities are, etc. We must still ask further boundary and scope questions and the ranking questions. Here are some examples of these questions:

▶ Do the graders need or keep records on whether students have previously tried to "copy" from one another? If so, do the graders write down which students are involved so that they may compare for undesired future cooperation in homework? Who has or should have access to that information?

▶ Are the analysis results kept with the class records? Are they attached to the grades?

▶ Do the class records contain more than the program grades and analysis results? What else do they contain? Where does this information come from? From whom must it be protected?

▶ Are there any shortcomings to the system besides those inherent in the analysis method? Who deals with these shortcomings? How? Is the system supposed to help? How? How important is that?

▶ Which of the activities and features should be automated, and how important is that? Why? What would be gained from it?

▶ What is the most inadequate part of the current system? Which feature or activity would help most?

When all these questions have been answered, we will be ready to draw a detailed abstract functional requirements diagram (which the reader may attempt as an exercise). Now there is enough starting information to begin the definition and analysis of the qualitative requirements.

Problems and Questions

1. Answer the open questions for the program analyzer (give reasons why your assumptions are valid) and finish the detailed requirements diagram.

2. Would the requirements diagram change if we had a system

▶ for more than one course?

▶ for more than one language?

▶ that can also support the analysis of output?

▶ If you think it will change, show how and where. Otherwise explain why it wouldn't change.

3.6. Alternative Methods to Derive Functional Requirements

Requirements diagrams with their data dictionaries are only one way to write functional requirements. They use graphics and tabular representation to illustrate how the system will work. They are static in the sense that we cannot execute them like a program. An alternative method would be to describe the functions of the system in English or another human language that users and developers understand. Sometimes a mathematical description of a system's functions is possible. We find some of that in the functional description of the program analysis and plagiarism detection example. As long as the set of methods and the means of expressing functional characteristics complement each other and cover the realm of functional requirements, it may be advantageous to use several methods in combination. In this section, we will describe two techniques, the previously mentioned PSL/PSA [Teic77] and Warnier-Orr diagrams [Orr77], to illustrate other ways to describe aspects of functional requirements.

For a concise description of the relationship between data objects and the functions that operate on them, we may consider PSL/PSA (a technique with automated tool support). PSL (*Problem Statement Language*) may be used to express a system's functional behavior and its performance requirements. PSL has language constructs to define objects and their attributes as well as functional relationships between objects. Hierarchical interdependencies between levels of refinement may be described. For every activity (process), the data used and the data generated may be described. This language helps us to write the three types of information that a good technique for functional requirements must describe: activities, their data, and their interrelationships. Statements in PSL are subsequently checked for errors by PSA (*Problem Statement Analyzer*). Inconsistencies and some missing object, activity, or relationship declarations may be found and pointed out to the user. Because it is a general system, it does not require a specific methodology.

PSL is a simple, keyword-oriented language. Its syntax is easy to learn and to analyze. Table 3.8 gives the main language features. With this language we can define activities and determine where they fit within the system's structure. The previous technique implied structure through its notation for activities and subactivities. Hierarchy and interface information were never explicitly described in one place. In PSL, each activity also explicitly states which major data objects (files) it is creating and which it is using as input. This way of describing a system emphasizes the hierarchical structure of the system more than the requirements diagrams did and may be used to complement them.

Table 3.8 Syntax of PSL.

Statement	Meaning
PROCESS ⟨name⟩	Process is defined with identifier ⟨name⟩
DESCRIPTION ⟨text⟩	English language description of what process does.
SUBPARTS ⟨name⟩, ... ⟨name⟩	A list of process names on the next lower level of the hierarchy that the process uses.
PART OF ⟨name⟩	Names parent process in hierarchy.
DERIVES ⟨file⟩	Process generates the set of data with name ⟨file⟩. This may or may not be an actual file.
USING ⟨file⟩	Process uses the set of data named ⟨file⟩ as input.
PROCEDURE ⟨text⟩	Algorithmic description of how process accomplishes task. This is filled in during a later phase

The tax preparation system is an example. We could describe activity 4 in PSL (as in Table 3.9) by using the information from Table 3.3 and Figures 3.3 and 3.4.

Table 3.9 PSL description of activity 4 (prepare tax forms).

PROCESS	prepare_forms
DESCRIPTION	This activity uses the tax relevant information, orders and sorts it, tallies totals in all categories, and puts the information on the proper line(s) of the tax form(s). Consistency checks are performed; when information is missing, it is requested. Tallies and detail information on the tallies are produced for record-keeping purposes.
SUBPARTS	sorting_activities, heading_preparation, forms_compilation
PART OF	taxrecording_and_preparation_system
DERIVES	IL1040_HIST, 1040_HIST, SE_HIST, C_HIST, B_HIST, A_HIST
USING	deduction_file, income_file, taxes_file

Furthermore, we could define activity 4.1. (called "sorting activities" in Figure 3.4) as in Table 3.10.

Table 3.10 PSL statement of activity 4.1 (sorting activities).

PROCESS	sorting_activities
DESCRIPTION	All tax relevant items are sorted into major and detail categories and put into piles. Totals are computed.
SUBPARTS	sort/add_taxes_paid, sort/add_incomes, sort/add_deduction_types
PART OF	prepare_forms
DERIVES	sorted/tallied_taxes, sorted/tallied_income, sorted/tallied_deductions
USING	deductions_file, taxes_file, income_file

Similarly, we can rewrite the requirements diagram of Figure 3.6 for the plagiarism detector and program analyzer in PSL. Table 3.11 shows the diagram on the highest level. We named the top level "program analysis."

Table 3.11 PSL statement of the plagiarism detector (top level).

PROCESS	program_analysis
DESCRIPTION	Analyzes student programs for plagiarism according to Ottenstein technique. Generates reports and computes similarity indices for a history file.
SUBPARTS	analysis, comparison, record keeping, report generation
DERIVES	cumulative_stats, student_files
USING	programs

We are assuming that the programs are in files that indicate student identifiers, assignment number, etc. Since direct user input is not in the files, it was not mentioned in the PSL statement. On a lower level, the activity **report generation** could be defined as in Table 3.12. It assumes that reports are filed as well as printed for the user.

Table 3.12 PSL statement of activity "report generation".

PROCESS	report_generation
DESCRIPTION	Generates all analysis reports, similarity statistic reports, correlations and historical profile reports.
PART OF	program_analysis
DERIVES	reports
USING	student_files

Writing functional requirements in PSL provides automated consistency and completeness checks such as the following:

▶ Are all SUBPARTS to a process defined?

▶ Do all SUBPARTS have a PART OF statement with the proper name of the parent?

▶ Are there processes with no PART OF statement other than the highest level one?

▶ Are files used that are never derived?

▶ Are files derived that are never used?

While automatic checks (through PSA) are possible, and the hierarchical structure of a system is understandably specified, the PSL statements are less capable than the requirements diagrams of illustrating the data flows.

There are other formal techniques that enjoy automated tool support, such as SREM [Davi77] and SADT (a trademark of SofTech, Inc. Waltham, MA [Ross77]. SREM (Software Requirements Engineering Methodology) consists of two parts. First, there is a language RSL (*Requirements Statement Language*). It describes the functional aspects of the system. Second, there is REVS (*Requirement Engineering and Validation System*). It checks whether the system described in RSL is consistent or whether there are contradictions, missing data objects, or unexplained activities. SREM could be used to develop a functional requirements description for the doctor's office (cf. Chapter 2), where the software will be embedded into the larger health care system and has to interface with it and its subsystems. The software system would play an important, but not the most important, part in the doctor's office. It will have a secondary, supporting role. RSL allows us to describe the data objects (data descriptors) and the activities (processing steps). Then we may refine them by decomposing both data and activities. REVS allows us to analyze the requirements statement by simulating aspects of the design and by supporting the user in a feasibility analysis.

SADT (Structured Analysis and Design Technique), although a manual technique may be automated with the proper graphics support. However, its verification must remain mostly manual. SADT lets us draw hierarchically structured diagrams. Boxes show activities (tasks) that are successively refined in the lower levels of the hierarchy. Different sets of arrows between boxes define relationships between activities. For example, the doctor cannot proceed to a diagnosis until the result of the lab test is back or the medication he prescribed has lowered the fever and the temperature has been taken by a nurse. In addition to specifying the relationships among activities, SADT assumes roles and specific responsibilities for members of the development team, including system analysts, system description authors, validation and verification roles (readers and commentators, technical review committee), the manager, the development secretary who keeps the project documents current, and even a teaching role for the SADT technique. SADT emphasizes relationships between system components.

Another technique for writing functional requirements for a system or program is Warnier-Orr diagrams [Orr77]. This diagramming technique is useful to structure both data and activities. It may be used instead of a data dictionary or to complement the requirements diagrams with a clear emphasis of the hierarchical structuring of the activities. Warnier-Orr diagrams are written in columns, where the next column to the right gives the next level of detail for the activities or data in the preceding column. Figure 3.7

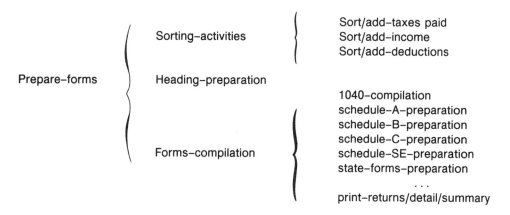

Figure 3.7 Activity Structure for "Prepare Forms."

shows a Warnier-Orr diagram for the PSL statement of Table 3.9, which shows the activity structure of the **prepare forms** activity. Figure 3.8 gives an example of data structuring with Warnier-Orr diagrams for the data object W2 from Table 3.1, which defined data objects for the tax preparation system.

Warnier-Orr diagrams are a good visual representation of data structuring and the refinement process. This refinement process provides the activity structure for a given system. Although a Warnier-Orr diagram does not give the detail of a data dictionary, it is a good complement to it. One problem with using this diagram as a replacement for a data dictionary is that Warnier-Orr diagrams cannot indicate optional versus nonoptional parts of a data object. The advantage of Warnier-Orr diagrams is that the same diagramming technique may be used later during design and implementation to denote program structure and implementation data structure. Instead of activity names, we would see names of procedures and subroutines or design modules. Instead of names from the data dictionary, we may find names of variables, records, files, etc.; depending on the level of detail of the Warnier-Orr diagram, it may be possible to code directly from it.

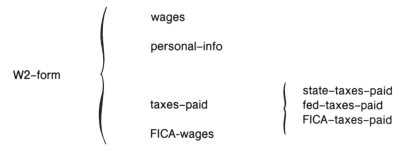

Figure 3.8 Data Object Structuring for W2 Form.

If we rewrite the program analysis process description of Figure 3.6 as a Warnier-Orr diagram, it resembles Figure 3.9. The structure of the analysis input and analysis output are shown in Figure 3.10.

Warnier-Orr diagrams have also been used to describe activities and their associated data flows in one diagram [Zieg83]. The leftmost column indicates the system name, the second column indicates the activities on the next lower level, and the third column describes input for and output from each activity with arrows to other inputs or outputs of the same name. It also indicates which storage medium they come from or go to. A short description of the format of these diagrams is given in Figure 3.11.

The item ⟨**dataname**⟩ may be any data object or file. The items ⟨**where from**⟩ and ⟨**where to**⟩ indicate the medium on which ⟨**dataname**⟩ is stored, or read from or written to. These may be disk, cards, user-input, hard copy, tape, or a named file or a logical device. While this modified Warnier-Orr diagram is very useful for grasping the input-output and processing characteristics, it may become unwieldy when lots of data flows

Figure 3.9 Warnier-Orr Diagram of "Program Analysis."

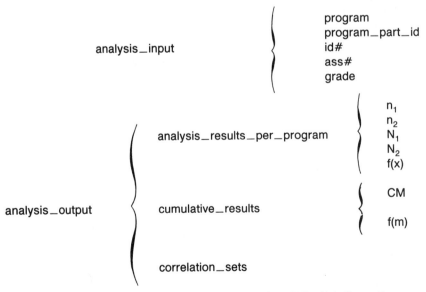

Figure 3.10 Warnier-Orr Diagrams of "Analysis Input" "Analysis Output."

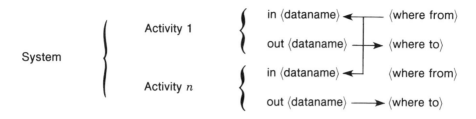

Figure 3.11 Modified Warnier-Orr Diagram.

between many activities. There may not be enough room for all the connecting arcs in the last column, and their multitude may interfere with readability. In principle, however, we may rewrite the requirements diagrams in terms of modified Warnier-Orr diagrams, one per level.

Figure 3.12 shows such a modified Warnier-Orr diagram for the program analysis ex-

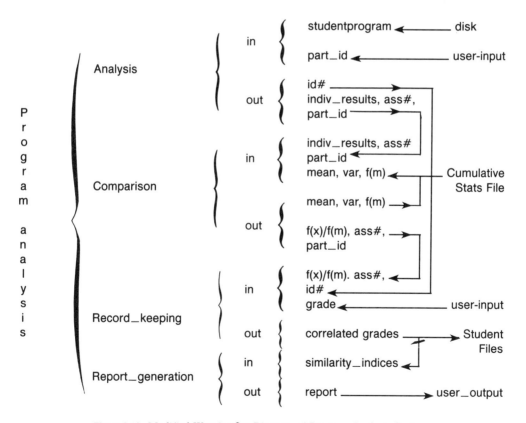

Figure 3.12 Modified Warnier-Orr Diagram of Program Analysis System.

ample. It provides the same information as the requirements diagram of Figure 3.6, except that the data object **studentprogram** was introduced in the modified Warnier-Orr diagram. It is a data object that combines the three data items (program, ID#, ass#) from Figure 3.6. The data objects were consolidated to keep the modified Warnier-Orr diagram simpler and more readable.

Problems and Questions

1.   Rewrite the requirements diagram of Figure 3.5 as a modified Warnier-Orr diagram. Hint: How can you best group and name families of data so that the Warnier-Orr diagram will not become unwieldy? Develop a separate list of explanations for the activities and data objects used in the diagram.

2.   What will the characteristics of a system have to be if you find that

▶   a requirements diagram with data dictionary is most suitable?

▶   a PSL description is best?

▶   a combination of requirements diagram with a data dictionary and a PSL description is most appropriate?

▶   a set of Warnier-Orr diagrams is sufficient?

▶   a functional requirements diagram and a data dictionary with Warnier-Orr diagrams is best?

Explain your choices.

3.   Is there a situation in which a combination of PSL and Warnier-Orr diagrams would give you more important information than one of them alone? Which? If not, why not?

4.   Under what conditions would you use modified Warnier-Orr diagrams? How will your answers to exercise 3 change if we substitute modified Warnier-Orr for Warnier-Orr?

3.7. Summary

This chapter described collection and analysis of functional requirements. We presented a range of techniques from prose to formal methods. Most of the chapter dealt with functional requirements diagrams, data dictionaries, and supplementary English prose descriptions for activities and data. This is an example of a diagramming technique that covers all aspects of functional requirements. Two other techniques were presented: PSL and Warnier-Orr diagrams.

Although this list of techniques is not comprehensive, the techniques address different aspects of developing and expressing functional requirements; thus, they complement each other nicely. Collectively, they provide good coverage of available techniques and the types of information that ought to be collected. Additionally, their principles are easy to learn (a definite plus).

The following are the methods presented and their characteristics:

1. **Requirements diagrams and data dictionary**.   We would use them when an understanding of the processes and the data that describe functional behavior of a system is important. Requirements diagrams and the data dictionary work well with data or object-oriented problems, such as the tax preparation system. The technique is less appropriate for the program analysis system. It works well for systems that process data, because it emphasizes processes and the data flow between them.

2. **PSL**.   We would use PSL if the structure of the processes and the relationships between processes and data are important (while processes and data are known). The focus in this technique is on interaction and interfaces between processes. This technique is appropriate for a system with a complex structure that is very important but not readily observable and when interfaces are crucial. PSL works well in this case because it highlights the structure of processes and the interfaces and dependencies between them. PSL/PSA provides automated checking for completeness and consistency of structure and interface information.

3. **Warnier-Orr diagrams**.   They describe data structuring and process refinement and are useful when concise information of this type is desired. Warnier-Orr diagrams are used when the functional requirements definition must describe all levels of data in one diagram (name only) and when all constituent levels of a process must be shown in one diagram (name only). Besides concise information about these aspects of structure, they have the advantage that the same diagramming technique can be used in several phases. They emphasize structuring and refinement information in concise diagrams without the extra explanatory information that functional diagrams and data dictionaries would provide.

The modified Warnier-Orr diagrams are applicable in the same situations and for the same reasons. In addition, they are useful when the analyst wants to describe a limited but important amount of input/output data for activities. However, the amount of such data must be limited; otherwise, the diagram will become too cluttered. Alternatively, we may have a situation where only important I/O data and connections between activities must be described concisely. Thus, modified Warnier-Orr diagrams are advantageous when the structure of processes and data is important and a limited amount of interfaces between processes exists and when this information must be represented in a concise form without additional information on what the data and the processes mean.

Other methods are provided by [Zieg83] and [Myer75]. Although presenting them would make this chapter more comprehensive in terms of a survey of techniques, the alternate techniques do not describe fundamentally different aspects of functional requirements when compared to the techniques chosen for presentation.

This chapter is complemented by the next one on qualitative requirements and the requirements analysis process. Together they constitute the full requirements collection and analysis process that is known as the requirements phase.

► 4

Qualitative
Requirements

4.1. Overview

Until now, development and discussion of requirements centered around the functions required by the proposed system or program. Such requirements are called functional requirements. They are used to describe the functionality of the new system. A functionality description details the desired functions of the new system and the possible degrees of functionality, if there are options. In addition to functional requirements, others describe qualities beyond the new software's functions. These are qualitative requirements. This chapter describes a checklist of potential software product qualities, constraints, and benefits associated with a planned project. The checklist serves as a frame of reference for requirements analysis and the trade-offs that often must be made with regard to costs and benefits.

The discussion starts with a description of the requirements checklist (Section 4.2.). Those requirements that describe product capabilities are explained in Section 4.3., and a discussion of constraints and benefits for a software product follows (Section 4.4.). These sections present the task from the viewpoint that users either derive requirements themselves or may be interviewed for the necessary information. Section 4.5. gives guidelines for situations where this is not the case.

Section 4.6. explains how to analyze requirements and establish technical feasibility for a software project. First, requirements, constraints, and benefits are prioritized and ranked. This information drives trade-offs that may become necessary for a feasible product. A benefits analysis compares pairs of requirements and benefits to see whether they are consistent and realistic. Then we explain a procedure to investigate technical feasibility for all functional and quality requirements, and we come up with feasible development options. This step uses ranking information and performs trade-offs. It also provides complexity and size information that management uses for cost and effort estimation.

Section 4.7. describes the deliverable of the requirements phase: the requirements document. Section 4.8. discusses phase testing activities for the requirements document.

Throughout this chapter we will explore further the two major examples: the tax preparation system and the program analyzer. Because the objectives for these two products are different, they are used to illustrate different aspects of requirements analysis.

Qualitative requirements are important because they describe how well the proposed system has to function. Without them, we cannot distinguish between good and bad systems that have the same functions. Quality requirements are also important because they relate to the objectives for the system that make it usable. Lastly, they provide information about user priorities, which is important for trade-offs, feasibility, and benefit analysis. Without collecting and analyzing functional and quality requirements, these analyses cannot be done.

Quality requirements describe in detail the functions the system will perform. Functional requirements (described in the abstract requirements diagram and data dictionary) form the basis for establishing qualitative requirements for all activities and subactivities and all the data objects listed in them. After collecting qualitative requirements, all requirements are analyzed for consistency and technical feasibility, including checking whether required benefits may be achieved. After a successful phase test of the requirements document, the requirements phase ends with freezing the requirements document. Then the specifications phase can start.

Qualitative requirements are collected by the same people who collect functional requirements. Requirements analysis requires knowledge in all areas that must be investigated for feasibility. The analysis may need more than the skills of a requirements or systems analyst. In that case, experts are brought in (e.g., performance or security experts): hardware or software experts determine whether the proposed product is feasible with specific hardware or software; financial analysts investigate cost-effectiveness; market analysts investigate the width of the market window and how long software development may take while remaining marketable.

At the end of this chapter, the reader will know how to collect qualitative requirements and analyze requirements and will have a basic understanding of technical feasibility analysis. The reader will also be familiar with methods to phase test requirements and how to structure a requirements document.

4.2.   Quality Checklist for User Driven Requirements

Qualitative requirements detail how well a system will work in key areas such as performance, storage requirements, generality, responsiveness, maintainability, and development and usage costs. Qualitative requirements also describe the quality of all functions that the new system will have, including an analysis of the levels of quality or sophistication of a useful system. It resolves deficiencies of the current system or manual procedure. All requirements are ranked to reflect the user's priorities for solution alternatives. The ranking may be based on the expected benefit of an alternative. User objectives direct the priorities or rankings of levels of functionality and quality characteristics, expected benefits, and cost.

It is often necessary to trade cost for quality. For example, the degree of sophistication in the user-machine interface is an important issue. There are three types of users: novices, intermittent, and expert users. The relative importance of these user types and the quality of human factors they require guide trade-offs and compromises. Compromising on human factors signifies that the budget is more important than having a three-level user machine interface for the three types of users. Maybe an agreement is made to have just one, probably the one geared towards intermittent users. This may affect other quality areas as well:

1. **User Productivity:**   Novices may not receive the guidance they need, and experts may find the system too awkward for their needs of speed, abbreviations, macros, etc. Both situations can reduce user productivity, often an important benefit.

2. **Performance:**   Potentially, less storage is necessary for faster execution time.

3. **Schedule:**   Only one interface must be implemented, which results in faster development.

4. **Reliability:**   One user machine interface makes the software less complex, so there is less room for making errors.

The functional requirements diagrams and other information collected during user interviews serve as a starting point for developing qualitative requirements. Usually it is easier to analyze requirements for a part of a system than for the whole, because the problem it solves or the function it provides is a smaller one. Because we already have a structured set of subsystems with several levels of refinement, we should use these results of system decomposition to guide us in the requirements collection.

Qualitative requirements may be established by answering a checklist of major items. For examples of such checklists, see [Myer76], [Shne80], [Gilb83], [Horo75], [Brow78], and [Horn83]. Some checklists are arranged as quality characteristic trees; they reflect several levels of quality where some lower level quality factors contribute to a higher level one. Because some of those lists or trees are more extensive than necessary at this stage, the following list (Table 4.1) of hierarchical quality requirements attributes are restricted to what the analyst most likely will need. They may be amended to deal with particular projects and problems. Not all items in this list are equally important for every software development effort, but it is good practice to ask the user whether they are and to ask him in what situations they are not to avoid misunderstanding. Table 4.1

Table 4.1 Requirements checklist.

I.   Product Capabilities
    1. Degree of Functionality
    2. Useability
        2.1. Reliability
        2.2. Performance (Efficiency)
        2.3. Security
        2.4. Human Factors
    3. Intended Use—Generality
        3.1. Extent of Solution
        3.2. Portability
        3.3. Compatibility
    4. Future/Lifetime Expectations
        4.1. Adaptability
        4.2. Maintainability
            Corrective
            Perfective
            Installation
    5. Documentation
II.   Constraints and Benefits
    1. Schedule
    2. Resources
        2.1. Physical Limitations
        2.2. Personnel Limitations
        2.3. Organizational Limitations
        2.4. Budgetary Limitations
    3. Benefits
        3.1. Tangible
        3.2. Intangible

---

is a structured list of the check items. The items are described in detail in the next two sections.

4.3. Product Capabilities

4.3.1. Degree of Functionality

If we describe the (abstract) system solution with a requirements diagram and data dictionary, we have a well-defined starting point for developing functionality constraints. Now we must add information on quality and its value. For each major function, we try to determine the possible levels of sophistication and quality. Then we ask how much each level is worth to the user? How important is it to him to have it automated? Requirements diagrams and the data dictionary are a structured outline for asking questions about the desired quality of the proposed system. How important is it to automate activity x, data object y? What is the most important aspect of this activity for automation? How useful would it be to automate x, but not y?

These questions elicit ranking information and desired degrees of computerization for the application and its parts. Based on this ranking information, options in functionality and possible versions of the automated system will emerge. To simplify the procedure only three priorities or rankings are suggested:

3—very important, absolutely necessary;

2—important, but not necessary; and

1—purely optional.

Starting out with only three priority levels is simpler and often clearer. More priority levels tend to be confusing rather than helpful. If greater discriminatory power is necessary, we can fine tune one of these levels (most probably level 2 or 1). This will only be needed if we have to distinguish between proposed or possible versions.

The result of this ranking is a set of versions or alternatives for the proposed automated system. These versions are ranked according to user priorities. The "core" functionality or "minimal" system would have the highest ranking, and more features would be added for the more extended versions of the system.

For example, in the program analysis system (PAS) from the previous section, we may assume the user ranks options as follows:

Activity 1: Analysis
　　　3: implementation of basic analysis algorithm for whole programs, user-specified program parts
　　　2: impurities of type one

1: other types of impurities, automatic selection of program parts, computerized output analysis

Activity 2: *Comparison*

3: computation of statistics such as means, variances, covariance matrix CM, $f(x)/f(m)$ as a similarity measure by program and program part

2: comparison with similarity indices in the past

1: same as 2 but for more than one course

Activity 3: *Record Keeping*

3: name, SSN, class number, grade, similarity index with back reference to other similarity indices for the same assignment and whether cheating in fact occurred (only programming assignments)

2: names of students with highest similarity to each other's assignment, compatibility with gradebook, which includes nonprogramming assignments also

1: cross-references to other courses, format compatible with sister systems, such as grade history of student, program of study, disciplinary history

Activity 4: *Report Generation*

3: simple histograms, cumulative data in table form, reports as summary or by student reports, interactive and hard copy

2: graphs

1: fancy output, such as colors, graphics, multiple figures on the screen, etc.

This list contains 3 * 3 * 3 * 3 = 81 possible versions. Table 4.2 lists only a fraction of them. The first is the minimal version; the last is the maximal one. In practice, evaluat-

Table 4.2 Some potential versions according to functionality priorities.

Version	Priorities by Activity				
#	1	2	3	4	
1	3	3	3	3	minimal version
2	3	2	3	3	
3	3	2	2	3	
4	3	2	2	2	
5	3	1	1	2	
6	3	1	1	1	
7	2	3	3	3	
81	1	1	1	1	maximal version

ing all possible options in detail is impractical. Requirements analysis reduces them to a manageable number, using the relative importance of functional areas, cost, and benefits. The user states which functional and quality areas he is willing to trade for others and how important they are in comparison.

The user of the tax preparation system may have the following priorities: analysis > comparison > record keeping > report generation, where ">" means "more important than." Often the number of potential versions is reduced by the fact that quality levels in one functional area or activity are required to obtain a quality level in another. For instance, level 1 for activity 2 (comparison) is needed for level 1 of activity 3 (record keeping). On the other hand, even a minimally acceptable functionality in the analysis area does not exclude maximum functionality in the others.

This approach works for the tax preparation system (TAP). The user indicated the following priorities for system functionality:

Activity 1:   *Tax data Entry/Update*
  3:   insert, edit capability, short keystrokes, variable format, individual entries
  2:   prompts for missing information, partial totals in categories, organized output
  1:   carry-overs from previous years
Activity 2:   *Extract Deduction Checks*
  3:   only deduction checks, no others.
  2:   all manners of checks, not just tax-relevant ones.
  1:   multiple banks/accounts, compatible with the sister system account balancing.
Activity 3:   *Sort/Add Deductions*
  3:   by type, fixed by user, does not change
  2:   choices of types, partial totals in deduction categories during the year
  1:   multiple years
Activity 4:   *Prepare Forms*
  3:   automate 1040, A, B, C computation, cross-check for inconsistencies, errors, what-if capability, correct format for forms, totals of income, taxes, etc. in categories, also partial accumulations during the year and detail reports
  2:   find optimal way to handle deductions through automatic selection of most advantageous schedules, automatic computation of taxes as opposed to table look-up by user
  1:   multiyear returns, highlighting of items with high audit probability

In this list of requirements, all output for individual activities is described with the activity. Another way of dealing with this is to define a separate requirements category for output. The omission of a report generation activity in the requirements diagram made it difficult to consolidate the output requirements, which indicates that the requirements diagram was not as perfect as it should have been. We must add another functionality area and describe its requirements:

Activity 0:   *Report Generation*

  3:    same format as forms, partially accumulated totals during the year to aid in tax planning, screen and hard copy, detail listing of items in all data categories.

  2:    printing onto the final tax forms

  1:    computerized record keeping according to IRS requirements.

We define versions based on these prioritized user requirements, associate costs and benefits to each version, rank the activities themselves according to the user's preferences, and augment the requirements in the functionality area with those of the remaining quality characteristics. There are less than the potential 3^5 versions, because more quality in activity areas 2,3, and 4 is correlated. Choices for typing deductions into several categories (Activity 3, level 2) are related to suggesting the most advantageous schedule (Activity 2, level 2).

There may be required ways of performing functions, such as a prescribed algorithm or required formats for data. In PAS, the algorithm for basic program analysis is prescribed. In TAP, the format of the schedules (sequencing of data for useful output) is fixed. The IRS also has rules how to keep records by computer.

By now, anything that requires specific ways of processing or assumptions about data objects and files must be known. We may assign priorities to the individual requirements and prioritize versions and options to rank them as mandatory (priority 3) or negotiable (priorities 2, 1).

Accuracy of the solution is part of the functional requirements which is especially important when no cost-effective or practically implementable algorithm exists and approximations or heuristics must suffice. For PAS, the solution is not totally accurate because of possible impurities in the code. What accuracy is required? Is the basic algorithm enough? Or is it mandatory to detect at least impurities of class 1? How about the more difficult ones?

Mathematical software usually needs to specify accuracy requirements. Expert systems are often based on guessing methods or Bayesian analysis. Their level of accuracy or expertise must be specified.

4.3.2. Effectiveness/Usability

This category includes the following subfactors:

▶   Reliability

▶ Performance

▶ Security

▶ Human Factors

The definition of these quality characteristics varies. We will define them in user terms.

4.3.2.1. Reliability

This is the degree to which hardware and software can perform user functions in the presence of hardware and software malfunctioning. Thus, it involves the frequency of failures and how they are dealt with. A reliability requirement may be elicited from the user with the following questions: What should or can happen to your software and your data when the hardware breaks down, when the electricity goes off, etc.? How should the system react when a necessary file does not exist, when there are insufficient access rights to a file, and when the operating system crashes or is brought down?

These questions target possible failures of the environment and how this may affect the software. Few users regard the application software as reliable when hardware or system software faults lose a day's work. Ability of the software to withstand or buffer external failure and the degree of loss of data or loss of computation are important requirements.

In a database system, for example, it is important that no data are lost and that data integrity is not compromised. Either one of these undesirable effects may occur when the operating system goes down (a failure) in the midst of a database update. To preserve the correctness of data in the database and to safeguard data are crucial elements of a database application. This will affect the selection of algorithms and the organization of data for the solution (see [Vand80] for crash-secure database design). Insufficient resources may also cause failures. Running out of storage is a very common fault. If this occurs, is it acceptable to have the program stop and "die"? Or should it stop gracefully, buffering the effect of the fault by closing all files, saving relevant data, reporting back to the user about what happened, making sure that no processing is lost, and *then* stopping?

Application failures violate constraints for proper software operation. Examples of failures within the application are

▶ erroneous use of the system,

▶ running out of capacity within the program, such as table or stack overflows, and

▶ time constraints violation in real-time systems.

The user is not interested in what precise technical problems cause those failure conditions; rather he wants to be sure that internal problems do not bring the application to its knees. How does he expect the system to react in the presence of such failures, and how often may they occur?

An example of a capacity problem that can detract from the reliability and usefulness of a word processor is the following (a true story). The word processor has a maximum number of pages that varies because of internal page organization, and therefore is not known to the user. When a document is full, it is reported to the user when he tries to save the current page. However, because the document is full, the page can no longer be saved, and data loss may occur due to lack of internal capacity. It is hard to imagine that a user would find this acceptable. Unless "no data loss when documents become full" was specified as an explicit requirement, the word processor can *not* be regarded as unreliable because of potential data loss.

Besides capacity problems, functional and logical bugs can make an application unreliable. Because it is a measurable quantity, reliability in this context is usually stated in terms of average number of failures over time, or as mean time between failures (MTBF). This number would only be useful after the fact if we didn't have models to estimate reliability during development. Some of these models are presented in the chapter on metrics. For a book on reliability models see [Musa87].

In summary, when we ask the user questions about reliability requirements, we want to define

▶ what are acceptable consequences of failure;

▶ what is the severity of errors allowed;

▶ what is the frequency of errors allowed (maybe by severity type);

▶ what is the tolerable amount of data loss or loss of computation;

▶ what are the functions required to detect, correct, or tolerate faults; and

▶ what are the requirements for the detection of or recovery from user errors, hardware and supporting software failures.

4.3.2.2. *Product Performance or Efficiency*

Performance constraints occur in several areas:

Response time. This is for interactive systems, and it measures the amount of time from request submission to return of the result on the screen.

Turnaround time. This is a performance index for batch applications, measuring the time from job submission to job completion.

Reaction time. This performance index is used for real-time systems, because one of their most important performance constraints is timely reaction to requests or data.

Units of work per unit of time. This is also known as throughput, but it is usually for the entire computer system not just one application. In transaction processing systems, it is often important to know and state how many transactions need to be completed by the application per unit of time.

Storage requirements. This prescribes the amount of main memory, disk space, or other storage media that is required or, if it is a constraint, that is the upper limit.

Transmission capacity. This is an important performance index for distributed systems, such as networks of workstations with a file server. A requirement for this quantity is derived from the amount of user work that involves access to the file server. Other examples are the amount of work or data transferred between workstations in networks, accesses to remote databases, such as in international airline reservation systems, or in billing systems for national or international companies.

Knowing what affects these performance indicators helps to formulate user-oriented questions. The performance indicators are functions of

▶ workload posed by the new application;

▶ existing workload that uses resources and is often not easily controllable or predictable; and

▶ system specifications for the system on which the application is to run.

To predict possible performance levels accurately, we need to know the characteristics of the input variables, i.e., workloads and system. The analyst must ask about quantity and arrival patterns of work with questions about

▶ the maximum number of work units at a time;

▶ deadlines for getting work done;

▶ volume of data generated/stored/used;

▶ size of the work unit the application will be processing, or size of the problem it is solving, frequency distribution of problem sizes (how often is what size problem solved);

▶ hard versus soft requirements; and

▶ factoring out other workloads.

Here are some questions that cover hard and soft requirements. Is the performance always to be within certain ranges or only a guaranteed fraction of the time, say 80%? If percentages are used, are their meanings explained precisely? What does 80% of the time mean? Does it mean 80% of the time the application is running or that 80% of the transactions submitted are to be handled within the required performance range? Is that range the same for all types of problems or requests the application is processing?

The size of the problem or work unit determines its computational needs; thus, it has an impact on performance. In the case of structural analysis package, the more nodes that the structure must analyze, the longer it will take and the more storage will be necessary. The number of nodes indicates problem size. If the user intends to analyze structures of less than 1,000 nodes, that provides a maximum on computational requirements and resulting performance. If a bigger problem is solved, and the performance is less than optimal, it is not a failure to perform adequately. In the tax application, the number of tax-relevant items and the number of categories for them determines the amount of necessary storage space needed and the time to process the items.

Factoring out the effect of other workloads, the sixth area, makes the requirement more precise. This may be done by qualifying the stated user requirement with a description of the other workload, such as in "80% of the time the response time should be below 5 seconds when the workload on the system is light to medium. Light to medium means less than 30 users logged on and no more than one batch job in the background."

There is a reason for collecting this amount of detailed information. Because the application is not developed yet, it is necessary to model its performance for the types of work it will process. Inputs to this performance model are estimates of resource requirements. They are based on the characteristics of the work units to be processed. For known algorithms, processing needs may be established through an analysis of algorithms. Models are fed with estimates of service times and number of I/O operations and system characteristics, such as processing and transaction speed. Model predictions indicate (roughly) what the resulting performance will be.

4.3.2.3. Security

Security requirements explain what should or should not happen when information that is supposedly private or protected is accidentally or purposefully referenced or destroyed. Operating system or system software failures may cause accidental destruction of user programs or data. This is a reliability problem. A lack of protection against other users who may not even be aware what they are doing may cause such destruction. The problem of accidental destruction is more frequent in applications where data and possibly programs are shared or partially shared between many users.

The user interview asks about areas where users interact or might share data or programs. Who has ownership of data or programs that are shared or mutually accessible? What rights should the owners and the users have to those objects? What happens when someone tries to violate those rights or has insufficient rights? For example, denying access to a file results in an access fault for the user who tries the access; what are acceptable system reactions for that user? What protection will prevent unauthorized access?

Other security requirements specify a degree of safeguarding for data or programs from planned misuse. Planned misuse can include

▶ unauthorized access to data (information that a user is not supposed to have access to, thus violating data privacy);

▶ unauthorized use of programs;

▶ unauthorized data modification (changing and deleting information); and

▶ unauthorized program modification.

Users must specify requirements in these areas, how important they are, and how important on-line versus off-line security is. On-line security includes all automated, computerized procedures, while off-line security encompasses procedures that are not automated. Examples of off-line security measures are locking up the personal computer with its diskettes, locking the computer room, tapes, and manuals that explain how to access private or sensitive material.

4.3.2.4. *Human Factors*

Often requirements in the human factors area say "the system should be easy to use, be user friendly, and be hard to misuse." It is impossible to measure the degree of compliance for this requirement. It is equally hard to assess the effort necessary to build a system that fulfills the user's requirement. What are "good human factors"? "Good" reflects what is good for a specific user community. What is it that the user community expects in terms of user productivity? Productivity is influenced by the following factors:

Training time. The longer it takes to train the user to become productive using a system, the more productive time is wasted. The same is true for relearning. If it is easy to forget how to use the system, then more time will be wasted learning it all over again. What does the user expect?

User performance. User performance measures how clumsy or elegant command language or menus are and indicates whether the user wants shortcuts to do some tasks quickly. During requirements collection we should determine the most important frequent usages and what the user expects in convenience and interaction speed.

Error rate. How often is the user willing to make errors using the system? How forgiving should the system be? How should the system react? Usually users make more errors with cryptic and inconsistent commands than with clear, simple, uniform ones. It is more important for beginners than for experts to have simple, meaningful commands.

User satisfaction depends significantly on the type of user. Shneiderman [Shne82A] defines three levels of users, each with their own requirements. Novices need a clear and simple interface with a small number of meaningful commands. Often, guided menus are the easiest. Error messages clearly point out the problem *and* how to deal with it. On-line help facilities are indispensable. Novices also need reinforcement when they succeed (e.g., completion messages, that indicate success). To learn easily, users need comprehensive learning materials covering the system and its environment. This may include a primer on how to log onto the system and how to edit files.

The more knowledgable user requires simplicity and meaningful operations that are easy to remember. With good prompting facilities that can overcome problems like forgetting sequence or nature of parameters, productivity is usually increased. On-line assistance is still important, however.

Frequent or expert users usually want high speed interaction with the system: powerful commands, reduced keystrokes, shortcuts, macro facilities, and brief messages.

More than one level of users may necessitate more than one type of human machine interface to fulfill their differing needs. This increases complexity and cost but may be accomplished as the four levels of a graphics system interface [Moze82] show. It supports the following user learning stages:

▶ trying to learn the basics;

▶ progressing toward independent use of the system;

▶ probing into subtle and difficult features; and

▶ producing quality results within known system constraints.

Each level poses different requirements for the human-machine interface. It is important to know what types of users will use the system and what their needs and expectations will be, because this may call for trade-offs during requirements analysis.

4.3.3. Intended Use/Generality

We must describe the generality of a solution and how or where the system will be operated and who will use it.

1. *Extent of solution.* The user describes generality and scope. The difference between degree of functionality and extent of solution is very slight and this far has depended

only on the technique used to describe functionality. Under functionality, we grouped all requirements that could be deduced with the aid of the requirements diagrams and data dictionary. Others may be listed under extent of solution. An example question is, do you see a more general version of the problem that you might want to solve? For instance, it should be asked whether TAP should keep multiyear records with carry-over data or whether it should estimate the likelihood of an audit. If extent of the solution was described under functionality, we need not describe it again.

2.   *Portability.* If the software will be used on different computers at multiple installations, it must be portable. Portability is a quality characteristic that describes the degree to which software can be run on different computers. If portability is an issue, the analyst must ask, what are the computers on which it is to run? What are their characteristics? The last question the user may not know or care to know, but it is important for analysis purposes. What operating system do they run? Several releases may exist.

3.   *Compatibility.* Compatibility requirements describe the systems and software with which the proposed application must be compatible. The types of compatibility are exchange of data between systems, providing or using data from other systems, and providing or using processing capabilities. If a new system must work within an environment of other existing systems, they must interface properly with each other. An example of such a compatibility requirement is to have the tax preparation system interface on-line with the account balancing system. At other times, compatibility with specific operating systems is required. For example, on machines with virtual machine operating systems kernels (such as IBM's VM), several operating systems may run concurrently. With which of these should the application be compatible? Another important issue is "upward compatibility," where the application must run on bigger machines of the same family. Is an upgrade planned? Possible? How important is it that the software be compatible?

It is also important to ask for the *degree* of compatibility. Must it be data compatible or processing compatible? When a variety of different pieces of software must be integrated into one set of tools to solve a problem, they are often too dissimilar to combine them into one software system. An example of such a situation is a set of automated tools for software development support. There are many types of processing and many types of information that are generated or used in various phases of software development. Procedure compatibility is possible in limited cases, where one tool directly calls for the execution of another. Usually their compatibility centers on a common database [Howd82].

Awareness of interfaces with other systems is crucial. In an unsuccessful implementation, the user may have to reenter data that one system has generated as input for another. This may negate the benefits of computerization. We must know the effects of degrees of incompatibility and whether the user is willing to live with them or not. Asking the user about what he does and does not want avoids misinterpretations and misunderstandings.

4.3.4.   Future/Lifetime Expectations

4.3.4.1. Adaptability

While the system is in operation, the problem it solves may change, and the environment within which it operates may also change. What are the users' requirements in the event of such changes? The software quality associated with such changes is called adaptability.

We may consider TAP's adaptability requirements. In the past, fundamental changes in tax laws caused significant modifications in preparing returns. Forms and computations changed. Further modifications are likely. Thus, a tax preparation system with a life expectancy of several years must be adaptable to such changes. The layout of the forms must be easy to change, because rules for tax computation and deductions change also.

How much flexibility and adaptability should the system have? Is the user willing to customize the forms himself every year and make his own changes in processing rules? Or will that task be done by system support? Should there be a front end to the system that will set up form layout and processing rules according to user specifications? Answers to these questions will determine the exact nature of adaptability constraints.

The number and type of schedules and forms may change over the years. Will the system be able to handle all possible scenarios with the predefined schedules and forms? What about the need for forms that are not implemented? Will the user prepare them manually, or is a feature required that helps to define new schedules or their interface with the currently implemented ones? As a third option, must system support modify the program accordingly? What is the importance and usefulness of each option? Answers to these questions define adaptability requirements, their relative importance, and possible options.

4.3.4.2. Maintainability

Maintainability describes how easy it is to keep a piece of software in operation when modifications to the code become necessary. It is usually stated in terms of the time and effort required to make those changes.

The requirements should state the maximum amount of time and effort necessary to maintain the software. Adaptability and maintainability are related. Adaptability requirements describe the ease of adapting the product for new uses, while maintainability requirements state effort and time for code modifications.

Maintainability requirements should address corrective, perfective, and adaptive maintenance:

1. No more than two hours of user time and three billing hours of maintenance time to customize the tax system for a given year.

2. No more than two hours billing time and no more than twenty-four hours to correct 90% of the errors.

3. No more than one man week to add a new schedule or tax form.

The user must specify installation requirements. They describe the characteristics of installations at which the user wants the software to run, as well as the maximum allowable effort and time to install the software on any of those systems. This requirement is especially important for operating systems that are installed on thousands of systems of the same type but with varying configurations and installation-specific characteristics.

4.3.5. Documentation

This part of the interview concerns the type of documents the user requires and their extent and quality. Often he wants a general user's manual that explains all the inputs, outputs and functions, and error messages and possible actions for them. The manual may include sections on how to log into the system (this may be different for different installations!), how to prepare data, and a syllabus of commands for quick reference. Which of these does the user want? How detailed?

There may be several versions of user manuals, such as one for novices and one for experienced users, or, one general user manual may be divided into introductory and advanced sections. Both fulfill the requirement of having material for novices and advanced users. The user may also require a tutorial for training purposes, written, on-line or both. Often parts of the user manual are on-line as a help facility. Some commercial software includes a training course and training material.

When the users maintain the software, they need development documentation. For installation purposes, a systems manual (which details the types of files, system support programs, minimal and maximal hardware configuration requirements, etc.) may be necessary to provide the proper run-time environment. For all types of documentation, the extent and quality must be considered.

4.4. Constraints and Benefits

This section describes the role of schedule constraints and resource limitations. It also explains various benefits that must be realized in a software product. Constraints and benefits are important information for trade-off and feasibility analysis.

4.4.1. Schedule

User requirements usually include schedule requirements. Software is worth developing only if it is still timely when developed (i.e., it will not be obsolete). Problem-oriented
deadlines pose additional schedule constraints. Some problems "go away" after a while,
even if they are not taken care of. Often they grow into new ones. Other time constraints
are imposed through outside market consideration; e.g., "we need an individual tax
preparation system on the PC market by next January because the competition will
have one by March." Still other constraints stem from limited availability of personnel.
Users or developers may be available only at limited times; e.g., "we have four people
available full-time for the next two months, but after that they will be busy with another
project." Interdependencies between departments and individuals involved in the development process must be clear in terms of schedule constraints.

New government regulations or corporate policies that go into effect at a certain date
pose further schedule constraints. Software that conforms to the new regulations or is
subject to new policies must be available by the deadline. A new government regulation
may, for example, require certain information to be furnished for tax purposes.

A company policy may require a high degree of computerization of operations by a
given date. Software may not be outdated or useless if delivered late, but serious trouble
may result. Strict deadline constraints exist when software development support tools
(testing tools, design or specification aids, project tracking systems, etc.) must be built
and used for a specific development effort. If support tools are not available when necessary, they become useless for that project.

Schedules do not always need strict deadlines; therefore, we must ask about an acceptable range. In evolutionary development, software systems become available in increasingly enhanced versions. What are acceptable schedules for them? While complete
functionality has not been reached, will the existing manual or computerized system
run in parallel? How long? Maybe there is a lease contract on the software that will ex-
pire. When should customer training begin, and when should it end? If there is prototyping, by what time must the prototype be available?

4.4.2. Resources

This category describes (limitations of) available resources: those that apply during development and those that refer to the operation of the software. The user will not always
describe both. It depends on whether he has to make them available or pay for them.
There are four major types of resource limitations: physical, personnel, organizational,
and budgetary. Depending on the degree of user involvement during development, some
of the constraints may or may not apply; e.g., in a situation where the user is involved

only during the requirements and specification phase, he would specify only budgetary constraints and the operational environment.

4.4.2.1. Physical Limitations

These describe constraints on computer and peripheral equipment, their capacity and the time available for use, development support software, availability of implementation languages, etc. This information must be precise enough for an analysis of requirements and constraints to determine the feasibility of performance requirements.

Access to the user's computer system may be limited; e.g., installation may take place only after working hours so as not to disturb regular operation, or it may not be allowed during the last week of the month when the system's full capacity is needed (payroll?). Access may require security clearance or U.S. citizenship. This is a common restriction for government contract work. In many companies the development team only has access to resources in the presence of an authorized representative of the user organization.

Computer capacity restrictions may require that only a given percentage of memory, processing power, or transmission bandwidth be used by the development team. Where software is developed on the user's computer system, development support may be limited.

Restrictions may exist for operational software. How much of the computer system's capacity may it use? What system software and other support software is needed? Is it available?

4.4.2.2. Personnel Limitations

There can be development and operations constraints depending on whether and how much the user's personnel is involved in software development. When are personnel available? What type of personnel is available? For what types of tasks? Experience level? Knowledge? How many are available? During which times? Which experience level?

When the user is not involved in implementation, the developer must answer these questions before a requirements analysis and feasibility assessment are possible. During the operating life of the software, personnel limitations determine the staff available to operate and maintain the software.

4.4.2.3. Organizational Limitations

Organizational constraints are the limitations due to the structure and type of support within the user organization during the operational life of the software. The developing organization adds its own constraints and limitations as they relate to organizational structure and support. Because these limitations usually involve management, they are detailed in Part 2 of this book.

4.4.2.4. *Budgetary Limitations*

The user will state what he is willing to pay for system development and operation. Amounts vary with the software's functionality and other quality characteristics. A user may be willing to pay a great deal for a reliable system or a fast one or one with many features. On the other hand, he may say, "I am willing to spend $5,000 for development and $500 a year to use it. Give me the best system you can build for that." The user's priorities for product capabilities and their relative importance describe what the user considers to be "best."

An acceptable cost range (budget) for development operation may be broken down further into fixed start-up costs (investment) and variable costs for amount of use. In case requirements are not user-derived, a budget range may be set by the developing organization. We must know the costs for items in cost categories for all alternatives.

> ▶ **System cost.**   This includes the cost for using existing hardware and software as well as buying new hardware and software. The analyst will ask the user how much he is willing to spend on system cost during development, e.g., for software development support tools;
>
> > ▶ for buying or leasing a compiler so that an appropriate language for the problem may be used;
> >
> > ▶ for adding sufficient hardware capacity to develop the software; and
> >
> > ▶ for computer use charges, such as for CPU time, main memory, disk and tape storage, paper, etc.

During the software's operational life, the same system costs may occur during development. Amortization over the system's lifetime also must be considered.

> ▶ **Personnel.**   Salary and benefits are the major components of this cost item. Usually it is adjusted for administrative overhead, which may be as high as 75%. Cost depends on the number and experience level of people available for development and on staffing alternatives. Personnel costs occur during development and maintenance.
>
> ▶ **Materials and supplies.**   This covers books, paper, pencils, mailing costs, etc.
>
> ▶ **Space.**   The cost of regular office space is often part of the administrative overhead. Offices for user representatives may not be included. Additional space to house a new computer system and peripheral equipment is an extra cost item.

▶ **Travel.** Software development for several sites may require a substantial amount of travel. Maintenance by a group that is remote from the site of operations involves travel, too. Travel may necessary for research purposes, e.g., to inspect a system elsewhere, to visit consultants, to train.

In summary, the following two cost constraints are established for all implementation and operation alternatives: overall cost or budget and cost ceilings for individual items as the user requests them. Contract work in the public sector often has ceilings on amounts that may be spent in specific cost categories. They may be expressed in percentages of the overall budget, as maximum dollars allowable for some cost items, or sometimes both. Travel expenses and equipment costs are most often restricted.

The outcome of requirements collection in the cost category is to specify the limitations the customer puts on resources and to describe available resources and their limitations.

4.4.3. Benefits

Benefits may be tangible or intangible. Tangible benefits, such as cost reductions in operations and increased profits, are quantifiable. A user may expect increased profit because more work is handled in the same amount of time: a high level of cost-effectiveness provides increased profit. Other expectations may center on by-products of computerization. These by-products may be organized, readily available information, such as mailing lists or salable software. Also, the user organization may now be able to analyze consumer behavior patterns, which allows them to forecast future needs for production and inventory more accurately. This improves cash management and decreases the cost of loans and investments.

In the tax planning example, increased accuracy in tax preparation and tax planning result in fewer penalties for underpayment of taxes or tax errors. Increased accuracy may be measured as the amount of error dollars (sum of the dollar value of each error). The following examples of such errors:

▶ unreported deductions,

▶ computation errors,

▶ filing errors, copying errors, and

▶ disadvantageous schedule choices.

The benefit of "less penalties" adds the following dollar values:

▶ penalties due to errors in return and

▶ penalties for underpayment of taxes

More sophisticated tax preparation systems may realize tax savings as the result of better tax planning (such as actions the system suggested for estimated taxes, selling of stock, etc.). This is a hybrid measure because it combines avoiding penalties with increased accuracy.

The program analyzer is expected to save grading time and improve its accuracy. The first can be measured in hours, and the second in number of successfully detected plagiarized programs.

Intangible benefits are not so easily quantified. Examples are

▶ staff morale,

▶ improved decision making, and

▶ better legibility, understandability.

The intangible benefits for the tax preparation system might include

▶ better organization and legibility of tax records;

▶ improved decision making in the areas of investment and acceptance of consulting activities;

▶ better planning for taxes (no more surprises); and

▶ less stress in the event of a tax audit, because everything is prepared.

A list of possible intangible benefits (some of which are secondary) for the program analyzer are

▶ deterrence from plagiarism;

▶ better organization of student records;

▶ identification of repeat subjects;

▶ more knowledge about predictive and analytic quality of the method;

▶ better communication between graders; and

▶ more knowledge about what makes programs similar and how that relates to problem-solving styles.

Both tangible and intangible benefits should be prioritized whether achieving them is mandatory (3), important but negotiable (2), or purely optional (1). These priorities facilitate comparative analysis and trade-offs.

Users often expect to see benefits within a certain time frame. What is that time frame?

Problems and Questions

1. If we develop an automated system for a doctor's office, what tangible and intangible benefits would we expect? Which quality expectations would the nurse, the doctor, and the secretary have? State them with a short justification.

2. You are asked to establish quality expectations for a Help Facility for your favorite sophisticated word processing system. As a user, what would you define as your quality expectations? How would you translate them into more technical terms so that you can give them to your colleague to see whether they are implementable?

3. What documentation would you suggest for the tax record keeping and preparation system? Why? What should it contain? (Hint: Keep in mind the user, the maintainer, and the quality expectations that were discussed in this section).

4. For evaluation purposes we have offered three levels of quality—mandatory [3], important [2], purely optional [1].

   a) Why should they be enough in most cases?

   b) Give an example of when more discriminatory power is needed.

(Hint: What happens in each of the following situations?

▶   tolerance for wrong decisions is small

▶   constraints are tight

▶   most options show basically the same evaluation)

5. What are the types of reliability? Give one example for each. They must be different than the ones in the book.

6. A lawyer wants to install a small computer system to keep track of his client files, to set up form letters and papers for court, and to remind him of deadlines for client cases. Which questions would you ask him about quality expectations? What options for each quality expectation can you think of? What are the tangible and intangible benefits of a legal office system?

4.5. Requirements Collection without User Interviews

Thus far, we have assumed that the analyst (or group of analysts) may interview the user. Requirements are user-driven, and their quality depends on the amount of knowledge that the analyst has acquired about the user's needs, goals, and problem solution constraints. During the collection of requirements and their subsequent analysis, two perspectives converge: the user's (which provides the broad picture by giving the context within which the software is to be used) and the developers' (which provides the detail). Developers must understand the context and intent of the system in detail in order to build it. This requires a reconciliation of these different perspectives and constitutes the objective of user-driven requirements.

The user organization may also develop the requirements. Developers usually have a contract with the user organization, and the requirements represent a major part of this contract. Where the user organization can develop requirements in sufficient detail for the developing (sub)contractor, this will not pose a problem. However, if the user organization fails to provide sufficient detail, it creates an information gap for the developers (a potential source of problems).

Just as the user organization can establish requirements on its own, the developing organization may do so without direct contact with a user. User-independent requirements are often developed for a generalized marketable product, such as new operating systems, compilers, word-processing software, etc. The emphasis is on marketability: will a large number of potential users want to buy and use the product? Without a specific user, we must identify the typical user types and their characteristics and needs. Often a market analysis establishes previous usage patterns and needs for a software system. Because the marketing department and, in the case of redevelopment, the technical support group or customer services know most about the potential users, they will probably be involved in establishing requirements for the new system. They take the part of the user.

For tax preparation software, a variety of systems exist with varying degrees of sophistication that were most likely developed without user involvement. Commercial development of tax preparation systems may identify the needs users in general are likely to have instead of concentrating on the needs of a particular customer. This will result in a system that attempts to give reasonable service to the widest range of users but probably not the most optimal service to any one of them (as a custom built system would do).

Regardless of which organization establishes requirements, someone is always needed to represent the interests of the user. While there may be more than one type of user and while the developers may interview several (potential) users to make sure that they know the needs of all classes of users, it is important to have a key representative with the final authority on a user need. Otherwise, the developers may have to reconcile differences and conflicts among users to arrive at one set of requirements. Another problem may occur when the developers deal with different user representatives. Each new representative may have his own ideas about requirements, so the requirements keep changing. It is desirable to have only one user representative who makes decisions when conflicts arise among user classes and user interests. Everything must be written down: the requirements and who has authority to make decisions about them.

The group developing the requirements, which may include the user organization, must always have a representative from the developing group or organization. As in the case of the user representative, stability is important. One person must have authority to make decisions and to state the developer's position.

To ensure smooth continuation into the next phase of development, there must be a person involved in the requirements analysis who plays a key role in writing specifications. As a result; we have representatives of three groups involved in establishing requirements:

▶   the user or user representative,

▶   the developer, and

▶   the group involved in writing specifications.

They cooperate to analyze the existing system, meet or conduct user interviews or market analyses, assist in or evaluate user interviews or market analyses, perform, direct or evaluate feasibility studies or parts thereof, and estimate benefits. Other reasons for involving representatives from three different areas are related to work satisfaction of the requirements group. People should see their work as contributing to an end product that is visible to them, to have some control over their work and its result, to get feedback on its quality, and to ensure that work scope is not narrowly defined (as to become boring). By involving representatives from the next phase and providing the challenge of user communication, we widen the scope and provide feedback. The next phase's work is visible through cooperation with the specifiers; the requirements analysts control how they do their evaluation.

Problems and Questions

1.   What makes it sometimes difficult to establish quality expectations that may be evaluated by a team of technical experts, if the quality expectations are given by

   a)   the marketing department

   b)   a non-DP end user

   c)   a DP end user

(Hint: Think about natural bias inherent in their position).

2. How would the quality expectations and functional requirements change if the tax preparation system was developed for a general market, but for single users only?

3. How would the quality expectations and functional requirements change if the program analysis system was developed not exclusively as an aid for plagiarism detection but also for course record keeping?

4.6. Requirements Analysis and Technical Feasibility

4.6.1. Priorities and Ranking

To facilitate requirements analysis and trade-offs, requirements are ranked in descending order of importance. A user may rank the following quality areas:

1. degree of functionality,

2. human factors,

3. reliability, and

4. performance.

All other quality areas are of lower but equal importance, i.e., ranked as "5." We can trade off *nonmandatory* requirements for the ranked areas according to these priorities. Negotiable quality levels of portability (5) may be sacrificed for same-level qualities in the area of performance (4), because performance is more important than portability. The result is that we will keep the most important quality areas at their highest potential level. Candidates for trade-offs are level 2 quality characteristics. There is a difference between ranking and level of quality of an attribute. Ranking defines importance among attributes. The level of quality measures quality of the attribute itself. We defined them earlier as having three possible levels: 3 (mandatory), 2 (important), 1 (optional).

In the tax preparation system, the relevant quality areas come from the checklist of Table 4.1. We assume that schedule and resources have fixed limitations; therefore, they are not included in the list, and neither are benefits. We will compare the effects of quality levels with expected benefits in a separate step. The user may have ranked the remaining quality attributes in the following order:

1. degree of functionality,

2. lifetime expectations (adaptability, maintainability),

3. reliability,

4. documentation,

5. human factors, and

6. compatibility.

   This ranking implies that negotiable parts of the collected requirements in the area of human factors may be traded for those in the documentation area. An example is on-line user help versus a glossary in the user manual. Adaptability ranks high, because tax rules and regulations change frequently, and any system that is useable for more than one year must accomodate that.
   If the schedule and the resource limitations are also negotiable, they must be included in the ranking, so that decisions can be made as to whether a higher level of quality in one area is preferable (though it may take longer or cost more).
   Going back to the second major example, the user may have given the comparative ranking of quality areas for the plagiarism detector as the following:

1. reliability,

2. degree of functionality,

3. security,

4. performance,

5. human factors,

6. adaptability, and

7. documentation.

   As before, we are assuming that schedule and resource limitations are fixed and not subject to negotiation. The user chose reliability as the most important quality charac-teristic because the amount of data makes it difficult to check plagiarism manually. There may be many users, especially teaching assistants, who tend to change a lot; they are not always familiar with the system and must be protected against their own mis-takes. The degree of functionality is second, partly because it is somewhat of a research or experimental system, where evaluating whether the basic approach works well is im-portant. Security comes next, because the privacy of the students must be protected. Likewise, it must be very difficult for an unauthorized user to gain access or even change evaluation data. Because some of the programs may be of significant length, perform-ance is important if analysis will be done interactively. Because of the relatively low fre-quency of use, the user interface must be supportive to such intermittent users, which is why human factors is next on the list. Adaptability refers to adding new programming languages that may be analyzed and to adding new insights into analysis procedures. Not all impurities must be dealt with, and the body of knowledge about efficacy of the analysis procedure is spotty. Both of these points emphasize the need for documentation, which is next on the list.

Problems and Questions

1. What is the difference between ranking of quality expectations and levels of quality?

4.6.2. Benefits Analysis

Benefits analysis compares pairs of requirements and pairs of benefits to see whether they are consistent. The objective of comparing stated product capabilities (functionality, useability, intended Use, future/lifetime expectations, documentation and Schedule) with benefits is to ensure that every stated requirement is accurately reflected in the expected benefits:

▶ All requirements have a corresponding benefit.

▶ Reaching each benefit is supported by specific quality requirements.

▶ Each requirement has the same level of importance as the benefit that it supports.

This cross-checking avoids mismatched requirements and benefits and misconceptions of what the system can do, and it spots inconsistencies and incompleteness between the requirements for the product and the benefits expected from it. Wherever such inconsistencies occur, they must be reconciled. Functionality requirements that do not support any expected benefits must be examined closely. They may be superfluous, or the corresponding benefit may be missing.

In general, there should be a reason for having requirements. If they are obvious, we may not have to do a formal evaluation. In that case, if the system is very complex, it may become difficult to assess the effect of trade-offs on expected benefits. It may be educational for the users to see that some of their "favorite" requirements don't bring them closer to realizing expected benefits. For the implementor, a formal analysis clarifies the motivation behind requirements and keeps an emphasis on the rationale for product capabilities.

For the plagiarism detector, we must inspect functional requirements to see which of the stated benefits they support. We can establish a matrix where the rows show the expected benefits with their associated levels of requirements ([3] mandatory, [2] important but negotiable, [1] purely optional). The columns represent the top-level activities to indicate the functions the system will perform. The entries in Table 4.4 state which requirements levels for an activity support a specific benefit. If all levels of requirements support a benefit, it is marked by an asterisk; otherwise, the highest level applicable is indicated. For the plagiarism detector, we must assume that the tangible and intangible benefits are as stated in Table 4.3 with their associated requirement levels. Table 4.4 shows the result of the comparison between degree of functionality and expected benefit.

Table 4.3 Program analyzer benefits.

Number	Priority	Benefit
		Tangible benefits
1	[3]	Save grading time
2	[3]	Improve grading accuracy
		Intangible benefits
3	[3]	Deterrence from cheating
4	[3]	Better organization of the grading process
5	[2]	Identification of repeatedly similar submissions
6	[2]	More knowledge about predictive/analytic quality of method
7	[3]	Better communication among graders
8	[2]	More knowledge about what makes programs similar and possible relations to problem-solving styles

Table 4.4 Functionality vs. benefit comparison.

Benefits	1 [3]	2 [3]	3 [3]	4 [3]	5 [2]	6 [2]	7 [3]	8 [2]
Activity								
1	*	*	*	−	−	*	−	*
2	*	*	*	−	[2]	*	*	*
3	*	−	*	*	[2]	−	*	−
4	*	−	*	*	*	*	*	*

Note (*) all levels support benefits; (−) does not support benefit; [2] level 2 supports benefit.

Table 4.4 shows that all benefits are supported by at least one activity, and the levels of requirements are compatible with each other. It also indicates the minimal functionality levels that support all mandatory benefits. In this example, we may restrict ourselves to the minimal system without losing a mandatory benefit. The only two entries lost are for benefit 5, activities 2 and 3, but they are not mandatory.

Problems and Questions

1. Do the Functionality versus Benefit comparison for the tax preparation system. Reference all the information from previous sections and state any assumptions you have to make explicitly.

2. Why is it useful and desirable to do a formal comparison of functionality versus benefits? Can you think of a situation when it is not necessary to do it formally? Explain.

3. What may be the reason when a stated expected benefit does not relate to any of the requirements? Give an example and suggest what should be done.

4.6.3.   Technical Feasibility

Technical feasibility examines the technical implications of user requirements and establishes whether a requirement item is feasible and where it might conflict with others. First, the degree of functionality requirements must be examined. Is it possible to implement a given functionality? Possible features in the earlier versions are ranked by implementation complexity. Together with stated priorities, they constitute the basis for trade-offs. If two functional features of a system are at the same negotiable priority, but one is less complex to implement than another, the simpler one is best.

A wide variety of factors have been identified that correlate with higher complexity of implementation. Boehm, in [Horo75], mentions size, implementation language, type of system (real-time, operating system, application, utility), and standard programming task versus first implementation of a new idea. On a detailed level, the IBM method [Swed72] distinguishes among three aspects of implementation: input, output, and processing complexity. Walston and Felix [Wals77] also list variables that correlate significantly with functional complexity. They include items such as user interface complexity, complexity of code developed, complexity of application processing, overall constraints on program design, performance, multiplicity of classes of data objects, size of documentation, and type of application (numerical, text, I/0). DeMarco [Dema82] also lists a variety of factors that influence the complexity and, hence, the feasibility of the functionality of the proposed system.

DeMarco's model is more detailed than the others. It is based on counting lowest level functions and data items and relations between functions as well as between data items. Thus, we can measure functional complexity, data complexity, and interface complexity. Because every requirements diagram has aspects of all three, one may be tempted to combine them into one overall metric. This, however, is fraught with error for two reasons. First, this is like adding apples and oranges, because numbers of functions and numbers of data items are not the same unit of measurements. Second, even if we use them as one complexity unit each, these three entities are not independent of each other. If their complexity measures are added, dependent complexity, which shows up as part of a score in both measures, is added more than once and biases the result. Therefore, it is advisable to concentrate on one principal indicator for complexity. We must decide whether complexity is primarily a result of function, data, or interface complexity. DeMarco suggests that for most systems the function count is an appropriate predictor of implementation complexity.

This function count needs to be adjusted for other factors that influence complexity. These include the following:

▶ It is influenced by the amount of data items used or produced by a low-level function. DeMarco suggests using Halstead's [Hals77] result that says function size is proportional to the number of data items times the logarithm (base 2) of the number of these data items.

$$size_{function} \sim data * log_2 data$$

Thus, if a low level function is associated with five different data items, its adjusted functional complexity indicator is

$$CI = 5 * log_2 (5) = 5.8.$$

▶ It is easier to implement a simple edit function than one that implements an I/0 device driver. DeMarco lists generic types of functions with their relative complexity factors. Because their complexity depends on the implementation environment (machine, operating system, support utilities, programming languages), such a set of weighting factors must be established for a given environment. We may define a set of standard generic functions and associate a complexity of unity with one of them. Any others of the set with equal complexity are assigned a complexity value of unity, which also provides a set of reference points. Starting from those, complexity indices for the other generic functions may be developed through a comparative ranking. Weighing factors for other types of primitive functions are developed by asking "How much more or less complex is this function than the others?"

Based on data complexity and inherent functional complexity, a revised complexity index may be derived that will drive the cost model and is considered a prime indicator of effort (cf. Part 2). The analysts identify technical factors relevant to effort, cost, and risk, but they do not relate them to management factors, such as schedule, cost, or risk analysis.

The next step evaluates the combined impact of functional requirements and requirements in the other areas, which entails a pair wise comparison of requirements for product capabilities. If it is sequenced according to relative importance of the quality areas, trade-offs may occur along the way, using the rule, "If the new quality area conflicts with a previous one of the same level, the new area under consideration loses out to the one already considered." One requirement area after another may be added. At each step we must determine whether the system is still feasible. The burden of quality requirements on feasibility is a cumulative one and, thus, must be evaluated for its compound effect. The effect on development complexity may be additive or multiplicative ([Dema82]).

Then we compare the quality expectations and their impact on technical resource constraints. This is a pair wise comparison and must be done for all alternatives that have remained technically feasible. We also must consider the feasibility of using and customizing off-the-shelf software.

The remaining technically feasible alternatives are listed with a comparison among these options. During our investigation of technical feasibility, we will not decide which system will be implemented, and we will not consider nontechnical resources. The objectives of this analysis are as follows:

▶ Pinpoint major areas of effort and indicate relevant factors.

▶ Provide the technical data for feasibility of alternatives.

▶ Identify technical risk factors.

This data is necessary for the feasibility study (see also the chapter on management aspects of feasibility in Part II).

For the tax preparation system, the activities and their levels of functionality (cf. Section 4.2.) may be ranked according to development complexity. We will do this by layer of degree of functionality, i.e., for levels [3], [2], [1]. Table 4.5 shows this relative complexity matrix for the activities of the tax preparation system by level. Complexity is on a scale of 1 to 4. This includes the complexities of the processing and the input and out-

Table 4.5   Relative complexity matrix.

Activity	1	2	3	4	0
Level [1]	1	2	2	4	2
[2]	3	1	2	4	4
[3]	3	2	2	4	3

put from an activity as well as its interfaces to others. The numbers were derived from a table, such as that suggested by DeMarco [Dema82], and reflect the complexity of these functions when compared to a set of standard generic functions for which the developing organization has established standard functional complexity weights.

Other methods to compute implementation complexity take into account the types of complexity and use the requirements diagram, the data dictionary, and the required level of functionality as a base. They develop the following indices:

▶ A processing complexity index (PCI) is a weighted sum of activities. They may be weighted by the complexity of an activity (cf. Table 4.5).

▶ An interface complexity index (ICI) is the number of interfaces weighted by their complexity in terms of data objects and data formats. An example of this is the Halstead formula mentioned above.

▶ An input/output complexity index (IOCI) is a weighted sum of data object complexity of input and output data objects.

Assuming that the important areas of quality for the tax preparation system are reliability, performance, and security (in that order), the following requirements have been specified for them:

1. **Reliability.**

▶ No data loss because of tax system errors beyond those data added since the last save operation. [3]

▶ Error isolation for user and system errors to the module where it occurs. [3]

▶ No more than one error per year in tax computation. [2]

2. **Performance.**

▶ For editing: response time no more than three seconds. [2]

▶ For forms compilation: no more than two minutes of computing. Printing may take longer. [2]

3. **Security.**

▶ User locks up personal computer and diskettes. [3]

▶ Encrypt data on diskettes and have user password, in case they get into unauthorized hands. [1]

Because of the importance of the reliability requirements, their impact on the complexity and feasibility of software development is investigated first. Fulfilling the reliability requirements at level [3] entails implementing a "save" operation that saves the file whenever the user wants to protect her data, other than when exiting the edit mode. This makes the save operation complex, but not impossible. Therefore, we increase the complexity index of activity 1 appropriately. In comparison to activity 4, which has a complexity figure of 4, adding the modified save operation does not make activity 1 as complex as activity 4, so we add only .5 to the score for activity 1.

The second reliability requirement on level [3] requires consistency checks at every module, which increases code complexity but helps to test the code. Therefore, there is no further increase of implementation complexity.

When we look at performance, all requirements are negotiable; there is no feasibility problem for level [3]. Likewise, mandatory security is a user responsibility. The minimum alternative is feasible in these areas. The overall complexity index for level [3] is the sum of all (adjusted) complexity indices for all activities:

$$CI([3] = (3+.5) + 2 + 2 + 4 + 3 = 14.5$$

For the level [2] system, we use the complexity indices for that level, add them to the ones from the previous level, and proceed as before to add the impact of the other quality requirements at level [2]. The new reliability requirement, although technically feasible, is a very strict one that increases the effort of development and its complexity. It affects activity 4 the most. The development experts decided that it would add 2 complexity points to activity 4 and one-half a point to activities 2 and 3.

At level [2] the performance requirement may become a feasibility problem. Because the editing module now has the intermediate save operation to implement, whether the response-time ceiling of three seconds can be held or not will depend on the amount of data to be saved and how that data is organized. There are actually two options:

▶ trading the response time for the save operation, because reliability is more important, and

▶ implementing the save operation in the background so that the response time experienced by the user consists only of initiating the save. This adds more complexity to the implementation of the save and to data consistency for continued editing while information is saved, increasing the complexity index of activity 1 by .5.

The second performance requirement is a function of the volume of data involved. We have to do a worst case analysis to determine whether the system would hit the performance ceiling at any time. Assume that

▶ compilation of a form involves at most 30 entries per form,

▶ there are no more than seven forms,

▶ no more than half of the entries are totals in categories, and

▶ each category has no more than 50 items.

Let *entry(x)* be the time it takes to enter *x* entries onto a form. *Add(n)* is the time needed to add *n* pieces of information. Then, per form, at most *entry*(30) time is used to enter information. Each *add* involves adding at most 50 items. Thus, it will take at most *add*(50) time. Therefore, the total time involved in compiling the forms is no more than

$$T(compilation) = 7 * (entry(30) + 15 * add(50)).$$

Assume that adding and entering any item takes no more than 1 msec, i.e., *entry(x)=x* msec and *add(n)=n* msec. Then

$$T(compilation) = 7 * (30 + 15*50) \; msec = 7 * 780 = 5460 \; msec = 5.46 \text{ msec.}$$

But this assessment assumed that the entries were sorted. If sorting must be done, as well, we have to factor in the amount of time it takes to sort them. With a bubble sort for 1,000 items this would take approximately $1,000^2$ msecs or about 1,000 secs. That is more than 10 minutes and not fast enough. If a more optimal sort is used, we may get away with order *N*log*N* or 1,000log1,000, which is about 10 seconds, making the total approximately 15.5 seconds.

Next, data retrieval, which involves searching for data items, is required. For 30 items per form this requires at most 210 retrieves. Assuming that one retrieval does not take more than 10 msec, the data retrieval time is about 2.1 secs. This results in a total time for forms compilation of just under 17 seconds. However, we still have not added the time for printing or putting the output on screen. This has been a performance analysis of the simple functions, but level [2] requires more sophistication, such as implementing the optimal way to handle deductions. If we are assuming that in the worst case there are seven different possibilities to handle deductions and they require at most the recompilation of the entire tax return for each of the seven possibilities, then the time to compile the optimal return is at most seven times the simple one:

$$T(opt) = 7 * T(compilation) = 7 * 17 = 119 \text{ secs}$$

The time needed to compile a tax return almost exceeds the performance requirements at level [2], indicating that this requirement needs to be closely watched because it constitutes a risk factor.

The above is a simple example of an analysis for a performance requirement. The analysis showed that some of the implementation options had to be ruled out for performance reasons (bubble sort). Often the situation is more complex than that. When the system will run on a multiprogrammed computer system, there will be the interference from other programs and there will be queueing for resources, such as CPU and disk I/O. Sometimes analytic models may be used; however, in other situations they are not powerful or accurate enough to answer the question with enough certainty. In that case, a simulation program is written. The most work-consuming way to determine feasibility is actual prototyping, i.e., implementing the module to see whether it is feasible to fulfill a mandatory requirement.

The complexity index increment for level [2] is determined by adding the adjustments to the relative complexity indices for each activity at level [2].

Activity	Level [2] adjustments					
	1	2	3	4	0	total
Relative complexity	3	1	2	4	4	
Adjustments	.5	.5	.5	2	–	
	3.5	1.5	2.5	6	4	17.5

The complexity index for level [2] is the sum of CI([3]) and the increment resulting from level [2]:

$$CI([2]) = CI([3]) + 17.5 = 32$$

When we analyze the feasibility of level [1], we must establish the compound effect of the new features and the reliability, performance, and security requirements to properly adjust the complexity index. Although there are no more new reliability requirements, and the level [1] features do not add more complexity to the existing solution, the increased degree of functionality will noticeably affect performance. For example, multiple-year returns and carry-overs must be searched or at least retrieved. The tight performance constraints of level [2] will be violated now, making a level [1] solution infeasible because of a performance problem. However, there is the possibility to trade off functionality for performance. But since level [1] functionality is ranked lower than level [2] performance, the latter is more important. This evaluation procedure may be described algorithmically.

1. Determine the Relative Complexity Matrix (RCM_{ij}) for all activities j ($j = 1, \ldots, a$) and all levels [i] ($i = 1, \ldots, k$).

2. $CI([k + 1]) = 0$ (necessary for boundary value to effect correct calculations in loop)

```
For i=k to 1 do
   CI([i]) = CI([i+1])
   For j=1 to a do
      determine adjustment factor f_j for current level (i)
      activity j as a function of qualitative requirements.
      CI([i]) = CI([i]) + RCM_ij + f_j
   end
end
```

At this point in the analysis we may add the additional complexity factor resulting from the data items that are used or generated by the various activities. The data dictionaries of Tables 3.1, 3.4, 3.5, and 3.6 were used to determine the number of data items for each major activity. For example, activity 1 uses the following data objects: **nonwages, noncheckdeds, personal–info, taxes, income**, and **deductions**. That totals six data items for activity 1. Some assumptions were made for the forms produced in activity O (Output): Table 3.6 stated that 10 entries were entered into Schedule A; this was taken as the average for all tax forms. We assumed that state forms add only 10 data items; this may be low. We are also making a high-level estimate of the complexity of implementation. Thus, our estimate combined the complexities of the functions at the lower levels. We did, however, try to fine tune the effect of data complexity. Table 4.6 gives the counts for data objects and complexity adjustment factors (CAF) for all activities.

Table 4.6 CAF for data complexity.

Activity	No. of data items (N)	CAF ($N*\log N$)
1	6	7.8
2	2	1.0
3	3	2.4
4	4	4.0
0	11	19.0

With these adjustments the complexity index is

$$CI([3]) = 3.5 * 7.8 + 2 * 1 + 2 * 2.4 + 4 * 4 + 3 * 19 = 107.1.$$

For level [2], the CAF adjustment results in a complexity indicator of

$$CI([2]) = CI([3]) + (3 + .5) * 7.8 + 1.5 * 1 + 2.5 * 2.4 + 6 * 4 + 4 * 19 = 241.9.$$

This is a "lumpy" indicator, because it does not differentiate between the sizes of the data objects. It shows, however, how much of the complexity of a function is caused by the complexity of its data. In environments where functional complexity has proved sufficiently accurate to predict efforts and cost, it is not necessary to include adjustments for data items.

If using ready-made, off-the-shelf software is an option, we must compare its capabilities to the user requirements. For tax preparation, at least 26 different software packages are available, starting at about $50 with varying degrees of sophistication and a variety of features. Some may not fit the requirements because they do not prepare state forms; others are geared toward businesses that prepare taxes for a variety of clients and thus are "overqualified" for our purposes. Both the undersized and the oversized packages should be weeded out quickly, but the remaining packages deserve a closer look. We may proceed the same way as before, except that now we do not have to worry about implementation complexity. It is useful to do some research and to check how relevant trade publications evaluate various systems that are on the market. For a discussion of tax planning and preparation software see [Huds84] and [Hein84].

If the software does not meet the requirements, it may be possible to customize it. Then we must evaluate the additional work involved and whether it is feasible. The same analysis procedure that we presented above may be used. This procedure uses a sequence of pair-wise comparisons that is directed by the relative importance of requirements areas and levels of priorities within them. There are correlations between the different requirements areas for all quality expectations. We have already seen the positive correlation between degree of functionality, performance, and reliability. What influenced them and caused the correlation was the complexity that resulted from more sophistication in the functions to be implemented.

To examine the possible correlations between all quality expectations, we will proceed in the order of Table 4.1 from degree of functionality to the last quality expectation, documentation. For brevity, only new pairs will be mentioned. The pair (degree of functionality, performance) is discussed under degree of functionality; it will not be mentioned again under performance.

Degree of Functionality

The previous example analysis for the tax preparation system showed that the complexity of solution and implementation rose as the number and sophistication of its features grew. However, the complexity is inversely related to a variety of other quality areas:

1. **Performance.** The more complex the solution is, the more computation and storage is needed. This has a negative influence on performance.

2. **Software reliability.**   The more complex a system is, the more difficult it becomes to reach a given level of reliability. Errors tend to be left in the system, and they are hard to find and difficult to remove without causing a ripple effect through other parts of the system.

3. **Maintainability.**   Complex systems are harder to maintain, unless special care is taken to increase maintainability, which may cause increased effort.

4. **Adaptability.**   When sophisticated solutions are general, adaptability of the system may not suffer; however, in complex interwoven systems, changes to accommodate solving a modified problem become harder and harder.

5. **Documentation.**   It is clear that the development of a system with simple functions is easier to document than one with more specialized and sophisticated ones. For user documentation, the degrees of functionality may also make a difference. For example, a system of multiple users is more complex functionally, but it also is in its documentation, because it must describe the system to more than one type of user.

The complexity of the human machine interface may, however, be inversely related to user documentation complexity, and the effort needed to achieve it. For example, a supportive system needs little said in the user manual. That, however, is usually compensated by the increased complexity of the human machine interface itself, which indicates that a trade-off has taken place.

Usability

Usability encompasses reliability, performance, security and human factors.

a)   *Reliability* is positively correlated with complexity because fault detection, fault tolerance, and fault correction all add more work to a system, thus making it more complex. This additional reliability work is overhead for processing itself and correlates negatively with performance constraints, due either to time or storage limitations. Reliability can be positively correlated to maintainability, because both are enhanced where problems are localized.

b)   *Performance* is often negatively related to human factors, because stepping a user through the process of using a system requires remembering the correct procedures. This includes helpful answers to user errors, which point out the problem, where it came from, and what to do about it. All of these items require more information that must either be kept somewhere (storage) or deduced (more processing). Security mechanisms are another area of potentially significant overhead as far as performance is concerned. Checking whether access is authorized or not and preventing unauthorized access to data and functions is extra work and needs time and storage space for authorization information. This overhead becomes especially prevalent when the agent controlling the security mechanism is centralized. Depending on the traffic intensity, long queues may form with requests for access. The central agent creates a bottleneck. The performance of the system is then primarily a function of how fast this central agent can process requests for service.

c)   *Security* is inversely related to human factors. For example, a very secure system may not be as easy to use as one with less stringent security requirements. Passwords need to be remembered, and the system may not tolerate repeated mistakes, because they might be an attempt at penetrating the system. Transitions between system states that favor the user are not possible directly, because they could undermine the security of the system. This problem is aggravated when there are several user classes with dynamically varying access rights to information and functions. Maintainability and adaptability can be severely affected when security requirements result in cryptic code that is purposefully hard to understand. It may protect the code from being compromised by unauthorized changes, but it also makes planned modifications that much harder. On the other hand, security mechanisms may localize access to specific data objects through well-defined functions and a set of possible access rights. This calls for clearly defined interfaces between systems and high degrees of quality (modularity) of the functions. Multiple entries to a module are much harder to control than single entries. Characteristics that aid security also increase maintainability and adaptability. Whether portability is facilitated or not with higher security requirements is not clear. There's no problem when existing security mechanisms on one machine can be used on another, but when a security mechanism makes use of nonportable features, it will. It is harder to port the security mechanism or to integrate a given security mechanism on another machine; sometimes it is impossible. Redeveloping one which provides the same security level is of course more work, adding to implementation complexity.

d)   *Human factors* influence every other quality characteristic, mainly because they introduce additional complexity. Jensen and Tonies [Jens79] indicate that there is difference of a factor of three, whether a piece of software is written for personal use (low human factor needs, because the user knows how it all works) or whether it is written for others to use (even harder still to develop it into a generally marketable product). This added complexity stems from higher expectations for the human factors. For similar reasons, high requirements in the human factors area correlate with high levels of maintainability. At times high human factors may be traded for higher requirements for user documents.

Intended Use

Intended use encompasses extent of solution, portability, and compatibility.

a)   Extent of solution highly correlates with degree of functionality, and, therefore, all arguments for that quality area apply.

b)   Portability requires separating portable from nonportable parts of the system, isolating and minimizing the nonportable ones so that modified parts that make the software run on the new machine may be plugged in easily. This requires a clear separation into dependent parts (or modules). Separating dependent parts into quasi-independent subsystems facilitates maintenance and keeping of accurate, up-to-date development documents, making both less complex. With many machine-dependent parts, however, maintainability and simplicity of documents are affected negatively, making them more complex.

c)   Compatibility requirements usually complicate matters further (e.g., when the tax preparation system must be compatible with the account-balancing system. Formats must be the same or routines must be written to convert them. Sometimes there is more information provided than is needed by a system. Then we need a filter that reduces the information to what is actually needed. In either case, extra work is required, which results in increased complexity for all other quality areas.

Some documents and human factors requirements may be simplified, if the user does not need to know about conversions. He merely sees that he can use several systems without copying information from one to another manually and that he does not have to convert his program to run it on the new operating system release.

Lifetime Expectations

They encompass adaptability and maintainability. Some of the positive and negative effects of other quality characteristics on development and maintenance have already been mentioned. Some of them center on complexity. How hard a problem is it? The more difficult the problem, the harder it is to maintain required levels of adaptability and maintainability. If it is possible to partition the problem into smaller ones that are only loosely connected and thus solvable almost independently from each other, changes in any of the problems and their solutions are easier. This is what modularity is about. Adaptability, as a quality, is highly correlated with modularity and also with maintainability. Both adaptability and maintainability are influenced positively by modularity, which reduces complexity. Complexity is one of the characteristics that determines how difficult it is to maintain a software system. Others include the quality and quantity of the documents that must be kept current.

The relations between quality areas and their levels revolve around two common characteristics: complexity, which makes attaining a desired level more difficult, and modularity, which decreases complexity and simplifies the problem of reaching given quality levels. All of the techniques throughout the software development life cycle are geared toward decreasing complexity by separating concerns, decisions, and solutions, i.e., modularizing in all these aspects.

Having explained the correlations between quality areas, we will go back and analyze the requirements for the second major example, the program analyzer. Its functional requirements were described in Section 4.3.1. We will proceed to determine whether they are feasible for all activities and all levels of degree of functionality.

Level [3] is feasible for the analysis portion of the system. We were given the procedure in Chapter 2. Level [2] is more complex than level [3]. Dealing with type one impurities is basically feasible, but difficult because it is doubtful that the program will be able to handle the many special cases. Some of the level [1] requirements are impossible. First, there is no expertise available for other types of impurities. Automatic selection of program parts will be possible only by subroutine. Because statements may be part of an I/O module or a processing module, automatic detection of I/O similarity is not feasible. Without natural boundaries implicit in the program for delineating program parts, it is difficult or impossible to automatically define parts or to compare them against each other. The technique has an implicit shortcoming: the same characteristic quadruple (n_1, n_2, N_1, N_2) may result for two programs doing totally different tasks. The underlying assumption for given programs or program parts must be that they are supposed to accomplish the same task. With an automatic search for program parts that must be compared, this assumption is violated and, thus, allows for erroneous results. In summary then, for the analysis portion of the program analyzer, option [3] is feasible, option [2] is hard and the algorithm is questionable, and option [1] is considered infeasible and is dropped. Table 4.7 shows the analysis results for the other activities.

Table 4.7 Analysis of functional requirements for program analysis project.

Activity	Analysis	Comparison	Record keeping	Report generation
Priority Item				
[3]	Feasible	Feasible	Feasible	Feasible
[2]	Hard	Feasible	Feasible	Feasible
[1]	Infeasible	Hard	Hard	Hard

Under comparison and record keeping, the option ranked [1] was judged hard, because there are interfaces to other departments and instructors. The systems involved deal with grade history, program of study, and disciplinary history and are controlled by other academic or administrative departments. Because report generation in color graphics also adds additional complexity and skill, it was judged hard. If we assume that infeasible and hard choices may be dropped because they are not mandatory, we may reduce the number of implementation options from 81 to 4.

Such a prioritization also serves as a good guide in selecting phases of incremental or evolutionary development. For example, the program analysis system may be implemented in the following steps:

1. Include all priority items [3] (mandatory).

2. Add comparison at level [2].

3. Add report generation at level [2].

4. Add record keeping at level [2].

If necessary, we may break up iteration 1 further. A breadboard approach would have rudimentary record keeping and output generation, while a mock-up would concentrate on those last two because much of the user interface is contained in these two activities. In this way we may show the prospective user what it will be like to use the system. (Because the instructor is interested in an exploratory system for program analysis, we must start breadboarding the analysis portion, and then add simple record-keeping and output-generation modules.)

This is an example of how to use user requirements as an aid in selecting implementation strategy. The advantage of an incremental approach in this development situation is that we may show that something works fairly quickly. If you must do this as a semester project for a course, this may be appealing to you and your instructor. The exploratory nature of the program analyzer for plagiarism detection also suggests an incremental approach to implementation. We can and must regard each iteration as a life cycle in its own right, with its own goals and constraints.

In a similar manner, the tax system may be implemented in successive versions. We may start with the most basic schedules and forms and add more forms successively. We may also use the relative complexity matrix (Table 4.5) together with levels of priority to guide us in sequencing the implementation. The first mandatory layer may be iteration 1. Of course, we may subdivide here into breadboarding versus mock-up to achieve two iterations for this step. Implementing the user interface first is probably a better choice, because this is the most crucial aspect of the system. After the mandatory functionality aspects, we may add level [2] functions for activity 1; in the next cycle, we may add level [2] functions for activities 2 and 3.

The advantage of an evolutionary approach to implementing the tax preparation system is that it is similar to reacting to new tax laws by implementing new schedules and forms. The disadvantage is that we might create more changes than necessary with this approach, although we will "keep expandability in mind." Because the basic set of schedules is small, it is probably better to implement the system in its entirety. We still may decide on a mock-up that we may give the user to "play with," so that inefficient organization of the user interface may be spotted before we have added function modules underneath and changes become more involved.

So far, we have tried to analyze two characteristics of quality expectations:

▶ their basic feasibility and

▶ the complexity of their implementation.

We demonstrated simple feasibility techniques for performance and relied on expert judgment combined with experiential data for a complexity assessment of quality areas. Published reports about functional complexity indices and tables of adjustment factors, such as the ones in [Dema82] may help; however, they must be augmented by tables for adjustment factors because of other quality requirements. In the absence of such tables, which are dependent on a particular environment as well as techniques to achieve them, we used a method called "guestimates" or "expert judgment." While this method, plus a conscientious effort at data collection, is appropriate for the beginning, methods based on historical data and the tables derived from it should replace it. How do we develop those tables? First, we start with a hypothesis for an adjustment table which is developed by defining gradations of complexities for the quality areas, such as performance, reliability, etc. Essentially, the expert formulating the hypothesis asks, "How much more complicated will it be to implement this additional quality requirement?" If that entails implementing specific types of additional functions, this may be estimated separately with the functional complexity model, and the complexity index is added to the basic one, weighted by the data CAF.

While Walston and Felix [Wals77] give ranges for productivity changes based on a few quality expectations, the ranges are too wide to be of use and must be associated with more specific definitions of the nature of the requirements. Literature is scarce on this topic; the best strategy is to develop one's own tables (one for each quality expectation adjustment factor). These are based on sets of expectations and techniques that are commonly encountered. Such quantifications provide clear and well-documented correlations between levels of quality and associated effort and complexity. They are, however, dependent on technique and environment. For this reason, no example tables are given, because they would inevitably be false. Rather, one may start with a comparative ranking of levels for a quality factor and then assign values between the ranked items through comparison. Those values are used as a starting table (as the working hypothesis) and are continually evaluated for their accuracy and effectiveness. Over time, they will change as new and better information becomes available or when the environment that they purport to model changes.

The last area of technical feasibility and complexity addresses availability of proper resources (feasibility) and the additional complexity introduced by less than optimal existing resources. First, there may be physical limitations on resources during development and during the software's operation. Computational capacity is one of the limitations that was addressed in the discussion of the feasibility of performance constraints (because the performance characteristics of the existing hardware and software are part of the performance model). This is true for component speed, storage capacity, or service rules for them.

There are other resources that may be necessary, e.g., the available language processors. How do they affect the feasibility or complexity of the project? If the project involves lots of text manipulation, a good language to use is SNOBOL, a bad one to use is FORTRAN. If only FORTRAN is available, the job will be complex, because the test manipulation routines, which would already be available in a text-oriented language, need to be written. The additional effort may be estimated by assessing the complexity indices of each additional support function that must be written. Similar effects result when a problem asks for a fourth-generation language, such as LOTUS 1-2-3™ or DBASE™, and only PASCAL or MODULA-2 are available. This causes additional work, because the language does not have sufficient power. The software developer must add the missing power in the language (i.e., the wheel must be reinvented). Sometimes that has been accomplished earlier. For example, a set of support routines for text manipulation may be available in FORTRAN at an installation. This, however, is additional support software that is not standard. That must be taken into account before deciding to use it.

For some quality expectations that we studied earlier, we implicitly assumed a given environment for which the system will be developed. When there are options, such as which language to choose, the effect of the implementation language on these requirements must be assessed. This entails a factorial analysis. The feasibility assessment that was described above is performed for every possible environment. To save time, one may rank the environments, depending on how supportive they are to accomplishing the stated requirements.

For example, we may assume that the requirements are ranked $R_1 > R_2 > R_3 > R_4 > R_5$. Let the operational environment options be E_1 to E_4. They represent a combination of levels for aspects of possible operational requirements (languages, support utilities and machines). We first select the environment that supports R_1 best; (assume it is E_2). Both E_1 and E_3 support R_1 to the same degree, but E_1 supports R_2 more than E_3. So E_1 will be selected as the next best environment. Further investigation reveals that E_4 supports R_4 better than E_3 but is less supportive of R_2. Therefore, E_3 is chosen next, and E_4 is chosen last. Knowing the relative importance of the requirements and how supportive of these requirements the different operational environment options are is enough to derive a ranking of the operational environment options. These may now be evaluated with respect to technical feasibility and complexity of implementation. Often operating environments that support the requirements of an application system cost more than those that do a less efficient job. Because complexity affects cost, one must evaluate more than the most supportive one (which makes operating and maintaining the software easiest). At other times, it is not clear which one is the best overall. Then, it is important to evaluate all of them with respect to the stated requirements. Fortunately, the choices are usually limited to one or two computer systems and a handful of languages. Theoretically, this still presents five to ten options. The ranking process, explained earlier, helps to reduce them further. This is called for when the problem of dealing with resource limitations involves reducing options rather than finding feasible ones.

The procedure for evaluating operating environments may also be followed for selecting and evaluating development environments. Here, the desired ranking is achieved by implementation complexity. For example, low-level languages increase the complexity (so do languages not suited for the type of application). They essentially become "low level" for the application. Development support software decreases complexity. Usually, only factors that differ from the standard development environment for the developers (which make the options different), must be considered for decision making.

In the standard effort estimators, factors that define the standard environment are known and their effect is already taken into account. The various tables that may be developed for deviations from the standard environment must only be developed and used for factors that may vary in a software development organization. Obviously, the more stable and standardized an environment is, the easier it is to keep predictive models for feasibility and complexity accurate and current.

Cost and effort models, which are used to estimate feasibility of budget and constraints, are driven by complexity indices. All three of these estimators for cost, effort, and complexity are based on a given development environment. For development environments, the development of a software system may be infeasible. For example, a language with parallelism may be necessary but the existing languages on the system may not have these features. Also, the user organization may require the use of development procedures that mandate automated software tools, but they may not be available; or, half the computer system options may not fulfill mandatory performance requirements. We may trade only options that fulfill mandatory requirements; all other options are infeasible.

In addition to the availability of hardware and software, the technical qualifications of the people who will develop and possibly maintain the application system must be taken into account. The first question is whether there is enough expertise to solve the problem. If there is, then we may ask how much expertise. If it is "standard," the current complexity indices developed for the project will remain. If expertise is higher or lower than "standard," the complexity of the project will decrease or increase accordingly. Higher expertise means more efficiency and less effort; lower than standard expertise increases complexity and resulting effort. Contributing factors to expertise are

▶ relevant education

▶ work experience in the areas required,

▶ motivation, and

▶ the ability to cooperate with other team members.

Only the first two are technical factors; therefore, only the first two are considered at this point. The last two are discussed in detail in Chapter 15. Like quality expectations, tables of correction factors may be developed over time for levels of expertise in key areas. They describe how knowledge about the problem, hardware, and software affects the complexity of its implementation. In the beginning, it is wise to restrict oneself to two guidelines:

▶ Use a small number of most important factors.

▶ Use a scale with few values to measure levels of experience in the factor areas.

Table 4.8 outlines an algorithmic description of how to establish complexity-adjustment factor tables. Table 4.9 explains how to use the tables to rank various development options and to reduce poorer options, so that only the better ones must be investigated further.

The results, either cumulative as overall complexity indices or as a set of complexity indices for various parts of the evaluation process, are input for the remainder of the feasibility study.

Table 4.8 Evaluation tool development.

---

1. Define standard development environment (SDE)
2. Develop complexity indicators and adjustment factors for SDE:
    a) Functional complexity table (FC_i)
    b) Data complexity adjustment factor (CAF_i)
    c) Quality expectation complexity adjustment factor tables (QE_i)
3. Develop complexity adjustment factors for SDE changes
    a) hardware (HW-SDE)
    b) software (SW-SDE)
    c) staff experience levels (SE-SDE)
4. Combine items 1 and 3 into development environment factor table (DE)
5. Develop complexity adjustment factors for operating environments (OE)
    a) standard is development environment (DE)
    b) deviation from DE are rated in tables, according to area and significance of change.

Table 4.9 Requirements analysis procedure.

---

1. Define set of DE-s as a function of hardware, software, and staff.
2. Define set of OE-s as function of hardware, software, and staff.
3. Rank DE-s, OE-s lexicographically with respect to stated requirements ranking.
   Result:$\{DE_j \mid j=1, \ldots, n\}$, $\{OE_i \mid i=1, \ldots, m\}$
   The lower the index, the higher the rank.
4. Reduce OE_i-s.
   Take OE adjustment table for one DE_j at a time.
   If OE_j has higher adjustment factor than OE_1 at DE_1
   $(j=1, \ldots, m)$
   then throw out OE_j
5. Reduce DE_i-s.
   Take SDE adjustment tables.
   If DE_i has higher adjustment factor than DE_1,
   then throw out DE_i.
6. Recompute rankings, reindex.
   Result: $\{DE_j \mid j=1, \ldots, k\}$, $\{OE_i \mid i=1, \ldots, g\}$
7. For i=1 to g
   For j=1 to k
     develop CI = f(FC, CAF, QE)
     adjust for DE_j, OE_i
       using HW-SDE, SW-SDE, OE tables.
   Result: final complexity index FCI(i,j)
     max = FCI(1,1)
8. Rank FCI(i,j) so that lowest FCI comes first and reindex FCI.
   Result: $\{FCI_p \mid p=1, \ldots, k*g\}$
9. Reduce options.
   top = k*g
   While $FCI_k >$ max do
     throw out FCI_k and its corresponding DE_j and OE_i.
     k = k−1
   end while

After consideration of technical, administrative and political factors, risk and benefit to the developers, and other nontechnical factors (as described in Part 2), an option may be selected. Its description uses relevant information on functional and quality requirements (requirements diagram and data dictionary, schedule and cost projections).

Problems and Questions

1. Given is a list of functions. Rank them according to functional complexity:

   a) changing a set of values in a data object

b) text manipulations (such as finding a substring, comparing one string to another, concatenating strings, etc.)

c) device driver routines

d) consistency checks in the system

e) splitting or combining data

f) tabular reports and simple figures

g) output formatting for nontabular reports

h) transfer data without change

i) user-interface functions (*not* total user-interface, but smallest constituent parts)

j) mathematical functions (e.g., computing an autocorrelation matrix, inverting a matrix, solving a system of equations)

k) simple computations (e.g., computing the mean of a set of numbers)

l) synchronization and sequencing control

m) initialization routines

n) data analysis (such as checking whether a bill has been paid and acting accordingly)

2. After you have done the ranking, take one function and assign unity (1) as a complexity weight. What complexity weights would you give the other functions in comparison, and why?

3. How does the requirements analysis procedure become simplified when there is only one development environment, when the development environment is also the operating environment, and when the quality expectations are standard and their complexity captured in tables?

4.7. The Requirements Document

The requirements document contains all functional and quality requirements for a software product. This document may be structured according to Table 4.1. Additionally, we must address versions, results of the requirements analysis as they pertain to the final requirements in the document, and types of acceptance tests of the final product. Although we may not give actual test cases until the inputs to the system are specified, we may describe the types of tests the software must pass. Table 4.10 summarizes an outline for the requirements document. This outline is only for the technical requirements document. It does not contain nontechnical information, such as the type of development contract and contract remedies. Nontechnical aspects of a requirement document will be discussed in Part 2.

Table 4.10 Outline for requirements document.

1. Overview
2. Product Capabilities (by version)
   a. functionality (hierarchically organized)
   b. useability (reliability, security, human factors)
   c. generality (extent of solution, portability, compatibility)
   d. lifetime expectations (adaptability, maintainability)
   e. documentation
3. Constraints (by version and overall)
   a. schedule
   b. resources (including hardware/software, staff, budget)
4. Benefits (by version and overall)
5. Summary of requirements analysis results
6. Acceptance criteria
7. Appendices

The section on product capabilities contains either requirements diagrams and the data dictionary or a description of the functions and data required by the software in an alternate notation. This must be included for all versions of the system. It helps to annotate the overall system description, indicating which version contains which functions and data or describing, in several system descriptions, successive levels of functionality. A description of the qualitative requirements follows. In Section 3, constraints are detailed, including schedule and available resources over time. Section 4 describes the expected tangible and intangible benefits that will be realized with the product. The next section gives a short summary of the requirements analysis results of the final requirements. Analysis substantiates why certain requirements are considered either difficult or easy and provides a summary of a feasibility study. It also points out options. The last section describes acceptance criteria: types of tests that will be run and what will be tested but not specifics of these tests. It does not describe particular test cases. This will not be done until the next life-cycle phase. Appendices may be added to explain some of the information gathered during requirements collection and analysis.

4.8. Phase Test of Requirements

The requirements document must be phase tested. The first step is to make sure that everything required by the outline is in the document (or that there is a good reason for something missing, e.g. that no performance requirements were imposed). It is important to catch errors early in the software development life cycle. Early on, they will be less expensive to fix, because less effort has gone into developing the erroneous aspect of the solution. There is less backtracking with the error correction. It is advisable to be quality conscious from the beginning and to establish workable procedures for acceptance of the first major document of the software development life cycle. Four dimensions of quality are

- ▶ clarity,

- ▶ comprehensiveness,

- ▶ consistency, and

- ▶ cost-effectiveness.

Each section and paragraph of the requirements document is reviewed and rated for each of these quality dimensions. Rating is a subjective activity and depends on the quality and experience of the raters, their preferences, biases, and objectives. We must choose the right people to examine the document. The "quality assurance team" consists of people with different but complementary views of the problem. We must include people who will be affected by the document. Those are the *users* or their representative or the marketing representative. Then we must consider the technical side of the development effort. There are people who must translate and refine the document into specifications. The *specification writers* must evaluate the document also, because the document must be understandable not only to the user, but also to the person who must work with it. For TAP, it will not help to write the requirements analysis entirely in tax terminology, unless the developer understands that. It is also necessary to involve the *managerial* level, because they must assess the quality of the document in the area of cost-effectiveness, and they must look at schedules, resource requirements, and personnel issues.

Thus, the "four C's" (dimensions of quality) are rated by three groups in the development organization:

- ▶ user organization (in the broad sense),

- ▶ technical staff, and

- ▶ managerial staff.

Although the writer may have done the best job possible we must require that another technical person evaluate the document to guard against tunnel vision on the part of the writer.

Another structured way of phase testing requirements is to check the document against "the seven sins" [Meye85]. Although they were originally meant to evaluate specifications, we have rewritten them slightly for requirements documents.

1. **Noise.**   Noise is irrelevant information. Or it may be relevant information but not for the problem, issue, or feature at hand. It is also called redundancy or remorse.

2. **Silence.**   Silence marks an omission. It occurs when a feature or aspect that is relevant and important is not covered in the specifications.

3. **Overspecification.**   Requirements are supposed to describe the needs of a solution not its implementation (unless, of course a particular implementation is a specific part of the requirements).

4. **Contradiction.**   A contradiction exists when a feature or aspect of the system is described in at least two different, incompatible ways.

5. **Ambiguity.**   An ambiguity allows the interpretation of a requirement in two or more ways. It is not clear how to interpret it.

6. **Forward reference.**   Features that are used before they are defined are instances of forward reference.

7. **Wishful thinking.**   This covers any statements about functionality and quality that cannot realistically be validated; i.e., there is no way of testing whether a requirement has been fulfilled.

In addition to these subjective testing activities there are other helpful testing guidelines:

- ▶ Make sure that all requirements diagrams and data dictionaries (or whatever other notation is used to describe functional requirements) meet notational rules. For requirements diagrams, this would mean to check whether data flow in more than one direction, whether data streams disappear or suddenly appear on a lower level with no indication of being a refinement, etc. This is similar to checking for compliance with coding standards and may be done in a walk-through. The diagrams also have to be cross-checked against the data dictionary: are all data in the requirements diagrams in the data dictionary and vice versa? Are all functional requirements represented in the requirements diagrams? For this we may have to cross-check with the requirements diagrams and the function table that explains what the activities do. Are the required levels of functionality represented?

▶ When quality of the requirements analysis is tested, we need to check whether all qualitative requirements have been analyzed. They should have been analyzed pair-wise against benefits and constraints (as described earlier in Sections 4.6.2. and 4.6.3.).

▶ Is one notation or method's result comparable with another's? This applies when several notations describe requirements; e.g., is the hierarchy developed through the requirements diagrams described in Warnier-Orr diagrams or with SADT code?

▶ Have all quality expectations been accounted for? This aspect of testing was mentioned earlier.

The areas of evaluation are essentially the same as the checklist (cf. Table 4.1) that helped us to develop the requirements document in the first place. Every evaluator must go through the requirements document and check the "four C's" of each item on the list. This type of evaluation can only be done successfully if the priorities of the project have been spelled out properly. To ascertain whether conflicts and trade-offs have been dealt with correctly and whether the document is consistent, we must know the priorities and goals of the project. Any contradictions (i.e., lack of consistency), ambiguities (i.e., lack of clarity), missing points (i.e., lack of comprehensiveness), and unrealistic expectations (i.e., lack of cost-effectiveness) must be pointed out.

In summary, a phase test for the requirements document uses the steps given in Table 4.11. These steps may have to be repeated several times when several versions of a software product are required.

Parts of this eight-step procedure may have been completed earlier, when collected requirements were analyzed for technical feasibility and for realization of required benefits, or when trade-offs were made (cf. Sections 4.6.2. and 4.6.3.).

It is advisable to collect this data from each evaluator and then let the document authors deal with the revisions. This requires clear and constructive evaluation. The revised version will be subjected to the same quality assurance procedure that was used for the areas that previously needed improvement. This process may require several iterations and renegotiations until the requirements document is ready for acceptance sign-

Table 4.11 Steps of the phase test for requirements.

1. Check contents against outline of document.
2. Review content for "four C's" and "seven sins".
3. Cross-check requirements diagrams against data dictionary and function descriptions.
4. Cross-check requirements diagrams against required (levels of) functionality.
5. Cross-check requirements analysis summary to determine whether all requirements have been analyzed, whether all benefits are obtained, and whether all constraints are met.
6. Check multimethod and notations in requirements document for consistency between methods and notations.
7. Determine whether all quality expectations have been accounted for.
8. Does the acceptance test strategy cover all functional and qualitative aspects of the software product?
9. Determine whether versions are sequenced properly and whether they comply with their budget and availability of resources.

off. Although we must be sure that all the user classes are satisfied with the requirements document and that the developers are confident of the feasibility of the project, we also must guard against "endless debating." After the document is accepted, it must be considered "frozen." Changes will require renegotiation of the project and an evaluation of ramifications of the proposed changes.

We also must not start the next phase prematurely with an insufficient understanding of the problem and its requirements. Although it may look as if we are spending most of the time in discussion and never seem to get any code done, many projects are fairly trivial and rely on common techniques and available packages for their implementation. The hardest part of development in these cases is often requirements and specification writing. Quite justifiably it will also consume a significant portion of the total development time.

In the example of the tax helper, the final product will most likely consist of a modified spreadsheet and accounting programs that are tailored to the tax forms used and, most importantly, to the record and tax needs of the individual or class of individuals. It is not difficult to implement an accounting or spreadsheet program or buy such a program; however, the crucial steps are to determine what forms and record keeping requirements are necessary and would constitute a significant help. This project relies heavily on the quality of the work in the early phases that lead to a short, almost trivial implementation. But we must know what will help and what will not; otherwise, we may provide a solution but not for the user's problem. Other problems require more effort in the later phases, and requirements are fairly straightforward. An example might be developing a compiler for a known language in its standard form. Other examples fall somewhere in between.

4.9. Summary

This chapter described requirements collection for qualitative requirements and their analysis. The requirements checklist in Table 4.1 organized requirements into either those describing product capabilities or those stating constraints and benefits. Product capability requirements include functionality, usability, intended use, future or lifetime expectations, and documentation requirements. Constraints refer to schedule and resources. Expected benefits may be tangible or intangible. The user must rank these requirements. This ranking constitutes the basic information for trade-offs that may become necessary.

We do not always have the opportunity to let the user describe requirements to the developer or contractor. When this is the case other tactics must be chosen. Section 4.5. described some of these scenarios.

After requirements have been collected, requirements analysis starts. One activity determines whether required benefits will be met. Each requirement must have a matching benefit at the same level of importance. We presented a tabular technique for this analysis. Technical feasibility analysis is presented as a five-step procedure: (1) check whether it is feasible to implement a given functionality; (2) identify and rank all complexity aspects of alternatives for a functionality; (3) evaluate combined impact of functional requirements in qualitative requirements areas; (4) compare quality expectations and their impact on technical resource constraints; and (5) list remaining technically feasible alternatives that compare options.

The presentation formalized this procedure through complexity indices of functions and complexity adjustment factors for the effects of complexity of data and of qualitative requirements. Other complexity adjustment factors address the effects of hardware, software, and staff experience, i.e., the development environment. Adjustments may be made for different development environments and differences between the development and operating environment. Table 4.9 summarizes the requirements analysis procedure.

This structured procedure has the advantage of predictable and objective evaluations. Its drawbacks are the potential initial overhead for development of complexity factors and how they relate to risk, cost, and effort models (cf. Chapters 12, 13). Reliable complexity adjustment factors must be developed. This effort may be unnecessary for small projects or rapidly changing project types and development methodologies. For such cases, we should follow the steps of the procedure, but we would not use formal complexity metrics. This, however, will make the use of estimation models for cost and effort more difficult (cf. Chapters 12 and 14).

The complexity assessment procedure is related to the one proposed in [Dema82]. It has been refined, and there is more emphasis on analysis and trade-off activities that use these complexity indices.

The requirements document describes all requirements for all proposed versions of the software, including product capabilities, constraints on schedule and resources, benefits, a summary of requirements analysis results, acceptance criteria, and other information that is deemed necessary by users or developers. A requirements document often forms the basis of a contract and, thus, has legal significance in addition to providing information for developers and their managers.

Like all other phases, requirements also should be phase tested. Because most requirements documents are written in natural language, we presented two strategies to find errors: looking for the "four C's" and checking for the "seven sins" [Meye85]. Table 4.11 outlined the nine steps of phase testing requirements. This reflects our emphasis on continuous phase testing throughout the software development life cycle.

► 5

Specifications

5.1. Overview

Requirements define the characteristics of an acceptable solution. Specifications, the deliverable of the specifications phase, give both the developer and the user a precise, concrete description of the proposed computer solution. Specifications of a software system describe functional and quality aspects. The functional part of the specifications describe the inputs, outputs, and functions of the system, as well as how the system changes state with different inputs. The quality aspects of specifications describe in more detail how the various quality requirements will manifest themselves in the system and how that will appear to the user. The same list of quality aspects given during the requirements analysis applies.

Specifications convert requirements to a description that enables the user and the developers to see what the system will look like and how it will behave. Without such a description, users do not know "what they are getting," and developers do not know "what to build." That is why the specifications phase is an important part of the software development life cycle.

Specifications bridge the gap between requirements and design. Its inputs are the requirements document and information from users and developers. The latter information is important for the following reasons:

▶ Specifications must describe a usable system. Therefore, it is imperative that the user or a user representative guide specification development and evaluate whether specifications indeed describe a usable system.

▶ The system as described in its specifications must meet requirements and be implementable, which usually requires design expertise.

Thus the software engineers who develop specifications must possess the communication skills to relate to users, enough application experience to understand the users' needs and language, and knowledge of specification methods and user interface design techniques. They also need design skills, at least to the degree of assessing the implementation impact of decisions made during the specification phase. Because of increasing specialization, these skills may be the cumulative skills of a team, not of a single individual.

Specifications describe the solution in all its aspects and with all functions and features it provides. Thus more precise estimates of effort, personnel needs, computer time, costs, etc. become possible.

A variety of specification methods exist and span the entire spectrum from formal, mathematical notations to informal descriptions in natural language. Depending on project objectives and goals, some will be more appropriate than others. Some techniques cover all steps and activities of developing specifications, others only a specific aspect.

Section 5.2. describes various types of functional specifications based on their objectives and goals. Section 5.3. illustrates the scope of specifications, describing inputs, processing, outputs, state transitions, quality aspects, and programming notes. Section 5.4. details the steps involved in developing specifications and the activities that are part of each step. Section 5.5. provides guidelines for user interface design, one of the aspects of specification development.

Formal methods are used when the advantages of mathematical rigor outweigh the disadvantages. Some of the advantages are the possibility of correctness proofs, easy or automatable checks for completeness and consistency, automatic code generation, and standard translation rules. Disadvantages of formal methods include complexity, limited practicality for large systems, and the need to learn a formal notation that may be foreign to users and developers alike.

On the other end of the spectrum are specifications written in natural language without any prescribed framework. Somewhere between these two extremes are techniques that use graphs or tables. They provide a formal notation for a specific aspect of specifications. The aspects that are used to structure specifications are inputs, processing, outputs, state transitions the system goes through, and quality aspects. Most specification documents are developed as a combination of natural language and formal description for specific aspects. This improves readability while maintaining verifiability for aspects that are described with a formal notation.

Section 5.6. presents a series of methods that cover the spectrum of specification techniques. Section 5.6.1. presents formal methods and notations. The first, Extended Backus-Naur Form (EBNF) can be used to describe inputs and outputs. The second, a notation suggested by Meyer [Meye85] is capable of describing relations between inputs, outputs, and functions. It is based on college-level math notations for functions, relations, and predicates and was chosen because it is one of the simplest to learn and use.

Section 5.6.2. gives a partial specification for the program analyzer as an example of natural language specifications.

Section 5.6.3. describes two formal notations that cover a specific aspect of specifications: decision tables and cause-effect graphs. Decision tables formalize the relationship between input and processing and define input classes that result in different processing. Furthermore, decision tables help in selecting test cases.

Cause-effect graphs are related to decision tables. They help prepare decision tables and test cases for specifications. They provide a link between natural language and decision tables and are therefore a useful aid in developing formal specifications.

Section 5.6.4. explains state transition diagrams, a formal method for describing the state transitions that a system may go through. State transitions occur, for example, when an editor goes from input mode to edit mode, where different commands apply or when the tax system goes from tax input to tax computation mode. State transition diagrams are described in tabular form with transition tables. Section 5.6.4. uses transition diagrams to describe state changes and what causes them.

Section 5.7. deals with quality aspects of specifications and assessing qualitative requirements. The system as specified must conform to all quality expectations in the requirements document, and the specifiers must match objectives, benefits, and requirements and reestimate resource needs. Section 5.8. describes the specification document, its organization, and its content. This is the major deliverable of the specification phase.

Section 5.9. consists of a first draft of the acceptance test, which is based on the specifications and thus implementation independent. Early planning for the acceptance test helps to clarify the user's and designer's understanding of the specifications to see what the finished system is going to be tested against.

Section 5.10. discusses phase testing of specifications. The specifications, like all other deliverables in the software development process, are subject to verification and validation (V/V). V/V includes all the techniques and procedures needed to ascertain whether a level of quality has been reached; this is sometimes referred to as *quality assurance*. A set of test cases is needed to test the functional specifications, some of which can be used for acceptance tests. The phase test checks whether the specifications match the requirements and objectives for the system. If not, a formal change request is submitted to revise the requirements document accordingly. If the change request for the requirements document is denied, the specifications themselves have to be revised to reflect all requirements and objectives.

5.2.   Types of Specifications

Different types of specifications are classified on the basis of degree of accuracy and precision of input, output, and essential functions of the proposed system. This description is done by the components of a system, which may be given through the activity structure of the requirements diagram. Specifications are usually developed by the developers and, at the top level, constitute the developer's interpretation of the requirements and its translation into a solution. The DACS glossary [Dacs79] states three degrees of precision for specifications:

1. **Very precise specifications.**   The description of what the software system does is completely and precisely defined. The implementor has to make only a few, if any assumptions, and it is almost impossible to arrive at an ambiguous interpretation of the system.

2. **Precise specifications.**   Inputs, outputs, and functions are well defined. There are some underlying assumptions which are not explicitly stated, but it is assumed that any programmer who works on the project has sufficient experience in this type of project and understands them. There is potential for ambiguity and misunderstanding, however, from mismatched assumptions, lack of experience, and lack of communication. To make these kinds of specifications work, the programmers must be at the same level, and newcomers must be properly initiated, guided, or formally instructed. Since questions will come up, good, reliable communication channels are needed. Development teams that have been working with each other for a while often develop informal standards and assumptions; this degree of accuracy for specifications will probably be sufficient. The same holds for set and known standards for software development. In cases where several new people come in, or when there are barriers to communication (such as multisite teams), precise specifications may be inadequate. It may be more cost effective to develop very precise ones in the first place. It is a trade-off between cost of accuracy (how much will it take to make the specifications very precise) versus cost of inaccuracy (what will it cost to resolve the effects of misunderstandings).

3. **Imprecise specifications.**   In this type of specifications, the inputs, outputs, and functions are only loosely defined. Much of what is required is assumed, not specified. The specifications rely heavily on experience and frequent communication. Such speci-

fications are analogous to "insider jokes" in the sense that outsiders may have a hard time getting the (fine) point. Therefore loose or imprecise specifications have no place in development situations with outside personnel, inexperienced people, and no instant mechanism to resolve questions. Imprecise specifications work best in small development groups that share an office or work in close proximity, so that the inevitable questions can be solved on the spot, in all their ramifications. No one is left uninformed or is without impact on the decision-making process. However, often the time that is saved writing precise specifications is used for resolving questions. Again, there is an obvious trade-off to be made.

The inherent risks must also be considered when deciding which degree of precision should be used. How much does it matter to have problems originating from precise or imprecise specifications? If the potential losses are small, it may not matter too much. If they are considerable and a conservative strategy is sought, the usual choice is "more precision." When human factors have a high priority, or when the user wants to review what the system will look like before its implementation, it is advisable to have a precise specification of the human machine interface.

5.3. Scope

Specifications describe input and its processing, the resulting output, any state transitions the system may go through along the way, and quality characteristics of the software. Occasionally, specifications may contain programming notes.

5.3.1. Input

The input description to the system details both syntax and semantics of any input given to the system. This includes formats of all inputs, which inputs are valid, which are invalid, default values when the user does not provide a value for an input variable, and how the system interprets that. Input ranges for all types of user input also need to be described because they impact the design and implementation of the system. Defining valid, erroneous, and default values creates three classes of inputs for a given input variable. There may be more when valid inputs are processed in various ways. In that case, the class of valid inputs can be divided even further.

When input is described in this way, it is defined as a set of classes where all values within a class have either processing or some other characteristic in common (such as being invalid for example). Every class is distinct from any other. As a result there must be boundaries between them. These are often described in terms of boundary conditions. For example, a boundary condition for the minimum size of a list to be sorted may be 1, and so the error condition for the list is "length smaller than 1." What about an upper limit for the length of the list? Fuzzy boundaries are a frequent mistake when specifying input classes. Unnecessary bounds are another. For example, if the user does not think there is a reasonable fixed upper bound then there shouldn't be any, no matter how convenient it might be for the implementation.

The number of parameters for an input command could be none, one, or two. This means that "number of parameters greater than three" is an error condition for erroneous input. The boundary is three parameters, which is still legal, versus four parameters, which is illegal. We have to pay close attention to what happens at the boundaries, because this is where many errors tend to occur. For example, one might erroneously specify that "number of parameters greater or equal to three" is the error condition. This is one of those famous "off by one errors" that happens at the boundary of input classes.

Another possible mistake is to leave the boundary value out, as in
  legal input: "number of parameters < 3"
  illegal input: "number of parameters $> = 4$"

Nothing was specified about how to handle three parameters. Because values at the boundaries are prone to either type of mistake, they require special attention.

5.3.2. Processing and Output

The associated processing is described for every class of input, together with the outputs the function will provide. Often these two are subsumed under the category output description. The output description of the specifications puts all outputs in their respective classes. This includes prompts and terminal messages, error messages and warnings, reports, graphs, computation results, etc. As with the input description, it encompasses layout ("syntax") and meaning ("semantics") of the outputs. The description relates outputs to the inputs that caused them, which is done by specifying associated processing. A good specification document should be precise enough so that the user can determine exactly what outputs are generated for any given input. As with inputs, there will be boundaries on the output classes as well. Care needs to be taken that those descriptions are complete. Note that inputs to the system can be made from files; output can be made to files. This means that general formats as to what (not how) those files will look like needs to be determined. Depending on how files interface with subsystems or modules, a specific format may already be determined. The subsystems or modules are independent from each other in this respect, and development can proceed without further specification and communication as to what the file interfaces should be.

5.3.3. State Transitions

Specifications describe how the system changes states. Some processing functions generate outputs to the user and put the system into a different state. These system transformations are part of the specifications and are a first cut at sequencing processing and functions in the system. System transformations are described from a user's viewpoint. For example, an editor usually has an input state, where information is entered by the user, and an edit state, where previously entered information is changed. There are commands or control characters that switch the system from input mode to edit mode. This is a system transformation. Within a given system state, usually only a subset of all possible inputs (e.g., commands) are legal. Some of the legal ones will change the system state again.

5.3.4. Quality Characteristics

Quality characteristics, which are refined during specifications, include reliability, efficiency, security, adaptability, etc. Under reliability, one would explain in detail the effects of any possible failure of the system as they manifest themselves in the system (system state, system data), the files (are they open, closed, compromised?), and the user. A section in the specifications could describe the overall approach. Detailed effects of particular (user) errors are described in the Input-Processing-Output descriptions throughout the functional specifications.

Efficiency constraints are more precisely analyzed, using the new, more detailed functional information that the specifications provide to reestimate turnaround or response time and storage requirements. Often they are classified by usage pattern.

5.3.5. Programming Notes

Occasionally, the specifications provide some ideas or suggestions on system design in the form of programming notes. This should be minimized so as not to unnecessarily constrain the implementation, thus precluding better designs. On the other hand, specifiers may have gained insights into the problem of how to build the system, and conveying that information can save the designers extra work. Or, when the programming notes point out a route to avoid, it may prevent the designers from going down a dead end street. While the specifications describe every possible input to the system (legal, invalid, or default) and the system's reaction to each input (outputs, processing, and system transformations), little or nothing should be implied about how the system is to be built. Specifications only describe *what* the system looks like and *what* it does, not *how* this is to be accomplished.

5.4. Top-Down Specification Development

Table 5.1 describes a top-down approach to writing specifications that begins with the requirements document and, where it is available, the requirements diagram and the data dictionary. "Level" corresponds to the levels in the requirements diagram and the data dictionaries. It is a good idea to structure specification information according to the levels the users will see when they use the system. A structured approach that follows the levels of the requirements diagrams and data dictionaries reduces cross-referencing between phases, and during maintenance and further development, implications of changes for different phases can be investigated more easily.

Table 5.1 Steps to develop specifications.

---

1.   Select overall approach
2.   *From* level ← highest-level *downto* lowest-level *do*
      2.1. Classify level's inputs and their boundaries
        - legal
        - illegal
        - default
      2.2 Refine those three major classes where they differ in the processing of input.
      2.3 Identify classes of outputs for that level.
      2.4. Identify conditions for different processing.
      2.5. Identify multiple and compound conditions and their processing consequences for level.
      2.6 Define system transformations for level.
    end step 2.
3.   Match with requirements. *
4.   Reestimate resources. *
5.   Approval process including quality assurance and V/V. *

Note: All steps marked with asterisks may involve iteration to previous steps and possibly to a previous phase.

    The first decision is to select the overall approach. Because specifications define (among other things) the user interface, requirements for human factors play an important role. Selecting an overall approach means selecting techniques for writing specifications, appropriate languages, and diagramming techniques. It also entails choosing the type of user interface. There are three major types: command languages, menu driven systems, and graphic-oriented systems.

    After the overall approach has been selected, the inputs for the top level need to be defined and put into an input class. For a command language, this means defining the top-level commands and their parameters. In a menu-driven system, the main menu is designed. In the requirements diagram, the data objects that are closest to the sources and sinks of the system are usually next. In the data dictionary, we can see how they are described in more detail. The data dictionary lists their constituent parts and options. Any lowest level data items which have not originated from a user type source (not necessarily directly) or are not ultimately going to a sink at the border of the system, do not have to be considered for specifications. In this way, we can use the requirements diagram and the data dictionary from the previous phase to help us in determining inputs and outputs and whether or not they have all been considered. The same is true for the files used in the system.

The input values for input data objects that are defined at a given level are then separated into three major classes according to whether they are valid, invalid, or default values. The classes are then examined to see whether the values within a class will result in different processing. For example, Form SE helps to determine whether additional social security tax should be paid for self-employment income. This form only needs to be filled in when there was self-employment income (an **SE–amount** > 0). When there was none (an **SE–amount** $= 0$), no Form SE needs to be filled in. Neither is Form SE necessary when there was a business loss (**SE–amount** < 0). The two conditions (**SE–amount** $= 0$ and **SE–amount** < 0) differ in other processing, however, because the first signifies no net income in this income category, while the second indicates a business loss. Zero would probably be a reasonable default value for **SE–amount** because it will keep tallies unchanged. Because 0 is the default, this value is in a different category than the negative ones. Note that there are no illegal ones; this was an example of refining valid inputs into further subclasses. Illegal inputs do not all generate the same error message and system response. Where they do not, they are put into different subclasses of illegal inputs. At this point, we have defined classes of input and associated processing for a given level.

The next step is to identify the resulting output classes for those (input, processing) classes at the present level of analysis. We work backwards from the sink of the requirements diagram and data dictionary. Specific output values belong to separate classes if they are generated through different processing steps. Which processing applies depends on a combination of input conditions. These are identified next and may be simple or compound. It is useful to identify the simple conditions per input data item first and then determine the compound ones for combinations of data items.

After input, processing, and output, we define the system states at that level and the conditions for changes in system states. This concludes *Input-Processing-Output-Transformation* or IPOT specifications for the given level. The top level is the user interface level, and the lower level specifications are not always totally visible to the user. In systems, these lower levels help to specify the nature of interfaces between subsystems (what, not how) and the lower levels of processing.

After the full IPOT description, the specifications must be matched against the requirements. Do they fulfill all functional requirements, i.e. are all features included? Do they fulfill the qualitative requirements in areas such as security, performance, adaptability, etc.? Are the estimated needs for resources, time, budget, etc. still correct? This applies to development and operation. If requirements differ from what is considered achievable now, and if resource estimates have increased beyond what is allowable, a change request for the requirements document needs to be submitted. This means an iteration back to the previous phase (the requirements) and, if not approved, may involve another iteration through the first part of the specification activity.

The last step in the specifications stage is the V/V or quality assurance activity. In this step the specifications are evaluated for correctness, completeness, and precision. When their quality is adequate, they are accepted and frozen. This general process of specification development is language and method independent.

5.5. User Interface Design

There are three types of user interfaces: command languages, menu-driven systems, and graphic-oriented systems. Usually command languages are preferred by the intermediate to experienced user because they offer the following potential advantages:

▶ They provide faster use of the system. This is true when commands can be abbreviated; bringing up menus tends to take longer. Some menu-driven systems provide a shortcut through their menus for experienced users (e. g. Lotus-1-2-3™, Multimate™). Instead of going from menu to menu through the hierarchy, complete "paths" can be entered (much like a command sequence) that switch to the last menu in the path without bringing up any intermediate menus.

▶ There are less required sequences of interaction between the user and the machine. Menus are often associated with required execution sequences where the user is stepped through the sequence. Opting out of a sequence often entails a return to the main menu, and going across levels is harder.

▶ Command languages, when chosen carefully, are amenable to macro construction, which makes it possible for the user to define execution sequences on a permanent basis, thus speeding up the system's use.

▶ Commands require command interpretation but less elaborate layout of the screens.

▶ Command languages lend themselves to interactive and batch use.

Menus on the other hand are favored for less experienced or intermittent users who tend to forget the fine points of using a system, even the syntax of commands. The potential advantages of menus are as follows:

▶ the user has to remember less about how to use the system, because every menu can explain the possible choices to him;

▶ sequences of menus are a convenient way to step the user through an execution sequence without him having to remember it; and

▶ there is no need to learn a command language that if not designed properly, can be cryptic and prone to user error.

These two approaches are complementary. The actual choice depends on the type of user and his preference as well as the usage patterns for the system. The third option, graphics, and possibly a mouse, can be used in either case but is usually reserved for situations which require icons and graphics capabilities in the user interface. It can easily become a much more work-intensive, and thus costly, interface than either of the others.

Regardless of which approach is taken, there are some guidelines which apply for all. First, the user interface should be uniform and based on one concept. This rules out mixing commands with menus or different approaches to an implementation of commands or menus. For example, if menu selections are numbered 1, 2, 3, . . . and the user is asked to type in the appropriate number, there should not be menus where selections are identified a, b, c. Exit selection in menus should always be the same for all menus (e.g., 9 or 99 or X when selections are made with alpha characters). For command languages, the syntax of the commands and their parameters should also be uniform. Commands that sometimes have three characters, sometimes five, or sometimes seven are not. Full length English language commands may be of varying length, but abbreviations may not be. Neither is it uniform to require parameters separated by blanks in one command, by commas in the next, and by vertical bars in the third.

In order to design a harmonious, uniform user interface, it is important to keep designers to a minimum; otherwise the user interface reflects a series of concepts that is anything but uniform.

Appropriate selection of the user interface hinges on the specifier's knowledge of the user's environment. This requires a clear understanding of the problems, needs, and usage patterns of the prospective users. Problem analysis and requirements collection provide this understanding.

In our examples, the tax preparation system and the program analysis system, we have two different types of users. The users of the tax preparation system are intermittent users; they may not use the system for weeks or months at a time. For them a menu-driven system that steps them through the execution sequences is probably the best. On the other hand, the program analysis system is going to be used by experienced programmers, teachers, and graders. When the programs are long, they may want to submit the analysis in a batch mode. For them, a command language is probably a better choice.

Ergonomics is an area of industrial psychology that deals with the most effective way of physically organizing work. Ergonomists use their knowledge about the psychology of man-machine communication to suggest features for a user interface or to evaluate one.

One of the underlying benefits of conceptual integrity is that it makes the user less prone to errors, because he can expect patterns for proper use of the system. Once he has memorized the major concept, it is easier for him to learn and keep proficient in using the system. The more exceptions and the more concepts buried in the user interface, the harder it will be to learn the system and to keep fluent in conversing with it. User productivity is very much a function of user knowledge of the system.

It is also a function of user error rate, which means minimizing user errors is another important guideline. This is furthered by inputs that are uniform in format, abbreviation, and underlying concept. Tailoring the interface to the training of the user is also important. If a system is overly hard for a beginner to use, he will get turned off and never learn how to use the system. Even if they do put up with the learning process, they will probably make a lot of errors. Help facilities and informative (never abusive) error messages are mandatory. An angry user is rarely productive and might even be destructive. Errors are made more frequently when long inputs are required from the user, because there is simply more opportunity for typographical errors. Another source of potential error and user aggravation is when user input is not acknowledged or flagged as erroneous until much later, requiring the user to input a whole series of inputs all over again. For these reasons, information that the user must type in should be brief, and the system should validate and acknowledge it immediately. Unwarranted assumptions about the type of input data can prove deleterious to a system. For example, if a system requires a yes/no response from the user but only checks whether the first character is a y (for yes), a user inputting a "yuk" may see a process initiated, which he did not want at all (such as the deletion of a file and with it an entire day's work). There are two lessons to be learned from this example:

▶ The system should have been able to handle any input data and detect user errors appropriately.

▶ when a sensitive or complex transaction is initiated, the user should have a chance to verify it and tell the system what he wants done. The input in this verification step should be validated just as carefully as the other inputs (point above).

When processing is more complex, results may not be shown to the user immediately, even in an interactive environment. Because of this, it is helpful to have the system show the user some indication that it is still working on the processing. Otherwise, the user may wonder whether something happened to the system, whether it accepted the input, whether it is hung up in a loop, and whatever else his imagination may dream up. Impatient users start playing with the keyboard. Is the system prepared to handle that? How?

Where the accuracy of an input is crucial, it may become necessary to require redundant information from the user. [Myer76] mentions the example of a banking system where accounts should be identified by name *and* account number. This way typographical errors will not cause incorrect deposits or withdrawals. Rather, an inconsistency between name and account number can be detected immediately before the change is made. A similar argument may be made for many other database systems with crucial data transformations (such as the tax payer data the IRS keeps or the customer data which is available to credit card companies). Other, nonbusiness examples include process control systems that give the user the possibility to reset important system control parameters. Usually this need for input accuracy is coupled with high reliability needs and high penalties (monetarily or loss of life) for potentially legal input values which might, however, be incorrect in a particular situation. Analogous to coding theory, redundancy in the input provides the system with the ability to spot incorrect input values through consistency checks.

A user interface with good human factors in all these areas can become rather complex. Whether to prompt the user for all missing input or to be a little more parsimonious can make a big difference in the complexity of the implementation. For one thing, the system has to be aware of details of the system state and provide this information in the form of analysis and helpful suggestions to the user. Furthermore, overly zealous prompting can actually confuse the user more than it helps. For example, take the following command:

    PUT address envelope

where **PUT** is a command with two parameters, indicating what (**address**) is to be put where (**envelope**). If the user forgets the format and just types in **PUT**, the system might prompt

    ? What:

and after **address** has been input, it comes back with

    ? Where:

to process **envelope**, the last required input. For the sake of argument, assume that the two actual parameters for **PUT** were a and e. The user did not hit the a key properly, and the *a* was not input, only the *e*. The system interprets the *e* as a "what" parameter and prompts for "where." At this point, the novice user might ask, "What do I do now? The system has the wrong impression!" What was meant as a help to the less knowledgeable user has backfired against him. It would have been easier to report

PUT needs 2 parameters, WHAT and WHERE.
Please repeat command:

User interface complexity is not minimized by global guidelines advocating "always prompt for missing information," or "never prompt for missing information." Rather, by analyzing the user, his needs, the commands, and the errors he could possibly make, a judicious choice avoids the shortcomings of prompting while preserving its advantages.

Error messages are important for a well designed user interface. They were already discussed in the section on human factors and reliability requirements, and the design of the user interface should reflect these requirements. Error messages are designed just as uniformly as the remainder of the user interface.

In summary, [Myer76] suggests that the most successful strategy in specifying a user interface for a reliable product is to provide a uniform and simple interface, to expect anything as input, and to immediately detect as many errors as possible.

Problems and Questions

1. Why was a menu-based user interface chosen for the tax preparation system?

2. What are the reasons for choosing a command language for the program analysis project?

3. Can you see reasons for combining menus and commands even though it violates the idea of uniformity? Explain why you see or do not see the reasons for doing it.

4. How would you prompt for multiple input in a command?

    a) consider long vs. short parameters

    b) consider criticality of input and function

    c) consider sophistication of user

    What are your choices in each situation? Explain.

5.6. Writing Specifications

5.6.1. Specification Languages

Specification languages span the entire spectrum from very formal, and thus mathematically verifiable notation, to English narrative. There is some disagreement whether natural language is to be used at all. [Meye85] considers natural language specifications neither precise nor rigorous enough. Therefore, such specifications give rise to problems due to ambiguities and misunderstandings. Moreover, they are hard to verify or validate. And lastly, in an era when more and more tools support software development, it is easier to build tools for a formal specification language, which makes the use of natural language less attractive still.

Natural language has the advantage of being easy to understand for the user. He does not have to learn another formalism to be able to read what his system will look like. One option then is to develop formal specifications for the developers and then translate them into natural language or figures for the user.

Formalism has the advantage of concise accuracy, allowing little room for ambiguities and vagueness. Because of its formality, it allows the use of formal verification techniques. Formal notations which have been used to describe the syntax of user input include BNF or Backus-Naur Form [Naur63] and its variations, the Vienna definition language [Jone80], and syntax graphs such as the ones used to describe PASCAL's syntax [Jens75]. An extended form of BNF and syntax diagrams work well for specifying input and output.

Backus-Naur-Form (BNF) and Extended Backus-Naur-Form (EBNF)

Command syntax is often described formally, because it simplifies implementation and verification. BNF is a very common type of context-free grammar that is often used even in user manuals to describe the syntax of command and programming languages. The alphabet of this grammar consists of terminal tokens (characters and words), non-terminals (items in ⟨ ⟩), and a special, nonterminal starting symbol. Terminals are characters and words which occur in the language as a predefined unit. Examples would be operator symbols, key words and reserved words, blanks, delimiters and brackets, and the character set for the language.

Beside the alphabet, there are rules how to derive valid sentences in the language that is defined in BNF notation. These rules state how a set of terminal symbols, called a sentence, derives from the starting symbol. All the sentences that the rules can generate form the language. BNF notation has been generalized to include operations in the rule descriptions that were not part of the original notation. Table 5.2 shows rules and transformations of this extended definition. Additionally, precedence in transformation rules can be expressed with parentheses.

Table 5.2 Extended BNF notation.

---

1. Basic Form of a Transformation Rule

   ⟨a⟩ ::= ⟨b⟩   the symbol on the left (⟨a⟩) is transformed into the expression on the right (⟨b⟩).

2. Other Right-Hand Side Expressions

   ⟨a⟩ | ⟨b⟩ | ⟨c⟩ ...   list of possible transformations, | indicating choice of one of the expressions listed

   ⟨a⟩ ⟨b⟩ ⟨c⟩   concatenation of element ⟨a⟩

   {⟨a⟩}   repetition (zero or more) of element ⟨a⟩

   [⟨a⟩]   element ⟨a⟩ may be present or not

   {⟨a⟩}^{k} element ⟨a⟩ is repeated up to k times, maybe less.

Application of EBNF

Table 5.3 defines a command language for the program analysis system. Note that syntactical correctness according to the BNF notation does not mean that a sentence makes sense, i.e., is correct or meaningful semantically. For example, the command

ANALYZE ABC.PAS (50,10)

Table 5.3 EBNF description of top level of command language for program analysis system.

1.	⟨command⟩	::=	⟨analysis⟩ | ⟨stats⟩ | ⟨reports⟩ | ⟨quit⟩ | ⟨compare⟩
2.	⟨analysis⟩	::=	(ANALYSIS | AN) ⟨an_parms⟩
3.	⟨stats⟩	::=	(STATISTICS | ST)
4.	⟨reports⟩	::=	(REPORTS | RE) ⟨re_parms⟩
5.	⟨an_parms⟩	::=	⟨file⟩ [⟨range⟩] [, ⟨an_parms⟩]
6.	⟨range⟩	::=	⟨module⟩ | ⟨lines⟩
7.	⟨module⟩	::=	⟨alpha⟩ { ⟨alpha⟩ | ⟨num⟩ | _ }
8.	⟨alpha⟩	::=	A | B | ... | Z
9.	⟨num⟩	::=	1 | 2 | ... | 9 | 0
10.	⟨number⟩	::=	⟨num⟩ { ⟨num⟩ }
11.	⟨file⟩	::=	⟨fname⟩ [.PAS]
12.	⟨fname⟩	::=	⟨alpha⟩ { ⟨alpha⟩ | ⟨num⟩ | _ }^{6}
13.	⟨lines⟩	::=	"(" ⟨number⟩, ⟨number⟩ ")"
14.	⟨quit⟩	::=	QUIT | QU
15.	⟨compare⟩	::=	(COMPARE | CO) ⟨co_parms⟩
16.	⟨co_parms⟩	::=	⟨id⟩ (* | ⟨st_file⟩) { , ⟨st_file⟩ }
17.	⟨st_file⟩	::=	⟨fname⟩ [.STA]
18.	⟨id⟩	::=	⟨alpha⟩ {⟨alpha⟩}^{9}

Note: To distinguish parentheses which are part of the language that the BNF describes from the BNF notation symbols, they are set in double quotes.

is syntactically correct but does not make any sense because the lower limit of the line numbers is higher than the upper limit. The example has been simplified by leaving out the delimiters between parts of a command. This is common practice and indicates that the separation of the input text into identifiers, delimiters, key words, etc. has already taken place by a lower level functionality. This subdivision into lexical items or lexical tokens is called *lexical analysis* and is a step prior to parsing. Parsing means to identify whether the lexical tokens form a syntactically correct sentence and to define what its parts are.

A representation in a BNF-like notation has the advantage that a parser may be easily implemented. For a description of how to implement the corresponding parser with a technique called top-down parsing, see the design chapter. Many user manuals use this notation to specify command syntax.

Syntax Graphs or Syntax Diagrams

The command language could also have been described as a *syntax graph* or *syntax diagram* [Horo83], [Jens75]. A syntax diagram is a graph with two types of nodes: circles and boxes. Terminal symbols (tokens) are represented by circles, nonterminals by boxes. Arcs are the equivalent of operators between these symbols. Figure 5.1 shows the

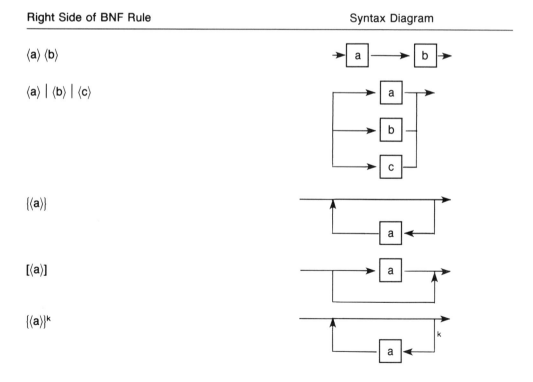

Figure 5.1 Elements of a Syntax Diagram.

translation of operators into arcs of the syntax diagram. Usually we draw one syntax diagram per rule.

Application of Syntax Diagram

As an example how to apply this technique, Figure 5.2 shows syntax diagrams for rules 1, 2, 5–8, 10, and 12 of Table 5.3.

Meyer's Notation

If the processing for a given input needs to be described formally as well, then BNF and syntax graphs are no longer sufficient. [Meye85] suggests a notation that consists of standard mathematical notation to describe sets, predicates, functions, and relations. The sets and predicates describe input and output classes. The functions and relationships, combined with rules for composing relations and functions, describe the processing of input into output. [Meye85] points out that his formalism is not necessarily difficult because he does not introduce concepts such as finite state machines, abstract data types, or attribute grammars (this doesn't mean he couldn't describe them). He does concede, though, that this formalism is used mostly for programs and less for systems. The notation is very close to the syntax for first-order logic. Because the notation is very formal and requires more work, it is reserved for situations when its precision is needed and warrants the effort, such as high reliability requirements for critical care systems in hospitals, reactor control software, and many military applications. Table 5.4 defines the notation.

With this notation, we can describe inputs and outputs in classes as sets, possibly satisfying particular predicates (conditions for being in a particular input or output class). It is also possible to define functions or relations that relate the input sets to output sets. These functions and relations can be simple or composite. In this way all the aspects of input, processing, and output can be described. System transformations can be included implicitly as predicates that change with the execution of functions.

Application of Meyer's Notation

Table 5.5 describes some of the EBNF rules to Table 5.3 in Meyer's notation. We are assuming that every variable s is a sequence of characters, fulfilling the predicate **SEQ(s)**. Furthermore, there is a functiong **length(s)** which returns as output the number of characters of the sequence s, and $s(i)$ denotes the ith character in the sequence. The predicate that is true when one item a is equal to another item b is written as $\mathbf{a} = \mathbf{b}$. $s(i)$ $...s(j)$ means the subsequence of s from the ith to the jth character in the sequence. If j is smaller than i, then the subsequence is undefined. If j is greater than **length(s)**, the subsequence function returns $s(i)...s(\mathbf{length}(s))$. If i is greater than **length(s)**, the function is undefined. The logical *or* operation is written as |, logical *and* is written as **&**.

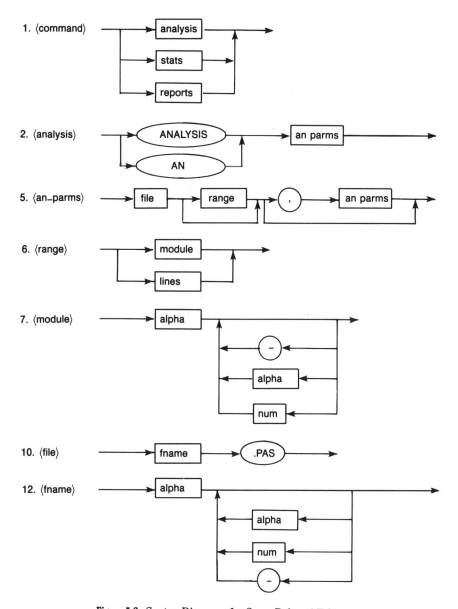

Figure 5.2 Syntax Diagrams for Some Rules of Table 5.3.

Table 5.5 shows a number in the first column that corresponds to the BNF rule in Table 5.3. The predicates that describe valid syntax do not worry about delimiters. We could take care of that by inserting a predicate **NEWTOKEN(j)**. It is true if, after all delimiters have been removed from the input string, the character string starting at position *j* starts a new token.

Table 5.4 Formal specification notation according to [Meye85].

Type	Notation	Explanation
Function	o = f(i) or f(i)=o	*i* is input, *o* is output, *f* is name of the function.
Relation	$\{\langle i_1, o_1 \rangle, \langle i_2, o_2, \rangle \ldots\}$	i_j are input, o_j corresponding outputs.
Sets	{a, b, c, ...}	Set of elements.
	a..b	Ordered set of elements from *a* to *b*.
Predicates	P(x)	*x* has property *P*.
	i ∈ A, i ∉ A	*i* in *A*, *i* not in *A*.
	∀i ∈ A, ∀i ∉ A	For all *i* in *A*, for all *i* not in *A*.
	∃i ∈ A	There exists an *i* in *A*.
	a⇒b	*a* implies *b*.
Definition	a==b	*a* defined as *b*.
Composition		
functions	g∘f (i) = g(f(i))	
relations	t∘r = { ⟨i,o⟩ | ∃ k: r(i,k) & t(k,o)}	

We can define error messages depending on where a part of a predicate is not true. This formal way of defining syntax also gives us an easy way to generate test data for testing the commands, because all we have to do is to find input data so that predicates or parts of predicates are or are not true.

A function that defines an error message for a wrong range could be

wrong–range(s) == { o | SEQ(o) &~range(s) &
             o = "incorrect module name or range of lines.
                Please repeat command" }

Note that in this case, { } does not indicate a set but a specific output together with properties for the inputs that cause the output.

This is not the most specific error message, because it does not tell us whether a module name was input incorrectly or whether it was a line number. We could refine this to define that a module was intended when the first character was an alpha character, and lines were intended when the first character was a (or a number.

wrong–range(s) ==   { SEQ(o) &~range(s) &
             [(~s(1)="(" ⇒ o = "incorrect module name.
                           Please repeat command") |
              (s(1)="(" ⇒ o = "incorrect line range.
                           Please repeat command") |
            (~alpha(s(1)) &~ (s(1)="(" | num(s(1))) ⇒
                      o = "incorrect module name or
                      line range.
                      Please repeat command")]

Table 5.5 Some of the BNF rules of Table 5.3 in Meyer's notation.

No.	Rule	
9	num(s)	== (s ∈ {0,1, ..., 9})
10	number(s)	== (∀ i ∈ 1 .. length(s): num(s(i)))
8	alpha(s)	== (s∈{A, ..., Z})
12	fname(s)	== (alpha(s(1)) & ∀ j ∈ 2 .. length(s): (alpha(s(j)) | num(s(j)) | s(j)="_") & length(s)≤7)
13	lines(s)	== (s(1)="(" & ∃ j ∈ 2 .. length(s): (number(s(2) .. s(j)) & s(j+1)="," & ∃ k: (number(s(j) .. s(k)) & k+1=length(s))) & s(length(s))=")")
11	file(s)	== fname(s) | (fname(s(1) .. s(length-4)) & s(length-3) .. s(length)=".PAS")
7	module(s)	== alpha(s(1)) & length(s)>1 ⇒ (∀ j ∈ 2 .. length(s): alpha(s(j)) | num(s)j)) | s(j) = "_")
6	range(s)	== module(s) | lines(s)
5	an_parms(s)	== ∃ j ∈ 1 .. length(s): [file(s(1) .. s(j)) & j<length(s) ⇒ ((~range(s(j+1) .. s(length(s)) ⇒ (j+1)="," & an_parms(s(j+2) .. s(length(s))))) | ∃ k ∈ j+1..length(s): (range(s(j+1) .. s(k))& (an_parms(s(k+1) .. s(length(s)) | k=length(s))))]
	rep	== {REPORTS, RE}
4	reports(s)	== ∃ j ∈ 1 .. 7: [s(1) .. s(j) ∈ rep & j<length(s) & reparms(s(j+1) .. s(length(s)))]
	sta	== {STATISTICS, ST}
3	stats(s)	== ∃ j ∈ 1 .. 10: [s(1) .. s(j) ∈ sta & j<length(s) & st_parms(s(j+1) .. s(length(s)))]
	ana	== {ANALYSIS, AN}
2	analysis(s)	== ∃ j ∈ 1 .. 8: [s(1) .. s(j) ∈ ana & j<length(s) & an_parms(s(j+1) .. s(length(s)))]
1	commands(s)	== analysis(s) | stats(s) | reports(s) | quits(s) | compare(s)

This is a little awkward to write. We could define the outputs of the function as a set union of outputs instead.

$$\textbf{wrong-range(s)} == \{\text{"incorrect module name or line range"} \mid \sim\text{range(s)} \,\&$$
$$\sim\text{s(1)="("}\} \cup$$
$$\{\text{"incorrect line range"} \mid \sim\text{range(s)} \,\&\, \text{s(1)="("}\}$$

This last definition is also a simplification of the error message, because it assumes only a character string starting with a (is to be an incorrect line range. Other wrong range indicators could be wrong module names or wrong line ranges.

These formal descriptions of the input constitute only one step towards formal specifications and are often supplemented by an English narrative to describe the functions that are invoked by the commands. For a complete functional specification we have to add a description of the system's reactions to the inputs (valid, invalid, defaults).

Problems and Questions

1.   When could you use a formal language like Meyer's? When would you not use it? Why?

2.   Translate the remainder of the BNF rules of Table 5.3 into syntax diagrams as in Figure 5.2.

3.   Rewrite Table 5.5 (Meyer's method) by

▶ inserting the **newtoken(j)** predicate in the appropriate places;

▶ using a subsequence definition
   subseq(s,j,k) $==$ s(j) . .$s(k)$; and

▶ defining a function **compacted(s)** which takes as input a line s, strips it from all delimiters between tokens, and sets predicates for newtoken.

5.6.2. Partial Specification for PAS

This section gives a partial functional specification for the commands of the programs analysis system using English narrative. In practice, there would be more sections to this part of the document, and they would be organized in levels, but for now we are only describing the **ANALYZE** command. The description includes all aspects of an IPOT specification.

Legal commands on the top command level would be listed as follows:

ANALYZE (see Section S.1)
STATISTICS (see Section S.2.)
REPORTS (see Section S.3.)
QUIT (see Section S.4.)

All commands may be abbreviated by two characters; the characters which are to be used as abbreviation are underlined. Commands and parameters are separated by an arbitrary number of blanks, unless a specific delimiter is specified.

Errors

When the first token of the command line does not represent a valid command, the system responds with

command *xxx* does not exist

please correct command

where *xxx* is the character string the system could not recognize as a valid command name.

Notation

Items in ⟨ ⟩ specify expressions, that are defined in more detail later. Where parameters are optional, they are enclosed in []. If a list of parameters can be input, the repeating parts are enclosed in {}. Where any of these characters are part of the command language syntax, they are enclosed in "". ""are not acceptable input.

S.1. The ANALYZE Command

Syntax

ANALYZE ⟨file⟩ [⟨range⟩] {, ⟨file⟩ [⟨range⟩] }

Description of Parameters

Valid parameters for the ANALYZE command consist of a valid file name (⟨file⟩), possibly followed by a range indicator (⟨range⟩). The file name gives the file in which the program that is to be analyzed is stored. The range indicator specifies which part of the program is to be analyzed. For multiple analysis, a series of file names and ranges may be given, separated by a comma.

At minimum, a valid file name consists of no more than seven characters. The first one must be an alpha character, but the remainder may be alphanumeric and underscore. If a file extension is given, it must be PAS and is separated from the first part of the file name by a dot.

The following are the errors:

1. When a syntactically incorrect file name is input, the system responds with
    incorrect filename xxx
    please repeat command
    where **xxx** is the character string the system could not recognize as a legal file name.

2. If there is no file with the given name, the system responds
    file xxx does not exist
    please repeat command
    xxx denotes the name of the nonexisting file.

3. When the file exists but is not of type PAS, the system responds
    file xxx does not have PAS extension
    please repeat command

A range is either a module name of the program or a range of line numbers. A module name consists of an alpha character that might be followed by an arbitrary number of alphanumeric characters or underscores. Note that the system will not reject module names, which are reserved words in PASCAL, if the program is to be analyzed does not use them as module names. A range of line numbers is specified as a pair of integers separated by commas and enclosed in parentheses. The first number indicates where analysis is to start and the second specifies the last line of analysis. The second line number must not be smaller than the first. If no range is given, the entire program is analyzed. The following are the errors;

1. When a module name starts with a character other than an alpha character or an opening parenthesis, "(", or contains special characters other than the underscore, the system responds
    incorrect module name xxx
    please repeat command

2. In case of incomplete parentheses, real numbers, missing comma or inappropriate delimiter between line numbers, or another syntactically incorrect of range of line numbers, the systems responds
    incorrect range of line numbers xxx
    please repeat command

3. When the second number is smaller than the first, the system responds
    incorrect range of line numbers
    second number xxx smaller then first xxx
    please repeat command

Function

The **ANALYZE** command performs a statistical analysis of the programs and/or program parts specified as parameters. The analysis is the same as the one described in Sections 2.4.2. and 3.5. It is assumed that the programs or program parts are syntactically correct. Up to 100 programs can be analyzed at a time. Analysis results are available as long as you stay in analysis mode. They can be saved between modes in the accumulator or permanently in a file. There is a limit of 100 results for nonaccumulated results in the accumulator.

Outputs

Summary results are displayed on the screen in the form

#	id	name	module	unique (optrs, oprds)	total (optrs, oprds)
⟨#⟩	⟨id⟩	⟨file⟩	⟨range⟩	(N1, N2)	(n1, n2)

⟨#⟩ is the sequential number of the set of programs or program parts, which was specified in the current **AN** command as items to be analyzed. ⟨id⟩ is the author identification code of the analyzed program or program part. ⟨**file**⟩ is the name of the file without the PAS extension in which the program resides, while ⟨**range**⟩ gives the module name or the line range. Module names are abbreviated to 13 characters, and line ranges are given as they were input into the system. *N1, N2, n1,* and *n2* are intergers.
The following errors may occur:

1. In case the analyst encountered an unrecoverable error, such as when the program was not syntactically correct, analysis is terminated and the following message is printed
    program ⟨file⟩ ⟨range⟩ cannot be analayzed.
    please check whether it is syntactically correct
    In this case, the output table shows * instead of numbers.

2. After 100 programs have been analyzed in one analysis session, the system has reached capacity and prompts.

> **Warning: Temporary storage capacity filled.**
> **No more programs can be analyzed and temporarily stored.**
> **If you do not save the results before further analysis,**
> **the current results are overwritten.**
>
> Results not in accumulator are overwritten first, on a least recently analyzed basis.

Next Lower Level Commands

After a set of program analyses, the user may invoke the following lower level commands:

▶ **SAVE**

▶ **ACCUMULATE**

▶ **COMPARE**

▶ **EXIT**

▶ **REPORTS**

SAVE saves all or part of the results in a user specified file name. **ACCUMULATE** adds the results to the current accumulated results and updates the means vector and the covariance matrix. **COMPARE** switches from **ANALYSIS** mode to **COMPARE** mode. This mode allows comparing similarity indices $f(x)/f(m)$ for specific programs (students) for different analysis batches (homework submissions). **EXIT** transfers the user to the top-level command interpreter. Any change of mode implies that all open analysis files are closed but does not save permanently any of the analysis results. The contents of the accumulator are available across modes. **REPORTS** switches over to report mode and prints a list of outputs.

Discussion of the Narrative

This English narrative showed another way to specify a user interface. It gave a short description of the function **ANALYZE**, its inputs, and its outputs. The function description is very short because it was already done when we looked at the problems. For the other functions we would have been more elaborate. Even if we hadn't described what the analysis does, it would have made sense to refer to a separate section or appendix here, because analysis is such an involved function.

The inputs are classified into valid and invalid. Default values are implied (i.e., the PAS extension for a file name or the lack of a range indicator). While this English narrative explains the same syntax as the BNF or syntax diagram before, it does more. Specifically, it detailed.

▶   classes of input values

▶   functions performed for them,

▶   resulting outputs,

▶   sequencing of functions and changes of system state,

▶   error processing,

▶   default actions, and

▶   semantics.

This type of description already reads pretty much like a user manual. The obvious advantage is that the user can see at an early point in development quite well what the resulting system will look like, and then provide feedback on the effectiveness of the proposed system at a time when changes are more easily incorporated.

The disadvantage is its lack of rigor for the designers and implementors. Additionally, it may be too wordy for the developers. To counteract this, one might have a more formal version of aspects of the system, such as the classes of inputs and associated actions they cause. A technique which concentrates on this are decision tables.

Problems and Questions

1.   According to the BNF notation in Table 5.3, state whether the following system inputs are syntactically valid:

```
ANK
AN K 10,0
ANALYZE K (10)
ANALYZE BEGIN
ANALYZE END (0,100)
ANALYZE PROG5 PRINT_IT
ANALYZE (10,30)
```

How does the system respond to these inputs? Do you think the specifications are accurate enough for multiple errors? If not, correct them. Which of the commands are syntactically correct but not semantically? What is wrong? How does the system respond?

2.   Give a list of test cases so that every possible class of error messages from the example in this section is generated.

3.   List all classes of default values for the example in this section with the action they provoke.

4.   Write functions in Meyer's formalism which specify all possible error messages for the **ANALYZE** command. (Hint: You will encounter ambiguities in the narrative. In each case, state your assumptions and proceed.)

5.   Somebody says to you, "When I write specifications, I try to translate them into a formal notation like BNF or Meyer's, because it shows me where my errors are." What do you respond, based on your experience with exercise 4 and the difference between syntax and semantics?

6.   Check whether the following issues have been addressed in the specifications of the **ANALYZE** command. Amend or correct the specifications to solve the problem or mistake, if there is one. Also give a set of test cases to check every one of the features you added and corrections you made.

   a.   More than one part (module and/or line range) is to be analyzed for a given program. What happens to the input file (or is that an implementation question? Do we have to decide on that now?) Do the module names or line ranges have to be in sequential order? What if they are nested as they can be in PASCAL?

   b.   How is the ⟨id⟩, which appears as part of the analysis output, entered?

   c.   How do you identify if the same analysis was done more than once? What if anything should be done about it? Why?

   d.   Is there a minimum length per program? What happens when a syntactically correct but pathological program is input (i.e., no executable statements, only a begin-end block)?

   e.   Are impurities handled or not? Should they be?

   f.   When is an empty accumulator generated or saved? What exactly happens? Is it desirable?

   g.   What are line numbers (line in the source file, number of statement, or what)? What happens when a statement is split over two lines?

   h.   Are commands in lower case recognized? Should they be?

   i.   What happens when the range of line numbers has a number for the upper limit which exceeds the highest line number in the program?

j. What happens when the range of line numbers does not contain any executable statements?

5.6.3. Decision Tables and Cause-Effect Graphs

Decision tables describe the conditions for individual input data and combinations of input data as well as the functional consequences of such data. Since conditions are either true or false, such tables partition the input data into complementary input classes. An example for the tax preparation system would be the filing status of a tax payer. The values this input can have influences the tax rate and standard deduction for the tax computation procedure. Table 5.6 shows the different values for filing status and the effects on the activities "select tax rate" and "compute standard deduction." Standard deduction values are based on 1987 figures.

Table 5.6. Input data "Filing Status".

Filing status (Input)	Single or divorced	Married filing jointly or qualifying widower	Married filing separately	Head of household
Select tax rate (Action)				
a. Single	X			
b. Married jt		X		
c. Married sp			X	
d. Head hshd				X
Compute standard deduction (Action)				
a. $3,760		X		
b. $2,540	X			X
c. $1,880			X	

Note that the four conditions for input applied different processing to compute the output. Sometimes the classes of input data have one data point as a member, sometimes a wide range of numbers. The table shows that for every input class at least one processing action applies. That is, we cannot "do nothing" as reaction to an input.

Another example of a possible decision table deals with the computation of social security tax. For the professional user for whom the tax system is developed, the following data determine whether additional social security tax (SST) is to be paid.

▶ total social security wages from forms W2 (SSW) (income for which social security tax has already been paid);

- ▶ earnings due to self-employment (SEI); and

- ▶ relationship to maximum amount of combined wages and self-employment earnings that are subject to SST. This amount is \$43,800 for 1987 and \$45,000 for 1988. We call it SSMAX.

The computation whether and how much additional SST needs to be paid is determined by a combination of values for SSW and SEI. Table 5.7 shows single and combined conditions for subclasses of the data items SSW and SEI. The processing for a class that stands for a single input data item (such as SSW) is done regardless of the value of other data items (such as SEI). We need not consider combinations of 1 & 3, 1 & 4, 1 & 5, 2 & 3, or 2 & 4, because at least one of the single conditions already specifies skipping Form SE. Therefore, no new processing is introduced through the combination of conditions. All subclasses with identical processing rules can be put into the same subclass. Table 5.8 shows the reduced decision table. We kept the numbering of the input classes as in Table 5.7 to simplify the names of the subclasses.

Table 5.7 Decision table for combinations of conditions for input data.

#	Data item	Condition	Processing
	SSW		
1.	Social Security Wages at least as high as maximum taxable SSW	SSW > = SSMAX	Skip Form SE
2.	Social Security Wages below maximum	SSW < SSMAX	
	SEI		
3.	no self-employment income	SEI < = 0	Skip Form SE
4.	Self-employment income under \$400	0 < SEI < 400	Skip Form SE
5.	Self-employment income at least \$400	SEI > = 400	
	Combinations		
6.	2 and 5	(SSW < SSMAX) & (SEI > = 400)	Fill in Form SE
7.	6 and difference of SSMAX and SSW smaller than SEI	(SSMAX − SSW) > SEI	Use (SSMAX − SSW) as base for additional SST computation
8.	6 and difference of SSMAX and SSW at least SEI	(SSMAX − SSW) > =SEI	Use SEI as base for additional SST computation

Table 5.8 Reduced decision table.

#	Name of subclass	Condition	Processing
6.	2 & 5	(SSW > SSMAX) & (SEI < = 400)	Fill in form SE
7.	6 & difference of SSMAX and SSW smaller than SEI	(SSMAX − SSW) < SEI	Use (SSMAX − SSW) as base for additional SST computation
8.	6 & difference of SSMAX and SSW at least SEI	(SSMAX − SSW) > =SEI	Use SEI as base for additional SST computation
9.	(1 or 3 or 4)	(SSW > = SSMAX) or (SEI < 400)	Skip Form SE

This example illustrates how a decision table describes conditions that imply variations in the processing of input. We defined subclasses that met combinations of conditions and had their own processing associated with them. In this way we can analyze precisely what is being done for all subclasses of input.

Defining a decision table proceeds in the following steps [Gilb83]:

1. We define a planned input and output class, which may be finite, infinite, valid, invalid, or default.

2. We determine each condition that causes processing to vary.

3. We determine for all conditions which we found in the previous step

    (a) the subclasses which a condition creates, including defining the ranges of values a condition has in a subclass, and

    (b) the results which the processing actions produce for all individual subclasses.

4. We look at combinations of conditions and determine their processing and the processing results. We consider all possible intersections of subclasses.

Note that we are concerned with what defines classes, not with how they are implemented. Likewise, the nature of processing is important, not which algorithm accomplishes it. Let us illustrate this process with another example from the tax preparation system.

Note that Table 5.9 is not complete. We did not subdivide subclasses (B1 & C1) and (B1 & C2) further, which should happen, because the difference of GSE and ESE determines whether Form SE needs to be filled in. The refinement is actually given in Table 5.10. As before, we should put subclasses with the same processing requirements into

Table 5.9 Sources of taxable work income.

1.	*Classes of Input.*		
A.	Number of employers		
B.	Gross self-employment income (GSE) before subtracting expenses and deductions.		
C.	Expenses and deductions for self-employment.		

2.	*Subclasses of Input.*		
	Name of Subclass	Condition	Processing
A1.	One employer	$|W2| = 1$	Take W2 data from W2 Form and proceed.
A2.	Multiple employers	$|W2| > 1$	Add W2 data per category.
A3.	Was not employed (D)	$|W2| = 0$	Set W2 data to zero.
A4.	Error	$|W2| < 0$	Report error A4.
B1.	Had additional nonemployee income	GSE > 0	Put GSE onto Schedule C (fill in part 1).
B2.	No additional nonemployee income (D)	GSE $= 0$	Skip SE.
B3.	Error	GSE < 0	Report error B3.
C1.	Had SE expenses	ESE > 0	Put on Schedule C, part II.
C2.	Had no SE expenses(D)	ESE $= 0$	Skip Schedule C, part II
C3.	Error	ESE < 0	Report error C3.

the same subclass. Combinations of subclasses of A with those of B and C indicate precise values to be used in the computation of the adjusted gross income on Form 1040. This computation also depends on the totals from other schedules and forms, notably A and B. The reader is encouraged to use Appendix B with the sample forms and schedules to determine further input classes he needs to consider for combinations. The table also shows the default values and their associated processing marked with (D). When there are many combinations of conditions to consider, the form of the decision table as we have used it in Tables 5.7 and 5.10 can become unwieldy. Another representation that represents the class B and C combinations, as in Table 5.11, becomes more practical.

Action 7 needs further refining. Whether it is equivalent to action 10 or to reporting a profit depends on the difference of GSE and ESE. Action 8 needs further refinement for the same reason.

Decision table development iterates until the proper refinement level has been reached, i.e., until each combination of conditions that is relevant to processing is explicitly considered. After the decision table is complete, we check whether there are any columns that result in the same processing. They can be combined or at least clustered together. Next we check that each possible input satisfies the conditions in exactly one column. If the classes were defined to be mutually exclusive and collectively exhaustive, this will be the case.

Table 5.10 Combinations of subclasses B and C.

B1 & C1	Some SE income, some expenses	(GSE > 0) & (ESE > 0)	1. 2. 3.	Fill in C. Determine net SE income to see whether Form SE needs to be filled in (cf.T. 5.7). Put results onto 1040.
B1 & C2	SE income, but no expenses	(GSE > 0) & (ESE = 0)	1. 2. 3.	Fill in C part 1. GSE is net SE income. Determine whether to fill in SE (cf. T. 5.7). Put GSE onto 1040.
B2 & C1	Net SE business loss	(GSE = 0) & (ESE < 0)	1.	Set ESE to net business loss on schedule C. Report on 1040 as net business loss.
B3&(C1vC2)	Error	(GSE < 0) & (ESE >= 0)		Report error B3.
C3&(B1vB2)	Error	(GSE >=0) & (ESE < 0)		Report error C3.
B3 & C3	Error	(GSE < 0) & (ESE < 0)	1. 2.	Report error B3. Report error C3.

Table 5.11 Alternate form of Table 5.10.

B C	B1 C1	B1 C2	B1 C3	B2 C1	B2 C2	B2 C3	B3 C1	B3 C2	B3 C3
Processing									
1. Put GSE onto Schedule C (part I)	X	X	X						
2. Skip Form SE				X	X	X			
3. Report error B3							X	X	X
4. Put ESE on Schedule C (part II)	X			X			X		
5. Skip Schedule C part II		X			X			X	
6. Report error C3			X			X			X
7. Compute net SEI income as SEI=GSE−ESE	X	X							
8. Put SEI onto 1040	X	X							
9. Determine whether to fill in SE	X	X							
10. Set ESE to net business loss on Schedule C and 1040				X					
11. Put 0 onto 1040 for SEI					X				

Sometimes conditions take precedence, and the action is performed no matter what the other conditions are. This often happens for error conditions, as we saw in Tables 5.9 and 5.11. Unless processing also occurs due to other values, we put a - or a * for condition values of other subclasses in the combination. This indicates that we do not care what the value is. If for a B3 error, the only result would be error processing for the B3 error regardless of all other condition values, columns B3 & C1, B3 & C2, B3 & C3 could be combined into one column (B3, *). Since decision tables can become quite large, generating all the combinations of conditions manually may not be feasible nor desirable. For example, if there are n conditions and each has m different values, then there are m^n sets of actions to consider. One could, however, write a program which can generate combinations of conditions. Second, we should try to determine which actions can possibly be combined with each other, because this also reduces the size of the table.

Whether we will and should use decision tables is a matter of scale, because of the sheer size of the tables when there are many related processing variables. While size can be a drawback for decision tables, it also has advantages. One is that the classification of inputs and input boundaries is clearly stated in terms of conditions. It is easy to see and check whether there are values of conditions for which no actions are defined. The same is true for erroneous condition values and defaults. In the tax preparation system example, we defined the default values for certain types of income. Examples of default actions state which schedules and which lines are to be filled in by default and with which values. Default values and default actions are best tailored to the most likely use of the system. Other criteria that help to select default values and processing actions assume that the default value is zero or a minimal legal value and that, unless specifically stated otherwise by the user, no action should be taken by the system.

Decision tables discourage vague input class boundaries, a potential source of error. It is more difficult to define a decision table for a vague input definition. However, decision tables do not prevent all vagueness. To illustrate this take a look at Table 5.9. Upper limits for the number of employers, for gross self-employment income, and for expenses and deductions due to self-employment are vague. In support of the table we should add, though, that the problem itself does not prescribe them. When doubts about an input boundary occur, we assume that the most general condition is intended. When restrictions need to be placed (such as on the number of employers the tax preparation system will be able to handle), the customer should get a chance to review them. All restrictions are stated explicitly in the specification document and later in the user manual. They should have corresponding diagnostics in the program that point out which of the restrictions was violated and caused the error message. Restrictions on input data should not merely reflect the programmer's convenience. If ease of implementation is the guiding force in determining restrictions for input values or for processing, we may end up solving the wrong problem.

Since conditions classify inputs with respect to the processing they trigger, decision tables are excellent sources for deriving functionally oriented tests. All we have to do is to select one set of input values for each condition and their combinations and we have a specification-oriented test. As an example, the following sets of input data satisfy all single conditions for Table 5.11, which we can use to test the specifications as well as the program:

Condition	Value	Condition	Value
B1	5,000.00	C1	781.99
B2	0.00	C2	0.00
B3	−55.17	C3	−17.81

Another technique to formalize natural language specifications and to derive test cases is cause-effect graphing [Myer76]. This technique is a link between natural language specifications and decision tables. It starts with a natural language specification and restates it in the form of a cause-effect graph, which is then transformed into a decision table. Causes are inputs, and effects are outputs. We can think of causes as conditions that define classes of inputs and their combinations. Effects are the equivalent of processing actions and what they produce. The cause-effect graph consists of the following:

1. *Nodes.*
   Nodes represent causes and combinations of causes and effects.

2. *Arcs.*
   Arcs are drawn to indicate which conditions are to be combined into a new condition. They are annotated with how the combination is to be done:
   OR   the new condition is formed through a logical OR of the conditions from which the arcs originated.
   AND   the new condition is formed as a logical AND of the conditions which have an arc going to the new condition.
   NAND composition of the new condition is according to the logical NAND function. This is equivalent to NOT (C1 & ... & Cn).
   NOR   the new condition states that none of the constituent partial conditions must hold.
   NOT   the new condition is the negation of the original condition.

In this way more complex conditions are formed, until we have a condition node that directly causes one or more effects. Then an arc is drawn from the condition node to the effect node.

Besides these logical rules for building conditions (connecting nodes in the graph), there may be constraints for invoking effects or conditions. They are as follows:

(E)   *Exclusive conditions or effects.* Only one of them can hold or be invoked at a time.

(I)   *Inclusive conditions or effects.* At least one will hold or be invoked but maybe not all.

(B)   *Multiple effects.* The invocation of one effect will cause the invocation of another.

(M)   *One effect masks another.* This happens, for example, in the case of errors.

Figure 5.3 shows an example of a cause-effect graph that uses some of the possible annotations for arcs and some of the constraint notations for arcs. The causes are on the left and the effects are on the right. Cause-effect graphs can be used for describing the effect of commands in command languages. They include as causes or conditions all the various ways in which syntax can be wrong and lead to different error messages.

A cause-effect graph shows the different ways that specific effects (processing and output) can be produced. This is then condensed into a decision table as follows:

1.   Pick one effect at a time;

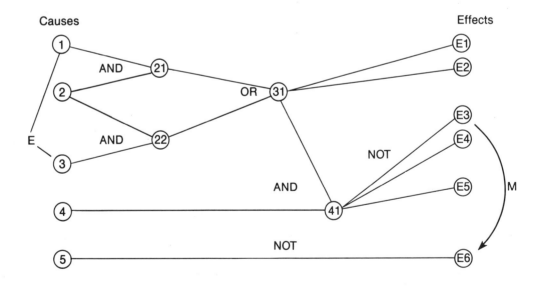

Figure 5.3 Cause-Effect Graph.

2.   Write down all combinations of causes that generate the effect; and

3.   Write down states of all other effects for the list of combinations of causes. If a combination of causes generates more than one effect, they can be combined in the analysis and in the testing.

These two steps give all the information that is needed to establish a decision table as in Table 5.11. The rationale behind using cause-effect graphing as an intermediate step is to reduce the decision table from all possible combinations to a more parsimonious number. We also encountered some rules for table reduction earlier in this chapter.

Essentially, the advantages of cause-effect graphs is that they provide a rigorous way of formalizing specifications and help to derive decision tables which are more parsimonious. This support is especially useful when no requirements diagrams and data dictionaries exist from the previous phase and the natural language specification is poorly structured; the step between the requirements document and natural language specifications to decision tables is too big. Cause-effect graphing has, of course, the same advantages as decision tables, i.e., generation of test cases is an inherent part of the technique. So is validation as the decision table is developed.

A major disadvantage of cause-effect graphs is that they are not always easy to construct. Layout and size can become a problem. And it is time consuming. Automated support is not available, and much of the technique relies on the intuition of the person who builds the graph. The second disadvantage is that a cause-effect graph is only able to express combinations of causes; it does not take into account their timing, iterations, etc. Lastly, while it provides a wealth of useful test cases, it does not provide highly destructive ones [Myer76], and test cases generated with a cause-effect graph need to be augmented.

Because of the significant extra effort, cause-effect graphs as well as decision tables should be used when this extra effort is worth it and the advantages outweigh disadvantages.

Problems and Questions

1.   Build a decision table for the **ANALYZE** command of Section 5.3.2. Define classes and subclasses for single input classes and define combinations of classes and subclasses. Define conditions for processing, and then reduce the decision table. Also give the alternate form of the combination table. Select a set of input data to cover every possible action.

2.   Build a cause-effect graph for the **ANALYZE** command. What do you think of the result of your efforts? Has the English narrative of the command shown shortcomings? Has it given you a better understanding of the command? Why or why not? How do the

test cases you derived from it compare to the ones you found in exercises 1, 2, and 4 of Section 5.3.2? Which test cases were the easiest to derive? Those from the narrative? Those from Meyer's notation, BNF, decision tables, or cause-effect graphs? Why?

5.6.4. State Transition Diagrams

The specifications methods thus far have described the functionality of the system as a partitioned view of what the system does, its inputs, and its outputs. What is still missing is a method to specify the different behavioral states that characterize the system and how it changes. State transition diagrams provide a convenient and fairly simple structured way to do that:

▶ Every state the system can enter is represented as a node in the state transition diagram.

▶ Arcs denote possible transitions between states.

▶ Labels on the arcs state the conditions for a change of system state. These conditions may coincide with the occurence of an event, or they may indicate the system's reaction to an input. Labels also can describe the output to an input.

▶ The state transition diagram is hierarchical, just as the requirements diagram was. For example, a command language often has top-level commands, as well as commands that are only valid within a specific system state. Take the program analysis example. We have listed the commands and when they can be invoked in Table 5.12. Note that this is a very brief description and therefore lacks the precision, detail, and completeness of full specifications.

Before we can draw a state transition diagram, we need to do the following:

▶ enumerate all possible system states in a hierarchical fashion,

▶ establish conditions for changing states, and

▶ describe the characteristics of the system while in a given state.

There are six possible states in this system: the operating system state (**SYS**), the top command level (**TOP**) and one for each mode (**AN, ST, CO, RE**). Table 5.12 describes briefly which commands change state for each mode. It also gives a short explanation of what the system looks like in a given state. Figure 5.4 shows the state transition diagram. The command to start program analysis is PAS. We can see that the first level command states are almost fully connected across. This means that the user can do a partial analysis, comparison, or whatever he has in mind. Then he can quit the system

Table 5.12. Hierarchical command language.

Name of command	Explanation
ANALYZE	Program (part) analysis, produces quadruple, author ID, file and module ID, output is list of IDs and quadruples for all programs (parts) mentioned in parameter list of most current AN command.
SAVE	Save analysis results held in accumulator permanently in a user-specified file.
ACCUMULATE	Accumulate all or parts of the latest analysis results into accumulator.
COMPARE	Switch over to compare mode. Only what is in accumulator is still available. Is equivalent to EX, CO.
ANALYZE	Further analysis cycle.
REPORTS	Switch to report mode and prints quadruple results as described in Section 5.3.2. Is equivalent to EX, RE AN * (AN stands for analysis reports, * for accumulator).
EXIT	Return to top-level command interpreter.
COMPARE	Compare for similarity indices to correlate previous submissions of same authors.
COMPARE	Keep doing it with new set of authors and/or analysis files.
ACCUMULATE	Accumulate comparison results.
SAVE	Save comparisons permanently.
REPORTS	Switch to print comparison report. Contains author and program ID, covariance, $f(x)/f(m)$, and summary information. Same as EX, RE CO *.
EXIT	Return to top command level.
STATISTICS	Compute statistics for one or more user. Specified result files and accumulator (puts all into accu)
SELECT	Select analyses that are to be part of statistics (files, accumulator)
TYPESTAT	Select type of statistic per quadruple, mean, mode, variance, median, min, max, covariance, $f(x)/f(m)$
ACCUMULATE	Put results of latest selection into accumulator
SAVE	Save contents of accumulator permantly
REPORTS	Print statistics reports, switch mode same as EX, RE ST *.
EXIT	Returns to top level command interpreter.
REPORTS	Print analysis, comparison, and statistical reports.
SAVE	Save the reports permanently.
EXIT	Return to top-level command interpreter.
QUIT	Exit system, save all results that are in accumulators, close all files.

and resume work at some other time (provided he saved results). The negative aspect of allowing a fully connected state transition diagram is that it does not step the user through a sequence. This can produce problems when the user tries to statistically evaluate the contents of an empty accumulator. It is also potentially dangerous when the user forgot to accumulate results before switching to another mode, or when he exits the system, because only accumulator results are saved.

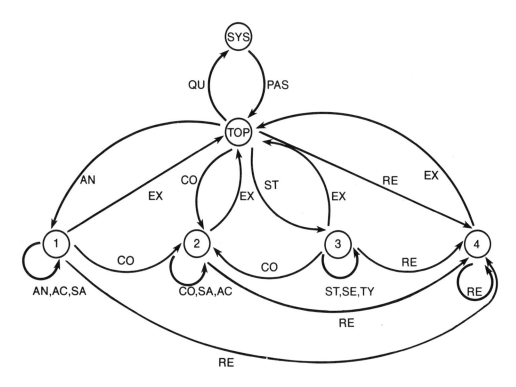

Figure 5.4 State Transition Diagram of Program Analysis System.

In this particular case, the advantages weigh more, because the user will have a need to do exploratory analyses, comparisons, and statistics without saving them all. The exploratory nature of the system makes it very likely that switches between modes will be frequent. And the users can always redo their analyses (short commands) if they inadvertently fail to save information they want after all.

In any case, the advantages and disadvantages of such a fully connected set of command states should be considered before deciding on a strict hierarchical structure or a weak one as we have here.

Once we have a state transition diagram, we can define test cases based on sequencing of commands; e.g., **PAS, AN, EX, QU** means that after starting the program analyzer, some programs were analyzed, the analysis mode was exited without saving anything in the accumulator, and the system was exited. Since the accumulator was empty, no analysis results were saved. Such command sequences can show what happens, and we can test whether it is what we expected to happen and whether it is desirable. Other example execution sequences are (for simplicity's sake we have left out parameters for the commands):

1. **PAS, AN, AN, AC, EX, QU**. This sequence saves the accumulator contents permanently.

2. **PAS, AN, AC, AN, SA, EX, QU**. This sequence saves some results permanently through the save command before exiting the analysis mode. Results in the accumulator are saved when the system is exited.

3. **PAS, CO, RE, EX, QU**. This sequence performs comparisons, prints some reports, then exits without saving comparison or print results.

4. **PAS, AN, AC, ST, AC, RE AN*, RE ST*, CO, RE, EX, QU**. This sequence performs a set of analyses, saves some in the accumulator, analyzes the results statistically, saves the statistics in the accumulator, prints analysis and statistical results, compares results, prints them, and exits the system, saving the accumulated results.

When we inspect what happens in these execution sequences, we see that it is possible to do analyses without saving any results. The same is true for statistics and comparison. As soon as results have been put into an accumulator, exiting the system will save them permanently. This, however, may not always be useful or desirable. One way to get around this is to require an explicit save operation; the **QUIT** will then no longer save the accumulator's contents automatically. However, if we do that, we should provide a warning when nothing has been saved. Another aspect of this command language is that so far, every file that is to be analyzed contains at most one program, meaning that there are many file names to type and to remember. We could either allow more than one program per file or have a feature that allows the user to list all relevant files in a directory. Because the main objective is to explore the usefulness of program analysis, we should consider a list feature a future enhancement. For now, the user can list the files in a directory before starting the system. For the same reason, we can still keep the restriction of one program per file.

Deriving these test cases for state transitions of the system not only helped us to see what the system does and whether it changes states as we expect it to do, it also gave us some more insight into how we should organize the system, its states, and transitions between states. A minimally thorough state transition test would try to cover all possible transitions between system states, i.e., all arcs in the state transition diagram. In addition, all possible classes of parameters should be considered, including none and the resulting default values.

Problems and Questions

1. Add a help command to the set of commands for the program analysis project. What are the conditions for state change? Should you allow help from anywhere in the system? What are the advantages and disadvantages of having a single new state in Figure 5.4 as a help state? What are the advantages and disadvantages of not having a single help state but distributing it throughout all states of the system? (Hint: Think about whether you want to return to the state you were in before the help command put you into the help state).

2. Someone tells you that sequencing tests that are derived from the state transition diagram should cover all arcs of the diagram. Is this enough to test for all possible sequencing problems? (Hint: What role do parameters and default parameters play?)

3. Develop a set of sequencing tests for the diagram in Figure 5.4 that covers all possible transitions in the diagram.

5.7. Specifications and Quality

One of the crucial aspects of specifications and their quality is how well they reflect the user's need. Because of this, attention to the human factors requirements is one of the most important ingredients for quality, as is user involvement or, where this is not possible, the involvement of a user representative. In the first section of this chapter we have outlined some guidelines on developing a user interface and what the reasons are for selecting one interface option over another. Sometimes it is not clear which human factors design will produce the most helpful or useful system. We might want to implement the best option and let the user experiment with it. The feedback from using the mock-up can then guide us in designing the final user interface. Unfortunately, this is not always viable. We may just have to get as much information as we can, make our decisions, and then go ahead and define what the system will look like.

Decisions on what the system will look like are guided by what the human factors requirements stated. During the specification phase, we can no longer look first at their functional aspect and then at their quality as we could do during the requirement stage; now they are intertwined. For example, when we make a decision as to what the command language looks like and how to sequence commands, we have to cross-check whether this decision will satisfy our quality requirements. Besides human factors requirements, reliability and performance are usually the most important factors that guide decisions about input, output, and function. Extendability and adaptability, however, can also influence the design of the user interface significantly. For example, the tax preparation system will have to design its menus so that changes in the tax law are easily incorporated. The basic classes of tax information will still be there, so a classification into income, deductions, and taxes paid is probably stable, but what types of taxes have been paid, what types of deductions we have, and what taxable sources of income are (and on which schedules they are going to be put) can change. Menus that deal with this type of information have to be designed in such a way that changes will not be too hard on the system or the user. Next, we must take into account that we may have to add additional schedules over time. Thus it must be possible to add menu screens for those other schedules. It might be a good idea to organize menus around schedules and forms.

The quality of human factors is closely related to user productivity. Therefore, when we think of sequencing menus in the tax preparation system, the ones most often used should be the most accessible and require the least input. For example, W2 Forms and personal information should be input only once, or in the case of several employers, a few times. Most often, the user would enter receipts for deductions. With that in mind, we could organize the main menu and the recording of tax relevant information as in Table 5.13. The most frequent choice is listed first. Selection 8 is used uniformly to return to the next higher level menu or to exit the system. We could have used ⟨esc⟩ but felt that a number was more appropriate because all other choices involve numbers.

There are some disadvantages to organizing the screens this way. First, the discriminatory power is very small with only three or four choices per screen. As a result, many screens need to be brought up before the user gets to the point where he can actually enter data. Second, some of the forms, such as the W2, contain information on both income and taxes. As it currently stands, we will need two different screen selections when we record its information—income and taxes—and possibly three if we record the per-

Table 5.13   Sample menu for tax preparation system (TAP).

TAP—Main Menu	
Recording	1
Computation	2
Reports	3
Exit TAP	8
Select and hit ⟨cr⟩:?	

Recording	
Deductions	1
Income	2
Taxes	3
Personal data	4
Return to main menu	8
Select and hit ⟨cr⟩:?	

sonal information at the same time. We will need four selections if, at some future time, tax deferred income is to be recorded also.

An alternative is to organize some of the recording around the forms from which they are to be recorded.

Table 5.14 Alternative organization of recording menu.

Recording Menu	
Deductions	1
Self-employment income	2
Interest-income	3
W2	4
Personal data	5
Return to main menu	8
Select and hit ⟨cr⟩:?	

This menu can be expanded by adding more choices when schedules (for dividend income, capital gains and losses, etc.) are added. The screen is still much bigger than the choices we have listed so far, and we could easily combine the main menu and the recording menu, thus saving another selection step. It makes the use of the system more transparent and also faster.

Table 5.15 Reorganized main menu of TAP.

TAP—Main Menu	
Recording	
Deductions	1
Self-employment income	2
Interest-income	3
W2	4
Personal data	5
Reports	6
Computation	7
Exit TAP	8
Select and hit ⟨cr⟩:?	

Deductions	
Personal	1
Self-employment	2
Checks	3
Other	4
Return to main menu	8
Select and hit ⟨cr⟩:?	

Later we can add other types of deductions, such as investment losses, deductions for married couples when both work, to the deductions menu. We can also eliminate some when the tax laws change and they are no longer applicable. We have added the "other" category for two reasons. The user might be unsure on which schedule to put a deduction; this way he can give it a name and later define it as a subcategory of one of the above. If it is a new category that will be made permanent, the system will bring it up as a separate category in the menu. This also keeps the system adaptable to changing user needs and tax rules. The way we have organized deduction categories states an implicit decision on which form or schedule the deduction will belong. Once a selection has been made, the deduction categories for the selection come up as a lower level menu; e.g., for personal deductions (Schedule A), there will be a list of categories with their full English names (we can take those from the data dictionary in Table 3.6, Section 3.3.). It is followed by a list with headings for deduction amount, deduction category, date, and purpose of the deduction. Table 5.16 shows the layout of that menu.

Table 5.16 Schedule A menu.

			Personal Deductions
Categories:	MED	-	medical
	TAX	-	local, state, real estate taxes paid
	INT	-	interest paid (mortgage, etc.)
	CON	-	contributions
	CAS	-	casualty/theft
	MIS	-	miscellaneous (union dues, education, etc.)
enter your deductions now:			

amount | categories | date | purpose

?

The user can step from column to column with tabs. The input is entered when a ⟨**cr**⟩ is entered at the end of the line. Two ⟨**cr**⟩ in a row switch the user back to the deductions menu. Errors for entries are handled the following way:

1.   For an invalid amount, an error message is printed and the cursor is put at the column where the error occurred. The user can type the correct amount and a ⟨**cr**⟩ to enter it. There is no need to type the entire line over.

2.   We have two choices for an unknown category name. First, we could accept anything as a category name, assuming that it is a new category for this type of deduction. This, however, is not friendly towards typos, because it automatically creates a new category for every typo. Assuming that typing errors happen a lot more frequently than naming new categories, it is more efficient to report to the user that an unknown category was

encountered and refuse to accept it. The user must now define new categories with the "other" option in the deductions menu. As in the case of an invalid dollar amount, the cursor is set to the category column. The corrected category name is entered followed by a ⟨cr⟩.

3.   If an invalid date is reported, the cursor is set to the date column, and the user has a chance to type the correct date. A ⟨cr⟩ enters it into the system.

4.   If the text which describes the purpose is too long, it is truncated and a warning is issued.

Based on our arguments which led to the current screen design, we can now specify exactly what has been done to achieve user productivity. We looked at the pattern of usage and designed the menus around them. We can also specify how we achieved adaptability—with the variable screens which we designed. Note that these were first rounds of defining the solution; the specification is still vague, e.g., what happens if someone defines many new deduction category names and the screen becomes too small? How exactly are the inputs "amount," "category," "date," and "purpose" defined? Are all always required? Which are optional?

How about changing entries afterwards because something about them is not correct? This requires an edit mode for the system. There are two basic choices—a full screen editor where the user points the cursor to the item he wishes to change and a change command of some sort. The first is a good deal more convenient and also fits in with the menu approach better than the second but, it also happens to be more complicated to implement. The next question is when and where should it be possible to edit entries? In any menu? What is brought onto the screen? Only the ten most recent deductions? Or is it the ten first ones and then we can scroll downwards? Another option would be to add an identifying number for each (deduction) entry and to implement a simple delete function to eliminate typos and entries that are in the wrong category. The corrected ones can be entered through the usual mode of entering information. This is a simpler but more cumbersome alternative.

Which of the options should we choose? The answer is whatever is more useful, exhibits the required qualities, and fits into time and budget constraints. When we make decisions as to what the system will look like, we have to keep the requirements and quality expectations in mind.

The menu description for TAP should not be considered complete or very precise. We have only tried to sketch the basic approach; the details still need to be filled in.

Reliability is another important quality to consider and specify more precisely during the specification phase, and we now must state how reliability manifests itself. Take, for example, the program analysis system. One source of reliability is how the system behaves in the face of user mistakes, both in syntax and semantics. From the specifications in previous sections, we know the following:

▶ The system does not lose data due to invalid user input.

▶ It recovers gracefully when command syntax is wrong and when a program that is to be analyzed is syntactically wrong. When semantically wrong file names are input, the system does not shut down either.

▶ Exceptions to not losing data and recovering gracefully from wrong user input are control character sequences that abort the PAS program using module names that are valid PASCAL keywords.

▶ It doesn't protect against failure to save data. If the option of not saving results is allowed, not much can be done to prevent inadvertent failure except the issuing of a warning.

▶ When the system goes down, PAS does not protect the user from loss of unsaved data. Everything that has not been saved is lost.

▶ When a user does the same analysis twice and tries to produce statistics with such a contaminated sample, the results will be computed, but they don't mean anything. Likewise, statistics computed for one program only are not meaningful, nor are they when applied to an empty accumulator.

There are also some limits of PAS that may affect reliability:

▶ PAS warns against too many programs before it overwrites results.

▶ Is it possible to have too many files open? What happens? (This is an omission in the specification so far, but should be addressed).

▶ What is the maximum number of program parts to be included in a statistic evaluation? What happens if it is exceeded? (Again this has not been specified yet, but it is an important aspect of reliability in the face of system limits).

▶ How many operators are there? How many operands (variable names) can the system handle? What happens if they are exceeded?

▶ Is the program or program part size limited for analysis? If so, what happens? Is analysis aborted? What are the results? Are they the same for a program that could not be analyzed because it was not syntactically correct, i.e.,* in the quadruple for the analysis results?

▶ So far, PAS does not have a feature we mentioned earlier that tells the user "I'm still at it" (something like "Analysis in progress" with a new "." every 15 seconds to indicate that it is still working). Omitting this may cause the user to add input while analysis is still going on. What happens then? Is this input ignored? Buffered? What happens when a user inputs the control sequence to abort a program?

In none of these situations (except for the control sequence to abort a program) do we want the PAS program to crash. Rather we would like to have it recover from the problem gracefully, reliably keep information which earlier steps have generated, and give the user a reasonable way out to deal with the problem. Now, during specification time, we have to decide what the system should do in each of these situations.

The last area of reliability was the reliability of the system implementation. In this regard, there is nothing new to report, we take the objectives as they were defined in the requirements analysis.

What input looks like, how much input we have, and what the system does with it, are all decisions that have an impact on performance. Both processing speed and capacity requirements are affected by that. Once we have defined the different fields of an input object and have a rough idea of how many of them we can have, we may use this information to compute storage requirements. For example, the program analyzer specified an accumulator. What is in it? How big will it be? It depends on how many programs and program parts are to be analyzed. What do the requirements specify?

The space requirements are related to the maximum number of programs and program parts for which analysis results are to be kept active. The specifications require that 100 such results fit into the accumulator. This means we need 100 * space (quadruple, #, ID, program name, module, or range ID). Next, we need a table to identify all the operands. How many are there? Then we need room for at least one line of program input. We cannot quite say how much, because that is implementation dependent. The statistics results also require space. Mean, median, mode, variance, covariance matrix, $f(x)$, $f(m)$, and maybe $f(x)/f(m)$ need to be stored for the analysis results. If we want to allow the ability to merge different sets of analyses, how many? It will have an impact on the space we need as well as processing.

Response time is another important performance quality attribute. Components of response time depend on the functions being performed. The time to analyze a program should be less than it takes to perform a syntactic analysis for it. We can check how long the compiler takes to do that for small, average, and large programs. This gives us an upper bound on the response time for the analysis function. If it turns out that this time can be substantial, it is better to define the possibility of submitting batch jobs for analysis and to perform the statistics and the comparisons interactively. A potential way to submit analysis as a batch job would be to define it as

```
PAS B
AN ⟨files⟩
SA ⟨resultfile⟩
QU
```

The user (professor, grader) submits a background job and lists all the (student) files to be analyzed as parameters for the **AN** command, saves the results in a ⟨resultfile⟩ and later looks at the results interactively. We might even analyze programs automatically as they are submitted from the students' to the professor's account. This is a bit more involved, because for every student submission a batch job needs to be generated. Then, after all programs have been submitted, the analysis results need to be merged. Another alternative is to wait until all programs have been submitted and then start a predefined batch analysis run. We could generate a list of file names based on the class roster and add the project number to distinguish between different homeworks. Any but the most primitive editor would easily handle changing the list of file names with a few commands. Such naming conventions are not unusual but tend to change from course to course and instructor to instructor. What happens if not all students submit their program by the deadline? The analysis program will encounter a missing file name. Should it give a warning, ignore the problem, and proceed to the next file name? In the interest of uniformity, should it react the same way in the interactive mode?

If we choose to implement a fully automatic analysis, we are locking the user into a specific naming convention for files for batch analysis. This may not give us the flexibility to analyze other, nonstudent, programs in batch mode. Therefore it is probably better (and simpler) to require unassisted preparation of a batch run and to skip any nonexisting file names with a warning.

Note that the program analyzer's environment and the usage patterns that we expect for its use are influencing the specifications. Usage patterns can be different for different environments and modes of operation. Somewhat different errors can occur and user reaction to them can vary also. We have to take that into account when we develop specifications. Sometimes the need for different modes of operation does not become clear until quality requirements, such as performance, are taken into account.

The next component of the PAS computes statistics. For the mean, we simply have a fixed number of numbers to add. The accumulator is restricted to 100, but other result files can be merged. What are the biggest samples we will be dealing with? Sometimes we have statistical results for the smaller sample. Could we merge those? Although there is a recursive formula for the mean, such formulas become difficult to impossible for higher order statistics (e.g., covariance matrix). That implies that we will compute statistics only after all items are in. This requires storage and a new round of computation for every set of statistics. These decisions have an impact on space and response time.

What is the maximum size of analysis results that we want to allow? What should happen when it is exceeded?

Search for comparisons also needs data in core, and its performance depends on the size and the search method employed.

The quality expectations from the requirements document guide decisions about what inputs, processing, and outputs ought to look like, and what system states we should have and how the system is to change states. They sometimes prescribe action and help to define what the system will accept as input and what it will do with it. As we specify more of the system, the quality expectations become more specific also. Robustness to user errors is one example. Specifications should state precisely what will happen when error *xxx* is made. This simultaneous consideration of functional and quality expectations happens before and during the process of developing specifications.

It can also be useful in evaluating specifications. We can relate functionality to quality expectations by asking, "Will the specifications fulfill quality expectations?"

Or we can start with quality expectations and ask, "How are the quality expectations reflected in the specifications?"

We should be able to answer this question for all quality expectations. If we can't, we have probably missed a requirement. As we have seen from the previous discussion about the PAS, we can further develop features in response to quality issues. The batch option for **PAS (PAS B)** is an answer to the performance problem we encountered when the system is used interactively for large numbers of longer programs. What batch option is specified depends on the environment and usage pattern for the proposed system, on the complexity of the various alternatives, and on how they relate to resource constraints for the system.

When quality expectations are specified, we can and should use them to generate test data, if not to test the feature now, then for inclusion in the acceptance test. In the TAP system, we had expectations of extendability and adaptability in terms of adding another schedule and responding to changes in the tax law. What we should test for is to

▶ update deduction categories,

▶ update income categories,

▶ update taxes categories, and

▶ establish or change cross-links between forms (when entries are made on more than one form and new forms need to be bound into the return or old ones changed or eliminated).

As far as reliability of the PAS system is concerned, we should test for

▶ invalid commands,

▶ wrong input files (source, analysis results, statistics, reports, comparisons),

▶ nonexisting files,

▶ aborting the program,

▶ exceeding the maximum number of programs allowed to be analyzed,

▶ exceeding the maximum number of result files in any category (analysis, statistics, reports, comparisons),

▶ empty files,

▶ input when PAS is working on a command,

▶ exceeding the number of operands,

▶ statistics when all programs are the same, and

▶ statistics when only one program was analyzed.

A stress test checks performance expectations. For PAS it includes

▶ analyzing the maximum number of biggest programs,

▶ analyzing the maximum number of open files (source, analysis results, statistics, reports, comparisons),

▶ analyzing the maximum set of statistics, reports, and comparisons, including the merging of previous results, and

▶ testing a set of "average" analyses (include definition of average).

For the TAP system, a stress test includes

▶ all schedules,

▶ maximum number of total items of each object type (income, deductions, taxes paid), and

▶ the maximum number of items in each category.

Specifications of software quality should be stated in a way so that we can derive test cases.

Problems and Questions

1. Update the specifications for the **ANALYZE** command of Section 5.6.2 to include the considerations of this section about quality expectations. Specify how quality expectations manifest themselves in PAS and give test cases for how you intend to test them.

2.   Develop specifications for the tax preparation system based on the discussion in this section about usage and quality expectations. Specify how quality expectations manifest themselves in TAP and give test cases for how you intend to test them. For each menu, specify possible user errors (syntax and semantics) and TAP's reaction.

3.   Why is it no longer possible during the specifications phase to specify function first and then analyze other qualities?

4.   What are the factors that influence developing and selecting alternative specifications?

5.   Why are human factors, reliability, and performance important quality aspects to consider during the specification phase?

5.8.   The Specification Document

All the functional aspects that need to be described in the specifications are finally put together in a specification document. How should this document be organized? One possible outline for the specifications document is given in Table 5.17. The first chapter includes an overview of the system, a definition of its general purpose, its users and what is to be found where in the specification document. The second chapter describes the user interface in detail. After a summary of all assumptions which are made about the system and its use, an overview of the user interface organization follows.

Table 5.17 Outline for specification document.

1.   Overview
2.   User Interface and System Specifications
2.1. Assumptions on System Use
2.2. User Interface and System Organization
2.3. Detailed Description of System by Layer (I-P-O)
3.   State Transition Diagrams
4.   Error Messages
5.   Output (Report and File) Layout
6.   Specifications of System Quality
7.   Task Assignments, Schedules
8.   Acceptance Criteria, Acceptance Test
9.   Appendices

An organization by level of functionalities is recommended. It can parallel the structure of the requirements diagram in terms of major subsystems (activities), their constituent parts (sublevel activities), and, down to the lowest level, individual small functions. We can use the structuring done during the requirements phase to make both documents more uniform. First are all the activities on the top level and for each activity, its lower level function descriptions. Next are the state transition diagrams for all levels. The functional descriptions for each processing action already included any error messages and warnings as part of the output description. Nevertheless, it is useful to have a centralized description of all error handling and error messages as well. The next section will do that. There is also a section that details all output reports. After the user interface description, the specifications of system quality are described in the next chapter. Then follows a list of task assigments and schedules for the members of the development group. The last chapter is devoted to describing the acceptance criteria and the acceptance test. There may be appendices for more detailed descriptions of items, related system descriptions, summaries of relevant literature, a sample session and a few programming notes.

Parts of the specification document can also serve as a preliminary user manual. This is very useful, because it can provide a user-oriented system description.

▶ Feedback from the user for evaluating scope, level, and quality of functions is facilitated;

▶ The user interface can be evaluated by future users;

▶ Preliminary training can start, which is especially useful when a mock-up of a user interface or a prototype is to be built and users have to learn how to use it; and

▶ Feedback on whether the organization of the manual is appropriate, helpful, understandable is available.

The specification document is the major deliverable of the specification phase. Another deliverable is the acceptance test document. This is discussed in the next section.

5.9. Acceptance Test

Acceptance test and acceptance criteria have to be related to functional and quality expectations of the system, because they are the instruments to measure the overall quality of the developed software. The objective of the acceptance test is to find discrepancies between the system and its requirements. Test cases of an acceptance test may also serve other purposes. Some of the test cases can be used during program test phases. They can be used to test the specifications themselves (indeed, quite a few good test cases are derived when specifications are phase tested), and they help to clarify the designer's understanding of the specifications.

An acceptance test should specify test data for all classes of anticipated system usage (correct and incorrect) and for possible variations in environment. It should test all features and combinations of features and all requirements of quality, which may be done through a set of benchmarks (Benchmarks are representative system usages or sample runs for programs). Sometimes a system is installed on a limited basis so that it can be tested by regular use. This temporary usage should be planned to get the most test mileage out of this time period. Sometimes both the old and new systems are in operation simultaneously.

Environments to be tested include all machines and all possible configurations (usually maximal, minimal, and some in between). If we assume that the tax preparation system is to run on a series of personal computers, it must be tested on every one of them, and the PAS system may have to run on all school computers that are used for programming classes. Environment testing also includes testing for installability and serviceability. The new system must be tested for compatibility with an old one or with sister systems. In new releases of a system, the user interface must often stay the same, and the system must be able to handle "old data." For example, a new release of a compiler must be able to compile correctly what the old one could, and a new release of a mathematical software package must be able to be bound into the old ways it was used before. This can pose quite a challenge and, naturally, must be tested.

Load and stress tests are included in an acceptance test to see how the system handles peak loads. So are volume tests to see how much data the system can handle over longer periods of time. All functionality and quality expectations need to be tested. In critical systems, security tests are vital and are sometimes performed by a professional "penetration team." Performance tests check whether the system works within the limits set for it (speed and storage capacity). Reliability and availability tests check whether the system reacts to user and system errors the way it should. This would also include recovery testing when the system goes down for some reason. Human factors are compared against objectives. Lastly, all user and system documents need to be checked for accuracy.

When we compare what an acceptance test involves and what information the specifications provide and how we tested them, we can see that there is already a fair amount of test cases available which can be used for an acceptance test. Acceptance tests are usually performed by any of the following:

▶ the eventual users or their representatives,

▶ key analysts and designers (i.e., people involved in developing requirements, specifications and design documents),

▶ psychologists (for human factors), and

▶ a separate group (for objectivity and specialized knowledge as in the case of security).

Table 5.18 lists the areas that the acceptance test usually covers. Some may not always be applicable. Whether they are depends on the size and type of software and its environment(s).

Table 5.18 Area covered in an acceptance test.

Area	Explanation
Functionality	All features in requirements.
Quality expectations	Everything applicable from the list of quality areas (cf. Chapter 3), e.g., performance, reliability, human factors, security, etc.
Environment	Machines, configurations, interfaces to other systems
Compatibility	To earlier versions
Stress test	Peak loads (short time).
Volume test	Maximum input (longer time).
Documents	All required, accuracy and correctness.

5.10.   Verification and Validation

How should we review a specification document? The first step is to check whether everything that was promised in the outline is actually included. Then we can go through the document to see whether it fulfills the four C's of quality or commits any of the "Seven Sins of the Specifier" [Meye85]. As an example of applying these quality evaluation techniques, we will now examine the specification of the **ANALYZE** command for the program analysis system from Section 5.3.2. for the "Seven Sins" (i.e., noise, silence, overspecification, contradiction, ambiguity, forward reference, wishful thinking).

1. *Silence.* The list of legal commands on the top level does not mention the COMPARE command that we know should be there (Table 5.12 mentions it).

2. *Silence.* The paragraph after the list of commands does not mention the role of carriage returns ⟨**cr**⟩ or line feeds ⟨**lf**⟩. Are they delimiters? Some commands have parameters. When they do, does a ⟨**cr**⟩ or ⟨**lf**⟩ act as an "end of command" indicator or assume the role of a delimiter between the command and the parameter list?

3. *Ambiguity.*   The term "token" assumes knowledge about parsing. Even then it is imprecise.

4. *Silence.*   The specifications state that the program to be analyzed should not use reserved keywords as module names. What are the reserved keywords? What happens, if someone uses them anyway? The list of reserved keywords would probably go into an appendix or a table, but the effect of using one as a module name should be specified here.

5. *Silence (Ambiguity).*   What happens, if the module name cannot be found?

6. *Noise, overspecification, and wishful thinking.*   In the function description, there is a reference to Sections 2.4.2. and 3.5. These contain noise, overspecification, and wishful thinking. First, only Subsection 2.4.2.2. and some information from 2.4.2.3. apply. Even then there is still some noise (general motivation and explanation of software metrics) and wishful thinking (impurities).

7. *Ambiguity.*   The section speaks of operators and operands but never defines what they are.

8. *Noise.*   The metric terms "vocabulary" and "length" and some of the general explanations about software metrics are noise for a specification.

9. *Wishful thinking.*   When dealing with impurities, we get a vague notion of what they are, but a solution that deals with them is not described.

10. *Forward reference, silence.*   Statistical quantities such as mean, median, standard deviation, covariance matrix, multivariate density function are mentioned but never precisely explained. This may be fine when the developers know what they mean, but it makes the specifications less than precise.

11. *Noise.*   There is noise in the explanation of what the quadruple values and the derived statistical quantities mean, but what precisely groups quadruples into similarity classes is left very ambiguous and vague. The list of the problems with the method is noise. While these things are fine and necessary for a problem analysis, they do not belong into a specification document.

12. *Noise.*   If we are willing to include the problem discussion (2.4.2.3) into the reference, there is noise in the beginning when the scope of the problem is explained.

13. *Contradiction.*   400 programs need to be analyzed, but the accumulator only holds 100 results.

14. *Ambiguity.*   This develops when we look at the need for analyzing 400 to 600 executable lines of code. How does that translate into how many operands we may have? We don't find anything on that in the specifications.

15. *Ambiguity.* Finally, when we look at the requirements diagram of Section 3.5, we have an inconsistency in naming, because the activity labeled "comparison" is related to the command **STATISTICS** while the **COMPARISON** command does not have anything related in the requirements diagram. At the very least, the choice of words is confusing.

By using the classification of the "seven sins" we have uncovered 15 problems with this specification. Some of them stem from the fact that a previous document was used indiscriminately. We have also found some inconsistencies with the requirements diagrams. The specifications are imprecise in some areas, because they assume knowledge about parsing and statistics that the reader may not have.

For further phase testing we can use decision tables to check for ambiguities, completeness, and redundancy in the input and processing descriptions. The cases we use to test input and processing we should keep as part of an acceptance test, or at least to test the implemented system against its specifications. To the same end we can also use cause-effect graphs. Because they provide a detailed analysis of the specifications, they help to find errors in the specifications and are an aid to generating optimal test cases.

The third step in checking specifications out is to cross-check the state-transition diagrams against the sequencing of commands as described in the function description of the specification document. What are the implications? Are they considered? Any contradictions?

Let us look at the state transition diagram for the PAS system. One question that is not quite clear is what happens to the accumulators? There seem to be different kinds: for analyses, for statistics, for comparison results. What are their sizes?

The fourth step cross-checks whether all data objects from the requirements diagram are still in the specifications. There should be good reason for it whenever data "disappear." If new data objects were "invented," were they necessary? Why? In PAS there are some new names when we compare the specifications to the data dictionary. This is a source of misunderstanding and should be avoided.

The fifth step checks whether the human factors are as they should be. Are errors handled correctly? Is the interface consistent? What about layouts of output, sequencing of commands, or menus? What about the amount of output? Of input? While not always possible, it is advantageous and extremely helpful for development to get feedback on this from the user.

Are all quality expectations accounted for? We have already discussed this in the previous section, so we will concentrate on an example here, the program analysis system. The first quality expectation on the list is degree of functionality. Based on earlier discussions during requirements analysis, we only need to have all mandatory features present. Analysis requires the implementation of the basic analysis algorithm without impurities. Analysis is to be done for whole programs and for user specified parts (module names and line ranges). The specifications also describe comparison with earlier statistical results, which we can remove for the moment and implement later, in a more enhanced version.

We have already tested the specifications of the **ANALYZE** command and have found several things wrong with it (Exercise 6 of Section 5.6.2, Exercises 1 and 2 of Section 5.6.3, exercise 1 in section 5.7., and the 15 sins). Because we did not specify details about the other commands, we cannot test them here. The intent of this step should be clear, however, even without that.

All required functions need to be reflected in the specifications. The specifications have to describe and deal adequately with minimal and maximal values and pathological cases. Not unlike our example, this is one area where many specifications are weak. They do not anticipate what curious input can befall a system, and the result is that products sometimes crash rather unexpectedly or produce peculiar results. It is more obvious to describe "regular" use of a system, but specifications should attend also to boundary conditions for inputs and the system's reactions to them.

Reliability describes what the effects of system failure and user errors are. Some effects of system failure were described in the previous section. The effect of user errors was also considered previously. A list of pathological or boundary uses of the system was given in Section 5.7, and the effects on the system are undefined for a number of them. This shortcoming of the specifications needs to be remedied.

Effects of capacity limitations are also described: the accumulator is overwritten. We have already mentioned that the effects of exceeding the number of operands is not yet specified. Other cases for a stress test were given in Section 5.7. The effects of most of them still await specification, however.

Has PAS considered the relative importance of quality expectations? Section 4.2. listed them as given in Table 5.19. This table also explains what the specifications have done to achieve the desired quality.

Benefits are related to the quality of the human interface and the quality of the analysis. For PAS they would be saving grading time and improving its accuracy. That, however, is a long-term goal, because there are still questions about the efficacy of the method. Understanding and gaining knowledge about program measurement through the use of PAS is a more realistic goal, requiring that we can do basic analysis and statistics and simple reports. PAS as described with its simple command language and features is quite able to provide that benefit.

What we have done in this step of phase testing is to show how quality expectations are reflected in the specifications so that we ensure that all aspects of quality have been addressed.

Does every task have someone assigned to it? How well are responsibilities spelled out? Is the schedule realistic? Is there more parallelism than there should be (because work that is prerequisite will not be completed by the time a task is to begin)? Are the

Table 5.19 Quality expectations and specifications for PAS.

Areas of Quality ====>	How they are reflected in the specifications
Reliability	Analysis method, protect user against mistakes, point out limits of PAS
Degree of functionality	Basic analysis enough (experimental system)
Security	Student grades and analysis results protected through security built into professor's account
Performance	Related to length of programs
Human factors	Very simple command language for intermittent users
Adaptability	For experimental version only simple features, not tailored to specific gradebook format or language, could have extra parameter for language selection, could conceivably collect other measurements during analysis
Documentation	Full set of development documentation, system manual and user manual, version plan for future enhancements (evolutionary approach)

tools and equipment available when they are needed? These questions are dealt with in Part 2 on management aspects of software development.

In summary, a phase test of the specifications uses the steps given in Table 5.20.

Who should test the specifications? First there is the possibility of an n − 1 + 1 review. In a review for the specifications phase, the authors of the requirements (previous phase) and the designers of the system (next phase) will review the specifications. This ensures that the specifications are correct and that the designers understand—and consider feasible—what the specifications describe.

Specifications can also be user reviewed. The analysts give the user the specification document and examples of system use. The user examines the document and either returns it to the analysts for revisions or accepts it.

Table 5.20 Steps of phase test for specifications.

1. Check content against outline of specification document.
2. Review content for "seven sins" or "four C's."
3. Use decision tables or cause-effect graphs to test for ambiguity, completeness, redundancy.
4. Cross-check state-transition diagrams against functional description.
5. Cross-check requirements diagrams and the data dictionary against functions, inputs, and outputs in specifications.
6. Test human factors (uniform, consistent, etc.).
7. Compare quality expectations against features in specification document.
8. Check budget and schedule for realism and against requirements.

The next technique is called manual simulation or specification walk-through. The person or group performing the walk-through starts with a set of test cases and the specification document. The test cases are inputs; the specification document describes their processing and what outputs they will produce. The testers see whether the document specifies the correct outputs for the inputs. The test cases should include valid, invalid, boundary, and default inputs. There should also be test cases for quality expectations.

A related phase test technique is terminal simulation. It is also called "the man in the hidden computer game." It is a variation of the manual walk-through. A mock-up of the system has been implemented so that the user can test how the system works. Whenever he enters data, it is conveyed to another terminal where another tester uses the specifications document to return the proper output to the user. The user has the impression that the complete system has been implemented when, in fact, only the human interface exists. This type of simulation needs a very precise specification. It is not always possible. Just think about the poor soul who tries to count operators and operands for a long test program when the specifications for PAS are phase tested this way.

Human interfaces are often tested without the second person simulating a system's functionality. The system responds with fake output to show what type of output it would generate. Either version is useful to find human factors flaws and to study how the system would support human productivity.

During phase tests, we find errors, and objectives, benefits, requirements, etc. may need changing. It is very important to update all documents consistently, and every change needs to be investigated. Before changes to documents of a previous phase can be made, (written) approval should be required. Strict change control keeps the complexity of the system manageable, increases reliability and correctness, and keeps previous documents useful. It also prevents running after a moving target because focus and/or requirements have shifted without proper readjustment of resource needs and schedules.

How does that relate to an evolutionary approach where the developers get feedback from the users and incorporate these changes before proceeding? We have seen such change in the system for plagiarism detection. Originally, the goals were much higher: simplification of grading, more accuracy. When it turned out that the analysis procedure was not sufficiently understood, the focus shifted to an exploratory system. That is a different goal. We should not and will not evaluate an exploratory system against the objectives we had for the original production system. We are now talking about a program analyzer, no longer about plagiarism detection. What should be done, then, is to update the requirements document accordingly. This does not mean that we throw out the assessment of the original goals; rather, in the analysis, we add a paragraph that states that there will be phases of evolution and what the first phase of evolution will be.

5.11. Summary

The specification phase describes precisely what the solution will look like, how we intend to test it once it is implemented, and what the steps are to achieve the desired implementation. The degree of accuracy and detail of specifications varies depending on the objectives for the specification phase, which influences the content of the specification document. We discussed the types of specifications from very precise to imprecise and the activities involved in developing specifications.

We gave a sampling of accepted or popular techniques that are capable of describing all aspects of functional specifications. The techniques were classified according to the aspects of specifications they describe, i.e., inputs, functions, outputs, state transitions, and quality characteristics. Table 5.21 shows the specification aspects that each of the techniques of Section 5.6. covers. All but natural language are considered formal notations or techniques. Some tend to become cumbersome as the size of the system increases: Meyer's notation, decision tables, and cause-effect graphs. Therefore means were discussed to keep descriptions in these notations manageable.

Table 5.21 Application of specification techniques/notations.

			Aspects			
	I	P	O	T	Q	Type
EBNF (syntax diagrams)	x					Formal
Meyer's notation	x	x	x	x		Formal
Natural language	x	x	x	x	x	Informal
Decision tables	x	x				Formal
Cause-effect graphs	x	x				Formal
State-transition diagrams				x		Formal

The spectrum of techniques and notations can be classified differently, namely into relational and state-oriented notations. The selection of notations and techniques presented in Section 5.3. covers this categorization as well.

Relational notations are used to describe objects, the relations between them, and functions and operations that can be executed on the objects. Thus the following ways to describe properties of a solution are all relational notations:

▶   mathematical equations and relations (x = y or b < a);

▶ recurrence equations such as recursive functions;

▶ axioms such as the fact that removing an element from the top of a queue and adding another at the end results in a new queue of the same length as the old one; and

▶ regular expressions.

The examples we used along the way were meant to illustrate common problems and shortcomings in specifications and how to recognize and deal with them. We also wanted to show how specifications can evolve through feedback from test cases. Various ways to generate test cases for specifications (and based on specifications) were explained. Because there are many alternatives to choose from when specifications are developed, some guidelines were given how to use requirements to pare them down. Once the specification document is accepted, a strategy for designing the solution can be developed.

Meyer's notation can be used to write all but the last of these relational notations, and extended Backus-Naur-Form is more powerful than regular expressions. Thus these two techniques cover the spectrum of relational notations.

State-oriented notations include decision tables, event tables, transition tables, and state transition diagrams. Since decision tables, event tables, and transition tables are of equivalent expressive power [Fair85], only one of these three (decision tables) is presented (Section 5.6.3.). Cause-effect graphs are a technique related to decision tables. They help in preparing decision tables and test cases for specifications. They provide a link between natural language and decision tables and therefore are a useful aid in developing formal specifications (cf. Section 5.6.3.). Lastly, state-transition diagrams are used to describe various states the system may go through. In tabular form they are described with transition tables. Section 5.6.4. uses transition diagrams to describe state changes and what causes them.

The reader who is interested in a survey of relational and state-oriented notations that are not covered here is referred to [Fair85] and [Geha86]. The latter reference is a very comprehensive collection of papers on basic and advanced specification techniques and environments. The relational and state-oriented techniques presented in Section 5.6., however, have comparable expressive power to those in [Fair85].

This chapter emphasized the role of quality expectations in shaping specifications. This cannot be covered with any of the formal techniques described in Section 5.6. Consideration of quality expectations, such as quality of human factors, reliability, performance, security, etc., influences what the specifications will look like, rather than how they are described. Quality expectations are often useful in guiding decisions when choosing between alternatives.

Section 5.7. illustrated how quality considerations permeate specification development and guide choices. Quality cannot be put into a product after it is defined; it must be engineered into it from the very beginning. Quality expectations, also, like other aspects of specifications, guide the development of test cases. In fact, all formal techniques facilitate test case generation for phase test of the specifications and for testing design and code against specifications. Sections 5.8. and 5.9. discussed the two deliverables of the specifications phase; the specification document and the acceptance test plan.

Phase testing is a major tool to assure quality of phase deliverables. We gave a seven step testing procedure for specifications that covers the techniques discussed in Section 5.6. Especially important are techniques to evaluate specifications written in natural language. They are the most prone to errors and least amenable to automatic verification. At the same time, they are still the most common. An example illustrates the use of the same testing technique that was used to test requirements ("seven sins"). This technique has the advantage that it can be applied to any natural language document no matter what the phase is. Thus one has to learn only one technique. Its shortcomings are that it is only as accurate as the evaluator, and badly organized documents make evaluation virtually impossible. This is why outlines for specification documents, such as the one in Section 5.8., help greatly. Other outlines can be found in [Glas88], [Pfle87], [Press87].

The examples in this chapter were meant to illustrate how to use the techniques presented and how to recognize and deal with common problems and shortcomings in specifications. We also wanted to show how specifications can evolve through feedback from requirements and specification test cases. Once the specification document is accepted, we can go on to developing a strategy for designing the solution.

Problems and Questions

1. The following are suggested output formats for the **REPORT** command of the program analyzer. Do they give all the information you think **REPORT** should give?

Program	range	n1	n2	N1	N2	N
main	(50,500)	21	18	331	215	715
. . .						

Table of statistical data

	mean	median	mode	stan. dev.	min	max
n1	12.55	13	12	1.77	3	25
n2	30.49	40	35	15.44	29	105
N1	176.23	172	175	12.95	132	201
N2	112.78	105	100	28.77	67	289

Suspect Programs	covariance	f(x)	f(m)	f(x)/f(m)
main				
adopt				
Summary				
prog35				
search				
qucksrch				
Summary				

Specify the **REPORT** command in detail.

2.   What must the files produced through **ANALYZE** and **STATISTICS** look like for the reports to be possible? Specify accumulator and file format.

3.   What do you think about the practicality of the following output description for analysis results? (Hint: If you have 50 programs in a batch, how many pairs of programs do you have? What will that do to output, run time, and the size of the result files that are to be saved?)

Analysis and statistics results

	mean	median	mode	std. dev.	min	max
n1						
n2						
N1						
N2						

```
prog-1 n1 n2 N1 N2 vol int
prog-2 n1 n2 N1 N2 vol int
  confidence factor: con
etc.
```

Besides the summary analysis and statistics results, a pair-wise comparison is performed for all program analysis results that are part of the statistical evaluation. The results of the comparison are printed for each pair with a confidence factor of 90% or more.

▶ 6
Design: Strategies
and Notations

6.1. Overview

The beginning of the design phase marks a transition from describing what the solution looks like (specifications) to how the problem is going to be solved. The design document that we will develop during this phase is the blueprint of the software. It describes how the solution to the customer's problem is to be built. Since solutions to complex problems aren't usually found in the first try, iterations are most likely required. This is true for software design as well. For this reason any design strategy, design method, or design language must be flexible and must easily accommodate changes due to iterations in the design.

Complex problems aren't usually solved in one step. Rather, they are solved using the principle of "divide and conquer," where the problem is divided into a set of subproblems that are solved more easily. These partial solutions are then combined to become an overall problem solution. Any technique for design needs to support and guide the partitioning process in such a way that the resulting subproblems are as independent as possible from each other and can be combined easily for the solution to the overall problem.

Subproblem independence and easy combination of their solutions reduces the complexity of the problem. This is the objective of the partitioning process. Partitioning or decomposition during design involves three types of decisions:

▶ define the boundaries along which to break;

▶ determine into how many pieces to break; and

▶ identify the proper level of detail when design should stop and implementation should start.

This decomposition process results in a set of design modules (the pieces) and a description of how they will interact (interfaces). In general, the term "module" has many definitions. We have used it to describe parts of functional requirements and specifications. We will now use the term design module, or module for short, to mean a well-defined, manageable unit with a single purpose. Thus a module may be, but need not necessarily be, a subroutine or procedure or the unit of work assigned to a software developer. The important characteristics of a module are its well-defined single purpose, its well-defined interfaces to other modules, and its function to the outside. A design module may or may not translate into an implementation module such as a subroutine. That depends on the capabilities and limitations of the programming language.

Design methods and strategies should also facilitate fulfilling specific quality requirements from the requirements document, such as degree of functionality, usability, intended use, lifetime expectations, schedule, etc. (see Section 4.2.). Where performance is an important quality criterion, it will require selecting data structures and algorithms that are efficient enough to satisfy the performance requirements; sometimes the most efficient solution needs to be found. Usually trade-offs have to be made between storage requirements and speed. For example, it is possible to read in an entire input file and then process it. Often, when information is scattered all through the file, having all of it in core enables much faster processing—at the expense of memory. On the other hand, we might only read in part of it and go back to get more information as we need it, but every time an I/O request is issued, processing is delayed while the request is pending. The second approach saves storage but is slower.

When reliability is a quality criterion, fault-handling techniques should be used. Usually one strives for an error detection mechanism that can pinpoint the error's exact location. The more we can isolate the error, the less it will perturb the rest of the system, and the easier it will be to fix it and have the system deal with it gracefully. A technique for error isolation is called "mutual suspicion." Each module assumes that its inputs may be faulty and checks them for correctness before processing them. This is also an approach that supports maintainability, because effects (desirable and otherwise) of changes can be traced more easily.

When we have adaptability requirements, we will choose data structures and algorithms that can be changed more easily, such as variable sizes for tables and arrays and simple self-contained functions. Let's assume that we want to implement the tax preparation system. There are several lines on Form 1040 that represent the result of filling in another schedule or form. Schedule A is an example. If we decided that we would implement Schedule A later, all we need at this point is a dollar amount for personal deductions. Later, this dollar amount would be the result of a processing activity that fills in Schedule A. If we want to be adaptable to changes for Schedule A, we should choose the data structure for the results of this schedule so that we will not have to make changes all over the place later. We could define **Personal_deductions** as a function that returns the sum of all personal deductions. In the beginning, it might ask the user for input or look it up in a data object that the function owns. Later, another function may be substituted for it. The processing step that needs the cumulative figure for personal deductions need never know that there was a change in how the figure is prepared.

Another example task could be to find entries in a table. Let's call the function we are looking for **find_entry**. Over time, the number of entries and the search algorithm may change. If we keep the table size variable and the definition of the search algorithm separate from the parts of the program that use the **find_entry** function, both types of changes will not be hard to accomplish. It is similar to removing one unit and plugging in another. What makes a program adaptable to changes is this containment of solutions to predictable, simple parts of the system. That is what we mean by modular.

Besides increasing product flexibility, a modular design is also easier to comprehend. It is possible to study the system or program design one module at a time. Furthermore, modules can and should be used as planning and scheduling units. Having a system organized into self-contained modules makes a project more manageable, reduces dependencies between implementors, and shortens development time significantly.

Every quality expectation from the requirements list has its own preferred algorithms and data structures that support it. We will encounter these later in this chapter. The examples we gave so far are meant only to emphasize that making design decisions is a requirements driven activity. The examples are neither comprehensive nor detailed enough. Fulfilling quality expectations is at least as important as providing proper level of functionality. We should also use our own knowledge of requirements when making design decisions. Otherwise the final software product is likely to lack those quality expectations that were left unconsidered.

Functionality is one last area of quality that we should explore before proceeding. Requirements and specifications clearly spelled out what features were required, what they looked like and what the scope of the solution was. When we look at how we can produce the solution and proceed to make decisions about data structures and algorithms, it often turns out to be simpler to implement a more general solution than is actually required. The solution to the problem that was posed in the requirements and specifications is only a specific case. We find an example of this in the tax preparation system.

This problem as it was presented to us specifies a fixed set of schedules and forms. In all of them it is determined what information is to go on which line. Likewise, all the categories of data, such as specific types of deductions, are fixed and known. As far as functionality is concerned, we can design and implement this information exactly. On the other hand, tax laws, schedules and forms, and lay-out often change from year to year. Adaptability was one of the quality expectations the user had for the tax system. If we take this into account, ultimately it will be easier to implement a more general solution. The more general solution allows the user to configure his or her own schedules and categories of data (especially when it comes to deduction categories). For a smooth start, there can be a subset of forms and data categories that are predefined. In this case, they should be redefinable when forms or data categories change. What makes the solution more general is that we added a configuration step to set up the current year's tax forms, schedules, and all the data that pertain to them. We now have the most generality for possible forms and data. This solution also exceeds the original problem scope. It makes the system easily adaptable and extendable—even for tax preparation in foreign countries.

During the design process, decisions are made step by step. How will the required functionality be implemented? How will functions or subsystems interact with each other? What are the data structures that represent the data objects and items of information the software system must handle? Design strategies tell the developer when to make which type of decision. It is much more difficult to answer all implementation issues at once rather than one at a time when they are independent. Ideally we would like them all to be completely independent. This requires decoupling of decisions. Maximizing subproblem independence and the decoupling of decisions is at the root of all design strategies. Next we need rules for decision sequencing. These differ for different design strategies.

Before design decisions can be sequenced, however, one has to determine which decisions need to be made. This includes decisions about software system or module structure, functions, interfaces between all parts on all levels, and data structures. Examples of design decisions are whether to use binary or general trees, singly or doubly linked lists, recursive or iterative algorithms, message or procedure based systems, etc.

When the decisions are known, they can be ranked according to their impact on the system and its design as a whole. Those decisions that affect the largest part of the system are to be made first. Usually they either constrain or prescribe parts of the design for subsystems. For example, the organization of the accounts file in the tax preparation system affects not only that system but the system that balances accounts as well. Selecting the representation of this file is an early design decision, because it has an influence on both systems. For the tax preparation system for example, it impacts how processing of deductions can be done.

Another type of high-ranking decision is one that partitions a complex problem into simpler ones. The third criterion for sequencing design decisions is first to make those decisions that entail the fewest restrictions or prescriptions for later decisions. This is important because it defers design decisions until they absolutely have to be made, a design principle. All of these guidelines affect the resulting structure of the software system, and they support the objective of separating concerns by decoupling decisions.

The design process essentially consists of a sequence of decisions about how to solve the problem within the constraints that were set by requirements and specifications. In this chapter we will encounter a set of basic design strategies that prescribe the order of decisions and what overall game plans are useful. Advantages and disadvantages of the design techniques help narrow the range of possible design methods. One example of a design strategy is top-down design (6.2.1.), where design proceeds from the most general to the most detailed. We also discuss iterative enhancement (6.2.2.). This strategy first designs solutions to a core set of functions. This minimal system is then enhanced in subsequent design steps until the full design exists. Design and implementation may be done at each step. The last strategy develops the design around abstract data types or monitors (6.2.3.). It designs major data objects and operations together and looks at them as an abstract data type module. Furthermore, the objects are classified at several levels depending on the level of detail they represent.

Section 6.3. looks at design notations. Section 6.3.1. introduces MIL, or Module Interconnection Language [Dere76], as a means to express structural aspects of a design. Next is an example of a language that is well suited to describe detailed design within modules. Its original version is called Program Design Language, or PDL [Cain75]. In its many variations, it is also referred to as Pseudocode, Metacode and is really a form of structured English. For parallel programs, synchronization needs to be expressed. We will describe a form of PDL called *path expressions* that can be used to express execution constraints for parallel software. These three languages can express three major aspects of a design: algorithms, structure, and parallelism.

In addition to languages there are many diagramming techniques. Traditionally, flow charts have been used to describe designs. They are very limited in their capability for modularization and structuring, and we will not even describe them here. Another diagramming technique, Warnier-Orr Diagrams, was introduced earlier. They are mainly useful to describe system and data structuring. They lack the ability to express algorithmic relationships (intramodule design). Structured flow charts or Nassi-Shneiderman charts are another useful diagramming technique [Nass73]. They serve the same purpose as PDL. As we proceed, we will encounter more informal diagramming techniques. Some have been formalized and named; others are *ad hoc* and used because they explain pictorially an idea that might be difficult to formalize using a language. Often language and diagrams complement each other. For those who are interested in concentrating more on diagramming techniques, [Mart85] describes in detail a variety of diagramming techniques. This chapter concentrates more on languages, because they are machine processable, easily read, amenable to formal verification, and, in combination with the diagramming techniques that we will encounter along the way, provide an excellent feel for structure. Unless automated graphics support is available for drawing diagrams, relying on them as a primary means to express design can become very unwieldy.

Designers are knowledgeable about design methods that structure a solution. They must also know how to develop a design in detail. They need to select the proper strategy and method, and they need to understand design methods to achieve various quality requirements. They must be able to assess the impact of design decisions on implementation and long-term product objectives. This requires expertise in design methods, the hardware and software environment, the implementation language, performance and security techniques, and design techniques that keep a product adaptable, testable, and maintainable. Often this expertise is distributed throughout a design group, where specialists can address specific questions in their area of expertise. As a result, designers also need communication skills to unify their efforts. This is especially true for large-scale efforts when several teams work on various parts or aspects of a design.

After finishing this chapter, the reader will understand what design is and have a working knowledge of three major design strategies that guide the order in which design decisions are made. The reader will also "speak" several design languages to describe design structure and algorithm design for sequential and concurrent software. He will know what their advantages and disadvantages are and will have seen examples of applying design strategies and design languages to the design of TAP and PAS.

Chapters 7 and 8 cover software system structure design (software architecture) and program structure (detailed design). Chapter 8 also includes a discussion of quality requirements during the design phase and discusses how to ascertain design quality.

Problems and Questions

1. What are the objectives of the design phase?

2. What influences how and when design decisions are made?

3. Which design decisions do you think are to be made first for

   ▶ the program analyzer?

   ▶ the tax preparation system? Why?

4.   Why is it a good design principle to defer design decisions until they absolutely must be made? What can happen when they are made too early? Too late?

6.2.   General Design Strategies

6.2.1.   Top-Down Design with Variations

6.2.1.1.   Top-Down Design

When a design is developed top-down, the designer starts with a description of the highest level manifestation of the problem and successively proceeds to add more and more detail. Design techniques using the top-down design principle differ in what they consider the "top." The top could be

▶ the user level (as opposed to the level at which functions that execute user commands are designed), the user interface, or what the user sees;

▶ the statement of the function of the program;

▶ the highest level of the requirements diagrams and, within that, the box(es) with input(s) from external sources; and

▶ the major control loop in a program.

   Top, then, is either the most general statement of a solution or the component closest to the user. The bottom, by contrast, is the most detailed statement of a function, the part of the design furthest removed from the user interface, or the lowest level of the requirements diagrams. Top-down design implies an ordering of the decisions made in the decomposition of the solution. It begins with a simple description of the entire process or system (top level) and proceeds with a succession of refinements of what has been defined at each level, specifying the next lower levels. Decisions that affect the entire system or more than one module are made early.

   We employed this strategy during the development of requirements diagrams and the data dictionary when we started out with the main activity of a physical system and refined it step by step into its constituent parts. First, design develops the overall control logic that drives the program and then details more and more precisely how constituent parts (modules, operations) are to be implemented. We are proceeding from the more general, the level closest to the user, to the more detailed and precise. This sequence of steps is called *stepwise refinement*. Each level of refinement implements a function or set of functions on a more detailed level than the level above it. It is possible to organize each level as an *abstract* or *virtual machine* that supports the next higher level.

An abstract machine is a logical entity that consists of a set of specific data objects of defined types and a set of operations that are allowed to act upon these data objects. The objects and operations fully present the capabilities and characteristics of the abstract machine to the next higher level using it. Designs that first identify abstract objects at a given level of abstraction, then define their associated operations, and subsequently develop a module that contains these data abstractions are called *object-oriented* designs ([Booc83]).

For example, a specific level may implement the data objects of type stack with the allowable operations **LENGTH, PUSH, POP**, and **EMPTY**. This and only this level implements the data objects and their operations. The next higher level may only use them with their name and perform those four predefined operations on them. Specifically, they could not reorder stack elements in the stack directly, reset pointers indicating the current top stack element, remove stack elements other than using the **POP** operation, or insert an element in the stack other than through a **PUSH** operation. Data objects together with their operations form an organizational unit or a module. Note that this definition of a module is different than some commonly used ones, such as defining a module to be a subroutine or a function. Indeed, it may be impossible to code the module that we have defined this way as one subroutine or function, especially when the implementation language is on a lower level (FORTRAN, for example). Modules in this context mean conceptual units, not parts of a program.

The level implementing the data object **STACK** provides it as an abstract data object to the next higher level, which in turn may use it to provide another higher level abstraction to the next higher level and so forth.

Top-down design does not require top-down implementation. The sequence in which design decisions were made does not have to parallel how the design is sequenced for implementation and testing. Implementation can be top-down, bottom-up, or a combination of both, called sandwich ([Myer76]). These implementation approaches indicate how coding of modules and thus (availability for) testing is sequenced. While design decisions are made mostly top-down with some variations depending on how critical certain design decisions are, an implementation sequencing strategy is selected based on a variety of considerations. These include schedule, how long it will take until a working program becomes available, what drivers and stubs will be needed, the degree of work parallelism, the ability to test structural aspects of the software, and the degree of control over the implementation process. These issues are discussed in the chapter on testing.

When implementation of a design is done bottom-up, modules at the lowest level are coded and tested first. They are used when the next higher level is implemented and so forth. Bottom-up implementation needs a minimal amount of scaffolding code. Scaffolding code is written to simulate modules or functions, for testing purposes, that have not been implemented yet. In top-down development, those would be modules on the next lower level. Bottom-up implementation is a good strategy when the problem and the human machine interface are well understood, because the customer sees the finished product rather late. It may then be difficult for him to suggest changes, maybe crucial ones, to make the system adequate.

6.2.1.2.   Variations of Top-Down Design

Where user interface and machine compatibility are crucial for success, a mixed or sandwich approach to design is the best compromise. Design and implementation is done partially from the top and partially from the bottom, and then the design efforts meet somewhere in the middle of the hierarchy. For example, the base-line diagram may have been constructed top-down as far as A, B, and C. The remainder may have been developed from the bottom up, i.e., starting with the lowest level modules ACA and ACB. If this is combined with a sandwich approach to implementation, the feasibility of the lower level modules can be ascertained and the amount of scaffolding code is reduced. At the same time, the user can still see the top level and the top-level interfaces early while changes or modifications in the user interface are more easily accommodated.

6.2.1.3.   Outside-In and Inside-Out Design

Top-down design is related to outside-in design. In outside-in design, design decisions start with the user level and work towards the implementation. If top is defined to be the user level, then outside-in is a form of top-down design. For the same reason, inside-out is a specific instance of bottom-up design. Bottom is defined as the implementation level.

Implementing a mock-up to test the feasibility and quality of the user interface is a top-down design that uses the functionality as provided to and seen by the user as the pattern along which design decisions are made. The major influence on structuring the system is provided by functionalities as seen on the outside. While this is an "obvious" design philosophy, it will not always produce the most maintainable system [Parn72]. The functional structure is not always the best design structure. If a system is structured along the functions it provides, some aspects about these functions may change, and others will not. When functions are structured around data objects, changes in data objects can percolate throughout.

For these reasons, some forethought is useful when a system is structured, even during the specifications phase. Optimal functional structuring when the specifications are developed will not necessarily be a good or even feasible precondition for the design effort. This is especially important when there are strict machine constraints (performance, memory space, instruction set, system software) or when other quality requirements can only be fulfilled within a narrow set of design options.

In some cases it may not be clear whether the preferred user interface is implementable on the target machine. A design approach needs to look at the interface software and user software at the same time. Implementable means that the software will work according to the quality expectations established for it, satisfying resource and schedule constraints.

Top-down design, however, is not always the same as outside-in design. Assume a high-level statement of an algorithm: "perform garbage collection." This can be refined by adding more precise, detailed design information about it (e.g., the algorithm used, how items to be kept are marked, how information is compressed, whether and how newly freed items are cleared of old information). This is top-down design but certainly not outside-in design, because garbage collection need not be transparent to the user at all. A similar argument can be made for the difference between inside-out and bottom-up design.

6.2.1.4. Tap

One way to design the tax system TAP in a top-down manner is to define the user level as the top and to see what functions are mentioned in it. Designing these is the next lower level of detail. Then the constituent parts of these functions would be identified and designed. This produces a set of more and more refined levels and a functionally oriented design. Tables 5.15 and 5.16 gave a layout of the functions of TAP's main menu and the deduction recording menu. The solution structure is very similar to it (Figure 6.1 and

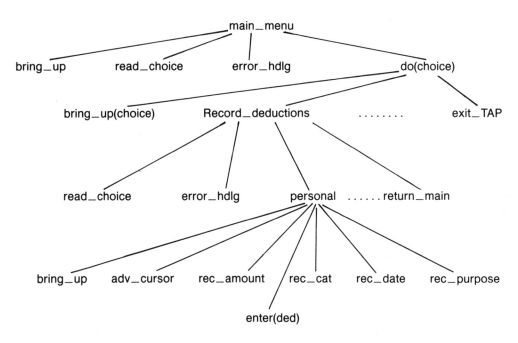

Figure 6.1 Initial Top-Down Design for TAP.

6.2). A top-down design that considers the main menu as the top would start by asking how the main menu is to be implemented. We bring up the screen, read a choice, complain about erroneous input, return, or perform the function of choice. The next level of refinement is to detail more precisely how the function of choice will be implemented. Let us assume the particular function of choice is to record deductions.

This next level down has some similarities to the previous one. Functions that need to be performed at this level include bringing up the menu, reading a user's choice on which type of deduction to record, processing errors, returning to the main menu, and actually recording deduction of choice. The next lower refinement level is to ask how we are to record deductions. Assume the choice was for personal deduction (Schedule A). We must bring up the proper menu, put the cursor to the amount column, read the amount, put the cursor to the category column, read the category, advance the cursor to the date, read it, etc. At some time we must put the entry into the list.

At this point we cannot refine the solution further without deciding what deductions should look like and how we will store them internally. Several of the functions will use at least some of the information in a deduction record. The design process needs to select a representation that is amenable to that. The following questions need to be answered:

▶ Should we have a fixed or variable list of deductions? A fixed list must be long enough so that it will not easily overflow. We must plan for maximum deduction size. The list is mostly empty in years with few deductions. A list of variable length involves links and makes the data structure more complicated. On the other hand, sorting is easy because we do not have to recopy elements, only reset pointers. Another consideration is the performance requirement for tax data entry (no more than two seconds).

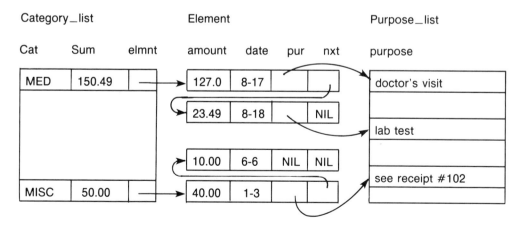

Figure 6.2 Sample Organization of the Deduction List.

▶ How should we implement individual deduction entries (the elements of the list)? They are dollar amounts (plus some explanatory fields like date, purpose, etc.). Should we try to find a record type that can take care of all the differences in the deduction elements or not?

▶ How should we enter information into the list? Should it be entered so that it is already sorted according to categories or not? Which category is to come first? Should it be lexicographic order or the order in which the summary amount of deduction categories will appear on Schedule A? Answers to this question will take into consideration what the list looks like (the first question). If it is a linked list, it is easier to enter them sorted, because we can place pointers at the beginning and ending elements each category and link the new one to the end.

If we do not enter them in the proper sorting order, should we put them into the next free element? If a linked structure is used and elements are to be entered so that they are sorted, is the new element the first or the last or entered so that the date is increasing? Figure 6.2 shows one of the alternatives. **Category_list** carries running totals for each category. This is not an ideal situation for decomposition. The entry and the delete function for deduction elements have to update the running total because entering or deleting an entry will change it. Entry and delete are two functions that are closely related. One operates on the deduction element, the other on the running total. This decreases module flexibility when one or the other of the constituent functions requires a major change. It is an example of how a design decision on a data structure can influence modularity and maintainability.

▶ What is the impact of these decisions on the file of checks from the bank account system? Are they sorted as the file becomes available or can we check periodically what is new and merge the checks that constitute deductions just as user input into the sorted deductions file? Checks are somewhat different because, in addition to the information on other deduction entries, they carry banking information. Can we put it into the purpose field defined above?

The data structures **deduction** and **deduction_list** are defined early because they affect the other functions in the main menu (computation and reports generation). While functional requirements diagrams, the data dictionary, and the specifications have an impact on the structuring of the design, they do not necessarily show the very same structure. The sorting function in the functional requirements diagram is a very low level part of data entry, when deductions are entered into the proper place in the list as the user inputs them. When we compare the elements of the data object deductions in the data dictionary with the elements of the data structure element deduction in the design, we see all elements covered in both instances but not necessarily the same way. We could use pointers or indexes to indicate categories or types, encode them with numbers, distribute the information of one data object in several lists in the data structure design, etc.

6.2.1.5. PAS

For the program analyzer, the top for a top-down design is the command handler; underneath is a parser for the language that identifies operators and operands. Yet underneath are routines that put operators and operands into a table so that they can be counted. On the same level as the parser is the module that computes statistics, because it is another step in the processing. On the next lower level of detail are functions that sum, compute means, or compute the covariance matrix. When we make each step in the process a module on the same level, we have a highly functional design. Top-down design is actually very well suited for such sequential problems.

Both TAP and PAS used mostly an outside-in approach. Neither applied it as a pure strategy. Pure strategies like top-down or bottom-up are rarely ever followed precisely. They are conceptual strategies, not rigorous positions. In most practical cases, we will end up with a mostly top-down, mostly bottom-up, or mostly sandwich approach. This way we can avoid the disadvantages and possible problems of a pure approach.

Problems and Questions

1.   Give an example where a design organized around user-visible functions in a strictly hierarchical manner will not be a good strategy, because it is not easily changeable.

6.2.2. Iterative Enhancement

Iterative enhancement, developed by Basili and Turner [Basi75], involves structuring the design into independent parts in such a way that a successively larger subset of the problem solution is designed and implemented. Iterative enhancement is a repeat process. It starts with a core (minimal) solution. Successively larger solutions are designed and implemented until the final product is delivered. This works especially well when successive versions can be described as distinct parts and when the user has already specified priorities on different degrees of functionality for the software system. If it is hard to partition into core functionality versus additional features, interfaces between modules may be more complicated than in the layered design structure. The advantage of this method is that prereleases can be done. A minimal running system is available early. It may only have minimal functionality, but it has at least some. Various design decisions can be tested early with such an approach.

Iterative enhancement is a type of evolutionary development. We design and implement a software system in successively enhanced versions. It takes into account feedback and adjusts product objectives accordingly.

Enhancement is not restricted to adding a previously nonexisting function. It also encompasses substituting a function with another one of higher quality, larger scope, better performance, etc. The new version of the software system is obviously an enhancement of the previous one.

Iterative enhancement combined with top-down implementation is advantageous when the schedule is late. With a late schedule, bottom-up implementation is probably the worst, because almost nothing can be shown to the user until the very end. Iterative enhancement requires the additional effort of scaffolding code to simulate nonexisting modules (also called stubs).

Iterative enhancement takes into consideration functional and quality expectations, priorities, and levels of functionality when successive versions of enhancement are defined. Often several alternatives exist. The tax system, for example could be designed and implemented according to the following three alternative enhancement plans.

Alternative 1

In this alternative, the user interface should be implemented (bringing up menus, sequencing, etc.; no actual function implementation; pure mock-up), and functions should be added in the following order:

▶ Store, update, and add taxes paid and income received.

▶ Implement Form 1040 since it is the major tax form. Any results that come from other forms and schedules are scaffolded as "user input." Then we mark the lines in the 1040 and prioritize them as to which form or schedule is to be implemented next. Let's assume the sequence is Schedule A, Schedule C, then Schedule B.

▶ Design and implement Schedule A, i.e., deductions and deduction types, sorting and adding them, storage, retrieval, and update.

▶ Implement schedule C.

▶ Implement schedule B.

▶ Whenever a new function is added, the required printing routines and the appropriate SAVE operation are added, too.

Alternative 1 is forms oriented in the way it sequences development. One form at a time is added.

Alternative 2

This alternative is fully requirements directed and uses what we said about priorities and quality expectations for the tax system in Chapter 3. Table 6.1 shows a list of functional, reliability, performance, security, and adaptability requirements for TAP. The number next to the requirement indicates which enhancement or version will partially or totally satisfy a particular requirement. The versions have been defined based on criticality and requirements priority (note that we have only considered mandatory levels of quality expectations, i.e., level [3]):

1. Use error detection and isolation techniques overall.

2. Implement full set of menus, mock-up only. No functionality.

3. Implement the most critial component to adaptability and functionality, i.e., the tax relevant items. This includes the following functions:

    ▶ insert item in variable format so that they are sorted,

Table 6.1 Requirements for TAP and version compliance.

Functional	Version	Adaptability	Version
Tax data entry/update		Changes in tax law	
Insert/edit capability	2,3	Categories, items	2
Short keystrokes	1	Forms layout	3
Variable format	1,2		
Individual entries	1,2	**Reliability**	**Version**
Extract deduction checks			
File only contains deds	2	No data loss due to system	
Sort/Add deductions by		errors beyond data added since	
type, fixed by user, doesn't	2	last SAVE	3
change		Error isolation to module	
Prepare forms and print		where it occurs	1+
1040, A	3		
B, C	4	**Performance**	**Version**
Check inconsistencies, errors	3+	Edit response time limit 3 secs	2,3
What-if	5	Compile responsetime limit	
Correct format	3,4	2 minutes	3+
Running totals in cats	2+		
Detail reports	2+	**Security**	**Version**
Summary reports/forms	3+		
Screen/hard copy reports	2+	Lock up computer	n/a

- ▶ ensure that individual entries are possible,

- ▶ read deduction check file, merge with other deductions, mark those in file which have been read, so that they are skipped the next time,

- ▶ allow predefined and user defined categories for items (tax, income, deductions),

- ▶ sum totals in categories, and

- ▶ print list of items per category and running totals.

This second version provides "minimal usefulness." The user can enter and sum any tax relevant information. He does already receive detail and summary information but still has to know on which form and line to put the information. No cross-check is performed whether data is correctly copied from one form or schedule to another, nor are range or rules checked. This is mainly a tax record keeping, not yet a tax preparation system.

4.   This enhancement adds the possibility to define forms with a system generation step and implements, as an example, Form 1040 and Schedule A. The following functions are provided:

- ▶ establish links that relate totals in categories to positions on forms and schedules (use with 1040 and A);

- ▶ establish limits for positions on forms and schedules (for example, wages must be positive);

- ▶ establish rules for computing entries for positions on schedules (such as maximum amount of charitable contributions that may be deducted without filling out Schedule A);

- ▶ use system generation module to define Form 1040 and Schedule A;

- ▶ compute taxes;

- ▶ print routines for 1040, A (correct format); and

- ▶ implement save operation.

This enhancement offers more than the required generality in some areas of functionality. The reasons are adaptability and extendability.

5.   This version configures the set-up and processing rules for Schedules B and C.

6.   The what-if capability is added.

In contrast to Alternative 1, Alternative 2 is computation oriented. Summing up items in tax, income, and deduction categories comes first, actual forms later. Adaptability and extendability had the biggest impact on the design. It is reflected in user definable categories for items and the system generation or configuration phase.

Alternative 3

This alternative implements the tax system as a self-guiding system with a configuration phase as the last enhancement. Note that we have to consider this last enhancement in how we design earlier versions. If we select a design that freezes schedules, forms, types of deductions, income, and taxes, this last enhancement might be difficult to add or may require rewriting parts of the system.

As far as implementation of schedules and forms is concerned, we can regard this alternative as a bottom-up implementation. Top is the forms configuration during system generation; bottom is the actual set of configured forms with their associated rules and links between them. Thus Alternative 3 has reversed the implementation sequence in Alternative 2 for schedules and forms. We would probably prefer Alternative 3 to Alternative 2 if time is a major risk factor and if we are not facing the problems of implementing a user directed forms generation module. If on the other hand, we knew that the ultimate goal was to add expert system capabilities, finding and testing a way to implement rules is a very good idea. Note that consideration of future use and user needs played an important part in the consideration of which enhancement plan to choose.

It is also possible to define successive versions of enhancement for all functional areas. Let us illustrate that with a set of versions for the program analyzer. It must be capable of the following functions: command interpretation, lexical analysis and parsing of the language, operator and operand identification, counting of operators and operands, and statistical results. Even the first, most restricted version can have a little of all the functional areas but still not have fully developed functions. With each successive enhancement, the function is more completely implemented. So we could, for example, choose to implement the command interpreter in a very rudimentary manner: it only recognizes and executes the analysis command with a list of full programs. Postprocessing prints results and saves them. An earlier version of the program analyzer might also be restricted to a subset of PASCAL instead of analyzing the full language. Operator and operand identification might be restricted to simple variable types and constants, no structured types are recognized yet. Counting is a simple enough operation. We probably would design and implement that in the first version. Statistical results might initially consist of means and the covariance matrix and be printed in a simple table.

There are other guidelines for sequencing design decisions. The first implements the most critical component first. This ensures that an infeasible strategy will not force the redevelopment of other affected components. This prevents lost time, because there is less chance that parts of the system that have been implemented already have to be redone. At times the most critical components are also the ones with the strictest constraints. We can also sequence our development by using the requirements analysis and developing the most constrained components first.

Problems and Questions

1. Develop a set of successive versions for the development of PAS.

2. Someone defines the following three types of prototyping for you [Free83]:

   ▶ **Traditional prototyping.** The system is implemented substantially like the desired one. It is only used by an "understanding user" and shows some inefficiencies. There is a fixed plan how and when to switch to the final system.

   ▶ **Concurrent prototyping.** The objective is to get something to the customer *quickly*! The final system and the prototype are developed in parallel.

   ▶ **Decision prototyping.** A prototype (reflecting the decisions to be made) is developed at each stage to help make decisions.

How are these three approaches to system design and development related to

   ▶ **evolutionary development?**

   ▶ **iterative enhancement?**

   ▶ **breadboards?**

   ▶ **mock-ups?**

Which types of design decisions are supported by them, if any? How do they function with top-down, bottom-up, and sandwich design strategies?

6.2.3. Abstract Data Types and Monitors
6.2.3.1. Abstract Data Types and Information Hiding

Many design methods consider the data object and its access mechanisms the crucial factors around which the entire design revolves. These strategies are object oriented. Requirements diagrams are object oriented, because refinements center around how activities process data objects. During a design that focuses on abstract data types or monitors, we again view the system as object oriented. The key to partitioning is to identify the most important data objects. Every type of data object has a fixed number of operations that can be performed on it. This is similar to predefined operations for a data item of type **INTEGER** in a programming language. The operations for an object of this type include addition, multiplication, and integer division but not shifting bits in its lower level representation nor concatenation (an operation defined for a different type—**CHARACTER**).

Based on this concept of abstract data types, a design module includes a data object and all functions and operations defined for it. It is a cohesive, well-defined unit with a single purpose, i.e., describing the abstract data type. This abstraction is provided to all other modules using it. It has a well-defined interface to these other units through the operations defined for the abstract data object.

Related to the concept of abstract data type is the concept of information hiding [Parn72] and abstraction [Dijk68]. The actual implementation of the data object and the functions operating on it are hidden from components using the object. The component only sees the object and its operations as an abstraction, a black box. For example, when we use information hiding for objects of type **INTEGER,** the actual machine implementation and any objects of this type is hidden to its user. For all the user knows, multiplication might be implemented using the current constellation of the stars.

If we use the concept of information hiding, nothing about the internal representation—how it is structured, how it is organized, or where it is stored—is shown to the outside. This prevents the user from making assumptions that can inadvertantly change. An example would be to assume that an integer variable is initialized to zero, therefore saving the initialization step in the program. If the system happens to change that, the program does not work anymore. Whatever we make known about a module's insides to the outside, will probably be used. The more we make known, the less we can change without "telling." For this reason, we should reveal as little as possible of the inner workings of a module. During design we should hide design decisions for a module from the rest of the system.

Modules, when we structure them around data types, need not and often do not conform to steps in processing. What then should be contained in a single design module? What should be hidden from the outside? Parnas [Parn72] lists the following reasons for putting items into a module and hiding them from the outside:

1.   Data structures and procedures that access or operate on the data structure should be put into the same module. That is why the stack module would contain the stack data object and all the stack operations. A module should not manipulate more than one major data structure.

2.   If a routine is called in a specific sequence of instructions, that sequence and the routine itself form a design module. The reason for this is that the calling sequence has information about how the routine works and should be hidden. Note that not all programming languages are capable of implementing this design module in one single code module.

3.   Information about particular lower level implementation of objects, such as character codes, alphabetic orderings, etc., should be hidden within a module. The higher level abstraction is enough and less prone to change.

4.   When an operation on a data object is done in a specific sequence, this processing sequence should be hidden from the outside (as far as practical). If we assume that the module using an operation will make use of all information it gets about the module, this would include sequencing information. That means that any change in the sequencing might affect this user module, which violates the concept of abstraction. Parnas was using this rule specifically with regards to operating systems where equipment additions and unavailability of resources make sequencing extremely variable.

How should we sequence design decisions that produce data objects and operations that are to be put into a module and hidden? We begin with a list of the most critical and difficult design decisions. For the tax system, one of those is how to organize the data objects **deduction** and **deduction_list**. Also high in priority are those design decisions that are likely to change. For TAP, this would be the question of schedules and forms design, such as data objects, the varying categories of deductions, and other aspects that are affected by changing tax rules and user needs. Those difficult and modification-prone decisions, once made, should be hidden in a module. Changes will affect that module only and not others. This approach to design will produce modules that do not correspond to steps in processing. Modules are not defined as a collection of one or more subroutines.

The concept of information hiding as Parnas describes it is a very useful design philosophy and serves as a criterion by which to evaluate designs. It is not a method or even methodology, because it does not, in itself, give much guidance in selecting what design decisions to hide nor how to best layer or group them. The way design units (modules) and design interfaces are defined does not provide a clear translation from design modules into programmable, interconnected modules [Booc83].

Hiding information in modules avoids the following obstacles when systems are to be adapted, either extended, shrunk, or otherwise modified [Parn79]

Obstacle 1.   Information is excessively distributed. Too many parts of the system assume knowledge about something that needs to be changed now. This would be the case if a part of the TAP system knew how the records were arranged in the list of deductions (for example that they are ordered by increasing date per category) and made use of this information.

Obstacle 2.   The second obstacles occurs when a sequence of components transforms data objects from one representation to another. When information is added to the data object later, or when information needs to be eliminated, the whole chain of transformations is affected. We can run into format clashes. As an example, take the tax system again. If we did not anticipate that there might be deduction receipts from cancelled checks, it is possible that changes have to be made all over the system. On the other hand, if we isolate the data object deductions in a module, changes are localized.

Obstacle 3.   Some components perform more than one function. This is common when one function is rudimentary or very easy, somewhat related in the chronology of processing, and thus "fits" with the other one. It may be very hard to separate them later, when the need arises. This can happen because now there are either more complicated ways of performing the function or more than one way to do so. All parts of the system that use that multifunction component rely on it as it was before; separating it into two different ones may be very hard. We have seen an example of this combination in TAP. When the decision was made to enter deductions "in the proper order," entry and finding the proper place was combined.

Obstacle 4.   The fourth obstacle occurs when components rely on each other heavily. This can be described as the situation where nothing works until everything works.

These obstacles may force redevelopment when systems cannot be changed. We avoid such a situation during design using a combination of techniques:

▶ Identifying subsets of functionality during the Requirements Analysis.

▶ Information hiding, i.e. hiding the insides of a module definition and how the interface of a module is implemented. We need to identify those items that are likely to change, put them into separate modules, and design intermodule interfaces so that they are insensitive to anticipated changes. We should not reveal any changeable aspects. It is an obstacle to product flexibility.

▶ The idea of abstract data objects should be augmented with a structuring concept such as the abstract machine or virtual machine concept (cf. 6.2.1 and 7.2). This way, every functionality (data object and operations on it) is defined on one level and provides functions to a higher one. The higher level does not and should not know how the lower level is implemented. Changes are localized and affect only small, known parts of the system.

▶ Reduce the interdependence of components. Two components are dependent if the correct functioning of one depends on the correct functioning of another. We should avoid loops in the dependence relation because it makes the system less changeable. A strict hierarchical structure prevents such loops. Dependence has nothing to do with one module invoking another. They can be dependent because they share data, because of timing constraints, or because they make assumptions about how the other works.

Dependence should only be allowed

▶ when it makes the dependent component simpler,

▶ when not allowing dependence would make a component more complex, and

▶ when we cannot find a useful subset of either component so that they would no longer be dependent.

A design that follows these rules will create a large number of relatively simple, single-purpose programs or routines on the lowest level. The upper level programs are implemented with the same goal of simplicity. This design strategy is aimed at producing adaptable, flexible software, where change is cheap and efficient. It is almost a truism that software is modified during its lifetime. Therefore, keeping the above rules in mind is always useful. This strategy of designing software structure can also be combined with iterative enhancement to design subsets and extensions.

6.2.3.2. *Monitors*

Designing software around data abstractions provides visible and enforceable control of a data object's use. Nowhere is this more helpful than during the design of concurrent or parallel programs, where access to shared data needs to be controlled and scheduled.

Monitors are an abstract data type that provides a useful abstraction for process communication. The monitor concept [Hoar74] views a shared data structure and the set of functions that access the data structure as an entity controlled entirely by the monitor itself. The data objects contained in or controlled by the monitor can only be operated upon using the functions defined for the data object. Even more, the monitor controls access to the data structure by allowing or disallowing execution of those functions, depending on synchronization rules for the data structure. Every time a process issues a request for an operation to be performed on the shared data object, the monitor is activated and checks whether the operation can be allowed at this point. Essentially, monitors are passive "watchdogs." The processes that issue a request for function execution do not know how the data object nor its associated functions are implemented. Synchronization is the role of the monitor. Thus monitors provide a mechanism to associate shared data with their critical regions. Critical regions are those parts of the design and code which allow access to a shared data object by one process at a time.

When we design a parallel program using monitors, critical regions in the processes' code are no longer necessary. The monitor provides the necessary synchronization. The operation or functions that are controlled by the monitor can be free to execute, or they can be blocked when their execution is currently prohibited by the monitor. In the latter case, the monitor will return a blocked indication and have the process wait for its turn. Waiting can be accomplished with a busy-wait or by putting the process into a waiting queue. The waiting queue is part of the monitor. Real-time systems sometimes allow the calling process to decide whether to wait or to give up and try later.

Shared data objects are no longer global, but local, hidden in the monitor. Because the object and rules for its use are centralized, we can check more easily whether the synchronization mechanism works correctly.

Taking this concept to its logical limit, we can design concurrent software as collections of processes and monitors. Every data object is local to a monitor if it is shared, and its access needs to be controlled, or local to a process, if it is not shared. Sequential and concurrent issues are clearly separated and allow an object-oriented decomposition of the system into separate parts. This simplifies the development of correct software and facilitates changes. Monitors make software flexible. When design and implementation of a shared data object change (such as a paging table, or the scheduling algorithm for a queue), the processes requesting functions need not know that anything has changed about the data object's implementation. They didn't know how it was organized to begin with. The addition of a new process will not create changes all over, because it is naturally bound into the system when it issues a function controlled by a monitor. An analogous argument holds for adding or modifying a monitor.

Monitors are a centralized synchronization strategy. Every request for function execution will go through the monitor on a sequential basis. When the monitor does not perform fast enough, it can become a performance bottleneck. Effects on performance need to be assessed before deciding on this concept.

Monitors are designed as abstract data types and do the following:

1. Identify the shared data objects—the entities whose access must be protected by the monitor.

2. Identify the operations and functions to access all or parts of the shared data objects.

3. Specify the conditions and rules for execution of any of the operations and functions. This includes rules for mutual exclusion and sequencing of operations such as in the producer-consumer problem. The producer-consumer problem deals with the synchronization of two processes. The producer produces data and puts it into a shared data structure in memory (usually a shared buffer). The consumer process takes data out when it is ready to do so and thus consumes it. Proper synchronization requires the following rules for sequencing of operations:

▶ Nothing is produced when there is no more room to store it (buffer full). The producer waits.

▶ The consumer waits when the producer is behind and there is nothing in the buffer.

▶ Access to the shared data structure (the buffer) is done under mutual exclusion to avoid inconsistent information.
Specifying rules for execution also includes scheduling rules for processes that must wait. To avoid starvation (a process waits for indefinite periods of time), sometimes more than a first-come-first-serve rule is needed. Priorities and dynamic adjustment of priorities may be called for. This makes the conditions more elaborate—on the next lower level. It has no effect on the top design level that states simply "wait your turn."

4. Design the operations and functions for the shared data structure. Use stepwise refinement where appropriate.

Let us take an example from [Hoar74.] He uses SIMULA67, an ALGOL-like language, to design a monitor for a single resource. Monitors are defined as data types, in the same way that **ARRAY** is a type. As we can generate objects of type **ARRAY**, naming them for example **A1, A2, A3** etc., we can also generate a series of monitors of the defined (and named) type that control access to data objects of this type. Figure 6.3 shows the general monitor type definition. Assume that *Rules* may be named and may

```
⟨monitor_name⟩ : Monitor
Begin    ⟨local data⟩;
         ⟨Shared data structure definition⟩;
         Rules ⟨rname⟩ ( ⟨formal parameters⟩ );
              Begin
                      ⟨body⟩
              End;
         Procedure ⟨pname⟩ ( ⟨formal parameters—interface to
                                              outside⟩);
              Begin
                      ⟨body⟩
              End;
         ⟨other operations and functions⟩
         ⟨initialization of monitor⟩
End
```

Figure 6.3   General Framework of Monitor Definition Similar to [Hoar74].

have formal parameters. This concept, while similar to Hoare's, is not the same. We separate rules from operations and procedures. Hoare's concept includes them as statements within procedures. During design, a separation of operations and synchronization rules makes more sense, because it makes the rules more obvious and transparent.

Figure 6.4 shows an example for controlling a shared data object through a monitor. The monitor type definition **port** defines what a port looks like. Then we can define instances of monitors as in Figure 6.5. **Port1** and **port2** are instances of monitors of type **port.** Two operations control execution: **wait** and **signal. Wait** means that the process executing this operation must wait until a **signal** operation will wake it up again and allow it to proceed. Either operation can be prefaced by a condition that indicates what the process would be waiting for or, when applied to the signal operation, that the condition is true.

Port: *Monitor*

```
Begin    M_out, M_in: Mailbox;
         Rules
             Begin
                     do not enter when full: wait until not full
                     do not remove when empty: wait until not empty
                     do not enter more than one item into same slot: wait until current
                     active entry completed
                     do not remove same item more than once: wait until removal complete
                     when enter is active for a slot, no other enter or remove is possible;
                     the same holds for remove.
             End;
         Procedure enter (item);
                 Begin
                         put item last into M_in
                 End;
         Procedure remove (item);
                 Begin
                         take first item out of M_out
                 End;
         Procedure connect (P);
                 Begin connect Port and P such that M_in of Port is
                         M_out of P
                 End;
         Set M_in, M_out to empty;
         Connect (Port);
End port
```

Figure 6.4 Monitor Example.

```
Port1, Port2 : Port;


Port1.connect(Port2);
Port1.enter (question);
Port2.remove(answer);
```

Figure 6.5 Usage of Monitor.

When shared data objects, operations, and rules for synchronization are concentrated in one place, it is easier to validate or verify that the monitor works as expected. We will discuss formal correctness proofs in the section on validation and verification.

While monitors were developed for structuring operating systems, there is increasing interest in concurrent application programs to utilize the full potential of parallel systems. This makes the concept useful beyond structuring operating systems. The rule aspect also shows promise for knowledge and rule-oriented programs, be they sequential or concurrent.

6.2.3.3. Generalizations

Monitors add synchronization, access rights, and restrictions that stem from synchronization needs to the qualities that must be described by the data abstraction. Policies for queuing for access (to procedures and hence to the data objects upon which they operate) have become part of the data abstraction but on a lower level. The abstract data type itself has become hierarchically structured.

The same is true for a further generalization of the concept of abstract data types. Monitors allow procedures to execute sometimes but not at other times. They protect access according to the rules embodied in them and according to a synchronization policy. In our example, any process that knows about a port and wishes to execute a connect operation for this port can do so. This is not always desirable and can establish connections that are neither wanted nor secure. We may want to prohibit some processes but not others from performing certain operations. Let's say only processes with certain rights can establish connections for their ports. Restrictions on execution of operations usually are made for security reasons, and monitors are not readily equipped to handle that.

The control problem generalizes to all kinds of security policies. They specify what needs to be protected from whom and when. On the lower level a protection mechanism will specify how it is actually done. There are two levels of abstraction: the level of mechanism and the level of policy, i.e., how to use the mechanism. This generalization is accomplished with capabilities. Each activity (operation, function), as part of an object within a data abstraction, has certain capabilities. In an operating system those can be read or write access to a file, ownership of a resource, the right (capability) of transferring rights to other subjects, the right to execute certain operations, and the right to acquire physical or logical resources.

The terms "object" and "subject" as they are used in this concept need to be defined more precisely. An object is anything to which access must be protected or restricted. This includes pieces of code. Subjects are active entities whose access to objects must be controlled. A currently active procedure or operation (a process) can be a subject. Because of chains in the execution, a subject from one viewpoint can be an object from another.

Capabilities provide a mechanism for accessing objects. Every access requires possession of a capability. A subject's capabilities to an object can vary across subjects and over time. Capabilities are manipulated by the lower level. When a subject becomes active, the universe within which it operates has to contain all objects that may be accessed and their particular access rights. This includes directly and indirectly accessable objects. Since capabilities specify whether, when, and by whom objects can be accessed, they have been used for addressing [Fabr74], and operating systems have been developed that are capability based (HYDRA [Wulf74], [Wulf81]).

If we look at capabilities as a flexible way of defining rules about creating, using, manipulating, and destroying data objects, their power extends far beyond operating systems and security. The capability concept is a generalization of the notion of abstract data types and is particularly appealing for concurrent and distributed software systems. Let us look at an example that shows how to use capabilities. Figure 6.6 presents a view of a business database, parts of which can be accessed provided the subject has the proper capabilities.

In this example, **Data_base** and **File** are object types and their capability list states all their capabilities. The specific database **Employee_database** only has a subset of these capabilities; only reads and updates can be done, but no information can be deleted or changed. **Employee_database** contains two files: the **Salary_file** and the **Employee_file**. The **Salary_file** can only be read, while objects of type **File** can have a wider range of capabilities defined for them. The **Employee_file** can be read and updated.

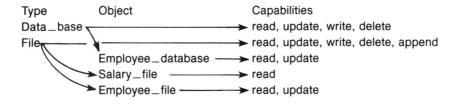

Figure 6.6 An Example of Using Capabilities.

Sometimes policies, stated in terms of capabilities, need to change. This is possible on the policy level and up to the user or subsystem who instituted the policy to begin with. The part of the system or subsystem that is concerned with policy is called the policy module. In distributed and parallel systems, policy change can affect the effectiveness of other parts of the system. It becomes advantageous to coordinate the setting of policies. Load-balancing in a distributed system is an example of that. This means that we need a third conceptual level above the policy level; let us call it legislature. Policy changes are brought to this level and decided upon based on what is considered good for the whole system. This provides maximum flexibility and avoids conflicting policies on the part of different subsystems. The extended capability concept is shown in Figure 6.7 with three levels of abstraction: legislature, policy, and mechanism. Legislature reviews and decides on policy proposals that are submitted from the policy modules. Policy modules use the functionality of the mechanism layer for policy enforcement.

Capabilities have the advantage of allowing multiple policies for different subsytems. They provide for universal and flexible access control and are easy to use. Objects are uniformly designed and handled. Protection and usage are controled separately. Capabilities have been used exclusively for operating systems and, even there, not fully. Some of the operating systems experience large overhead for initial access when the access rights are first checked and pointers are set to all the accessible objects.

Problems and Questions

1. How are abstract data types, monitors, and capabilities related?

2. When is it allowable to have a dependency relationship between modules?

3. How is the term module to be defined in this section? Does it correspond to a procedure or a subroutine? Why or why not?

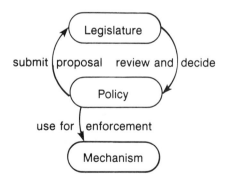

Figure 6.7 Extended Capability Concept.

4.   In some programs functions are more complex than the data they operate upon. In others, the functions are mostly trivial, but how to organize the data objects and their relationships to each other is not. Into which of the two categories do TAP and PAS fall? Would you suggest the same design strategy for both? Why or why not? What else, besides function or data orientation are you considering for your argument?

6.3. Notations

6.3.1. Module Interconnection Language (MIL)

MIL75, a *Module Interconnection Language*, was developed at the University of California, Santa Cruz, in 1975 by DeRemer and Kron [Dere76]. It was conceived as a language to aid in system design, to break the system into manageable modules, and to organize them into a useful efficient structure. Design structure and its interfaces between the parts of the structure are crucial. This information is often needed without the additional information of how the modules work internally, and having to collect it from all over the design is not an efficient way to describe structure. MIL attempts to concentrate this structuring information through a graph that represents a partial ordering.

MIL encourages structure before detail. It emphasizes the design of a correct environment for modules. MIL allows specification of all structural aspects of system levels and their interconnection. Because it does not encourage intramodule detail, it promotes information hiding. The partial ordering is very conducive to designing a system as a set of abstract machines. MIL also separates the description of module interconnection from the module itself.

MIL, as a graph description language, defines system structure and module interfaces as sets of tuples.

1.   The first tuple describes system hierarchy in terms of a system "tree" (actually a partial ordering). The system tree is defined as a quintuple consisting of

   ▶   a set of nodes,

   ▶   a special node called the root node,

   ▶   a set of node names,

   ▶   a mapping of node name to nodes, and

   ▶   a mapping such that for every node in the tree except the root, this parent function returns the name of the parent. This establishes the system hierarchy.

2.   This system tree can be augmented by resources. For every node there is a list of the resources it provides and which resources it expects the children to provide. There are

restrictions as to which resources can be provided. Siblings must not be expected to provide each other with resources. The flow of resources goes upward. In the graph they are drawn with dotted arrows.

3.   Next, we can determine for each node what accesses there are to resources of other nodes. This includes sibling accesses for nodes on the same level and inherited access rights for any node. Solid arrows between two siblings A and B indicate that A has access to all resources provided by B. This is not a transitive relation. Children of B are invisible to A (information hiding). Inherited access rights are based on the rule that children inherit, by default, the access rights of the parent. The parent can restrict access rights by giving only a subset, or none, of its access rights to its children.

4.   Finally, there may be derived access. A parent has access to resources provided by its children but does not have any knowledge of grandchildren or any other nodes further down. In this way we can structure a system as layers of abstract machines.

With these four sets of information, MIL describes the system tree, the resource and access augmented tree, the set of modules, and several functions. These functions determine the module name for a given node, which module originates a resource, what the derived resources are that are used in a module, and what the nonderived resources are that are used in a module. While we have made our examples in terms of annotated graphs with rules for node connections, MIL's graphs actually can be expressed as a language. The basic language constructs used are given as follows:

```
SYSTEM ⟨name⟩
AUTHOR ⟨name⟩
DATE ⟨date⟩
PROVIDES ⟨list of resources⟩
CONSISTS OF
  ROOT MODULE
    ORIGINATES ⟨list of resources⟩
    USES DERIVED ⟨list of resources⟩
    USES NONDERIVED ⟨list of resources⟩
  SUBSYSTEM ⟨name⟩
    MUST PROVIDE ⟨list of resources⟩
    HAS ACCESS TO ⟨list of resources⟩
  .............⟨further subsystems⟩
END SYSTEM ⟨name⟩
```

Let us give an example for a design structure using MIL. We will take the top two levels of nodes of the design structure for TAP in Figure 6.1. The annotated MIL graph for it is given in Figure 6.8.

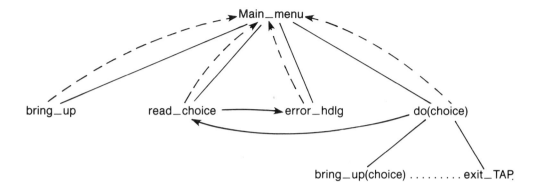

Figure 6.8 MIL Graph for TAP (cf. Fig. 6.1).

The dashed arrows indicate resources provided by a child to the parent; the solid arrows indicate sibling access, and solid lines denote system hierarchy. This design structure can be written in the MIL language as follows:

```
SYSTEM main_menu
AUTHOR smith
DATE      sept 1985
CONSISTS OF
     ROOT MODULE
       ORIGINATES main_selection
       USES DERIVED top level menu, choice, error messages, switcher
       SUBSYSTEM bring_up
                MUST PROVIDE top level menu
       SUBSYSTEM read_choice
                MUST PROVIDE choice
                HAS ACCESS TO error_hdlg
       SUBSYSTEM error_hdlg
                MUST PROVIDE error messages
       SUBSYSTEM do(choice)
                MUST PROVIDE switcher
                ORIGINATES switcher
                USES DERIVED action of choice
                HAS ACCESS TO read_choice
       SUBSYSTEM bring_up (choice)
                . . . . . . .
       SUBSYSTEM exit_TAP
END_main_menu
```

Note that the constructs **USES DERIVED** and **MUST PROVIDE** identify parent and child. There is no need for nesting.

The advantages of MIL are as follows:

1. It forces the designer to state structure and module interfaces and therefore explicitly increases reliability, at least in this area of the design.

2. MIL provides a concise and readable language to describe structure. Because of this, it serves as an understandable communication vehicle.

3. Because structure and interfaces are defined early, their early testing is possible.

4. MIL, being a formally defined language, lends itself to more rigorous validation techniques that approach semiformal proofs. Restrictions on providing or expecting resources and on their access can be checked easily.

5. When combined with a language processor, MIL can defer some of the consistency checking, completeness verification, and transcription into graphical form (for easy readability) to the language processor. This facilitates design considerably.

6. Because of the partial ordering MIL posits, starting out with a root node and then proceeding to lower levels, MIL supports top-down design, modular decomposition, and provides a formalized method of abstraction.

Its major disadvantages come from the fact that it concentrates exclusively on structure. It does not have any constructs to specify function. Data abstractions are only implied, not explicitly defined. As we will see in the next section, if we compare the advantages and disadvantages of PDL and MIL with each other, the two languages are complementary. What PDL lacks, MIL has, and vice versa. Therefore, it is best to use MIL in connection with a program design language. They both are practically useful. PDL and MIL are two different vehicles to describe how to abstract from the complexities of a system.

Problems and Questions

1. Check and correct the example in Figure 6.8 for violation of access rules. Is there any way to simplify the structure and its accesses? How?

2. Add the other modules of Figure 6.1 to the MIL description (graph and language) of Figure 6.8 (Hint: It helps to determine the resources first for each node. Then determine which are needed at the next level. Finally, determine what sibling access rights need to be granted.)

6.3.2. Program Design Language (PDL)

Program Design Language (PDL) was introduced by Caine, Farber, and Gordon in 1975 [Cain75] and has since appeared in a variety of dialects under a multitude of names. The motivation behind PDLs is to provide a form of language to implement software design in the same way programming languages implement an algorithm. And because the objective of structured programming is to build understandable and correct programs in the target programming language, design methods aim for well structured, comprehensible designs—which we can write in a PDL. The formal nature of a PDL hopes to increase rigor and thereby reduce errors and facilitate formal verification. PDL uses the concept of functional and data abstraction and stepwise refinement. It is possible to isolate the basic design concept from implementation detail, referring it to lower design levels. We can describe abstract machines in PDL.

Program design languages should have the following features to be maximally useful:

1. **Structuring capabilities**.   Features for structuring a design should correspond to the steps of the design technique chosen. It should be possible, for example, to write designs for which step-wise refinement was chosen as a general design approach.

2. **Implementation hiding**.   The program design language should be able to hide the details of lower design levels and their implementation. This reduces design complexity and promotes the understandability and modifiability of a design.

3. **Formality**.   The design language should be formal enough to expose ambiguities, inconsistencies, and other errors. It also should be formal enough to enable some degree of verification. The advantages of formality were one of the prime reasons for developing design languages.

4. **Ease of construction and modification**.   The idea behind wanting these characteristics is that designs are frequently changed; therefore a design language must be able to accomodate changes easily. Construction should not be difficult or time consuming; otherwise the old "napkin approach" is still too attractive.

5. **Ease of understanding.**   Another reason for writing designs is to make everybody understand what the design is all about. A design language must facilitate this understanding. When the language does not promote better and more streamlined development, nobody will want to spend the time reading and understanding the design.

PDLs usually consist of two types of components, the outer syntax and the inner syntax. The outer syntax is stated in formal statements, much like a programming language (albeit on a much higher level). It can be parsed, and it expresses the flow of control through a design. The inner syntax is application dependent, informal, and often in plain English. The earlier PDL dialects included data structures and operations on data. PDL, as developed by Caine, Farber, and Gordon, adds to this the possibility to organize PDL statements into segments (units or modules). If we design the software as levels of abstract machines, we will have a tree of segment references that give the structure of the software.

Besides these functional or flow segments there are three more types of segments. Text segments are like comments in a programming language. They allow for design documentation, introductory material, etc. Data segments provide a means of explicit data definition. There is also an implicit data definition capability, using an underscore when a data object is first used. This, however, has problems similar to implicit variable declarations in programming languages: it can obscure intent and logic and lead to less reliable software. External segments specify segments that are either not part of this design or whose design is to be hidden.

An additional feature is the data reference index. It is the design equivalent of a cross-reference list, which is a common option for compilers. It shows where in the program which data object is used. The segment index is the functional analog to the data reference index. It lists which segments use which others. The tool that Caine, Farber, and Gordon built also formats source statements automatically.

Other variants of PDL are not automated. The languages vary in their specific syntax but usually provide all or a subset of the following outer syntax statements:

Sequence

Statements are sequenced by separating them with semicolons. Statements can be PDL statements or an English statement of the function to be performed as in

```
Handling(command);
Read_next_program_file;
```

Selection Statements

There are two kinds; the **IF** statement and the **CASE** statement. They are defined as

```
IF ⟨condition⟩ THEN ⟨statement_1⟩ ELSE ⟨statement_2⟩;
ENDIF;

CASE ⟨expression⟩;

⟨value_1⟩: ⟨statement_1⟩;
⟨value_2⟩: ⟨statement_2⟩;
. . . . . . .
⟨value_n⟩: ⟨statement_n⟩;
OTHERWISE ⟨statement_n+1⟩;
END CASE;
```

Here the outer syntax is typed in upper case. The inner syntax is enclosed in ⟨ ⟩. Conditions, expressions, and values for the expression in the **CASE** statement can be in English or semiformal. How formally defined depends on the level of detail. The construct ⟨statement_1⟩ can be another PDL statement, an inner syntax statement (i.e., English), or a sequence of them. The following is an example of using the selection statements:

```
IF command valid THEN determine command_type;
ELSE report error;
get new command;
ENDIF;
CASE command_type;
      AN: perform analysis;
      ST: provide statistics;
      RE: provide reports;
      SA: save information;
OTHERWISE report system error;
END CASE;
```

Not all variants of PDL provide a **CASE** statement. Those that do not provide it can simulate it with the selection primitive.

Repetition

Here we can find a variety of constructs. Some of the more frequently used are

```
WHILE ⟨condition⟩ DO;
      ⟨statement⟩
ENDDO;
```

The statement (or the list of statements) is executed as long as the condition remains true. If it is more logical to evaluate the condition in the end, we could use

```
DO
      ⟨statement⟩
UNTIL ⟨condition⟩
```

The design equivalent of a **FOR** loop in a programming language is defined as

```
FOR ⟨variable⟩ = ⟨expression_1⟩ TO ⟨expression_2⟩ STEP ⟨expression_3⟩;
      ⟨statement⟩

ENDFOR;
```

Constructs to Leave a Loop

There are two ways to exit a loop: when the condition is evaluated and the current value causes the loop exit and from within the body of the loop. In the latter case, control passes to the first statement after the loop statement. This control statement is called **LEAVE.** A related statement that does not necessarily exit the loop, but transfers control to the point where the looping condition is evaluated, is called **CYCLE.** For example,

```
WHILE there are more programs to analyze;
       analyze (program);
       IF analysis successful THEN compile statistics for program; ELSE CYCLE
       ENDIF
       IF no more room in accumulator THEN LEAVE;
ENDWHILE;
```

Assignment

This is the design equivalent to the assignment statement in a programming language. It reads

⟨variable⟩ := ⟨expression⟩

A variable can be a defined name or a qualified name in English, such as in

```
first entry := name of project;
next free element address := relative address + base register;
```

Procedures, Operations, and Functions

For procedures we simply write their name, followed by actual parameters. As an alternative we could use the form **CALL** followed by the procedure's name and the parameters enclosed in parentheses. Functions are used within expressions in a similar way to variables, because they return values. They contain a **RETURN(⟨value⟩)** statement within their function body. If we adopt the monitor concept described in Section 6.2.3, we execute an operation on a data object by prefixing the name of the operation with the name of the data object. Examples of these types of design statements are

```
Handle(commands)
CALL parser(line)
token := next_token(line)
port1.connect(port2)
```

Type, Variable, and Constant Declaration

Types of data objects are defined with a **TYPE** statement, instances of a type with a **VAR** statement, and constants using a **CONS** statement, as in

```
TYPE semaphore;
      special variable with two operations P, V.
      only use for synchronization
END_TYPE;


VAR sem_driver, sem_queue : semaphore;
CONS size_of_symboltable, queuelength;
```

Before we list the advantages and disadvantages of PDL, let us make a more extended example. We will try to design the command-handling module and some of the lower level modules that provide part of the checking for valid parameters. The basis for the design is the EBNF from Table 5.3. Figure 6.9 shows the design for the command-handling module. Figure 6.10 refines the **get_an_parms** statement, which obtains and checks all the parameters expected by the AN command. Analyzing the file name is described in Figure 6.11. Figure 6.12 details a routine that checks whether the file name is valid or not.

The advantages of a program design language (PDL) are

1. It supports functional abstraction. All operations, procedures and functions are abstractions at the place where they are used.

```
command_handling:
   WHILE TRUE DO;
     read_next(command);
     strip first token off command;
     token := first token of command;
     CASE token;
        AN, ANALYSIS   : get_an_parms; analysis;
        ST, STATISTICS : statistics;
        RE, REPORTS    : get_re_parms; reports;
        QU, QUIT       : LEAVE;
        CO, COMPARE    : get_co_parms; compare;
        OTHERWISE report_error(unrecognized cmd_name)
        END CASE;
   ENDDO;
   save_accu;
END_command_handling;
```

Figure 6.9 PDL of Command Handler for PAS.

```
get_an_parms:
  get_file;
  get-range;
  get-comma;
  get-an-parms;
END-get-an-parms;
```

Figure 6.10 PDL for Analyzing Parameters for AN command.

```
get_file:
  token := advance token(command);
  IF NOT file(token) THEN report_error(file_error);
                          backup_for_correction;
  ELSE open_file(token)
  ENDIF;
END_get_file;
```

Figure 6.11 Refinement of get_file from Figure 6.8.

```
FUNCTION file(token) RETURNS(TRUE/FALSE):
  IF last_4_digits_of_token = .PAS
    THEN fname = token_last_4_digits;
    ELSE fname = token ENDIF;

  IF length(fname) > 7 THEN report_error(long fname);
                          return(FALSE);
  ENDIF;
  IF first digit of fname not_equal alpha
    THEN report_error(fname);
         return(FALSE);
  ENDIF;
  WHILE another character to look at in fname DO;
        CASE next_digit(fname);
             alpha, num, underscore: CYCLE;
             OTHERWISE report_error(fname);
                       return(FALSE);
        END CASE;
  ENDDO;
  RETURN(TRUE);
END_file;
```

Figure 6.12 Checking for Proper File Syntax.

2.   We do not need to define the contents or formats of the data in their precise implementation. Only the conceptual parts need to be known and not always at the highest level. We can defer design decisions until later.

3.   PDL is capable of defining what the system does and in which order the individual functions are performed. Condition, sequence, and control information is added to the information from previous phases.

4.   Because we can define yet undesigned functions and use them at higher levels, PDL coordinates well with top-down design. Only well structured control statements are available. This encourages structured design. The way inner syntax (the yet undesigned parts of the system) can be refined and stated in PDL, gently pushes it toward modular decomposition. This is not to say that unfortunate ways to decompose a problem are not possible or that the resulting design must be structured. It merely becomes a little harder to do so in PDL.

5.   As in the [Cain75] version of PDL, there are restrictions on how long a design unit or segment can be. Usually the limit is one page. This avoids long, convoluted, interdependent modules that represent more than a function or logical unit.

Even with these obvious advantages, PDL does not meet all objectives of a program design language. Its shortcomings and disadvantages are

1.   PDL is a purely linear description. There is no capability to describe concurrency or multitasking. We could add the monitor definition and the statements how to use the monitor as additional language features as Section 6.2.3 introduced them. We still would need a construct to define potential parallelism of design parts. One way to do this is to add something like

PARALLEL PARTS ($\langle$name_1$\rangle$, $\langle$name_2$\rangle$, . . . , $\langle$name_n$\rangle$)

Then parts named in parentheses can (when executed) become parallel processes. They execute in parallel and may or may not have to communicate or synchronize their activities. In a sense they are all on the same design level with each other. They may all be at the top level or they may have been initiated by a single or several parallel levels above them. An example for using this construct is

```
PARALLEL PARTS (producer, consumer)
  PART producer            PART consumer

      produce_item             consume_item
      END_producer             END_consumer
```

2.   There is no facility for a detailed description of module interfaces and of how modules communicate. This is a serious deficiency because a big part of design errors occur in interfaces. Therefore it is crucial to describe interfaces in one cohesive place. It increases understanding of the design and helps in its validation and testing. It also facilitates translation into proper code and serves as a convenient, efficient reference when questions occur.

3.   There is no construct for decomposing data abstraction into further detail, and thus PDL is only marginally useful for object oriented design.

4.   Unless we add the monitor or an abstract data type definition as another language feature, we cannot describe a full abstract data type, because the operations allowable on a data object are not bound to the data object. We could, for example, define abstract data types with the following schema:

```
CLASS ⟨abstract⟩;
      VAR ⟨data_object⟩ : ⟨type⟩; /*may have list of them*/
      OPERATION ⟨op_1⟩ ( ⟨parameters⟩);
                  BEGIN
                  ⟨statements in PDL⟩;
                  END;

      .........
      OPERATION ⟨op_n⟩ (⟨parameters⟩);
                  BEGIN
                  ⟨statements in PDL⟩;
                  END;
      ⟨initialization of data_object⟩
END_abstract;
```

Then we use this abstract data type definition to define objects of this type and perform operations on them as in

```
VAR ob_1: ⟨abstract⟩;
ob_1.⟨op_i⟩(⟨parms⟩);
```

In summary, design languages of the PDL variety have been very popular because they increase comprehensibility. Their semiformal structure allows checks for design ambiguities and defects, even though no formal, built-in proof mechanism exists because it is not a formal language. Writing a design in a strictly defined form reduces the number of errors. When combined with a support tool as in [Cain75], formatted listings can be produced automatically. Design thus becomes more readable. It is easier to keep track of data references with the data reference list. A PDL design provides a useful source of design documentation. It must however, be augmented with further syntax or with other languages or diagramming techniques to cover the aspects in which it is deficient. These are data object structuring, design structure and module interfaces, and parallelism.

Problems and Questions

1.   The example about the program analyzer and its command handling module did not address the question of checking whether the system was in the proper state to accept the command, even though it might be legal. Design a module that checks for proper state transitions. Use the state transition diagram of Figure 5.4 as a model of what is valid.

2.   Identify the data objects, their parts, and the operations performed on them to form modules that contain the data abstraction. Name the abstract data type, and rewrite the PDL example to use them.

6.3.3.   Path Expressions

Section 6.2.3.2. introduced a RULES part for the monitor definition. The rules for the desired synchronization properties are not written in any formal notation at all but in natural language. This lack of rigor makes validation and further implementation more error prone. It would be very useful to have a kind of PDL that can formally specify the synchronization properties of design modules. Then it would be easier to understand, and we might even be able to come up with a formal or quasi-formal technique to verify desired synchronization properties of our design.

Path expressions ([Habe75], [Camp74], [Flon75]) define as part of a type definition (similar to the RULES part of the monitor definition) the order in which named parts of parallel processes can execute. By writing path expressions, a designer specifies restrictions on the execution of potentially simultaneous operations on shared objects. The shared object may be thought of as a monitor or an abstract data type as described in Section 6.2.3.2. The path expression is part of the internal structure and describes permitted executing sequences of operations on the shared objects. While there are only a couple of implementations of path expressions as an implementation language, they are well suited for design purposes. They allow the designer to specify the synchronization between operations on a shared data object without having to know how the synchronization is actually implemented. This makes designs more understandable and consequently helps to reduce errors. Having separated the synchronization rules from the operations that need to be synchronized also facilitates changes to synchronization rules and makes construction of designs faster.

A path expression is enclosed by the pair **path end**. Thus a path expression has the form

path ⟨expression⟩ **end**

The expression specifies the particular rules for synchronization for the operations, procedures, or functions named in it. They are the operands. The operators in the expression define the precise nature of the synchronization rules and describe in which order the operations mentioned in the path expression can be executed. Compliance with the rules is checked along the path specified in the path expressions. Once the end of the path expression is reached, one execution path is completed and we start all over. The **path end** brackets form a loop structure. The operators in the path expression are

1. Sequence operator ";"

    Example:
    path A ; B ; C **end**

    This path expression states that the operations A, B, and C have to be executed in sequential order as stated; i.e., before an execution of C is allowed, one must have had an execution of B after an execution of A. None of the operations A, B, or C can be executed in parallel. The permitted execution sequences are

    $$A\ B\ C\ A\ B\ C\ A\ B\ C \ldots$$

    In between the parallel to the execution of A, B, and C, any other function not mentioned in the path expression can execute. A, B, and C are called factors of the expression.

2. The Kleene star "*"
    Like the pair **path end** this operator means that an arbitrary number of sequences (to which the operator "*" is applied) may be executed sequentially. That number may be none.

    Example:
    path A ; B* **end**

    After an execution of A, an arbitrary number of sequential executions of B may be executed before the next invocation of A. Examples of valid execution sequences for this path expression are

    $$A\ A\ A\ B\ A\ B\ B\ B\ A\ B\ B\ A\ A \ldots$$
    $$A\ B\ A\ B\ A\ B\ A\ B\ B\ A\ A\ B\ B \ldots$$

3. Parentheses "( )"
    They group the expression within the parentheses together to form a factor. With this operator, nesting becomes possible.

    Example:
    path A ; (B ; C)* ; D **end**

The parenthesis causes the Kleene star operator to be applied to the sequence (B; C). Thus the sequence

$$A\ B\ C\ D\ A\ D\ A\ B\ C\ B\ C\ D$$

is valid, but the sequence

$$A\ B\ D\ A\ C\ D$$

is not.

4. Exclusive selection "+"
This operator requires a choice between the two or more operands that are separated by "+." Only one of them may be chosen. For example, the path expression

$$\textbf{path}\ A\ ;\ (\ B+C\ )\ ;\ D\ \textbf{end}$$

means that either B or C, but not both or none of them, must be executed between an execution of A and an execution of D. A valid execution sequence is

$$A\ C\ D\ A\ B\ D\ A\ C\ D\ldots$$

but the following sequences are invalid:

$$A\ B\ C\ D\ldots$$
$$A\ D\ldots$$

B and C are called terms. They can be expressions formed by use of parentheses.

5. Conditional
The conditional has the form

$$[\langle cond\_1\rangle{:}\langle elem\_1\rangle,\langle cond\_2\rangle{:}\langle elem\_2\rangle,\ldots,\langle cond\_n\rangle{:}\langle elem\_n\rangle,\langle elem\_n+1\rangle]$$

The conditional element is set to the leftmost element for which the preceding condition is true. The $(n+1)$st element is optional and provides for the "otherwise" case. The variable operands in a condition may only be changed by operations in the path in which the condition occurs.

Example:
path A ; [n>k: B , n<k: C, D] ; E **end**

After an execution of A, B is allowed to execute if $n > k$. C may start its execution if $n < k$. If $n = k$, D may start. After an execution of B, C, or D, an execution of E is allowed and must have occurred before another invocation of A can be granted. Only the procedures B, C, or D may change the values of n or k. This keeps the interfaces and side effects simpler.

6. Concatenation of paths "&":
This operator concatenates two paths into one; i.e., only one function named in the concatenated path can be executed at a time.

Example:
path A ; B & C ; B **end**

Each execution of B must be preceded by an execution of A and C. The order is arbitrary. A and C may not be executed in parallel. The difference between the concatenated path expression and the parallel path,

path A ; B **end**
path C ; B **end**

is that the connected path does not allow parallel execution of A and C whereas the parallel path does. When paths using conditional elements are connected, the variable operands in a condition may only be modified by operations in the path in which the condition occurs. As this has to hold for parallel paths, it will surely hold for concatenated ones.

7. Simultaneous execution "{ }"
Enclosing a factor in { } brackets permits several processes to execute a given operation or procedure simultaneously. These brackets may not be nested. With this operator as many instances of the bracketed expression are generated as there are requests for it while there is still at least one incomplete execution of the bracketed expression. The bracketed expression has been fully executed when the last such request has been completed.

Example:
path A ; { B } ; C **end**

This path expression permits simultaneous execution of B. Once a process starts to execute B, other processes may do so, too, provided that there is at least one incomplete execution of B. As soon as the last is finished, expression evaluation advances. An execution of a C and an A is required before the next request for an execution of B can be granted.

The difference between {B} and **B*** is that {B} allows simultaneous execution of an arbitrary number of instances of B, whereas **B*** requires these instances to be executed one after another.

These operations allow a description of synchronization by stating all permissible execution sequences. Sometimes only a restricted set of operators is used; e.g., no simultaneous execution operator or no concatenation of paths is permissible. If the set of operators only comprises operators 1 through 4, path expressions may also be translated into nondeterministic automata. The arcs in the graph for the automaton represent the operations, functions, or procedures. The nodes represent the initial state, the final state, and the intermediate states, corresponding to the semicolons in the path expression. For example, the path expression

path A ; (B + C)* ; D **end**

can be represented as

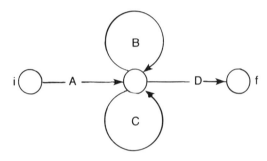

where *i* is the initial state and *f* is the final state.

The advantage of path expressions is that they allow us to specify synchronization properties on a higher level without the need for detail on how the synchronization will actually be implemented. They support information hiding and separate concerns, thus promoting understandability and modularity. Synchronization rules are easily changed, which is important for design languages. An algorithm exists that can translate a path expression design into a set of parallel program parts using P/V synchronization [Laue75]. It was implemented in a design tool [Dhes82]. The formality of path expressions lends itself to formal proofs of synchronization properties. The chapter on verification and validation of designs explains how to derive assertions about the behavior of path expressions and how to use these assertions to prove various synchronization properties such as mutual exclusion, freedom from deadlock, and starvation.

Path expressions are not without shortcomings. They do not provide any means to describe timing constraints for its operands. This is a serious deficiency for real-time systems for which accurate timing is the key to correct synchronization. We will have to express and analyze timing constraints using other means. The operations for an abstract data type or the functions and procedures mentioned in the path expression must be named to specify their synchronization. While path expressions certainly are not a panacea for curing all design problems in concurrent and distributed software, they are very useful for the scope of issues they are able to address. They are easy to read, write, and understand, even for the beginner.

Problems and Questions

1.   Write a path expression for the reader-writer problem, i.e., only one writer is allowed to access a resource at any given time, but an arbitrary number of readers can access it as long as no writer is active.

2.   What is wrong with

path {reader}; writer **end**

or

path reader*; writer **end**

as a solution to exercise 1? Distinguish between a solution that complies with the access restrictions but is too restrictive and one that violates some restrictions.

3.   Assume that there is a producer and a consumer process. The producer puts items into a buffer that the consumer can take out. So a path expression like **path {producer; consumer} end** looks appealing but is no longer sufficient to describe the situation when the producer can generate an arbitrary number of items at a time and the consumer may need to consume more than one item at a time. If we assume that the producer knows how many he is producing and the consumer knows how many he is consuming, how can we use the conditional operator to rewrite the solution?

6.4.   Summary

This chapter discussed general design strategies, which suggested how to sequence design decisions. Since different types of software have different needs for their design, it is not reasonable to expect one design strategy to work for all. We explained top-down and bottom-up design and related strategies such as sandwich (a combination of top-down and bottom-up), outside-in, and inside out. The latter two are specific instances of top-down and bottom-up design. Top-down design does not require top-down implementation. Indeed, there are reasons to couple top-down design with bottom-up or sandwich implementation. An analogous argument can be made for the other strategies. They relate to the amount of scaffolding code that may have to be written, the criticality of certain system components, and how soon or late the user will see anything working. These considerations are the primary reason why pure strategies likc top-down or bottom-up are rarely ever followed precisely. They are conceptual strategies, not rigorous positions. In most practical cases, we will end up with a mostly top-down, mostly bottom-up, or mostly sandwich approach, etc. This way we can better take care of the disadvantages and possible problems that stem from a pure approach.

Iterative enhancement was the next design strategy. It consists of a sequence of enhancements, starting with a core set of functions. There are several guidelines for sequencing enhancements and the design decisions associated with them. The most critical component is implemented first. This ensures that an infeasible strategy will not cause redevelopment of other components that have been developed before the infeasibility was discovered. Such an approach prevents losing time, because there is less chance that the parts of the system that have been implemented already have to be thrown out and redone. At times the most critical components are also the ones with the strictest constraints. We can also sequence our development using requirements analysis results and develop the most constrained components first.

Iterative enhancement combined with top-down implementation is advantageous when the schedule is late. With a late schedule, bottom-up implementation is probably the worst, because almost nothing can be shown to the user until the very end. Iterative enhancement requires the additional effort of scaffolding code to simulate nonexisting modules.

The third design strategy, abstract data types, is object-oriented and supports information hiding and the concept of abstraction. We discussed abstract data types and extensions to the concept that consider parallelism (monitors) and policy issues (capabilities and extended capabilities). Information hiding is a very crucial concept during design, because it keeps complexity down and maintainability high. In particular, it avoids the list of problems discussed in Section 6.2.3.1. The concept of information hiding as Parnas [Parn79] describes it is a very useful design philosophy and serves as a criterion with which to evaluate designs. It is not a method or even methodology, because it does not in itself give much guidance in selecting what design decisions to hide, nor how to best layer or group them. The way design units (modules) and design interfaces are defined does not provide a clear translation from design modules into programmable, interconnected modules [Booc83].

Problems with maintainability can be avoided by using a combination of design strategies with the following guidelines: identify subsets of functionality during requirements analysis; practice information hiding; augment the idea of abstract data types with a structuring concept, such as the abstract machine or virtual machine concept (cf. 6.2.1. and 7.2.); and reduce interdependence of components.

The second part of this chapter introduced design languages. The first was MIL, or module interconnection language [Dere76], to express structural aspects of a design. The next language, PDL, is well suited to describe detailed design within modules [Cain75]. In its many variations, it is also referred to as Pseudocode, Metacode and is really a form of structured English. We also described a form of PDL called path expressions to describe execution constraints for parallel software. These three languages can express three major aspects of a design: algorithms, structure, and parallelism.

Let us summarize the advantages and shortcomings of MIL, PDL, and path expressions. MIL's advantages are its emphasis on design structure and interfaces over design detail. Being a formally defined language, it lends itself to more formal validation methods. When combined with a language processor, MIL can defer some of the consistency checking and completeness verification to it. MIL supports top-down design, modular decomposition, and abstraction.

MIL's major disadvantages stem from its exclusive concentration on structure. Functions cannot be designed, and data abstractions are implied. MIL's shortcomings are PDL's strengths. It is a vehicle to describe design of functions in a structured manner. Like MIL it supports top-down design without requiring yet undesigned detail and is amenable to formal analysis. PDL's shortcomings lie in its lack of design structure and interface constructs (these have to be inferred and are not obvious), its lack of data object structuring, and its inability to express synchronization. To deal with the last problem, path expressions were introduced.

The advantage of path expressions is that they allow us to specify synchronization properties without actual implementation detail. Thus they support information hiding. They also separate concerns and thus promote understandability and modularity. Synchronization rules are easily changed. An algorithm exists that can translate a path expression design into a set of parallel program parts using P/V synchronization [Laue75]. It has been implemented in a design tool [Dhes82]. The formality of path expressions lends itself to formal proofs of synchronization properties. In the chapter on verification and validation of designs, we will explain how to derive and use assertions about the behavior of path expressions to prove various synchronization properties.

Path expressions are not without shortcomings. They do not provide any means to describe timing constraints. We will have to express and check out timing constraints with other means. The operations for an abstract data type or the functions and procedures mentioned in the path expression must be named. Path expressions are no panacea for curing all design problems with concurrent and distributed software, but they are very useful for the scope of issues they address and—one of their most obvious advantages—they are easy to read, write, and understand, even for the beginner. This is a striking difference to other competing languages to model synchronization behavior, most notably Petri Nets.

We did not describe flow charts, because they are limited in their capability for modularization and structuring. Other diagramming techniques are Warnier-Orr diagrams (introduced earlier) and Nassi-Shneiderman charts [Nass73]. They serve the same purpose as PDL. We will also encounter in the next few chapters various informal diagrams and tables that are used *ad hoc* to describe an idea pictorially that would have been hard to describe in a language. Often language and diagrams complement each other. [Mart85] describes in detail a variety of diagramming techniques. This chapter concentrated more on languages, because they are machine processable, easily read, and amenable to formal analysis. Unless automated graphics support is available for drawing diagrams, relying on them as a primary means to express design can become unwieldy.

▶ 7

Software System Structure Design

7.1. Overview

Software system structure design, also called system architecture, is the process of partitioning a software system into smaller parts. The parts can be programs, subsystems, components, or modules. We have already heard that it is possible to structure a system as an abstract machine when the system is decomposed into levels of abstraction. Sometimes we can identify sequences of processing (phases). In this chapter we will encounter some more ways to decompose a system into parts and more detail for those methods introduced earlier.

To design the structure of systems, we have to identify what the distinct problems are and how they relate to each other. We will use a combination of strategies, such as top-down or bottom-up, information hiding, and the concept of data abstraction, to arrive at a system structure.

Different problems respond to different design techniques. Appropriate techniques include a method based on levels of abstraction as defined in the previous chapter. It is called abstract machine design (Section 7.2.). We also discuss systems that can be structured around communication needs (message-based systems of Section 7.3.). Still other systems show clearly identified sequences of processing. The output of one step is input to the next. This, too, lends itself to structuring (phases of Section 7.4.).

Many systems are data driven. Such systems can be structured around how data flows between various processing activities. A diagramming technique for software system design is the data-flow method with its resulting data-flow and organizational diagrams (Section 7.5.). This technique combines both system and program design. Another technique focusing on data objects is object-oriented design (Section 7.6). The system is structured around major data objects.

Section 7.7. discusses quality and phase testing of the design structure. Section 7.8. gives a sample outline for the system structure document. The summary provides suggestions for using the different system architecture techniques.

System architecture uses different techniques because systems are different from programs. This difference is not only one of size—systems are usually bigger and more complex—but also of scope. A software system represents a set of solutions to a set of distinct but related problems [Myer75], while a program is a solution to one single problem. A program can be part of a system. PAS, the program analyzer, once developed, is a program. The tax preparation system, on the other hand, is a system, albeit a small one, because it represents a solution to two distinct but related problems, namely tax record keeping and tax preparation. If we add the what-if module, there is even a tax consulting component. Other examples of systems are operating systems, banking systems, airline reservation systems, electronic switching systems, manufacturing control systems, or administrative systems.

System structure design is necessary to keep the complexity of large-scale software development manageable. Subsystems are not identified arbitrarily. Each subsystem consists of highly related features, functions, and data, while the relationships with other subsystems are fewer and simpler. This increases the independence of subsystems and facilitates implementation by different, independent groups or people. It also increases reliability, maintainability, and adaptability. It is usually simpler to design and implement a subsystem than an entire system. This is another argument for system structure design.

System structure is designed after specifications have been frozen. This does not mean, however, that no structuring work can happen until then. In fact, it often does. When a user interface mock-up is implemented, some system structuring happens as a matter of course.

When we build a system oriented around its user level functions, we often have very little to do during the system architecture phase, because the abstract requirements diagrams and the data dictionary already provide the decomposition framework quite nicely. They show functional structure and data structure at various levels. Functional boundaries show where to break the system into components, and the functions themselves identify structural boundaries. Looking at the lowest functional level we can determine whether the level of detail is fine enough so that we can start implementation. It is not true, however, that abstract requirements diagrams and data dictionaries constitute the result of a system architecture process and give us a system design structure. They only structure what the problem looks like, not how the implementation of the solution is structured. When problem structure does not parallel solution (i.e., design and implementation structure), then the two can and should look very different. Maintainability requirements, in particular, can create structures that look different than the problem's [Parn72].

What we can and should do is use the structure of the requirements diagrams, its associated data dictionary, and the functional specifications to see how we can incorporate them into a possible design structure. The emphasis has shifted from "what" to "how."

We conceptually place the system structuring phase between specifications and detailed design. After structuring the system into components, programs, or modules, we use structured design techniques, such as stepwise refinement ([Wirt71]), to develop the system parts. Some of the same strategies used for systems apply, but what we apply them to is on a smaller scale.

System structure design is usually done by designers who are familiar with structuring methods and their implications on design constraints. These designers also must have a view of the "big picture." While they have to be able to define system interfaces precisely, they cannot get themselves bogged down in design details. These are the domain of developers who do detailed design and implementation.

As in previous chapters, we did not intend to cover all system architecture design techniques exhaustively. Rather, this chapter tries to present a representative sample of techniques that cover important classes of techniques. It is hoped that the reader will be able to classify other techniques he or she encounters within the framework set in these design chapters. After working through this chapter, the reader should be able to identify types of systems and the most appropriate structuring technique or combination of techniques. Then he or she should be able to apply an appropriate technique and develop a sound system structure design. Next, the reader should have the skills to phase test this structure design and put the information into a document form.

Problems and Questions

1. Is it correct to say that systems are more complex than programs? Why or why not? Give examples and/or counterexamples.

2. What is the role of requirements diagrams, the data dictionary, and functional specifications for system design? Do they prescribe design structure? Why or why not?

7.2.   Abstract Machine and Levels of Abstraction

The concept of levels of abstraction was originated by Dijkstra [Dijk68]. It represents a way to structure systems into separate, distinct hierarchical pieces. These pieces have very strictly defined, restricted ways of communicating with, and functionally depending on, each other. Restricted communication and functional dependence help to decompose the system into pieces, many of which are independent. Existing dependencies are highly controlled, totally predictable, and in one direction only. This avoids loops in the dependence structure that can pose obstacles to maintainability (see Section 6.2.3.). The system is structured in a strict tree hierarchy. The nodes at any given level or layer form an abstract machine.

In order to achieve maximum independence, the following restrictions apply:

▶ Each level is a group of closely related modules. This is precisely the reason why they can form an abstract machine. An abstract machine was defined as a set of data objects and all the operations that can be performed on them. This set of data objects and operations provides a functionality to any module that uses it.

▶ The module that uses functionality from the next lower level is not allowed to know how the functionality is actually accomplished (information hiding). We hide the properties of lower level objects such as resources and data representations, and then each level represents an abstraction of these objects to the next higher level. This makes modules highly independent of each other and minimizes complexity of module interfaces.

We can construct the hierarchy either bottom-up or top-down. If we decide to follow a bottom-up design strategy, we start at the lowest level, say level 0. Basic data structures, functions, and operations are found at this level. Then we design the next higher level (1) using only the abstract data types and their functionality of level 0. On top of level 1 we again build the next layer with the help of the previous one. We continue this until the top level is reached. In the process, it is expressly forbidden to use any components or modules of a level j-2 at level j. Only the ones at level j-1 may be used directly to build level j. This is the level immediately subordinate to level j. Dijkstra requires that if a function or module is to be used by two levels (say it is defined at level k and both levels k + 1 and k + 2 wish to use it), it must be provided explicitly as a level k + 1 function or module and thus as a separate entity to level k + 2. In practice, this may mean that a module m at level k + 2 calls a module n. The only thing that module n does is to call a module o at level k that m cannot call directly. Since this is a cumbersome procedure, it is not often followed.

Alternatively, we can design a system structure as a set of abstract machines, one on top of the other, using a top-down technique. We start with the highest level abstract machine and see how we can build it using a somewhat simpler abstract machine on the next lower level. This is advantageous if we wish to postpone decisions about whether and how specific functions will be implemented until late in the design process. One reason for this is that design and performance studies can be made. The same restriction as in the bottom-up design apply: only use the modules on the level immediately below, none on levels further down. It is also forbidden to use modules on the same level. Figure 7.1 shows a hierarchical structure that represents a design in levels of abstraction. Dependencies that are not allowed have double dashes through their arcs.

A variation of the pure concept of levels of abstraction is to allow any level to reference any or all of its lower levels. This is not a complete abstraction, because higher levels are allowed to peek into the insides of lower levels. However, like top-down or bottom-up design, this structuring method makes design less complex by reducing potentially difficult and nonmaintainable interfaces and dependencies. Therefore, we can, very judiciously, break rules of strict abstraction. The advantages of this are usually due to qualitative requirements (performance for example), or they fall into one of the categories of Section 6.2.3., which detailed when modules can be allowed to be dependent on each other. Dependence loops were a no-no; a hierarchical structure of abstract machines prohibits them. Thus it is a structuring technique that complies with this design philosophy.

The desired properties of each level of abstraction are as follows:

1.   Each level knows nothing about the properties or the existence of any higher levels. This eliminates dependency loops as described in Section 6.2.3. It decreases connections and system complexity.

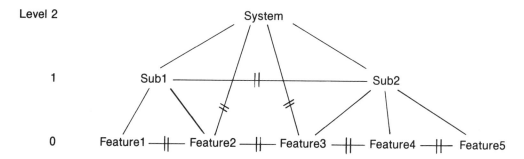

Figure 7.1 Levels of Abstraction.

2. Each level knows nothing about the insides of any other level. They communicate, if at all, only through predefined, rigid mechanisms. They know data abstractions as types and which operations can be performed. Such information hiding reduces connections and complexity.

3. Each level consists of a group of modules whose internal make-up is neither known nor can be referenced. Their external characteristics, such as names, are known by higher levels only.

4. Each level contains local and global resources. Local resources are hidden to the outside, while global resources are provided as an abstraction to the higher level.

5. Each level can support the abstraction of a functionality. This ensures that modules are functionally cohesive units and not random conglomerations of data and procedures.

6. Each level tries to minimize assumptions it makes about other levels. Assumptions can be made about data representations, relationships, time dependencies, etc.

7. Connections between levels are limited to explicit arguments. In particular, levels avoid sharing global data.

8. Each level is a highly cohesive functional unit providing a single functionality. Coupling between levels should be as loose as possible (single data items such as parameters avoid big data objects such as sets of related tables).

This system structure makes changes easy, because they are isolated to specific, well-known parts of the system: the modules in which the change is made and the interfaces to other modules. Usually only a minor part of them is affected, if any. Levels of abstraction show precisely which part of the system needs to be altered. This is due to information hiding [Parn72] and data abstraction. When changes are easy, the system is better maintainable, more adaptable, more extendable, and more shrinkable. Portability is also positively affected. To port the system from one machine to another only requires the lowest level of abstraction to change, because it sits on top of the machine or operating system.

This approach has been used in a pioneering effort by Dijkstra when he implemented the THE operating system. It initiated an important branch of research in multilevel systems architecture. THE showed that hierarchical modularity is a powerful approach to organize large systems. THE is designed as a hierarchy of nested abstract machines. Each layer of software extends the instruction set, and thus the functionality of the machines below it, and hides the details of its resource management from the levels above. THE has five levels of abstraction [Dijk68]:

0.   The lowest level is responsible for processor allocation, for processing interrupts of the real-time clock, and for priority rules for scheduling. Above this level the number of processors that are shared is no longer important; it is hidden from the higher levels. The higher levels deal with the activity of different sequential processes.

1.   The segment controller is at level 1. This level deals with all the bookkeeping that results from having automatic backing storage. At all higher levels, identification of information can take place in segments; the detail of pages is hidden.

2.   Level 2 contains the "message interpreter." Console (operator) and higher level processes communicate via the message interpreter. The abstraction at the next higher levels appears to the processes as if each one of them had its private conversational console, when in fact there is only one. The message interpreter takes care of the details.

3.   This level contains all sequential processes that are associated with buffering and unbuffering I/O streams. Logical communication units are the abstraction level 3 provides.

4.   At level 4 we find independent user programs.

Level 5, which, in its conception, was meant to deal with the operator, was never implemented. The implementation followed this hierarchy strictly. A process in level i may only begin another process in $i-1$. This resulted in a high degree of integrity and security. Implementation found only trivial errors. The error rate was about 1 error per 500 instructions, and debugging took no more than 10 minutes. Testing started at the lowest level and proceeded upwards. Some aspects of the desired functionality were formally verified, and techniques to reduce the number of test-cases through identification of predefined states for testing were used. Besides new insights into how to structure large software systems, THE also pioneered new concepts in the area of operating systems (semaphores, Banker's algorithm), but that is beyond the scope of this book.

Since THE, a level-oriented operating system structure has been well accepted and is widely practiced (e.g., MULTICS, UNIX). Often it is referred to as "onion skin structure." Levels of abstraction can also be used to implement virtual machines. The Venus operating system is such an example [Lisk73]. A virtual machine operating system provides one or more virtual machines to its users. Every user uses its virtual machine as if it were its own and a real one. The operating system takes care of the translation process into real resources, their scheduling, etc. In this sense, every abstract machine can be thought of as providing a virtual machine to the next higher level. On the other hand, not every virtual machine need be structured in levels of abstraction. IBM's VM operating system is an example of that.

In conclusion, structuring a system as a hierarchical set of levels of abstraction is a good approach for initial structuring of large systems.

Problems and Questions

1. How is Dijkstra's concept of levels of abstraction using the following strategies:

    ▶ information hiding

    ▶ abstract data types

    ▶ top-down design

    ▶ bottom-up design

2. Is it possible to use iterative enhancement with Dijkstra's levels of abstraction? How? Give an example.

3. Can we use an evolutionary development cycle and structure a system with levels of abstraction? Why or why not? If so, give an example how. (Hint: Levels can provide simple or sophisticated functionality. Because only the abstraction is known and their implementation is hidden, how is the next higher level to know?)

7.3. Message-Based Structure

Much of the early insight into message-based or port-driven systems comes to us through experience with operating systems. When we base system structure on the messages that parts of a system will interchange, communication becomes the focal point of structuring. Message-based structure looks at proper communication techniques between components of a system, between its subsystems, and on a smaller scale between parts of a program. In contrast, the previous structuring approach, levels of abstraction, was concerned with the proper distribution of functions among hierarchical levels of a system. [Laue78] calls the first message-oriented, the second procedure-oriented.

Parts of a system can be connected through passing control, data, or both. Passing control without explicit data transfer happens when one process relinquishes control to another as is the case in interrupts, **GOTO**s, and supervisor calls. Procedure and subroutine calls pass control and data. When only data are passed between system components, a message passing mechanism is needed. Mailboxes are established where processes can put or receive data they wish to communicate. Such inboxes or outboxes are sometimes called ports. Each port is associated with a queue and contains a list of messages to other subsystems or processes. We can divide the system into a set of input ports, one for each subsystem. Output ports are connected (identified with the input port of the target subsystem to which messages are to be sent). Basic communication operations are **SEND** and **RECEIVE**. When subsystem S_1 issues a **SEND**, it places a message in its output port which, due to its connection to the input port of S_2, places it on the input port of S_2. Similarly, S_2 can issue a **RECEIVE** operation to read messages from its input port and process them.

Subsystems can communicate directly with each other, setting up communication channels, or they can do so indirectly. Indirect port configurations allow the subsystems to send messages to their output ports. They are connected to input ports of other subsystems, but the sender need not know how this is done or where these other subsystems or their parts are.

Such mechanisms increase the independence of subsystems. Not only are they independent in terms of flow of control, they need not even be aware of each other's location. Only the **SEND/RECEIVE** mechanism knows. In effect, the port-message concept provides a level of abstraction. The abstraction provided is the port as it appears to the subsystems using it. The **SEND/RECEIVE** level owns resources, the physical ports, but their implementation, their physical characteristics, and the location of the subsystems to which messages are sent, is hidden.

Basic characteristics for a message-oriented system include the following:

▶ Facilities exist so that messages can be passed among system components easily and efficiently.

▶ Because the speed of reacting to messages does not always equal the speed with which they are sent, messages are queued at the destination until the subsystem acts to receive them. When messages are not sent fast enough, the system component at the destination must be able to wait for messages. Synchronization between system components is implemented via message queues.

▶ When data objects are to be shared by more than one process or system component, they are passed explicitly or via pointers in messages. The sending process takes responsibility for synchronization.

▶ Important primitive operations for a message-oriented system should include

    ▶ **SEND** a message,

    ▶ **WAIT** for any or a specific kind of message, and

    ▶ **EXAMINE** the state of the message queue.

▶ In cases where priorities are important, such as in operating systems, it must be possible to preempt another executing system component, when a higher priority process has just received a message it has been waiting for and wishes to continue. Priorities usually are assigned statically to the system components when the system is designed, and they correspond to the needs of the resources that the system components provide and manage.

Messages themselves can be data items, sent directly, or pointers to larger data structures, which is more economical than sending a big data object. Messages usually have a message identifier. Input and output ports must have been connected. We can have more than one output port for a system component. The **SEND** operation has to identify which output port the message is to go to. It usually returns the message identifier so that the sending process can identify answers as pertaining to a particular message. The sender can also explicitly wait for a reply with an **AWAIT_REPLY (message_identifier)**. This operation returns the other party's reply as a message. A system component may wait for a new message on any of its message ports by issuing a **WAIT_MESSAGE (set_of_ports)**. This operation returns the first message with a message identifier, a message body, and an indication of which port it came from. If the receiver wants to send an answer to a message, it can issue a **SEND_REPLY**, identifying the message for which this is an answer and the answer itself.

A message-oriented system must be able to define message ports and connect them. This is part of the system initialization phase. Setting up ports when processes are created and taking them back down when processes are destroyed is significant bookkeeping work. Therefore, message ports tend to be long lived and are established during system initialization. For the same reason we usually find a small, relatively static number of large processes. It is difficult to delete a process, because it may have a large number of messages waiting in its mailboxes.

Let us contrast these message-based systems with procedure-oriented systems ([Laue78]). Procedure-oriented systems usually consist of many small, short-lived processes. Synchronization is implemented by means of semaphores or monitors. When a priority scheme is implemented for the semaphore queue or the monitor queue, preemption occurs when a process completes its critical section or a monitor controlled function.

Procedure-oriented systems operate with global data. Global data is shared but also protected through procedural interfaces that control all access. Monitors, when they implement abstract data types and hide details of implementation, provide such procedural interfaces. They are activated when an operation that is controlled by the monitor is called. Since no communication channels need to be created and taken down, it is easy to create and delete processes. Subsystems do not have to keep track of others in order to communicate with them, because shared data are the communication medium. Processes share data directly. Because processes are small, they tend to do only one function.

Procedure-oriented systems rely on the following facilities:

▶ procedure definitions with local data, parameters, facilities to return results (these are within the scope of a module);

▶ asynchronous and synchronous procedure calls (**FORK** and **JOIN** operations that start a procedure executing as a new process and finishes independent execution of a child process respectively, are important means of structuring execution flow in the system);

▶ monitors as special control modules; and

▶ a new instance of a procedure execution (a process) with allocation, initialization, and binding between the other parts of the system.

Table 7.1, which is an adaptation from [Laue78], shows the relationship between message-based and procedure-oriented systems.

Table 7.1 System structure duality.

	Message based	Procedure Oriented
Communication	Message passing	Shared variables
Control	Process	Monitor
	Message	Process
Mechanism	SEND; AWAIT_REPLY	CALL/RETURN
		FORK/JOIN

Lauer and Needham claim that it is possible to transform one type of system into the other using the duality table. The systems will perform the same functions. Neither approach is inherently preferable and the main consideration for chosing one over the other (for operating systems) is machine architecture. This claim has come under fire more recently [Stan82]. The main issues are greater distribution of system parts, both logically and physically. Greater distribution and increased parallelism of systems requires a different approach. The basic choice of system philosphy, and hence structure, depends on how components of a system need to communicate.

If system components operate in a master/slave mode where the slave is available at all times, there is no need for messages. A procedure-based system is quite sufficient. As soon as there is dialogue, as in the case where a user has to acquire permission to use a facility (database access, for example), communication patterns change. The activity (such as looking up information in the database) is triggered by the user but controlled by the facility. The connection between user and facility is temporary. If implemented as a procedure-oriented system we have calls back and forth between the user and the facility. This no longer suffices when many parties dialogue or the parties are distributed. Then a message-oriented system is preferrable. It avoids the problems of sharing global variables and buffering.

If the parties to the dialogue do not converse directly, but their communication needs to be sent via intermediate stops, a mailing system becomes necessary. Senders may operate in burst mode; processing can be delayed so that buffering becomes a necessity. Procedure calls do not support a mailing system. Message-oriented is clearly the way to structure such a system. Messages are also preferable when system components must, for whatever reason, be environment independent. This is the case in distributed systems.

Another mechanism to structure and implement parallel systems is the coroutine. Coroutines (as implementable in SIMULA 67) allow a partial execution of the procedure body, which can be resumed later. Thus a coroutine **A** can suspend itself when it activates coroutine **B**. **B** may partially execute then return control back to **A**, which resumes where it had stopped. Later, **A** may again suspend itself and activate **B**. **B** now resumes where it stopped the last time. It does not start its execution at the beginning as it would in a procedure call. An example of using coroutines is the producer-consumer problem. In the producer-consumer problem, the producer relinquishes control to the consumer when it has produced its share of items. The consumer consumes the unit(s) and proceeds until it needs an item that the producer has not produced yet. Then the consumer suspends itself and transfers control to the producer. The producer then continues where it had suspended itself earlier.

When should we structure a system as procedure oriented, and when are messages more advantageous? Messages are superior in situations that require communication between loose entities, such as mailing and dialogue systems. They also are better when subsystems or system components are physically distributed, as in the case of computer networks, or when procedures need to migrate between hosts.

Problems and Questions

1. Use the monitor example of Section 6.2.3.2., which defined a port and sent messages through a mailbox. Redefine it so that all operations that a message-oriented system is supposed to possess are included and show that your solution defines a level of abstraction. (Hint: Use a language construct that defines an operation that is part of a monitor as a local operation; i. e., it is not known outside of the monitor. Prefix such an operation with **LOCAL**.)

2. In this section an interpreter was said to be structured as a set of two major coroutines. Would you suggest the same for a compiler? Why or why not?

3. What are the major differences in structure between a message-oriented and a procedure-oriented system?

7.4. Phases

Sometimes it is possible to determine sequential parts that form tasks in their own right and can be implemented as a series of programs whose execution follows one another sequentially. Examples of such systems are UNIX™ pipes, multipass compilers, and the compile-link-load/execute phases for programs. In the latter, the entire process of getting a program ready for execution has been divided into a set of three phases. They form independent parts of this system in the following sense:

▶ The later phase knows nothing about the earlier ones. In fact, those earlier ones have disappeared.

▶ If we want to make the phases maximally independent, assumptions about previous phases should be minimized.

▶ Each phase hides system resources from the others.

Phases or passes are a good structuring technique for systems involving a series of data transformations. The output of one phase is used as input for the next. The last phase need not know what the data looked like in any of the previous phases. Phases are appropriate when the problem is inherently sequential and data that has to be transferred between phases is relatively simple. Sometimes it is possible to overlap parts of phases. If it is possible to assign phases to several parallel systems (which might communicate via messages or shared data), performance can be improved due to the higher degree of parallelism. On the other hand, we do not have a set of sequential programs any more, and we must look at one of the other structuring approaches for guidance.

Problems and Questions

1. What are the trade-offs involved between overlapping a sequence of phases and implementing them sequentially? (Hint: Look at how the interfaces between phases change, what effect that might have on quality expectations, and the effort needed to reach them)

2. Assume that someone wants to structure the program analyzer as a series of passes. The first pass through the system will extract all operands, the second all operators. Then, after all programs have been so analyzed, statistics can be computed, and, as the last phase, reports are generated. How do you evaluate this proposal? If there is anything that you find objectionable, state why and give an alternative.

3. Is there a need for a message-oriented system if it is organized as a sequence of phases? Why or why not?

7.5. Data-Flow Method and Organization Diagrams

The data-flow method, which uses data-flow diagrams to develop designs, is an object- or data-oriented technique. This section concentrates on the method as it is presented in [Gilb83]. Other related methods are described in [Your79] and [Jack75]. It is used for systems that center around data and their collection, transformation, and update. Business systems are a good example. Data objects are entities that are acted upon and represent resources. They exist in time, are created, destroyed, copied, shared, or updated. The structure of the data is the principal issue during design. Data structure is defined first, and then program units are structured based on data structure. Actions define processing for the data object. When such data-oriented systems communicate with each other, the format of communications is also a vital design issue. The tax preparation system (TAP) is such a data-oriented system. In TAP, tax records are stored, evaluated, updated, then combined to a tax return. The processing of data items is rather simple. It consists of additions, subtractions, and multiplications. The most complex part is how the records of income, tax, and deductions are decomposed and then transformed into the tax return. This makes it a good candidate for the data-flow method.

Three types of objects exist in a data-flow diagram:

▶ input objects (what enters the system through files, terminal input, etc.)

▶ output objects (reports, messages, etc.), and

▶ storage objects (they may be temporary or permanent and include all data structures which store data, e.g., arrays, records, lists, tables, variables of all types).

In the diagram, objects are drawn as bubbles, actions as boxes. Arrows between an object and a processing action indicate that the action reads the data object. Arrows between an action and a data object indicate that the action writes or deposits information into the data object. For example, the data-flow diagrams corresponding to the requirements diagram of Figures 3.3 and 3.4 are given in Figures 7.2 and 7.3.

In the diagrams, each action is one processing activity, a logically independent, self-contained unit. Sequencing of actions is not explicitly stated, but in cases where an action 1 needs a data object that is put into a storage object by another action 2, an implicit sequence is clear: action 1 is performed when the data object is available, i.e., after action 2 has done its job. Data-flow diagrams parallel requirements diagrams pretty closely, and the same levels and structure can be used as a starting point. This does not mean that system structure will always and at all levels parallel the structure of the requirements diagram.

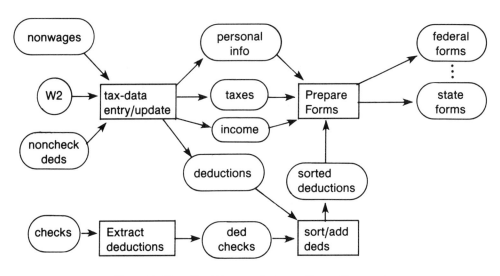

Figure 7.2 Data-flow Diagram Corresponding to Figure 3.3.

When different actions are performed based on the values of a data object or a condition value, they can be shown explicitly. For each condition, a corresponding data object is introduced. These conditions may be taken from the decision tables of the specifications and can represent a complex condition. Table 5.7 would produce two condition variables for simple conditions (the amount of social security wages and their relationship to the maximum amount of that is taxable and whether or not there was self-employment income). These combine to more complex conditions. Too many conditions can lead to a cluttered diagram. Adding condition variables or flags is therefore suggested only for important ones. Figure 7.4 shows how the input class A from Table 5.9 affects some of the solution activities for dealing with the W2 Form. Input class A stands for the number of different employers and thus W2 Forms.

Data-flow diagrams are derived from requirements diagrams by asking repeatedly which data objects are needed for the system, what type they are, and how they are transformed by the system. As in Myer's composite analysis [Myer75] we look at three aspects of our design problem:

▶ the inputs.

▶ the outputs, and

▶ the transformations on inputs and outputs.

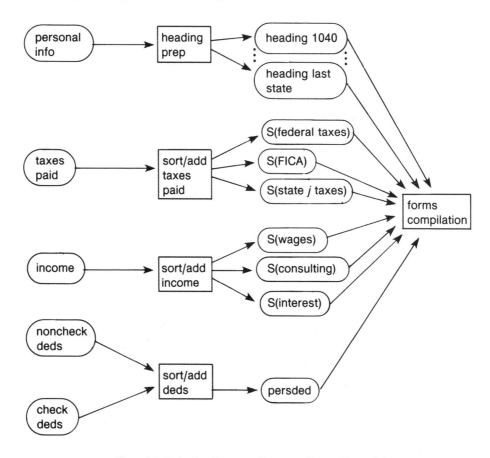

Figure 7.3 Data-flow Diagram Corresponding to Figure 3.4.

We start with the input data, deciding what data objects are needed to store them. Where are they moved to? Then we do the same for outputs. From which objects are output data produced? What are the immediate moves or transformations at the input and output boundary? This partitions the system. Now we can apply the same process again to the next inner layer. This way we can work horizontally through layers and vertically across levels.

In Figure 7.2 the input data consists of

▶ nonwages,

▶ W2,

▶ noncheck deds, and

▶ checks.

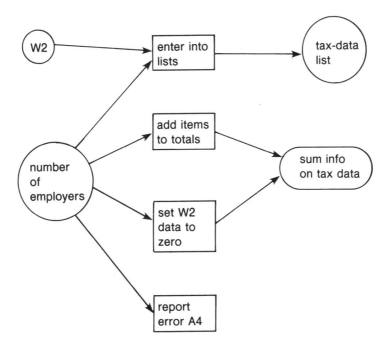

Figure 7.4 Effect of Input Class A of Table 5.9 on the Data-flow Diagram.

The first three, when entered, are transformed by the tax-data entry/update activity into

▶ personal info,

▶ taxes (paid),

▶ income, and

▶ deductions.

The last (checks) is transformed into **ded_checks** through the extract deductions activity. The data dictionary indicates that the constituent parts of the input and output objects for these two activities are not the same. This is called a structure clash. One type of data object is transformed into another. Usually we have to divide the data objects into their constituent parts to arrive at the parts that they have in common.

All items marked with an asterisk can exist in multiples; i.e., there can be a list of these objects. The contents of the object include a dollar amount for taxes and income, the source from which income is derived (name of bank, employer, etc.), and some others (see Table 7.2) for deductions. According to the constituent parts of the input data

Table 7.2 Structure transformations.

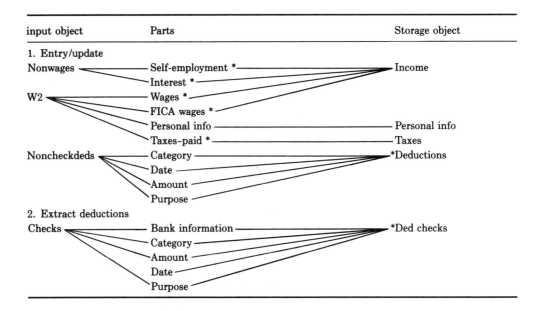

input object	Parts	Storage object
1. Entry/update		
Nonwages	Self-employment *	Income
	Interest *	
W2	Wages *	
	FICA wages *	
	Personal info	Personal info
	Taxes-paid *	Taxes
Noncheckdeds	Category	*Deductions
	Date	
	Amount	
	Purpose	
2. Extract deductions		
Checks	Bank information	*Ded checks
	Category	
	Amount	
	Date	
	Purpose	

objects, we would have to split the tax-data entry/update activity into as many separate processing boxes as there are different parts to enter into different lists (**enter_wages, enter_self_employment, enter_interest**, etc.). We will leave this as an exercise to the reader. The data objects deductions and ded checks have the same form, which suggests that the two lists could be merged; i.e., the activities entry/update and extract deductions would deposit their transformed deduction objects into the same list of deductions. Figure 7.2 consolidates **deductions** and **ded_checks**.

The next refinement (Figure 7.3) looks at the storage objects for the activity **sort/add_taxes_paid**. Taxes paid are of three types: federal, FICA, and those paid to different states. Since we may have more than one, there may be lists of each type. Similar to income types, each tax object consists of the dollar amount paid and a link to the next object in the list. The number of tax types is flexible, because we do not know beforehand just how many different states the person has worked in.

The **checks** data object is an entry in the file that is provided through the sister system banking and has banking information, too. This we will strip, putting some of it (check number and bank Id) into the purpose field for cross-referencing.

Personal information is entered and stored. We can defer the decision on the best procedure until later because, no obvious transformation takes place—the prepare headings activity will require us to determine that. Looking at the data dictionary, we do know, however, that this information includes name, address, filing status, and social security number.

Why did we have to separate income into three different types? Because all three go onto different schedules or are distinct entries in schedules and forms: for example, wages appears on Form 1040, self-employment income on Schedule C, and interest on schedule B. All three are output objects, and their form influences how intermediate objects are designed. (While we did not state this explicitly, we have taken the structure of the output object, tax return, and its constituent parts, forms and schedules, into account). The reason for needing several types of taxes paid objects is the same: they, too, appear as separate entities in the output objects. Because, apart from their type, they have the same form (a list of amounts), we can consolidate the types into one overall type for the entities and have the same types of lists for all. Thus we have singly linked lists for types of income and taxes. We can design deductions as in Figure 6.2 of Section 6.2.1. The design of the other storage objects is given in Figure 7.5.

We added a component **from** to the income element to store from whom (employer, bank, self-employment activity) the income is. This is required for Schedule B; for the others it is a good piece of information to have for the detail reports. This design decision is once more influenced by output objects. While we used only three letters to designate the origin of income, we could easily define it as a text variable to accomodate full names.

We could also have defined the data objects income and taxes paid with a type of PDL as in Figure 7.6. It is a notation that parallels PASCAL pretty closely. Since we hit

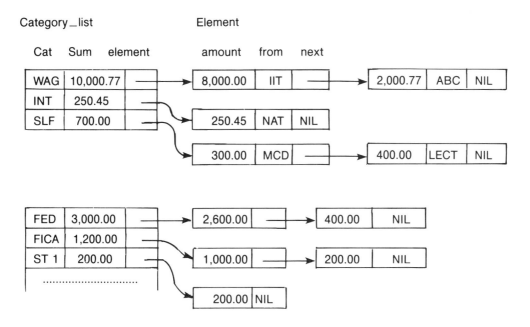

Figure 7.5 Sample Organization of Taxes Paid and Income.

```
TYPE income_list = LIST OF RECORD
                     cat :  income_types
                     sum:   dollar_amount
                     list :  pointer(element)
                     END;
```
where income_types, and element are defined as

```
TYPE income_types = ONE OF (WAG, SLF, INT);
TYPE element = RECORD
                 amount:  dollar_amount;
                 from    :  text;
                 next    :  pointer(element)
                 END;
```

the taxes paid list could be defined as

```
TYPE taxes_list = LIST OF RECORD
                    cat :  tax_types;
                    sum:   dollar_amount;
                    list :  pointer(entry);
                    END;
```

where tax_types and entry are defined as

```
TYPE tax_types = ONE OF (FED, FICA, ST_1, . . . , ST_n)
TYPE entry = RECORD
               amount:  dollar_amount;
               next    :  pointer(entry)
               END
```

we now can define variables of these types:

```
VAR income: income_list;
VAR taxes_paid: taxes_list;
```

Figure 7.6 PDL for Income and Tax Paid Data Objects.

PDL's limits in terms of data structure design capabilities already, you will notice that we are using new language constructs, which we did not define in the section on PDL: **LIST OF, RECORD, ONE OF, pointer(..)**. This data structure design does not yet prescribe how the list is to be implemented. Naming sets of categories as we did with **income_types** and **tax_types** makes it easier to add or delete some, because only the named set will change.

　　How are the data objects accessed? The two activities in question are **tax data entry/ update** and **extract deduction checks**. First we should separate the **entry/update** activity into two different processing units.

Enter: 1. Determine type of information to be entered.
           2. Put information where it belongs.

Update: 1. Find type of information to update.
           2. Substitute new information for old.

The phrase "where it belongs" needs further refinement. It could include sorting in the sense that whatever information is entered is inserted into the list so that the list is always sorted. Then the sorting activity is subsumed under entry. The second structural question is whether adding the individual dollar amounts should happen when a new entry is made or after all entries are complete. While it does not affect functionality, a decision on this affects sequence. Updating the sum at every entry supports quality expectations (reliability, partial results). The design structure subsumes sorting and adding as a processing step, which is on a lower level than data entry or update. Here the design structure departs from the structure of the requirements diagram. We assume that error processing is done according to the specifications and leave this aspect out for the moment to concentrate on the basic processing steps. PDL for entry and update is given in Figures 7.7 and 7.8.

Entry and update are not symmetrical: while the tax data entry module deals with the input data object, the update module organizes input around the storage data objects. This is because the granularity of this information is finer and allows partial updates (such as for the wages part of the W2) easily. Tax relevant information cannot always be reconstructed from the original input (such as a full W2), which the user may want to update immediately. Because the format of the storage elements is somewhat different, different substitute functions perform the update. If we assume that we are going to implement the tax information elements as variants of a record type, we could consolidate the functions into one. But instead of having one **CASE** statement in the **update_tax_ info** module, we would have a case statement and different lower level actions depending on the record variant. This can make the program harder to change, and, because changes are likely, we decided against that. Separate substitute functions also have the advantage that they only operate on one of the lists. This simplifies the function and makes it a more cohesive unit.

Data object definition goes beyond drawing bubbles around names for data objects in the data-flow diagram. Starting with the information from the data dictionary, we have to define what the data object's parts are; as a new piece of information, its structure is defined as to whether it is a table, an array, a record, a tree, etc. Next, methods of access for the elements in the data object are given. This may be field selection, such as for a PASCAL record, subscripting for an array, or a higher level access function, such as finding a data item based on some key. The kind of information an element holds is also defined. This list of data object definitions is an extension and further development of the data dictionary. Now implementation structure and implementation information

```
PROCEDURE enter_tax_info:
          determine type_of_info;
          CASE type_of_info DO
               nonwages        : WHILE more nonwages DO
                                      read(cat, amount, from);
                                      enter_income(cat, amount, from);
                                 ENDWHILE;

               W2              : WHILE more W2 DO
                                      read(amount, from);
                                      enter_income (WAG, amount, from);
                                      read_personal_info(personal_info);
                                      enter_personal(personal_info);
                                      FOR type = FED, FICA, STATE DO
                                           read(taxes);
                                           enter_taxes(type, taxes)
                                      ENDFOR;
                                 ENDWHILE;
               noncheck_deds : WHILE more deductions DO
                                      read(cat, date, amount, purpose);
                                      enter_ded(cat, date, amount, purpose);
                                 ENDWHILE;
               checks          : WHILE more checks DO
                                      read(cat, amount, purpose,
                                           bank_info);
                                      extract(bank_info, checkno,
                                           bnk_id);
                                      merge(purpose, checkno, bnk_id);
                                      enter_ded(cat, date, amount,
                                           purpose)
                                 ENDWHILE;
          ENDCASE;
END enter_tax_info
```

Figure 7.7 PDL for Entry.

has been added to it. The example above used the list of items for the tax system in the data dictionary of Table 3.1 to arrive at the design of its data objects as in Figure 7.6. The design decisions were influenced by the need for augmentable data structures (in particular, the lists and categories of information) as opposed to fixed lists. Qualitative requirements also influenced our choices. It is not difficult to come up with more than 10 ways to design and implement any of the above data objects. Which of the alternatives we choose depends on how well they support qualitative requirements. Whenever a design decision is made, how well (or badly) it supports qualitative requirements should be checked. Our example supported adaptability, maintainability, and performance requirements.

```
PROCEDURE   update_tax_info;
            find type of info to update;
            CASE type of info DO
                  personal_info  :  read(p_id_old, new_personal);
                                    IF exist(p_id_old, loc)
                                       THEN sub_pers(loc, new_personal)
                                       ELSE error(not found);
                  taxes_paid     :  read(t_id_old, new_tax);
                                    IF exist (t_id_old, loc)
                                       THEN sub_tax(loc, new_tax)
                                       ELSE error(not found);
                  income         :  read(i_id_old, new_income);
                                    IF exist(i_id_old, loc)
                                       THEN sub_inc(loc, new_inc)
                                       ELSE error(not found);
                  deductions     :  read(d_id_old, new_ded);
                                    IF exist(d_id_old, loc)
                                       THEN sub_ded(loc, new_ded)
                                       ELSE error(not found);
            ENDCASE;
END update_tax_info;
```

Figure 7.8 PDL for Tax-Data Update.

The example also augmented the activity description of the requirements diagrams. First, we listed in an action list how the action is to be accomplished. Then we refined that into PDL (Figures 7.7 and 7.8). Design provides an action list for every corresponding action in the data flow diagram. This action list explains exactly how the action is performed and defines its parameter arguments precisely, if it is a procedure. The example did that as part of its PDL. The corresponding parameter list is given in Table 7.3.

Read( ) does not show. It is assumed that **read** is a predefined input function that allows arbitrary arguments as long as the types of data that are read match the type of the input variable in the input list. Otherwise we would be forced to distinguish different types of read. This becomes necessary if **read** is a more sophisticated function that provides the user-software interface, checks for valid input, organizes switches between menus, etc. The current level does not in any way know or need to know how **read** is accomplished. It only knows which variables contain necessary information.

Examining the parameter list of Table 7.3 there are two open issues.

▶ There are several parameters of undefined type. In this regard, the design is incomplete. The question is whether it is necessary to define the type exactly right now or whether it is sufficient to name it for the moment and to define it later. The arrows in Table 7.3 indicate which parameters are, while as yet undefined, to be of

Table 7.3 Parameter list for PDL of Figures 7.7 and 7.8.

Action/Procedure	Parameter	Type	IN	OUT
enter_tax_info	N/A			
determine	type_of_info	undef		x
enter_income	cat	income_types	x	
	amount	dollar_amount	x	
	from	text	x	
read_personal_info	personal_info	undef		x
enter_personal	personal_info	undef	x	
enter_taxes	type	tax_types	x	
	taxes	dollar_amount	x	
enter_ded	cat	undef	x	
	date	undef	x	
	amount	dollar_amount	x	
	purpose	text	x	
extract	bank_info	undef	x	
	checkno	integer		x
	bnk_id	text		x
merge	purpose	text	x	x
	checkno	integer	x	
	bnk_id	text	x	
update_tax_info_	N/A			
find	type_of_info	undef		x
exist	p_id_old	undef	x	
	loc	pointer		x
sub_pers	loc	pointer	x	
	new_personal	undef	x	
error	not found	undef	x	
exist	t_id_old	entry	x	
	loc	pointer		x
sub_tax	loc	pointer	x	
	new_tax	entry	x	
exist	i_id_old	element	x	
	loc	pointer		x
sub_inc	loc	pointer	x	
	new_inc	element	x	
exist	d_id_old	undef	x	
	loc	pointer		x
sub_ded	loc	pointer	x	
	new_ded	undef	x	

the same type. Their use in other parts of the system will determine how to define them. We should ask, for example, how **date** will be used elsewhere and how **bank_info** will be used by the sister system, etc., before decisions on the data object's structure are made.

▶ There are several operations which carry the same name but have parameters of different types; the operation **exist** is one of them. It takes an entry in one of the lists for income, taxes, personal information, or deductions, searches whether it is contained in the appropriate list, and returns its location and a success indicator (or reports that the entry does not exist in the list). Because each of the exist functions searches different lists, not all of which have the same type of entries, either we can have different exist functions for every list, or we can parameterize the entry function so that it is able to search any of the lists. The first choice produces several functions with almost identical code, and the second requires redefining types for the entries in the list as records with variants in PASCAL or as a type that encompasses all variations.

In this way, feedback between the data-flow diagram, the data structure definition, PDL for processing steps, and parameter lists influences design iterations. While at any but the last iteration we do not have to define all component parts of the four aspects of the design, we should postpone a decision until we can determine what will influence it. "Holes" in the design should be clearly marked. One might even annotate them with the parts of the system that determine design decisions for them.

For emphasis, let us repeat again that the example design step is only one of the steps in the design for TAP. The fact that it is not complete at this point does not mean that it is faulty; it's fine as long as the design is not finished. However, when it is finished, there should be no holes. The way we chose to express the design, clearly shows the unresolved issues, and we can choose the appropriate one for the next design step.

When we follow the rules for developing data-flow diagrams, we have to create

▶ a new object for each new storage requirement and

▶ a new action for each new processing requirement.

Doing this mechanically often produces actions that are the same or conceptually similar. These we can condense. Sometimes they can be parameterized. Such condensed action boxes will become subroutines in the implementation. In the diagram we use vertical lines for an action box as shown in Figure 7.9. The **read** action is parameterized, because it works on different types of data. So are **enter_income, enter_taxes**, etc. In fact, in order to save time and reduce the number of diagrams, we went to the consolidated description as given in the PDL. The **read** action resolves the structure clashes between the user objects that come into the system by dividing them into their constituent parts and storing them in individual variables. The **enter_ded, enter_income**, and **enter_taxes** activities on the other hand build the new structure from these individual parts as it is needed in the system. This data-flow diagram shows condition variables: **type_of_info** and **cat. Type_of_info** is a condition variable that regulates

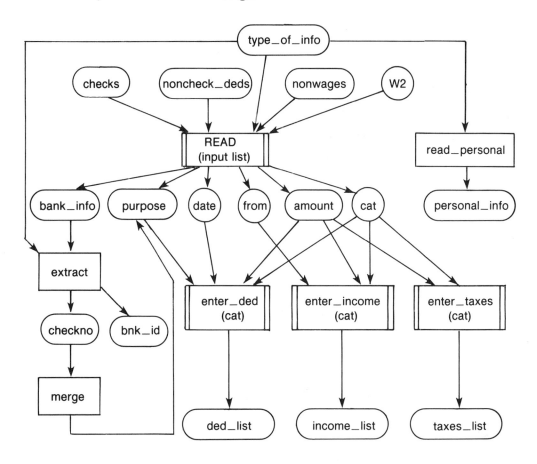

Figure 7.9 Condensed Actions and Objects for Tax-Data Entry.

which of the enter functions is to be executed. It should connect to all boxes of type **enter** and to the boxes labeled **extract** and **merge**. Since this would result in too much clutter, we chose to draw bubbles only to those boxes that are not also affected by the value of the condition variable **cat**.

It is often possible to consolidate objects. Different objects of identical form, such as deduction of different categories in the tax system, can be consolidated. When the objects were consolidated, sometimes a new dimension was added so as to specify which category was applicable. This was the case with categories of income and taxes paid. Also, the seemingly different data objects really can be reduced to the same type of storage object as became evident in the case of deductions and deduction checks. They are both transformed into the same type of entry for **ded_list**. Because they have been split into their constituent parts when read in, they no longer appear in the diagram of Figure 7.9. Note also that Figure 7.9 only shows the consolidated data-flow diagram for tax-data entry. We did not include the update activity.

The data-flow method consists of a sequence of design steps. The sequence is dictated by the hierarchy of the requirements diagram and is usually top-down. For all tasks, we need to determine what type of information must be stored, how will the software need to use this stored information, and what is the form of the data objects that support its use. The focus of the design is clearly on the data objects. Actions are data moves and transformations. All action boxes in the example in Figure 7.9 transform data before storing them.

For actions we need to determine what they need to accomplish and how this action will be accomplished. This depends on the type of information, how it is stored, and how the software uses it. In the TAP example, the structure of the various lists had a major impact on how the entry functions for tax data operate.

As design proceeds, we identify further actions and data. We should strive for a minimal system and avoid proliferating data objects and actions. This is why, in the TAP example, data objects and functions were consolidated. Our example began with the input and designed the first layer into the system horizontally. The next step is to work backwards from the output towards the input. In TAP, this means designing the tax forms and schedules and the actions that construct them. The goal is to connect the storage objects that are designed as we go from the output directly to the input via a series of simple and obvious data transformations. If this connection cannot be made simply, another intermediate design step is needed.

Data objects can serve several storage functions: they can contain data, such as the objects **purpose, from, amount, date**, etc. in Figure 7.9. Or they store groupings, and combinations of data such as an income element or a tax entry. They can also store relations between elements. The lists for deductions, income, and taxes in TAP have a part that identifies which category of deductions, income, or taxes the elements or entries belong to and arranges those of the same type in a list. That stores relations between data. Another set of important relations is that which relates tax data to the forms and schedules on which they appear. We have two choices: we can decide to put these relations into the flow of control—i.e., express them as functions—or we may store them in data objects. The second is more amenable to change if we are successful in designing a **build_new_relation** functions. Then we can combine the forms and schedules virtually any way the user wishes without any code change at all. The first approach would have necessitated code changes.

Our example also showed that the design process can run into structure clashes. We resolved them by splitting the input objects into their constituent parts (intermediate object) and then constructing the new data object from them. Another possibility is to separate actions into actions for one type of structure and actions for another. The TAP design did that for the two types of read functions, **read** and **read_personal**, and also for the different types of enter: **enter_ded, enter_income**, and **enter_taxes**.

We can use the data-flow method for systems as well as programs. For systems, we would start with the top-level requirements diagram, which shows the different systems as actions with the data they share flowing between them. Starting with the top level will require that interfaces between systems be defined early, which is a crucial part of system design because it renders further design of system components independent. The design of the interfacing data objects is, however, influenced by how the system components use them and what they need them for. Thus we have to consider at least the next level of detail.

Besides the data-flow diagrams, we need explanations of the functions that have been designed, data structure design, and an interface description. Structure is indicated by the organization and hierarchical ordering of the data-flow diagrams. The design items are developed in several iterations. We used PDL for describing individual functions and operations, and we extended PDL for data structure definition and a parameter list that defines the order and type of each parameter. The critical functions should be designed in detail with a PDL description. Critical can refer to functionality, efficiency, or other quality expectations. Not every function is critical enough to need this detailed design.

The data-flow method is an object-oriented design technique and suffers from the resulting disadvantages described earlier. Object-oriented design can have problems when a system is large and deals with many data objects. The data-flow method is appropriate when the software or software system is not too large and is data dominated. Function-oriented problems (such as a mathematical optimization routine) do not seem that well suited for the method.

Problems and Questions

1. In the TAP design example we omitted dealing with FICA wages (i.e., the amount of wages for which FICA tax was paid). Add this component to the design. Provide data flow diagram, data structure design, and PDL.

2. In the TAP design example, the data-flow diagram for the tax-data update module was omitted. Develop this diagram in a consolidated form similar to Figure 7.9.

3. Develop a set of relationships that relates the deduction, income, and taxes information to the tax schedules and forms. Propose at least two ways to implement the relationship and discuss the advantages and disadvantages.

4. Write the system structure for the **taxdata_entry** design of Figure 7.9 in MIL. Include the sister system for balancing bank accounts, which produces checks in the checks file.

7.6. Object-Oriented Design

Purely object-oriented techniques tend to suffer from a common problem: when the size of the system increases, there may be too many data-objects. It may become too difficult to relate and interface them all, and instead of making design more understandable, it becomes less so. Booch [Booc83] claims that, therefore, object-oriented techniques, such as the one we discussed in the previous section, are not good for larger systems.

To cope with this problem, he suggests the following object-oriented design methodology [Booc83]. It combines principles of abstraction, information hiding, and abstract data types. Each object in the system is an instance of some type. This means it has a set of possible values, a set of operations that can be performed on it, a view of it from the outside (as it is used), and a view from the inside (how it is designed internally). Modules are formed around objects. Design proceeds in three steps. First, the problem is defined. This corresponds to requirements and specifications. Then an informal strategy is developed. The basic approach to the problem and its solution is described in English. In the last step, the solution strategy is formalized.

This formalization is based on the English description of the informal strategy. Because the design will center around objects, the first step is to extract nouns from the informal strategy description. The types of nouns that will become abstract data types are common nouns and mass nouns or units of measure. Common nouns describe classes of entities such as schedule, form, deduction, tax, and income (for the tax system), or operand, operator, covariance matrix, and source program (for the program analyzer). Mass nouns and units of measure describe a quality or quantity or an activity associated with a noun, such as deduction category, self-employment income, or set of analysis programs. Next we have proper nouns and nouns of direct reference that identify specific data objects of a data type. Examples from our two major examples, TAP and PAS, are medical deductions, tax return, first analysis result, and first token of the command line.

After identifying the abstract data types and data objects, we have to find the operations that are defined for these objects. To this end, we underline verb phrases for objects. Operations can have attributes; there may be time relationships or required sequencing of operations, and sometimes the number of iterations is important. These types of information are usually contained in adverb phrases.

Then we need to establish relationships between objects and between user and design objects. We have to describe the scope and the visibility of each entity. This completes the design on a particular level. We can then either try to implement the operations or repeat the definition process until the detail is fine enough.

Let us look at PAS to see which information we can use at the start. We have the specifications document and the data dictionary (which should give us an excellent source of what the user data objects are). In addition, we have the paragraph in Section 6.2.1.5., which is reproduced in a slightly modified form below. Nouns are enclosed in ⟨ ⟩ and verb phrases are italicized. Adverb phrases, if there were any, would be enclosed in { }.

"For the program analyzer, the top for a top-down design would be *handling* ⟨commands⟩; underneath there would be *parsing* of the ⟨program⟩. The parser *identifies* ⟨operators⟩ and ⟨operands⟩. Yet underneath would be routines that *put* ⟨operators⟩ and ⟨operands⟩ into a ⟨table⟩, so that they may be *counted*. On the same level as the parser might be the module, which *computes* ⟨statistics⟩, because it is another step in the processing. On the next lower level of detail we can find functions that *sum* ⟨counts⟩ and *compute* ⟨means⟩ or the ⟨covariance matrix⟩."

The objects for this section of solution description are

1. command

2. program

3. operator

4. operand

5. table

6. counts

7. means

8. covariance–matrix

9. statistics

There are several operations or functions that operate on these objects. In the text they are underlined. Table 7.4 lists the functions and the objects they operate on.

The narrative did not describe sequencing explicitly, which is why we did not find any useful adverb phrases. Nevertheless, the function list gives the proper order of functions. Table 7.4 shows how they can be grouped as belonging to major system states based on the specifications. If we consider the states in which the objects will be used, we have to add the reports state to this set. But let us concentrate on the states that produce these objects for the moment. Later we will consider the needs of the components that

Table 7.4 Operation-object relationship.

System component	Function (Operates on)	Object no.
PAS	1. Handling(commands)	1
Analysis	2. Parsing(program)	2
	3. Identify_operator	3
	4. Identify_operand	4
	5. Put_table(operator),put_table(operand)	3+4
	6. Count_operator	3
	7. Count_operand	4
Statistics	8. Compute_statistics	5+6, 9
	9. Sum(counts)	6
	10. Compute_means	5+7
	11. Compute_cov_matrix	5+8

use the objects, because they have to be designed properly for the needs of all components.

We need to establish relationships between the objects and between user and design objects. For example, ⟨**operators**⟩, ⟨**operands**⟩, and ⟨**counts**⟩ are related to the design object ⟨**table**⟩. ⟨**Operators**⟩ and ⟨**operands**⟩ are user objects, while ⟨**table**⟩ is a design object. ⟨**Means**⟩ are related to ⟨**counts**⟩, as is the ⟨**covariance–matrix**⟩.

There are two types of relationships: temporal and comprising. A temporal relationship indicates that an object is needed to compute another. A comprising one states that some objects are part of another object. The list of objects above shows the following relationships:

Temporal		Comprising	
command	- program	operator	- table
program	- operator	operand	- table
program	- operand	counts	- table
counts	- means	means	- statistics
counts	- covariance_matrix	convariance_matrix	- statistics

The next refinement step could be to expand on **handling (commands)**. In effect, here we do not need to use the narrative extraction approach that Booch suggests. We can use the formal description in terms of syntax diagrams, BNF, or even Meyer's formalism, all of which we described in Chapter 5. Sometimes it may be necessary to expand on how to implement the function or predicate specified in the formalism, but when specifications have been described in proper detail, those narratives will be relatively short and relations between specification objects and design objects should be straightforward.

As an example, let us look at the description and syntax diagrams for handling commands for PAS. They were specified in section 5.6.1. When PDL was explained in section 6.3.2, an example presented the design of parts of **handling (commands)**. This design derived from Table 5.3, which is the BNF equivalent of syntax diagrams. There are algorithmic methods that are able to derive a PDL design from a BNF type grammar, as long as certain restrictions on the type of grammar are fulfilled. One such method is called recursive descent. The example of Figures 6.9 to 6.12 used a variation of recursive descent that is a top-down approach to parsing. More detail on this technique can be found in [Prat83].

In recursive descent, each box in the syntax diagram corresponds to one procedure in the parser. The diagram must not be ambiguous. We have to be able to make a choice. Left recursion in the diagram is not allowed either, because it would cause endless recursion. Left recursion occurs when the leftmost box in the diagram has the same name as the diagram itself. Because that corresponds to a recursive call to the procedure without a plan for final resolution of the recursion, it leads to endless recursion. Recursive descent works on a token at a time. We assume that there is a function **get(token)** that assigns the next token in the command line to token. Tokens are separated by blanks (which are skipped by **get(token)**) or by commas, which are tokens themselves. With these rules, the design for the parser looks as in Figures 7.10 to 7.11.

Thus, when other algorithmic methods are available, such as in the case of parsing most command languages, the general, nonformal approach of Booch is not always necessary. There may be more direct, specialized ways of developing a design, which build on the work of earlier phases. As in the case of parsing, there may even be direct translations from specifications into design. However, we wrote down assumptions about how to deal with **get(token)**. We refine the description of the solution and apply Booch's method: We assume that there is a function get(token) which *assigns* the next ⟨token⟩ {in the ⟨commandline⟩} to ⟨token⟩. A ⟨commandline⟩ is a ⟨string⟩ of ⟨characters⟩ which ends with an ⟨EOC⟩ (end of command) character (we will, for the moment, defer the decision as to what EOC is exactly). Before get (token) operations can be issued, the commandline has been *read in*. ⟨Tokens⟩ in the commandline *are separated* by ⟨blanks⟩, ⟨linefeeds⟩ (both of which *are skipped* by get (token)), by ⟨commas⟩, or by parentheses which are ⟨tokens⟩ themselves.

Get (token) *checks* whether the ⟨end of the commandline⟩ has been reached. If so, there is no token to return. Otherwise, get (token) *takes* the ⟨first character⟩ in the ⟨commandline⟩ {which has not been processed yet} and *accumulates* ⟨characters⟩ for the ⟨token⟩ until it *encounters* an ⟨end of token character⟩. Then it *returns* the {accumulated} ⟨token⟩.

An ⟨end of token character⟩ is a ⟨blank⟩, a ⟨linefeed⟩, a ⟨comma⟩, a ⟨parenthesis (left or right)⟩, or an ⟨EOC character⟩. Some of these are tokens themselves, namely the comma and parentheses. ⟨Blanks⟩ *are skipped* until the ⟨cursor⟩ *points* to the ⟨first character⟩ of the ⟨next token⟩. {In the beginning}, the ⟨cursor⟩ *points* to the ⟨first character⟩ of ⟨the commandline⟩. {Whenever a character is processed}, the ⟨cursor⟩ *is advanced* to the ⟨next character⟩ in the ⟨commandline⟩.

```
OPERATION command;
           get(token);
           analysis;
           IF not analysis statement
              THEN stats
                    IF not stats statement
                       THEN reports
                            IF not reports statements
                               THEN error(unknown statement) ENDIF
                    ENDIF
              ENDIF
END_command;


OPERATION analysis;
           IF token NOT EQUAL "ANALYSIS" AND token NOT EQUAL "AN"
              THEN return(not analysis statement)
           ENDIF;
           get(token);
           CASE token_type DO
                EOC          :   return(okay);
                comma        :   an_parms;
                OTHERWISE    :   range
           ENDCASE
END_analysis;


OPERATION an_parms;
           file;
           get(token);
           CASE token_type DO
                end_of_command: return(okay);
                comma:          an_parms;
                otherwise:      range:
           ENDCASE
END_an_parms;


OPERATION file;
           fname(token);
           get(token);
           CASE token DO
                EOC: return(okay);
                .PAS: return(okay);
                OTHERWISE: return(wrong extension);
           ENDCASE;
END_file;
```

Figure 7.10 Recursive Descent Parser for Syntax Diagrams of Figure 5.2.

```
OPERATION range;
          IF module(token) THEN  get(token);
                                        return
                          ELSE lines;
          ENDIF;
END_range;

OPERATION module(token);
          char:= first character of token;
          IF NOT alpha(char) THEN return (bad modulename)
             ELSE CASE char_type DO
                      alpha, num:CYCLE;
                      OTHERWISE:return(bad modulename);
                  ENDCASE;
                  get(token)
END_module;

OPERATION fname(token);
          char:= first character of token;
          IF  NOT alpha(char)
             THEN return(wrong fname);
             ELSE FOR char = second TO last OF token DO
                      CASE char_type DO
                         alpha, num, _: CYCLE;
                         OTHERWISE: return(wrong fname);
                  ENDCASE;
                ENDDO
              ENDIF
END_fname;
```

Figure 7.11 Recursive Descent Parser Design for Figure 5.2 (cont.)

This further detail on the **get(token)** description yields the following information:

1. command line: type: string of characters.
                    operations: **get_char (commandline)** yields **char.**
                    read_cmd_line yields **commandline.**

2. character: type: elementary
                subtypes: **end_of_token:** blank   action: skip
                                              linefeed   skip
                                              comma
                                              parenthesis

                           EOC

3. token   type: string of characters
              operations: **get(token)** yields **token**
                           accumulate(char, token)

4. cursor   type: selector for **commandline**
              operations: **advance (cursor)**
                           point_to_first

The English narrative can be translated into the design of Figure 7.12. The way a narrative describes a solution can support or hinder the development of the design. This is both a weakness and a strength of this method. Weak solution descriptions will usually make design difficult. Passive tense and conditions, such as until or while, may not indicate the best way to deal with conditions. It would be better if the design used **IF** constructs or **CASE** statements as the next example shows. The description order in the narrative does not always parallel design sequence. Structure needs to be deduced. In

```
OPERATION get(token);
   token:= EMPTY;
   WHILE TRUE DO
        CASE char_type DO
                blank, linefeed:       skip_them;
                                       LEAVE;
                comma, parenthesis:   IF token = EMPTY
                                        THEN token:= char;
                                               char:=
                                                  get_char(commandline);
                                       ENDIF;
                                       LEAVE;
                EOC:                   LEAVE;
                OTHERWISE:             accumulate(char, token)
            ENDCASE;
            char:= get_char(commandline);
   ENDWHILE;
   RETURN(token);
END_get;

OPERATION skip_them;
   WHILE more char left DO
            char:= get_char(commandline);
            IF char NOT EQUAL blank OR char NOT EQUAL linefeed
              THEN LEAVE;
            ENDIF;
   ENDWHILE;
END_skip_them;
```

Figure 7.12 Design of Get(token).

the narrative, phrases that indicate order, conditions of operation, and adverbial phrases are enclosed in { }.

The design of the data objects **commandline** and **cursor**, as well as the types of character that we chose, are crucial to the entire parsing process. All other operations that are involved in **get(token)** operate under the assumption that the data variable **char** holds the first character of the next token to be assembled. The abstraction of **commandline** with the operations **read** and **get(token)** helps to provide the abstraction of a string of tokens for the parser. At the higher levels the actual implementation of the command line, how the cursor works, etc. need not be visible. If we decide to change what a command line is (such as several lines or a ";" as an end of command indicator), this need not affect the rest of the system. Therefore, structurally, the **get(token)** operation is on a lower level in the design architecture. Figure 7.13 shows the structure of the

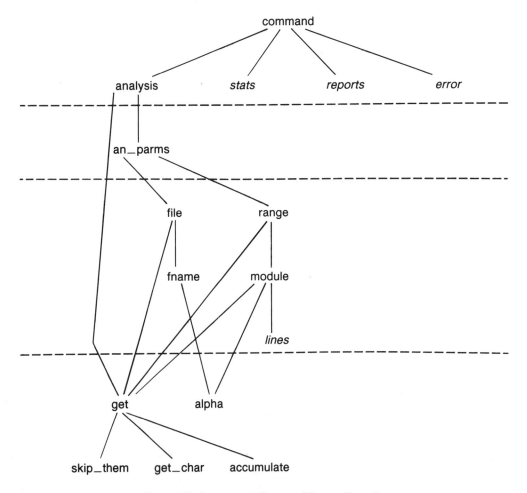

Figure 7.13 Structure of Command Parser (Partial).

parser for PAS commands. Only the subtree for the analysis command is fully developed. Parsing the other commands is designed analogously. Parts that have not been refined fully are underlined.

How we design **token** and the operations that are to be performed on it affect other parts of the system: token type must be determined to be able to identify and execute the commands. This particular case has two types of parsing: parsing of the command language and parsing of the source program language (we chose PASCAL). We should use analogous types of data objects (**sourceline** instead of **commandline, token, char, cursor**) for getting tokens for parsing the source code. The actual function **get(token)** for parsing PASCAL will look somewhat different because the rules differ for what separates tokens, what constitutes tokens, what is an end of statement indicator, etc. The basic approach to design and structure of the parsing function is, however, the same.

Instead of starting with the narrative from Section 5.6.2, we could have started with the state transition diagram for PAS and annotated which data objects are exchanged or shared between different system states. For simplicity, let us concentrate on a subset of states and transitions, namely those which are involved in analysis, statistics, and reports. There are some major data objects that are exchanged between those states or stages of processing. The MIL description of Figure 7.14 mentions them as resources. The object numbers of the previous approach (cf. Table 7.4) are given in parentheses.

Based on this structure and what is known about the data objects, only a small portion of the major design objects have been defined so far. To complete this phase of the

```
SYSTEM PAS
AUTHOR smith
DATE oct, 1984

CONSISTS OF
ROOT MODULE
   ORIGINATES commandline(1), source_file(2)
   USES DERIVED fname
   SUBSYSTEM   analysis_parser
               MUST PROVIDE fname, range, modulename, lines
               HAS ACCESS TO commandline
   SUBSYSTEM   source_code_parser
               OWNS symbols_table (3_5)
               MUST PROVIDE accu (6)
               HAS ACCESS TO range, modulename, lines
   SUBSYSTEM   stats
               MUST PROVIDE means, covariance_matrix (7,8)
               HAS ACCESS TO accu
   SUBSYSTEM   reports
               MUST PROVIDE an_reports, st_reports
               HAS ACCESS TO accu, means, covariance_matrix
```

Figure 7.14 MIL Structure of System States.

structural design, all data objects that are designated as resources in the MIL language need to be designed with all operations that act upon them.

An important data object between parts of the program analyzer is the accumulator in which analysis results are collected. Both the analysis and the statistics module use it. It contains cumulative information and is related to the symbols table. When the parser for the source program has recognized a token as an operand or operator, it needs to be entered into the symbols table (if it is not there already) and the count for it is incremented. The statistics component on the other hand looks at the cumulative counts of several such tables and computes statistics for them. How should we organize these tables, namely the accumulator and the symbols table? This is a top-level concern, because several parts of the program will be affected. Let us first list what we know about how analyses are performed:

▶ The **AN** command allows several programs and parts to be analyzed for one command.

▶ The accumulator needs to be able to collect analysis results not just for one **AN** command but for up to 100 individual analyses.

▶ information must include per program or program part

the number of distinct operators,
the number of distinct operands,
the number of uses of operators, and
the number of uses of operands.

As a result, the accumulator table needs to have 100 entries, one for each analysis result. Since the specifications stated that the oldest result is to be overwritten, it can work as a circular buffer. After tokens have been identified as operators or operands, information about them is entered in the accumulator. What and how? Because we have to be able to distinguish between distinct operators and operands, we could consider the following information for a single analysis entry:

▶ the identifier for the operator or operand,

▶ the number of occurrences for it, and

▶ the totals for operators and operands.

The number of occurrences for each individual operator or operand is not strictly needed. The number can, however, provide more microscopic information if we decide to compare the same program but different parts. However, because it increases the amount of storage needed significantly, we will drop this information. We need the data objects given in Figure 7.15.

While analysis needs all the information in the symbols table, the statistics module only requires cumulative information. Based on this, the following operations are performed on the data objects (cf. Figure 7.16).

We still have not decided on the detailed organization of the symbols table or its entries. This is not necessary when we consider the interfaces between the phases of PAS. The next lower level of the design effort deals with this, because the symbols table is purely internal to the analysis component. Between analysis and statistics, the top structuring level concentrates only on the data objects that form interfaces between

```
symbols:     TABLE OF unknown length WITH sym_entry.
sym_entry:   undetermined, must contain identifier for operator or operand, and which
             type it is
tot_optr:    nonnegative INTEGER initially 0
tot_opnd:    nonnegative INTEGER initially 0
accumulator: TABLE OF 100 WITH analysis_result
analysis_result: RECORD
                        prog_id:unknown
                        dist_optr,
                        dist_opnd,
                        tot_optr,
                        tot_opnd:nonnegative INTEGER
            END
```

Figure 7.15 PAS Analysis Data Objects.

```
1. symbols:   search, enter (operand or operator)
              add(distinct operands or distinct operators) RETURN (dis_optr
                 or dis_opnd)
2. tot_optr, tot_opnd:
              increment
              assemble_an_res(tot_optr, tot_opnd,...)
3. analysis_result:
              assemble_an_res(tot_optr, tot_opnd, dis_optr, dis_opnd)
                            RETURN (analysis_result)
              enter_accu(analysis_result)
4. accu:
              enter_accu(analysis_result)
              statistical functions that compute means, covariance matrix
```

Figure 7.16 Operations on PAS Objects.

phases. The same is done for the interfaces between analysis and reports and between statistics and reports. We also need to consider the type of information that has been read in from files. The next step down would have to consider the files themselves, the read and write operations for them, how to fill the accumulator from an external file, and how to write from the accumulator to the external (history) file.

The example design step for PAS has done the following in order to identify and design structure (which is one of the aspects of design that this method is supposed to be good for):

▶ It has decided that PAS has phases (most prominently there is analysis, statistics, and reports).

▶ It has identified the information which flows between phases and which data objects are the source of this information. In our case it was as follows:

source	information between phases
symbols, tot_optr, tot_opnd dis_optr, dis_opnd	analysis_res in accu

Knowledge about how source information is used in other phases helped to determine its form. This necessitated the design of a fairly low-level module (such as **get(token)**) several times, because it impacts the design of two parsers (the one for the command language and the one for the PASCAL source program).

▶ It has organized individual phases hierarchically using levels of abstraction.

The requirements diagrams, the data dictionary, and the specification document helped to determine the crucial data objects that need to be designed first. Object-oriented design is greatly helped by using information gained during previous phases, in particular the requirements diagram, data dictionary, and functional specifications. Their structure provides initial guidance on how to sequence the design effort. The fact that the requirements structure guides the design effort need not result in an architectural design that mirrors functions and their structure on a requirement or specification level. Our example showed that it is sometimes necessary to approach object-oriented design in a sandwich manner. After identifying the critical data objects, overall system structure may or may not be immediately apparent, unless we base it on previously gained information. The example used phases and levels of abstraction.

When combined with other structuring techniques, object-oriented design supports system as well as program design. The author's claim that his object-oriented design is equally successful at system and program design raises several doubts and reservations.

1.   Selecting the proper data objects for interfaces presupposes that some decomposition has already taken place. If we build on the requirements diagram, data dictionary, and functional specifications, guidance for such decomposition exists. Those documents, however, are not part of the method as suggested. Depending on which document is selected, decisions are sequenced differently as the PAS example shows. Design philosophies and structuring techniques, such as abstract machines, sandwich design, most critical component first, layers of abstraction, or phases, provide the guidance to sequence decisions, which the technique itself does not provide.

2.   The result is not explicitly designed structure for data objects *and* functions; it is for data only. Functional structure or design architecture is provided implicitly where needed and needs to be deduced. It should be mandatory to write it down in MIL.

3.   The process of developing a design comes more naturally with smaller entities. As the reader will undoubtably have realized, the examples are small, and some of them are carried to a very detailed level that goes much beyond designing system structure. Centering design around important design objects will invariably produce some such functions, because they are part of the data abstraction. Structural and detailed design become intertwined.

4.   The complexity of bigger systems may still make it very difficult to develop the proper structure and not get all tangled up with too many objects.

5.   The quality of the narrative is crucial in this process. The narratives that work best should really be guided by the specifications. Think of the specifications as a WHAT-narrative that is now being augmented with HOW-annotations. Not all narratives are easy to analyze; in fact, some of the ones that were used in the example did not provide a whole lot of information. For measuring a narrative's information density we could look at the density of markings (i. e. $\langle \, \rangle$, $\{ \, \}$, and underlining) and see what proportion of the narrative is marked in any paragraph.

In summary, object-oriented design is a very useful technique that combines the advantages of the data-flow technique with the structuring capability of functional design. It can provide high quality system and program designs. Object-oriented design profits greatly from incorporating other design philosophies and techniques to give it additional guidance in sequencing decisions. And, as many other design techniques, it works better when it is incorporated into the overall framework of software development and uses the results of earlier phases.

Problems and Questions

1.   Compare the sequencing decisions for the PAS for the following different design techniques:

294 Software System Structure Design

▶ object-oriented design with phases,

▶ data-flow design, and

▶ layers of abstraction with top-down design.

2. What are the data objects that are fully or partially shared between the reports module and the analysis module or the statistics module? What does each module do with them? Based on this information, how would you design those data objects as abstract data types? How are the top levels of the functions that operate on them designed?

3. Which of the following designs for the symbols table is better? Why? Give their advantages and disadvantages:

   a. The symbols table is an array of text variables from 1 to **SYMSIZE**. There are two pointers, **opnd_count** and **optr_count**. The table is filled from the top with operand identifiers and from the bottom with operator identifiers. Search is sequential. New operators or operands are entered where the appropriate pointer points. The table overflows when we try to grow into the other type's entries. Then **opnd_count** and **optr_count** are equal. **Opnd_count** is initialized to 1, **optr_count** is initialized to **SYMSIZE**.

   b. The symbols table is a linked list. Each record consists of an identifier, the type (operator or operand), and a link to the next entry. Search and entry is sequential. A **last_sym** pointer points to the last element in the table.

   c. The symbols table is actually two tables, one for operands and one for operators. Search and entry is sequential for both. Each has their own pointer. When the table with the operands overflows, an overflow routine is activated. The same is true for the operator table.

   d. This is same as c, but it uses a hashing function and appropriate fields in the table to resolve collisions.

   e. This is same as b, but it has a set of pointers to sublists for faster indexing.

7.7. Quality Issues and Metrics for System Architecture

The system-structuring phase decomposes the system into independent pieces and defines clearly the connections between the parts. A measure of quality for system architecture is a function of component dependency and interface complexity.

Quality also depends on how well we were able to follow the type of structuring technique we chose. How often were the rules "bent"? For example, we could count negative scoring points for each violation of the strict hierarchy for a design based on abstract machines. Or we can see whether and how many times the uses relationship exists without a reason, which Parnas allows. The degree of information hiding (or lack thereof) is another indicator of quality in interfaces.

While there may be good reason to violate a particular rule, those instances should be marked, because

▶ they make the effort more complex,

▶ they need to be watched to prevent problems,

▶ they may influence work assignment for implementation, and

▶ they may influence maintainability, extendability, and adaptability.

The evaluation of interfaces and architectural structure should consider the number of levels, the extent of sharing of functions, and the average complexity of the interfaces between functions (the simplest way to measure complexity is in terms of number of atomic parts of each data object). There should be a standard against which the measures are compared. These standards will vary with development environments and the type of project. Next, we can compare the complexity of the design structure with that of the requirements and/or specification structure. Again, there should be historical data to indicate whether there is unusual growth in complexity for the design structure. Any structural complexity that varies from the standard or exceeds the average for the current design significantly should be cause for investigation. Could the structure or the interface between system components be simplified? If not, the affected system components are more prone to develop interface problems.

The two most important quality issues at design structuring time are structure (of data and functions) and external interfaces between system parts (both data and function). Table 7.5 shows the quality issues and suggested metrics for structuring techniques discussed in this chapter. The structure tree for the analysis portion of PAS is an example of levels of abstraction (Figure 7.13). When we count the times that the strict hierarchy is violated, there are four violations for **get(token)**, one for **get_char**, and one for **alpha**, for a total of five violations. With the relaxed hierarchy rules, there are none. From what we know about the internals of the functions in the tree, proper use of **get(token)** is very crucial to correct analysis. This shows how much more complexity is introduced when strict rules of hierarchy are violated. It helps that the data objects involved are fairly simple. Each time, one token is involved for the **get(token)** function on the higher levels. On the lower ones, **cursor** and **commandline** exist, but they are known to less functions. To measure functional simplicity of the external interface,

Table 7.5 Quality issues and metrics for system architecture.

Method	Structure		External Interfaces	
	Issue	Metric	Issue	Metric
Levels of abstraction	Adherence to strict hierarchy	# arcs that violate it in graph	Simplicity (data)	# data items per function (out + in)
			Simplicity (function)	1. # functions sharing object
				2. per function: # functions to which it is connected (data or calling)
Message	Spread of messages from given unit: connectivity	# ports each component has (input, output)	Simplicity	1. # data items per message
				2. per function: # of messages scored by item
Phases	Info/work redone,	# similar functions in different phases	Simplicity	# different data items passed to next phase (history)
	passed thru	# data items unchanged		
Data flow, object oriented	Spread of data objects through system	# components accessing same data object: for all objects	Simplicity	1. # different data items per object
				2. # distinct functions per object

there are seven functions that share **token**, three that share **char**, and two that share **commandline** and **cursor**.

Let us illustrate scoring a message-based system's structure with an example (cf. Figure 7.17). The connectivity measure for C1 is 4, and for C2 to C5 it is 1, making C1 the central component in the system. Looking at the messages that are to be exchanged, assume that M1 consists of a table entry that in turn has three parts to it. Thus M1 scores 3 points for every component that sends or receives it. If M2 and M3 are single data items, the data complexity for C1 sending messages is $2 * 3 + 2 = 8$. Its receiving complexity is 1. Using these measures, we can target the more complex functions and those that interact heavily with their environment.

An example of a phased system structure that exhibits high connectivity between phases, is a compiler that makes several passes through the same source during parsing.

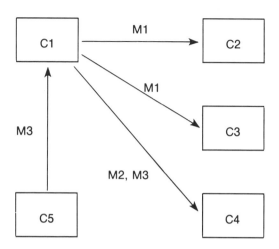

Figure 7.17 Example of a Message-Based System.

In PAS, we could have picked out operators in one pass, operands in another. This structure is more complex than necessary.

In the previous section one part of the PAS structure was designed using object-oriented design. Assume we want to measure the spread of the data object **token** in the design. In the analysis subtree there are 13 functions. The function **get (token)** appears in five of them, **accumulate (token)** in one. Almost half (6 out of 13) functions are connected through this data object. We have not even counted the statement "first character of token" as another function. **Token** has two distinct functions defined for it: **get** and **accumulate**. While the spread of the data object **token** is wide, the actual interface is simple because there are only two functions defined for it.

With the metrics defined in Table 7.5 we can evaluate the connectivity and the simplicity of design structures for any design method. High scores indicate that the functions and their interfaces with other system components are likely to be more complex. The use of data objects with a high index of spread needs to be watched and tested very carefully. They can also be used as input for an estimation model to correlate them with the amount of effort required in later phases.

Problems and Questions

1. Take Table 7.3 and measure the degree of connectedness and the simplicity of the interfaces for all action entries in the table. Use the following rules to determine scores:

   ▶ Data items are atomic entities that are either simple types such as **INTEGER** or take on values from a set of predefined values. They score 1.

▶ Pointers have a score that is determined by the size of the data objects to which the pointer points.

▶ Records have a score that is equal to the sum of the scores for their constituent parts.

Based on your evaluation, which are the components that are the most connected? Which data objects show the widest spread?

7.8. The System Architecture Document

After the software system has been structured, the resulting system architecture is described in a document that becomes part of the design document. The architecture part describes the decomposition of the system into its major parts. Depending on the method used, the document describes system components, subsystems, programs, processes, levels of abstraction, passes, or phases. For each part we have to describe its function or functions (i.e., what it does) and its precise interfaces with all other components. The system structure document includes the following information:

▶ Control-flow hierarchy details calling structure.

▶ Data-flow hierarchy is especially important for message-oriented systems. Data-flow diagrams are an explicit technique to describe it.

▶ Task hierarchy is important for parallel processes as they were described in the sections on abstract machines and message-oriented systems.

▶ In case memory overlays and multiple storage regions are required, we have to specify which parts of the system can be overlayed or which parts of the system are in the same or separate regions. This defines memory structure on a system-wide basis.

▶ For measurement and estimation purposes, we should include complexity and quality measures for the architectural design and point out the areas that scored as more complex or lower quality and thus need close attention.

▶ An evaluation of estimates for this part of the design phase should be added, too. This should include an assessment of accuracy and reasons why deviations occurred. Such an evaluation is indispensable for improving estimates over time. For large projects, a reestimate of the remainder of the project should follow, using effort indicators derived from measurements of the architectural design. For smaller projects, reestimation may be deferred to the end of the design phase.

Because some of the techniques develop structure and detail alongside each other, we often find a need to describe some details also. How to organize them in the design document is described in the next chapter on program design techniques.

7.9. Summary

The purpose of all the structuring techniques that were discussed in this chapter is to support the following goals of the design process:

▶ Identify the structure of the problem solution. Structure includes functional as well as data object structure. On the architectural level, the emphasis is on top-level key data objects and functions and on those whose use is spread throughout the system.

▶ Create external interfaces between system and program parts. There are interfaces between functions (calling patterns and hierarchy) and between data (sequence of parameters, who owns which object, etc.).

▶ Identify the most complex parts of the system, measure structural quality, and determine components with high connectivity.

▶ Sequence further steps of detailed design and implementation. In the example for PAS, we presented the basic approach to command parsing. Then the analysis component was investigated and structured. The next steps in the structuring process could be as follows:

   ▶ Define data objects that interface with statistics and reports but are not totally local to them.

   ▶ Define operations that are performed on them and by which component. Outline the resulting structure and precise interfaces.

   ▶ Add other components based on command language and state transition diagram.

A similar sequence is reasonable for PAS's detailed design and implementation. Usually one takes the full structure description and marks and sequences the parts for detailed design and implementation. When the structure is developed, we have to compare its capabilities to the requirements and functional specifications. This ensures that none of the functional and quality requirements have been left out.

▶ Select major algorithms and data structures. If they are predefined and self-evident, we only need to give the name of the algorithm, such as **quick-sort, bubble-sort**. Sometimes it is not necessary to mention the particular flavor of an algorithm; a statement like **sort** is sufficient. If it is not evident whether one or another algorithm in a class will work, we either have to check it out immediately or plan for a set and design the interfaces accordingly. Mathematical optimization tends to fall into the latter category, since there is no one optimization algorithm that works well all the time. Success depends very much on the type of problem and how well or ill conditioned it is for the algorithm at hand. If the type of problem cannot be characterized narrowly enough, plans have to be made for experimenting with several to see which one works best.

The structuring techniques presented in the previous sections provided either explicitly or implicitly both an external definition of the components of a program or system and interfaces between them. This they did either stressing the functional aspect or the data aspect of the solution. Techniques that stress function are also called process oriented, while those that emphasize data are object oriented. Table 7.6 gives a short overview of the techniques and classifies them as either process or data oriented.

Some of the techniques relied more heavily than others on the results of earlier phases, most notably the requirements diagrams, the data dictionary, and the functional specifications. It is indeed a good strategy to start with the structure of the problem as it was determined in the earlier phases to try to create system structure in a similar manner. The examples did find, however, that while it is a good starting point, the resulting architecture for the design does not always resemble the problem's structure. Forcing design to comply with that may even be counterproductive.

Since different design philosophies and techniques stress different aspects of a system, it should be clear that many different design structures can result for the same problem. All, however, attempt to decompose the system into modular parts. Information hiding and data or functional abstraction are key concepts to a good design structure.

Some of the techniques combine structure with detailed design. In effect, they develop structure concurrently with detailed functions and data. Often this happens with data-oriented techniques and for crucial parts of the system. While all structuring techniques were introduced with systems in mind, the techniques work with programs as well. Not all of them are equally good for large systems. Table 7.6 lists the maximum size for which a technique should be used.

Table 7.6 Comparison of structuring techniques.

Technique	Emphasis	Aspect	Languages/Diagrams	Max size
Levels of abstraction	Process	S (D)	MIL, PDL, structure charts, interface lists	Large
Messages	Data	S	PDL & message operations, diagrams	Large
Phases	Process	S	PDL, interface lists	Large
Data flow	Data	S, D	Data-flow diagrams, PDL, MIL (derived)	Medium
Object-Oriented	Data	S, D	PDL, MIL (derived), data definition table	Medium

Note: S - Structure; D - Detail.

The examples were written down in a variety of languages and diagramming techniques. Some were *ad hoc* or so simple that they did not warrant special definition in the chapter on languages. Examples also used PDL, MIL, etc. Table 7.6 lists the languages and diagramming techniques that work well for these structuring techniques.

▶ 8
Detailed Design

8.1. Overview

The previous chapter concentrated on system structure and suitable methods for designing software systems; this chapter is about designing programs and algorithmic details. Of course, the structuring techniques of Chapter 7 are also applicable to programs and support more detailed design, as we have already encountered. This chapter, however, formalizes methods for detailed design and emphasizes those techniques that aim primarily at designing programs.

Program structure design includes the definition of all modules, their hierarchical structure, and their interfaces. The information upon which program structure is built consists of the external specification for the program, its functional specifications, and the system architecture when the program is part of a system. The external specification of the program would specify its name, the major functions it performs, and any parameters needed to start the program or system components. The order, type, and number of parameters is given. Any other inputs, the valid domains of input data, and their format and type are also part of the external design. The same is true for outputs and other externally visible effects, such as printing messages, reordering a queue, etc.

While these are the minimal pieces of information with which to start program design, we often find many more at the end of the system structure phase. The simple reason is that more detailed information is needed to specify data objects that are part of a program's parameters or its inputs. Thus the distinction between system structure, program structure, and detailed design is often a matter of concept rather than the position in the sequence. As evidenced by some of the techniques we encountered, system structure can be developed alongside a good deal of program structure and detailed design. The difference lies in what is emphasized and the goal of the activity. Furthermore, the objective of loosely coupled subsystems usually necessitates some design of their relating parts, which may require some detailed design. The distinction between structural and detailed design is also helpful for documentation. Documentation usually describes the structure of a program or system separately from the design of its modules, even if the design was intertwined.

Section 8.2. describes two methods suitable for program and detailed module design and illustrates them with some examples. The two methods are Source-Transform-Sink (STS) Analysis or Composite Design [Myer75] and Stepwise Refinement [Wirt71].

Source-Transform-Sink Analysis or Composite Design [Myer75] coordinates well with object-oriented design techniques. It is a top-down, iterative reasoning process that analyzes problem structure and how data are transformed as they flow through the program. Problem structure (as given in the requirements diagrams) and data transformations are used to decompose the problem into a layer of modules. For these, external design is developed. Then the process is repeated at the subproblem level until the degree of detail is fine enough.

Stepwise Refinement applies a top-down design strategy to the internal design of modules. We begin with a first, top-level statement of what the solution might look like (PDL is a good medium), both in terms of function and data. Then we refine one or more of the instructions of the current solution into more detailed instructions. This may entail developing and refining the data objects on which they operate.

Section 8.3. introduces measures for design quality to measure module strength and module independence. Module strength is high when the design managed to isolate one conceptual function in one module. Module independence tries to maximize the data relationships that are internal to a module and minimize those that are external to it.

At various decision points, we choose alternatives, because they support one or more qualitative requirements. Usually the most important ones are maintainability, reliability, and performance, but we may have to deal with any of the quality expectations of Table 4.1. Whenever a design decision is made, the alternatives must be evaluated to see whether they support or hinder any of the quality expectations. Some alternatives may even make it impossible to achieve the level of quality that the requirements mandate. Besides guiding decisions, quality requirements may also prescribe specific algorithms that must be used to achieve a level of quality. Section 8.4. goes through the list of quality expectations and discusses how to go about fulfilling them.

Designs are proposals at first and then are frozen into a design document. Section 8.5. addresses both types of design documentation. It explains how to organize the detailed design document and then suggests how to organize the design document as a deliverable. This document is the input to the coding phase.

Validation and verification of designs are the phase-testing activities for the products of the design phase. The degree of formality of the design determines whether testing and a concomittant validation or a verification procedure can be used. Section 8.6. discusses three types of phase testing, one of which is a verification method. After successful phase testing of the design, the design document is frozen, and development proceeds to the coding phase.

Detailed design involves most of the skills of higher level design, albeit with a different emphasis. We need more expertise in the area of algorithms and data structures and how to select and develop them for the problem at hand. Overall structuring skills, while required, do not have to be as high as they do for system architecture. The degree of expertise depends on how well specified the design structure and interfaces are when detailed design starts. Design expertise in qualitative areas, such as security, performance, and reliability, is also important. Again, we may use specialists in areas where designers do not have the expertise. Oral and written communication skills are also still important. The designer may have to present design alternatives and argue for the best one. Some phase-testing methods require interaction with other people. The design document must be readable. If formal verification methods are used to phase test a design, the designers must have expertise in this area. They should also know how to select an appropriate phase-testing method.

After reading this chapter, you will be able to design programs with two detailed design methods. You will be able to measure the quality of a design, you will know how to organize detailed design documentation and the final design document, and you will know structured methods to validate and verify designs.

8.2. Program Structure and Detailed Design

8.2.1. Source-Transform-Sink (STS) Analysis

Source-Transform-Sink Analysis or Composite Design [Myer75] coordinates well with object-oriented design techniques, particularly data-flow diagrams. It decomposes a program into a set of modules and defines their interfaces and the relationships between modules. It is a top-down, iterative reasoning process. It starts with analyzing problem structure and how data are transformed as they flow through the program. Problem structure (as given in the requirements diagrams) and data transformations are used to decompose the problem into a layer of modules. For these external design is developed. Then the process is repeated at the subproblem level until solutions are obvious.

The initial decomposition is a so-called STS decomposition. STS stands for Source-Transform-Sink. A diagram is partitioned into three kinds of subfunctions:

▶ those that acquire data (they are at the source);

▶ those that transform data, i.e., alter its form; and

▶ those that deliver data; such functions are connected to sinks.

The initial STS decomposition uses a short outline of the problem as a sequence of three to ten processes that are based on the data flow through the problem not on a procedural relationship. A requirements diagram or a data-flow diagram are valuable because they suggest how to outline problem structure.

Next, the major sources of input and output are identified. They become the guide along which to decompose the program into modules. First, the major input stream is traced through the problem structure. At the point where the input stream changes its form and seems to disappear, we mark the border of a module. This point is called the point of highest abstraction. We move backwards for the output stream to determine where the structure of the output first becomes visible. That marks the border between data transformation and sink functions. The two borders divide the problem into its most independent parts. They can be individual functions or modules that can, in turn, be decomposed further. Iterative application of this technique identifies the structure of the program. At each point of decomposition, interfaces between the parts are defined.

After the initial decomposition step (always an STS decomposition), there are two more possibilities for further decomposition: *transaction decomposition* and *functional*

```
STS decomposition WITH problem RETURNS 3 subproblems;
    define their external interfaces;
    while logic of subproblems not obvious DO
    CASE subproblem characteristic
        STS:          break into 3 subproblems as STS
        transaction:  break into peer functions;
                      regard them as subproblems.
        functional:   break into functions according to
                      their data transformations
    ENDCASE
    define their external interfaces;
    select next subproblem
ENDDO
```

Figure 8.1 STS Decomposition.

decomposition. Transaction decomposition breaks a piece into peer functions that process unique types of transactions. For instance, decomposing a command handler would use transaction decomposition and identify the various commands as separate functions. Functional decomposition, on the other hand, breaks a piece into functions that perform individual or otherwise connected sets of data transformations. The type of decomposition depends on the characteristics of the subproblem, and the choice between transaction and functional decomposition is often intuitive. Decomposition stops when the logic of the resulting functions is obvious.

Writing design structure and module interfaces is easier if we have a standard way of doing so. Structure can be specified with *organization diagrams* [Gilb83], parameters, and other interfaces with interface tables, such as the one we introduced informally in the previous chapter. Organization diagrams [Gilb83] consist of boxes for modules and preexisting programs. Preexisting programs have a second set of vertical lines along both sides to distinguish them from module boxes. Named sets of data elements are enclosed in round or oblong bubbles. Links between components are indicated as follows:

1. *Reference.*   A little box marks the component from which data is referenced.

2. *Call.*   The component that is called is marked with a dot.

3. *Include.*   A little triangle marks the component that is included in the other component.

Not all links are allowed nor desirable. Some reflect undesirable or pathological linking structure and should be avoided. A module referencing data or another module constitutes ordinary usage, but data referencing a program or other data is pathological. Similarly, a program module usually can call other program modules but not data, and data should not attempt to call a program module. These are pathological links. A module may include another module or data and data may include other data, but data including a function is pathological. However, merely avoiding pathological structure will not necessarily guarantee good structure.

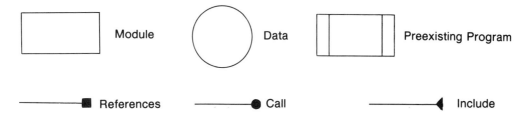

Figure 8.2 Organization Diagrams.

Interface descriptions can be as simple as the interface table of Table 7.3. Sometimes it is important to specify their use: whether they are parameters that are referenced (**REF**), modified (**MOD**), merely passed through to a subordinate module unchanged (**THRU**), used as a variable that controls execution (**CTL**), or passed through to a subordinate module but then modified there (**SMOD**). What the parameter means in user terms, or as a design entity, may be important to record, too. Then the simple interface table (Table 7.3) has two more columns: one for use of the parameter and another for its significance. Note that these should only be added when there is a need to do that; otherwise we only provide "noise" and additional possibility for error and inconsistency.

It is useful to have a list of data accesses for every called module that also mentions which other module contains the data (if it is not contained in that module itself). A table of direct data accesses and ownership is especially important when they are to be implemented as global data structures and do not show as explicit parameters in module calls. Pass-through parameters (**THRU**) do not show, because they do not access the data they pass to a lower level. This table can also save lines in the organizational diagram. Use this table to avoid too many lines. Lines that specify which module contains a data object are no longer necessary, because they show up in the data access table.

Lastly, patterns of module calls and usage descriptions of modules may be important to record, especially if deviations from it would imply erroneous behavior. We can even annotate the usage of modules with test data that cause a given pattern. To describe patterns of usage we can use operations similar to those defined for EBNF.

It is not always necessary to use every type of table described, and it is possible to use organization diagrams and interface tables with any structuring method. Detail should only be recorded where it is needed. As with all descriptive tools, be they languages or diagramming methods, it is useful to define conventions or standards. This facilitates fast access to information in a document.

Table 8.1 Patterns of module calls.

Meaning	Syntax
Single call for M	M
Any number of calls	{M}
A specific number of calls	{M}^{k}
Sequence	$M_1 \, M_2$
selection	$M_1 \mid M_2$
form composites from M, M_1 and M_2. $\langle op \rangle$ is any of the binary ops	($M_1 \langle op \rangle M_2$)
	({M})

Example 1: PAS

Let us see what STS decomposition can do to help us design the statistics component of the program analyzer. The input to the statistics module consists of the accumulator (**accu**), which holds a series of analysis results (**an_result**), and possibly files storing analysis results. The outputs of the statistics module are means, **covariance_matrix, f(x)_list, f(m)**, and the similarity indices **f(x)/f(m)** in an accumulator for statistics results. Its form is still to be determined. We can also save the outputs in a file.

An STS decomposition defines the point where the accumulator of analysis results first starts to disappear. Some of the processes that make up the statistics module are:

A	open_file(file_id) read_accu merge(file, accu) to form the basis for statistical computations
B	compute means compute covariance matrix compute f(x), f(m), f(x)/f(m)
C	store statistics results in st_accu select and file statistics results

When **an_result** entries in the accumulator and those in the file are merged, the input stream given by **accu** and the file disappears. Therefore, the first module (subproblem) contains the first three processes listed above. The output first appears when the system puts it into **st_accu** and gets ready to save it in a file. Therefore, the next line of decomposition is drawn before those two operations. Those are the points of highest abstraction. We now have three subproblems: those marked A, B, and C above. The next step is to define their interfaces. Between A and B there is the merged set of analysis results, which will be called **st_base**. This list of analysis results forms the basis for statistical computations. We do not need all the information contained in the accumulator during the computation of statistical quantities. We only need the numbers not the identifiers for the numbers. They are not needed until output is prepared in module C. We therefore must choose whether to pass that (unneeded) information through B or whether to store it in a data object accessible to C. While the accumulator contains both identifiers and numerical results, **st_base** would only contain those numbers. A matrix four numbers wide and long enough to accommodate all entries in the accumulator is all that needs to be passed. Order in the accumulator determines order in **st_base**. That way **st_base** can actually be regarded as a part of **accu** which can be passed as a parameter in its own right.

The interface between B and C consists of four means, the number of distinct operands (**m_dis_opnd**), the number of distinct operators (**m_disoptr**), the total number of operands (**m_tot_opnd**), and the total number of operators (**m_tot_optr**). Then there are the covariance matrix, a list of **f(x)** for all analysis results, **f(m)**, and a list of **f(x)/f(m)**. We must organize them so that they can be identified with the particular program or program part analyzed. If the identifier has been passed through to module B, we can link this information with the identifier; if not, the correct order will suffice.

After this initial decomposition for the statistics module, we need to see whether A, B, and C are obvious enough so that no more decomposition is necessary. Let us start with subproblem A. All three processing actions in A are related in terms of processing: they all furnish data and put it in a form to be used by B, but they work on different input objects (**file** vs. **accu**) and do different things (reading vs. putting information somewhere). This makes A nonobvious and a lesser quality module, because too many different things are going on. We can split A into three different parts, using functional decomposition this time:

```
open_file(file_id)
read(an_result)
put_accu(an_result)
```

Merging is actually accomplished by adding analysis results to the accumulator. The interfaces between them are obvious and given as parameters. We could have done it by adding the numbers in all four categories as they are read in. This would generate one more data object as a basis for computing statistical quantities. However, module A would be doing part of module B's job, which complicates the interface and decreases A's inner cohesiveness.

Subproblem B also contains several functions that depend on each other sequentially and therefore can be decomposed into separate functions using functional decomposition:

```
Compute_means
Compute_covariance_matrix
Compute_f(x), f(m), and similarity index f(x)/f(m)
```

The next step defines their interfaces. **Compute_means** uses the **st_base** and returns a means vector of four means, i.e., **m_dist_opnd, m_dist_optr, m_tot_opnd, m_tot_optr**. The function **compute_covariance_matrix** uses the means vector and **st_base** as input and returns the covariance matrix.

How should the means vector and the covariance matrix be organized? It helps to consider the design of **st_base**. If it is a **matrix[1:4, 1:no_analyses] OF** positive **IN-**

TEGERS, we can design the means vector as **vector[1:4]** of positive **REAL**. The covariance matrix has individual entries **cov(x,y)** where **x** and **y** are elements for which we want to establish covariance. **Cov(x,y)** is commutative. Therefore we do not store the entire matrix, only the upper triangle. The diagonal contains the variances.

The means vector, **st_base**, and **covariance_matrix** are needed to compute **(f(x), f(m))**, and the similarity indices **f(x)/f(m)**. There are as many **f(x)** and **f(x)/f(m)** as there are analyses results in **st_base**. We can store them in a vector of that length and **f(m)** in a separate variable. Those are the outputs of the third function we have identified as a subproblem.

The computation of the means vector is straightforward. We need not decompose this function any more. So let us look at the computation of the covariance matrix. The formula for the covariance of two random variables X and Y is given by

$$cov(X, Y) = \sum_{i=1}^{n} (X_i - M)(Y_i - N) / n$$

where M is the mean for X, N is the mean for Y, and n is the number of observations. If we have more than two variables for which we want to determine covariance (as is the case here), we will need the differences between measured values and mean more than once. It would be a waste of computation to recompute them every time around the loop all over again. Therefore, we compute these lists of differences first for each random variable and then use them to compute the covariance matrix. On the other hand, if memory is scarce, we may have to trade off speed against the extra storage for the differences of values against the mean. Apart from this deliberation, computation of the covariance matrix is straightforward.

In a similar manner, computation of the similarity indices can be investigated. This is left to the reader. It will most likely require another decomposition step, because it involves several activities.

Example 2: TAP

The tax preparation program can be decomposed into the following subproblems using the STS decomposition:

Subproblem input: **Taxdata_entry** takes input from menus and stores it according to data categories. At this point the input stream has disappeared. The stored data are the output of the input module. Further organization and data objects involved in this module are given in Figure 7.9.

Subproblem output: The print module provides the tax forms and prints the forms and schedules. The output in this form first appears when the internal representation of the forms has been established (links between lines on a schedule or form) and data values have been entered and checked for consistency. This constitutes the boundary between transformation and sink.

Subproblem transformation: The forms compilation module encompasses all the processing actions that have to be finished before the print module can start:

▶ establish internal representation of forms (what goes where);

▶ sum entities by categories and enter the sums (we decided earlier that this should happen right when data is entered. Logically, however, this is a data transformation that produces new data and thus is part of the subproblem transformation.);

▶ compute unknown lines on schedules and forms (sometimes percentages need to be computed, differences evaluated, etc.) and fill in information; and

▶ cross-check between forms for consistency.

The inputs to the forms compilation module are **ded_list, income_list, taxes_list** and either data that describes location or hard-coded information about how to compile schedules and forms. If we want to be totally flexible in terms of what goes on which form or schedule and how to compute it, we must be able to describe those rules with data values and compose forms with them internally. Since this is dependent on the rules for the current list of schedules and forms, we might want to wait for a lower level of decomposition and defer the design of rules until we have more information on their use.

The general procedure is to write out all rules for a given form and then try to abstract the following from the particular rules:

▶ WHAT data is involved (single items from one of the lists, sums, maximum or minimum amounts, etc.)?

▶ HOW do we combine that data (sum, percentage, subtract, smaller or bigger of two numbers, etc.)?

▶ WHERE do we put this information (one or more schedules, lines)?

▶ What are the CONSISTENCY conditions (positive, negative)?

An example of this process is to look at the 1040 Form. There is a line for entering wages. We must look up wages in **income_list**, take the sum, and enter it on the 1040 (where else is this information needed?).

Based on information provided through this procedure, we can decide which rules to hard-code and which to represent as data to control computation. These decisions influence TAP's adaptability and extendability. We might, for example, contemplate adding a module that lets the user "define" a form. This would not be difficult if the system is already designed so that rules governing forms compilation are considered data. We have not detailed the exact sequence when rules for forms are established. They could be established before tax-data is entered, but they must be available when entries for forms are computed.

Example 1: PAS

The recursive descent parser, which was designed with a structure as given in Figure 7.13, has all module links marked with dots at the module on the next lower level, because the graph reflects calling structure. The data objects on which the modules operate are marked with a reference link (a little box next to the data object bubble), while modules that contain data objects show an include link (a triangle next to the bubble).

The STS decomposition for the statistics module is given in Figures 8.3 and 8.4. We decided to physically include the input modules in the statistics module Stats, while modules B and C are separate subprograms called by Stats. The design structure does not always coincide with the structure of the implementation, i.e., the code. We might

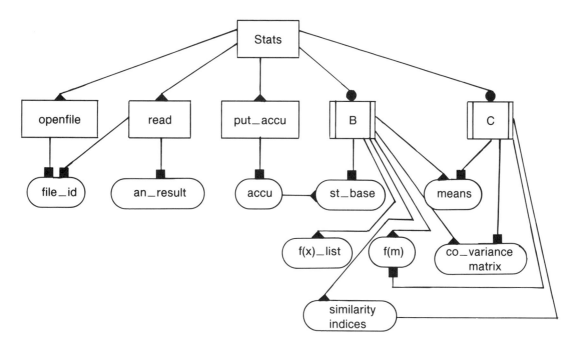

Figure 8.3 Initial Decomposition of Statistics for PAS.

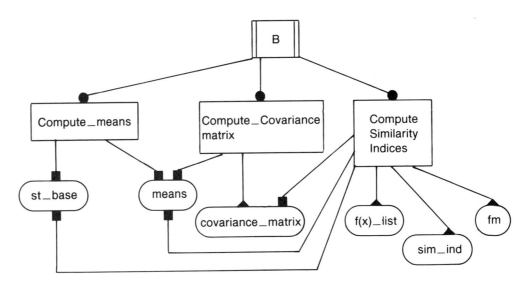

Figure 8.4 Further Decomposition of PAS.

require that during design the module that originates a data structure also includes it, while modules that only use it never include it. This works well when there is a clear differentiation between providing values for a data structure and referencing it. In the implementation that data structure may be an import item in languages like MODULA or a global data structure with specific access rules for languages like PASCAL or FORTRAN.

Example 2: TAP

When drawing an organization diagram for TAP, we should take into account the refinement that we already developed in Figure 7.9. Figure 8.5 shows the corresponding organizational structure. The smaller data items from Figure 7.9 are missing in the diagram (e.g., purpose, amount). Only those that constitute interface data are mentioned. The print module is drawn as an independent subprogram. The interfacing data structures are rather sizable entities. This tells us that we should decompose more to simplify the interfaces further. The lists show reference links but not which modules include them. We have the option of defining a data module for them or an abstract data type for each major object.

Tables 8.2 and 8.3 show examples of interface lists that use the results of the STS decomposition. Most of the time we have **REF** or **MOD** parameters, where **REF** is often an input and **MOD** is an output. Much less often do we encounter **CTL, THRU,** or **SMOD** parameters. To keep the tables simpler, type definitions for the parameters are left out.

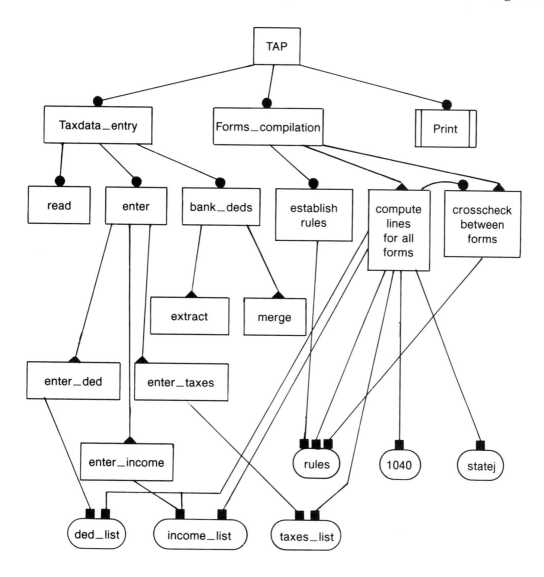

Figure 8.5 Organization of TAP.

Tables 8.4 and 8.5 show direct data accesses for the modules of Tables 8.1 and 8.2. Table 8.6 shows patterns of module calls for TAP.

An STS decomposition stops when the resulting subproblems are "obvious." Obvious subproblems may often be categorized as one of the following types:

▶   sorting and searching

Table 8.2 Parameter description for PAS.

Module	Parameter	In/Out	Use	Significance
openfile	file_id	In	REF	Identifies file to be opened to read an_results
read	an_result	Out	MOD	an_result is read from open file
put_accu	an_result	In	REF	Contains one an_result
B	st_base	In	THRU	Raw data for statistics used in lower level modules
compute_means	st_base	In	REF	Data from which means are computed
	means	Out	MOD	(m_dis_opnd, m_dis_optr, m_tot_opnd, m_tot_optr)
compute_means		In	REF	See above
similarity_	covariance_matrix	In	REF	Covariances
indices	st_base	In	REF	See above
C	means	In	THRU	data for
	covariance_matrix	In	THRU	printing
	similarity_index	In	THRU	used in lower
	fm	In	THRU	level modules

- ▶ merging of data
- ▶ inserting or deleting data
- ▶ checking for validity, consistency, etc.
- ▶ storing
- ▶ reading data
- ▶ initializing data

When a function is nonstandard and its implementation is nonobvious, it is a candidate for further decomposition. While we may not be able to give the precise algorithm yet, we should be able to point out the types of actions that form a solution. These kinds of functions or subproblems are called critical and are, in effect, what detailed design centers on.

As design progresses, some of the structuring data may change because modules were rearranged and grouped together differently. In presenting STS, we have combined it with some diagramming and tabulating methods to illustrate the results better and to enhance their readability. STS also benefits from the information provided by data-flow diagrams, because it is also a data-oriented technique. When structuring decisions are made, it is beneficial to keep the concept of abstract data types in mind. Modules can

Table 8.3 Parameter description for TAP.

Module	Parameter	In/Out	Use	Significance
forms— compilation	—	—	—	No parameters
establish— rules	rules	Out	MOD	Data representation to fill in tax forms
compute—lines for—all—forms	rules	In	THRU	used by
	ded—list	In	THRU	lower level
	income—list	In	THRU	modules to assemble
	taxes—list	In	THRU	lines on forms/schedules
crosscheck— between—forms	rules	In	REF	Uses rules to check consistency
	problem—report	Out	MOD	Identifies problem, if any

Table 8.4 Direct data accesses for modules of Table 8.2.

Module	Data access	Contained in
Compute—means	st—base	stats
	means	stats
Compute—covariance—matrix	means	stats
	covariance—matrix	stats
Compute—similarity—indices	means	stats
	covariance—matrix	stats
	sim—ind	stats

Table 8.5 Direct data accesses for modules of Table 8.3.

Module	Data Access	Contained in
Enter—ded	ded—list	TAP
Enter—income	income—list	TAP
Enter—taxes	taxes—list	TAP
Establish—rules	rules	forms—compilation
Compute—lines	rules	forms—compilation
	ded—list	TAP
	income—list	TAP
	taxes—list	TAP
Crosscheck	rules	forms—compilation

Table 8.6　Patterns of module calls for TAP.

Calling module	Pattern for calling other modules
TAP	{Taxdata_entry} {Forms_compilation} {Print}
Taxdata_entry	{Bank_deds Enter} {Read Enter}
Enter	Enter_ded | Enter_income | Enter_taxes
Bank_deds	Extract Merge
Forms_compilation	{Establish_rules}
Compute_lines	{Crosscheck}

be grouped around a data object. One detailed design technique that we have used informally in previous design examples is stepwise refinement [Wirt71]. The next section will discuss it in more detail.

Problems and Questions

1. How would the design of TAP change if we centered organization around the following major design objects and access operations:

   ▶ **ded_list**

   ▶ **income_list**

   ▶ **taxes_list**

2. Describe the rules for Schedule A and Form 1040. How would you fill in these forms

   ▶ when rules are given through data values or

   ▶ when rules are coded in modules **fill_in_A** and **fill_in_1040**?

3. How would the design of PAS change if we centered organization around the following major design objects and access operations:

   ▶ **accu and st_base**

   ▶ **means**

   ▶ **covariance_matrix**

   ▶ **similarity_indices**

What would stay the same?

8.2.2. Stepwise Refinement and Detailed Module Design

Stepwise refinement [Wirt71] is a technique that has been around for a while and, while it is not always acknowledged, has become a part of most design methodologies. It was initially introduced as a program design technique and is quite useful to determine the internal design of modules, which includes the algorithm, how the module will accomplish its task, how it will use parameters, and which local data objects it will need to accomplish its function(s). Stepwise refinement answers these questions in a gradual, top-down manner. The solution is gradually developed through a series of refinement steps.

We begin with a top-level statement of what the solution might look like (PDL is a good medium), both in terms of function and data. Then we refine one or more of the instructions of the current solution into more detailed instructions. This may entail developing and refining the data objects on which they operate. Along the way, we may construct trial solutions or use loops or recursion to break the current instruction level into a set of simpler ones. How refinement proceeds is the result of design decisions made along the way. There were usually some options as TAP and PAS gradually developed. Objectives or requirements helped to decide which one to choose. As refinements proceed, particular design decisions can lead to a dead end. It becomes necessary to back up and follow another path of refinement. We can regard the options and solutions as a tree of possible solutions. We try to follow the path from the root (top-level solution statement) to those leaves (fully detailed solution) that represent the most advantageous solution for the requirements and product objectives.

One goal of refinement is to decompose the current solution statement into a set of simpler ones. This is greatly facilitated when we decouple issues and decisions. When we defer designing detailed algorithm and data structure representation until the latest possible point, design and the software built from them usually is more adaptable and maintainable.

None of this should be unfamiliar; previous design deliberations used these concepts already. The parser for PAS is an example of stepwise refinement, especially when the lower level algorithms were developed; these determined whether a token was a parameter for a command, obtained the next token from the command line, or extracted a character from a token.

Another example is the gradual development of TAP, its data structures, and the operations performed on them. **Taxdata_entry** was developed gradually, going from a top-level solution statement to the internal algorithmic aspects of its modules. Along the way, data structures were designed in more general terms, such as the **ded_list, income_list, taxes_list**, and especially the **rules** data object. As more became known about the details of the solution, more decisions could be made about these data structures. Sometimes additional information causes changes, because a somewhat different data structure design has become more appropriate. In general, we would like to defer decisions that will lock us into a specific solution. For example, we did not design what the **rules** data structure is all about. This necessitates deciding which part of the rules is going to be represented with instructions and which aspect is translated into data, their categories, and links between data objects.

For the program analyzer PAS, the design of accu is ultimately very crucial, but the first try at design needed to be more precise. We realized that **st_base** was a part of **accu** and making it into a matrix would facilitate computing statistics. That would influence the detailed design of this data structure.

PDL is the perfect language for stepwise refinement. It offers us the possibility to distinguish nonrefined (those enclosed in ⟨ ⟩ and function or procedure names that don't have further explanation) from the refined parts. When we contemplate stepwise refinement, the starting point is most conveniently the general structure or calling pattern. It might have been developed with STS decomposition or any of the other structuring techniques. Remember, however, that not the entire structure needs to be designed first before stepwise refinement is possible. Interleaving both activities is certainly an option as we have seen in previous chapters.

Detailed module and algorithm development begins with the critical modules in the program or system. There may be one or more known types of algorithms, in which case we have to pick the one best suited for this application. It may be the fastest one, the one that needs the least storage, the most obvious and simple one, or the one that is the easiest to change. When there is no known algorithm for exactly the purpose needed, an heuristic often needs to be developed. In order to determine this, we must look at the following issues:

▶ What are the rules for using the module, and what is it supposed to do?

▶ What are the assumptions that users of the module make about its functioning? Less is better, of course, because assumptions constitute a source of interdependency and increase the possibility of error (by ignoring them).

▶ Would it be easier to make the solution more general? Easier can refer to the algorithm itself but also to the expectations for the software. A less general algorithm may suffice right now but not in the future. If the less general algorithm would lock us in it might be better to select the more general to begin with.

▶ Have we encountered similar modules in the past? Can we use or adapt the solutions?

▶ What are the conditions that describe the use of the module and the data supplied to it?

For every module or function that does not have a known algorithm, we must develop one. For this, we use stepwise refinement. First, we try to write a coarse-grain solution that becomes more precise in subsequent steps. Data that is accessed in a module will influence how to design the next refinement for it. Conversely, internal design will influence the design of a module's data structures. Data and function are developed in parallel.

As an example, we wish to design the stats part of PAS using stepwise refinement. What do we know about the solution so far?

```
    PROCEDURE Stats(accu, ⟨maybe other things⟩);
/* include component A */
      WHILE ⟨there are file_ids to include⟩ DO
        openfile(file_id);
        WHILE NOT EOF DO
            read(an_result);
            put_accu(an_result)
        ENDDO;
      ENDDO;
/* call parts of component B */
      compute_means(st_base, means);
      compute_covariance_matrix(means, st_base, cov_matrix);
      compute_similarity(means, st_base, cov_matrix);
/* call component C */
      print(⟨all⟩);
    END_stats
```

At this point, there are a number of unresolved parts that need refinement. We can attack them by logical part (note that stats contains parts **A, B,** and **C** from the STS decomposition, at least in terms of calling parts of them if not actual inclusion of instructions). Another method is to determine which is the crucial decision that must be made now and to refine around that.

The first unresolved part is ⟨**maybe other things**⟩ in the parameter list. Because this is probably contingent on some future insights, we'll leave it for the moment.

Next is ⟨**there are file_ids to include**⟩. It should give us the **(valid) file_id** with which to open the file of analysis results. It will return a success or failure indicator so we know if more files need to be read. We have:

```
FUNCTION files(file_id) RETURNS(success)
success: BOOLEAN;
⟨gets: file_id⟩;
⟨check: validity(file_id)⟩
RETURN(success);
END_files
```

This is not PDL yet because the following are missing: what happens if it is not valid (does files try again?) and how does files know when to stop trying (a "no more files" indicator?).

What we do have is the precise definition of the external interface of the function files: the first and last statement and the return statement. Some of the interface data (i.e., the Boolean variable success) have also been defined. **File_id** is the other one that still needs to be defined. What it will look like and what are valid and invalid **file_ids** is in the specification document. Next, important local data need to be defined (in our case the "no more files" indicator is one of them. As the solution is refined, more precise data will emerge). Once all PDL has been written, coding may start. This will be the subject of the next chapter, and we will not discuss it here.

In summary, detailed design proceeds in these steps:

1.   Select the general algorithm and high level data definition for it. Usually the simplest tends to be the best.

2.   Determine whether coding the solution is obvious or whether more refinement is appropriate.

3.   Define a refinement where the interfaces are precise (first/last statement, multiple entry statements, parameters); the insides may still be fuzzy.

4.   Determine insides of the new function or procedure in PDL. This includes data and actions. If implementation is obvious, stop detailed design, otherwise put the nonobvious parts into the queue of subproblems that need refinement.

5.   Evaluate the design step, which includes checking whether the solution will always work for any input data to the module, function or procedure we just designed. If it doesn't work for all, what are the conditions when it will work? Is that enough? If it is, do we have to check for them and report the failure? If it is not enough that the algorithm works under those conditions only, what causes the failures? Is it imperfect strategy (can we improve it?), or is it that no solution is possible? When evaluating an algorithm, it is useful to try to find as many unusual, even pathological cases as we can imagine, because they might provide a counterexample—the algorithm really doesn't work for all cases.

Let us continue to refine the stats procedure. The **open(file_id)** is usually a system function, which means that this is obvious. There can't be any more problems, because we checked the validity of the **file_id** already.

Is the read function obvious? That depends. Assume that the algorithm reads in one **an_result** at a time. Under which conditions will this work? It will work when there are valid **an_result** entries in the file, which means we must worry about error conditions and define types of errors and what to do about them. Two are obvious: we opened the wrong file (it does not contain **an_results**) and there are no entries left to read (a special case is when the file is empty). Should we check this in **stats** or in the **read** procedure? We can make an argument for either. If **read** is supposed to take care of its own error processing, then it would include dealing with these conditions. But it then has to return an error indicator (a CTL variable for **stats**) so that **stats** knows it should leave the loop. Or **read** is considered a system function and dealing with errors is up to **stats**.

   Put_accu is a procedure that knows what to put into **accu** but not where. If the number of analyses in **accu** is known, then the slot one higher than that number should be free (assumption: sequential organization of **accu**). The implication of this is that **stats** needs another parameter, **no_analyses**, which it passes (**SMOD**) to **put_accu** so that the routine knows where to put the entry and can increase the number of analyses whenever a new entry is made. What about error conditions for **put_accu**?

   Refinements often have to consider error conditions. Overflow of the accu or semantically incorrect **an_results** are two of the more important ones. Refinements add them to the design. How the module will deal with them is determined by the specifications, unless it is a system error.

   After these refinements, the design for stats could look like the following:

```
    PROCEDURE Stats(accu, no_analyses, ⟨maybe other things⟩):
/* include component A */
     WHILE files(file_id) DO /here are file_ids to include*/
          openfile(file_id);
     WHILE NOT EOF DO
           read(an_result, cond);
           CASEcond DO
                no_err: put_accu(an_result)
                EOF:     LEAVE;       /*no more entries*/
                invalid: error(invalid an_result in file)
                                      /*trying to read data
                                      of wrong type*/
                OTHERWISE: problem /*program error*/
           ENDCASE;
        ENDDO;
     ENDDO;
/*call parts of component B */
     compute_means(st_base, means);
     compute_covariance_matrix(means, st_base, cov_matrix);
     compute_similarity(means, st_base, cov_matrix);
/* call component C */
     print(⟨all⟩);
   END_stats
```

Note that we used the English statement of the previous level of refinement as a comment for the current one. This, together with descriptive names for data and functions, makes a design easier to understand. This example also illustrates how design architecture from the diagrams can be reflected in the design for procedure stats: we indicated both the type of link and the module names as comments. The way we earlier chose to select names for the results of an STS decomposition emphasizes again how helpful it is to choose descriptive names: someone who hasn't read the structural description is probably puzzled by the component names **A,B,C**. We could and should have chosen better names.

Stepwise refinement for **stats** could continue step by step and thus resolve all the open issues in the design. The final result is a design in PDL or even the program itself if the programming language is a very high level one. As refinement proceeds, design decisions need to take into account the programming language more and more. This is an indication that design is done and coding should begin. Other indicators of sufficient design detail are that all functions and procedures are obvious. Obvious means that

▶ They are implementable by a standard algorithm.

▶ There is a formula for it.

▶ There is a PDL description for it.

▶ All interface data (parameters and global) have been defined.

▶ All major data objects and operations on them have been drafted (e.g., it is a list or a table with certain types of entries but no details about how it is going to be represented internally. In this case we need a description of access functions).

Design grows and changes as more about the solution becomes known. It is important to include and integrate new knowledge with the existing partial design. Often this requires comprehensive changes. For this reason, a design should be written so that it is easy to change and changes can be made in a consistent manner. Designs need to be evaluated. There are two aspects of this: evaluating the algorithm (we discussed that earlier) and evaluating the module structure. This is the topic of the next section.

Problems and Questions

1. Why is it not necessary to refine **compute_means, compute_covariance_matrix**, and **compute_similarity_indices** any further? Based on what you know about the uses of **accu** and **st_base**, how would you design those two data structures? What are your options? Which do you consider superior? Why?

2. Refine the print module for PAS.

3. How would you connect the user interface for PAS with the **stats** module?

4. Get a copy of the 1040 Form from the library and determine all the rules for filling it in. How would you design it if it is to be data-driven? What would the data objects and PDL look like if it were control oriented?

8.3. Measures for Structural Quality

When we apply any of the previously mentioned methods we have a set of modules that are connected in some way. While the ideal is to have modules that are highly independent of each other, in reality designs often fall short of that. In particular, modules often exhibit the following three classes of problems:

1. They mix and merge functions. When a module does too many related, but different things, it tends to obscure the logic and constitutes an impediment to maintainability and reliability.

2. Several modules perform some of the same functions. In such cases common functions have not been identified and extracted.

3. Data shared by modules can be rather complicated, and the interaction pattern sometimes determines what modules do. They may be data driven through nonobvious shared or common data, and the modules tend to interact on shared or common data in unexpected ways. Needless to say, such complexities stand in the way of reliability and maintainability.

The first two problems are related to the functional cohesiveness of a module while the third is a problem of module independence, or rather lack thereof. The objective is to maximize module independence and module strength. Module independence tries to maximize the relationships that are internal to a module and minimize those that are external to it. Module strength is high when the design isolates one function in one module. Module independence is related to data relationships within and between modules and can be thought of as the degree of coupling through data within and between modules. Module strength, on the other hand, has to do with the functions one or more modules perform.

If we can measure module strength and degree of data coupling, we have a means for evaluating the quality of a design. Before we do that, however, let us introduce the various degrees. The terminology used here is that from [Myer76]. A somewhat different terminology is used in [Jens79] without any change to the meaning of the quality levels. We will proceed from the lowest to the highest level of quality.

Types of Module Strength

1. **Coincidental strength**. There is no meaningful relationship among the functional elements within a module nor between the different modules and components. The module does not perform an identifiably meaningful function. This lowest degree of functional strength for a module usually goes hand in hand with a close relation to the modules that call the one with coincidental strength.

2. **Logical strength**. At each invocation, the module performs one of a set of related functions that are contained within it. These functions are explicitly requested by the calling module, such as passing a function code as parameter. The problem with such a module is that, depending on which function is to be executed, there may be different interface needs. Yet they are all contained in a single interface because the functions are all contained in one module. This leads to complex interfaces. It may also lead to errors when one or more of the functions is changed and necessitates interface modifications. Changes in the interface are much more complex in modules with logical strength.

3. **Classical strength**. The module's functions are related sequentially, and one might have functions that initialize and terminate data objects, files, processes, in the same module. These functions are related sequentially, but the module does not necessarily sequence them according to execution sequence. The problem with such modules is that they often have implicit relationships with other modules in the program, such as the ones that do the actual processing, and they assume that one or another computation or action has taken place.

4. **Procedural strength**. The module's functions sequentially perform a class of related functions. The functions are related through the procedure they use to solve the problem. The major difficulty is that the functions may be intertwined in the design. Changes in one of these functions necessitates changes all over the module. It may be very hard to locate these necessary changes.

5. **Communicational strength**. A module with communicational strength also has procedural strength, and all its functions are related in how they use data. This does not do away with some of the complexitites of intertwined functions, but it reduces it in the sense that they all work on a common set of data.

6. **Information strength**. This is the kind of strength we achieve when the design is based on information hiding. A module performs several functions that operate on the same data structure. Each function is represented by its own unique entry point. The functions are grouped together in a module to achieve information hiding.

7. **Functional strength**. A module has functional strength if it performs a single, specific function. This is the highest degree of strength.

These measures of quality are something we should keep in mind while designing and structuring modules. When evaluating a design, we should know whether modules are high-level or low-level design units. On a high level, a module may be viewed as one function, and thus show functional strength, but on a lower level, it can appear as a conglomeration of functions with a much lower score for strength.

As an example, let us evaluate the **stats** module as it was designed in the previous section. It consists of the following parts:

▶ ***Stats***.   This module shows at least classical strength, because all functions in it are related sequentially. They are related in terms of function (providing statistics) and thus show procedural strength. Moreover, they relate in how they use data, which gives it communicational strength. We can even make an argument that the module provides information hiding, because the functions in it work on the same data structure that is hidden to the outside. That makes stats a module with informational strength. Because it obviously contains more than one function, it does not possess functional strength.

▶ **Compute_means**.   This module performs one function only and thus shows functional strength.

▶ **Compute_covariance_matrix**.   This also possesses functional strength.

▶ **Compute_similarity_index**.   Similarly, this possesses functional strength.

▶ **Print**.   This module has not been fully designed yet. There are two possibilities. If **print** is designed essentially as a big **CASE** statement that selects the proper lower level print routine, then **print** possesses functional strength. If on the other hand, it includes all print routines, then it shows merely informational strength.

This means that the design for **stats** shows at least informational strength and that the majority of its modules possess functional strength.

Types of Module Coupling

Coupling indices measure the data relationships among modules. The fewer and simpler the connection, the better. Connection between modules can be established through defining mechanisms to pass data and through the attributes of the passed data. The best, i.e., lowest, degree of coupling is when all data are passed in explicit, simple parameters.

1. **Content coupled.**   This is the worst. A module is content coupled when it directly references the contents of another. The biggest problem with this is that almost any

change of the referenced module will introduce an error in the other, unless it is changed properly, too. That may not be easy or obvious.

2. **Common coupled.**   Two or more modules are common coupled if they reference the same global data structure. When global data structures are shared, controlling access to them becomes impossible. The modules sharing them can do whatever they want with it. This binds modules, reduces readability (we have to know what every one of the sharing modules does), and consequently poses problems for reliability and maintainability.

3. **External coupled.**   Modules are external coupled when they reference the same global data item. This simplifies the problem, because the shared data is less complex.

4. **Control coupled.**   This degree of coupling usually occurs with logical strength and denotes that one module explicitly controls the functions of another, such as through a function code. As in the case of logical strength, the main problem is that we have a single complex interface.

5. **Stamp coupled.**   Stamp coupled modules reference the same nonglobal data structure. That is, they pass a data structure as a parameter. Because the called module often only uses part of that data structure, this type of coupling tends to create unnecessary connections. It can be puzzling to figure out what part of the data structure is really needed.

6. **Data coupled.**   One module calls the other module. All inputs and outputs between the two modules are data item parameters. This is the simplest and loosest degree of coupling.

7. **Noncoupled.**   One module calls the other without parameters or sharing global data.

Let us examine the degrees of coupling for the design of **stats**. **Stats** is called with two parameters, **accu** and **no_analyses**. The first is a data structure, the second a data item. This means that **stats** is stamp coupled to the modules that call it. If **accu** were a global data structure, **stats** would be common coupled. If, on the other hand, it is possible for the lower level functions to import **accu** and **no_analyses** from another module (as is the case in **MODULA**), then **stats** is noncoupled. Thus the degree of coupling depends as much on the organizational structure as it does on the implementation. Or, to put it another way, we can design **stats** without those data objects as parameters, even though the implementation might have to use them. Thus the degree of coupling depends on the language used. We might give credit for lower coupling inherent in a **THRU** or **SMOD** parameter to the module that passes it, because the language requires it.

For the same reason that **stats** is stamp coupled, the modules **compute_means, compute_variance**, and **compute_similarity_indices** are also stamp coupled: they all have data structures as parameters. The **print** module is stamp coupled, if it uses the previously generated data structures as parameters, or it is noncoupled, if the lower level print routines import the data structures they need on their own.

How can we use the two sets of scores (range one to seven for functional strength and for data coupling) as an evaluation tool? The higher the score is, the better the design. But how good is good? This can be determined by measuring standard quality programs after the fact to determine their scores in both areas. Ranges, means, and standard deviations should be computed for both. This forms the basis for a standard. Every new design is then compared against the standard. If it is substandard, it must be improved.

Even if a design meets the standard, low scores are identified, because they indicate increased complexity. Actions to preserve reliability are determined. One action might group data and all its access functions into a module. This will decrease coupling and thus increase the quality score for this aspect of design. It will, however, decrease functional cohesiveness but only by one point. If that is not possible for the implementation and data structures need to remain global or need to be passed as parameters, it helps to determine which modules may access the data structures and which may not. This must be enforced during implementation and maintenance, and it is not difficult to build a tool that checks compliance with these rules.

Besides these actions, it might be necessary or desirable to revise the design to increase its quality.

It appears that there is often a trade-off to be made between functional strength and data coupling. However, there is no clear-cut empirical evidence how the two relate and what effect that has on setting reasonable standards. Standards might change with type of software, application language, and probably with design methodology. As yet, there is no empirical investigation as to how they are related statistically. The value of high scores in functional and data areas is self-evident, because it indicates a high degree of module independence. Just exactly what can be expected and how this can be quantified has not been established empirically. It would provide a useful basis for combining this metric with others to predict output variables such as cost, time to completion, or software reliability.

Problems and Questions

1. Evaluate the quality of the parser design for PAS using the two metrics above. Which are the modules with the lowest scores? What should be done about it? Compute mean, mode, and variance for both types of scores.

2. Evaluate the quality of the design for TAP using the two metrics above. Which are the modules with the lowest scores? What should be done about it? Compute mean, mode, and variance for both types of scores.

8.4. Design for Quality Requirements

At various decision points during the design we chose alternatives, because they supported one or more qualitative requirements. Usually the most important ones are maintainability, reliability, and performance, but we may have to deal with any of the quality expectations of Table 4.1. Whenever a design decision is to be made, the alternatives must be evaluated to see whether they support or hinder any of the quality expectations. They may even make it impossible to achieve the level of quality that the requirements mandate. Besides guiding decisions, quality requirements also prescribe specific algorithms that must be used to achieve a level of quality: if a database organized around b-trees is to be used, but it must be crash resistant, then we must find such an algorithm. (e.g. [Vand80]). If large lists of items have to be sorted very efficiently, then a simple bubble sort is out of the question; something like Heapsort or Quicksort is more appropriate. Let us go through the list of quality expectations to see how and if they are fulfilled.

8.4.1. Degree of Functionality

Complying with this requirement means that we find an algorithm to implement any of the functional characteristics of the proposed system. The design techniques that we presented try to ensure that. Sometimes algorithms are fairly straightforward; at other times the designer may have to develop one. Books on data structures and algorithms, such as [Knut68], [Knut73], [Horo78], or even the collected algorithms of the ACM are a big help. Library routines exist for many well-known algorithms. It is, however, much more common to need to implement than to borrow, because most problems are in some sense new.

When algorithm selection is completed, a cross-check is necessary to ensure that the required degrees of functionality are in fact present in the design. This we can do in two ways. One is to compare the functionality of the design to that of the specifications; every function mentioned in the specifications should be accounted for in the design. The other way is to compare the design against the degree of functionality as it was laid down in the requirements. While it seems that the first method is enough, because the specifications conform to the requirements, the second is also recommended. It provides an additional consistency and completeness check. Redundancy, in this case having two different documents to cross-check against, is a basis upon which we can build higher reliability.

8.4.2. Usability

Since usability comprises reliability, performance, security, and human factors requirements, each will be discussed in a separate subsection. Some concentrate on techniques, others more on evaluating the design with respect to a particular quality attribute.

8.4.2.1. Reliability

Reliability usually requires the application of techniques that deal with different types of errors. The question during design is, "how should we implement the reliability requirement *xyz*?" For example, the requirement may state that no saved data should be lost when the system goes down, the specifications may indicate that the system provides a **SAVE** operation for data, and the design must decide how the **SAVE** operation is to be implemented.

Another important issue is dealing with user and program errors. The specifications indicate what the system's reactions should be. This section of the specifications supplies the designer's basic information. Specifically, we must ensure that

▶ all error messages stated in the specification document are accounted for;

▶ the required fail-safe procedures have been planned for (i.e., the system reacts to failures the way it is supposed to); and

▶ there are well-defined actions for all instances when the software experiences problems. Because the specifications cannot predict how the solution will look, some of these "system errors" will not have been defined. Such error conditions can and do occur, and the system's reaction to them needs to be described. It is good practice to consolidate all error handling parts of the design in one section, because it makes reading easier. We need, however, cross-references to those parts of the design where the error occurs.

Myers [Myer75] describes a series of design practices that increase reliability and address fulfilling reliability requirements. We will summarize them.

Basically there are two important parts to providing reliability. Faults must be detected and isolated, and the system has to react to them. Sometimes they need to be corrected. Design must consider both aspects. Whether they are user or internal errors, they need to be detected and isolated, and dealt with according to the specifications. Because the design principles are the same for internal errors and user errors, we will describe them together.

Isolating errors is easier if input to the software and input to modules is immediately checked for validity. If a user types in a wrong command, the program should recognize and deal with it and, if stated in the specifications, allow the user to correct his or her mistake. If data that is input to the software or passed to a module is checked for validity immediately, the software is built according to the "mutual suspicion" principle. The occurrence of an error is pointed out where and when it happens, making error isolation and proper reaction to errors easier. It also adds code for checking and makes modules more complex. This tends to reduce software reliability and performance. When performance is critical, trade-offs may have to be made.

Sometimes it is not easy to determine whether an error has occurred. This happens when the range of a variable is wide yet restricted for particular cases (such as income, the amount of a check, etc.). Then we might add redundancy, either implicitly or explicitly, to make error detection easier. The tax preparation can use these techniques by looking at more than one data item at a time, cross-checking entries in more than one form, etc. Related to this concept are techniques that require confirmation before actions that cannot easily be "undone." We could also require additional confirmation before deleting entries from the list of tax data (category *and* amount *and* date). This avoids deleting entries by mistake. It has a negative effect, however, on user performance when he or she doesn't make a mistake. An employee database might require name and social security number before making changes to an employee's record. Since both name and social security number are easily misspelled, the system has a chance to catch such an error when name and social security number don't match.

A variety of strategies can be pursued to detect errors. It is important that whatever strategy is adopted, it is followed consistently throughout the system. These particular measures include

▶ checking data attributes such as type, length, and sign (no negative wages for TAP, and no negative counts for the number of operands or operators in PAS);

▶ checking whether the data is within range (e.g., interest is between 0 and 400 dollars in order to be able to avoid filling in Schedule A, or a module that accesses **accu** checks whether the pointer is actually pointing at an entry in the accumulator or is out of bounds).

▶ using the **OTHERWISE** clause for all **CASE** statements. This avoids errors that are propagated because the program assumed that because the data value wasn't one of the first K values, it must be value $K + 1$, when in fact there are more than $K + 1$, and the wrong assumption was made. We can even see an example of this for specification: the user is asked to answer "yes" or "no" to decide whether a data set should be deleted. If it is implemented as

```
If no THEN skip ELSE delete(dataset)
```

then a typo like "nno" will delete the dataset—a very undesirable level of reliability with regards to user error, and

▶ adding extra fields, keys, or other information to enable consistency checks.

After an error has been identified and located, the system must react as prescribed in the specifications. In cases where no recovery is possible, it will terminate with an appropriate message and enough information to indicate what was wrong and why (snapshot of system state is very helpful). Termination usually has to be "graceful," because we do not want information destroyed. Files need to be closed, results may have to be saved, etc. If the system does not have to terminate, then a recovery action needs to be started. The designer must figure out what needs to be done and how to do it. Usually we will deal with undoing the damage an error has caused, not with correcting the error itself. An example would be to go back to the user and request another (valid) input instead of the system trying to correct the error without the user.

Reliability also relates to errors in the software. The design techniques are geared towards increasing software reliability, and thus, quality indices for structure and module quality will give us a reliability indicator for the finished software. Designs with poor modularity have been shown to be hard to comprehend (cf. Woodfield's Comprehension Study [Wood81]). Another study by Troy and Zweben [Troy81] showed that both complexity of module interface (degree of coupling) and complexity of modules correlates with error counts. Therefore we can safely say that a design with poor modularity usually exhibits poor reliability.

Another way to improve reliability of the system is to determine possible error conditions for all data structures and see to it that the design has provisions for how to deal with it. Examples of such cases are

▶ overflow and underflow of tables, arrays, etc.;

▶ mismatch of input variable types and data which are read in; and

▶ algorithms that don't apply to particular ranges of data values.

8.4.2.2. Performance

Performance is one of the most important design factors, because performance requirements influence algorithm and data structure selection and decisions about architecture and modularization. If performance is put off until after implementation when the program or software system is tuned, it may well be too late to meet requirements. How a program or system is structured has a big impact on its performance. Proper selection of data structures and algorithms is another very crucial aspect of performance during the design stage. This aspect deals with intramodular structure. Details on data structures and algorithms and their evaluation go beyond the scope of this book. Good books on data structures and algorithms are [Stan80], [Knut68], [Knut73], [Aho74], and [Horo78]. The last two also address the issues of algorithm design and evaluation, e.g., whether an algorithm has a complexity of order N or N^2, exponential, etc. "Of order N" means for example that the time to execute the algorithm or the space the data occupy grows linearly with N. N can be the size of a list or an array, the number of items to be processed, the number of nodes in a graph, etc. It is an indicator of the magnitude of the work provided to the algorithm. If an algorithm has complexity of order N, then we can describe it as a linear function of the form

$$complexity = a * N + b.$$

When N is small, the value of these constants can make a big difference in performance. When selecting an algorithm we should therefore not only consider what order the algorithm is in terms of execution and space requirements ("Big O" evaluation), but we should also try to estimate the constants. Note that more sophisticated algorithms usually have a higher overhead, which translates into bigger constant factors. We must determine what value of N is the break-even point when we compare the efficiency of two or more algorithms. Then we can select the most efficient solution under the circumstances.

How the algorithm will be used has a big impact on what the most efficient solution is. Sometimes it is possible to classify the problem into subproblems and have classes of easier solutions for them. Then we must be careful about the boundaries. Sometimes it is more efficient to work with bounds instead of the precise solution. Special cases may be precomputed by hand more efficiently. Which route to go in improving performance depends on the problem at hand and on the frequency with which subclasses of problems occur. Cases that occur often should receive high priority and be made most efficient. The pay-off is biggest. Cases that will never occur should be pointed out and stricken from the solution if that would make it more efficient.

The performance of every design should be evaluated. We can model performance with simulation or analytic models or use the evaluation technique that assesses an algorithm's complexity as described in [Aho74] or [Horo78]. Performance evaluation during design serves several purposes:

▶ We want to determine whether the expected performance of the design is satisfactory.

▶ We want to determine whether the computational resources are satisfactory.

▶ We want to determine what the impact of the new application is on the current system's performance, as well as what the performance of the new application is going to be when it competes with the current workload.

▶ We want to find out which components or modules are critical for performance and therefore need to be watched closely. Identifying such critical components will affect the implementation plan (they should be built first) and provides the basis for more effective management of the development process.

▶ We want to compare design alternatives with respect to their performance. This is a very important aspect of performance evaluation and prediction during design, because it allows us to weed out bad design alternatives early. This saves time, because the designers will not continue developing a bad design alternative further.

▶ We want to determine the performance limits of the design. At which point will performance degrade? What is the largest problem the algorithm can handle while preserving reasonable performance? Many algorithms are exponential, which indicates that their performance can be very bad for big problems. Therefore we would like to know at which point approximately performance requirements will be violated and whether this will pose a problem in practice. If we only expect to run problems smaller than the cut-off point, we don't have a problem.

▶ For time-critical and real-time systems, how will the system react when performance constraints cannot be met? An example of such a situation is when data signals are coming into the system faster than they can be processed. Will the system lose them or ignore them? If so, which ones, and what effect will that have on proper system functioning? Can the situation be improved through a (bigger) buffer? Note, that buffers can only address short-term overloads, not a long-term constant imbalance. When data are coming in constantly at a higher rate than the system can handle, they will keep overflowing. In order to determine what the buffer size should be, we should compute the average or most probable queue length. If losing data is not acceptable, the maximum queue length corresponds to buffer size.

How should performance be estimated? This depends on the level of available detail. On the highest level we need the following information:

▶ We need a description of the usage pattern or workload for the system that is being designed. We can start with a user interview or a questionnaire. Often this information is already available, because we needed information on usage patterns to design the user-machine interface. If we did terminal simulation of the user interface, we may have collected data on typical usage patterns for the system. This will come in very handy now, because it can also form the basis for workload specification for the system. Also helpful are the tests that were developed for the specifications. For some models (those that take into account queueing delays due to competing workloads) we also need to determine what the other workload on the system is.

▶ We need a description of the design structure. This, combined with the usage pattern, allows us to determine how often components are executed, in which order, how often I/O requests are made, and how much data is transferred.

▶ We must know installation characteristics. This tells us how fast hardware and the operating system are processing work, what the overhead is, whether the system is paged or not, and other pertinent facts.

Using modeling tools such as CRYSTAL [Bgs83] or PAWS [Ira83], we can determine what the projected resource requirements and performance characteristics are. These two modeling packages take queuing and the effect of other workloads into account.

Another useful evaluation technique is to perform a best case and a worst case analysis (straight-line analysis). We determine how long it would take to execute the example scenario, which we developed earlier at best (no contention from other workloads) and how much storage it would take. If that indicates that performance is unacceptable, this design alternative can be discarded immediately. On the other hand, if a worst case analysis (biggest problem, maximum projected delays) still falls within performance requirements, then the design is likely to conform to those requirements.

If we know the probabilities with which transitions between system components occur and how long it takes on the average to execute one of them, then we can use the program graph model [Triv82]. This model determines the average time to execute the program represented by the graph. It is a big help if we try to learn from past designs. Keeping records of how design items translate into time and space requirements on a specific installation is a good way to improve the predictive quality of models. If we have PDL code, we might implement specific types of statements and measure how long they take; from there we can determine how long a module coded in PDL takes and build time estimators bottom-up (bottom-up estimation).

Because some of the quantities used in the predictions are estimates, they are prone to change. Sensitivity analysis can determine what the effects of such changes are on performance indicators. Changes in system parameters (CPU speed, OS overhead, paging rates), workload, and usage pattern are common.

It is much beyond the scope of this book to provide more than a glimpse at modeling techniques. The interested reader should consult [Triv82], [Ferr78], [Ferr83], [Smit81], and a special issue of the *CMG Transactions* from September 1985, which contains an extensive bibliography on software performance engineering by C. U. Smith.

8.4.2.3. Security

The requirements describe what level of security is required, and specifications describe what security looks like. Now we have to consider how to implement it. Security is an entire field of computer science in its own right, and we can only give a short overview of the problems and techniques involved in it. Suffice it to say, security problems have gained increasing publicity and importance. Networks, distributed systems, and multiuser systems have contributed to the complexity of the problem. Those systems and the information that is accessible through them cannot simply be locked up any more, as we could do with a personal computer and its diskettes. While specific types of computers and applications have their own particular security needs, there are a series of general issues that are part of computer and software security [Land81]:

▶ Information must be kept secret (nondisclosure requirement).

▶ Unauthorized modification of information must be prohibited.

▶ Unauthorized withholding of information (denial of service) must be avoided.

The problems with these security requirements are as follows:

▶ **Aggregation.**   While access to a complete record in a file may be prohibited, it might be possible to look at other information that is not classified and piece the (secret) information together. Databases are especially prone to that when they provide statistical information. It helps the person who wishes to access secret information to ask questions that narrow cumulative information to the item he or she is looking for.

▶ **Authentication.**   This problem has to do with making sure that the person who accesses information is who he says he is. If the access key is a password, then anybody who happens to know what the password is is authenticated through use of that password as the person who owns it.

▶ **Browsing.**   It may be convenient to be able to browse through directories, even if file access is not allowed. This can compromise information through inference. Someone may browse through all files that are at a lower security level than he or she is, but again, this can compromise security. This is why access is often restricted to those who have a need to know. Access can be restricted to a tree-like structure that allows only the relevant subtree to be examined. Other subtrees belong to a different class of information that the particular user cannot access.

▶ **Integrity.**   When a file is shared, modifications may be made to it without anyone's knowledge. Similarly, data that is sent (even when it is encrypted) from one part of a computer network to another, might have been changed. This can render the information useless or damaging. It is not necessary that the subject that makes the change knows or can decipher the contents of the information whose integrity is compromised.

▶ **Copying**. Unless proper security measures are taken, this can become a major source of security breach.

▶ **Denial of service**. Hardware and software are not always reliable, and that can result in denying service to an authorized user. Any of the above security problems may actually lead to an algorithm that denies service according to the principle of "if you guess at the password, I will not let you try again." In fact, it may have been a typo. On the other hand, it is a means to increase safety.

▶ **Confinement of information**. Leaking information to other processes can be done in a variety of ways:

   ▶ through legitimate or storage channels (e.g., passing a file from someone who is authorized to someone who isn't or using the printer to convey information); and

   ▶ through covert channels or timing channels, which are channels not intended for conveying information. A program might loop 1,000 times in a specific loop to convey information A, 5,000 times for information B, and once for information C.

▶ **Trojan horses and trap doors**. These are programs that pretend to be something they aren't and use that pretend status to circumvent security mechanisms to leak information.

▶ **Wiretapping**. Unless information is encrypted, there is little chance to prevent leakage. Even with encryption it might be possible to decipher it.

Based on these classes of security problems, we can identify those that we must deal with in the software we are designing. Then an appropriate solution needs to be selected. The problems and solutions are somewhat different for different types of software and systems.

In networks, data security is very important. *Computer Magazine* devoted its February 1983 issue to this aspect of computer security. Important techniques to achieve data security in networks include public-key cryptography [Denn83], secure protocols [Demi83], and digital signatures [Akl83], which are a secure means for validating and authenticating messages.

In multiuser computer systems, basically all the problems described above can potentially be a security risk. [Land81] describes a series of formal models of computer security that try to deal with these problems. In a later article [Land83], he addresses the importance of considering security early in the design phase. Security cannot be an add-on. It influences design philosophy and structuring technique. Capabilities are a good concept that has been successfully implemented, as are secure kernels ([Ames83] and

[Sche83]). They can impose significant performance costs, however. It is useful during design to study the information flow of a system (as we can do with a data-flow diagram) and to determine which authority is needed for which information. At all stages of design (a hierarchical set of design specifications is proposed in [Land83]); security needs, authorization mechanisms, and levels need to be considered. To keep performance costs low, it is important to take into account how well a security mechanism is suited to the hardware.

While there are a variety of security models and mechanisms, every serious penetration study that attempted to defeat the system has succeeded. This means that on a theoretical level it may not be possible to build a system that is totally secure in all aspects, because not all aspects can be controlled. How much security we should build into a system depends on the risks of having some aspect of security compromised. Before we decide on a very expensive (speed and space) security mechanism, we should consider which information needs to be protected, what the potential threats are, and how vulnerable the system or software is to them.

In our example problems, both TAP and PAS require that data be kept confidential. In the case of the tax preparation system, we can do that by locking up the diskettes—the design of TAP does not have to worry about implementing security any more. PAS, however, being run on a school computer, has a much higher risk of having information not only accessed by unauthorized users, but also modified. The least that must be done is to investigate the built-in security system. For the "research system" that PAS is meant to be in the beginning, existing system security is adequate, but if a later production system is developed and integrated with grade information, risks of compromising information increase, and this calls for a reassessment of the situation. The data-flow diagrams show where sensitive information is exchanged and who should be able to have what kind of access to it. Based on that we can determine what type of security mechanism would best suit our needs.

8.4.2.4. Human Factors

Human factors are usually taken into account at specification time. At design time, we have to cross-check whether the qualities have been preserved and negotiate changes if they have become necessary. Since the user interface is often defined during the specifications phase, this material was covered in Chapter 5. Design of helpful user-interfaces and support tools is one of the most rapidly growing areas in software engineering.

8.4.3. Intended Use—Generality

This aspect of quality requirements relates to the extent to which a solution has been provided, to portability and to compatibility. The algorithms that the design stage develops may be more or less general than what the requirements stated. Sometimes a more general algorithm may be easier to implement than the solution requires. This should be stated. It is important for maintenance and possible future extensions. It is equally important to describe what doesn't work, why no solution could be found, and what it would take to meet the expectations. Sometimes other quality requirements, in particular performance restrictions, preclude a full solution. It may only be a small aspect of the problem that is difficult, inefficient, or prone to security problems. These may be easily overcome through user interaction. If that is the case, it should be stated and a case made why a less extensive solution was designed.

Portability considerations during design require that design philosophies be chosen to support portability. Levels of abstraction are particularly well suited for portability. When the level closest to the machine (or the system software interface) is isolated in the lowest level, then only this level needs to be designed for portability. If total portability cannot be achieved, then we still have to change only those modules that interface with the different systems on which the software is to be run. It is clearly possible to identify the parts that have to be changed to port the system when those modules can be isolated, because they have been designed that way. In order to have an easily changeable modular design, the design has to make an effort to isolate the necessary modules from the rest of the system.

We also need to consider whether those modules can be implemented on the target machines without major sacrifices in performance. This can necessitate selecting different algorithms and data structures, file formats, storage management strategies, etc. than we would if we did not have to consider portability. For example, a structural analysis program will work with very large matrices. On a system that is organized in storage regions, it will be important to keep the current matrix (or part thereof) in a storage region. Once it is in core, we do not have to worry about the particular access pattern too much (more details when to worry about it come in the next chapter on efficient coding). If we intend to port this program to a paged system, we more than likely will not have the entire matrix in core at any time. The access pattern will, however, influence paging behavior and overhead and thus performance. For example, if a matrix is stored by rows in successive pages but the program references matrix elements by columns, many more page faults occur than if program references were made by rows also. This causes overhead and, in case of memory contention, may adversely affect performance. The impact of different operating system strategies can be very detrimental when not taken into account. For an evaluation see [Vonm81]. Other issues which need to be considered are as follows:

▶ Differences in I/O need to be considered. This affects file formats, file structure and accesses to files, blocks and record structure, and all types of input/output routines. Even on a system of the same type, particular installation parameters can vary. We must take that into account.

- ▶ We must consider interfaces to the operating system (supervisor calls), whether assembly language code is necessary, and whether it is possible to translate one assembly code easily into the other.

- ▶ Storage and its management, overlays, and paging are important. The design should make an attempt to facilitate implementation that is suitable for any of the target systems. If no such algorithm can be found, it is important to try and isolate the dependent parts and vary their algorithms. Sometimes decisions affect many parts of a system (e.g., matrix layout, access to matrices) and cannot be isolated. Then a decision needs to be made whether the implementation on one of the target machines is allowed to be less efficient.

- ▶ We must consider standard or common subset of a programming language. When a program is to be developed that is portable between a mini and a microcomputer, the smaller machine may only have a subset of the implementation language available. If the design makes use of its knowledge about powerful commands (possibly nonstandard) on the bigger machine, it may be hard or impossible to port the software to the smaller one.

Because compromises need to be made in the interest of portability, we may not always get the most efficient system. When such compromises are made, we need to consider their effect on the other quality expectations. There is a trend towards common or standard operating systems, which tends to simplify portability because only installation specific differences need to be taken into account.

Some of the same considerations that need to be made for portability also affect compatibility. When a compiler is a new release of a previous one, the programs that would compile with the previous one should still compile with the new one. The same holds true for software and different versions of an operating system. This means that the differences between the previous version and the new software have to be considered. This may affect data formats. Transformation algorithms can become necessary. As in the case of portability, we have to identify the differences and design ways to deal with them.

8.4.4. Future Lifetime Expectations—Generality

This aspect of quality deals with adaptability and maintainability. These, too, are not add-ons after the fact. Throughout the design process, decisions were made that tried to satisfy adaptability and maintainability requirements. The reader is invited to look back into Section 6.2 and Section 7.6. The single most important contributor to maintainability is a modular design with high scores for functional cohesiveness and low data coupling. All of the design techniques try to support that. Standards in how to document the design also facilitate maintainability, because they make a design easier to read and to comprehend. Adaptability is also greatly aided by modularity. In addition, some knowledge as to what is likely to change is necessary to design those aspects in a flexible manner. We may not be able to say just how changes will come about, but if we isolate the data objects and operations on them in modules, changes will not affect the entire system.

Besides these four major quality expectations, the design must take into account what the requirements stated about the documents that are to be provided as deliverables for this phase. The schedule deserves a close look. Is the version plan that was made during the specification phase still feasible? How does that translate into implementation of the design? Usually the most critical components are implemented first so as to make sure that they all work, before money and time is spent on inconsequential parts.

For PAS, the critical parts are program analysis and computation of the statistics. They should be implemented first at the level that the first version requires. For TAP it depends on which design option we decide to go with. If the data-driven design is selected, then composing forms properly is the crucial part of the system. If rules for forms are to be represented with an algorithm per form, then starting with the forms of the first version is appropriate.

Based on how one decides to proceed, the effect on available resources needs to be assessed. Is there enough (or too much) personnel available? How about computer time? The list of resources needs to be gone through all over again and matched against the needs that are known at this point. Lastly, the design also has to consider benefits. How does each design alternative realize the required benefits? Because a design involves identifying alternatives and then selecting one, trade-offs may need to be made that reflect the decision-making procedure described in Chapter 4 and, more extensively, in Part II. The difference now is that the object of trade-offs are design decisions and their effects.

Problems and Questions

1.   Pick a system you work with. Analyze its security with respect to all the potential security problems which were explained in this section.

> ▶ (How) does the system deal with each one?

> ▶ How secure do you think it is in this regard?

> ▶ What are the specific mechanisms it employs to accomplish that?

Next, assume that the plagiarism detector is implementable on the system whose security you just evaluated.

> ▶ Which threats do you see for various types of information (programs, analysis results, grades, etc.)?

▶ What would likely be done to them and how could one go about compromising security? Stay in the categories you defined in the first part of this exercise.

▶ Suggest improvements to the security problems in question and order them according to their importance. What can you say about the effects?

Note: You will need to do some research, both on your system and on the methods described in the articles cited in this section.

2. Where in the partial design for TAP and PAS do you see redundancy that can be used to detect errors? How would you use it and why can it be beneficial? Where would you add redundancy to increase reliability? Why?

3. Some programs that PAS tries to analyze cannot successfully be analyzed. How would you deal with this error condition in the design for PAS with regards to **accu, st_base, statistics**, and **reports**? Why?

4. Evaluate in which respect the following two design alternatives support, hinder, or potentially violate any of the quality requirements for TAP. Be very specific.

▶ Filling in taxforms are data-driven to achieve maximum flexibility and implement a forms configuration step.

▶ Filling in taxforms are control-driven; i.e., for every form and schedule there is PDL that states where on the form the data belongs.

8.5. Design Documentation

8.5.1. Detailed Design Documentation

Design documentation should include an introductory section that describes the scope of the solution and its major assumptions, restrictions, and design objectives. Then there should be an index so that structure and detail information on any data object or module can be found quickly. This is especially important with a large design document.

The next section should provide an overview of the program or subsystem, its basic structure, and references where more detail can be found. During the working stages of the design, a loose-leaf binder is appropriate to accomodate changes easily. The design document for the entire system may have to be split into a master document with several program or subsystem design documents. In this case, the program design manual should contain references on how it relates to the overall system.

The design structure of the program should be detailed next. Any consistent language, diagramming methods, and tables from the previous chapters can be used. Examples are data-flow diagrams, organization diagrams, interface tables, function and data descriptions in PDL, and graphical representation of data objects (cf. Figures 6.2

and 7.5 for the lists of tax data). Organizing the information in a top-down manner is helpful.

Sections on detailed structural design for the modules are next. Critical algorithms and conditions for execution and quality are explained.

Test cases may either follow the section they test or be grouped together in a chapter of their own. Results of design evaluation, design metrics, and current scores are analyzed. Actions to be taken and standards to be observed in later phases of development are described, when they relate to the quality of the design and its impact on later phases.

Next follows the test plan for the code. It includes a refinement of the version plan, test cases, and metrics to be taken to measure software reliability, quality of production, and productivity. After that follows a description of deliverables—which programs, on which medium, what types of documentation, what types of manuals, completion of training courses, etc.

Last is a refinement or possibly a revision of the schedule. This includes personnel, time, and resources per phase and per subsystem. It also includes a statement of resource usage to date and an assessment of how realistic the schedule has been so far, i.e., whether the project is on schedule and if not, where it slipped.

We have yet to discuss some of the issues described for the later chapters of the design document. They will be explained in separate chapters, but it is still important to know now that these items all belong into a design document. As mentioned before, a design document is a growing entity; often a variety of different options are possible when decisions need to be made. Because of this, the design document usually is a proposal in its first version. The style should reflect that.

We should structure the design document so that it can evolve easily. The people who are reviewing the design sometimes need to be talked into the solution. Because of this it is not sufficient to merely state the design; the process of how the design came about has to be made transparent. Design alternatives should include a rationale explaining why one alternative is superior to another. Otherwise, the reviewer might run down the same dead alleys that the designer did. Rationalizing a design also helps to find errors in it, when the rationale or the assumptions upon which design decisions are based do not make sense.

8.5.2. Putting It All Together: The Design Document

The design document covers the information in Chapters 6_8. The actual contents of the design document vary depending on the size of the project, design approach, and the particular design techniques and notations chosen. In its minimum the document describes system architecture, module design, and data object design, and how quality expectations are going to be met. Table 8.7 gives the outline of a comprehensive design document.

Table 8.7   Outline of design document.

---

1. Introduction
    Scope of solution
    Constraints (hardware, interfaces to other systems)
    Limitations
    Relationship of this document to previous deliverables
    Organization of remainder of document
2. System architecture
2.1. Overview
2.1. Structure by levels/phases/subsystems/components
    For each level (including top)
    2.i.1. Component identification
    2.i.2. Links and interfaces
    (state transitions, calling patterns, definition of parameter sequences, shared data objects)
    2.1.3. Files and databases
2.*. Design rationalization
3. Modules and data by component/level
3.i. Module design component i
3.i.1. Data objects
3.i.2. Function/processing (algorithms)
3.i.3. Interfaces
3.i.4. Metrics
3.* Design rationalization
4. Quality expectations
    All areas of Table 4.1.
4.*. Design rationalization
5. Test plan
5.1. Architecture
5.2. Modules and data
5.3. Quality expectations
    Note: a detailed test plan is given in Section 10.7.
Appendices

The introduction describes the scope of the solution and any major constraints and limitations. These may be due to hardware, other software, or organizational constraints and limitations. The relationship to previous documents (deliverables) is also stated. The introduction must explain how the remainder of the document is organized.

Software architecture describes the structure of the software, how components are linked, and what the interfaces between components are. It includes state transitions, calling patterns, and how parameter sequences are defined. It also explains any shared data objects, files, and data bases. This part of the document may be organized by design level, component, or subsystem.

Sometimes the rationale for major design decisions is stated. This tends to help during evolution and maintenance.

Modules and data are described by component or level to preserve a uniform structure throughout the design document. For each module design component, the document describes its data objects, the algorithm, interfaces to other algorithms, and subsystems. Metrics for design quality may be listed. Sometimes the document contains design rationalization arguments.

The section on quality expectations describes design decisions related to all quality areas of Table 4.1 and argues why they assure that quality expectations are met.

The test plan describes all testing activities for system architecture, modules and data, and quality expectations. Appendices may explain material that is important but does not fit into any of the other categories.

Problems and Questions

1.   Develop an outline for the design document for PAS. Which parts have been designed and which design information is still missing? What were the specific alternatives for PAS? What others do you see?

2.   Develop an outline for the design document for TAP. Which parts have been designed and which design information is still missing? What were the specific alternatives for TAP? What others do you see?

8.6.   Validation and Verification of Designs

8.6.1.   Introduction

Validation and verification of designs are the phase-testing activities for the products of the design stage. Whether testing and concomitant validation or a more formal verification procedure is used, depends on the formality of the design. We will discuss several techniques to phase test design deliverables. The most commonly known is the walkthrough (8.6.2) or review, of which three major variants exist. A quality assurance technique, which also facilitates maintenance and redesign, is design rationalization (8.6.3). Then a verification technique is presented for path expressions (8.6.4).

Phase testing for design proceeds along the outline for the design document (cf. Table 8.7). The actual contents of the design document vary depending on the size of the project, design approach, and the particular design techniques and notations chosen. At its minimum, we have to test system architecture, module and data object design, and whether quality expectations are going to be met:

▶ **Software architecture**.   Here we test the structure of the software, how components are linked, and whether the interfaces between components are defined correctly. The test covers state transitions, calling patterns, how parameter sequences are defined and whether they are used correctly, consistency of shared data objects, etc.

▶ **Modules and data**.   Intramodule evaluation checks out whether the algorithm works correctly for all classes of data, i.e., normal operating cases, boundary cases, invalid ones, and, because the objective of testing is to try and make the object under test crumble, as many hard and "impossible" cases as the tester can dream up. This also applies to testing data structures. We try the inner range of values, invalid values, and boundary values, if there are different classes (distinguished by different functional processing requirements). We can reuse test cases from the specification phase test and augment them.

▶ **Quality expectations**.   Here we test whether the quality expectations are met even under the harshest of conditions. Invalid input, no input, maximum load, unusual system states and transitions between them, and start-up and termination should not only be tested with regard to functionality (that includes the cases above) but also with regards to whether the design will conform to the quality expectations in these situations.

Another way to look at the question what to test for is to check for the "four C's": clarity, completeness, consistency, and correctness. Because clarity is one of the most important contributors to achieving software quality, areas where the document is not clear are marked for improvement. This can be done editorially and factually. Editorial clarity concentrates on style, layout, and organization of the document. Factual clarity pinpoints vagueness and holes in the content of the design. This is usually done while one tries to find errors and tries to establish whether the design represents a correct solution. The design is a major supporting document for building the software and for future modifications. Also, if the document is not clear, it will be hard for the maintenance team to understand what certain parts of the design mean and how they work (together). We can check readability against Meyer's seven sins.

Completeness is checked with regards to the following:

▶ Have all functions that were described in the specifications been designed? Are they all present?

▶ Have all quality expectations been met (performance, reliability, etc.)? Do we have specific evaluations? This requires a cross-check with the requirements and the quality expectations section of the specification.

▶ Have all constraints on resources and schedule been considered (functional and quality constraints were addressed in the previous two steps)?

▶ Does the test plan provide test cases or scenario descriptions that cover all functions, modules, interconnections, algorithmic behavior, valid and invalid data, etc.? Does it show all stages of testing and what is to be done during those stages?

▶ For the design itself, are the test cases able to evaluate what the design does or doesn't do in all areas mentioned above? Try to reuse test cases from the specifications, because they represent typical, atypical, and erroneous uses of the system. Additional test cases focus on the particulars of the design and how the solution deals with functionality aspects, data objects, etc. Classes of data for user (specification) objects do not always parallel those of design objects. This necessitates test cases that focus on design classes and the differences between user and design objects.

Completeness evaluation evaluates whether the translation from specification into design was comprehensive. A consistency check is often performed in parallel. Consistency needs to be established between specifications and design. In the design document, consistency is important in the following areas:

▶ **Basic approach**. It is very confusing and detrimental to a reliable and maintainable system when design approaches are mixed. An example of an inconsistent design approach could be how error handling is designed. When half the error messages are consolidated in a module and the rest is done all over at the point where they occur, errors are treated inconsistently. This is not only confusing to someone who may be maintaining the software later (What am I to do? Can I do anything I like or is there a secret to doing it this way which I don't understand?), it is also error prone (Are all errors accounted for or not?).

▶ **Between system or program components**. Levels of abstraction must be consistent. Descriptions of building blocks for the system and the links between them are checked for contradictions. A component cannot be physically contained in two different components. A module cannot be part of two different levels of abstraction. The structure diagram should not show a calling link between A and B when the PDL does not show such a call.

▶ **Between data structures**. It is especially important for those shared between modules. Usage of a data structure in one module must not contradict usage in another. Inconsistencies can occur with regards to ranges, special values, and boundary values.

▶ **With the implementation language**. Designs look different for different classes of languages. In the designs that we have seen, one of the high-level general purpose programming languages was tacitly assumed as a target language. If SNOBOL were the target language for the parser of PAS, there would have been no need to develop PDL. We could have coded from the syntax diagrams and the formal specifications of Chapter 5 after ensuring that no infinite recursion occurs. The TAP design would be different if we had decided to use a special purpose "language" like Lotus 1-2-3 (Reg. Trademark) or DBase III (Reg. Trademark). The tax-data entry and retrieval functions are source language operations in the database software, and calculations on classes of data are easily performed with a spreadsheet program. The emphasis of the design would have been to interface between the two products. During phase testing, consistency between the design and the target language needs to be established; i.e., can the design be translated into the code and will it use the language features to advantage?

Last, but most important is correctness. During testing we do not so much try to find that the design is correct, rather we focus on finding as many errors as we can; i.e., we attempt to show that the design is incorrect. These efforts target all aspects of the design: functional correctness, quality expectations, and resource and schedule constraints. They test design architecture, module design, and evaluations of quality requirements and investigate the feasibility of the further implementation plan.

It is not recommended to postpone all test efforts until the entire design is complete, unless it is a small project. There are natural break-points in the design: when architecture is complete we can review that part of the design, and as module designs are completed, they can be tested. This is advantageous because the knowledge learned here can be used in the next step. It also describes the design structure to the people who will be involved in module design and thus have to understand what the overall structure looks like. Because the whole (design) is not the same as the sum of its pieces, another step needs to be added to test how it all fits together. Any of the verification efforts for an individual aspect or for any of the design components will be limited in size, which reduces the complexity of the effort. That is a major advantage of doing design validation this way.

Designs should be tested by those who built it, those who wrote specifications, and those who will be involved in implementing the design into code. This does not mean that all people in these respective capacities get involved. We have a representative from each group. If there are major subcomponents to the system, then the representatives from the specification and implementation team are responsible for a particular subsystem. Both have a natural interest in contributing to the testing effort, because it is the specifier's work for which a design has been developed, and it is the implementer's job to translate the design into code. One might say that the implementor on the test team has more at stake than the person from the specification team, because specification work is over. This is only true if they do not have to deal with changes and revisions and if they are not held responsible for the results of their work. On a more positive note, positive feedback contributes to job satisfaction, and if we rob the specification team of that, they are working in a vacuum. They will not know how well they have done, and they will not learn, because they never know about their mistakes.

We may also need performance specialists, reliability experts, a penetration team to test security, systems programmers, and hardware specialists. A separate testing team would be involved in developing and/or checking out the test plan. For big development projects there may be experts on scheduling, administrators, management, etc. to do those aspects of the design phase.

The following sections discuss several approaches to design validation and verification. Variations on these techniques are possible and many other techniques are suggested or practiced. The ones that were chosen reflect basic approaches and explain them in specific categories.

Problems and Questions

1.   List three reasons why the specification team and the implementers should have at least one representative involved in phase testing the design.

2.   Take PAS specification test cases that were developed in earlier exercises. Which aspect of the design do they test? Which aspects are not tested? Why? Add test cases that test these aspects explicitly.

8.6.2.   Design Walk-throughs

Design walk-throughs can be an informal, semiformal, or formal affair. Informal walk-throughs get a bunch of people together who look through part of a design and see whether it will work or not. They can be held over lunch or over a beer. We may turn around to an office-mate and show him the work, or we may call someone with a question to ask his advice. These kinds of walk-throughs are very useful during the development of a design when simple questions arise. However, this is not appropriate for reviewing bigger pieces of design and certainly not for approving it.

A semiformal walk-through is more structured and usually involves more than two people. The participants agree on walk-through procedure. People read the material before the walk-through meeting and come back with what they think are the basic flaws of the design. Because much of this is based on good will, it does not always work. Its pitfalls are

▶ too much other work, not enough time to prepare;

▶ the wrong people agree to participate (not qualified, personality clash);

▶ wrangling about decisions stymies the evaluation process; and

▶ design on the fly can be very error prone.

For these reasons, walk-throughs are often a formal structure with assigned roles for participants. This makes the whole process a bona fide development activity (which can be scheduled and is part of the participants' work responsibility). It makes it more efficient (rules are known; they don't have to be fought or negotiated for) and thus more economical (the right people are involved).

The roles of the people involved are as follows:

▶ **Moderator.**   This is an independent person, maybe from another project, who directs the discussion and makes sure that everyone gets a chance to voice opinions. He need not be an expert on the project but must have people skills. The moderator must also organize the meeting, distribute materials, set dates, find a meeting room, procure an overhead projector, and visual aids, a blackboard, etc. Afterwards, he distributes the results of the walk-through to all participants.

▶ **Designer or presenter.**   This is the person (or persons) whose work is being walked through or reviewed. Sometimes they make a presentation. At some walk-throughs the participants have done their review at home and have questions. Because of this, the designer need not always make a presentation (sometimes it is feared that this can bias the walk-through), but it helps when the designer is present to field questions. This group also includes other designers who are asked to review the presenter's design.

▶ **Specification specialist.**   This person (or persons) is responsible for determining whether the design constitutes a valid translation from the specification and whether it reflects the specifications correctly, completely, and consistently.

▶ **Implementer, coder, or language specialist.**   The design must be implementable in the target language, and the role of the implementer is to review the design in this aspect.

▶ **Performance analyst.**   This person makes sure that the performance requirements are met.

▶ **Security specialist.**   This person is responsible for checking how well the design fulfills security requirements.

▶ **Tester.** This person is responsible for reviewing the test plan, the testability of the design, and he may be asked to prepare a few representative test cases for walking the design through during the meeting. When the correctness of a part of the design is questioned, he should be able to find a test case that would find the error. Thus he must be familiar with the test cases for the design under review.

▶ **Standards bearer.** This person is responsible for pointing out all violations of standards for the document and for development procedures. This ensures that standards are kept where necessary but not slavishly.

▶ **Maintenance specialist.** This person reviews the design document with respect to lifetime expectations for the software, i.e., adaptability and maintainability.

▶ **Secretary.** This is the person who takes notes about the meeting, the problems found, where, and what they are. Some reviewers' irrelevant comments need not be recorded, and a clerical secretary usually cannot distinguish between the two. Therefore, the secretary for a walkthrough should be a person knowledgeable about the project, maybe a team member. The secretary would typically record all the errors with

> ▶ type of error (they can be interface errors, missing or inconsistent parts in a data structure, performance, reliability, intramodule logic error, standards, etc.),
>
> ▶ severity (minor, major),
>
> ▶ where it occurs,
>
> ▶ what is wrong,
>
> ▶ who is responsible for correcting it, and
>
> ▶ the time frame for correcting it.

The goals of a walk-through are to find as many errors as possible. It is not the goal of a walk-through to correct the errors or make design decisions. A walk-through identifies and classifies errors. It may start with an overview and an agenda, and then the inspection begins. After the errors have been recorded, the persons responsible for the rework will deal with the errors that were found. The result is reported in a follow-up to the original walk-through. This follow-up may be another walk-through, if the document could not be accepted as is, or via mail to show all participants that the required changes have been made.

The walk-through itself should not exceed two hours. If it is important to have a longer walk-through, there should be a break, so that participants can recuperate. Otherwise the success rate of the group will drop with their attention span. The roles of the participants are not necessarily limited to one role per person; sometimes more than one person of a role may be needed, but the group size for a formal walk-through is usually around five or six. If the group becomes too big, it easily loses effectiveness and can degenerate into a committee meeting [Your79].

The concept of a walk-through is easily applicable to other parts of the software development process. [Free82] describes in minute detail all the things to do and to avoid in a walk-through, how to make it succeed, how to deal with problems, how to keep people motivated, and when not to have walk-throughs.

It is important to measure the effectiveness of a walk-through. Success should be documented, and it should be noted when people came unprepared. How can we measure effectiveness? One way is to use the recorded error data. This alone is not enough, however. It must be compared against the number of errors that could have been detected during that walkthrough but weren't discovered until later. We can develop a standard by recording the number of errors per size over a period of time in both categories. When a walk-through turns up an unusually high error rate, either the quality of the design is low or the participants did a very good job. The analysis will determine this and provide the necessary feedback to the participants. Similarly, when the error detection rate is unusually low, then either the design is very good or the walk-through group didn't do their job.

Error data can be used in other ways [Faga76]. They point out which part of the design is error prone and needs to be improved. Over time, we can learn which errors are commonly made by fitting a distribution to the error types. This lends guidance to the error finding process. We can target the most common and most critical ones.

A walk-through should never be a basis for staff appraisal. If the authors of a design are evaluated by the amount of errors they made in their design, the participants will be faced with a dilemma. They must find errors (some) to satisfy the work requirement but can't embarrass the designer. This can kill the spirit and the effectiveness of a walk-through and transform it into a congratulation society.

Problems and Questions

1.   Take the design for PAS or TAP. Assume you have gotten it in the mail to prepare for a walk-through. Assume each role of the walk-through group except moderator and secretary. For each of these roles

   ▶   What do you do to prepare for the walkthrough?

   ▶   what errors did you find?

   ▶   what methods and test data did you use?

2.   Organize and perform a walk-through of the design of a project (part) with you as the moderator and participants that may come from your class or your project. What was difficult? What was easy? Why? What would you do differently next time?

3.   You try to organize a walk-through of TAP. The agenda should emphasize most critical issues first. What would your agenda look like?

8.6.3. Design Rationalization

Design rationalization is a technique suggested in [Free75] to increase the understandability, maintainability, and adaptability of a design. As design problems are solved they are broken down into smaller subproblems. Each subproblem usually has a variety of solutions, and each serious alternative needs to be evaluated. Design rationalization is the reasoning that led to the selection of a particular alternative, and it is left as part of the design documentation. This shows anybody who evaluates or for other reasons (implementation, redesign, maintenance, extension, adaptation, etc.) needs to work with the design, why certain decisions were made. The reviewers on a walk-through are now not only able to evaluate the design, but they also may evaluate the decision-making process behind it. They can see whether all alternatives have been taken into account and whether these were evaluated correctly.

Similar arguments can be made when redesign or maintenance requires a second look at design decisions. Again much time can be saved if the alternatives are still documented. Maybe the situation has changed and other alternatives have become more attractive. If we have documentation, we are already a good ways down the road to redesign.

Of course, documenting design rationalization takes more effort and increases the design document. It is only used when there is a need for it, such as long projected software life with a good deal of anticipated changes. It is possible to only document some of the reasoning behind design decisions, such as the most crucial ones and the ones where evaluation took considerable effort. [Free75] suggests design rationalization only for routine design and not for exploratory or discovery designs. Regardless, it facilitates the job of the people who have to review a design and, thus, is a technique that supports the design validation process.

Problems and Questions

1.   For which of the design decisions for TAP would you document design rationale? Why? Which would you omit? Why?

2.   For which of the design decisions for PAS would you document design rationale? Why? Which would you omit? Why?

8.6.4. Verification

Verification of designs ranges from formal proofs to checking algorithmic behavior against assertions. Assertions describe, in mathematical language, conditions for reasonable states of a system, data structures, and algorithmic behavior. An assertion about a stack might state that at the end of a push operation the stack must be nonempty. For parallel software it can state what valid synchronization states are, such as "only one writer or several readers or none of the above can be active at the same time." When we walk through the design that has been annotated with assertions, they have to be true when manual simulation encounters them. Otherwise, there is an error. Since these methods are formal, they require that the design be stated in formal language. Developing assertions requires thought. We have to think beforehand what valid states are and how to describe them formally with logic conditions. Formal proofs are mathematical reasoning about correctness and often lengthy. Proofs themselves can and do contain errors. Not everybody likes or cares to understand formalisms, and consequently, proofs have not been very popular in practice.

The advantage of proofs is that a design component, once proven correct, is correct, while the best we can say from inspection techniques is that we couldn't find any more errors. There is also some computerized support through theorem provers. Because of the advantages and disadvantages associated with proofs, they should be used under the following circumstances:

▶ the amount of work is not prohibitively large,

▶ expertise exists,

▶ the pay-off is reasonable (i.e., the design component that needs to be proven correct is crucial and complex enough so that the investment in time and skill is justified); and

▶ other, cheaper methods will not do an adequate job.

Let us explain a scenario where formal proof is desirable. Parallel software is highly complex, because in addition to the sequential characteristics of each individual parallel process of a parallel program, synchronization properties like mutual exclusion or absence of deadlock must be inspected. Parallel execution may interleave statements in arbitrary order. On the other hand, computed results depend on the order in which statements were executed. Any test of a design has to consider many possible cases depending on the ordering of statements over time. The combinatorial explosion of all possible execution sequences is often prohibitive for testing. Moreover, testing may not uncover all the errors, because special interactions in which errors would become apparent may not occur during the manual walk-through of the code.

An understandable formal method to prove desired synchronization properties of designs for parallel software seems to be more appropriate than inspection methods. A number of approaches exist. Some are for programs ([Owic75], [Owic76A]_[Owic76C], [Lipt75]), and others can be used to verify designs. Parallel programs and some design aspects that use the monitor concept can be proven with [Howa76] and [Owic77]. They all require expertise in formal methods and can be rather tedious. Therefore we describe a method [Amsc78], which is easier to use, concentrates exclusively on synchronization aspects, and proves synchronization properties for designs written using path expressions (6.3.3).

We will show how to derive assertions about path expressions and then how to prove sychronization properties for them using a few simple theorems. The assertion at the heart of this technique is called the monitor invariant (we assume that path expressions are developed for use within monitors). It describes, in terms of the function names mentioned in the path expression, all reasonable and possible states of the design component. For each function **F** in a path expression, three counters are needed to describe

▶   the number of requested calls for F: $r(F)$,

▶   the number of active instances of F: $a(F)$, and

▶   the number of finished executions of F: $e(F)$.

As an example, if there are five not yet granted requests for the procedure **WRITE**, one running instance of **WRITE**, and three fully executed **WRITE**s at one time, the values of these counters are

$$r(WRITE) = 5; \; a(WRITE) = 1; \; e(WRITE) = 3;$$

For the operators in a path expression the following invariants describe the characteristics of the monitor design at different points in time during its execution. For now **A** and **B** denote function names, later they can be factors or expressions.

1. Sequence operator: ";"
For a path of the form *path* **A ; B end**, the following hold:

1.1. $e(A) \geq e(B)$
1.2. $e(B) \leq e(A) \leq e(B) + 1$
1.3. $a(A) = 1 \Rightarrow a(B) = 0 \;\&\; a(B) = 1 \Rightarrow a(A) = 0$
1.4. $a(A) \leq 1 \;\&\; a(B) \leq 1$

Condition 1.1 states that at least as many A have been executed as B. This condition alone is not sufficient to describe the path expression fully. 1.2 states that, at any instant in time, the number of executed A must never exceed the number of executed B by more than one. A B must be executed before the next execution of A is allowed to start. 1.2 includes 1.1. Formula 1.3 asserts that A and B must not run in parallel. 1.4 ensures that only one instance of A or B may be active at any time.

2. Selection operator "+"

For a path expression of the form **path A + B end**, the following hold:

$$2.1.\ a(A) = 1 \Rightarrow a(B) = 0\ \&\ a(B) = 1 \Rightarrow a(A) = 0$$
$$2.2.\ a(A) \leq 1\ \&\ a(B) \leq 1$$

which merely states that A and B have to exclude each other in time and may not be executed in parallel.

3. Parallel execution   "{ }"

For a path expression of the form *path {A} end*, the following hold:

$$3.1.\ a(A) \geq 0.$$

This states that parallel execution of A is permitted. A stronger condition is

$$3.2.\ a(A) > 0 \Rightarrow r(A) = 0.$$

As long as there are uncompleted executions of A, other calls to A may be granted at once. This is part of the characteristic of { }. On the other hand, if there are unfulfilled requests for A, then no instances of A can be currently executing or else the requests could be fulfilled instantaneously. Another function F different from A must be active and prevent A from executing. This leads to the assertion

$$3.3.\ r(A) > 0 \Rightarrow (a(A) = 0\ \&\ (\exists\ F)\ [a(F) > 0\ \&\ \neg(F = A)]).$$

4. Kleene star "*"

For a path expression of the form **path A ; B* end**, the following hold:

$$4.1.\ a(A) = 1 \Rightarrow a(B) = 0\ \&\ a(B) = 1 \Rightarrow a(A) = 0$$
$$4.2.\ a(A) \leq 1\ \&\ a(B) \leq 1$$

An arbitrary number of B can be executed between two subsequent executions of A, but A and B must not be executed in parallel. Note that in 4.2 $a(B) \leq 1$, because the Kleene star permits only one instance of B active at a time (but an arbitrary number of B can be executed sequentially.)

5. Conditional

For a path expression of the form **path [n>k : A, B] end**, the following hold:

$$5.1.\ (n > k) \Rightarrow (\ r(A) = 0\ or\ a(A) = 1)$$
$$5.2.\ (n \le k) \Rightarrow (\ r(B) = 0\ or\ a(B) = 1)$$

Because A and B are allowed to change the values of n and k, a fourth variable needs to be introduced to specify where in the execution of the path expression the system is at the moment:

$$f = \begin{cases} \textit{1 if execution is at the beginning of the path before the conditional (or after it)} \\ \\ \textit{0 otherwise} \end{cases}$$

This allows the stronger assertion

$$5.1'\ ((n > k)\ \&\ f = 1) \Rightarrow (r(A) = 0\ or\ a(A) = 1)\ \&\ a(B) = 0$$
$$5.2'\ ((n \le k)\ \&\ f = 1) \Rightarrow (r(B) = 0\ or\ a(B) = 1)\ \&\ a(A) = 0$$

If the execution is inside the conditional ($f = 0$), then in general, no statement can be made, because either A or B may be executing and may or may not have changed the values of n and k.

6. Path concatenation

The path expression has the following form **path P_1 & P_2 end**, where P_1 and P_2 are expressions for paths. An assertion for the concatenated path expression is constructed by using the assertions $I(P_1)$ and $I(P_2)$, which have been derived according to any of the above rules. A new variable is introduced to indicate which of the two subexpressions is currently being executed.

$$f(P) = \begin{cases} \text{1 if } P_1 \text{ is executing} \\ \text{2 if } P_2 \text{ is executing} \\ \text{0 if neither } P_1 \text{ nor } P_2 \text{ are executing} \end{cases}$$

At the beginning (end) of the path expression both $I(P_1)$ and $I(P_2)$ have to hold. The invariant assertion for the concatenated path is

$$I(P) = ((f(P) = 0) \Rightarrow I(P_1)\ \&\ I(P_2))\ \&\ ((f(P) = 1) \Rightarrow I(P_1))\ \&$$
$$((f(P) = 2) \Rightarrow I(P_2))$$

7. Parentheses "( )"

This operator forms a factor that may be used within a path expression as a regular function name. The assertion for the expression in parentheses is derived in two stages. First the parenthesized expression is substituted by a unique new name F (without loss of generality, F does not occur as a function name). For the resulting path expression an assertion is derived according to the above rules.

Example

path A + (B;C) end is substituted by **path A + F end**. This yields the assertion

$$a(A) = 1 \Rightarrow a(F) = 0 \ \& \ a(F) = 1 \Rightarrow a(A) = 0 \ \& \ a(A) \leq 1 \ \& \ a(F) \leq 1.$$

The next step derives an assertion for $\mathbf{a(F)} = 0$ (i.e., one instance of F is active) and $a(F) = 0$ (i.e., one instance of F is active). Inactivity of F means that no functions in the subexpression are allowed to be active and that the execution of the subexpression has not yet completed B. So the first deduction is

$$a(F) = 0 \Leftrightarrow a(B) = 0 \ \& \ e(B) = e(C).$$

Likewise, activity of F means that either B or C is active or that the execution of the subexpression F has just completed an execution of B and not yet started an execution of C:

$$a(F) = 1 \Leftrightarrow (a(B) = 1 \text{ or } a(C) = 1 \text{ or } e(B) = e(C)+1).$$

The subexpression $(B;C)$ renders the second part of the assertion (rule 2):

$$I(B;C) = e(C) \leq e(B) \leq e(C) + 1 \ \& \ a(B) = 1 \Rightarrow a(C) = 0 \ \& \ a(C) = 1 \Rightarrow a(B) = 0 \ \& \ a(B) \leq 1 \\ \& \ a(C) \leq 1.$$

The assertion for the sample path expression then reads

$$a(A) = 1 \Rightarrow (a(B) = 0 \ \& \ a(C) = 0 \ \& \ e(B) = e(C)) \ \& \ (a(B) = 1 \text{ or } a(C) = 1 \text{ or } \\ e(B) = e(B)+1) \Rightarrow a(A) = 0 \ \& \ a(A) \leq 1 \ \& \ I(B;C).$$

These deduction rules apply only if the function names in the path are all different. When function names appear in different places, deriving an assertion for the path expression is more complex. We need to introduce auxiliary variables to keep track of the current state in the execution of the path expression and of the history of previous executions. Sometimes this is possible by splitting up the variables that control the number of active (a) fully executed (e) and required (r) executions of a function that occurs more than once in the program: for each of the m occurrences of a function F in the path expression, counters $a(F_i)$, $e(F_i)$, $r(F_i)$ ($i = 1, \ldots, m$) are introduced (m new function names). The sum of $a(F_i)$, $e(F_i)$, and $r(F_i)$ has to add up to $a(F)$, $e(F)$, $r(F)$.

Example

$$path \ (A \ ; \ B) + (A \ ; \ C) \ end$$

has the following counters for multiple occurrences of A: $a(A_1), e(A_1), r(A_1), a(A_2), e(A_2)$ $r(A_2).A_1$ refers to A in the first subexpression and A_2 refers to A in the second subexpression. $a(A)$, $e(A)$, and $r(A)$ are as follows:

$$a(A) = a(A_1) + a(A_2); \ e(A) = e(A_1) + e(A_2); \ r(A) = r(A_1) + r(A_2).$$

We derive the path expression invariant by substitution:

$$S_1 = (A;B) \ and \ S_2 = (A;C).$$

The new path reads **path S_1 + S_2 end**. From the selection rule we get

$$I(P_1) = a(S_1) = 1 \Rightarrow a(S_2) = 0 \ \& \ a(S_2) = 1 \Rightarrow a(S_1) = 0 \ \& \ a(S_1) \le 1$$
$$\& \ a(S_2) \le 1.$$

For the subexpression S_1 the sequence rule yields

$$I(S_1) = (e(B) \le e(A_1) \le e(B) + 1) \ \& \ a(A_1) = 1 \Rightarrow a(B) = 0 \ \&$$
$$a(B) = 1 \Rightarrow a(A_1) = 0 \ \& \ a(A_1) \le 1 \ \& \ a(B) \le 1.$$

This invariant can be stated even more strongly. Because only one instance of the functions mentioned in the path expressions can be active, $a(A) <= 1$, and because $a(A) <= 1$ implies $a(A_1)$, we can replace all occurrences of $a(A_1)$ except the first one by $a(A)$. $I(S_2)$ is analogous to $I(S_1)$, with A_2 and C substituted for A_1 and B. The next step is to determine assertions for $a(S_1) = 0$, $a(S_1) = 1$, $a(S_2) = 0$, and $a(S_2) = 1$ in terms of the subexpression. This is done the same way as in the previous example.

$$a(S_1) = 1 <=> one(S_1) := (a(A_1) = 1 \ or \ a(B) = 1 \ or \ e(A_1) = e(B) + 1)$$
$$a(S_1) = 0 <=> zero(S_2):= (a(A_1) = 0 \ \& \ a(B) = 1 \ \& \ e(A_1) = e(B))$$

$one(S_2)$ and $zero(S_2)$ are analogous to $one(S_1)$ and $zero(S_1)$ with A_2 and C substituted for A_1 and B. The invariant assertion for $P =$ **path (A ; B) + (A ; C) end** then reads as follows:

$$I(P) = (one(S_1) \Rightarrow zero(S_2)) \ \& \ (one(S_2) \Rightarrow zero(S_1)) \ \&$$
$$a(A) \le 1 \ \& \ a(B) \le 1 \ \& \ a(C) \le 1 \ \& \ I(S_1) \ \& \ I(S_2) \ \&$$
$$a(A) = a(A_1) + a(A_2) \ \& \ e(A) = e(A_1) + e(A_2) \ \&$$
$$r(A) = r(A_1) + r(A_2)$$

While this appears to be a rather long expression, it is usually possible to simplify. These expressions state conditions that hold for the execution of path expressions and thus describe possible states of execution for the monitors that contain these path expressions. We will use them to prove synchronization properties about designs written with path expressions.

Example

Cars coming from the north and south must pass a bridge across a river. The bridge has only one lane, which means that cars from only one direction at a time can pass the bridge. It is supposed that these cars, though crossing the bridge simultaneously, drive one after another on the bridge or else the one lane requirement would not be modeled correctly. The monitor that controls access to the bridge reads as follows:

monitor: bridge
path {cross_north} + {cross_south} *end*
procedure: cross_north

    .
    .
    .

end cross_north;

procedure cross_south

    .
    .
    .

end cross_south;

⟨other parts of the monitor⟩
end monitor

Every process of type **car** that wants to cross the bridge must issue a call **bridge.cross_north** or **bridge.cross_south**. The deduction of the monitor invariant proceeds as follows:

1. **Substitution**.

$$S_1 = \{cross\_north\}$$
$$S_2 = \{cross\_south\}$$
$$P' = \text{path } S_1 + S_2 \text{ end}$$

An invariant for this type of path expression was developed before. It reads

$$I(P') = a(S_1) = 1 \Rightarrow a(S_2) = 0 \ \& \ a(S_2) = 1 \Rightarrow a(S_1) = 0 \ \&$$
$$a(S_1) \leq 1 \ \& \ a(S_2) \leq 1$$

2. **Determination of activity for the two subexpressions.**
S_1 is active as long as there are cars on the bridge crossing northwards. More formally, S_1 is active as long as {**cross_north**} is being executed. This is the case if there is at least one incomplete instance of **cross_north**. S_1 is active if **a(cross_north)>0**. Thus

$$one(S_1) = a(cross\_north) > 0$$
$$one(S_2) = a(cross\_south) > 0$$

S_1 is not active as long as there are no instances of **cross_north** executing. Thus

$$zero(S_1) = a(cross\_north) = 0$$
$$zero(S_2) = a(cross\_south) = 0$$

3. **Invariants for the two subexpressions.**
From the parallel execution rule the following invariant is derived:

$$I(S_1) = a(cross\_north) > 0 \Rightarrow r(cross\_north) = 0 \ \&$$
$$r(cross\_north) > 0 \Rightarrow (a(cross\_north) = 0 \ \&$$
$$\Rightarrow (\ \exists\ F)[a(F) > 0 \ \& \ \neg(F = cross\_north)]$$

$I(S_2)$ is analogous to $I(S_1)$ with **cross_south** substituted for **cross_north**.

4. **Determination of the condition that no more than one subexpression can be active at any time.**
The invariants **I(S_1)** and **I(S_2)** do not bound the number of **cross_north** and **cross_south** which can be active. An arbitrary number of active **cross_north** or **cross_south** times one is still arbitrary. Therefore this condition can be dropped altogether.

5. **Complete invariant for the original path expression.**

$$I(P) = one(S_1) => zero(S_2) \ \& \ one(S_2) => zero(S_1) \ \&$$
$$I(S_1) \ \& \ I(S_2)$$

After substituting the formulae into this expression, the invariant reads:

$$I(P) = [a(cross\_north) > 0 \Rightarrow a(cross\_south) = 0 \ \& \ r(cross\_north) = 0] \ \&$$
$$[a(cross\_south) > 0 \Rightarrow (a(cross\_north) = 0 \ \& \ r(cross\_south) = 0)] \ \&$$
$$r(cross\_north) > 0 \Rightarrow (a(cross\_north) = 0 \ \&$$
$$(exist\ F)[a(F) > 0 \ \& \ not(F=cross\_north)]) \ \&$$
$$r(cross\_south) > 0 \Rightarrow (a(cross\_south) = 0 \ \&$$
$$(exist\ F)[a(F) > 0 \ \& \ not(F=cross\_south)])$$

We can remove the existential quantifier, because there is only one possible function F to substituted. The invariant can then be used to prove properties of programs calling the procedures **cross_north** and **cross_south**. This path expression does not prevent starvation (a request is delayed indefinitely without apparent deadlock), because there is no constraint for the time or the number of cars that may pass in one direction before directions are switched. Cars from one direction may pass over the bridge all the time while the other direction is blocked. For this to happen one new car must arrive at the bridge and start crossing while another is already on the bridge.

These invariant conditions are used to prove properties about path expression designs. The theorems are adaptations of mutual exclusion and deadlock theorems originally developed by Owicki et al. ([Owic75], [Owic76A]_[Owic76C]) for programs written in an ALGOL-like language.

8.6.4.1. Mutual Exclusion

Mutual exclusion must be proven for objects shared by parallel processes if these objects require exclusive usage. All shared objects and any access to them are controlled by the monitor. Therefore only calls to the monitor procedures in the parallel processes have to be checked.

a)   Let S_1 be a call for a monitor procedure F_1 and S_2 be a call for monitor procedure F_2 made by two different parallel processes. To prove mutual exclusion of the calls to the monitor, it has to be shown that simultaneous execution of F_1 and F_2 are impossible. An active execution of F_1 (F_2) is denoted by $a(F_1) > 0$ ($a(F_2) > 0$). The legitimate states of the monitor R are described in its invariant $I(R)$, which is derived through the path expression rules defined earlier. Thus if

$$a(F_1) > 0 \ \& \ a(F_1) > 0 \ \& \ I(R) \ => \ FALSE,$$

F_1 and F_2 exclude each other.

b)   This result can be generalized. Let FP be a monitor procedure call in process P. Let Q be another process parallel to P. If, for all calls FQ to monitor R in Q,

$$a(FP) > 0 \ \& \ a(FQ) > 0 \ \& \ I(R) \ => \ FALSE,$$

then FP and Q are mutually exclusive.

c)   Finally, let P, Q be two parallel processes within a program. If for all calls FP to monitor R in P, FP and Q exclude each other (cf. b), then the processes P and Q are mutually exclusive with respect to monitor R.

Example

In the bridge problem it has to be shown that a call **cross_south** issued by a process of type **southern_car** and a call **cross_north** issued by a process of type **northern_car** exclude each other. The first theorem (a) yields

$$a(cross\_south) > 0 \ \& \ a(cross\_north) > 0 \ \& \ I(bridge) => FALSE.$$

After substituting the invariant for the monitor **bridge**, the left side of the implication arrow gives us

$$
\begin{aligned}
&a(cross\_south) > 0 \ \& \ a(cross\_north) > 0 \ \& \\
&a(cross\_north) > 0 \Rightarrow \quad (a(cross\_south) = 0 \ \& \ r(cross\_north) = 0) \ \& \\
&a(cross\_south) > 0 \Rightarrow \quad (a(cross\_north) = 0 \ \& \ r(cross\_south) = 0) \ \& \\
&r(cross\_north) > 0 \Rightarrow \quad (a(cross\_north) = 0 \ \& \\
&\qquad\qquad\qquad\qquad\qquad (\ni F) [\ a(F) > 0 \ \& \ \neg (F = cross\_north)]) \\
&r(cross\_south) > 0 \Rightarrow \quad (a(cross\_south) = 0 \ \& \\
&\qquad\qquad\qquad\qquad\qquad (\ni F) [\ a(F) > 0 \ \& \ \neg (F = cross\_south)])
\end{aligned}
$$

This simplifies to

$$a(cross\_south) = 0 \ \& \ a(cross\_north) = 0 \ \& \ a(cross\_south) > 0 \ \& \ a(cross\_north) > 0,$$

which is obviously FALSE.

This verifies that **cross_north** and **cross_south** exclude each other. Since both **cross_north** and **cross_south** are the only calls for procedures controlled by monitor **bridge, southern_car** and **northern_car** processes are mutually exclusive with respect to monitor **bridge**.

8.6.4.2. Deadlock

Let $P_1, \ldots, P_n$ be n parallel processes sharing monitor R. Let $I(R)$ be the monitor invariant. Let $\{F_{kj} \mid j=1, \ldots, n_k\}$ be the calls of procedures controlled by monitor S_k. Let D_1 be the following predicate:

$$D_1 = (forall \ k = 1, \ldots, n) \ [\ post(P_k) \ or \ (\ni j)[r(F_{kj}) > 0]].$$

D_1 defines the possible synchronization states of the program: any process P_k is either finished, which means that its postcondition $post(P_k)$ holds (a postcondition describes with a logical expression the finishing state of the program in terms of values for its variables and states) or that there is a call for a monitor procedure, which prevents P_k from continuing its execution. In this case an execution of a monitor procedure has been requested. One possible postcondition for process P_k is that none of its monitor procedure calls is currently executing:

$$(\forall \, j = 1, \ldots, n_k) \; [a(F_{kj}) = 0].$$

If the number of executions for one or more of the monitor procedures is known, say procedure F_{kj} is executed t_j times, then

$$(\forall \, j, j = 1, \ldots, n_k) \; [a(F_{kj}) = 0]$$

will also hold at the end of process P_k. Thus

$$post(P_k) = (\forall \, j, j = 1, \ldots, n_k)[a(F_{kj}) = 0] \; \& \; e(F_{kj}) = t_j].$$

If the number of possible executions of function F_{kj} is not known, the statement $e(F_{kj}) = t_j$ is omitted. Let D_2 be the following predicate:

$$D_2 = (\exists \, k) \, (\exists \, j) \; [r(F_{kj}) > 0].$$

D_2 states that there is actually a waiting process. Then if

$$(D_1 \; \& \; D_2 \; \& \; I(R)) \Rightarrow FALSE,$$

$P_1, \ldots, P_n$ cannot be deadlocked with respect to monitor R, if the execution of program P started in a legitimate state (i.e., the initial assertion is true). Note that this modified deadlock theorem needs only information about the synchronization (i.e., assertions about active, requested, or executed function calls). And it only states absence from deadlock with respect to the monitor R whose path expressions are investigated.

Example

For the bridge problem the following assertions are determined:

a) **post(southern_car)** = **a(cross_south)** = **0**
   The statement about the number of executed **cross_south** is missing, because it is not known how many times the function **cross_south** is executed.
   Similarly, **post(northern_car)** = (**a(cross_north)** = **0**).

b) D_1 = [a(cross_south) = 0 or r(cross_south) > 0] &
        [a(cross_north) = 0 or r(cross_north) > 0] &

c) D_2 = [r(cross_south) > 0 or r(cross_north) > 0]

d) **I(bridge)** is the same as above.

Thus,

D_1 & D_2 & I (bridge) =
    a(cross_north) = 0 & a(cross_south) = 0 &
    [a(cross_north) = 0 & a(cross_south) > 0 or
    a(cross_south) =   & a(cross_north) > 0] ⇒ FALSE

This means that no deadlock occurs, in the sense that the program as a whole is blocked. It does not ensure termination, however.

8.6.4.3. Termination

Termination can be proven through the following adaptation of the termination theorem in [Owic75]. A process P terminates conditionally with respect to R if it can be proven to terminate under the assumption that it cannot be deadlocked with respect to a monitor R. Let T be a parallel program whose parallel processes access a monitor R. If T is not deadlocked with respect to monitor R and if each of its parallel processes terminates conditionally with respect to R, then T terminates with respect to R. The program T terminates if it terminates with respect to all monitors in the program.

In the bridge problem freedom from deadlock for **southern_car** and **northern_car** processes has been proven above. As mentioned before, the starvation problem occurs when there are northern cars crossing the bridge endlessly, and in consequence, southern cars never get their turn (or vice versa). Endlessly means failure to terminate the creation of **car** processes going in an active direction. The solution for the bridge problem is free from starvation (and the program terminates with respect to monitor **bridge**) if that part of the program that sends cars to one side of the bridge terminates, at least long enough so that the switch can be made.

Path expressions focus on the flow of control and on the synchronization rather than on the assignment of values to variables that are used to implement a desired synchronization structure. The invariants derived from the path expressions are a formal statement of conditions that cause the occurrence of events like procedure calls. Combined with the theorems for mutual exclusion and freedom from deadlock, they provide useful reasoning tools to ascertain required synchronization properties of a design. We have stated the method and the parts of proofs as gently as possible without taking away from their logic. What distinguishes this verification technique from others for parallel software is that it explicitly separates the parallel from the sequential aspects of the design and concentrates on the parallel aspects. After proving synchronization properties of a design, we can use manual walk-through techniques for the sequential parts.

This type of decomposition is supported very nicely by designing around monitors, because all synchronization procedures are gathered in one place in the program. We will later discuss how to develop a program from the design construct path expressions and how to build an automated tool to support this development process. As pointed out in the beginning, verification is usually a costlier process than other phase-testing methods. But that is not always true, as this little excursion into formal procedures shows. Often we can simplify matters through a "divide and conquer" approach for testing procedures, not just for the design construction. Specialization paid off, giving us a relatively simple method.

Problems and Questions

1.   Determine the proper path expression for the message and port monitor in Section 6.2.4. (Figure 6.5). Use it in an example that has several ports and processes. Determine whether deadlock around ports can occur and whether mutual exclusion for reading and writing messages is preserved.

2.   Develop invariants for the following path expressions:

> path (A + B) ; C ; {R} end
> path [n = 1: A, n = 2: B, C] ; (D + A); B* end

8.7. Summary

This chapter concludes the three chapters on software and program design. It explained methods for program and detailed design and how to measure design quality. Design must ensure that quality requirements are met. Section 8.4. discussed techniques that support various quality areas. As the last of the design chapters, it also discussed the contents of the design documents, as a proposal and as a base-lined document. A phase test of design documentation assures quality of the design.

The two methods for detailed design are STS analysis and stepwise refinement. We introduced organization diagrams to describe structure. Organization diagrams hold more information than structure charts or base-line diagrams. Interface tables describe parameters, data access, and calling patterns. We have combined STS with these diagramming and tabulating methods to better illustrate results and to enhance readability. STS also benefits from the information provided by data-flow diagrams, because it is also a data-oriented technique. When structuring decisions are made, it is beneficial to keep the concept of abstract data-types in mind. Modules can be grouped around a data object.

Together with the methods from Chapter 7, STS and stepwise refinement cover a spectrum of design methods, ranging from function oriented to data oriented. The list of design methods include STS analysis, stepwise refinement, object-oriented design, and data-flow diagrams.

Methods that have not been discussed include JSD or Jackson Structured Design [Jack83], Warnier-Orr [Orr77], Yourdon's Structured Design [Your79B], and Transactional Analysis [Zieg83]. Transactional analysis is essentially the same as STS analysis. Yourdon's structured design and JSD are related to functional requirements diagrams and data-flow diagrams. Warnier-Orr was explained as a method to describe functional requirements of a system in chapter 3. We pointed out then that it can also be used to structure functions and data during design. Nassi-Shneiderman Charts ([Nass73]) are an alternate to PDL and Warnier-Orr notation. They must, however, be combined with a design strategy, because they are notations, not techniques.

The reader who is interested in a comprehensive book on design should consult the IEEE Computer Society Press *Tutorial on Software Design Techniques* ([Free83]). Other books on design include [Zieg83], [Gilb83], [Jack83], and [Booc83].

Section 8.3. introduced measures for structural quality of designs. They measure module strength and module coupling through a simple rating scale. These measures can be used to identify modules with high interface complexity and low functional cohesiveness as candidates for improvement. Sometimes these measures serve to highlight modules that will require more attention during coding and testing because of their low scores. These measures can also be used to set standards. Other metrics that could be used to measure design quality are given in [Cont86].

Section 8.4. surveyed design approaches to achieve quality requirements in areas such as reliability, performance, security, maintainability, etc. Such requirements affect the choice of algorithms and data structures as well as the overall structuring approach. Section 8.4. also discussed necessary trade-offs between quality areas. Some quality areas are specialties in their own right, e.g., performance and security, but it is beyond the scope of this book to provide more than an overview of important issues in these areas. The interested reader was referred to relevant literature in these areas for more detail.

Section 8.5. discussed design documentation. A design document is a growing entity; often a variety of different options are possible when decisions need to be made. Because of this, the first version of the design document usually is a proposal, and the style should reflect that. We should structure the design document so that it can evolve easily. Design alternatives should be mentioned with a rationale why or in which respects one alternative is superior to another. During the working stages of the design, a loose-leaf binder is appropriate to accommodate changes and additions easily.

The base-lined document has different needs. We discussed a possible outline for it (cf. Table 8.7.). Specific documents vary depending on the design techniques used and the notation. At a minimum, the design document describes system architecture, module design, data object design, and how quality expectations are met.

Section 8.6. discussed three methods for validation and verification of designs, the design walk-through, design rationalization, and design verification for designs using path expressions. Walk-throughs have been accepted as a valuable tool to catch errors early and cost-effectively. They are not without risks, however. Unprepared participants, personality clashes, and design on the fly are some of the problems that can make walk-throughs ineffective. Giving walk-throughs formal structure aims at preventing such problems. [Free82] offers a comprehensive handbook on walk-throughs that should answer just about every question one might have.

Design rationalization, another validation technique, increases the understandability, maintainability, and adaptability of a design and thus makes it easier to validate. Design rationalization documents the reasoning that led to the selection of a particular alternative. This shows anybody who evaluates or for other reasons (implementation, redesign, maintenance, extension, adaptation, etc.) needs to work with the design, not just that certain decisions were made but why. The reviewers can assess whether the reasons for a design are valid. They see whether all alternatives have been taken into account and how these were evaluated.

These advantages of documenting design rationalization do not come easily. It takes more effort and increases the design document and therefore should only be used when there is a need for it. Long projected software life with a good deal of anticipated changes can constitute such a need. Design rationalization facilitates design review and thus is a technique that supports the design validation process.

Section 8.6.4. described a verification method for path expressions to illustrate the concept of verification. It is based on [Amsc78] and is easier to use than [Owic77] and [Howa76] because it concentrates exclusively on synchronization aspects. It proves synchronization properties for designs using the path expression notation. We used a few simple theorems about the monitor invariant.

Formal proofs are often lengthy and require lots of work, not the least of which is to express the design in mathematically provable terms. Proofs themselves can and do contain errors. Not everybody likes or cares to understand formalisms, and consequently, proofs have not been all too popular in practice.

The advantage of proofs is of course, that a design component, once proven correct, is correct, while the best we can say from inspection techniques is that we couldn't find any more errors. There is also some computerized support through theorem provers. On the other hand, proofs can be tedious, and require knowledge of the proof process, designs must be stated in provable language, making proofs often expensive.

The verification method we presented is a compromise to keep the need for tedium and formality to a minimum. We did this at the expense of proving comprehensive properties of the design. This verification technique explicitly separates sequential and concurrent aspects of a design and concentrates on the concurrent aspects only. The pay-off is a simpler verification procedure.

▶ 9

Coding

9.1. Overview

The main activity of the coding phase is to translate design into code. We have tried up to now to structure our work products so that they facilitate understanding, and we have tried to blueprint a well thought out solution with good inherent structure. If we translate this structured design properly, we will have a structured program. Structured programming has been a buzzword for over a decade and many articles and books have described "structured code." It is surely more than the absence of GOTOs. A structured program doesn't just "happen." It is the end product of a series of efforts that try to understand the problem and develop a structured, understandable solution plan, i.e., the design. It is all but impossible to write a good structured program based on an unstructured, poor design. So the minimum premise for a well structured program is a well structured design that was developed through the structured techniques from the previous chapters.

This chapter is organized around the steps in which code is developed. The next section (9.2.) presents principles of design-to-code translation. These include guidelines for writing code that is simple, readable, well documented, changeable, and predictable. It should show consistent handling of input and output, preserve module independence, and emphasize good structure. These are the major qualities that make code testable and maintainable.

Section 9.3. concentrates on programming style and standards, documentation, and how to write structured code, even in an unstructured language. Examples present a variety of languages from old ones, such as FORTRAN, to newer, modern ones, such as MODULA-2. The reader who is not familiar with some of the high level languages in the examples should nevertheless be able to understand the code examples, as long as he or she has been exposed to at least one modern high level language like PL/1, PASCAL, MODULA-2, ADA, ALGOL, etc. In the interest of European readers some examples are written in SIMULA67, an ALGOL-like language.

Section 9.4. deals with quality issues. We concentrate on two important quality aspects, reliability and performance. The section on reliability presents error-prone coding practices and shows how to avoid them or improve the code. It also explains useful reliability techniques. Section 9.4. is important because it helps the reader to build reliability and performance into their code and illustrates the necessary trade-offs between performance, reliability, and other code qualities.

The section on performance highlights the impact of data structures and algorithm selection on performance, and it explains what types of trade-offs can be made. Examples include stacks, trees, and recursive functions. Instruction types that cost time are discussed.

Section 9.5. addresses methods to improve code. Code improvement has two major objectives: better clarity and structure and improved performance. The first can prolong the life of software, and coding practices to achieve better performance may be indispensable to meet requirements.

Section 9.6. deals with code walk-throughs, the major phase-testing technique for the coding phase. This assures quality of the code that can then undergo testing.

Sometimes detailed design, coding, and unit testing is done by the same person. Sometimes coding is one person's sole responsibility. Testing is done by a separate test group while designers provide the coders with detailed design specifications. The range of responsibilities varies as much with the expertise of the coder as it does with development philosophy and organizational structure. We will discuss the latter in the chapter on personnel issues. Testing may be separated from coding because it is felt that implementors cannot test their own programs; they have tunnel vision (cognitive dissonance, [Wein71]). Knowledge and expertise vary with the extent of the job description.

Somebody whose job responsibility is coding must be able to interpret design into structured code. He must be able to assess reliability and performance impact of coding choices and perform trade-offs. This requires knowledge of data structures and algorithms, not just in what they do but what their performance characteristics are. He must know coding standards and the implementation language. He must know techniques for improving code without compromising readability.

While most readers have been exposed to at least part of the material in this chapter, it is presented as a refresher and to emphasize its importance. The chapter is kept short and serves as a review of coding issues—it does not intend to teach the reader how to code. Rather, we explain how and why standards and rules are developed. We hope that readers will be inspired to develop some of their own based on their individual needs. The reader will know basic rules for writing reliable code and how to assess performance trade-offs when coding. He will be familiar with several methods to improve clarity, structure, and performance of code. He will also know how to organize and participate in code walk-throughs.

9.2. From Design to Code

Structured coding practices translate a structured design into well structured code. PDL statements come in four different categories: sequence, selection (**IF-THEN-ELSE, CASE**), iteration (**WHILE, REPEAT-UNTIL, FOR**), and parallelism. Data statements included structure definitions and monitors. Programming languages may have special purpose statements: pattern matching in SNOBOL; process creation and generation of variates for some probability distributions in simulation languages such as SIMULA67; and creating, appending, or querying a database file in DBase (Reg. Trademark). Even special purpose languages have at least the first three types of statements.

The goal of the coding effort is to translate the design into a set of Single-Entry-Single-Exit (SESE) modules. We can explain this by representing a program as a directed graph where every statement is a node and possible transfers of control between statements is indicated through arcs between nodes. Such a control flow graph shows one input arc, one output arc and for all nodes in the graph a path starts at the input arc, goes to the output arc, and passes through that node.

PDL design modules are SESE modules if the design is well structured. We translate them into code using the following algorithm:

```
⟨design unit is single function node⟩
WHILE ⟨more PDL⟩ DO
        ⟨replace PDL statement by SESE code module⟩
END WHILE
```

A structured program shows the following basic characteristics.

1.   Control flow is constructed from three types of constructs:

   ▶ sequence,

   ▶ selection (**IF** statement, **CASE** statement in PASCAL), and

▶   interation (**WHILE, REPEAT-UNTIL, FOR** loops in PASCAL).

2.   **GOTO**s are rare. However, in languages like FORTRAN, there is often no way to get around them, because they are used to implement a higher-level construct such as a **CASE** statement. **GOTO**s that branch backwards are to be minimized. They reduce readability and understandability, often to the point that code becomes nearly unintelligible ("spaghetti bowl" programs). Therefore, if **GOTO**s need to be used, use them to branch forward not backward. Exceptions are general **WHILE** and **REPEAT-UNTIL** loops.

3.   SESE modules exist. Multiple entry points (PL/1 is one of the languages which provides that) or exit points are not allowed. When a situation "looks" as if it needs this, the coder should try to decompose it into two single entry routines, use a control parameter with a case statement for a single entry, or consolidate exits into one **RETURN** statement.

4.   Judicious exception handling is the norm. During program execution, any of a number of conditions may arise that represent events suspending normal program execution. Examples of such events are end of file, undefined file, overflow and underflow, subscript out of range, attempt to divide by zero, or operations that are attempted with illegal data values or lack of available space in primary or secondary memory (maximum number of pages, alloted disk space, etc.). Good defensive programming practices anticipate possible exceptions and define appropriate actions through an exception handling procedure that executes when an exception is raised. Not all programming languages provide the possibility of user defined exception handlers. Some require the programmer to use exception handlers that are part of the run-time support system. Exception handling can be classified into two categories: those that allow resumption of program execution at the point where the exception is raised after executing the exception handler and those that return control to the calling module after execution of the exception handler. PL/1 is an example of the first type, and ADA is an example of the second.

5.   The solution is readable and looks simple and straightforward. Choose the first obvious algorithm that solves the problem, and keep the data structures simple. If you have to use a more involved algorithm, put its more complex functional aspects into one routine. This way you can change to a simpler one any time and it aids comprehension. Consider for example a hashed table entry and search, instead of a simpler, sequential procedure. In this case, computing the index should be a routine, so that the thoughts on hashing do not clutter up the routine, which needs to have the entry index for the table. Don't use too many levels of pointers; they become hard to understand.

Even a program constructed from these elements is not necessarily a good program, nor need it be readable, efficient, or reliable. We need good programming style. It is also important to use an appropriate programming language. The higher the level of the programming language, the closer to the problem we stay. With a high level language (or a special purpose language) we spend our time problem solving, instead of fighting low level details. This costs time.

Higher level languages eliminate several levels of software, hide machine details, and thus make software more understandable, easier to change, and (depending on the coding style and quality) somewhat self-documenting. This is especially true when design terms are used as comments and names for routines and data structures. Higher level control structures also tend to make code more understandable. When language processors or compilers are available on several machines, high level languages enhance compatibility and portability of programs. Often it is enough to stick to the common subset of a language or to the official language definition. When system calls are allowed, they can be identified and their compatibility or portability is established. That is different from considering vast passages of system dependent code. Even with a structured approach, portability can be treacherous. Consider, for example, "standard" I/O packages that really aren't. Using a high level language does not guarantee portability, but it does help. Higher level languages also allow the programmer to express and manipulate complex data structures that are close to the problem data object.

It is claimed at times that high level languages are not as efficient as lower level ones and that code absolutely must be programmed in machine language to be efficient. This can be true or false, depending on the situation. The major ingredient to an efficient algorithm is to choose an appropriate algorithm and data structures for the problem. If a programmer chooses to implement a bubble sort in machine language to make it faster, he will not have as much success as someone who programs an inherently faster algorithm such as quicksort or heapsort in a higher level language (we assume that the lists are large). Choosing an inherently superior algorithm and data structures is more important than second order efficiencies gained by using machine language. Secondly, we should use an optimizing compiler for a higher level language to gain much of the efficiency using machine language.

Attention to data structures is very important. Coding brings the data abstraction down to the code level, and it can still use abstract data types and information hiding: restrict knowledge of the data structure to one (or few) modules that control access. When anything about that data structure changes, only those modules are altered. This concept of data abstraction on the coding level is at the heart of object-oriented programming, which focuses on code objects and their access functions as opposed to control-oriented programming, which focuses on what to do next. In such programs the control flow is clear, but the effect on data isn't. We use object-oriented programming when objects are crucial (a data-oriented system) and when there are many. We use control-oriented programming when the flow of control is more important and the data objects are relatively few and simple.

Consider an example of an abstract data type in SIMULA67. Such types are called **CLASS**. The format of a class definition is very similar to the PDL for an abstract data-type or a monitor (cf. 6.3.2).

```
CLASS ⟨abstract type⟩
      BEGIN
        ⟨declaration of objects⟩
        PROCEDURE ⟨operation 1⟩ ( ⟨parameters⟩ );
          ⟨body of operation 1⟩
        END;
        PROCEDURE ⟨operation 2⟩ (⟨parameters⟩ );
          ⟨body of operation 2⟩
        END;
          .
          .
          .
        ⟨initialization code for object⟩
      END
```

Figure 9.1 Syntax of **CLASS** Object in SIMULA67.

We define the token that is used for PAS during recursive descent parsing as a class in SIMULA67 (Figure 9.2). This is a type definition. Another operation creates an object of this type. When the object is generated, the initialization code is executed. Operations on the object are done by prefixing the name of the operation with the name of the variable pointing to the object. We still have access to components by prefixing the name of the component with the name of the class variable.

We had to encode token types with integers, because there are no sets in SIMULA67. We achieve flexibility of use for the token class through having the command that refers to the current command line. Comments in SIMULA67 are preceded by the word **COMMENT** and ended with a dollar sign (**$**), a semicolon (;), or a period followed by a comma (. ,). This can become unwieldy for in-line comments.

The usage is as follows:

1. Define the variable that can point to an object of type **tokenclass**.

    REF (tokenclass) tkn;   COMMENT declare token variable$

2. Generate a new object of type **tokenclass**. **tkn** points to it, and the initial values are **NIL** for the token component and **notype** for the **token–type** component.

    tkn :- NEW tokenclass (command);   COMMENT generate an empty token$

3. Perform operations on **token**.

    tkn.get;   COMMENT gets new token$
    tkn.accumulate(chr);   COMMENT add chr to token$

4. Access components of **token**.

    tkn.token   COMMENT refers to text component$
    tkn.token_type   COMMENT indicates type of token$

```
CLASS tokenclass (command); REF (commandclass) command;
  BEGIN
    TEXT token;
    INTEGER token_type; COMMENT encoding of tokentypes:
                              < 0   invalid           7   text (alpha, num,_
                                0   notype            8   numeric
                                1   ANALYSIS          9   parenthesis
                                2   STATS            10   comma
                                3   REPORTS          11   asterisk
                                4   QUIT             12   EOC
                                5   COMPARE        > 12   invalid
                                6   SAVE
                       $
    PROCEDURE get;
      BEGIN
        COMMENT describe how to get token using PDL
                   from Figure 7.12$
      END;
    PROCEDURE accumulate (chr); CHAR chr;
      BEGIN
        COMMENT describe how to accumulate token$
      END;
                                      COMMENT initialize token $
        token :- NIL;                 COMMENT token is empty $
        token_type := 0              COMMENT empty token has no type $
  END_tokenclass;
```

Figure 9.2 The Token as a **CLASS** in SIMULA67.

Another example of a **CLASS** used in PAS is the accumulator. Partial code for it is given in Figure 9.3.

```
CLASS anresult;
   BEGINTEXT prog_id;
         INTEGER dist_optr, dist_opnd, tot_optr, tot_opnd;
                                          COMMENT nonnegative integer$
   END;


CLASS accumulator;
   BEGIN
      REF(anresult) ARRAY accu(1:100);
      INTEGER ptr;                        COMMENT<0 or >100 invalid
                                                  initially 0, points to last
                                                  entry in accu$

      PROCEDURE enter(result) REF(anresult) result;
         BEGIN
           COMMENT body of enter$
         END;


      PROCEDURE comp means(means) REAL ARRAY means(1:4);
         BEGIN
           COMMENT body of compute_means$
         END;


      PROCEDURE comp_var(means, covarmtr) REAL ARRAY means(1:4);
                                          REAL ARRAY covarmtr (1:4,1:4);
         BEGIN
           COMMENT body of compute_variance$
         END;


      COMMENT initialization of accumulator $

      FOR i:=1 STEP 1 UNTIL 100 DO
         accu(i) :- NIL;                  COMMENT initialize accu to nothing$

      ptr := 1;                           COMMENT point to first free entry$
   END accu;
```

Figure 9.3 The Accumulator as a **CLASS** in SIMULA67.

Usage is as follows:

1. Definition and generation of an **accu** data object:

    REF (accumulator) a;   COMMENT accu variable$
    a :- NEW accumulator;   COMMENT a points to new, initialized
                                           accumulator$

2. Access and operations:

    a.accu
    a.ptr
    a.enter(result);
    a.comp_means(m);
    a.comp_covar(m,covarmtr);

SIMULA67 itself does not forbid access to the **ptr** component of the accumulator. We would probably disallow access to it outside of the class as a matter of standard. It prevents uncontrolled changes to the variable and assumptions outside of the class as to what particular **ptr** values mean.

A language that supports abstract data types and modules better than SIMULA67 is MODULA-2 [Wirt83]. It allows the definition of explicit interfaces between modules. A **DEFINITION** module describes what a module looks like to the outside, while an **IMPLEMENTATION** module describes the internals of a module. We describe the structure of Figure 8.3 of the statistics component of PAS in Figures 9.4 to 9.7. What has been defined in the definition module need not be redefined in the implementation module.

The names for the computation routines have not been spelled out; instead, shorter abbreviations are used, because studies have shown that shorter mnemonic names are superior for code comprehension. The optimal length ranges between five and nine characters [Duns85]. Conte et al. [Cont86] surmise that shorter names are probably not

```
MODULE b;                                  (*computation of stats*)
   FROM accumulator IMPORT compmeans, compcovar;
   FROM similarities   IMPORT compsim;
   compmeans;                              (*compute_means*)
   compcovar;                              (*compute_covariance matrix*)
   compsim;                                (*compute similarity indices*)
END b;
```

Figure 9.4 The Statistics Component in MODULA-2.

```
IMPLEMENTATION MODULE similarities;
    FROM accumulator IMPORT covarmtr, ptr, stbase, means;
    PROCEDURE compfm;
    PROCEDURE compsim;
    PROCEDURE compfxlist;
END similarities;
```

Figure 9.5 Module Similarities.

rich enough to help memory and comprehension, while longer names may be hard to re-member exactly. This also seems to indicate that names should be as dissimilar as possible.

The module **similarities** is still rudimentary, because we have not yet coded its indi-vidual functions. Details follow in Section 9.3. to illustrate coding style.

Good programming practices and coding standards help to develop code that is reada-ble and understandable, a functionally accurate representation of the design in the pro-gramming language, and exhibiting required qualities. Usually the most prominent qualities are reliability and performance. Complexity and maintainability are also im-portant. Complexity influences all other qualities, because they become harder to achieve.

```
DEFINITION MODULE accumulator;
    EXPORT QUALIFIED enter, compmeans, compcovar, means, covarmtr;
    CONST covmax = 10;
          novars = 4;
    TYPE    anres = RECORD
                       progid: idrec;
                       quad:   ARRAY[1..novars] OF CARDINAL
                    END;
    VAR means:      ARRAY[1..novars]  OF REAL;
        covarmtr:   ARRAY[0..covmax] OF REAL;
    PROCEDURE enter(result: anres);

    PROCEDURE compmeans;
    PROCEDURE compcovar;
END accumulator;

DEFINITION MODULE similarities;     (*computes similarity indices*)
    EXPORT QUALIFIED compsim, fxlist;
    VAR fxlist : ARRAY OF REAL;
    PROCEDURE compsim;
END similarities;
```

Figure 9.6 Interface Definitions in MODULA-2

How and where do we start coding? Usually we have made a plan. Parts for which feasibility is questionable are coded on a trial basis first (this may happen as early as feasibility study). Code can be written for approved design parts. Critical aspects of the design are coded first to make sure they work. We can implement top-down or bottom-up or use iterative enhancement or any of the development philosophies discussed in Chapter 6. If the user interface was implemented to let the user evaluate its quality, that part was probably coded first. We should have a plan, however, that tells us how and in which sequence to go about implementing the design. This helps to schedule meetings for reviewing code, for planning for integration testing, and for necessary communication of programmers working on interacting modules. Coding a design unit usually begins with selecting data structures and algorithms. Then the first and last statements (entry, exit and multiple entry/exit statements) are coded. Next, all interface data are declared, unless they have been declared already. In that case they are coded accordingly. After that, local data are defined. Then the code inside a routine is written and refined. Comments reflecting the design intentions are affixed. We may use the PDL from the design for that. Then comments are added to describe the module and its data to the outside (for more on commenting see the next section). Then the code is verified with an appropriate method (cf. Section 9.6.). The last step is to compile it. The goal is correct compilation the first time around.

Problems and Questions

1. Take two languages that you know which are as dissimilar as you can make them. What statements do they provide to express

▶ sequence,

▶ selection, and

▶ iteration.

What are their special features (e.g., statistical routines, graphics, or database capabilities)? What capabilities do they offer to structure data objects? For which types of programming problems would you use the language? Which problems are hard to do in it? The following are example languages: PASCAL, PL/1, MODULA-2, SNOBOL, ICON, FORTRAN, BASIC, assembler, ADA, LISP, SIMULA67, SIMSCRIPT, PROLOG, and even packages such as LOTUS 123 (Reg. Trademark) or DBase II or III (Reg. Trademark).

2. Describe how MODULA-2 supports abstract data types and information hiding. Code the **CLASS** definition of Figure 9.2 in MODULA-2.

```
IMPLEMENTATION MODULE accumulator;
FROM errors IMPORT error;

CONST accmax = 100;
VAR    accuid:    ARRAY[1..accmax] OF idrec;          (*prog_id part of the accu*)
                                                      (*idrec has not been defined
                                                      yet: deficiency in code *)

       stbase:    ARRAY[1..accmax] [1..novars] OF CARDINAL;

                                                      (*list of quadruples in accu*)
       ptr:       [0..accmax];                        (*points to last filled slot in accu, initially zero*)
PROCEDURE enter(result: anres);                       (* put-accu *)
BEGIN
  IF ptr >= accmax
    THEN error(accuoverflow);
    ELSE ptr                := ptr +1;
         accuid[ptr]        := result.progid;
         stbase[ptr]        := result.quad;
         END

  END
END enter;

PROCEDURE compmeans;
  VAR i,j: CARDINAL;
  FOR i:=1 TO ptr DO
    FOR j:=1 TO novars DO
      means[j] := means[j] + stbase[i,j]

    END
  END
  FOR j:=1 TO novars DO means[j] := means[j]/ptr END;
END compmeans;
```

```
PROCEDURE compcovar;
    VAR i,j, indij:     CARDINAL;
        diffs:          ARRAY[1..ptr] [1..novars] OF REAL;
        sum:            REAL;
    FOR i:=1 TO ptr DO                                          (*compute list of differences to*)
        FOR j:=1 TO novars DO                                   (*mean for covariance formula *)
            diffs[i,j] := stbase[i,j] − means[j];
        END
    END
    indij := 0;                                                 (*linearization of upper triangle*)
    FOR i:=1 TO novars DO                                       (*of covariance matrix *)
        FOR j:=1 TO novars DO
            sum := 0.0;
            indij := indij + 1;
            FOR k:= 1 TO ptr DO
                sum := sum + diffs[k,i]*diffs[k,j]
            END
            covarmtr[indij] := sum/ptr
        END
    END
END compvar;

BEGIN
    ptr := 0;                                                   (*initialization of accu *)
    FOR i:= 1 TO accmax DO
        accuid[i] := noid;                                      (* noid has not been defined yet *)
        FOR j:=1 TO novars DO
            stbase[i,j] := 0
        END
    END
END accumulator;
```

Figure 9.7 Implementation of Module Accumulator.

3. Suggest some ways how to get around the limitations of FORTRAN and PASCAL to implement abstract data types. Code the abstract data type of Figure 9.2 in PASCAL and in FORTRAN. Which language is better suited? Why?

4. Take the PDL for the recursive descent parser for PAS. Sequence the coding actions and state what you would have to do first, second, etc. Then state how you are doing it (i.e., what the resulting code looks like in PASCAL or another high level language of your choice.

9.3. Programming Style

Why is programming style important? A well written program is more easily read and understood both by the author and by others who work with that program. Not even the author will long remember his precise thoughts on a program. The program itself should help the reader to understand what it does quickly, because only a small fraction of the developers, if any, are maintaining the programs they wrote. Others will, and they must be able to understand what the program does. Bad programming style makes a program difficult to understand, hard to modify, and impossible to maintain over a long period of time, even by the person who coded it originally. Good books on programming style are [Kern78], [Vant78], and [Bent86].

A good programming style is characterized by the following:

▶   simplicity,

▶   readability,

▶   good documentation,

▶   changeability,

▶   predictability,

▶   consistency in input and output,

▶   module independence, and

▶   good structure.

We will discuss each one of these qualities in more detail, explain what they mean, and give guidelines how to achieve them and what to avoid.

Simplicity

This is what many call the KISS principle (*keep it simple stupid*). The logic of an algorithm should be stated in simple and direct terms. Convoluted solutions often have temporary variables, sometimes to "save time." The question is whose time? It won't help the programmer who scratches his head for days to find out just what initializing some, but not all, elements in an array to zero is supposed to do? Or why was an expression split apart into four parts, three of which were assigned to temporary variables that were only used once?

Tools that allow business to be stated simply and directly and then take this simple program and optimize it are best. Let the support software do the dirty work, at least at first. After the program works properly, we may determine through measurement that a particular part of it needs to be faster or must fit into less space. It is still early enough to sacrifice clarity for efficiency. It doesn't pay to improve the performance of code that has little impact on overall run time or storage requirements. Even when a piece of code is a major contributor to overall run time and storage requirements, we should only do improvements if the optimizing compiler can't do them. Find out which types of improvement it can or cannot do. For example, avoid run time type conversions. That is a maxim of defensive programming style anyway, because default type conversions can be rather unpredictable. A piece of code such as

```
Y = (a/b)**2 - (b/a)**2
```

is an obvious formula, while

```
T1 = a/b
T2 = 1/T1
Y = T11 - T22
```

means the same thing but is a lot harder to read. At the very least, put the first formula as a comment next to the last statement. Exponentiation takes longer than multiplication, and referencing the result is faster than recomputing it. An optimizing compiler optimizes such expressions for us.

Use off-the-shelf routines and software packages, i.e., libraries, and built-in functions. A well written program does not reinvent the wheel. Why does a run-time system have **LOG** and **SORT** routines, if we insist on inventing our own? Often such routines are coded in-line (hard to read) and just as often, there is a bug in them. For most widely used programming languages there are mathematical and statistical libraries with a host of functions that can be used while keeping the program that uses them very simple. There is PLMATH for PL/1 programs, and IMSL and SPSS or SAS work well with FORTRAN programs. Many libraries interface with several higher level languages. If we want to interface routines written in different languages, we should test with a small program to see if the interface works the way we think or hope it does, before using such "foreign language" routines in a big program. A test program is cheaper, and errors are more obvious.

When we use library routines, we should make sure that the specifications of the routine we intend to use are applicable to our problem. This holds especially for mathematical software. Let's take optimization routines as an example. There are gradient search techniques (such as steepest descent), methods that do not need a function to evaluate the gradient but, instead, approximate it (such as Rosenbrock's method), and heuristic pattern-search techniques. They all have their strengths and shortcomings. Some problems are ill-conditioned for one technique but work beautifully with another. It is very important to understand what a canned program can and cannot do for you, before you use it.

Readability

Making and keeping a program readable is related to making it simple. Avoid temporary variables. Repetitive expressions also detract from readability. After reading the fifth or sixth similar expression, intent may no longer be clear.

```
X = a*a − b*b
Y = b*b − c*c
Z = c*c + a*a
```

Is this correct code or is there actually a typo in the last assignment, i.e., the "+" should have been a "−"? Is this to produce all pairs of differences between a set of squared numbers, leaving out the ones which are negatives of each other such as (a * a − b * b) and (b * b − a * a)? If we extracted a common function or a loop with data arrays, the code would be more readable and less prone to undetected typos. We could rewrite generating permutations of differences for **VARSIZE** squares of numbers as

```
FOR i:=1 TO varsize DO
    FOR j:=i+1 TO varsize DO
        x[i] := a[i]*a[i] − a[j]*a[j];
```

If we need to make it faster, because recomputing squares and indexing the array elements takes too long, we compute all squares and store them:

```
FOR i:=1 TO varsize DO
    sqr[i] := a[i]*a[i];

FOR i:=1 TO varsize DO
    FOR j:=i+1 TO varsize DO
        x[i] :=sqr[i] − sqr[j];
```

One of the most important factors contributing to a readable program is choosing meaningful names. The names in programs are for variables, constants, functions, procedures, and labels. Names shouldn't be easily confused. Avoid names with predefined meaning in a language. Abolishing defaults can cause undesirable surprises or confuse the reader. Neither is desirable. Names that look very similar such as **TTT** and **TTTT** or **RECEIPT** and **PRECEIPT** are hard to read and understand. This is confusing and error-prone. The American penchant for inventing unusual spelling can also wreak havoc such as **FONE** instead of **PHONE**. Maintainers tend to use the second. This is also an example of two words that sound alike; such names don't work well either, especially when they are used together. We should also stay away from characters that are easily confused on the printout or the screen: zero (0) versus the letter o and one (1) versus the letters I, i, or l, especially in the middle of a name. Put numbers at the end of a variable name, not in the middle. Sometimes meaning can be overdone. [Vant78] uses the example **FOUR** = 12/5, which is certainly not four.

We already have a whole list of names from naming activities and data objects in the data diagrams, the data-flow diagrams, and the various levels of design. Using them has two advantages:

▶ It states the program in terms of what variables and functions mean on a problem level, and

▶ it establishes the connection between design and code, which is very important for readability and maintainability.

Some languages have default prefixes for type. FORTRAN assumes variable names whose first character ranges from **I** to **N** to be **INTEGER**, unless declared otherwise; all other default types are **REAL**. An **IMPLICIT** declaration can be used to define character ranges as implicit types, which are the choice of the programmer. This has both advantages and disadvantages. The advantage is that we know the type of a variable, whether it has been declared or not. Combined with a rule such as "all integer variable names start with an I," or "all **COMPLEX** ones with a C," we have a uniform way of making other programmers understand types of variables. The disadvantage is that it is prone to error. While some programming languages do not require declaring variables, it is usually much safer to do so explicitly, because implicit declaration may not be what is intended. Type conversions may not preserve needed accuracy. An implicit type may not coincide with the way a design item has been called. The first character of an explicit declaration may contradict its implicit type. While the compiler handles these matters beautifully, it is confusing to the human.

Even if variable names do not have to be prefixed, they might have to be abbreviated. Let us assume that the name we have in mind is

COVARIANCE_MATRIX

but only six characters are allowed. First, take out vowels from the right:

CVRNC_MTRX

This is still too long. Suppress consonants starting from the right, until the name is short enough (an underscore as the last character does not make sense, so we kept the M in, for matrix):

CVRNCM

We might use a special designation as a prefix or postfix to indicate whether the variable refers to a simple type or a structured type. This is usually far more effective and useful in languages that allow longer variable names.

MTR_COVARIANCE, COVARIANCE_MTR

It is harder to confuse two variable names that look very similar if they differ in the first letter rather than the last. Because of this, it is better to use

A_matrix, B_matrix

instead of

matrix_A, matrix_B

Numerical expressions become hard to read when they exceed more than five to seven items and span more than a line. It might be advantageous to partition a formula. Because not all languages have the same precendence rules and because precedence rules in people's minds do not always coincide with those of a language, use parentheses.

They avoid ambiguity and errors resulting from it. They also make the code more readable, because they clarify order of evaluation.

A similar point holds for logical expressions involving conditions on numbers. "Equal" (EQ) is the negation of "not equal" (NE). "Greater or equal" is the negation of "less than" (LT). We can express the same condition in either form by inversing the arguments. This type of inversion slows reading comprehension and is best avoided:

```
(SALARY .GE. SSNMAX .OR. FICA .LT. FICA_PAID)
```

reads better when both parts of the condition use the same relation operator:

```
(SALARY .GE. SSNMAX .OR. FICA_PAID .GE. FICA)
```

Also avoid inverting any of the two relations later in the program. It is easier to understand when conditions are expressed consistently.

Logical expressions can be hard to understand. DeMorgan's Laws are used to transform them into something simpler. The condition

```
(A .AND. B) .OR. (C .AND. A)
```

can be transformed into

```
A .AND. (B .OR. C)
```

Logical expressions that control execution must not be hidden in branches, such as an arithmetic **IF** statement in FORTRAN. It obscures logic, making it a matter of tracing execution flow instead of showing it explicitly. That makes a program harder to understand. The following FORTRAN segment makes a variety of mistakes. It uses arithmetic **IF** statements, confusing flow of control through jumps backwards and forward and inversion:

```
         IF (salary - ssnmax) 10, 40, 40
10       fica = ssn(salary)
60       IF (ficapd - fica) 30, 20, 20
20       due = 0.0
         GOTO 50
30       due = fica - ficapd
         GOTO 50
40       fica = ssn(ssnmax)
         GOTO 60
50       CONTINUE
```

An improved version is

```
IF (salary > ssnmax) salary = ssnmax
fica = ssn(salary)
due = 0.0
IF (fica > ficapd) due = fica − ficapd
```

But this is still clumsy. It uses the maximum of two pairs of numbers but reinvents the **MAX** function. We could have said more simply

```
fica = ssn(MAX(salary, ssnmax))
due = MAX(0.0, fica − ficapd)
```

Simplification is not always this obvious. Let's go back to the module of Figure 7.6. Computation of $f(x)$ (**compfxlist**), $f(m)$ (**compfm**), and $f(x)/f(m)$ (**compsim**) is done according to the following formula ([Ash70], p. 281):

$$f(x) = (2\ )^{-n/2}\ (det\ covar)^{-\frac{1}{2}}exp[\ -\tfrac{1}{2}\ (x\ -\ m)^t covar^{-1}(x\ -\ m)],$$

where

▶ *covar* is the covariance matrix,

▶ x is a quadruple of analysis results,

▶ m is the means vector,

▶ the superscript t denotes the transpose of a vector, and

▶ *det* is the determinant of a matrix, in our case the covariance matrix.

The formula only applies for a nonsingular covariance matrix. Otherwise, we have to use this formula with the maximally linearly independent subset of vectors in the covariance matrix.

This formula also determines the value for $f(m)$. The factor that involves exponentiation disappears, because the exponent reduces to zero:

$$f(m) = (2\ )^{-n/2}\ (det\ K)^{-\frac{1}{2}}$$

The formula for the similarity index $f(x)/f(m)$ is simpler, because the first part cancels out:

$$f(x)/f(m) = exp[-\tfrac{1}{2}\ (x\ -\ m)^t\ covar^{-1}\ (x\ -\ m)]$$

Before we implement the three functions **compfm, compsim,** and **compfxlist,** we need to determine whether we actually need all these quantities or whether it suffices to compute the similarity index. Since *f(x)* and *f(m)* are determined so that we can subsequently compute the similarity index, their computation is not essential. Then we do the following:

▶ Determine whether the determinant of the covariance matrix is sufficiently close to zero to indicate it is singular.

▶ If it is indeed singular, reduce the covariance by the minimal number of rows (and corresponding columns) to make it nonsingular. Call this matrix **newmtr** of dimension **newptr,** and compute its determinant.

▶ Invert the matrix.

▶ Multiply it to the right and left with the vector **(x-m).** We must remove any components whose corresponding rows and columns were removed from the covariance matrix to make it nonsingular.

▶ Substitute the result into the formula for *f(x)/f(m).*

```
IMPLEMENTATION MODULE similarities;                    (* computes similarity indices *)
   FROM accu    IMPORT covarmtr, covmax, means, novars, ptr, stbase;
   FROM mathlib IMPORT det, reduce, invert, vecmtrvec;
   VAR    inverse: ARRAY[ ][ ] OF REAL;

   PROCEDURE compsim(x: ARRAY[1..novars] OF REAL);
      WHILE ABS(det(covarmtr)) < 0.0001 DO
             reduce(covarmtr, x, means)
      END;
      invert(covarmtr, inverse);
      FOR j:=1 TO ptr DO
        FOR i:=1 TO novars DO
             diff[i] := x[i]—means[i]
        END
        fxlist[j] := vecmtrvec(diff, inverse);                (*diff*inverse*diff *)
      END;
   END compsim;
END similarities;
```

Figure 9.8 Module Similarities.

A program's readability also depends on layout. Layout affects declaration, executable code, and comments. In the declaration parts of the program, it is good to list variables alphabetically and to put them into columns (they are much easier to find); it is also good to cluster the declaration of variables with similar uses. An alternative is to sequence declaration according to when a variable is actually used the first time. Whatever you decide, be consistent in the way you lay out your program.

Many programming languages have grouping statements such as **BEGIN-END, DO-CONTINUE,** etc. Blocks of statements enclosed by these grouping statements should be indented (usually three to five spaces, consistently). Even FORTRAN code should be indented. The first and last of the grouping statements should align. An **IF** or a **CASE** statement is best put onto a line alone. All statements conditioned by it are indented to show their dependence on the condition expressed in it. Another way to group logical units of statements together visually is to separate them by blank lines from the other parts of the program.

Putting more than one statement on a line may save space, but it is harder to read and to change. Spacing helps readability, both for items in a list of variables and operators, such as +, −, and =. If parentheses are not necessary, spaces can be used to indicate operator precedence visually. The program layout must not contradict the way the program actually does things.

Some languages, such as FORTRAN, have statement numbers. A program should show statements numbers in increasing order. Use a standard increment (10 is frequent). Labels for **FORMAT** statements are often put at the end and start with the highest base number to indicate that they are different from other statement labels. Having standard increments for labels makes it easier to insert new ones without violating the order, and it helps readability, because the target of a **GOTO** can be found more easily. Higher increments set off partitions of code (e.g., all statement numbers in a loop are 5xx numbers, afterwards they are 6xx for the next partition of code, and so forth. **FORMAT** statements are 1000 and higher). This way the reader can tell whether a GOTO leaves a partition of code or not and even which conceptual part it is going to.

When programming assignment statements, readability is increased when statements line up at the equal sign. When a line must be broken, the next line with the remainder of the statement starts to the right of the equal sign.

It is customary to have only one module (procedure, function) per printed page. When procedures are nested, it should be indicated in the procedure name. We can prefix the nested procedure with the name of the procedure in which it is nested. How well this works depends on the length of the procedure names and the maximum length allowed in a language. Set the prefix off with an underscore. For the **stats** module in PAS we could define the following function and procedure names, assuming they are all included in the **stats** module:

```
PROCEDURE stats;
  FUNCTION stats_mean;
  PROCEDURE stats_covar;
  PROCEDURE stats_simind;
END stats;
```

Standards in programming help to understand code faster. They increase the reliability of the code. A program is read, maintained, and modified by a series of programmers during its lifetime and thus should conform to expectations. This is the main reason for standards. Standards prescribe how to indent code for readability, how to segment code on a listing (one module per page), the maximum nesting level for **IF-THEN-ELSE** structures (because complicated nesting structures obscure code), and how to deal with unavoidable **GOTO**s.

Standards often describe additional rules that the language itself does not enforce or support. If a language does not support a concept, such as abstract datatypes or structured programming constructs, the design must be implemented as well as the language allows, and rules must be established for usage of data structures and procedures. Useful programming conventions and standards are explained in [Vant78] and [Jens79].

Program Documentation

It consists of the code itself and the comments in the code. Proper commenting is vital to a maintainable program. This does not necessarily mean lots of comment; rather it means enough comment to understand what the program does. Code and comments must agree. Any change in the code also needs change in the comments. Because comments clarify what the program does, they are a way to establish a connection between code and design. Often PDL makes very useful explanatory comments in the source code. They give a natural narrative account of the data flow and the logic of a program. A comment that says in English what the program does, such as

```
X := X + 1; /*increment X */
```

is useless parroting of the code. Anybody familiar with the language can see that **X** is incremented. The reader would like to know why and what this action means (maybe pointing **X** to the next free slot in a table?). A reader must be able to discern from the comments what the program is doing. Comments should not clutter the code. Shift them to the second third of the line and align them properly. Figure 9.9 shows commenting and alignment in PASCAL.

PASCAL has no **LEAVE** operation. A flag variable simulates leaving the loop. Another option is to use **GOTO**s. Leaving loops is often done this way if **LEAVE** is not part

```
TYPE tokenrec = RECORD
                  txt: ARRAY[1..maxlen] OF CHAR;
                  len: 0..maxlen
                END;
VAR C:         CHAR,
    char type: SET OF  (blk,                      {blank}
                        lnf,                       {linefeed}
                        com,                       {comma}
                        par,                       {parenthesis, left/right}
                        eoc,                       {end of command}
                        oth),                      {other}

    cmdline  :  cmdrec;                            {commandline}

PROCEDURE get(token: tokenrec)                     {returns next token}
  init(token);                                     {set token.txt to empty
                                                     token.len to zero}

  leave := FALSE;
  REPEAT
    BEGIN
      CASE char_type OF
      blk, lnf:  BEGIN
                   skip_them;
                   leave := TRUE                   {end of token}
                 END;
      com, par: BEGIN
                   WITH token DO
                     BEGIN
                       IF len = 0 THEN             {if token empty}
                         BEGIN
                           len     := len + 1;     {token is comma or}
                           txt[len] := C;          {parenthesis}
                           c        := get_char(cmdline)
                         END
                     END
                   leave := TRUE;                  {end of token}
                 END;
      eoc:      leave := TRUE;
      oth:      WITH token DO
                   BEGIN
                     len      := len +1;           {accumulate token}
                     txt[len]  := c
                   END;
      END;
    IF leave = FALSE THEN get_char(cmdline);
    UNTIL leave = TRUE;
  END {get};
```

Figure 9.9 Commenting and Alignment in PASCAL.

of the language. It becomes difficult to read when the design shows many **LEAVE** instructions or flag variables. **IF** statements are another choice, one per character type. We can remove from the loop those character types that always result in leaving it the first time. It also helps to rearrange type values in the **CASE** statement.

Besides in-line comments there are so-called prologue comments [Vant78]. These are at the top of a module and describe one or more of the following:

▶ What the program or routine does. We can use functional description or a high level solution descriptions, such as those with which object-oriented design starts out.

▶ How to call or use it. This specifies calling sequence and an explanation of conditions external to the routine.

▶ A list and explanation of important data structures, both parameters and local ones. Here we would find specifications for the parameters, their type, size, what they are used for, whether they change values due to the call, etc.

▶ If applicable, instructions on I/O. Does the calling program have to provide file names, open files, close them, how many, predefined names? Specific types?

▶ Support routines used by the module. This is important because we may have to link to another library.

▶ Type of algorithm or solution method. Sometimes the type of method is mentioned or a reference is made to a publication. Where the algorithm is not a general solution, specific restrictions help the user to determine what the solution can do for him.

▶ Performance. Time and space requirements are listed as a function of the complexity of the problem (e.g., number of elements to be sorted, number of variables for a set of equations, number of nodes or arcs in a graph, etc.).

▶ Author, Date, and Owner. This indicates version, who has the authority to make any changes (the current owner) versus who originally wrote the code. Authority for changes is important for large software that is developed in increasing functionality. This avoids uncontrolled changes causing unanticipated ripple effects for *ad hoc* changes to previously developed modules.

For bigger programs or software systems, we also need to know where to find a particular module and what its location and function in the hierarchy is. A prologue is often set off in a box of asterisks or with vertical and horizontal bars. IMSL offers a set of mathematical and statistical routines that have prologues similar to what we have just described. Table 9.1 shows a predefined layout for a simplified module prologue.

Table 9.1 Comments in module prologues.

⟨declaration of procedure or function⟩			
*			*
* Purpose:		⟨short description of procedure/function⟩	*
* Parameters:			*
* ⟨name⟩	⟨type⟩	⟨meaning and purpose⟩	*
* Global variables:			*
* ⟨name⟩	⟨type⟩	⟨meaning and purpose⟩	*
* Local variables:			*
* ⟨name⟩		⟨meaning and purpose⟩	*

Legend: ⟨name⟩   is the name of the variable. It may be a list, if meaning and purpose are the same.
⟨type⟩   may be I (Input) and/or O (Output). Input indicates no change in value, while Output means that through this variable values are exported from the module.

Changeability

Programs change during their lifetime. The simplest way to start building changeability into a program is to keep quantities flexible, i.e., use named constants and variables instead of hard-coded constants. Such quantities are more like parameters that allow changes to sizes of tables, arrays, and lists easily. In the TAP example, we should not use constants such as .30 as a tax rate. Rather, the tax rate should be defined as a variable that is changed when taxes change. Figure 9.8 defined the length of a command line and of a token with a named constant. This is easy to change. Scientific constants are another such example, and so are I/O device designations. Standard input and output units tend to change from installation to installation. It is so much easier and less error-prone to change one parameter than dozens all over.

When a program is starting to be used more, its workload often increases. This usually impacts its data structures. Tables overflow, queues become too small, and buffer space runs out. We can avoid the problems associated with it by leaving space in tables and arrays or planning for increasing queues or the number of buffers. Some algorithms, such as hashing, work more efficiently when tables aren't close to being full. Keep all parameters that are prone to change in one place to locate them easily. We may combine that with developing a subroutine that initializes all the parameters that determine table sizes, system constants, etc.

Predictability

The factors that make a program easier to change can also make it more predictable. Uninitialized variables do not always have predictable values, or those values may not be the same on two different machines. A program that relies on specific default values needs modification when the values change. "Official" initialization routines for all variables are more predictable and reliable.

Consistency of the I/O format enhances predictability. Switching formats is not only confusing and hard to remember, but the user usually ends up reading or writing data incorrectly, a source of considerable user frustration.

Standards have a positive effect on predictability. They make a program more readable and understandable, because they ensure that certain aspects of coding are done in a uniform way. They prevent inconsistencies. Examples of standards include documentation formats for the code, indentation practices, commenting, order of declaration, etc.

Readability of Output

All output must be understandable without reference to other sources, without having to retype it, and without much further work. Computer output, therefore, must specify what it is and what it is for (e.g., detailed listing of medical deductions) and the date when it was compiled. Pages should be numbered and items should be labeled or named (no columns after columns of numbers!). Use tabulation and blank lines to increase readability.

Preservation of Module Independence

A coded module should be independent from its input source, from the modules that get its output, and from its use in the past. This is necessary so that the programmer can determine whether a module works correctly without relying on its context. Such modules can also be added to a program or changed more easily. Independence was the goal of the design effort and the corresponding code must preserve it.

A good design module can be described to the outside in terms of its domain of permissible input values, the range of its possible output values, and potential side effects. The inside of the module states the algorithm. To keep the code module as independent as the design module, we should not add any more interfaces to the outside; we should just define in code its interfaces and the algorithm that makes up the actions inside. A module should be implemented as an SESE with a minimum of paths. Each routine should do its own housekeeping and perform one logical task (this is assured through proper design). Many systems have a mainline routine or driver that directs the flow of control and data to all other processing routines. For TAP or PAS, this is an implementation of the state transition diagram or the command handler, in PAS, that invokes the proper processing for a command.

When a design module is too big, coding modularizes with subordinate procedures. Avoid repetitive code sequences. It is better to put them into a function or procedure. Its argument list summarizes the irregularities found in pieces of similar code. The function or procedure itself states its regularities. This is similar to procedural extraction during design, which consolidated similar actions into procedures. In Figure 9.9 the sequence of code for adding a comma or parenthesis or a character of type **oth** is the same. We could have defined a procedure or a function for it as the PDL did (that makes it more uniform, but a little slower).

Good Structure

Good structure comes from a well-structured design. Coding practices that stress using structured programming constructs support a good structure. The tenets of structured programming were described in the previous section. In addition, deeply nested **IF** statements can become very unstructured. We might pick them apart through reevaluation of the condition. If a language does not have a **CASE** statement, multiway branches can be implemented with a nested **IF** statement, provided it is not nested too deeply. Then we would use the first technique.

GOTOs should only be used to implement a fundamental structure but should be avoided altogether if the program is still readable. They are useful to implement **LEAVE** in a design (leaving a loop), provided that any looping parameters get redefined to predictable values.

A design that seems to warrant too many **GOTO**s often has been unstructured or undisciplined to begin with, showing too many paths from one point to another. **GOTO**s should not be used when a procedure call or a function call could have sufficed.

Not all languages provide the full range of structured programming constructs. And indeed as Jensen and Tonies [Jens79] point out, "It is strange that the popularity of a programming language is inversely proportional to the power of its progam control statements." In particular, FORTRAN, BASIC, and COBOL are widely used languages, but they certainly are deficient when it comes to structured programming constructs and modularization capabilities. While we would like to implement designs in a high level structured programming language, we do not always have the luxury to do so. Some of the many reasons are

▶ a more advanced version of the language, such as FORTRAN77 as opposed to FORTRAN, is not available on a particular machine,

▶ enhancements are needed to code originally written in an unstructured language,

▶ maintenance of old programs is needed, and

▶ there is no choice in the selection of languages.

Any of these reasons can create the need to use an "unstructured" language. This does not allow us to throw good programming practices out the window. Rather, we need workable strategies to deal with the problem. We can still design the software in PDL, but then we need additional rules that help us to translate PDL *uniformly* into code. These rules in effect define a standard. They help to make the code in a less than perfectly structured language predictable, readable, and ultimately more reliable. [Jens79] gives a variety of such translation rules. Here we are more concerned with how to define such rules. Assume that PDL has the following statements at its disposal, **IF-THEN-ELSE, CASE, WHILE, DO-UNTIL, LEAVE**, and that we are trying to find rules to translate the PDL statements **CASE** and **LEAVE** into FORTRAN.

PDL		FORTRAN *framework*
CASE ⟨item⟩ DO		IF (.NOT. item = it1) GOTO 100
it1: ⟨S1⟩;		S1
		GOTO 1000
it2: ⟨S2⟩;	100	IF (.NOT. item = it2) GOTO 200
		S2
		GOTO 1000
it3: ⟨S3⟩;	200	IF (.NOT. item = it3) GOTO 300
		S3
		GOTO 1000
OTHERWISE: ⟨S–other⟩;		Sother
	1000	. . .

This case statement assumes three possible values and an otherwise clause, but we can easily generalize it to more cases. The terms **item, it1** to **it3**, and **Sother** are code implementations of the corresponding PDL terms. **S1, S2**, and **S3** are code equivalents of ⟨**S1**⟩, ⟨**S2**⟩, and ⟨**S3**⟩. We may have to encode the type of item and its values **it1, it2,** etc. as integers, because FORTRAN may not provide the data type of the item. Then direct comparisons may not be made. Similar encodings can become necessary for the implementation of **FOR** loops where counting parameters can be sets or other countable types. We may want to establish a standard translation procedure for those.

The **LEAVE** statement can be implemented by a **GOTO** statement that transfers control to the first statement after the loop. Another alternative is to use a flag variable. Initially it is set to **FALSE** and checked as part of the condition so that the loop is left properly as soon as the flag variable is set to **TRUE** (at the point where the **LEAVE** statement occurs in the PDL).

These coding rules on how to translate PDL constructs into code need to be thought about for every programming language that does not provide one or more of the PDL's constructs. The above example in FORTRAN was made mainly to emphasize the point that we must give the translation process some thought, as opposed to "translating on the fly." It is too prone to error and too often results in bad quality.

Not all languages have the same module structuring capabilities of the design medium. What can we do about structuring a software product in a language that does not have the capabilities of MODULA-2? If adherence to interfaces is crucial, we can define "definition modules" that describe the items and only the items that other modules are allowed to use. Violations can be detected through comparisons (sometimes a good compiler will do this). Code writing is easier because we have a well established pattern for the interface to match.

So far we have encountered hints on how to translate PDL into design and how to ensure compliance with the design interfaces. Translation rules have only covered the sequential aspects of PDL. We also need to know how to translate the parallel constructs into code. Our parallel PDL are path expressions. Translating a path expression into a program using P/V operations on semaphores proceeds in the following stages [Camp74], [Laue75]:

A path expression of the form **path** ⟨**expression**⟩ **end** requires, as a first translation, a new unique semaphore **sem_1**, which is initialized to 1:

path	⟨expression⟩	*end*
P(sem_1)	⟨expression⟩	V(sem_1)

In stage two, we examine ⟨**expression**⟩ and select iteratively one of the following translations, depending on which operations are to be performed first in ⟨**expression**⟩. This divides ⟨**expression**⟩ into subexpressions that can be dealt with using the same rules of stage two over again, until all operations in the path expression have been taken care of.

▶ **Sequence.**   ⟨**expression**⟩ has the form ⟨**exp1**⟩;⟨**exp2**⟩. In this case we select a unique semaphore **sem_2**, initialize it to 0, and rewrite ⟨**expression**⟩ as

⟨exp1⟩ V(sem_2) P(sem_2) ⟨exp2⟩

▶ **Selection.**   At this point ⟨**expression**⟩ is flanked by semaphore operations to the left and right:

SO(l) ⟨exp1⟩ + ⟨exp2⟩ SO(r)

SO(l) stands for the semaphore operation to the left of ⟨expression⟩, and **SO(r)** designates the one to its right. We translate such a form into

SO(l) ⟨exp1⟩ SO(r) SO(l) ⟨exp2⟩ SO(r)

▶ **Simultaneous execution.**   When we encounter simultaneous execution, the ⟨**expression**⟩ enclosed in { } will look something like

P(sem_i) {⟨expression⟩} V(sem_j)

This is replaced by

PP(count_1, sem_3, sem_i) ⟨expression⟩ VV(count_1, sem_3, sem_j)

where **count_1** is a unique counter variable (initially 0), which is used to count the number of active instances of ⟨**expression**⟩. **sem_3** is a unique semaphore variable that assures mutual exclusion for incrementing and decrementing the counter. The first time **PP** is called, the operation **P(sem_i)** is executed (as it should be). When the counter reaches zero (no more active instances of ⟨**expression**⟩), execution has reached the end of the simultaneous execution and **V(sem_j)** is invoked. The synchronization operations **PP** and **VV** implement the counting process:

```
PP(count_1, sem_3, sem_i)           VV(count_1, sem_3, sem_j)
  P(sem_3);                           P(sem_3);
  count_1 := count_1 + 1;            count_1 := count_1 - 1;
  IF (count_1=1) THEN P(sem_i);      IF (count_1=0) THEN V(sem_j);
  V(sem_3)                           V(sem_3)
END PP;                             END VV;
```

▶ **Procedure names.** We include the synchronization operation to the left of the procedure name in its prologue and the synchronization operation to its right in its epilogue.

Let us make an example which uses these translation rules. The path expression that we will translate is

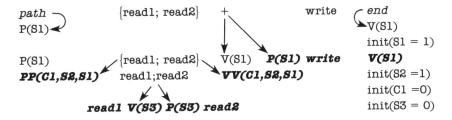

The last level of refinement is italicized and can be written consecutively as

PP(C1,S2,S1) read1 V(S3) P(S3) read2 VV(C1,S2,S1) P(S1) write V(S1)

Based on this, we can write the monitor with the above path expression as in Figure 9.10. The "language" used is similar to ALGOL or PASCAL. It can be considered a detail-level design language. Note that this methodical way of translating synchronization into code provides a predictable, structured code. All synchronization statements are either at the beginning or the end of the operations in the monitor. The situation is a little more complicated when we try to translate some of the other operations within a path expression. For the Kleene star, there are three cases we have to distinguish:

▶ The expression that has the Kleene Star is between other procedures, as in

   path A; B*; C *end*

▶ The expression that has the Kleene Star is the first in the path expression, as in

   path B*; C *end*

```
MONITOR example;
  SEMAPHORE S1=1; S2=1; S3=0;
  COUNTER    C1=0;
  PROCEDURE read1;
    BEGIN
       PP(C1, S2, S1);
       ⟨body of read1⟩
       V(S3)
    END read1;

  PROCEDURE read2;
    BEGIN
       P(S3);
       ⟨body of read2⟩;
       VV(C1, S2, S1)
    END read2;

  PROCEDURE write;
    BEGIN
       P(S1);
       ⟨body of write⟩
       V(S1)
    END write;

.....
END example;
```

Figure 9.10 Translation for Path Expression Example.

▶ The expression that has the Kleene Star is the last in the path expression, as in

path B; C* *end*

The first two can be solved with a combination of **P** and **V** operations, but the last one needs an operation similar to the **PP** and **VV** operations we have encountered earlier. We must have an equal number of **P** and **V** operations (developing a translation process is an exercise, cf. problem 8).

Developing structured coding rules in combination with translation mechanisms is a powerful means to make code more predictable and more reliable, and it can help to automate the coding process with tools. Even if such automation is only partial, it still provides some support for the less creative parts of the coding process.

Problems and Questions

1. Which rules does the following piece of code follow? Which are violated? Improve the code. Does it work?

```
C-      Compute additional FICA tax due, if any
        IF (salary-ssnmax) 10, 60, 30
60      CONTINUE
30      fica = ssn(ssnmax)
        GOTO 20
10      fica = ssn(salary)
20      IF (ficapd-fica) 40, 40, 50
40      due = 0.0
        GOTO 70
50      due = fica-ficapd
70
```

2. Try to improve the PASCAL code of Figure 9.8 using other suggestions and options mentioned in the text.

3. Code the operations **accumulate, skip_them,** and **get_char(commandline),** and define **commandline** as a type in PASCAL. You may want to use Figures 7.12 and 7.13, because they describe the parsing process in PDL.

4. Recode the SIMULA67 example of Figure 9.2 in MODULA-2.

5. Code the similarities module in FORTRAN. Which, if any, math routines (SAS, IMSL, etc.) would help? When would they work? How would you deal with the cases when they don't work? What checks and actions are reasonable to preserve the reliability of the routine?

6. Develop a set of standards for coding in PASCAL. They should include rules for

    ▶ indentation,

    ▶ implementing constructs the programming language does not have (think about abstract data types for example),

    ▶ commenting, and

    ▶ interfaces.

Do you think it is reasonable to require certain types of design objects (e.g., lists, queues) to be implemented in specific ways? Why or why not? When and when not? Illustrate your argument with examples.

7. Assume you are to translate your design into BASIC. Develop translation rules for PDL constructs that BASIC does not have.

8. Develop a set of structured coding rules for translating path expression into code. In addition to those developed in this section, develop rules on how to translate the Kleene star and the conditional into **P/V** and extended **P/V** operations. Make sure you consider cases.

9.4. Quality

9.4.1. Reliability

Much of the error isolation techniques (mutual suspicion, range checking, providing an action for all possible values of a variable, etc.) were already designed into the software. Housekeeping needs may introduce objects into the code that were not in the design. The same principles for reliable design apply here. Guidelines for achieving well written code also support software reliability: use PDL to write the algorithmic aspects of a module, test whether the basic approach works, and translate it into code. This separation into specifics of the algorithm versus specifics of the code increases reliability. Modularity also increases reliability.

Next, we will discuss error-prone coding practices and explain some useful reliability techniques.

Loops

Many errors in loops occur at loop boundaries:

    ▶ There is no execution of the loop. Can it happen? Does the code deal with it correctly? Some programming languages require extra work to circumvent a **DO** loop. FORTRAN is an example.

▶ There is only one execution of the loop. Can it happen? Is processing the same as in higher number of executions of the loop?

▶ Are there any special cases with abnormal loop exit? Does the code take care of it? Reset all loop parameters and variables properly before the loop is executed again. If abnormal loop exit (**LEAVE**) is implemented, will the next statement after the loop be executed properly no matter whether the loop exit was through normal execution or a **LEAVE** construct?

▶ There is maximum number of executions. Make sure that no arrays or other data structures overflow or that the loop "forgets" the last set of data to process. Both problems are "off by one" errors.

▶ If a loop is never supposed to exit normally. Make sure that it never does. Inspect the variables that govern flow of control through the loop and check whether there are values for them (albeit invalid ones) that cause an (undesired) normal loop exit. Is this what you would like to see or does it cause problems? Make the code deal with such cases.

Size

Write and test programs and systems in small pieces. Modular design was aimed at defining such pieces for us. Implementation strategies suggest possible sequencing of the coding process. Coded modules are usually no more than a page in length (although this alone is certainly *not* a sign of quality). Smaller units of code can be phase tested more easily and therefore tend to be more reliable.

Input

Users make errors; this simply cannot be avoided. A program reduces the error rate by making it harder to make errors and by giving the users feedback on the validity of their input immediately.

▶ Before using any user input or input from a file, tape, etc., code must check to see whether it is valid, and if valid, whether it makes sense. The specifications point out the input domain for any input variable and describe necessary actions. Program them.

▶ Input data is often open-ended, either because it is not known beforehand how many items need to be read in, or because the input file has a mistake in it (too many or not enough data). A FORTRAN statement such as

```
READ (iunit, 1000) noanal, (stbase(i,j), j=1,4), i=1,noanal)
```

that tries to read in how many analyses were saved during an analysis of PAS and then reads in that many quadruples, can

▶ cause the program to abort, if there aren't enough quadruples;

▶ overwrite the values of other variables stored after **stbase** without so much as an overflow message, if **noanal** exceeds the dimensions of **stbase** (This violates the concept of detecting errors where they occur. Some languages abort with an error if array boundaries are exceeded); and

▶ compute statistics with only part of the collected data when **noanal** is smaller than the number of quadruples to be read in. The results of the statistical evaluation are useless because they do not consider the entire sample.

Terminate input with an **EOF** indicator, or use a construct that allows error processing in case the file is at an end. PL/1 has **ON** conditions expressly for that purpose (**ON ENDFILE**...), and most languages let us ask whether the end of a file has been reached (SIMULA67, PASCAL, etc.) to condition reading input on the status of the input file.

▶ The above example does not check whether the input is valid. After detecting an error, the program should attempt to recover. Even if validity of the analysis results in **stbase** is checked later (negative ones don't make sense, the number of distinct operators or operands cannot be greater than the total number of operators or operands), recovery is more complicated: should we erase the analysis result? Then we have to reorganize the **stbase** array. It would have been easier not to enter it in the first place. Should we substitute a corrected set of values? Then we have to do user I/O during statistics computation. That's not desirable from an organizational viewpoint. Therefore, check input immediately.

▶ Many errors occur because of mixed formats and data types in the input stream. FORTRAN lets the programmer do all manner of strange things in this regard. Reading in real numbers in fixed format and then switching to float, or reading in integers over five columns and later switching to six is not just confusing to read about, it is very error prone to use. Formats should be uniform if they must be prescribed at all. Even better is input in any format, as long as the types of the data match. We have tried that for the command language of PAS.

▶ Input for TAP follows another maxim of reliability: it is self-explanatory and easy to prepare.

▶ Whether input is prepared for an interactive system or a batch system, it should be easy for the user to determine whether it is correct. The following

```
copy [adt.ebg1675] ourfile.pas 200:350 shr b
```

is not. If a data file is prepared, allow the user to line up numbers and text in columns. It is more orderly, easier to proofread, and more reliable, because less input errors will be made. If defaults can be used to shorten the input less errors will be made. If defaults are invoked, the user should be made aware of them (echo the system's understanding back to the user).

▶   Ideally, all input should be echoed back to the user. This is mandatory if the system does not do any consistency and validity checks. Otherwise the user does not have any indication that something might be amiss until the (wrong) output appears. This is too late. We may be more conservative about echoing user input back if there is a command that the user can invoke interactively before processing to check the input data. When the system thoroughly checks validity and plausibility, less echoing is necessary. Echoing user input makes a program more testable and improves reliability.

Declare and Initialize all Variables

Default types and values improve coding speed. They also make more assumptions and are more cryptic. They can have undesirable side effects. Default types can hide typos that a strongly typed language would have flagged. This is a problem in FORTRAN and PL/1. The results of using such undeclared, often uninitialized variables can cause erroneous program behavior which is hard to analyze. Cross-reference listings indicate which variables were declared and which were not, even what their initial values were. This is a valuable aid in dealing with such problems. Using undeclared values is undesirable for another reason: it is often used for programming "on the fly."

While some languages provide default values for variables, it is dangerous to rely on them. They can vary between machines. They can vary at random if the tacit assumption is that the programmer is supposed to initialize his own variables, but the run-time system doesn't enforce it. Constants are usually initialized with specific initialization statements, such as **INIT** (PL/1), **DATA** (FORTRAN), **CONST** (PASCAL). Variables, whether they are simple or structured types, often have their own initialization routine or at least a partition of code (in the beginning of a procedure or function) where they are set to initial values.

Boundaries

The specifications and the design determined classes of values for data objects that were associated with different processing actions. The boundaries between such classes are especially prone to error. When data values at the boundary are put into the wrong class, processing misses the last data value, tries to exceed array boundaries, sends payment notices to customers demanding a payment of $0.00, tries to compute means of zero or one analysis results, etc. It is one of the causes of "divide by zero" errors. Code must be checked whether it deals correctly with values along functional boundaries. Such boundaries are often established in conditions in **IF** statements or loops.

Accuracy

Never compare floating point or real numbers for equality. To compare for "approximate equality," state an epsilon area above and below which two machine numbers are "equal."

Hand calculations do not work the same way on the machine. While **a * (1/a)** is exactly 1 when it is calculated by hand, this is rarely true for code. On the other hand, we should use algebraic properties of formulae to make computation easier or more accurate. Scaling sometimes helps to avoid overflows and underflows. For example, the normalization constants H_m and H_{m-1} are used in analytic modeling to compute throughput and response time. For a network of k single servers and a network population of m jobs, the formula is

$$H_m = \sum_S x_1^{i_1} x_2^{i_2} \ldots x_k^{i_k},$$

such that

$$S = \{ (i_1, \ldots, i_k) \mid m = i_1 + \ldots + i_k\}.$$

If m is big, we can have underflows and overflows, depending on whether the x_i are smaller than one or bigger than 1. This results in big errors for the reciprocal throughput H_m/H_{m-1}. The solution to this problem is scaling. We can scale, because

$$H_m(ax) = a^m H_m(x).$$

For the reciprocal throughput this means

$$H_m(ax)/H_{m-1}(ax) = (a^m H_m(x)) / (a^{m-1} H_{m-1}(x)) =$$
$$= (a^m/a^{m-1}) (H_m(x)/H_{m-1}(x)).$$

Therefore

$$H_m(x)/H_{m-1}(x) = (1/a) H_m(ax)/H_{m-1}(ax).$$

We can compute the reciprocal throughput for the vector ax instead of x and divide by a for the desired result. The symmetry of H_m with respect to the x_i allows us to sort them in order, which makes it easier to determine the scaling factor a (we want the x_i to be as close to 1 as possible).

Avoid mixing different types of data and variables. In most cases they trigger conversion, which does not always give results of the desired accuracy. Sometimes calling explicit conversion routines will do better. Find out what your run-time system does when it encounters mixed data types. Don't use them if you cannot predict how they will work. You may find truncation instead of rounding. This can quickly add up to substantial errors in accuracy. If data types have to be mixed, group like types together so that subexpressions can be evaluated in one type and only the result is converted.

This is certainly not an exclusive list of guidelines to increase reliability. The worst thing that can happen is that a module accepts incorrect input but returns output which, while incorrect, looks correct. At worst, the user believes wrong results; at best, he realizes that there is a mistake, somewhere. A technique called "defensive programming" [Myer76] isolates such errors: every module checks its input data (parameters, global data, user input) whether they have the proper attributes, whether they fall within the expected domain, whether they are complete, and whether they make sense on a problem basis when associated with the current system state and the values of other related variables. This can lead to a lot of defensive code, slow execution, and increase the volume of code and its complexity. To determine how much defensive code is needed, [Myer76] suggests we make a list of all possible checks. Then the programmer considers how easy or difficult it would be to check, how probable individual errors in data values are, and what would happen if the data weren't checked. Important, easy checks for likely errors are implemented. Difficult errors that are not likely to occur and would not make much of a difference if they were not checked, are crossed off the list. Some languages do some of the checking for us and even provide possibilities for reaction (e. g. **ON** conditions in PL/1).

Reliability is not free. It cannot be built into the code without having been built into the previous work products. It can affect complexity and performance of software. We usually have to consider the effects of increased complexity and lesser performance.

Problems and Questions

1. Examine the parser for the PAS command language (cf. Figures 7.12 and 7.13) and determine

    ▶ which variables need to be checked for validity and plausibility;

    ▶ what the possible effects of not checking are

▶ how difficult it is to isolate and cope with the error (define range of possible error actions);

▶ based on this information, which checks should be made, which should not be made; and

▶ the program. How much longer is the code now than it was before defensive code was added?

2.   Code the design for the statistics module of PAS in PASCAL or another strongly typed language of your choice. Then do the following:

▶ Add the prologue and in-line comments.

▶ Determine and add the amount of defensive code.

▶ List boundary values for all variables and loops and the proper action required.

▶ Which of the rules for loops are followed, which are not? Why?

▶ Look at your largest (smallest) module for five minutes. Then put it away and try to reproduce it from memory. Compare the two versions. How many errors have you made for the large one (the small one)? What does that tell you?

3.   Code the statistics module of TAP in FORTRAN. Check it for compliance with all guidelines to enhance reliability. Pay particular attention to

▶ declaration and initialization of variables;

▶ type conversions and mixed data types in expressions;

▶ accuracy;

▶ input; and

▶ boundaries and loops.

4.   Code the PAS parser in SNOBOL. What makes this language so elegant but also error prone? Hint: Look at all the reliability techniques in this chapter and apply them to SNOBOL code.

9.4.2. Performance

Selecting a good algorithm and appropriate data structures yields the best performance. Using machine language cannot make an exponential algorithm nonexponential. It only decreases the constants in the formula for time or space requirements. The same is true for "clever" coding. It reduces the readability, reliability, maintainability, and adaptability of the code. Many "clever" coding practices are unnecessary. An optimizing compiler can do the same job (reducing computations within a loop, rearranging operations, introducing auxiliary variables to prevent multiple computations of the same expression, etc.). Programming such microefficiencies can actually outsmart the compiler and prevent it from performing its optimizations.

How should we select data structures and how should we implement efficient design algorithms? The answer is to look at the types of operations that are performed on the design objects and match them to the available data structures. List the types and frequencies of access to a data structure and use this information to select a representation that is efficient for the most often used operations (and maybe less efficient for the lesser used ones). The most important data structures on an abstract level are lists, tables, queues, stacks, sets, and graphs.

Graphs come in a variety of shapes. They can be directed graphs, such as binary trees or generalized trees, they can have cycles, or they can be nondirected. The more specialized the graph, the more efficient the algorithms can be made, because they can make assumptions about the graph. A general directed graph with many arcs between nodes is often stored in an adjacency matrix (binary) **m**. Element *m[i, j]* is 1 if the graph shows

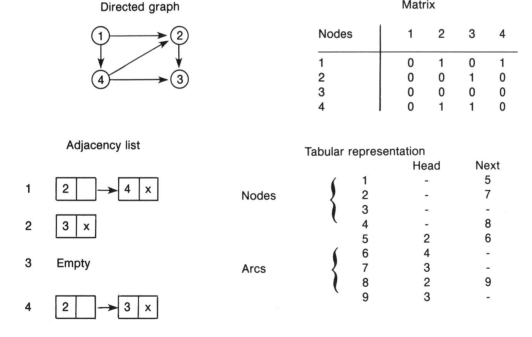

Figure 9.11 Graph Representations.

an arc from node i to node j; it is 0 otherwise. Storage for such an implementation is of order (N^2) where N is the number of nodes. So is the time to initialize the matrix. If the graph tends to have few arcs, we may be better off implementing the graph with an adjacency list for each node that gives the indices of all nodes to which a given node has an arc. Storage is of the order $(N + A)$, the number of nodes and arcs. We could simplify the linked list representation into a two column table, one column for the number of a node connected to the current node by an arc, the other for an index to the next entry in the table that has a node to which the current one is connected. Figure 9.11 shows these different ways to represent a directed tree.

Things are easier for graphs where the arcs are not directed, because only the upper triangle of the matrix needs to be stored; $m[i, j] = 1$ implies that $m[i, j] = 1$ also. We can actually store the matrix in $(N-1) + (N-2) + \ldots + 1 = N(N - 1)/2$ places. This is an approach that we can also use for other symmetric structures such as the covariance matrix for TAP.

Tabular representation simplifies further when the graph is a binary tree. We can store it in a table that has two entries for every node, one for the left son of a node, the other for the right son (cf. Figure 7.12). Alternately we could implement the binary tree using elements that have two types of links to each other: **left_son** links and **right_son** links. Depending on the stability or dynamic nature of the tree (adding and deleting elements or establishing the tree once, then searching it) we may find the first or the second representation preferable. Higher level language implementations often prefer linking elements directly—it is a more direct and obvious approach.

Most algorithms follow a balanced divide and conquer strategy to solve problems by cutting them approximately in half. Partial solutions are combined to an overall solution. Besides this basic solution philosophy there are several other categories for algorithms. For a more detailed discussion see [Zieg83]. Some algorithms compute solutions through successive approximation. Many numerical algorithms fall into this category, such as numeric integration, anything that can be expressed mathematically in terms of an infinite sum that converges ($\sin(\mathbf{x})$, Taylor series expansion, square root computation), optimization of functions and solving some types of sets of equations (differential and otherwise). Often they involve successive iterations which approach the true solution more and more closely. If the method is based on an accurate mathematical solution, they are often guaranteed to reach it (convergence to the solution). If they are heuristic, they may not.

Mathematical optimization sometimes uses so-called hill-climbing methods, which are based on knowledge about the function. Steepest descent uses knowledge about the gradient to minimize a multivariate function. Heuristics on the other hand do not assume or need such knowledge. Therefore they sometimes reach dead ends and have to backtrack. This happens also in situations when the program can apply one of a set of

Graph   Tabular

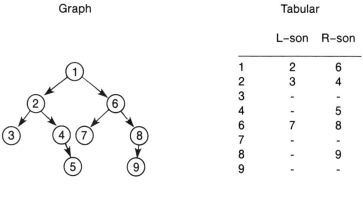

	L-son	R-son
1	2	6
2	3	4
3	-	-
4	-	5
6	7	8
7	-	-
8	-	9
9	-	-

Linked list

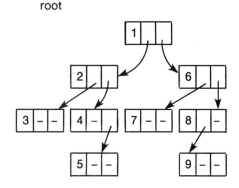

Figure 9.12 Tree Representations.

rules to proceed but is not guaranteed that the rule selected will lead to success. Finding a path through a maze or determining strategy and a set of moves in a game fall into this category. The algorithm guesses and, if the guess was wrong, backs up to try another venue. Enumerating or evaluating all possibilities before selecting the best one may be too expensive or take too much time and storage.

Some algorithms solve a problem by working backwards from the solution to the problem. We determine the path through a maze going from the exit to entry as opposed to the other way around. In TAP, we might work backwards from the tax forms to the tax data. We should check whether it would actually be easier to work backwards than forwards. This is not a new technique. Many mathematical theorems are proven that way. In fact, we could go backward and forward at the same time, meeting somewhere in the middle (STS works exactly this way). Such algorithms fall into the category of dynamic programming.

A powerful and elegant way to implement many problem solutions is recursion. Recursion states the solution in terms of a transformation into a simpler variant of the same problem. We find it not just in programming but in mathematics as well. F is a recursive function, iff

1. $F(n) = G(n, F(n - 1))$ for a known function G, and

2. $F(1) =$ some known value.

An example of a recursive function definition are Fibonacci numbers:

$$F(n) = \begin{cases} F(n-1) + F(n-2) & n > 2 \\ 1 & n = 1,2 \end{cases}$$

We could translate this directly into a recursive function. However, if we look at how the solution is actually computed, we find out quickly that it is very inefficient; most intermediate Fibonacci numbers are computed more than once in separate subtrees of the recursion. It is more efficient to implement it with a loop. The lesson from this example is that obvious recursion is not always efficient. We should investigate whether it is before programming. As a general rule, recursively defined data structures (such as trees) most often fare best with recursive algorithms. If a recursion has to be transformed into a nonrecursive solution, there are several methods:

▶ store precomputed results to avoid duplicating effort;

▶ transform the recursion into a loop (most mathematical recursion can be dealt with this way); and

▶ use a stack.

Let us explain the principle of removing recursion with the example of a tree traversal. The recursive version of a tree traversal is

```
traverse(tree);
visit root;
IF exist THEN traverse(left subtree);
IF exist THEN traverse(right subtree);
```

The stack solution pushes the entire tree onto the stack. As it pops one element at a time, it pushes its subtrees onto the stack (in reverse order, so that the subtree at which you want to look first will come up first) as the further problems to be solved:

```
push(tree);
WHILE not empty(stack) DO
  BEGIN
    pop(last element);
    visit its root;
    IF exist THEN push(right subtree);
    IF exist THEN push(left subtree)
END;
```

When translating a recursive solution into a nonrecursive one using a stack, we take the recursive solution and push the entire "problem" onto the stack. Then, in a loop, we pop the topmost (sub)problem, perform the computations as stated in the recursive design, and push the next lower subproblems onto the stack in *reverse* order (so that they can come up in the correct order when the next set of pop operations is performed).

Our discussions about efficient algorithm and data structure implementation did *not* change the basic data or algorithm, such as a tree traversal or the covariance matrix and its computation. What we did was follow efficiency guidelines on how to code them. Recursion is often expensive, because for each successive recursive call to a function or procedure, the full instantiation record has to be saved (registers, variables, return addresses). Often the nesting level is deep (try the recursive version of computing the 100th Fibonacci number). The overhead involved in nesting procedure calls and restoring states on the way back can be considerable and must be worth it. When it isn't, we may state the design using recursion but transform the recursive algorithm into a nonrecursive one. Some languages do not allow recursion (FORTRAN). Then we also have to transform a recursive solution into a nonrecursive one.

Removing recursion when it is too expensive for storage and/or time considerations is only one of the guidelines for efficient code. [Kern78] and [Vant78] state a variety of others. Those books, too, stress the importance of readability over efficiency. First, the code must work correctly, satisfy reliability requirements (robustness in the face of system and user errors), and be understandable. Avoid overly complex algorithms, especially those that are exponential or polynomial if they work on large amounts of data.

After implementing and testing the most appropriate algorithm, instrument the program and find out which parts are worth making more efficient. Programmers have been notoriously bad at predicting which part of the code consumes the most time ([Bent82]) without measuring it.

It is important to estimate how much storage and execution time a module will need when we make decisions about how to code the design. When we have options, choose the one that fits the performance requirements best. When storage is scarce, investigate whether overlays would help. A design structured around phases is a good candidate. Temporary variables and data structures can be reused (careful! This needs comments because it is easily confusing). Consider the trade-offs between storage savings and increased execution time due to linking instructions and data and the increased amount of I/O.

In virtual (paged) memory systems, overlays are hardly ever necessary, but we need to consider locality of reference. The bigger and more volatile a program's working set is, the more time will be spent paging. Avoid jumping around in a program. It can trigger many page faults. The same is true for global or **COMMON** data. They may be stored in one page but referenced in a variety of others; then all of them are part of the working set. When different modules define different global data, it aggravates this situation. Data references should preserve locality of reference. For example, assume you want to initialize a very large matrix that will take up n pages in memory. You can initialize all m entries on page 1, then all entries on page 2, and so forth. This incurs n page faults. If the algorithms initialize the matrix so that one entry on each page is initialized in the loop, there are $m * n$ page faults. While this is an extreme example, loops should be constructed to minimize page faults. We have to know how the program stores data structures such as matrices. We should also reference data in the order in which they are stored internally (declaration often indicates order).

A very important point concerns the arrangement of modules and how they are linked. Procedures and functions that call each other in sequence during execution should be called together. Sometimes they might even fit onto the same page. This reduces page faults. Cluster analysis ([Ferr78], [Spir77], [Frei72]) helps to determine how to organize and link parts of a program to minimize paging overhead. In the same vein, parts of a module that are only executed rarely should be removed. Those parts reduce the space that could hold more frequently called code. Such rarely executed parts of a module include more involved error handling routines and treatment of special (rare) cases. We might also need to violate some rules on when to initialize data: instead of initializing them at the beginning, it can save paging overhead to initialize them before they are used. This increases the density of reference and reduces page-outs and page faults.

It increases efficiency to initialize as many variables and constants as possible during compile time. We may also save space by ensuring that storage alignment for the declared variables does not waste space. [Vant78] suggests declaring the larger types first.

Loops can cost time because of the organization involved (looping parameters, checking conditions). Therefore they are often avoided unless their bodies are small with few iterations. Take all invariant parts out of the loop to avoid repeated calculation of the same quantity. Addressing through subscripts takes longer. They should not be used in loops when a single variable is possible. Sometimes we can reduce the number of subscripts by storing a multidimensional matrix into an array. That speeds up execution, too. A compiler capable of global optimization will do this.

Mixing types can also cost time due to the necessary conversion. Some types have faster operations altogether. Depending on the hardware, fixed point arithmetic may be faster than floating point arithmetic. Some arithmetic operations are faster than others: multiplication and division are faster than exponentiation and trigonometric functions. We save time by reducing the amount of reevaluation. In conditions, elements that appear more than once are eliminated using deMorgan's laws. Where this is not possible, precomputation of results can save time. The same is true for frequent calculations. This requires more space and must be assessed carefully. Some run-time systems stop evaluating a condition as soon as it is clear what its logical value is. We can use this to make our program faster, stating the most likely conditions first. Nesting **IF** statements also avoids repeated calculation of conditions but it reduces clarity and readability.

I/O also costs time. The program has to wait until a path to the I/O device is free, wait for a connection, wait until the data are found on the device, and possibly wait for a reconnect and data transmission. Depending on the amount of data and the congestion of the I/O subsystem, this can take a significant amount of time. It is faster to transfer as much data as possible at any one time. The total time spent waiting for transfer will be lower, because it happens less often. On the other hand, more storage or more buffers are needed. A trade-off is made between block size and storage available. An I/O-bound system usually is better off with more buffers and smaller block sizes. These issues must be considered during the coding phase. Sometimes performance measurements need to be taken, and sometimes data are known and hand calculations suffice.

Some of the guidelines for improving performance contradict those for clarity and good structure. Therefore, it is important to consider the effect on clarity before we follow them.

Problems and Questions

1. Assume we decide to store the upper triangle of a symmetric adjacency matrix (nondirected graph) in an array of length $N(N - 1)/2$. How do we access the element $m[i, j]$? Now assume that we want to store the covariance matrix for PAS. We need to store the diagonal elements, too. How long will the array be? How do we access the element $m[i, j]$?

2.   Which of the rules and guidelines of Sections 9.2 and 9.3. are violated through effi-ciency rules of Section 9.4? How would you trade off one against the other? Make examples.

9.5.   Code Improvements

9.5.1.   Clarity and Structure

Before improving code, we must determine whether it needs it. Have we violated any of the rules about good structure and clarity? Why? Sometimes there was an important reason for it. Is there a better way to code what we want the program to do? Relatively simple improvements are to follow rules about commenting, indentation, layout of program parts, naming of variables, etc.

Lack of good structure is a much harder problem. If it seems impossible to improve the structure of the code, the best approach is usually to rewrite it. In less severe cases, restructuring the code can help. Some structurally based problems with code are due to an unstructured language. We have already encountered suggestions on how to write structured code in an unstructured language (Section 9.2.).

Even with a high level language, we are sometimes faced with poorly structured code. There are three methods to restructure code:

▶ node splitting,

▶ adding variables, and

▶ procedural extraction.

Let us consider the following program:

```
MORE: IF (valid(new_request))                    {cond_1}
           THEN
               BEGIN
                   add(new_request);             {stmt_1}
                   read(new_request);            {stmt_1}
                   IF (new_request ⟨ ⟩ EOF)      {cond_2}
                       THEN GOTO MORE
                       ELSE close_file           {stmt_2}
               END;
```

This program contains a loop that is conditioned on **cond_1** and **cond_2**, except for the first time around the loop. We could split the loop, one part dealing with the first execution of the **IF** statement (which only depends on **cond_1**) and second part consisting of the remainder of the iterations. This results in the following code:

```
IF (valid(new_request))
  THEN
    BEGIN
      add(new_request);
      read(new_request);
      WHILE (valid(new_request) & new_request 〈 〉 EOF) DO
        BEGIN
          add(new_request);
          read(new_request)
        END;
      IF (NOT new_request 〈 〉 EOF) THEN close_file
    END;
```

The new code is structured and does not have a **GOTO**. But is it "better" or more readable?

Node splitting duplicated the code of **stmt_1**. If it is the major part of the code, its size almost doubles. We might consider making it into a procedure call. Secondly, the conditions are evaluated more than once. This will only work if **cond_1** and **cond_2** do not have any side effects (no variables are changed due to the evaluation of the conditions). If a program contained many **GOTO** statements, removing these **GOTO**s could increase the program exponentially in size. This is clearly not desirable. Node splitting is not always a useful technique. A program with **GOTO**s may be more readable than its "structured" alternatives.

We can eliminate **GOTO**s by adding variables. This happened when we translated the design of the **get (token)** procedure into code (cf. Figure 9.9). Because PASCAL does not have a **LEAVE** construct, we avoided a **GOTO** using a flag variable (**leave**). It is possible to translate every program that has **GOTO**s into one without [Zelk79]. Number each statement. Then add code that sets the appropriate next statement number after each execution of a statement. The execution of every statement is conditioned on whether the statement counter has the proper value. All statements but the last are enclosed in a **WHILE** loop, which is executed as long as the statement counter has not reached the value that identifies the last statement. Let us take an example.

For a program of length n, we add about n statements and that many new conditions. This will slow down execution significantly. While an algorithmic possibility of eliminating **GOTO**s is possible, it need not result in a well structured and understandable, nor an efficient (time and/or space) program. On the other hand, adding variables judi-

```
        x := x+1;                          {stmt_1}
        . . . .
L:      y := f(x);                         {stm_10}
        . . .
        IF y < 100 THEN GOTO L;            {stmt_25}
        . . .
        END;                               {stmt_57}
```

Figure 9.13 Example Code with GOTO.

ciously can eliminate **GOTO**s and still be readable if we don't overdo it with flag variables.

Methods of **GOTO** removal are not automatically any clearer than the original code. When redesigning code is too expensive or we want to avoid the tendency to extend the capabilities of the existing design and code ("beware of second system" [Broo75]), we try to restructure. Restructuring software that uses **GOTO** removal techniques is commercially available, e.g., the Structuring Engine ([Deba75A], [Deba75B]), or RXVP/R ([Mill75], Melt75]). Sometimes we have to redesign but can use parts of an existing system as building blocks. The more independent modules are, the easier this is. When we have to restructure, we should analyze the existing structure first (as done in the previous two methods). Control flow graphs (cf. Figure 9.15) are a valuable aid. We usually find three different types of blocks of code:

▶ SESE (single entry single exit). Those are okay.

▶ SEME (single entry multiple exit). The example with the **LEAVE** construct is an SEME block. Transform it into an SESE block by introducing additional Boolean variables.

```
WHILE (stmt ⟨ ⟩ 57) DO
  BEGIN
    IF (stmt = 1) THEN BEGIN x:=x+1; stmt := 2 END;
    . . . .
    IF (stmt = 10) THEN BEGIN y:=f(x); stmt := 11 END;
    . . . .
    IF (stmt = 25) THEN IF y < 100 THEN stmt := 10;
    . . . .
  END;
```

Figure 9.14 Example Code Without GOTO.

```
        stmt_1;
        GOTO L2;
        . . . .
        stmt_2;
        GOTO L1;
        . . . .
L1:     stmt_3;



        IF (cond_1) THEN GOTO L3


L2:     stmt_4;
        GOTO L4;

L3:     stmt_5;


L4:     stmt_6;
        . . .
        GOTO L1
        . . . .
        GOTO L1
```

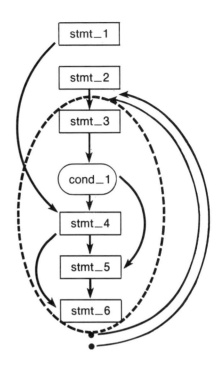

Figure 9.15 MEME Block and its Flow-graph.

▶ MESE (multiple entry single exit). This type of undesirable code block can be restructured through node splitting. Sometimes we can avoid MESE code through procedure extraction such as in the following example.

Extract the portion marked in the bubble as procedure **proc_1**. Then the code is rewritten as in Figure 9.16. It is an SESE block. There is some code duplication because there is more than one control path through the part of the flow graph that was extracted as **proc_1**.

Improving the quality of the code through restructuring is not only an activity for the coding phase. The need for restructuring occurs more often during maintenance when patches to the code and adding, eliminating, or changing features resulted in badly structured code. It is, of course, better to avoid badly structured code to begin with. Structured redesign is one of the better approaches to reduce the need for code restructuring.

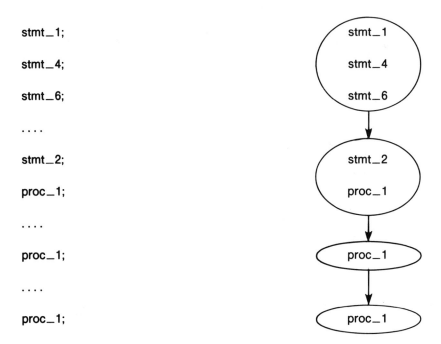

<table>
<tr><td>

```
stmt_1;

stmt_4;

stmt_6;

. . . .

stmt_2;

proc_1;

. . . .

proc_1;

. . . .

proc_1;
```

</td></tr>
</table>

Figure 9.16 SESE through Procedural Extraction.

Problems and Questions

1. Restructure the following piece of code using

    ▶ code duplication

    ▶ procedure extraction:

    ```
        stmt_1;
        GOTO L1;
        . . . .
        stmt_2;
    L1: stmt_3;
        IF cond_1 THEN GOTO L2;
        stmt_4;
    L2: stmt_5;
    L3: stmt_6;
    ```

2. Use a Boolean variable to restructure the following block of code:

```
        stmt_1;
L1:     IF (NOT cond_1) THEN GOTO L4;              {first exit}
L2:     IF cond_2 THEN GOTO L3;
        stmt_2;
        GOTO L4;                                   {second exit}
L3:     stmt_3;
        GOTO L1;
L4:     END
```

9.5.2. Performance

After the code has been written and tested, we sometimes have to improve its efficiency, in either storage or execution time. Because some of the methods for improving code efficiency can also help when writing code with better performance, we will discuss these methods here. Please, consider however, that we want to improve code that is working correctly (has been tested). Optimizing programs is also a maintenance activity. The procedure to optimize the performance of a program consists of the following steps:

▶ Partition the program into measurable parts.

▶ Measure those parts. This might be timing their execution or measuring their storage needs over time. This might require instrumentation. Code is added to measure time through calling the system clock at various points in the program. Sometimes measurement tools can be used.

▶ Establish an execution time and space profile. This is the basis for analyzing what various parts of the software are doing and why they are doing it. A profile could tell us for example that particular parts of the software are never executed. Then we should find out why. Maybe they are inaccessible. Maybe the data they would be dealing with are very infrequent, and performance for those cases is not crucial. Then we don't have to worry about improving those parts of the code. When a profile involves counts, we should see whether and to which degree there is a relationship between them. It may be worth our while to improve the performance of several parts simultaneously, because execution counts for those parts are related. Analysis of the execution profile addresses both time and space. We should also determine to which degree time and space could be traded off.

▶ Target the parts of the program that consume the most resources (time, space) and estimate the degree of possible improvement.

▶ Estimate the effort necessary to improve their performance. We can use a formula from [Vant78]:

$$\frac{\% \text{ of time} * \% \text{ of improvement}}{\text{effort needed}}$$

Those parts of the system with the highest ratio are the ones we should select as candidates for improvement first.

Let us look at measurement in more detail. Before we start to measure, we should do a little planning of our measurement experiment. What is it that we want to measure, why, and how should we go about it? We want to measure timing behavior of software, let's say, when representative problems are solved with it. This set of representative problems is our workload for the software. We can use test cases from the acceptance test for it. We usually want to figure out in more detail in which routines the software spends most of its time or the percentage of time of total execution time spent in each module. Sometimes it is possible to measure data directly; at other times we need to establish measurements indirectly. We can usually measure how often a routine is entered and how long it takes to execute it each time. If we add all such times, we get total time spent in it. This is a derived measure. It is also the result of a data reduction process. We often take a series of measurements and then reduce them by computing a derived quantity of interest. At times we use the reduction process to filter out the effects of events in the system that would bias the measurements, such as measurement overhead.

After we have determined which performance indices we need to measure, we need to determine how to do it. Should we measure when certain events occur such as invocation of a procedure, or should we sample? Sampling measures in fixed or variable time intervals, but it does not necessarily measure the occurrence of all events. If we were interested in the average execution time of a procedure, we could measure every tenth or fifteenth execution, form an average, multiply it with the number of invocations and get an estimated total execution time. Such sampling is often used when it would be too costly or too inaccurate to measure all occurrences of events.

Usually we measure the program's behavior through calls to self-built, off-the shelf, or system software. Such measurement tools are called software monitors. Since they are software themselves, they take up system resources (time to execute, storage, and I/O contention for measurement data). This can cause interference. The measured software runs more slowly than its uninstrumented counterpart. It may also take up more space. This can result in inaccuracies. Because of this, we often must measure the degree of interference and subtract the effect of measurement from the data. The time interference of software probes or checkpoints is proportional to the execution time of the code that they call. Space interference is often much harder to determine.

Another source for measurement inaccuracy are variations in the workload on the system due to other programs. We should try to measure when the system is stable and not when workload changes happen. A sudden surge in demand for resources changes system behavior and usually invalidates measurement in progress, unless it is independent from such interference.

Besides the degree of interference and its effect on measurement data, there are other issues to consider before we select a specific tool. Its accuracy must match the required degree of accuracy. Its resolution must be such that measurements can be taken at the frequency that events happen or sampling needs to be done. It must be able to measure what we need to measure. This is called scope. We should also look into a tool's prereduction capability. Reduction done by the tool on-line reduces the number of data that need to be stored for later off-line reduction.

Software tools are capable of measuring how often variable or data structures have been accessed, whether values have been changed or whether they have specific values, and how often which types of instruction were executed. Often we can use accounting information that is supplied to a charging algorithm to collect performance data. Probes that access the system clock are another way to collect timing information. A tool that can recognize the beginning and end of procedures can be built to insert probes or calls to a measurement routine. The instrumented program is then executed. Afterwards the collected data can be analyzed. This is the basis for determining which parts of a program are crucial to performance and why that is so.

Now let's assume that we know which routines are the most time consuming and which data structures and parts of code take up the most space. [Bent82] describes techniques that can be used to trade space against time and to improve performance characteristics of programs. We will describe some of these rules here. For those readers who wish to get a more detailed understanding of code improvements, Bentley's book is warmly recommended. There are several ways to improve software. We can modify data structures, the executable part of the code (control structures, logic, and arithmetic expressions), and program structure (procedures). We will relate the most important of Bentley's rules.

Data Structures

Often we can save time when we can find or modify information in a data structure faster, usually we must augment it. Pointers are a good way to target parts of a data structure. The way we organized the data structure for the deductions list is such an example. We had a list of pointers for various deduction categories. They can hint at the location of the data. Sometimes hints are not as obvious and may not locate a data item. Then we should have an alternate (slower, but robust) algorithm to fall back on. On the other hand, if space was at a premium, we could get rid of the list of pointers, store all deductions sequentially, and spend a lot more time on searching through it. It is often possible to save space by getting rid of information in a data structure that can be deduced, searched for, or recomputed.

Conversely, we can save time by storing precomputed results. This we have also done in the deductions list by keeping a running total of deductions in categories. Alternately, to save space, we could do away with this item and recompute the totals as needed.

We can use buffers and big data structures to keep data in core so that we do not have to wait for I/O that often. This can speed up execution time if the waiting for I/O is a big part of execution time. It costs more space, though. It will not work well if what is in the buffers is not used and we often need something that is not in core (poor locality). Matrix access should be analyzed carefully in this regard.

If we are not sure that we will always need a quantity, we may not compute it until it is needed. For example, in PAS's similarities module, we may compute similarity indices only on demand as opposed to computing all of them. Then we store each one and never recompute it. This reduces time for evaluation but adds time when it must be checked to see whether it has been computed. We have to trade-off one against the other.

Code

Loops are a source of wasted time. As a first approach, all computations in the body of a loop that are not dependent on loop parameters should be removed to the outside of the loop. This eliminates repeated computations of the same quantity over and over. We should also investigate whether we can simplify tests. It is faster to have one test with one category than several. Often we can achieve that by inventing "special values" for data. [Bent82] suggests avoiding repeated tests for whether we have reached the end of a data structure by adding a sentinel at the boundary, which will cause the search through the data structure to stop when we have "found" what we were searching for. This simplifies the condition

```
item_found OR end_of_list
```

to

```
item_found
```

It makes the code less understandable and less robust. We must make sure that there is room for the sentinel.

We can also apply what we have said about moving computations out of the loop to the computation of conditions. Then we only have to check for its Boolean value inside but do not have to recompute it every time around the loop.

Loops require initialization and checking for loop conditions, and thus they create overhead compared to straightline code. This is why it may pay to "unroll" loops. This is easy and does not detract too much from readability unless it is done often when the loops are short. We could unroll all the loops in the code that have as loop indices **FOR i:= 1 TO novar** (in the code we have written for PAS). **novar** is only four, and while it will make the code less elegant and readable, it is still not too bad. Even for big loops, we can gain some time by partially unrolling the loop and doing a fixed number of steps at once. Loop unrolling makes a program longer but faster. If we don't know how many times the program will have to execute a loop, we might try to use the sentinel trick again for indicating the end of the data structure.

In lower level languages that do not have high level looping constructs, it may pay to rotate a loop with an unconditional **GOTO** at the bottom of the loop to get rid of an unproductive **GOTO**. We should *not* apply this technique in higher level languages because it outsmarts the compiler.

There is another useful way to save on loop overhead. When two loops work on the same set of looping elements or data structures, we may be able to combine the two loops. While this reduces loop overhead, it can be confusing to the reader.

When writing conditions and logical expressions we should use deMorgan's laws to make their evaluation less costly. We can also use a simpler equivalent condition. Instead of asking $(\mathbf{a} + \mathbf{b}) * (\mathbf{a} - \mathbf{b}) > 0$, we can ask $a > b$ if we know that a and b are positive quantities. We can also use knowledge of a function's mathematical properties to simplify conditions (convexity, monotonicity, positive definiteness, etc.). This can also help to short-circuit computations when thresholds have been reached. We should make sure, however, that side effects will not cause mistakes.

Some languages evaluate tests in order and stop evaluating as soon as the expression is known to be **TRUE** or **FALSE**. If we order tests so that successful ones or inexpensive ones come first, we can save time, too. We can also do a space-time trade-off by precomputing and storing the function results of a complex logical or other function in a table for quick look-up. The domain of such a function should be small and finite. Conversions, **CASE** statements, and other multiway branches can be implemented this way.

Sometimes it is possible to reduce the number of Boolean variables, especially flag variables, by using an **IF-THEN-ELSE** statement instead. The **THEN** part of the statement specifies the code to be executed in case the Boolean variable is true, the **ELSE** part when it is false.

Execution time can also be saved by declaring constants and initializing variables at compile time. We can save time by replacing arithmetic expressions by their algebraic identities, which are cheaper. $\mathbf{X} * \mathbf{X}$ is cheaper than $\mathbf{X}^2$. In loops, adding a quantity repeatedly is less expensive than multiplying it with the loop parameter. We should be careful, however, to find out which of these reductions the compiler can do on its own. These we should leave alone. Otherwise the result may be worse. Sometimes expressions have parts that are used in several places. If we evaluate them once and assign them to an auxiliary variable, we can save time. Many compilers, however, can recognize and optimize such common sub-expressions.

Structure

During design and implementation we were striving for small independent modules. We have implemented them in procedures and functions. Every procedure call means overhead; one of the first things we can do is to write the code of a procedure in line, if

▶ they are performance bottlenecks and called often, and

▶ they have been designed as operations for an abstract data type.

It helps if they are only called in one place (no code duplication). Sometimes we can reduce the number of parameters and make the routine more specialized and faster by breaking it up into several. We should also try to identify which are the cases a procedure should handle most efficiently because they occur the most often and try to improve those. Next, we should determine whether a less general algorithm would be faster (it may not be) or whether the opposite is true. As we discussed before, recursive routines can cost dearly, and it may be faster to implement them using iteration or a stack. Iteration is often easy if the last thing a recursive procedure does is to call itself. We should also investigate precomputation and support routines as a way to make things faster. Parallelism is a powerful tool to speed up execution as long as we keep synchronization and precedence rules in mind.

Some of the suggestions are dependent on a particular system or compiler. That is why it is so important to know what your system and compiler does before embarking on low level improvement activities. Often we can determine, without actual execution, the approximate run time of alternatives on a comparative basis. We need to know estimates of the instruction time for all high level language constructs (for explicit timings see [Shaw79], [Ferr78]). If we assume the instruction of type i takes t_i units of time and that it is executed n_i times, we can predict its execution time as

$$t = \sum_i n_i t_i.$$

If we have a series of executions of each instruction of type i and can determine the time and the frequency of execution f_i, we can compute the average instruction time as

$$t = \sum_i f_i t_i.$$

Either can be useful to predict whether one improvement option is better than another. Since this simple model does not include queueing delays, it will not accurately predict execution time. Contention with other workload on the system can make a considerable difference in the actual numbers. For more detail on performance models see [Leve77], [Ferr78], and [Triv82].

While there are some modeling techniques that help to assess the effect of code improvement, the only way to find out for sure is to test an option. It is indispensable to know what the system and compiler do with the code. All the rules for transforming a program into a faster or ⌐maller one should (almost) never be used during design or the first coding. When we do make changes, we should make sure that we do not make code overly messy just to make it fast. It will cost dearly during maintenance. Sometimes it pays to leave the old understandable code as a comment, but only if it doesn't confuse more than it helps. The transformations that were explained are not a substitute for a clean design and proper algorithms and data structures. [Bent82] gives a series of caveats about his transformation rules:

▶ Some of them can backfire. Make sure a rule gets you the improvement you need.

▶ Go for the biggest improvement (that's why we identified the critical parts of the system first).

▶ Don't go overboard with the rules; it makes code unintelligible.

▶ Thoroughly retest the parts of the system that were changed.

▶ Measure whether you got the hoped for improvement. You may want to keep a set of notes to learn which actions work the best with your compiler and system and which actions work on more than one system.

▶ Carefully document the changes.

In the next section we will encounter several methods for reviewing code before it is formally accepted into the testing process. Some of what has been explained in this chapter are activities that occur during maintenance, during and after the first code review, and during the coding phase proper. We have included this material here because it is a coding activity. We invite the reader to compare the code transformations to the rules of developing structured, readable code.

Problems and Questions

1. Find out for your system and a compiler you work with what transformations are favorable and unfavorable for performance. Which of the code improvements can the optimizing compiler do without you?

2.   Measure the execution times of the language constructs for an HLL of your choice (PASCAL, PL/1, SIMULA67, ALGOL68, MODULA-2, etc.). Include the following:

▶   assignment,

▶   **IF-THEN-ELSE** with various complexities in the condition,

▶   loops (**FOR, WHILE, REPEAT–UNTIL**),

▶   expression evaluation $(+,-,*,/,**,...)$,

▶   subscript calculation, and

▶   parameter calls with various types and numbers of parameters.

Estimate the execution times of a program segment of your choice. Then try to improve its execution time. Before you run it, reestimate. Compare actual and estimated improvement.

3.   Determine which measurement facilities your system has for inserting probes into a program, for measuring timing characteristics, for reducing data (and deal with interference), for analyzing such information at relative frequencies, and for histograms, fractile diagrams, correlation coefficients, significance levels, ANOVA, etc. Put together a list of tools and how to use them so that you have defined a methodology for performance evaluation of programs on your system.

9.6.   Code Walk-throughs

Walk-throughs are the major phase-testing technique for the coding phase. Some are called code reviews, which can be done in a static or dynamic manner. During a static code review the code is read like a book. Items that are checked include [Myer76]

▶   Documentation. Is it complete and accurate?

▶   Readability.

▶   Conditions in **IF-THEN-ELSE** and **WHILE** statements, loop termination in **FOR** loops. It is a common source of error to confuse conditions that are closely related, such as $<$ instead of $<=$, especially when a design condition was inverted for coding. Off-by-one errors may leave the last or first element in a data structure unconsidered or may exceed array boundaries. Complex logical tests need to be checked, too. If they are not readable, that should have been flagged previously.

▶ Interfaces. Is the number, order, and type of parameters (**COMMON** blocks, etc.), matching with all usages?

▶ Overlays. **EQUIVALENCE** statements are a common source of error. Faulty overlays can cause a lot of trouble if not detected early.

As in other walk-throughs, errors and deficiencies are only recorded, not corrected. In a dynamic code reading session the code is executed "manually" by walking a representative set of test cases through the code under review. The review group usually consists of a small group of people and a moderator. They may include specialists like "code inspectors" whose task is to spot violations of standards, often made errors (interfaces), etc.

In a dynamic code walk through, the execution flow for a number of representative test cases is walked through. We should cover cases to test invalid and boundary input as well as default values (use ones developed earlier). When the design does not specify in detail the algorithm and how to code it, it may be necessary to explain part of a module's logic (fusing loops and other transformations to increase performance). Explaining how a piece of code works is often enough to make us aware of an error we have made. When programmers are involved in their work, they often suffer from "tunnel vision" or what psychologists have called "cognitive dissonance"; i.e., they have a hard time discovering their own mistakes. A review team or "buddy system" may help. The buddy system is less formal than a walk-through. Programmers exchange code with each other and cricitize it constructively. This works well when there is a common interest for doing it. It will not work when it can be used to put someone down and threaten his or her self-image.

Why don't we just throw our code at the compiler to see whether it works and where the problems are? There are several good reasons not to. First, a compiler will not detect all problems. This is particularly true for weakly typed languages (FORTRAN, PL/1) and those that accept almost anything as a legal statement (SNOBOL). Second, even if they are good at detecting syntax errors, they cannot detect semantic ones. It would be like publishing a book without reviewing or proofreading it. Thirdly, the combination of syntax and semantic quality control through code inspections has been shown to save a considerable amount of money. [Myer76] reports a huge difference for costs per line of code.

Besides the code itself, the documentation needs to be checked, too. We also must establish that the code actually is a transformation of its design and preserves its functionality. For this we need the module's external specifications as well as the PDL that was written to describe the inside of a module. In essence, we can have another $n - 1 + 1$ review: a representative of the design team can pursue the interests of the designers. Someone who will be involved in testing the code should inspect it, too. We can use the techniques that were introduced in previous phases in this one as well. The aim is to deliver source code that compiles correctly the first time, has (based on inspection) the capabilities the design blueprinted, is testable, and complies (with its associated documentation) with standards.

Problems and Questions

1. Take Figure 9.8 with a sketch of how to implement the **similarities** module.

    (a) What is wrong with it? (Hint: Are all variables declared? Is **covarmtr** changed anywhere and, if so, is this desirable? How about the **means** vector and **ptr**?

    (b) Is there enough commenting?

    (c) What would **mathlib**'s imported procedures have to be able to do in order for the module to work? Which variables do they need?

    (d) What can you say about the structure and how **similarities** is embedded into the rest of the system?

    (e) Are there any cases the module is unable to handle. What (if anything) will it do?

2. Take the answers from question 1 and improve the code. Add all necessary variables and comments, and if you deem it necessary, restructure the code or redefine interfaces (do you want parameters? which kind? which other modules are affected? which parts of the design need to be changed if any?).

9.7. Summary

This chapter presented pronciples of design-to-code translation. Characteristics of structured programs were reviewed. These included desirable programming constructs, commenting guidelines, standards, use of library routines, selection of variable and procedure names, construction of logical expressions, and the like. The reader who wants more depth in these areas may want to consider [Kern78], [Vant78], and [Bent86].

Not all languages provide the full range of structured programming constructs. When faced with an "unstructured" or structurally deficient language, we can still design in PDL, but then we need additional rules to translate PDL uniformly into structured code. We presented some translation rules and discussed how to define them. [Jens79] gives a full set of such rules for a variety of sequential programming languages. As an example of how to translate concurrent PDL into code, we described how to translate path expressions into a program using P/V operations on semaphores. More detail can be found in [Camp74] and [Laue75].

Next, we discussed aspects that make code more reliable. These include rules about how to handle loops and class boundaries for data, rules about the size of a code module, rules about input and output, rules about declaration and initialization of variables, and rules how to preserve accuracy of computation. We also discussed trade-offs between reliability and other qualities such as simplicity and performance. A good overview of these issues can be found in [Myer76].

The next section considered performance issues. We discussed various representations of abstract data types like stacks, trees, lists, and tables, and their access operations and the resulting space and time trade-offs. The importance of proper analysis of algorithms and measurement was emphasized. We mentioned the effect of overlays, shared data structures, locality of reference, mixing data types, and the performance impact of I/O and loops. The reader who is interested in more information on performance-oriented implementation is referred to [Bent82], [Ferr78], [Vant78].

The counterpart to well structured code with acceptable performance is code whose structure needs improvement and whose performance characteristics are deficient. Section 9.5.1. presented methods to restructure code: node splitting, adding variables, and procedural extraction. These are primarily techniques of **GOTO** removal.

While of some help, methods of **GOTO** removal are not automatically any clearer than the original code. Restructuring software that uses **GOTO** removal techniques is commercially available, e.g., the Restructuring Engine ([Deba75A], [Deba75B]), or RXVP/R ([Mill75], [Melt75]). The need for restructuring occurs more often during maintenance after repeated patching of code. It is, of course, better to avoid badly structured code to begin with. Structured redesign would start one level higher and avoid code restructuring, because old code is thrown out and new code is developed based on a modified design.

We sometimes must improve the efficiency of code, either in storage requirements or execution time. Section 9.5.2. presented a procedure on how to optimize the performance of a program. It includes partitioning the program into measurable parts, measuring to identify parts that are costly in terms of performance, establishing a time and space profile, identifying candidates for improvement, estimating the cost of improvement, making the improvement, and measuring its actual pay-off.

Techniques to make trade-offs between space and time were summarized. The reader who is interested in more detail should consult [Bent82]. These transformation techniques should (almost) never be used during design or the first coding. They make code less readable. When transformations are made, make sure that you do not make the code overly messy just to make it fast. It will cost dearly during maintenance. Performance transformations are no substitute for a clean design and good algorithms and data structures.

Walk-throughs or code reviews were discussed as the major phase-testing technique for the coding phase. They can be static or dynamic and include code and associated documentation. During an $n - 1 + 1$ review, design documentation and test plan are part of the information against which the code is compared.

This chapter tried to provide an overview of important coding issues. It was not meant to be an introduction to coding. It is assumed that the reader is familiar with good coding practices. Thus, this chapter served as a short review with references of where to find more detailed information.

▶ 10
Testing

10.1. Overview

All past chapters on phases in the software development life cycle had a section on phase testing. They dealt with applying quality control procedures to uncover any errors. Now that code is written, it, too, must undergo a quality control procedure. There are several steps to this, and the process is involved enough to warrant the definition of a phase of its own: the testing phase. This chapter discusses techniques and methods of the testing phase.

Section 10.2. explains the elements of the testing phase. It begins with a definition of the terms testing, validation, verification, certification, and debugging. Then the types of errors found through testing are listed. Next follows a definition of the elements of testing, including test preparation through a test plan, test case development, test execution and monitoring, and test evaluation. Different categories of testing methods are introduced.

Section 10.3. describes techniques for unit and program testing. It covers testing based on the code and its structure, which is known as structural testing or white-box testing. Section 10.3. also describes testing based on abstractions of the code, in particular on functional specifications. This is called specification-based testing or black-box testing. We also discuss a hybrid, functional testing as Howden [Howd87] describes it. It unifies white-box and black-box testing. Fault injection (or bebugging) is based on seeding a program with artificial errors. The rate at which both types of errors are found forms the basis for software reliability estimates. This can be used to control the testing process.

The next sections explain integration and system testing (10.4.), and acceptance and field testing (10.5.). A section on debugging describes how to deal with errors (10.6.). Section 10.7. defines (based on the knowledge of the preceding sections) what a test plan is and what it contains.

This chapter on testing contains both pragmatic and experimental material on testing techniques showing where the limits to testing support are. Some techniques have been successful in the research community but have not gained global acceptance. Reasons are given why this is so.

Unit testing is often the responsibility of the programmer while the later stages of testing (integration, system, and acceptance testing) may be done by independent testing groups. Testing requires a "destructive mind" in the sense that the tester must come up with test cases that are likely to break the software, i.e., uncover an error. If there is something wrong with the code, a good tester will find it.

A tester must also be familiar with a spectrum of testing techniques, their advantages and shortcomings. He must have an analytical mind and be able to extrapolate from detail into higher levels of abstraction. He may have to deal with significant code complexity when systems are large without getting overwhelmed. He must be patient and detail-oriented. A "sixth sense" about where there might be a problem also helps. These are high expectations that few people can meet. In spite of many testing techniques and organizational structures for testing groups, testing is still both art and science.

After reading this chapter, the reader will be familiar with complementary techniques to test units and programs, methods to assess testing progress, and integration test methods. The reader will also know several debugging techniques based on classes of anomalous behavior. He will also be able to develop a test plan.

10.2. Elements of the Testing Phase

Testing is a term with varied meanings, there are other related terms, such as validation, verification, certification, and debugging.

The literature is not always in agreement as to what these words mean: [Zelk79] define that validation aims to show by testing that a program performs according to specifications. Because specifications have been derived from the requirements (they describe how the software realizes its requirements), it is conceivable that other authors replace specifications with requirements. What is tested against is different, but the intent is the same: to show that the software delivers what was promised. How that is shown is not necessarily a mathematically rigorous method.

The second definition is from [Myer76]. He says that validation is finding errors by executing the program in a real environment. The emphasis here is not necessarily showing what works but finding what doesn't. This represents a totally different testing philosophy, namely that we cannot show the absence of errors, only their presence, and therefore testing should aim at uncovering errors.

The last definition by [Jens79] describes validation as ensuring that each end item product functions and contains the features as prescribed in the requirements and specifications. This is a somewhat extended version of [Zelk79]'s definition. It specifically states requirements as something to be tested against. None of these definitions require mathematical rigor as we would find in program proofs.

If a program or part thereof is mathematically proven correct, [Zelk79] defines that as verification. [Myer76] on the other hand understands verification as finding errors by executing the program in a test or simulated environment. [Taus77] includes, under his definition of verification, the following five demands:

▶ The program's responses fall within acceptable limits of functionally specified behavior (this is a less rigorous version of a previous definition, because it goes beyond yes/no comparisons when the program is tested against its specifications; it allows "acceptable limits").

▶ Requirements and project standards are met. This means that software is not successfully verified unless all project standards are shown to be met.

▶ Test procedures are generated. This is called test planning by other authors.

▶ Anomalies for corrective action are identified. This is Myer's [Myer76] notion of testing and validation.

▶ The program is ready for operation.

This definition for verification does not require any mathematical proof methods per se, rather it is a concise description of all activities of the testing phase. The last definition of verification is from [Jens79]. Verification assures that each level of requirements or specifications correctly echoes the intentions of the immediately superior level of requirements. All four of these definitions are decidedly different and it is advisable, therefore, for developers to agree on the definitions to avoid conflict and misunderstandings.

Certification is also understood differently by different authors. [Zelk79] sees certification as an overall process that includes validation and verification activities.

[Myer76] defines certification as an authoritative endorsement of program correctness. How it is done and who does it is up to particular development scenarios. Until such endorsement can take place, validation and verification activities are needed. Standards and procedures are often involved. Some countries have instituted "quality seals" for software tested by independent boards (e.g., Guetegemeinschaft Software e. V. in West Germany), and some contemplate instituting the equivalent of "underwriters laboratories for software." These are all efforts to establish a qualified authority, without which certification is a dubious activity. [Jens79] extends certification to the operational environment. Certification assures that a data processing system properly interacts within the total system context and performs specified functions in it.

Testing is often confused with debugging. Debugging starts when testing has uncovered an error. It involves locating the source of the error (the bug) and eliminating it. This means that the testing process is an iteration of test runs, followed by a debugging process when a test run uncovered an anomaly.

If there are that many definitions, which ones should we select for the remainder of this book? In principle, we could choose any one of them, even though some are more unusual and not included in the DACS Glossary [Dacs79], which lists those that have passed the scrutiny of a panel of international experts. However, we must stick with whichever one we do choose. Anything else breeds confusion and problems. In the remainder of the book, we will use the following definitions for testing, validation, verification, certification, and debugging.

Testing

"Testing is the part of the software development process where the computer program is subject to specific conditions to show that the program meets its intended design. It is the process of feeding sample input data into a program, executing it, and inspecting the output and/or behavior for correctness" ... (testing is) "exercising different modes of computer program operation through different combinations of input data (test cases) to find errors." [Dacs79]

Validation

"The process of determining whether executing the system (i.e., software, hardware, user procedures, personnel) in a user environment causes any operational difficulties. The process includes ensuring that specific program functions meet their requirements and specifications. Validation also includes the prevention, detection, diagnosis, recovery and correction of errors. Validation is more difficult than the verification process since it involves questions of the completeness of the specification and environment information." ... (validation is) "the process of ensuring that specific program functions meet their detailed design requirement specifications." [Dacs79]

Verification

"The process of determining whether the results of executing the software in a test environment agree with the specifications. Verification is usually only concerned with the software's logical correctness (i.e., satisfying the functional requirements) and may be a manual or a computer based process (i.e., testing software by executing it on a computer)" ... (verification is) "the process of ensuring that the system and its structure meet the functional requirements of the baseline specification document." [Dacs79]

Certification

"Certification extends the processes of verification and validation to an operational environment; confirms that the system is operationally effective; is capable of satisfying requirements under specified operating conditions; and finally guarantees its compliance with requirements in writing. Certification usually implies the existence of an independent quality control group for the acceptance testing of the overall system. The acceptance testing may be accomplished by operational testing, laboratory testing, and/or placing the system in simulated operation." ... (certification is) "the formal demonstration of system acceptability to obtain authorization for its operational use." [Dacs79]

Debugging

"Testing is the process of determining whether or not errors/faults exist in a program. Debugging is an attempt to isolate the source of the problem and to find a solution. . . . Debugging is only required in the event that one or more tests fail. It is the process of locating the error/fault that caused a test to fail." . . . (debugging is) "the identification and correction of software discrepancies." [Dacs79]

If the declared goal of testing is to find as many errors as possible, it can be helpful to determine the different classes of errors. The most common are logic errors. They may happen at any stage along the way or late, when detailed program logic and code are being developed. Logic errors also are those that constitute a misunderstanding of the applicability of a method. This can happen when a piece of software does not provide sufficient accuracy for some or all of its input values (problem classes) or when a formula or algorithm does not extend to specific values (usually singular values and those at a functional boundary). Such errors can be made in any of the development stages, not necessarily in the coding phase.

Errors that occur in the coding phase are typically typographical errors and violations of standards (modularity, documentation, nonstandard programming constructs, etc.). Quality errors include overload errors (i.e., buffers or tables overflow, signals are not processed fast enough, or a transaction system is unable to process the maximum number of possible transactions when they occur at the same time). Timing errors are another source of erroneous system behavior. They are especially tricky because they often depend on purely coincidental nonobvious combinations of events and on timing conditions. Because those possibilities are vast if not infinite, timing errors cannot easily be repeated in most cases. Other quality errors relate to performance and reliability problems. If response time or throughput are below requirement level, that is an error. We must try, through testing, to see whether we can force such an anomaly. Reliability errors can occur when the system or program fails and the required back-up is not performed or files get damaged. Sometimes there are restrictions as to how long recovery may take. This is another area for test. While we can categorize errors according to type, the development phase in which they are made (and not recognized), and whether they are functional or qualitative in nature, this only gives us a list of test areas; it does not indicate how easy or difficult it will be to test, classify, or remove these errors.

Testing involves running a set of experiments (the test cases) to determine whether or not there is an error in a particular part of the code. Thus we must plan for testing the same way we would for other experiments. The first part of test planning involves determining what philosophy and general testing strategy to use. Is it our aim to make the code fail by devising the most devious test cases we can think about? Or is it to concentrate on the most likely usages of the code, with only a cursory treatment of special cases and "freak" usages? This will influence which test cases and testing methods we select. Strategy defines, among other things, how to sequence tests, i.e., what to test for first, what later. Methodologies help to select test cases and guide their execution and evaluation. They can combine several testing methods, such as those based on program structure with those based on function (specifications). Test planning should be done early in the development life cycle. We developed test cases for various phase tests as early as the requirements phase. These should be included in the test plan. We should never invent a new test case when a previously developed one would do just as well.

When a master document for test planning has been developed, we can proceed to test case design. Test cases should *never* be on-the-fly but be well-defined, preferably rerunnable, and computer-stored. This entails that the test cases themselves have been planned, serve a specific purpose, are justifiable and necessary, and do not have to be reworked when code changes necessitated retesting (regression testing).

Test execution should be monitored, and the results of a test need to be evaluated. This is especially important because, if we do not evaluate whether a test uncovered an error or if we stop at only one, the knowledge will be lost. Cursory test evaluation often misses an error that the results of a test run would have pointed out quite expressly if all test output were checked. Such a test case is a waste of time and, what is worse, gives the erroneous confidence that the code is working when it is not.

Methods that can be used to test and validate software fall into five categories ([Fair78]):

1. **Structured walk-throughs**. This method is used to phase test code before testing starts as we describe it in this chapter. We dealt with its methods in Section 9.6. Code is not executed. It is therefore a static method.

2. **Static analysis**. In static analysis the structure of the code is analyzed (control flow and data) but without code execution. We may develop lists and tables (or use a static analyzer, cross reference compiler, or other appropriate computerized tool) to in-

dicate whether there are inaccessible parts of code, variables that are never used, variables that are used but not declared or initialized, or whether any error-prone coding practices have been used (mixed types or any of the "don'ts" from Chapter 9). Static analysis may or may not be incorporated in a structured walk-through.

3. **Dynamic analysis**.   In this method code is actually executed. This presupposes a test plan and test case design. Then test cases are executed, usually in a test harness or with the aid of a dynamic test analyzer that can measure which parts of the code where executed how often and which can trace values and provide other valuable information. Specifically it can help to

▶ identify dynamically dead code,

▶ control the correct number of loop iterations,

▶ target which are the most frequently used parts of the code and thus a prime target for optimization, and

▶ measure test coverage and identify parts that have not been executed as candidates for further tests.

Dynamic analysis is often used with testing criteria that are based on program structure [Stuc73].

4. **Symbolic execution**.   In this technique the program is not actually, but symbolically, executed. This usually means that no values for input variables need to be given. Rather, the code and its value assignments are traced as formulas along a predefined path ([King75], [King76], [Boye75], [Howd75], [Huan75], [Mime75]). Let us take an example.

```
read(a, b);
x := a + b;
IF (x > 0) THEN WRITE(x, a, b);
```

The symbolic values are a and b (we do not know the actual values of those two variables because they are read in and we do not have a test case defining their values). The second statement assigns the symbolic value "$a + b$" to the variable x. If we assume that the write statement is to be executed, then the code condition $x > 0$ actually translates into the condition

$$a + b > 0$$

for the input variables a and b, because x has the symbolic value $(a + b)$ at this point. In this way we can determine what is called path predicates, for any path through a module, by concatenating individual branching conditions of symbolic expressions. This helps to determine values for test cases and executability of paths and for comparing conditions in programs to the corresponding conditions in specifications.

There are two ways to produce path predicates: forward substitution or backward substitution. Forward substitution symbolically executes a path from beginning to end, assigning expressions (symbolic values) to variables and picking up path conditions at branching points. Backward substitution starts at the end of the path and works its way to the beginning. In practice, forward substitution has proven more successful, because it does not encounter as many problems with loops, subscripts, and pointers. Let us give another example for symbolic execution using forward substitution. The program graph is given in Figure 10.1.

Assume that a and b are input variables and that we are trying to find conditions for their values so that the statement **a:=−a** is executed once. Symbolic execution proceeds as follows:

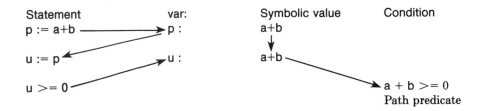

Symbolic Execution is a technique that can and has been implemented in programs (e.g., SADAT [Voge80]). It is considered experimental ([Deut82], [Glas79]) and "does not now appear to be feasible for mass application to large software projects. Some selective application to critical software units would, however, be advantageous . . . " ([Deut82], p. 313). Human testers follow a similar procedure when they methodically select test cases to execute parts of their modules. The difference is that they often "think" about their code on a higher level. This is called "chunking." They might reason for example that a test case is needed with more than one W2 Form to test the part of the tax system that deals with multiple employers (the loop in the module that processes W2 Forms).

5. **Proofs of Correctness ([Floy67], [Hoar69], [Hoar73], [Ande74], [Owic75]).** These are mathematically rigorous proofs of the correctness of code. They may use pre- and postconditions (mathematical description of conditions that are to be true before and after program execution), mathematical induction, or predicate calculus. We start out with a formal description of the initial state of the code (precondition) and then pro-

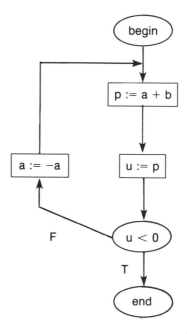

Figure 10.1 Code Fragment as Program Graph.

ceed in a set of steps, using axioms about the effect of program statements, to deduce the postcondition.

These five validation methods have their advantages and disadvantages as we will see later. Which one to choose depends on the complexity of the method, its reliability of uncovering certain errors, its cost, whether tools are available to support it, the size of the code to be validated, and the standards against which testing and validation are performed.

Either requirements and specifications or design (or both) may be the entity against which we need to test. Consequently, we find two categories of errors: what-errors (code does not meet requirements/specifications) and how-errors (code does not implement the design properly). Ideally, if we have followed the techniques and phase-testing prescriptions of the past chapters, we would have explicit, complete, correct, unambiguous, and readable documents and deliverables against which to test. In practice, however, shortcuts are often taken, changes are not documented, and the entity against which we test has become fuzzy. This is not a good starting point for testing and contributes to many a testing disaster. How can we hope to achieve a goal, if we don't know what it looks like?

For these reasons disciplined control is necessary. We support that through a comprehensive and precise test plan (and quality deliverables in earlier phases) and through a methodical execution and evaluation of the test plan. For larger systems, the testing phase itself can be partitioned into smaller testing activities. These should have their own small milestones and associated deliverables. It is important that we be able to measure testing progress and its quality quantitatively. Tool support is required for all but the smallest development efforts. At the least, a tracking system, test coverage analyzers, and means to store and rerun tests are needed.

Testing and software delivery usually entails the following testing activities: unit testing where the modules are tested alone; integration testing where modules are tested together to see whether they interface properly; and system testing where the software is tested to see whether it works within the bigger system environment. When new systems are developed, the modules and programs are put together step by step to determine the functioning of the entire system. Sequencing of unit tests and integration tests depend on the testing strategy. Bottom-up testing tests the modules that are lowest in the design hierarchy first and builds composite modules from the bottom upwards; top-down starts with the top modules in the hierarchy and works downwards. Top-down testing avoids "big bang" integration. Lastly, we can also combine top-down with bottom-up to test software in a sandwich manner. These strategies are analogous to the top-down, bottom-up, and sandwich design that we encountered earlier.

Often a field test follows. A newly developed software system is installed on a test basis at one or more actual sites to check it in production mode before selling or leasing it, or before its final turnover to the customer.

Which of the testing strategies and sequencing of testing actions is used depends on goals and strategies used and defined earlier in the development process. We have talked about sequencing versions and about incremental development and its impact on development plans earlier (Chapters 3 to 5). This, of course, affects how code is written and tested. Besides that, those parts of the system that are considered crucial, whether at the top or the bottom, are usually tested first. The rest is added incrementally (one at a time). We should aim at following the planned sequence of versions, but the parts of the code that deal with the most frequent usages of the system should be tested first. The amount of processing required for input classes also influences how testing and integration are sequenced.

Problems and Questions

1. How are the various definitions (given in this section) of the following terms similar? Where do they differ?

   ▶ validation

   ▶ verification

▶ certification

▶ debugging

2. How are validation, verification, and debugging related? In order to answer this question you have to give a set of definitions. You may choose the set from [Dacs79] or any other set derived from the material in this section.

3. According to the error classification in this section, which types of errors can be found at the phase tests for

▶ specifications,

▶ design, and

▶ coding?

Which method would you use?

4. What are the advantages of using test cases from earlier phases during the testing phase? Can you think of any disadvantages?

5. Take the following program graph and perform symbolic execution for both the yes and the no branch:

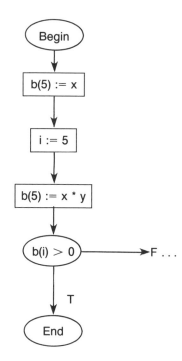

10.3. Program and Unit Testing

10.3.1. Introduction

Unit testing is concerned with the software flow pattern and the functionality of individual modules or units. Unit testing strategies often strive to exercise as many paths through the code as are feasible, because they are an indicator of software flow. The definition of feasible depends on the testing objectives and the time scheduled to do the testing as well as the complexity of the code.

10.3.1.1. Categories of Unit Testing

Structural Testing

Such testing is based on the structure of the code. We can use the structure of the control flow to guide testing efforts by using the number of logical paths that test cases have traversed. This is one reason why it is also called logic testing. We can also use the percentage of executed statements as an indicator of test coverage, and we can look at the structure of the data to derive test cases and guide our testing. Then the number of possible input classes to be tested compared to the ones we already have tested gives us an indication of how far testing has progressed. It also helps us select test cases (one from every class of values). Such approaches to unit and program testing have been developed to detect a large percentage of errors at minimal cost, without having to go back to previous phases for test case development.

Functional Testing

Also called Black-box testing, it is based on functional specifications, quality specifications, and requirements (if they can be used to derive unit and program test cases). Design documents may prove helpful for testing functionality that is not transparent to the user. If those documents are well structured and organized, it is usually not too difficult to derive test cases for unit or program tests. In addition, we should see which of the test cases that were developed for all or parts of the specification document apply to a module or program that needs to be tested. Here is one important area where we can save time and effort by saving previous test cases. Functional testing does not depend on the structure of the code. Therefore, mechanizable ways to develop functional tests for units or programs must be based on formal descriptions of specifications (specification languages). In most practical situations, creativity is required. This is the most important level of testing. It must be complete, even if structural testing is not. Black-box testing is not usually advocated for small modules (e.g., subroutines or functions) but is appropriate for larger modules (subsystems or components) and programs.

More recently, one type of functional testing has been described that uses structural knowledge of how elementary program functions are synthesized into code segments, modules, subsystems, and overall software products [Howd87]. The functions are described via input-function-output descriptions, but their synthesis into higher level functions requires structural knowledge of the type of composition. This puts testing based on function synthesis into the category of white-box testing. When it is only concerned with testing functions at the specification level, without regard to structuring of function synthesis, it qualifies as black-box testing. Note that the term functional testing as defined by Howden [Howd87] is more comprehensive than functional testing as referred to in other texts (e.g., [Fair85]). In those other texts, functional testing is synonymous with black-box testing and specification-based testing. Howden claims that a functional testing approach that considers functional synthesis on all levels includes both white-box and black-box testing.

Random Testing

This can mean generating test data at random, even the use of a random number generator [Gira73]. The advantages of such a technique are that the tester does not have to develop the tests. It is useful for testing telecommunication systems, real time systems, and transaction-oriented systems, when unpredictable workload needs to be processed and thus random requests need to be generated. Sometimes the behavior of requests can be captured in a probability distribution that then forms the basis for a random generation of requests, transactions, or workload. The common distributions are normal, negative exponential, Erlang, Poisson, Weibull, and Student T. As a unit testing strategy, random test data generation is less promising, because it cannot guarantee a comprehensive set of tests; actually, in its ignorance about the problem characteristics, it may test the same functionality repeatedly.

Researchers and practitioners have been more successful in using probabilistic assumptions about software faults and failures to direct the testing process and to evaluate its results. Testing aims at uncovering faults through causing failures in the software under test. Thus, generating test data based on probability distributions is tantamount to assuming that

▶ failure patterns can be described probabilistically over (execution) time and

▶ the distribution of errors (or faults) throughout the software can be described in probabilistic terms.

These assumptions help to construct a model of the testing process that allows an assessment of the effects of different testing (and debugging) strategies in different situations (e.g., [Down85], [Curr86], [Musa87]). It also serves to estimate the optimum allocation of test effort and the resulting reliability of the software. Some models even allow the assessment of effects of imperfections in the debugging process (e.g., [Down85]).

The second random testing technique is usually called "bebugging" [Gilb77]. In this technique, errors or bugs are artificially introduced into the program or unit before testing starts. The assumption is that the proportion of real or indigenous errors found is the same as the proportion of artificially introduced ones. This provides a means for measuring testing progress and confidence in the reliability of the program or unit. This technique combines testing with gathering data for estimation purposes. It can be used with any of the testing techniques discussed.

A variation of this technique is mutant testing [Budd78]. In this technique, a set of operators is defined that can be used to modify the existing program. Examples are interchanging variable names, modifying arithmetic or other program operators, adding expressions to existing ones, etc. When the operators are applied, a set of mutants (the modified programs or units) is created. Running both the program or unit and its mutants with the same set of test cases should provide differing results. Differences and the lack of different behavior are clues to errors and bugs. As [Howd85] points out, there are two problems with mutant testing. One is the potentially enormous number of mutants that can be generated with even a small set of mutant operators. The other is that there exists no procedure that can decide whether identical behavior of program (unit) and mutant(s) is due to a deficient set of test cases or whether the two programs are equivalent.

The last type of "random" testing is testing-on-the-fly or SOP (seat of the pants) testing. The tester arbitrarily runs tests as they enter his or her mind. The problem with this kind of testing is that it may test basically the same situation or set of conditions in a unit more than once (which is a waste of time) and/or may leave out parts of the program (unit) that should have been tested (possibly a serious testing deficiency). Because testing for all possible combinations of input values is practically impossible, testing strategies partition the set of input values or possible test cases into a finite set of equivalence classes such that it suffices to test only one representative (set of values) out of any class. All others would cause the program to behave in the same way. Then we have to run as many tests as there are classes for possible sets of inputs to the program (unit). Testing-on-the-fly does not guarantee that a representative from each class is chosen as a test case, nor does it guarantee that only one such test case per class is selected. This makes it a wasteful and inadequate method.

Computational Testing

This type of testing tries to find problems in the accuracy of solutions, with possible underflow and overflow problems. Let's assume that the following formula needs to be evaluated:

$$F(X,Z) = \sum_{i=0}^{m} X_i \{ Z^{m-i} / (m-i)! \}$$

Accuracy will be much better if we evaluate the expression in {} as

$$ZFAC(1) = Z$$
$$DO\ 100\ I=2,M$$
$$100 \qquad ZFAC(I) = ZFAC(I-1)\ *\ (Z/FLOAT(I))$$

instead of evaluating it directly as

$$DO\ 100\ I=1,M$$
$$100 \qquad ZFAC(I) = Z**I\ /\ FAC(M-I)$$

where **FAC(M-I)** returns **(m-i)**!

This solution is less prone to overflow and underflow for bigger values of *M*. Note also that we included explicit type conversion for integer quantities into real. When we test for accuracy we define a test case that taxes the algorithm in a module. For numerical algorithms, it is often not possible to compute the result manually. On the other hand, we can compare the results of an exact algorithm with that of an approximation and use mathematical knowledge about the quality of an approximation to determine whether a module has an accuracy problem or not. Similarly, we would define a test case with values towards the lower or upper boundary to test for underflow and overflow. In the above example, we could define a large value for *Z* (or a very small one). If underflows or overflows cause inaccuracies, it may become necessary to scale, as we have seen earlier, for the throughput formula for a queueing network.

Computational testing can often be combined with logic testing or any of the other testing approaches above, because we can select a representative test case from a class, which allows us to test for this class and for accuracy.

Data Handling Testing

This type of testing checks out whether input data is properly read in and processed, whether output is produced in the right location and format, whether data is converted correctly, whether erroneous or bad input is handled adequately, and (where appropriate) whether timing constraints are met. Again, this area of testing can be combined with any of the four testing approaches above.

A summary of the five approaches to unit and program testing is given in Table 10.1. Note that they are not to be considered exclusive of each other. Rather, they are complementary and should be used in combination.

10.3.1.2. Stubs and Drivers

After test cases have been determined with one or another of these strategies, the program or unit needs to be executed with the test data. A unit under test may call subordi-

Table 10.1 Approaches to unit testing.

Type	Measure	Generated from
Structural	No. of logical paths traversed	Code
(logical)	% of statements executed	Code
	No. of possible inputs tested	Code
Functional	% of specification items tested	Specifications
(black-box)	% of requirements items tested	Requirements
	% of design items tested	Design
Functional	No. of functional synthesis operations	Code
[Howd87]	present and tested	Design
Random	Random number generator: confidence interval sufficient	Prob. distribution
	Proportion of artificial errors found and resulting confidence interval	Code, art. errors
	Mutants and their behavior	Code, mutant operators
	None for on-the-fly testing	Code
Computational	Degree of accuracy	Design, code, requirements
Data handling	Proportion of cases tested	Specifications, design, code

nate units that are not included in the unit under test, and it may be called from higher modules that, likewise, are missing. The subordinate modules need to be stubbed in; the superordinate modules need to be replaced by a driver.

Stubs are simple versions of a module that is called by the unit under test but is not part of it. They either exit immediately without any action or return a predefined or a randomly generated value to be used by the calling unit. Sometimes the stub prints out that the (missing) module has been called. A stub may also execute for a specific length of time, busily doing nothing, to simulate timing behavior. More sophisticated stubs can perform a simplified version of the module they replace, calculate an approximation, read results from a result file, or ask the tester for input to be passed on to the unit under test. Stubs are necessary for top-down testing.

Drivers on the other hand simulate the missing module(s) that provide input to the module or unit under test. They usually make sure that the module under test gets all the data and the proper environment it needs. The driver also receives all output from the module under test. When writing stubs or drivers, it is important to make all test cases self-checking, because test cases themselves may contain errors. Driver or stubs should echo data that has been passed to them, echo input, and indicate success or failure of a test. Drivers are necessary for bottom-up testing.

Stubs or drivers can sometimes be rather complicated code and the temptation is great to alter the program or unit under test to make testing easier. This, however, is not advisable. Once that is done, the modified code is no longer the code that was supposed to be tested. Secondly, any code alteration brings with it the possibility for further introduction of errors. Therefore, stay away from changing code to make testing easier.

10.3.1.3. Human Objectivity

It is often useful to have someone else do the testing on the modules. It has been pointed out that it is much more difficult to find errors in one's own code than in somebody else's. The reason for this is called cognitive dissonance, a phenomenon that makes conscious acknowledgement of one's own mistakes more difficult. For the testing process, it means that there is a good chance that testing by an independent party will produce a more thoroughly tested program. The down side of this is that the coder no longer receives the feedback on how good the code is while doing his or her work. Unit testing would have provided this feedback. Its lack can result in reduced work satisfaction and lower productivity. Part II provides a more thorough discussion of these human factors issues.

For reasons explained before, you should avoid on-the-fly-testing. Besides being wasteful and inadequate, it also doesn't allow test cases to be reused easily. And the changes brought about by testing and debugging will very likely necessitate retesting.

10.3.1.4. Criteria for Test Completion

At its simplest, one could describe the criteria for unit and program test completion as "when all test cases in the test plan have been run without causing failure." This reduces the question of test completion to one of test data generation: what types of test cases are to be generated? Because this varies between methods, no general answer is possible. All methods have their own criteria and will be discussed in the respective sections. One important guideline for testing states, however, is that it is important to use complementary testing methods (e.g., white-box and black-box testing). This avoids the disadvantages of any one method and capitalizes on their combined strengths.

In the following sections, the testing methods based on code (10.3.2.) and those based on function and specifications (10.3.3.) will be discussed in more detail. Measuring quality and progress in the testing process are detailed using the bebugging technique in Section 10.3.4. The last section provides a comparative evaluation of the advantages and disadvantages of the various techniques.

Problems and Questions

1. Take two programs you developed recently. Explain how you tested them or their units or modules before integrating them into the overall program. According to Table 10.1, what kind of testing did you do? Why? How do you evaluate your efforts? What types of errors were found during the programs' operation? Why do you think you didn't find them during testing?

2.   Testing a program by units or modules requires extra work through writing stubs and possibly drivers. Why do you think it is still advisable to do unit tests? Can you think of a programming problem when you would not do that?

10.3.2.   Code-Based Testing

10.3.2.1.   Principles

Static and dynamic analysis and testing is often based on the code and its structure. Static analysis does not require code execution and is often done as part of, or instead of, a structured walk-through, with the aid of static analysis tools by the individual programmer. It provides global information about the program structure, such as program graphs. In a program graph every node corresponds to a statement in the code, and every arc reflects a possible transfer of control between two statements. Other pieces of information that can be derived through static analysis are number, type, histograms of statement types, usage of variables (reference, modification, parameter formal or actual, subscript, etc.), routines called by the unit under test, cross reference lists, and the like. The types of problems and errors that can be detected through this information include syntax errors, variables that have never been initialized but are used (or those that, although declared and initialized, are never used), unreachable code for any input values (such code is isolated from the rest of the program graph), and violations of coding standards and erroneous use of shared variables. The latter includes incorrect uses of global variables and mismatches of parameter lists (wrong types, wrong order, input parameters don't have a value yet, output parameters never receive one, etc.). Static analysis is not a testing technique that can or should be used in the place of other techniques. Rather, it should be used to discover the errors it is equipped to unveil, which can decrease the number of test cases for dynamic testing. It is also useful for test planning and bound to increase testing confidence [Fair78]. Errors and problems that cannot be revealed without actually or symbolically executing the code are difficult or impossible to recognize through static analysis. Dynamic analysis and testing becomes necessary to uncover those errors.

Each test case is a pair (input, expected output). The input causes a specific path through the program to be executed. The results of this execution are to produce the expected output if the program works. Dynamic analysis monitors run-time behavior by recording exactly what happens to variables and conditions along that path. Dynamic testing may uncover whether a module computes output values correctly and whether detailed program logic shows errors.

We have pointed out before that testing will not be all encompassing. Otherwise we could execute the program for all possible combinations of input values, record and check all results, and never have to run the program again, because we could look up all results in a table. This is clearly impossible. Testing merely executes a representative subset of all possible input, the test cases. Every test case is a representative of a whole set of possible inputs. They are in the same class because they show essentially similar program behavior. For example, they might cause the execution of the same statements and might even branch the same way. Testing methods and their associated test data generation differ in how classes of possible inputs to the program are defined and hence test data selected. It is possible therefore that classes of test data are defined erroneously; they are too big for the required discrimination that detects errors or not comprehensive enough, i.e., some possible inputs are left out. Because of this, testing can only discover the presence of errors, not their absence.

In this section we are talking about testing methods and criteria based on knowledge about the code and its structure. Because the code can be thought of as a processing box in a system diagram and because we consider what is in that box (the code, its structure, its variables, etc.), this type of testing is also called "white-box testing." This is in contrast to testing strategies that do not consider the code's structure but merely its function as seen from the outside. Such testing is called "black-box testing." These two types of testing were defined earlier as structural and functional testing.

In the following we will review three different strategies and testing criteria that are based on knowledge about the structure of the code. We will proceed from the simplest to the more involved [Mill74].

10.3.2.2.   Test all Statements Once

Each statement in the code must be executed at least once after all test cases have been run.

This criteria is clear and gives an unmistakable means to measure testing progress. The problem with it is that erroneous or missing transfer of control between statements cannot be detected. Nor will it detect errors that are present, but masked, because particular input values don't make it apparent. Let us make an example (cf. Figure 10.2.).

As long as **cond** is true, the incorrect transfer of control between the **IF** statement and **part2** (the statement should have read **IF cond THEN BEGIN part1; part2 END**) will never become apparent. We pay the price for a testing criterion that does not require all possible transfers of control to be executed and requires fewer test cases; errors can be overlooked, because they are not tested for.

The second problem is illustrated with the following example: the correct statement should have been written

$$A := B/C$$

but instead was written as

$$A := B*C$$

IF cond THEN part1;

part2;

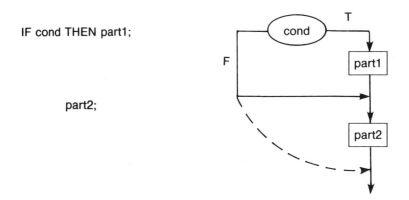

Figure 10.2 Erroneous Transfer of Control

As long as C is equal to one, the error in this statement will not become apparent, even though it is there. What does this imply for testing using the criteria that every statement should be executed at least once? Try not to use test data that result in variable values that are insensitive to operator changes such as − and + (avoid zero), / and * (avoid one), and the like.

10.3.2.3. Control-Path Testing

This testing strategy requires that a minimally sufficient set of paths in a module under test be executed at least once. For the program graph associated with the code it means that every arc is traversed at least once. We need a set of test data whose execution will cover all branches. Note that we are restricting ourselves to paths within the module, disregarding paths in subordinate modules. This is done to reduce the number of paths for which we need to run test cases, because it can be prohibitive. If a module has two paths, calls one module in every path each of which has five possible paths, then the number of paths is ten as opposed to two. We have to execute five times the number of test cases if we consider subordinate modules and their paths. This can quickly become intractable. The second restriction on paths is made for the same reason: two paths are the same if they exercise the same branches, which need not be in the same order or an equal number of times. If we didn't have such a restriction on what a path is, loops can easily drive the number of test cases skyhigh, as we can see in the following example:

```
FOR I:=1 TO 100
   A(I) := B(M-I);
   IF (A(I) > AMAX) AMAX := A(I)
END;
```

Without the branching there are 100 different paths through the loop, depending on when **A(I)** becomes greater than **AMAX**. Then there is the case of regular loop termination when no array element exceeds **AMAX**. If we only require every branch to be executed once, we only need two paths, instead of 101.

Thus stating that unit tests should perform control path testing means that every arc in the program graph (every branch in the program) needs to be executed at least once. A set of test cases with this property is "minimally thorough" [Huan75]. Note that the criteria of strategy 1 is weaker and will produce a subset of the test cases this second criteria requires. Control-path testing takes care of erroneous branching, but missing conditions and erroneous operators (cf. second example for method one above) are still not covered. This makes control path testing more comprehensive than exercising every statement at least once, but it is still not sufficient.

Before discussing remedies for this, let us explain the procedure in more detail. The first step is to select a set of paths that cover all branches of the program graph. A program graph or a tool that develops it automatically is the starting point for this. Next, a path predicate is derived for every path in the list. A path predicate is a condition that the input variables must satisfy to ensure execution of a particular path. The path predicate defines membership in a class of test data. That means that classes are defined around paths. There will be as many classes as there are paths. Then we test correctness of each class by testing with a particular member (set of test data). This method is good if the classes are representative of desired system functioning.

The number of possible paths, even with the restricted definition based on which arcs are executed (no matter how often and in which sequence), is on the order of 10^5 to 10^7 for reasonably sized programs [Mime75]. This tends to restrict control path testing to modules and smaller programs. The proper selection of paths becomes important to ensure efficiency in the testing process. Since we usually want to spend as little time as possible testing, we would like to run as few tests as possible. Then we need a minimal covering set of paths for the program graph:

▶ Each path goes from the entry to the exit statement for the module or unit under test.

▶ Every arc is traversed.

▶ No proper subset of paths exists that has the same properties.

While there are algorithms that can determine such a set of paths, they are very time consuming, and practice often resorts to an "almost" minimal covering set ([Krau73], [Amsc76], [Sloa72]). A reasonable strategy is to make the paths as different as possible. A graph representation of control flow is very helpful in determining test paths.

After having executed a set of test cases, how do we find out whether each arc was traversed at least once? One way to measure test coverage is to instrument a module by inserting a call to a counting routine at every branching point [Stuc73]. The counter is incremented each time the counting routine is called. After all tests have been run, the counter values from all runs are added for each counter. If all counter values are non-zero, the test covered all arcs and was minimally thorough. Figure 10.3 shows instrumentation points for an example program graph. There are commercially available tools (e.g., RXVP/80, SADAT for FORTRAN programs, CHECKOUT by Programming Aids Inc., SOFTOOL by Softool Corp. for COBOL and FORTRAN) that perform this instrumentation automatically.

Every instrumentation point causes extra code to be executed, which generates overhead and space and time interference. Performance will likely be degraded. These instrumentation tools should only be used where code performance during the testing process is not adversely affected.

Note that no counter is necessary to mark the transition from **statement_3** to **cond_1,** because this arc is executed **count_3** + **count_4** times to equal **count_2** times. We could even do without **count_2,** because nonzero values for **count_3** or **count_4** imply that **count_2** is nonzero also.

If we assume that we have defined a set of paths that need to be traversed, we still must determine test cases for all paths. This is called test case generation. It implies that we must find a minimal set of test cases such that the number of tests we run with them turns out to be minimally thorough. The procedure consists of the following steps:

▶ Find a minimal (or almost minimal) set of covering paths (This is what we started out with).

▶ Find path predicates for each path. For this we use symbolic execution as explained in Section 10.2.

▶ Find a set of values for all variables mentioned in the path predicate that satisfies it. This last step gives us a set of values for input variables that will drive execution down a given path.

The above procedure is well-defined, and its symbolic execution part is certainly automatable. There are some serious problems, though, which gives us some of the reasons why such analysis systems have not become part of everyday testing tools and why testers hardly ever rely on control path testing exclusively nor start unit testing with this method:

▶ The number of paths may be very large, resulting in a great deal of effort if we start out with the idea to do minimally thorough control path testing. Convoluted programming style adds additional complexity to the task.

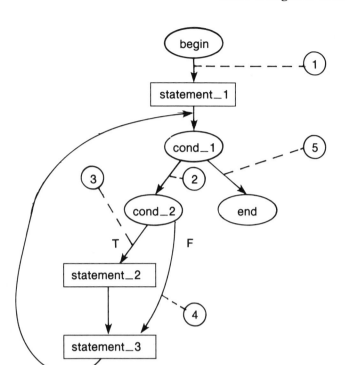

Figure 10.3 Instrumentation Points for Program Graph.

▶ Some paths may turn out to be nontraversable. The tester can look at a path predicate and simplify it manually, but an automated system may not be able to determine nontraversability without help.

▶ Because we have defined a path in terms of the arcs it traverses in the program graph, loop executions that differ only in the number of times the loop is executed result in the same path. The question is open as to how many times a loop should be executed.

▶ Let's assume that I and J are input variables and that a condition along the path reads

$$A[I] < A[J].$$

Then we do not know which elements of the array A the condition refers to. While it may be possible for a human to resolve this problem, a program usually cannot.

▶ Block structure, scope, and procedure calls and **EQUIVALENT** and **COMMON** variables are a problem. Any values that can be influenced from other modules or are possibly changed during execution of a path can falsify subsequently collected conditions for the path predicate. Again, a human tester may be able to cope with this in a particular case, but a program that must be able to deal with "any" case won't, unless helped by the user of the tool.

▶ Path predicates with floating point variables in the conditions are hard to solve automatically.

While this list of potential problems seems to indicate that control path testing is practically infeasible and certainly test case generation by an automated tool impossible, we should not forget that there is a theoretical reason behind the problem: the general test data generation problem is equivalent to the halting problem ([Howd87], [Huan75]): an algorithm that could detect the feasibility of any path would be capable of determining whether data existed that could cause an arbitrary program to halt.

Because of this, we cannot expect control path testing to be without difficulties, and any tool we might want to build to help us generate test data will never always be able to do so. The problems inherent in control path testing have led to changes in using it:

▶ Control path testing is not done as the first effort in unit testing. Other, functionally defined tests are often executed on an instrumented version of the unit first. If all branches were covered, the test was minimally thorough and no more test cases need to be developed. If not, paths for the uncovered areas are determined and test cases for them are derived. This reduces the number of paths for which path predicates and test cases need to be derived.

▶ All tools based on symbolic execution allow or should allow user involvement to compensate for the limits of the algorithm.

▶ To cope with the loop problem, additional test criteria are used. We will explain one particular set of such additional test criteria.

10.3.2.4.   Extended Structure Criteria [Howd75]

To overcome the problem of different numbers of loop executions in control path testing, we need to discriminate between paths whose execution traverses the same arcs but in a different number of times. To go back to the concept of classes of test data and their associated paths, we need to develop a refinement of the classification of paths. The first step is to distinguish between boundary and interior test paths for a loop. A boundary path is one where the loop is entered but not iterated, while an interior path is one which enters and iterates the loop. When two paths are the same except in traversals of loops, they are put into different classes (each requiring a testing representative) if

▶ one is a boundary and the other an interior test of a loop;

▶ they enter and/or leave the loop along different entry/exit branches;

▶ they are both boundary tests but follow different paths through the loop; or

▶ they are both interior tests but follow different paths through the loop on their first iteration through the loop.

In addition to these refinements on paths through loops and the testing required for them, the following testing criteria are helpful in finding errors:

▶ Test the loops for zero iteration, for single iteration, and for the maximum number of iterations possible.

▶ Inspect code for sensitivities to particular input variables (special cases).

▶ Test the boundaries of the domain for input and output values, and test for invalid inputs.

▶ Test for invalid conditions.

▶ When a condition consists of several terms, test for all logical combinations, not just for the truth or falsity of the composite condition.

$$(W2 = 0) \ \& \ (sched\_C > 0)$$

has four possible combinations. In doing so, we can reduce problems due to errors masked by specific values. If we assume that the income from W2 Forms and from self-employment is stored consecutively in a list with the wages first, then we could get to the Jth income from self-employment indexing

$$I := J + W2;$$

INCOME[I] contains the jth self-employment income.

If we assume that we typed $I := J - W2$ by mistake, a test case where $W2 = 0$ would not reveal the error, but if we test for all combinations of the condition above, it will be found.

▶ Test for overflow and underflow of values in numerical algorithms and for overflow of tables and lists and whether they cause array boundaries to be exceeded.

▶ In loops, test for possible sequences of conditions.

▶ The order in which program branches are executed are important [Fair85]. Thus, coverage of all arcs of the program graph in just any set of paths will not uncover as many errors as a judicious selection of paths (e.g., [Wood80]).

10.3.2.5. Comparative Example

We will look at an example to see how all three testing criteria can be applied. The **get(token)** procedure of Figure 9.9 contains a multiple branch (the **CASE** statement) and a loop. Execution is determined by sequences of characters in **cmdline**, the first of which is assigned to the character **c**. The following three sequences of characters will execute all statements in the procedure:

```
"a "
" "
"b,"
""
```

We have put the character strings in double quotes to make blanks and empty character sequences clear. The associated character types for the first character in the sequences are

```
oth
com
oth
eoc
```

This set of test cases not only executes all statements but also fulfills the criteria for control path testing. It does not comply with all extended structure criteria. Let us see which of the extended structure criteria are fulfilled with the test cases given to see which other test cases need to be designed to fulfill them:

▶ "a " interior test (interior tests all follow the same path the first time around the loop).

▶ "b," interior test but follows different path on second iteration

▶ "," boundary test

▶ "" boundary test but follows different path

New test cases are as follows:

▶ "a " interior test but follows different path on second iteration (**eoc** is flagged when the end of the command line is reached)

▶ " " boundary test but follows different path.

The next cases to consider are invalid inputs. Syntactically and semantically invalid user inputs are recognized at a higher level and we need not concern our testing with them. The only problem we might have is connected to a fundamental deficiency in the programming language we have chosen. If, by some mistake, **char_type** happens to be of a value not mentioned as a case, the program aborts. Because we did, however, mention all possible values in the definition of **char_type** in the **CASE** statement, this cannot happen. Therefore, a zero iteration through the loop is impossible. We have defined test cases for one or more iterations. Now we have to find a test case for the maximum number of iterations possible. This will be the length of the longest token possible. What is the longest token? The declaration lists the length of the token array as **maxlen**. This is not used to constrain loop iterations that can and will cause problems of array overflow for tokens longer than **maxlen** characters. This is clearly a case of missing functionality and thus, as happens in the course of test case design quite frequently, we have uncovered an error that would not have been uncovered through control path testing alone.

Because the **CASE** statement has multiple conditions (**blk** or **lnf, com** or **par**) we need to add tests for the parts of the condition that we have not tested so far in the test cases: **lnf, par**. Next we must test for sequences of conditions to see which are possible and which aren't: **eoc** and any other type that sets **leave** to **TRUE** cannot be followed by another, because it causes the loop to be exited; **oth** cannot be the last character type, because it will not set **leave** to **TRUE** and thus cannot cause an exit from the loop. When we examine sequences of conditions we also must consider whether there are any that cannot occur as the first ones in the sequence. Right at the beginning there are **blk** and **lnf**. This will result in skipping characters without returning a token, which is another error.

The point to be made with all the extra criteria for a code-based test is that if we had restricted ourselves to a control path oriented set of test cases, we would only have uncovered these errors by chance, not as a necessary consequence of the method.

10.3.2.6. Summary

Clearly, a purely control path oriented test can have serious deficiencies and will not uncover a great deal of possible errors in a program or unit under test. We therefore added other criteria that also are based on the code. Even with those additional testing criteria, we cannot test whether the unit under test has functional deficiencies (missing code) or behaves as the specifications describe. For that we have to compare the test results to what the specifications state. The next section will describe a testing method that is complementary to control path testing in that it starts from a different base: it develops tests from the specifications and some design aspects, with no regard to what the code looks like.

Problems and Questions

1. The text pointed out that it is important to consider possible sequences of conditions in paths to determine whether the code contains errors. For the code in Figure 9.9, what possible sequences of branching conditions (character types for the current character in the command line) are possible? Which represent desired (valid) sequences, which should not occur (represent invalid input)? Consult the design to see whether this represents an error. Design a set of test cases to cover both control path and extended structure criteria. Test the code with it. Determine whether it works with those test cases or not. Modify the code to remove the errors. Retest the modified parts. Can you still use the same test cases? Do you need additional ones? Why or why not?

2. Determine a covering set of paths through procedure **compsim** (Figure 9.8). Add paths to cover extended structure criteria. Determine test data, manually walk through the code with them and record any errors (and their type).

10.3.3. Functional and Specification-Based Testing

10.3.3.1. Method

Either the specification or the design document is now the starting point for developing test cases for a program or unit we wish to test. Since the tester does not use any knowledge of the code to select test cases or guide the testing process, the code remains a "black box" for testing. Therefore such testing is also called black-box testing, in contrast to structure-based or white-box testing. The key to this testing strategy is that a mapping between specification (or design) and the unit under test can be established; i.e., one needs to define the abstract functionality of a concrete piece of code. This requires at minimum the existence of a precise and well-organized specification document and/or design document. After a module's function has been abstracted (the mapping between specification or design and code exists), one can test whether the code possesses full functionality.

The unit test has long been said to elude functional or black-box testing (e.g., [Pres87]). Howden's approach [Howd87] unifies white-box and black-box testing into what he calls "functional testing." It is based on looking at testing the same way one would at design: using levels of abstraction, where each level contains functions that are combined to make one of the (composite) functions at the next higher level. Once a level of functions is tested, higher level functions composed from them can only incur errors through improper composition. Thus functional composition is the target of testing. At low levels, functional testing uses specifications of code and algorithm functions (detailed design), while functional testing at successively higher levels turns into specification-based or white-box testing. Thus functional testing bridges the gap between white-box and black-box testing.

In case of a composite function in a unit under test, we may have to decompose the overall function into its constituent subfunctions and the constructs used to synthesize a higher level function with them. [Howd85] distinguishes four types of elementary functions that are used as constructs to build higher level abstract functions:

▶ **Arithmetic function synthesis.** This includes the use of arithmetic, Boolean and relational expressions (function operators), string manipulations, and other low level operations on entities (matrix, list, stack, and possibly operations on lowest level design objects if we have an object-oriented design). Errors include wrong constants and operators, which requires the use of test cases that would uncover operator and operand anomalies.

▶ **Conditional synthesis.** Based on the evaluation of a condition (simple or composite), one lower level function is selected from a set of possibilities for computation. If we assume bottom-up testing, then there cannot be any error in that function, only in the evaluation of the condition that triggers the selection of the function. Test cases must check out the condition and the selection mechanism.

▶ **Iterative synthesis.** A higher order function is an iteration of the execution of a lower order one, and there is a condition that controls the iteration. If we assume, as before, that the lower order function cannot be at fault for an error, we must test whether there is an error in this looping condition, which would cause an inappropriate number of evaluations of the (test) function (body of the loop).

▶ **Control synthesis.** As we know from developing specifications, programs may change states. State transitions involve the computations of (lower order) functions. Errors that can be traced back to inappropriate control synthesis cause functions to be computed in unexpected sequences (interchanged functions, missing functions, missing conditional branches). Test cases for a function developed through control synthesis need to define what the expected state transitions and function sequences are and then test whether the coded module performs them or not. As before, we assume that the functions from which the higher order function is synthesized are error-free.

This approach to constructing a module and ultimately a program or software system from testable parts into levels of testable entities and testing parts successively covers, according to [Howd85] a wide variety of programming and design errors, including subtle and difficult to find missing code errors. It is obviously a bottom-up testing strategy, because we are starting with rather detailed code units and building higher level functions from them that are subsequently tested.

In the beginning, at the microscopic level, we usually need the design document to help us to abstract functionality. As we get to higher level modules, the specification document often becomes more involved in determining a unit's abstract function and appropriate test cases to test it. For example, to test proper state transitions for PAS or TAP on the user level, we need to consult the specification document. There may also be state transitions (function sequences) that are necessary for correct functioning but not necessarily transparent to the user.

Once a (composite) function has been identified, test cases need to be developed. For each condition and processing option, a test case is developed. A test case is necessary for the following aspects of a program or unit function:

▶ boundary points of input domains and output ranges,

▶ interior points of input domains and output ranges,

▶ invalid input values for each possible input,

▶ valid and invalid conditions,

▶ functional boundaries of algorithms and processing steps,

▶ "regular" cases of functional behavior, and

▶ cases that cannot be handled by the algorithm to see whether the program or unit behaves as stated in the specifications (reliability in the presence of failure, graceful termination, etc.).

It is now time to reuse test cases from earlier phases. Note that we used the input-function-output and the state transition model to help us define test cases for the specifications. This is analogous to how functional testing views the code. Consequently test cases will be reusable. If the specification and design document and their test cases are well organized, we can develop a matrix that shows us which test case tests which aspect of design or specifications. We can develop a test matrix that relates specific parts of the specification to particular unit tests in which aspects described in those design or specification paragraphs are tested. If, for example, Section 1.2. is tested in test 1 of unit 1 and test 2 of unit 2, this is marked with an * in the test matrix. Table 10.2 is an example matrix. We already might have such a matrix relating parts of the specification document to test cases for phase-testing specifications. Then reusing such test cases becomes even easier. An analogous procedure holds for developing a test matrix for the design document.

Because we have yet to test single units, not all paragraphs in the specifications or design document will be applicable to a particular code module but rather to a set of such modules. Those testing activities need to be deferred for integration tests (subsystem or system). Some aspects may only become testable during the acceptance test. In any case, the same concept applies. Taking all types of tests together in a set of test matrices,

Table 10.2 Specification test matrix.

Unit test no. spec. paragraph	Unit 1 1 2 3....	Unit 2 1 2 3.....	....
1.0		*	
1.1			
1.2	*	*	
2.0	* *		
2.1		* *	
.			
.			
.			

we should come up with a small ("minimal") covering set of test cases so that each paragraph (aspect) of the specifications or the design is covered in at least one test case.

We can simplify this matrix, if a covering set of test cases for the specifications already exists, because we can list in the matrix the number of the test case horizontally and the name of the program unit, module, etc. vertically. The test cases that apply to testing the code are marked with asterisks.

10.3.3.2. Example

In Section 5.3.2, exercise 1 listed seven (valid and invalid) ways to state **ANALYSIS** commands for PAS. Any of them can form a test case for **get(token)**. We can also use them as test cases again to see whether or not the procedures **command_handling** (cf. Figure 6.10 for its PDL), **get_an_parms** (cf. Figure 6.11 for its PDL), **get_file** (cf. Figure 6.12 for its PDL) and **file(token)** (cf. Figure 6.13 for its PDL) work properly. The test cases are numbered as follows:

```
#1:     ANK
#2:     AN K 10,0
#3: ANALYZE K (10)
#4: ANALYZE BEGIN
#5: ANALYZE END (0,100)
#6: ANALYZE PROGS PRINT_IT
#7: ANALYZE (10,30)
```

They all cover aspects of specifications for the **ANALYZE** command and its parameters and error messages. Table 10.3 shows a specification test matrix for this partial set

Table 10.3 Test matrix for partial PAS example.

Test no. → unit name ↓	1	2	3	4	5	6	7
get(token)	*	*	*	*	*	*	*
command–handling	*	*					*
get–an–parms	*	*	*	*	*	*	*
get–file		*	*	*		*	
file(token)		*	*				

of specification derived test cases for the PAS example. Thus we can reuse one set of test cases to test a whole set of modules. Note that not all test cases are necessary for every module. On the other hand, as exercises 2 to 6 of Section 5.3.2 indicate, this set of seven test cases is hardly comprehensive.

10.3.3.3. Summary

From the explanations and the test matrix of Table 10.3, it is obvious that a specification or function-oriented test is not just applicable to testing individual modules, but it works with groupings of modules as well. In fact, Howden's ([Howd87]) approach is one where the lowest level of functionality is tested first and, after that, the next higher levels are tested as compositions of the lower ones where errors can only come through the composition process, not through errors in the previously tested units. Thus, we can regard functional testing as a method suitable for unit and integration testing.

Problems and Questions

1. Assume you have done the exercises at the end of Section 5.3.2. Augment the specification test matrix of Table 10.3 to include those tests. Then determine the testing coverage for **get(token)** and the other units mentioned in the matrix. Have all control paths been exercised? Have all extended structure criteria been fulfilled? Which other test cases need to be added to test the remaining cases?

2. Based on control path testing and extended structure criteria, do we need all seven test cases to test **get(token)** as indicated in Table 10.37? Why or why not? Which, if any, would you not run for **get(token)**? Why?

10.3.4. Fault Injection
10.3.4.1. Method

One of the more difficult aspects of testing is to determine when to stop testing. One approach involves the injection of artificial errors or bugs into the code under test. It is called "bebugging" ([Gilb77]) and uses the knowledge gained from the error discovery pattern to predict the likely quality of the tested code. Before testing starts, a known number of artificial bugs are inserted into the code. The program is then tested for a while. A record is kept on the errors that are discovered, both artificial ones and those that are indigenous to the code. This data is used with statistical assumptions to compute an estimator of the errors still left in the program and the confidence level of having a certain number of errors left in the program. The formulas used to compute these inference statistics use estimators with the following statistical properties:

▶ they are "on target,"

▶ the estimators' variances are small, and

▶ they estimate the estimators with maximum likelihood [Triv82].

The most important assumption that is made about the relationship of indigenous ("real") to artificially injected errors is that they are found at the same rate. This means that if the tester has found 50% of the artificial errors, he or she also has found 50% of all real errors. So, if at this point 10 real errors have been located, the module or program still has another 10 indigenous errors left in it. How well this technique works depends on a number of things:

▶ The number of artificial errors should be large. The law of big numbers tells us that a bigger sample yields better results.

▶ The type(s) of artificial errors that have been inserted should be representative of the kinds of real bugs the code has. If all are of a similar type or concentrated in a particular area, this will likely cue the tester into finding them faster, which is not a good predictor for finding the indigenous errors. We can make artificially injected errors more representative if we base the error generation procedure on solid error statistics. This provides a typical error profile for the application in question. Moreover, types of errors can be correlated to the types of statements used [Gilb77]. This suggests inserting artificial errors in proportional frequency to such statement types.

▶ The statistical assumptions for reliability measures assume that the probability of finding an error is constant, regardless of the number of errors previously found. This does not always coincide with reality nor the rule of thumb that advises us that "where there's a bug, there's likely to be another." Another statistical assumption states that one error at most can be found during a test run. This is a very low yield. Testers try to develop their test cases so that they get the most errors revealed by them.

▶ When an error is taken out, no new errors are inserted. This assumption also is not quite realistic, because it is well established that especially in complex software it is all too frequent that new errors are introduced when existing ones are removed.

Even with these "unrealistic" restrictions, the predictive quality of the model is quite remarkable. We should, however, look at its results as an approximation, possibly an optimistic one.

What are these estimators of software reliability good for? First, they give us an estimate of the total number of (indigenous) errors in the code. Then we can compute, with confidence, that there are no more than **x** errors left in the program. Next, using intermediate data, we can develop testing or debugging curves [Gilb77] that relate the percentage of artificial errors found to the time it took to find them. Such curves will vary for different types of projects, for the quality of the programmers, for the quality of the design, and for the degree of testing and debugging support. It is unlikely that such curves can be developed for a more general purpose than a given development group and environment. While they may not be totally accurate, they can be accurate enough to provide useful scheduling and time planning information for the testing phase of other projects.

The kinds of errors that are inserted into the code cover all error types that were classified in Section 10.2. Artificial bugs are often inserted to interchange lines or variables, to change parentheses and operators in expressions, to fake "typos" by changing characters, to duplicate or delete lines, to modify looping parameters, to change the order of items in a parameter list, etc. A log of errors can be kept to provide lots of good ideas on how to put bugs into a program. If this is done for a while, a fairly representative picture of the most frequent types of errors will emerge.

We also should record where every artificial bug was inserted and what the original state of the code was, so that it can be restored. Whenever a bug is detected, an arbiter who knows about all the artificial bugs will state whether an actual or an artificial bug was found. The tester does not know where the artificial bugs are.

Now that we have defined the basic rules, let us explain how to compute the estimators of the total number of errors and the confidence factor ([Gilb77], [Myer76]).

The maximum likelihood estimator N for the total number of indigenous errors in the code is

$$N = \frac{i * A}{f}$$

where

N estimator of indigenous (real) errors in the code,
A is the number of artificial errors injected,
i is the number of indigenous errors found, and
f is the number of artificial errors found.

This formula is a rephrasing of the assumption that the proportion of artificial errors inserted to those found $(\mathbf{A/f})$ must be the same as the proportion of real errors to real errors found $(\mathbf{N/i})$. The consequence of this is that when all artificial errors have been found $(\mathbf{A = f})$, all real ones have been found also $(\mathbf{N = i})$.

The confidence factors represent the probability that they correctly reject a false statement about whether or not the program contains no more than $\mathbf{E}$ errors. They are computed as follows ([Gilb77], [Myer76]):

1. Not all artificial errors have been located yet, only f of them.

$$conf(\leq E) = \begin{cases} 0 & i > E \\ \dfrac{\dbinom{A}{f-1}}{\dbinom{E+1+A}{E+f}} & i \leq E \end{cases}$$

2. If all A artificially inserted errors have been found, the formula reduces to:

$$conf(\leq E) = \begin{cases} 0 & i > E \\ \dfrac{A}{A+E+1} & i \leq E \end{cases}$$

10.3.4.2. Examples.

Assume that the history of finding errors during test is as in Table 10.4. If we know that $A = 12$ artificial errors were inserted into the unit under test, the estimated number of errors changes, as given in the second row of Table 10.4. Note that the variance of the es-

Table 10.4 Error estimation example.

Detection pattern	f	i	f	f	f	i	i	f	f	i	i	i	f	i	f	f	f	i	f	f
N	0	12	6	4	3	6	9	7.2	6	8	10	12	10.3	12	10.5	9.7	8.4	9.6	8.7	8
conf(8)	.00		.00	.00	. . . .			.00	.01				.02		.07	.08	.17		.31	.57

timator is much bigger for smaller values of f and i. As more errors are found it stabilizes.

Note that the confidence factor **conf(E≤8)** is maximally .57, which is not very high. This is the confidence factor of no more than eight indigenous errors in the code after all (artificial and real) errors have been found. We can use the formula to determine how many errors we have to inject into the program to get a confidence of x that no more than y real errors are in the program, by rearranging the second formula for the confidence factor:

$$A = \frac{(y + 1)\, conf(y)}{1 - conf(y)} = \frac{(y + 1)\, x}{1 - x}$$

If we want a confidence factor of 90% that after finding all planted and indigenous errors in the code of the above example, there are none left, we have to inject

$$A = (8 + 1)\,.9\,/\,.1 = 81 \text{ artificial errors.}$$

As Table 10.5 shows, the confidence factor drops as the number of indigenous errors assumed in the code increases and as the number of artificially introduced errors decreases.

Table 10.5 Relationship between N, A, conf(N).

conf(N)	1	2	3	4	5	6	7	8	9	10	15	20
Artificial errors												
1	.33	.25	.2	.17	.14	.13	.11	.1	.09	.08	.06	.05
2	.5	.4	.33	.29	.25	.22	.2	.18	.17	.15	.11	.09
4	.67	.57	.5	.44	.4	.36	.33	.31	.29	.27	.2	.16
6	.75	.67	.6	.55	.5	.46	.43	.4	.38	.35	.27	.22
8	.8	.73	.67	.62	.57	.53	.5	.47	.44	.42	.33	.28
10	.83	.77	.71	.67	.63	.59	.56	.53	.5	.48	.38	.32
12	.86	.8	.75	.71	.67	.63	.6	.57	.55	.52	.43	.36
14	.88	.83	.78	.74	.7	.67	.64	.61	.58	.56	.47	.4
16	.89	.84	.8	.76	.72	.7	.67	.64	.62	.59	.5	.43
18	.9	.86	.82	.78	.75	.72	.69	.67	.64	.62	.53	.46
20	.91	.87	.83	.8	.77	.74	.71	.69	.67	.65	.56	.49
30	.94	.91	.88	.86	.83	.81	.79	.77	.75	.73	.65	.59
40	.95	.93	.91	.89	.87	.85	.83	.82	.8	.78	.71	.66
60	.97	.95	.94	.92	.91	.9	.88	.87	.86	.85	.79	.74

Note: N—total no. of indigenous errors assumed

Once we know what the target confidence factor is, we can look up in the table how many errors need to be injected into the program. With A known, we can generate those A errors by randomly determining the location of the error. A random numbers are generated between 0 and 1 and multiplied with the total lines of code and rounded to the nearest integer. This gives the line numbers where errors need to be inserted. We can work with a list of possible errors by type and choose the error we are injecting at the line at random, either uniformly random or using a probability distribution inferred through empirical data. This would presuppose, of course, that error logs have been kept reliably and have been statistically evaluated.

10.3.4.3. Post-test Confidence Factors

We can also compute so-called "post test" confidence factors to refine the confidence estimate after I indigenous errors have been found. The formula is given as follows [Gilb77]:

1. Only f artificially injected errors found:

$$conf(\leq E \mid I) = \sum_{i = I + 1}^{E} \frac{\binom{E + 1}{i}\binom{A}{f - 1}}{\binom{E + A + 1}{i + f - 1}} \times \frac{A - f + 1}{E + A + 2 - i - f}$$

2. All artificial errors have been found:

$$conf\ (\leq E + 1 \mid I) = conf(\leq E \mid I) + (A/(E + A + 2))[1 - conf(\leq E \mid I)]$$

If we use the previous example, we can compute the post test confidence factors as follows:

$A = 12;\ I = 6;\ E = 8$

$$conf\ (<= 8 \mid 6) = \sum_{i = 7}^{8} \frac{\binom{9}{i}\binom{12}{6 - 1}}{\binom{8 + 12 + 1}{i + 6 - 1}} \times \frac{12 - 6 + 1}{8 + 12 + 2 - i - 6} = .11$$

This is a much higher figure than the corresponding pretest confidence factor of Table 8.5. If all artificial errors have been found, post-test confidence increases to

$$conf(\leq 8 \mid 6) = .94.$$

If we stop testing before all artificially injected errors have been found, the effectiveness of the test is reduced, which becomes apparent by the formula

$$conf(no\ error) = f\ /\ (A\ +\ 1).$$

For the example this means that instead of a .92 level of confidence (no errors), we only attain .46, after f = 6 artificial errors have been found.

10.3.4.4. Summary

Fault injection does not prescribe any particular testing method to be used. It can be used in conjunction with control path testing or functional testing. It also is not restricted to testing modules or programs. The methods works just as well with subsystems or systems. While no data was available to the author, it seems that this technique would be useful to perform a comparative evaluation of the time needed and the estimated quality of different testing methods.

Fault injection, while providing us with statistically well-founded evaluations of the reliability of the tested software, has its drawbacks.

▶ It requires more effort to test and to record testing progress. The programs or units under test have to be prepared for test by an independent party who also must monitor testing progress to distinguish between artificial and indigenous errors.

▶ The statistical assumptions may not hold well in individual cases, which makes the estimators approximations. Too little is known on their quality.

▶ "Messing around with code" or "making it worse than it was" does not go over too well with authors who painstakingly try to provide the best code they can. It takes a special attitude to appreciate or to like working with such code. The psychological barriers are considerable.

It is not surprising then that fault injection has not caught on significantly in practice, even though the first two difficulties can be overcome with a statistically sound empirical database.

Problems and Questions

1. Determine successive estimators similar to Table 10.4 for the following error detection pattern:

$$f\,f\,i\,f\,i\,f\,f\,i\,f\,f\,f\,f\,f\,i\,f\,f\,f\,i\,f\,f\,f\,f\,f$$

What can you say about the variation of the error estimator? Compute the number of artificial errors that must be inserted so that

a)   conf(E≤6) = .75.

b)   conf(E≤0) = .9.

c)   conf(E≤5) = .75

d)   conf(E≤200) = .75

2.   Compute post-test confidence factors.

a)   Assume that A = f = 9, I = 2.

$$conf(E≤2 \mid 2) = ?$$

b)   Assume that not all, but only f = 8 errors have been found.

$$conf(E=0) = ?$$

How does that compare to the case when all A = 9 errors have been found?

10.3.5.   Comparison of Methods

Let us quickly illustrate the advantages and disadvantages of the three major types of testing methods that we have described for unit testing. The biggest advantage of code-based testing strategies is that there is a well-defined method to derive test cases and measurable, clear criteria for how far testing has progressed and which parts of the code still need to be tested. Its biggest problems are in the difference between specifications and intended function versus structure of the code. This causes "holes" in error discovery. Examples of such untargeted and often unrecognized errors are missing functionality, missing conditions, insensitivity of test cases to special values, and erroneous program functions for some sequences of execution (looping conditions and branching conditions within loops). Another fundamental difficulty is the impracticality of code-based testing where large numbers of paths and conditions are involved. Extended structure criteria can cause an even greater explosion of test cases. Because of the size and number of paths, such code-based testing is better restricted to testing individual units of code (modules such as procedures, functions, and subroutines).

Function-based or specification-oriented testing has as its biggest advantage the re-usability of test cases from previous phases. Its negative points are its dependence on the quality of specifications and test cases, as well as the lack of a well-defined, rigorous method. This type of testing can also show "holes" in its coverage:

▶   Not all functionally important aspects may be tested if the documents used to derive test cases do not show them.

▶ Not all code may be exercised. This happens because code is a translation of, but not a one-to-one mapping from, specifications and design. Differences require extra testing.

Besides having "holes," relying on previous test cases has other potential problems:

▶ Wasteful retesting of the same aspects of code may occur because while functional aspects may be different, the underlying code may be able to treat them the same.

▶ Test cases from previous phases can be deficient, too. Reusing them without questioning their adequacy can cover up and delay the detection of a previously existing deficiency.

An advantage of function-oriented testing is its applicability to unit and integration testing, thus providing a unified approach to the testing process. Code-based testing, as described for the unit test, does not provide that.

So it appears that both major techniques have their own deficiencies and strengths. Coming from two different starting points, they compensate for each other's weaknesses through their complementary strengths. This means that the issue is not "choose one of them," but rather "when to choose which of the two methods." The answer is simply expediency. Because function and design-based test cases are usually available when testing starts, we should include at least a subset of them for unit tests. As they are executed, we measure test coverage for them (and assess performance of critical units using a software monitor). Then code-based test cases are added where the function-based ones proved deficient. This way we have the best of two worlds—neither black-box nor white-box but "gray-box" testing to accomodate the advantages of both approaches.

If desired and appropriate, we can augment the testing process with a bebugging step. This third method requires people who monitor and prepare testing as an independent group. It is more work, so its advantages must be worth it and be reflected in development goals or be required in development standards and procedures.

10.4. System Integration Testing

10.4.1. Integration Sequence

The functionality of every unit needs to be tested, and then larger functional entities are built from these units. It is done one step at a time until the entire program, subsystem, or system has been assembled. This process is called program or system integration. The assembled units also need to be tested to see whether they function properly when put together. This type of testing is called system integration testing. It focuses on testing the interfaces and interdependencies of the units that have just been combined. Different module integration strategies differ in how they approach and sequence the combination and integration of modules into the ultimate program or system that is to be built.

If we remember what has been said about project planning and the sequencing of steps in developing the software as a project, there were two important planning steps:

▶ Planning for versions, either using iterative enhancement or prototyping or defining parts of the final system to be developed in a particular order. This version plan or development sequence will guide us now when we have to decide how to integrate modules to form bigger units.

▶ Critical algorithms and program or system parts. Code could be critical for a variety of reasons. Design wasn't quite certain whether the overall approach would work, whether particular algorithms work in specific, important cases, whether access to files or databases would function as desired and needed, whether existing software interfaced properly with the one to be developed, whether performance was going to be as required (speed of processing, memory requirements, traffic on communication lines, etc), or whether there were questions about any other qualitative aspects. In the course of development, important, but questionable issues need to be resolved as early as possible if they could influence other decisions. In such cases, code was written earlier to make sure that approaches to implementation were feasible and met requirements. As a result, we may have, at the outset of the "testing" phase, a variety of modules that have been coded and tested already. The test plan will have to mention those and plan for their implementation and unit testing accordingly. This is one other reason why test plans need to be made early, at least in an overall manner, so that both software testing during other phases and software testing as part of the regular testing phase can be accommodated.

When we plan for software integration and its testing, we must consider those two constraint areas before we can define the order in which to specify integration of modules. In general, critical modules are unit tested and possibly integrated into their system environment first. And version plans need to be followed.

A decision on how to put modules together will influence the order of coding (modules have to be coded before they can be tested, but not all coding has to be done before unit and integration testing can start), the form of the test cases, the tools to be used for testing, and last, but not least, the type and amount of support code or scaffolding code that needs to be written to support testing (drivers and stubs). Therefore it should be an early decision on a project-wide basis. In the beginning we may only have a version plan and a comparative prioritization of the parts of the software that need to be developed. As more detailed information (and test cases) become available, the plan becomes more precise. In any case, it must not contradict the two areas of sequencing that we have discussed above, i.e., version plan and testing critical aspects of the software first. The two constraints need to be complied with.

How modules are put together can be done using one of two approaches: we can either add them "in bunches" (phased, according to [Jens79], or we can add them one at a time (incremental, according to [Jens79]). When we add "bunches" of modules, fault isolation during the integration test can be rather difficult, because the error can be in any of the interfaces to modules just added or (when untested modules are added) in any of the untested modules themselves. The sources of possible error are manifold. That complicates testing in test case generation, test coverage, and debugging. This is the main reason why adding bunches of modules to form an integrated piece of software with them is only recommended when the modules are very small and simple, when their degree of coupling is low, and when individual modules have been unit tested before.

Modules that are more complex in function or interface should be added one at a time. Depending on how complex their function is and what degree of testing went into design and code reading, we may unit test them before or not. [Jens79] advises unit test, and [Myer76] allows to add tested or untested modules. Adding one module at a time focuses the testing process on the source of new errors: any error must be either in the interface to the newly added module or, in case an untested module was added, in the module itself. This contains the range of possible errors and facilitates error isolation.

Another necessary decision is where to start combining modules. We can begin integrating modules from the top down, starting with the main routine and working our way down the module hierarchy level by level. This means that we need to write stubs for all called modules that have not been added yet. Stubs, as pointed out before, can be quite complicated when modules have complex interfaces (many parameters, side effects), and thus writing them can be a lot of work. On the other hand, when the modules are simple enough to allow adding them without unit testing them first, we can combine unit and integration test. Another advantage of this approach is that it allows us to check the adequacy of the major design approach (good for nonstandard, research, or innovative projects) before all modules have been implemented or tested. Because the top modules usually also contain command handling or menu sequencing, we often see a top down approach in user directed development where the user interface is developed very early to test the adequacy of specifications and the quality of the human machine interface.

The antithesis of top-down integration is working from the lowest level modules to the highest level ones. Bottom-up testing needs a driver for all but the top module, but it makes sure first that the lowest level upon which all others build is feasible. No stubs are needed when untested modules are added. This can simplify test preparation significantly. It is also a natural technique for functional testing as [Howd85] defines it, because higher level functionality (the integrated set of modules) is based on previously tested lower level functions. A good abstract machine design facilitates this type of testing even further. Depending on the number of modules at the lowest level, there is a good chance of being able to work in parallel. This enables schedule compression. How to sequence integration is well defined and dictated by the code hierarchy. If we have versions, such as in iterative enhancement, we can work our way up from the bottom to the top integrating the current version's modules. The disadvantage of bottom-up testing is that the user and the testers see a working program or system rather late, i.e., when they have reached the top. It may also reveal problems with those top modules (user interface?) when it is too late to do anything about it, because so many things further down in the hierarchy would have to be changed. Furthermore, the cost of building drivers can be higher than the cost of building stubs.

If we are concerned about feasibility at the bottom, the machine and operating system side of things, as well as about the major design approach and the user interface, we may opt for a two-pronged approach, integrating both from the top down and from the bottom up, meeting somewhere in the middle. This is a good approach for very large systems, because it combines the advantages, but also some of the overhead for scaffolding code, of both approaches. Because work starts from both ends of the hierarchy, there is even more potential parallelism built into the testing process. That makes the schedule more flexible and allows schedule compression where more people work on more modules to get testing done faster. Planning is a little more complicated, because the exact sequence of what modules to add when is not predetermined. There are more degrees of freedom, but there is also the constraint that testing has to meet at a specific point in the middle. At that time all modules below and all modules above must be integrated.

[Myer76] suggests bottom-up integration for small to moderately sized programs, while sandwich integration using unit tested modules is the most appropriate way to integrate large systems. In practice, with the other constraints, we rarely find any of these integration approaches in their pure form. Instead, problem-based constraints tend to modify and soften the basic integration direction.

10.4.2. Examples

TAP

Section 6.2.3. on iterative enhancement gave three different alternatives how to plan for successive implementation of TAP. Accordingly, the system and its code become available in that order. Let us look at the first alternative to see what testing constraints are implied by it.

This first one involves the user interface (mock-up). Within this portion of the system we will probably implement and test the code top-down. If the modules are simple, we might add them without unit testing them first. At the lowest user interface level we need stubs to tell the tester (and the user) which (unimplemented) functions have just been activated. Menu choices bring up previously stored data on the screen and will probably show a previously stored script to indicate that they are functioning properly.

While coding and unit testing the main routine can go in parallel with coding and possibly unit testing the next lower level ones, integration testing happens sequentially. Thus the degree of parallelism is limited. Note that in case the user has to agree to the user interface, the mock-up would be available at specification time as one of its deliverables. This means that we have to plan for adequate testing time at this point in the development cycle.

The second constraint is the order in which functions are developed. The first set of functions to be developed store, update, and add taxes paid and income received. Whether we test these functions from the bottom up or the top down doesn't make much difference, because it is hardly more than a couple of levels and involves testing the lowest level object anyway (representation of income and taxes). On the higher end, it connects to the user interface (data input from the user).

Testing for the other functional capabilities also can proceed either bottom-up or top-down while we follow the prescribed sequence. Another aid in determining integration sequence is the processing order of data and data transformations.

On the macro level, we find the implementation and testing sequence top-down, because after the top (user) level, the functions below are added one at a time. At the micro level (within a step), we can test and integrate top-down or bottom-up. The drivers and modules under test will include major data structures, accesses to which constitute major functionality.

Sequencing of integration is directed by "object and function precedence," i.e., which function or object has to have been made available to add others without scaffolding code, even though from a design standpoint modules may be on the same level (but possibly in different subtrees). Note that this integration sequence directs itself around complete functional features. One could call it a specification driven integration sequence.

Alternately, we could start with a code hierarchy analogous to Figure 6.2 and decide to implement and test from the bottom up, beginning with the deduction list and the operations performed on it. Then we test the recording of different types of deductions, advancing the cursor on the deduction menu and bringing up the deduction menu. Parallel to this we might test the lowest level modules for dealing with income and taxes paid. This would not require testing, making the mock-up of the system available first. Therefore we would not use such an integration sequence with the first alternative for TAP.

If the organization of the deduction list is perceived as crucial, then we would implement and test it as soon as possible after the mock-up has been completed.

PAS

Now let us go to the (partial) structure of the command parser for PAS (Figure 7.13). We can test and integrate this part of the program top-down (starting with the command module), working our way down to the functions that operate on the command line and provide basic building blocks for syntax recognition. Since the objects that are handled by them are crucial for command recognition, it makes sense to work bottom-up. The modules **skip_them, get_char,** and **accumulate** are very small (code may actually write **skip_them** and accumulate in-line into **get(token)**, because they are used only once). Therefore we assume to add them without unit testing them first. The **get(token)** module is one used heavily by a number of other units on higher levels. Stubbing it in can be awkward. We would test this part of the command handler bottom-up. Note that we included in the decision-making process the type of usage units experience and the usefulness or complexity of stubs.

Next we might add the (untested) unit **alpha** to test the combinations of **fname** and **module.** The unit module uses a stub for the missing unit lines. This builds up to the set of modules having **file** and **range** as their topmost units. At this point the next level of abstraction (**an_parms**) has been reached. Adding the unit **analysis** gets integration testing up to the command level.

With this plan we need the following drivers and stubs for the modules in Figure 7.13.

We need a driver for **get(token)** (no stubs, because lower levels are added untested), a driver for **fname, module** (stub for lines), **file, range, an_parms, and analysis. Analysis** needs stubs for functional aspects of program analysis. The **command** level needs stubs for the missing components **stats, reports,** and **error.** Note that we do not unit test the next higher level unit before integrating it with those on the lower levels (which are already tested as an integrated set). This we do because none of the units calls more than three other units and they all are fairly simple.

A third integration sequencing strategy is best used for object-oriented systems. We integrate and test collections of units that revolve around objects and their functions (data abstractions). Isolated object/function conglomerates can be tested and integrated first. Functions accessing more than one object at a time need to stub in the functions for the "untested" or "not yet integrated" object. We test the most critical objects and their functions first. In TAP, tax, income, and deduction list come first. Then, if the most adaptable design is chosen, the data object that embodies rules for forms generation and its functions is the most critical.

Note that we can decide on integration sequences fairly early. In no case did we have to use code to determine integration sequence. Design was always sufficient. Version plans even allow earlier determination of integration sequence (albeit on a macro level) and testing philosophy during specifications or early design.

10.4.3.   Testing Module Interfaces

After determining the sequence of integration, how do we test each subsequent set of modules? If untested modules are added, unit test approaches for generating test data for the untested module in the set apply (cf. 10.3.). In addition, we need to test the newly added module's interface with the remainder of the set accumulated (integrated) so far. Interface testing has two aspects: data and control interfaces. Data interfaces are parameters that pass data between modules and any common or shared data areas. Often a protocol of access to such shared data areas is needed. Because data are the key point in this first class of interfaces, their functional significance (classes of functional behavior for the passed or shared data objects) determines test data generation. Therefore, we must determine which different actions or action sequences should happen for different values of data. This is similar to what we have done during the specifications phase when we associated different functional behavior with classes of input values. As we had to pay attention to special values and boundary values, we have to do so here as well. And we have to do it from two perspectives:

▶ Can the module(s) that provide the data provide all classes of values? What about other values (we just found a potential problem)?

▶ Can the module(s) to which the data is passed react to the data appropriately? This includes not just whether it does the right processing of the data but also whether it actually accesses the proper data.

The second aspect of testing interfaces revolves around their control aspect. Here we have to determine test cases for all possible classes of invocation of a module, for all possible entries and exits from a module (isn't it an incentive to write single-entry-single-exit modules?), and for possible calling sequences of modules and combination of modules. This often reflects higher level functionality and possible state changes within a program or system. In both cases, reusing specification test cases can be very productive.

System integration can go beyond program integration, because the software is often much larger and because system components can include hardware and software parts. System integration has to combine physically, electronically, and functionally all elements specified for a system [Dacs79]. This then may require not just software testing activities as we have described them so far but also testing the interfaces between hardware, firmware, and software, setting and defining parameters to accomodate the three, and making sure that the system parts cooperate and interact as specified.

10.4.4. System Test

Once the program or system has been fully integrated, we need to test it as a whole. During system test the testers try to find any discrepancies between the system and its original objectives [Dacs79]. This means that we now have to test the system against its specifications and requirements. In order to do that, we need to have the system assembled, we need system documentation (user manual, system manual, installation manual) and quantified, agreed upon objectives and requirements drawn from them (cf. chapters 3 and 4) and the specifications derived from them. If we assume that functionality has been tested during system integration, we have the following qualitative tests to perform:

Useability

This aspect includes (cf. Chapter 4) performance, security, reliability, and human factors.

1. **Performance.**   This includes a load and stress test to see whether the system performs as required for peak loads. Maximum number of transactions submitted at the same time is an example of a peak load definition. A related aspect is how much data it can handle over long periods of time. This is called volume testing. Usually these two are combined with performance requirements: no more than five seconds response time for peak periods. A stress test must try to find a set of test cases that will see whether this performance requirement has been exceeded. Volume and performance tests may be combined through restrictions on the amount of memory (primary or secondary) that may be used for temporary or permanent files; the system may only be allowed to take up a certain amount of storage. Response time and throughput may have constraints that have to be checked with a volume test when even the processing of large amounts of data may not take more than a certain amount of time. Besides performance considerations, there may be functional ones: can the system handle that much data? Benchmarks need to be defined and run, and performance statistics must be collected and evaluated to see whether performance objectives are met even for large amounts of data. Where performance constraints specify "average" or "typical" behavior, a set of typical uses of the system needs to be defined as benchmarks and monitored as they are run. We also have to take care that the system environment is typical in the sense that other expected workload is run together with the system under test. Because it competes for resources with other active programs or systems, we have to consider the degree of competition (light load, medium load, peak load) when preparing the benchmark.

Because benchmarks are rather expensive to prepare and to run, it may be advisable to use other performance analysis techniques (modeling, in particular) to predict system behavior under various loads. While it does not eliminate the need to run some benchmarks to collect basic performance data, it can reduce the number of such benchmarks. If the issue is to test the performance of a new system, performance and resource requirements for existing loads are usually known to the performance analysts and capacity planners who assist in projecting the new system's performance.

2. **Security.**   The security requirements describe the degree of security required. We now have to test whether the security mechanism can be penetrated. For systems with strict security requirements, a professional "penetration team" may perform this part of the system test. When we discussed security mechanisms in the design chapter, it was pointed out that a totally secure system is well nigh impossible, so the evaluation of the system's security often must focus on the difficulty of penetrating the system and the effort and time it would take to do so.

3. **Reliability and availability.**   Here we must test whether the system shows levels of reliability that were required in the presence of system or user faults. This includes recovery testing and all aspects of reliability discussed in Chapter 4.

4. **Human Factors.**   In case they were not tested with a mock-up at the specification stage, the user interface must be tested now. What was said about evaluating human factors at the specification stage applies here.

Intended Use—Generality

This aspect deals with portability and compatibility. In case of a new release of a previously marketed system, the user interface must stay the same. This needs to be tested. Note that we can use some of the scripts for user interface testing for this, too. In order to test efficiently, we should try to test more than one quality aspect at a time or reuse test cases. A system may also be written for upward compatibility and be run with a variety of possible configurations. These need to be tested also. At minimum, if an exhaustive test is not possible or desirable, we need to test for the minimum and maximum configuration, for any class of device or interfacing component, and for an "interior" configuration (maximum and minimum configurations are "boundary" ones in the sense we have used the term during unit testing in Section 10.3.).

Lifetime Expectations

This includes maintainability and, as part of that quality aspect, installability, serviceability, and procedure testing. In particular, systems that can be installed at several sites and on several machines usually have parameters that can be used to customize a system to a particular surrounding and to particular customer needs. All such options need to be tested.

In order to fix errors, identify sources of problems, and take corrective or adaptive action, it is important to have correct diagnostics; otherwise a system becomes quickly unserviceable. All facilities for tracing the system once it is installed, for diagnostic messages, for symbolic or hexadecimal dumps, and for fault isolation need to be tested, too. Some systems have messages to tell the user possible alternate system usages to get around a problem. That also needs to be tested (whether the correct message is displayed in such a case *and* whether the advice actually works).

Procedure testing goes through the procedure of preparing the system for execution and supporting it during its operation. This includes operator actions, tape or disk-pack set-ups, printer paper changes, etc.

Documentation

Every publication that accompanies the system needs to be tested for accuracy. This includes user manuals; lists of warnings, error messages, and suggested corrective action; installation manual; procedure manual; system manual; and all other publications pertaining to the system. It is very useful to check publications while a system's functional or quality aspects are tested. Test cases can make useful examples for the manuals, explaining features and special characteristics often better than a dry, but accurate technical description. Such examples also provide patterns of usage for novice users and tend to reduce "freak" usages, which none of the developers foresaw and therefore were not planned nor implemented correctly.

A system test should be performed by an independent system test group, i.e., a group that was not involved during the implementation phases (design, coding, and testing so far). Some organizations have specific groups whose charter it is to test a system before it goes out the door; others turn this job over to the key analysts and high level designers. Some testing aspects require special knowledge and experts in specific areas: performance analysts, capacity planners, security specialists, telecommunication experts, users, or psychologists (for the human factors). In many cases, these experts will have been involved in the specification and design of the quality aspects they now try to test. This is, however, not an ideal situation, because it is hard to find errors in your own work. This characteristic led to the institution of quality assurance and testing groups, which are independent of the development itself and whose declared work is to find everything that is wrong with a system. If very few errors that are uncovered during the operational life of the software can be traced back to oversights during system test, they did a good job.

While system test reaches its full complexity when it is actually a system that is being tested, most of the areas that need to be tested apply to programs as well. We may not have to test for several configurations, but it still has to run for a particular one. We may not have to worry about interfacing with several different hardware components, but we may have to test whether the program is portable to a variety of machines. Thus the term "system test" can be somewhat of a misnomer, which is the reason why it is important to give a definition of what it means and which activities it entails. When planning for it, we should use the description of activities as a checklist to see which apply and which do not.

The activities involved during system testing are not and need not be sequential. The key is often to overlap as many aspects of testing as possible, because it compresses the schedule. Large projects often need and do take advantage of that. Another issue is the effort it takes to bring up a system version that can be tested. Sometimes the work of hundreds of people needs to be combined into a test version of a system. It may not be possible to do that more than a dozen times. This means that we cannot afford to go back to the drawing board with every single error that we find. In addition, not every error is worth fixing. For these reasons, we test as much as we can with every system version, keep a list of the errors and the affected parts and then, when no more testing can be done, we go back to fix the errors.

System testing is completed when all classes of system capabilities (functional and qualitative) have been tested and enough problems have been corrected for the testers to be confident that the system will pass the acceptance test [Hetz84]. This is really a very open-ended definition of when to stop testing as well as what to test. A competitive marketplace often puts rather tight schedules requirements on a software development project. This may prevent testers from coming anywhere close to exhaustive testing of a new software system. What has been proposed instead is a selective testing approach that essentially says, "If the user is not likely to use a feature or will use it so infrequently that a bug in it is not likely to show up, don't spend a lot of time testing it." Systems are then tested based on an operational profile. An operational profile describes the typical uses for a software system. The test cases that represent the operational profile test only those aspects of the system that are deemed typical. Of course, testing will be only as good as the operational profile it is based on. This makes it all the more important to know what the user or customer wants and how the system will be used. Note that this information is solicited during the prototype and specification stages. This means that we can and should go back to the information gained with and about the user to determine what a cost-effective system test should be.

Problems and Questions

1. Determine which units of TAP (PAS) need to be unit tested before integration. Then select, based on a version plan of your choice, the integration sequence for TAP (PAS). Determine which drivers and stubs you will need and how you will implement

them. Will it be simple loops for drivers or a more sophisticated set-up? Do stubs call for user input, or will they prompt the user to input data? Give a rationale why you chose a particular integration testing sequence and its associated drivers or stubs. For each interface state the data and control issues that need to be tested and provide test cases. Where possible, reuse ones from previous phases. Develop a test matrix similar to the one of Table 10.2 or Table 10.3 to indicate which test case tests which set of units.

10.5. Acceptance and Field Testing

After the system test has been completed, a system is often used internally so that developers can learn and experiment with the system before releasing it to the customer. A firm that builds software to support performance analysis and capacity planning may first use a newly developed software component in its performance evaluation software for consulting customers about sizing their computer systems. Another company may use a new operating system internally first. Similarly, compilers, software libraries, and development support tools are often used in-house before being released to customer sites. This type of usage of a new system is also called a beta test.

During this experimentation and learning phase, the soundness of the software can be tested with actual production workload without the risk of turning off customers when errors or badly conceived human factors are detected. It is also much easier from an organizational standpoint to recall the system when serious flaws are found; there is no problem with several customized versions, or product warranty. Maintenance (corrective) has an easier job, because the user base is smaller and localized. New software is said to show a burn-in phase of about six months [Dema82] during which the biggest share of residual errors is found. If the software is used under close supervision during those months, it will most likely result in a more reliable system. However, market considerations and competition may not always allow such luxury.

During internal testing, facts on the experience with the system are collected and, where warranted, a revised system version is prepared. It must go through another testing phase in which the changed parts of the system must be retested (regression testing). All development documentation has to reflect the system changes as well. Here we encounter in a nutshell the first aspects of maintenance work.

Instead of an in-house use or in addition to it, the system may be released to specially selected customers for trial use. Such a period of learning and experimentation is called a field test. It may follow, substitute for, or run parallel to an in-house test. Its objectives are the same as for in-house usage: to learn and experiment with the system in a low risk environment. This is why customers usually do not have to pay lease or purchase costs during such a time. They also may run their old system (manual or automated) in parallel, because the new one is still "experimental." The customers are expected to report on any errors and to fill out a product evaluation. They may or may not have the right to demand certain changes.

After the field test, the system and its documentation is turned over to the users. Final user training is done. Maybe it is repeated whenever there are enough new customers or new users to warrant teaching another course. Regular operation and maintenance commences.

Sometimes there is an acceptance test after the field test. It is certainly recommended if there were changes to the system as a result of the experiences with the field test. If there was no field test, an acceptance test should be mandatory for the developer and the customer. What it entails was discussed in the section on requirements and need not be repeated here. It is the final verification step before user and developer agree that what was ordered has been delivered. To skip it or to do a cursory job on it is neither in the interest of the developer (he has no assurance that the user knows how good the software is) nor in that of the customer (who did not check properly whether what they are to pay for is what they wanted in the first place). Inadequate acceptance testing only leads to misconceptions and misunderstandings between developer and customer. When conflicts occur, usually both lose, which is not a very desirable situation.

Problems and Questions

1.   What is the difference between an in-house trial operation and a field test? What are the criteria to opt for a field test? When would you not want to have one? Do in-house trial operations or field tests substitute for a formal acceptance test?

2.   Review the previously developed acceptance test for TAP (PAS). Based on your current knowledge, would you add any more test cases? Why or why not?

10.6. Debugging

10.6.1. Analyzing Anomalous Behavior

The declared goal of testing is to find errors, but what happens when a test case does reveal erroneous program behavior? It is one thing to know that something is wrong, another to locate where the underlying cause is, and still a third to correct it. While there is a body of heuristic knowledge to help in debugging, many professionals concede that locating and removing the source of erroneous software behavior is still very much an art [Pres87]. Heuristics are usually bound into a structured, methodical approach, and debugging is no exception. Structured approaches (cf. [Myer79], [Brow73], [Brad85]) are preferable to brute force tactics such as loading the program with write statements and wading through the output afterwards. The latter becomes quickly impossible as program size grows.

Backtracking

This technique attempts to trace execution backwards from the point where an error became apparent. When done manually, the number of possible paths can become unwieldy. Diagnostic output statements, the tracing of data and control flow, and the setting of conditional breakpoints are helpful characteristics of state-of-the-art tools that support backtracking. Modern tool features include handling of assertions (logical predicates that describe program states), symbolic execution, and tracing (backward and forward) of program runs (live or post-mortem). Debugging tools that use debugging knowledge are still in the experimental stage. Those that support backtracking include VIPS ([Isod87]), PECAN ([Reis84]), PUDSY ([Luke80]), and MTA ([Gupt84]). According to Seviora ([Sevi87]), all but the first of these systems are experimental and not yet usable in the field.

Cause Elimination

Cause elimination can be done by induction or deduction. Induction sometimes uses binary partitioning. During fact finding, data are put into groups as they are associated with potential causes for an error. Then hypotheses for each error cause are formulated. One may rank them from most plausible to least plausible. Test data are then used to prove or disprove it.

Deduction relies on the formulation of possible causes and on tests to eliminate those that are not true. Those that cannot be eliminated need to be refined further to isolate the bug.

In both cases, necessary corrections need to be determined and implemented. One must verify, then, whether the correction works. This includes rerunning the test data that caused failure previously. Regression testing of earlier test cases is also usually necessary to make sure that the bug fix has not introduced new problems. In case it has, the method iterates.

Tool support for this approach includes debugging compilers, automatic test case generators, cross-reference maps, and the like. Systems that support debugging by representing programs and their behavior through graphics are Blit [Carg83], Incense [Myer83], and Balsa [Brow85]. More advanced knowledge based systems that facilitate bug isolation and correction are Proust ([John85]), Talus ([Murr85]), Laura ([Adam80]), and Falosy ([Sedl81]). As mentioned before, knowledge-based debugging support tools are experimental, limited to small programs, and usually incur high execution costs. There is much room for improvement in supporting debugging with knowledge-based tools.

The following are some suggestions on how to trace a fault from the point of detection to the point where an error originated. They are grouped into categories of debugging cases ([Vant78]):

▶ The program does not compile, but there are syntax errors. In this case we analyze the syntax errors and correct them. Often parentheses are not matched and termination indicators for statements, expressions, lists, strings, etc. are missing or unduly duplicated. Types used as indices are wrong. Variable names are mistyped. We may have ordered statements incorrectly (e.g., declarations before executable statements). Code reading at the end of the coding phase tries to minimize such errors. Programmers who throw a program together and expect the compiler to find their bugs often get a message at the end of their program: "maximum number of syntax errors exceeded." Then the known syntax errors have to be removed, before the programmer even gets to see the next batch of them. This is not our goal.

What the compiler marks as wrong need not be the original cause. If a variable of the wrong type is used as an index into an array, this may be because it is mistyped and therefore declared by default with the wrong type. Or it may be that while the name is typed correctly, the variable has never been declared and received a default and type that is not permissible as an index for an array—hence the syntax error. A missing comment termination can cause the compiler to regard a series or part of a statement as a comment. Depending on where such an error occurs, it can cause all kinds of syntax error messages, from missing declarations to unrecognized command. It can result in a whole series of such messages that were all triggered by that one error.

The error message gives only the symptom but not the underlying cause. It is useful to consider all the possible messages and warnings by the compiler to trace the symptom to the cause. Where available, a static analysis can help, too, because it gives summary information on the use (or lack of use) of variables, labels, etc. Cross reference lists are very helpful, especially if they combine a list of usages with variable types and location of declaration.

▶ The program compiles and executes correctly, but there is no output and no error messages or warnings. This situation indicates that for some reason the execution never encountered an output statement. Examine the conditions that cause branching around output statements or branching to the end of a program or module. Sometimes they occur when conditions for executions of loops cannot be met (default values for uninitialized variables? Wrong final value or step size for looping parameters?). Or is it a missing call to an output function? Does the output or format statement contain an error? The list of possible causes is long. As a first try at isolating the error we can trace possible execution flows that can cause a "no output" condition. If that does not solve the problem, we should judiciously add tracing statements to determine what values those variables have to control the flow of execution. Using a built-in tracing facility or a check-out compiler might be a good idea, too. We should not put print statements into potentially long loops, because it can produce "wallpaper."

▶ The program compiles correctly, executes, but produces no output. There are system error messages. Find out what they mean, and then find out where the problem described in the error message occurred. This is sometimes not easy when only an address is given. We may need linkage information to determine the unit in which the problem occurred. Errors that cause such termination include

  ▶ missing files or incorrect filenames when the program tries to open a file;

  ▶ wrong unit numbers for input or output units in FORTRAN; and

  ▶ exceeding array bounds—note that the error message can be all kinds of things if array bound options are not set: from trying to access statements or format definitions to using an incorrect value that can result in underflow or overflow errors.

It is sometimes difficult to determine the underlying cause from the reported error. As before, it helps to keep a list of previously encountered problems as a reference in addition to available manuals. Manually tracing your test data through the code to isolate the problem, and mistrusting your abilities for setting pointers correctly, indexing array elements properly, and writing compatible interfaces is a good strategy. Maybe, just as you have your own style of developing programs, you also have your own "preferred" mistakes. It can be very educational to keep tabs on the type of error one tends to make as well as how it manifests itself, how it is recognized, and how it can be eliminated.

▶ A corollary to the previous problem is when the program executes but aborts or does not seem to do all it is expected to. The reasons and remedies are similar to those in the previous situation.

▶ A program that executes without blowing up but still delivers incorrect results can have any of the classes of errors that have been described in the introduction to this chapter (Section 10.2). The best strategy is to figure out in which part of the program the error occurred. The testing strategies already give us an indication where things can have gone wrong: in the module under test, in the interfaces to other modules if it is an integration test, in the input procedure (reading the wrong data or reading the data the wrong way), or in the output procedure (printing or storing the wrong item or printing or storing the right item the wrong way or in the wrong spot). Consequently, we should determine the following first:

▶ Which module(s) are affected? It is much easier if the number of possibly affected modules is small, hence the philosophy of incremental testing. If we can, we might try to narrow the number of suspects down further by examining them one at a time for the issues mentioned below. We would start investigating the most likely candidate for an error first.

▶ Does data enter and exit the modules correctly? We might echo all input and print data in the calling module before it is used as a parameter in the module call. Likewise, we can print results before and after they the leave the module.

After such transference errors have been taken care of, we need to establish whether the test data took the expected execution path and examine whether all conditions and computations have been dealt with appropriately. We can use selective tracing to see what the variable values are when certain crucial points in the execution are reached. Some programming languages provide print statements for selective snapshots of variable values (e.g., the **PUT DATA** statement in PL/1 or a comparable statement in SNOBOL). Because many errors involve iterations around loops, it may pay to print out how many times a loop has been iterated. Logic tracing is also interested in the value of conditions at branching points.

▶ A program exceeds its run time and does not produce results commensurate with the CPU time consumed. The programmer may have miscalculated the time needed for the program to finish, but more likely, the program contains an infinite loop. If we suspect a specific loop, but are not sure, we can add print statements before and after the suspect or suspects, if there are several. Do not add indiscriminate print statements inside of suspected infinite loops. Printing from inside such a loop will indicate that this loop executes fairly often. It will also provide you with a nice fat stack of wallpaper, a bill for paper (if the computer center charges separately for it), and some weight-lifting experience. Hundreds or thousands of data values hardly ever solve the problem. We usually need only a few clues to find out what is correct and what is not. More printout only confuses. It is more important to think about what you really need to know than to tell the computer to spit out all its information. Precious time is spent wading through all the data.

Use the hints on good coding practices and error prevention as indicators of what errors to look for. If that doesn't help, it might be good to talk to others. It is amazing how often the error jumps out at you when you try to explain the problem to someone else.

The mutual suspicion principle, also called defensive programming, helps to contain bugs and facilitates error isolation and therefore their correction.

Lastly, do not dig yourself into the program. Debugging is hard mental work and can be exhausting to the point that your efficiency is highly diminished. When that happens it is better to go to lunch, go for a jog, watch some TV, walk your dog, do dishes, or bake bread. All of these activities are considered stress relievers, and, at least, they provide a change of pace. They even allow you to have your little debugging problem ruminating while you are occupied with something else. At times a good solution pops up precisely because you have taken a step back from your work. If you have to finish your regular work day and cannot walk away to leisure activities, you can change pace in other ways. Maybe there are adminstrative things that have been sitting in your in-basket, or maybe you had promised to explain something to a new colleague, which you put off because you had too much work for this program. It can even help to work on another aspect of the project for while: to write code for another module or prepare for the walk-through. Finding this particular bug is hardly ever the one and only thing that needs doing. Some people (those who are *always* organized) even have daily plans where they consider the need for a change of pace between mentally demanding and less demanding duties.

10.6.2. Error Logs

We have stressed before the importance of keeping your own error logs as a means to compile knowledge about your strengths and weaknesses and as a fast, efficient private reference work. Project error logs (as opposed to your private ones) are important for other reasons.

▶ They track testing progress. The error log should be able to distinguish between types of errors and indicate how many errors of which type have occurred.

▶ They form the basis for the development of error histories and error curves and through those make an evaluation of software reliability and software quality. A variety of metrics have been introduced that try to quantify the significance or severity of an error or the inherent effort to remove it. If we posit, for example, that an error costs more effort the longer it is undetected in the program, then we can develop a metric for total error removal effort (an indicator of lack of quality); for each error found, we determine the time it was introduced (during design, during coding, etc.) and the time it was found. The difference is the time the error existed. These times we sum to get the total error-time product. If we divide by the total development time, we get a normalized quantity that we can use to compare different projects with. To get an average, we can even divide by the number of errors found. Based on this last quantity, standards can be determined.

▶ They can conceivably be used for employee appraisal. This, however, has distinct disadvantages, unless error recording can be done by an objective party, which poses logistic difficulties. In the absence of that, using error statistics for assessing an individual's performance only leads to cheating on the official error logs. That defeats the purpose of having them.

▶ The rate at which errors occur can be used in software reliability models to predict software reliability and a variety of indicators that are important in project planning and maintenance [Musa87].

▶ They facilitate maintenance. First, the maintenance programmer sees which errors have been made and which decisions about dealing with them were rejected and why. He or she does not need to make the same error twice nor reintroduce a fallacious concept. Maintenance may also discover that the error that was supposedly removed during testing really wasn't.

▶ They provide the basis to make decisions about changes. When changes go beyond rectifying an error made during coding, corresponding changes need to be made in other documents. Because those are "taboo" to protect against wild, unreviewed, and incorrect alterations, errors that reach farther back than the coding phase usually initiate change control activities.

▶ They prevent forgetting about an error in situations where many errors are collected with a big test module and all errors are fixed afterwards, resulting in a long turnaround. This situation has been mentioned earlier and is quite frequent for large scale systems.

▶ They keep track of the yield of a test case.

▶ They keep track of when an error was fixed, by whom, and whether it was on schedule or not.

Because of these possible benefits of using error logs, the following information should be contained in them:

▶ testcase identification (number, date run);

▶ how the error manifested itself;

▶ underlying cause;

▶ modules affected;

▶ module(s) that contained error;

▶ error category;

▶ which documents or other pieces of code need changing;

▶ when was change applied for and what are the reasons;

▶ whether and when approved;

▶ person responsible for testing, debugging, and modification, deadline; and

▶ when was error removal and regression testing completed.

The layouts of error logs differ, and sometimes part of the information we suggest is contained in the related change control sheets. In order to keep the paperwork manageable, we should keep error logs to one sheet per error. Some forms try to fit all errors per module onto one sheet. Whichever way one decides to arrange an error log form, it should be easy to fill in. Otherwise the logs cost too much time and people won't want to do it, because they feel that it takes time away from their "productive work."

10.6.3. Change Control

As it was for previous phases, change control is important during the testing phase also, maybe even more so. The objective of change control is to avoid discrepancies between documents and deliverables from different phases. The code should reflect the design and not contradict it. The specifications should accurately describe what the code implemented. The code should provide a product that fulfills the stated requirements. Whenever changes to any deliverable would introduce discrepancies to previous work products, they need to be changed to reflect those changes and preserve a consistent set of documents. This requires change control. During the testing phase, three different actions can be taken when changes are proposed: now, later, or never.

Changes can be made on the spot if they only involve one person's code, do not affect previous documents, can be done without affecting the schedule, or are so critical that not making them would upset the schedule as well or worse.

Some errors can be collected for later resolution (they do not affect primary functionality, can be included in a later revision, there is slack time in two weeks to deal with the problem but not now, etc.). It is imperative that there is a procedure to keep track of such "deferred action." Otherwise, it is too easy to forget about it, error logs or no error logs. Therefore, when a change has been postponed, there should be a date for either a review of the postponement or work on the change. In case of successive versions, dealing with the change should be made part of the actions for the next version. The exact date is part of the plan for developing the next version, and material on the change should be formally included in the working papers for it.

Some proposed changes may be turned down. This happens more often with qualitative aspects rather than functional ones. A proposal for change could also include making an important part of the code faster. While that is a positive thing, it may not be necessary if the system is fast enough for its specifications. And, if improving its speed would make it harder to maintain, or would make the schedule tight, such change should not be allowed.

Any change that affects other documents needs to be reviewed by people who have the right to approve or disapprove of the change. We could set up a change control group whose charter is to make sure that all documents are consistent and to evaluate all proposed changes that require document changes. On smaller projects, a large group may be overkill. We could designate a person involved in each of the phases to deal with changes that affect that phase. This provides feedback to the people who developed that document in the first place. Knowing how well you did in your work (designing, specifying, developing requirements) is an important part of learning and job satisfaction. We should use opportunities to provide such feedback.

Any change needs to be reviewed for its ramifications and the scheduling and cost impact it will have on requirements, specifications, and design. If this duty is not taken seriously, the project is set up for a maintenance problem. It can be slight, or it can be a debacle. As with other oversights, any single, small change will not affect the consistency and therefore the usability of development documents much, but the combined effect can make them worse than useless: misleading. Then maintenance has only the code to go by. And for any medium-sized system that just isn't good enough.

Even during development, it is important to control changes that impact the boundary between two or more people's work. Otherwise an uncommunicated change can cause painful surprises as well as irreparable damages to working relationships. Take this scenario. Several people work on a system together. One night, late, A decides to change the sequence of parameters in a module he is responsible for but fails to communicate this to the people who need to use it. When B and C come in the next morning to build a new test run for integrating another module, it won't run. Because the error can only be in the new module or its interface to the existing ones (so they think), they try in vain to find the error there. Several days later, after much overtime work, they finally discover that the problem must lie in the interface to that module tested long before (the one A is responsible for). Would you want to work with A?

10.6.4. Summary

Testing then is a development phase that not only requires finding good test cases and running them but means finding errors and organizing necessary changes in an efficient manner. Testing therefore requires a good deal of planning and organization. The necessity for an organized and controlled approach to the testing process has prompted error logs and change control. The essence and purpose of this work is to guarantee technical quality of the resulting product, not to give us more paperwork to do.

Problems and Questions

1.   Develop an error log form for yourself. Then develop one for a group development effort.

2.   Try to generate all system error messages that pertain to a missing input or output file, to a wrong file, or to logical output unit usages. Go to the system manual and determine whether there are any that you could not generate. Try to find out why. Use any (or all) of the programming languages that you know.

3.   Take a program that you developed earlier. Insert errors from all error classes that were mentioned in this section (not necessarily all at once). Write down what you think should happen when you run your program. Then run it. What happens? Did you get the errors you expected?

10.7.   The Test Plan

While test plans are usually made much earlier, discussing the test plan was deferred until now, when there is enough detailed knowledge about the testing phase to put it all together and to realize what aspects about testing need to be planned and why. The test plan must answer the following questions about testing: What, when, how, by whom, with what, why, and how well. Let us elaborate on those one at a time.

1. **What.**   What needs to be tested. There is unit, integration, system, field, and acceptance testing that needs to be planned. The test plan must address every single one of them. In the beginning all cannot be planned for in minute detail, because that would presuppose knowledge about detailed design, which we just do not have in the beginning. The acceptance test will be planned and specified first. When enough design knowledge is ready, we can detail system and integration test. Field tests can be planned for on a preliminary basis at the time acceptance tests are prepared and planned for. Planning for a unit test, because it involves the most detailed knowledge, comes last. A test plan, therefore, is not a static document. Items are added as information becomes available. We know, however, when such information becomes available and can plan for making additions and decisions about testing efforts at specific points in the software development process. If we wish to classify phase testing for earlier phases as being part of testing, we need to include those into the plan as well. They can be planned for even earlier. Because they are natural parts of other phases, have predefined activities, inputs, and

outputs, and involve fewer phases, we do not include them in the test plan. The test cases, however, that they generate are part of the testing phase (depending on the method used for testing).

2. **When.**   A test plan must specify schedules and deadlines for all testing activities. Those can be in a hierarchical manner, determining deadlines for the larger steps first (unit testing done, integration testing done), and later they are refined to reflect activities on the next lower level. Note that the relationship between testing and debugging can be one to four for many kinds of bugs, even approach one to "infinity" for hard bugs. Time requirements like these need to be taken into account when planning for testing. Error logs from previous projects can provide average time frames, as well as variation and standard deviation for these quantities.

3. **How.**   The test plan also must state which testing strategies and methods need to be used (top-down, bottom-up, sandwich, constraints on testing sequences because of priorities and feasibility questions, control path testing, functional testing, or combination of the two). Here we also find reference to test cases from previous phases, test matrices, reference to test cases, test case libraries. Again, the "how" portion of the test plan gains in specificity as information becomes available. If we have not developed test cases to test the state transitions of a system, for example, we cannot include those test cases in the test plan. Sometimes specific test cases are not included in the test plan but referred to as a separate "testing workbook." In either case, the development of the test cases and time and manpower for that has to be planned into the schedule.

4. **By whom.**   Clear responsibility needs to be assigned for execution of testing activities and their supervision. If this is not done, it opens the door to "finger pointing" ("I thought you'd take care of that . . . "). Because people can only do one thing at a time, task assignment has an impact on schedules. We can take advantage of the parallelism inherent in the testing process to compress the schedule, but there should be enough time built in so that time for changes and coordination of work with other people is accomodated.

5. **With what.**   The test plan must describe and plan for all necessary resources. This includes planning for computer time and test support tools and also various testing configurations (such as we would need for a configuration test). The type of scaffolding code needed and when it is to be developed (drivers and stubs) must be included.

6. **Why.**   A test plan should also list the objectives of testing. This can be at a detailed level (test criteria) or at a more global level (testing state transitions, functional capabilities, performance according to rules, standards, regulations, etc.).

7. **How well.**   Answers to this question are related to the previous question. Usually, we give testing criteria (white box, black box, extended white box, gray box, etc.) any

metrics that we wish to use to evaluate the testing effort. A definition of error logs, their purpose, and a reference to where they can be found is also part of this aspect of the test plan. How to monitor tests and how to convey the debugging status is part of this aspect of the test plan as well.

The fact that we must address these seven areas does not mean that we describe our test plan in that order. The overall organization of the test plan would be first. Then we proceed with rough plans for unit and module test, integration testing, system testing, field testing, and acceptance testing in that order. In each category, the seven questions about testing and test planning must be answered. If there are areas common to all or at least a few of the testing steps, they need not be duplicated, but can be defined once in a separate chapter. An example would be resources, test facilities, support software, and the like, if they are used for several parts of the testing process. The same holds for test cases. In practice, it is often easier to describe the test cases in the section where they are first used.

The first available parts of the test plan are the version plans, the first criticality assessments, and the acceptance test. These should be incorporated into the test plan skeleton immediately. At this point, other parts of the test plan may only contain prescriptions of methodology and general strategy. This information, together with specifications and high level design, form the basis for the integration test. When the design approaches completion, unit test plans should also be finished. When the code is written, any control path tests need to be generated to complete the test objectives required in the plan.

Problems and Questions

1. When and where would you describe testing of critical modules in the test plan? At what point in time do you plan for testing against specifications? When are its test cases developed? How do you select them?

2. Indicate the earliest and latest times when each element can be finished. What are the deadlines you would set? Why? Does your answer depend on the testing method used? Which? How do your answers change with particular methods?

10.8. Summary

This completes the chapter on testing software. It is very important to plan for proper testing, to work with objective testing criteria, to combine functional and structure-based testing, and to control the testing process as any other phase in the development life cycle. As testing is completed, we have the following deliverables: the fully tested software, ready for turnover; all development documents consistent with each other and with the code; all user documentation consistent with the code; a signed acceptance agreement; and an evaluation of the testing process. This may or may not include quality estimations of the finished product.

Section 10.2. defined testing, debugging, verification, validation, and certification as terms related to the testing phase. It explained the activities of the testing phase. It also categorized testing methods (structured walk-throughs, static and dynamic analysis, symbolic execution, and proofs of correctness).

Three types of testing were introduced for program and unit testing. Code-based testing includes testing all statements once, control-path testing, and testing based on extended structure criteria. The last overcomes some of the shortcomings of the first two methods. The concept of minimally thorough testing was introduced.

Even these additional test criteria will not uncover functional deficiencies (missing code). This explains the need for a complementary set of techniques: functional or specification-based testing. We selected Howden's functional testing approach, because it can be used for unit and integration testing.

Fault injection helps to determine quality of testing and when to stop testing. It does not prescribe any particular testing method and works with programs and systems. It provides a statistically well-founded evaluation of software reliability but requires effort. It is not clear how robust the results are when statistical assumptions do not hold. Psychological barriers to "messing around with the code" can be detrimental to the acceptance of this technique.

System integration testing usually follows a strategy. We explained the advantages and disadvantages of top-down, bottom-up, sandwich, incremental, and phased integration. We also provided guidelines for when to use which approach. After determining the integration sequence, module interfaces need to be tested. This may not only include software but also hardware interfaces.

Section 10.4. described system test activities after integration of parts is complete. These include testing functionality as well as all quality requirements. We emphasized the need for an independent testing group. System testing is often based on an operational profile. Its quality determines the quality of testing.

After the system test is complete, the system may be put into a field test or used internally. This helps to take care of residual errors without the maintenance complication that large scale distribution would entail. Formal acceptance of the product by a customer happens after the product passes the acceptance test. Its details were described in Chapter 4.

Testing causes failures, and debugging locates the underlying fault. The section on debugging discussed two approaches to debugging—backtracking and cause elimination—its advantages and disadvantages, and currently existing tool support. Structured approaches to debugging are described in [Myer79], [Brow73], and

[Brad85]. In spite of a body of heuristic debugging knowledge, debugging is very much an art [Pres87]. Debugging tools that use debugging knowledge are still in the experimental stage [Sevi87]. They are usually limited to small programs and have high execution costs. There is much room for improvement.

Section 10.6.2. emphasized the importance of error logs to track testing progress, to establish error histories, and to estimate software reliability. They also serve to track the yield of test cases, who fixed an error at what time, and whether work was on schedule. Large scale software development needs error logs when errors are collected before they are fixed. To prevent programmer resistance, error logs must be simple and fast to fill out. Removing errors may necessitate changing base-lined documents. This requires change control procedures. These were discussed in Section 10.6.3.

Testing is an activity that requires a great deal of planning. It uses information from all previous phases. Therefore the test plan is a crucial document in the software development life cycle. Section 10.7. described its contents. The test plan answers the following questions: what, when, how, by whom, with what, why, and how well to test.

While this book cannot discuss all possible testing and verification strategies, the material explains some of the more important methods, why a test plan is necessary, what testing can do and what it cannot do, and how to go about developing a test plan. The reader who is interested in more depth in the techniques presented or in other approaches to testing, should consult [Basi87], [Chan81], [Demi87], [Deut82], [Dunn84], [Gelp88], [Gilb77], [Glas79], [Haus84], [Hetz84], [Howd87], [Haun75], [King75], [Mill74], [Mill81], [Mime75], [Myer79], [Ostr88], [Perr83], [Quir85], [Rapp85], and [Weyu88].

▶ 11
Operation and
Maintenance

11.1. Overview

Before a software system or program can be put into operation, we have to make sure that all the necessary documents and manuals for training and reference have been developed and are correct and consistent. McClure [Mccl81] added a documentation phase between development and operation and maintenance to emphasize this point. We include these activities under operation and maintenance.

The major issues to be discussed in this chapter are as follows:

▶ How do we ensure continued user satisfaction?

▶ How do we define and implement change request procedures?

▶ How should we deal with various classes of changes, such as errors, versions, and new releases?

▶ How can we understand the software product and its development documents to ease maintenance?

▶ How should we best go about assessing the impact of change?

▶ How do we integrate and validate the changes?

▶ How do we update the documentation?

Section 11.2. defines various types of maintenance and explains the elements of the maintenance process. Maintenance is classified into corrective, adaptive, or perfective maintenance. We also find enhancements as an objective of maintenance activities. The goal of maintenance is to keep a software product viable over time as environment and user needs change and as problems with the software surface.

Section 11.2. discusses the activity flow during maintenance and how maintenance is related to other phases of the life cycle. Maintenance activities are contrasted with development activities. The fundamental difference is the fact that maintenance must work with existing code and documents, which constrains options significantly. When changes are to be made, maintenance requires an understanding of all ramifications of a change. Between changes, maintenance activities encompass the training of users, operations staff, and maintainers and the management of the operational system.

Training and reference manuals were mentioned in previous chapters. Section 11.3. describes in detail what they contain and how to organize them. They are used during the operational life of a software system and should facilitate understanding. Therefore, quality expectations for these documents are best derived from the needs and uses during operation and maintenance. The same applies to training for various aspects of the software's operational life: user, system support, maintenance group, etc.

After a description of how to write various manuals and reference documents, we will delve into the details of the maintenance activities. Section 11.4. deals with user feedback and associated maintenance procedures when maintenance personnel evaluates and processes user requests for maintenance actions. It discusses various feedback options and develops a form for a formal user request for changes. A structured analysis procedure uses explicit priorities to trade off requests, to assess their impact on the product, and to estimate resource requirements.

A description of maintenance techniques (Section 11.5.) follows. This includes procedures for analyzing the impact of a proposed change on all documents of the life cycle. Section 11.5. also discusses change control, regression testing, and multiversion, multisite maintenance.

The last section (Section 11.6.) deals with software obsolescence and death. It discusses symptoms of software obsolescence and death and how to determine proper responses (major overhaul or replacement).

Maintenance can be a demanding job that should not be left to novices. It may require understanding of all development documents, of the techniques that were used to develop the product, and of the application area. This requires a well-rounded person, not a specialist in debugging.

After reading this chapter, the reader will know common maintenance activities and how they are driven by user requests. He will be able to evaluate such requests and use maintenance techniques to make changes to existing software. He will also be able to assess how viable a software product is. He will know how to structure various manuals and what information they should contain.

11.2. Elements of the Maintenance Process

Maintenance encompasses all activities that keep the system operational and meet the users' needs. Maintenance activities can be classified into corrective, adaptive, and perfective maintenance. We also find enhancements as an objective of maintenance. Let us define each of these types of maintenance.

Maintenance can entail fixing newly found errors, in which case it is called *corrective maintenance*. It can require adaptation activities. *Adaptive maintenance* happens when there are changes to the use or environment of the software system or program. Examples of such adaptive maintenance activities follow.

▶ **Changes to input data.**   This may involve format changes or changes necessitated by different ways of dealing with data altogether. New postal zip codes that involve nine instead of five digits fall into this category. The tax recording and information system will also encounter a great many adaptive changes, because tax rules and design for schedules and forms tend to change between years.

▶ **Changes to the system environment.**   Adaptive changes also need to be made when the operating system or the software's run-time environment changes. In real-time systems sensor technology can change and require conversion to deal with such equipment differences. A personal computer user may need to have his system adapted when he switches to a hard disk or buys a new type of printer. All system conversions fall into this category.

▶ **Functional changes.**   Usually such changes mean system enhancements. This is why this type of adaptive maintenance is sometimes classified separately as *enhancement*. Sometimes little used software functions are removed, especially when it will improve bad performance. More often, however, new and/or more sophisticated versions of existing functions are added as a maintenance activity.

Sometimes improvements to existing software become necessary. This is the focus of perfective maintenance. *Perfective maintenance* seeks to eliminate inefficiencies in existing functions, particularly performance and reliability problems. It may entail improving convergence in numerical software, upgrading security mechanisms, or any of the other qualitative aspects of the software that were first discussed in Chapter 4. This is usually required because the software does not live up to its qualitative requirements or the requirements have changed. Thus perfective maintenance can be corrective (when qualitative requirements are not met) or adaptive (when qualitative requirements have changed).

Maintenance consumes 40 to 80 percent of the software life-cycle cost and hence is not cheap. Functional and quality enhancements consume by far the biggest share of these costs (about 60%), corrective maintenance only a little more than 7%. The remainder is due to adaptations and other maintenance activities that are hard to classify ([Mccl81], [Lien80], [Fjel79], [Pari83]).

Because most of the maintenance work is really further development, its cost depends on how much further development is necessary and how hard it is to satisfy existing constraints (i.e., the software and its requirements). Getting right down to it, maintenance is often a misnomer. This is what is at the heart of the controversy between the waterfall model of software development and the evolutionary life cycle model (cf. Chapter 1). A development cycle in the evolutionary model encompasses going through any or all of the following phases: problem analysis, requirements, specifications, design, coding, and testing. If maintenance indeed encompasses all further cycles through development phases, then cost will depend on

▶   the number of such cycles,

▶   the degree of change in each cycle (which phases need to be gone through again), and

▶   the complexity of effecting the change within the constraints of the existing cycle, due to current objectives and existing software.

Whether we eliminate maintenance and call it further development activities, evolutionary cycles, or whether we stick to the traditional term maintenance is not important. What is important is to realize that during its operational life, software undergoes

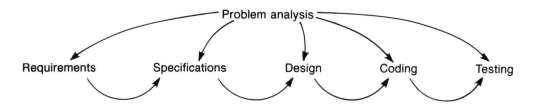

Figure 11.1 Activity Flow during Maintenance.

a series of further development cycles. They require going through one or more of the original development phases over again. Because every phase involves documents, their preparation and consistent update is very important. In addition, we have training activities.

Much of the maintenance work requires reevaluating the status quo, and an impact assessment of the effort required to achieve the objectives of the current cycle. This may require the need for a budget, scheduling, and planning of current cycle activities. Whether such planning is done "by default," by the maintainer, or by the manager and needs approval, depends on the nature of the current maintenance activities. It is determined, to a great extent, when problems or user requests are evaluated and classified.

Maintenance work is based on the existing software. Therefore, it revolves around understanding existing programs and all associated documents. More often than not, maintainers need to improve understandability through upgrading documentation. Maintenance often encompasses what is commonly called "technical support": answering questions of users and/or operations staff, finding and correcting bugs, managing multiple versions of an operational system, etc.

As software gets older, the effects of changes make themselves felt. Obsolete functions need to be purged, and adaptations and conversions are more likely and leave their mark (i.e., patches). Over time, software approaches a stage where restructuring and rewriting are in order to keep it viable and productive. We discussed restructuring in Chapter 9.

Why is maintenance so costly? If we look at what operations and maintenance people are doing, we quickly see that theirs is a rather complex, challenging, and encompassing job. Survey results have shown that more than half of their time is spent merely trying to understand the software. This involves not just the code itself but also all other development documents. In order to keep the software useful, operation and maintenance must keep training and retraining users and sometimes operations staff. They must answer questions, manage versions of the software, and make, understand, and document the changes in all related documents.

In order for a software system to be useful, it must continue to serve the users' needs. The maintainers' job is to make sure that it does. Because such needs are dynamically changing over time, the software will have to change as well. Further development or redevelopment is necessary, with one major constraint: the software already exists. This makes the "development" work that maintainers do considerably harder. They do not have the degrees of freedom that the first time developers had. They must stick to the existing basic design and implementation approach if they want to avoid patchwork and detrimental effects on maintainability. If they switched from an object-oriented design to a function-oriented one, the result would be confusing and much harder to understand. New error messages should still follow the same layout and principle. Coding style should stay the same if it was qualitatively adequate, using the same conventions.

Switching to different coding styles will only be confusing and make the code less clear, because our expectations of what to find where and how it will look are continually thwarted. That can create big problems for the next person who needs to understand the code.

Maintenance always involves making changes to the code and to documents. It is important to determine which changes are to be made, to make sure that those changes do not engender any undesirable effects, and that they be made cost-effectively. Thus, when change requests come in from the users or the operations staff, they have to be assessed (this is similar to problem analysis and feasibility study), objectives and requirements have to be adapted, designs need to be modified, and code (re)written. New parts require testing, and old parts that are affected by changes need to be regression tested. Manuals should be brought up to the current state. In essence, we go through another cycle in the software's evolutionary life. A prerequisite to successful maintenance or evolutionary development is that the software and its associated documentation be understood by the maintainer(s). This requires considerable skill and experience. Unfortunately, the task is often relegated to junior level people because it is perceived as less gratifying than new development and therefore boring and unchallenging. While it may be more fun to "build from scratch," we should recognize that, just as with houses, a renovation can require more skill, pose bigger challenges, and be more functional, useful, and cost-effective than tearing the house down and building it over. Because of the multiple skills and knowledge required in maintaining software, we need experienced people, not novices, to do this job. They have to be familiar with techniques from the entire software development life cycle.

Most often, maintenance activities are started through a user request. It may fall into any of the categories of maintenance that were just described. In order to deal with them properly, we need a change request procedure, not unlike the change requests we may have had during development, with one difference. During development, change requests were mostly due to errors or inferior ways of doing things (less than perfect design decisions or clumsy user interface design, for example). Now they most often originate from changed needs and thus involve applying for a change in requirements.

It would be too inefficient and confusing to immediately react to every request as it comes in, especially when a software system exists in multiple installations in several versions. Therefore, requests are usually batched. We need a decision-making procedure on how to put them in batches and how to determine in which order the requests are to be processed. An ordered batch of requests is the result of request processing. We need to do an impact assessment to determine the extent, consequences, and feasibility of changes. This involves understanding the existing system as well as the exact nature of the changes. Researching requirements document, specifications, design, and code is usually necessary.

Before a change can be accepted, it should be reviewed. This includes a review of all documents that are affected by the change. Next, the changes are made in the code, which is followed by testing of new parts and regression testing of existing ones. *Regression testing* means to rerun all or some of the previous tests for a piece of software to assure that no errors have been introduced through the changes [Pres87] or to verify that the software still performs the same functions in the same manner as its older version [Pfle87]. Testing is done in the same sequence of stages as during development: unit testing, integration testing, system testing, acceptance testing. The difference is that only the software parts affected by the changes need to be retested. Sometimes it is hard to know exactly what parts of the software need retesting. Then it may be more cost-effective to rerun all previous tests.

All manuals and reference documents need to be reviewed and modified so that they are consistent with the new system.

Factors such as modularity, consistency in design and implementation, coding standards, and a programming style that enhances understandability support and facilitate maintenance. So do choosing extendable and adaptable algorithms and data structures. The completeness and consistency of documentation and how it is organized also make a big difference. Nevertheless, software often deteriorates over time. There will come a point when it will be cheaper to replace the existing software rather than update it one more time. We will discuss how to determine whether this point has occurred or not. It is

Maintenance activities	Development activities
Understand software and documents	
Feedback evaluation:	
User request analysis	Problem analysis
Reassess objectives, impact assessment	Requirements analysis
Identify precise nature of change	Specification
Redesign and design modifications	Design
Code changes and additions, restructuring, improvements	Coding
Regression testing	Testing

Figure 11.2 Maintenance vs. Development Activities per Change.

1. Understand software.
2. Training and counseling of users, operations staff, new maintainers.
3. Manage operational system (multisite, multiversion).

Figure 11.3 Maintenance Activities between Changes.

also important to know whether all of the "old" software is to be thrown out, or whether parts of it can be salvaged, and, if so, which. Section 11.6. will deal with this.

Not every program needs a lot of maintenance. Some software is rather short-lived, of the "throwaway" type: it is used once and then scrapped or, more likely, stashed away some place. For such programs, many of the development activities (documentation of every phase!) and maintenance don't apply. On the other side of the spectrum is long-lived software like compilers, utilities, operating systems, mathematical and statistical libraries, etc. For these, there is a definite need for a structured, methodical approach to maintenance so that we can avoid the problems [Pari83] so eloquently describes:

▶ the software is not understood,

▶ documentation is missing or contradictory,

▶ proliferation of uncontrolled changes leads to structural decay of the software, and

▶ high turnover in the maintenance group with associated lack of expertise, aggravates and cements the previous three problems.

This chapter will describe how to prevent or alleviate the first three of these problems. Chapter 15 deals with the human factor of maintenance.

Problems and Questions

1.   Which types of maintenance are there? Which type is most frequent? Why is maintenance a complex activity?

2.   Do you think it might be possible to use or adapt the change request and approval procedure from the testing chapter so that it can be used during maintenance? Explain why or why not and what changes are necessary in your opinion.

3.   Two developers have a disagreement about whether the next development step in an iterative development plan falls under maintenance or is to be regarded as another development cycle in the evolutionary life of the software. What do you tell them when they ask you to be the arbiter?

4.   (student) How often have you used a program that you developed yourself more than once? Which programs/systems do you use most often? How long have you used them? How have they changed during this time? Which changes would you like to see in them? Which of those would you consider hard, which easy? Why? If someone asked you to make some of those changes, how would you go about doing it?

5.   (professional programmer) How many programs or systems are you maintaining now? Do you have data to determine how much time you spend per week on maintenance related activities? If so, make an evaluation of your development versus your maintenance efforts.

For the next month, keep track of how much of your time is spent on maintenance vs. development. For each maintenance task determine what type of maintenance task you were performing, which activity (understanding, changing, testing, updating documents), and whether you considered it "busy work," "unnecessary problems," or a needful activity.

What have you learned? (How) would you like to change things?

11.3. Documentation and Training

As mentioned earlier, we include a section on documents because they are

- ▶ a primary source of information for the users, the operations staff, and the maintainers,

- ▶ often updated during maintenance,

- ▶ used by operations staff and technical support personnel as reference works or to teach from, and

- ▶ not part of the testing phase, and we did not, like [Mccl81] include a separate documentation phase.

We will concentrate on manuals that are used by users, operations staff, and technical support during the operational life of the software. The contents of documents during development have been discussed in each specific phase before. Here we are only concerned with issues as they relate to consistent updating of material. The reader who wishes more extensive explanation on how to write manuals should consult [Brow84B].

The objectives of documents that are primarily used during the operations and maintenance part of software life are as follows:

- ▶ They should provide factual knowledge on all aspects of the software and its use. Documents differ in terms of what constitutes use. A novice or prospective user would need a training or beginners manual. Similarly, operator training manuals introduce operations staff to the basics of a software system's operation. They usually include a description of manual procedures as well.

▶ They should provide in depth information. Full reference manuals with cross reference lists for important items describe the software and its features, its environment, its manual and automated procedures, its trouble-shoot procedures, and an explanation of all error messages and recommended actions. We may have a user reference guide, a systems manual, an installation manual, an operator procedure manual, or a maintenance guide. Whether they are each separate documents or (partially) combined depends on the size and complexity of the software. For big software systems we may have separate documents for various subsystems. Information intended for different classes of readers should be packaged separately.

▶ They should provide fast access to information. Very few users are willing to read a manual from cover to cover, and even then, they may not know how to react to a particular sequence of events when they use the software. Usually they want to accomplish a particular function but need to find out how to do it, establish the proper parameters, etc. The same is true for operations staff. Maintainers also have to find information that is often nonobvious, intricate, or involves several development phases (and their associated documents). In order to enable effective use of the software and its effective maintenance, all documents not only need to be accurate and consistent with each other, but also well organized in order to speed up finding material.

▶ They should accomodate levels of knowledge. For user manuals, it is often beneficial to organize documents around levels of knowledge, starting with the basic and most common uses first, then proceeding to more intricate and advanced material.

When we prepare material, it is important to keep the following ideas in mind.

Identify the Reader(s)

Users, unless they do setups themselves, do not need to know detailed setup procedures, but operators do. Maintainers need detailed design knowledge, and users don't. Users need to know what an error message means and what recourse they have to deal with it, while maintainers also need to know what exactly triggers it and where in the code it is activated. Maintainers need more detail knowledge on system error messages than users. If you know who the readers are, you can make assumptions about what they already know versus what you need to explain to them. You can narrow down the material to what you really need to tell the readers. You might refer them to a different manual or section for material that is rarely needed. Duplicating that material is not recommended because it bears the risk that in the next update of the related document the parts that are duplicated elsewhere will not be properly updated, creating an inconsistency and opening the door to a mess of useless and contradicting information.

Identify the Documents

A user manual (introductory or reference) often uses the specification document as a start. Because the specifications describe what the software system looks like, this makes eminent sense. We would reorganize the material for a tutorial and add an introductory section that explains how to use the software, but the basic information is the same as in the functional specifications.

The design document can provide a valuable basis for the systems and operations manual; the test plan and the testing documents, especially system and installation test, will also do this when it comes to describing how to install and operate the software. For the system manual we can start with the design summary, followed by a specification of system tests to guide us in defining basic contents and structure. System test specifications describe what was tested, why, what was expected as output and what can serve as valuable information on what needs to be described, why, and how it should work. The installation test specifications constitute the basis for the installation procedure description. All test cases have potential to serve as examples. They also have the advantage in that we don't have to reinvent examples, they demonstrably work, and they are convenient because they already exist. It is important to keep examples simple and focused on the point we wish to explain. This is why some test cases may not qualify. Then we should construct a new example, sacrificing time savings for simplicity.

Identify the Basic Structure

It helps if you can parallel the structure in the existing documents, but if that should not be possible, make sure you have a detailed outline. Structure of documents differs for tutorial and reference materials.

In a training document it is important to describe material in logical order of use. We can use the flow of information from the high level requirements diagram to determine logical order of use. First, we describe how to activate the system (include information on how to log onto the computer, even to switch on the terminal if you can't depend on the users' knowing this). It is very annoying to have to find that information elsewhere. Be aware, however, that these passages are prone to change when new equipment is added and when new releases of the operating system or other supporting software come around. This part of the manual then becomes obsolete and needs to be replaced.

On the maintainer's desk should be an index card (you may substitute an electronic mechanism) stating that the manual's introductory section needs to be checked whenever operating system, equipment, or supporting software change. Ideally, one would like to have a computerized, automated reminder, but in most shops this is futuristic. Such a system would consist of a database cross-referencing all documents and identifying passages for reexamination when changes occur in specific, named objects, functions, and system environments.

In essence, a link between documents of two successive development phases is established during phase testing when two sets of documents (previous and current phase) are checked for consistency and completeness. If we had a reliable way of cross-referencing items from the user level all the way down to the code level and between manuals, a lot of the dogwork of "impact assessment" and "documentation update" would become a lot easier; we would simply follow the reference chains between documents.

In cases where we must duplicate material from other documents, we should make a reliable maintenance entry for the original document stating which parts of that document are duplicated in which other documents. This is work and more paper, but it avoids problems later. Even so, it is advisable to revalidate the consistency of documents when a sizeable number of changes have been made. This could be part of a major facelift for software when there are enough indicators of decay (changes involving all documents in the development cycle, system conversions, enough changes to warrant new release, etc.).

Whether the essentials of getting onto the computer are duplicated or not, the use of the most essential features should be described in the sequence the user would activate them. Since defaults were selected to facilitate the use of the system, you will probably explain simple versions of commands or menus that do not require many input parameters. The tax system would probably begin by explaining how to input and delete tax data items and then describe how to start computation of built-in schedules. Saving information might involve simple file names or default file names. In the most sophisticated version of the tax system, the one that allowed user definition of schedules and rules, this topic would probably be considered advanced and left for later sections.

Figure 11.4 shows the contents of and major rules for developing a training manual.

For TAP, the introductory section would include the features for which the reference manual should be consulted. This establishes intent and readership of the manual. Next we would describe how to start TAP, give a short explanation of what each section contains, and describe syntax and other conventions that we are using in the descriptive material.

The rest of the outline depends on the approach we are taking. We could structure each section of the outline in one of three ways:

1. Introduction
    product philosophy
    hardware/software environment
    how to start product (incl. prepare for start)
    how to use manual—progressive steps
2.-k. Successive learning steps
    steps in logical order of using and learning, not alphabetically
    most basic features or usages first
    increasing sophistication
    goal of learning in each section.
    whole work units
    error messages and how to deal with them
    examples
Appendices.
A.1. glossary of terms
A.2. index
A.3. short alphabetical reference section of commands (maybe to take out as a fold-a-card)
A.4. collected error messages

Figure 11.4 Training Manual.

▶ According to the three major types of data, i.e., income, deductions, and taxes that need to be computed. This is a data-oriented structuring approach. Schedules and forms are introduced when specific types of data are introduced.

▶ Around the forms and schedule hierarchy. We would start with Form 1040 and then add further sections on how TAP deals with increasingly complex tax returns involving other forms and schedules such as B, C, A, etc. This approach is also object-oriented, the object is now the completed tax form or schedule. Sections are sequenced according to the structure inherent in the actual tax forms and schedules.

▶ According to the logical sequence in which the tax system would be used. This is a function-oriented way of organizing material. The sections would start with an explanation of how to input or edit data of certain types, then schedules in increasing order of difficulty would be added, each learning step involves information on output (print routines).

If we follow this structure, the first section on features could describe simple data entry followed by 1040 computation, print routines for 1040, and the list of entries by type. This constitutes a whole work unit. The next section adds information on how to update tax data (modification and deletion) and introduces other schedules and forms that are predefined together with their associated print routines.

The last sections would describe the most intricate usage of the system: how to do rule-based forms generation. Note that this kind of structure is patterned very closely to the user needs pattern and the stages of evolutionary development that was identified during requirements analysis.

It is very important for the training manual to have an index of topics and questions so that the user who is still learning can find the answer to a question fairly quickly. We should emphasize user level terms in the index. It is considered motivating if each section contains a whole work step from beginning to end (from tax entry to a completed form and its printing), because the trainee can see that he or she can actually do something useful with the system. Equally important is a section on error messages. Because that user will have error messages in front of him or her, the emphasis is not only reproducing them in the manual but, much more importantly, on

▶ explaining what they mean,

▶ what the effects on the system and the user's data are, and

▶ what action options the user has at this point to minimize any damage (loss of data for example).

A reference manual, on the other hand, would describe everything there is to know about a feature or command in one place. We can still organize the material in chronological order of software execution, but it is often structured alphabetically around commands, language features, or major topics. Some people prefer to describe commands in alphabetical order, because it makes finding them so much easier. In this case, there should be a section that describes possible state transitions between different parts and functional aspects of the system. Another difference between training and reference manuals is in the amount of detail in which functional features are described. The reference manual must list all relevant material in full detail with default values, full and partial range of values, maximum and minimum usages, etc. The contents of a reference manual are given in Figure 11.5.

If we try to apply this outline to the program analyzer PAS, the introductory section contains the following:

▶ philosophy: experimental system, capabilities, and limits of program analysis;

▶ overview: structure information from specifications and state transition diagram (cf. Table 5.12, Figure 5.4), explanations;

1. Introduction
    product overview and philosophy
    product component/feature overview and interfaces
    state transitions between system states
    hardware/software environment, interfaces
    structure of manual
2.–k. Components and features
    (in alphabetic order) description of commands (features) in *detail* with all default
    parameters
    error messages
    examples
Appendices
A.1. error messages, explanations, effects, system status, possible actions.
    Cross-reference to section that explains system component or feature.
A.2. index
A.3. short, alphabetically ordered reference card for commands for quick reference.

Figure 11.5 Contents of Reference Manual.

▶ hardware/software environment: operating system on which it runs, files needed, how to start PAS, how to clean up afterwards;

▶ syntax and other conventions: how command syntax is described in the manual, what syntax is expected for programs to be analyzed, error message conventions; and

▶ structure of manual: whether alphabetic according to commands, alphabetic according to top commands, or ordered in hierarchical function sequence as in Table 5.12.

If we assume that further sections are organized according to function and alphabetically in order of top level commands, we get the following order:

▶ **ANALYZE**

▶ **COMPARE**

▶ **QUIT**

▶ **REPORTS**

▶ **STATISTICS**

Lower level commands would be described alphabetically as subsections of the major section above. The other option is to describe all commands in alphabetical order, regardless of their level in the hierarchy. Then we get the following order:

- ▶ **ACCUMULATE**
- ▶ **ANALYZE**
- ▶ **COMPARE**
- ▶ **EXIT**
- ▶ **QUIT**
- ▶ **REPORTS**
- ▶ **SAVE**
- ▶ **SELECT**
- ▶ **STATISTICS**
- ▶ **TYPESTAT**

The advantage to the second method is that we can find the particular command under its section heading. The disadvantage is that the structure information is lost. From which system state the command was invoked can be quite important in determination what it will do. In either case, the three ways of structuring information are all function oriented. Whether a function or data oriented structure for the reference manual is chosen, often depends on the method used for developing requirements and specifications and on the type of human machine interface.

The three appendices of the reference manual for PAS consist of error messages and possible remedies, an index, and a command syntax table.

Define All Terms

Terms should be defined the first time they are used. If the reader is likely to consult another document as well, cross-reference. Because changes in the manuals are likely, a continuous numbering system for the document is not wise. Rather, pages should be numbered with two items: the section number, followed by the page number within the section. The fifth page of the third section would then have the number 3-5. When changes occur, only those pages that belong to the changed section need to be changed. This makes it easier to keep track of changes. It would be even better if we could use a section name followed by the page number within the section. Unfortunately, short one word headings are rare.

Cross-Reference

Cross-reference between phase documents (e.g., specifications, design, and requirements) and between tutorial and advanced material. This is especially important when their organization differs. The page numbering method just described will also help to keep those documents current in the face of changes.

Group Material

In a reference manual, related material should be centralized in one section (e.g., error messages, file definitions, what the user needs to know about starting and stopping the software and related operating system particulars—you don't want them to never use the software, because they get so frustrated trying to figure out how to get started or to prepare input and output files). You can organize related material around objects (this works well if you used object-oriented design) and/or major higher level functions. If you need all or part of this information later, you either cross reference (make sure it applies to the new situation) or you extract the common information into a separate section.

Index

Use a methodical approach for the index. [Brow84B] describes two types of indices, the standard index and the instant index. The standard index is the extensive index by keywords, important concepts, and issues that we find in the back of reference books. They help the reader to locate specific information quickly and thus are a major ingredient for a usable manual. Browning [Brow84B] suggests the following procedure to develop a standard index:

1.   Take a full final version of the manual. This is important because the page numbers where you find the keywords for the index have to correspond to the actual pages that the manual will have when the readers use it.

2.   Highlight all words or concepts that are worth putting into the index. This will give you a rough cut of your index. A sizable number of highlighted words will be related.

3.   Organize the list of words. The first simplification arises when we identify main items and subordinate items, as in

tax
  forms
   1040
   A
   B
   C
   D
  schedules see tax forms

We can avoid duplicating subordinates for related or synonymous terms by referring to the main entry as we have done in the example above. The main advantage of an index, i.e., finding things fast, disappears when a term shows a long list of page numbers. Where should the reader look for the information? It may help to precise the entry more, adding (different) subordinate attributes. The main reference to a term should always be boldface. Sometimes an index term is a common item that runs throughout the book and shouldn't be part of the index at all (such as "program" in a book entirely about programming, or "software engineering" in a book on software engineering). Figure 11.6 shows an alphabetized list of index terms based on the narrative about the **ANALYZE** command for PAS from Section 5.3.2.

Besides a standard index, it may help the reader to find information fast if we provide an instant index [Brow84B], which can go inside the back or front cover or be a separate card that can be taken out of the manual or be acquired separately. Main categories for an instant index come from the structured keyword outline that was the starting point for writing the manual. Often-used categories are

▶ commands,

▶ statement types for languages,

▶ data attributes and types, and

▶ major functions and features.

We can switch from a function-oriented outline to a data-oriented instant index. This way there are two means to locate major items of information, and the instant index gives us information that the outline and table of contents do not. An instant index for PAS could be built on the hierarchical set of commands of Table 5.12. For each major and subordinate entry we give the page number where the information can be found. Figure 11.7 shows some options with simulated page numbers.

For TAP, on the other hand, we can build an instant index on schedules and forms (where to find what information on schedules) and on data types (deductions, income, taxes). Another basis for an instant index are the data dictionary and the function names of the requirements diagrams.

ACCUMULATE
accumulator
ANALYZE
- input
- function
- results
- errors
author identification code
commands
- conventions
- level
- mode
- types
  - ACCUMULATE
  - ANALYZE
  - COMPARE
  - EXIT
  - QUIT
  - REPORTS
  - SAVE
  - STATISTICS
COMPARE
covariance matrix
errors
- ANALYZE
  - capacity
  - file name
  - function
  - range indicator
  - syntax
EXIT
file name
f(x)/f(m)
means vector
output
- screen
- print
QUIT
range indicator
- line numbers
- module name
REPORTS
SAVE
similarity index
STATISTICS
storage
- permanent
- temporary

Figure 11.6 Partial Index for PAS.

1. Commands

ACCUMULATE	5-2	QUIT	7-2	STATISTICS	10-2
ANALYZE	5-6	REPORTS	8-1	TYPESTAT	10-10
COMPARE	6-2	SAVE	9-1		
EXIT	7-1	SELECT	10-1		

2. Parameters

files	analysis	5-7	accumulator	5-2
	results	9-1	module range	5-8
	statistics	10-3		

3. Reports

| analysis | 8-1 | comparison | 8-4 | statistics | 8-2 |

4. Statistics

covariance	10-5	mean	10-3	mode	10-4
f(x)/f(m)	10-6	median	10-4	variance	10-5
max	10-3	min	10-3		

Figure 11.7 Instant Index for PAS.

Training

Training follows the structure of the training manual, starting with the simplest and most straightforward usages of the system and advancing to the most sophisticated. The manuals should be augmented by other teaching materials, such as visuals, hands-on exercises, and the like. The preparation of teaching materials can parallel manual writing and use some of the same examples. When writing a training or reference manual, we can start out with the current form of the specifications. We then rewrite it as a user manual (training or reference). There is some material that we have to add: how to invoke the system and other technical details. Some of this information we can get through system test specifications and installation test descriptions. Ongoing training is very important for the following reasons.

▶ It keeps the user base big enough to allow productive use of the system.

▶ It prevents efficiency losses for maintenance personnel when inadequately trained users make errors and come asking about things they could have learned in a training course. It is more efficient to answer questions once to a group of people than to repeat the question and answer process on an individual basis.

As the number of questions about the same material grows, it is time to announce another training or refresher course. They need not be big formal affairs, nor last very long. We can also determine the need for training through analyzing user questions and requests. As you collect them, keep a tally of what was most often talked about and make sure you teach that. In this way the user-maintenance interaction can become useful as a feedback mechanism for training materials.

▶ It keeps the users up-to-date about changes and enhancements on the system or its working environment. There are many ways to accomplish that. Multiuser systems often have electronic newsletters or message boxes. When a user activates the software system, the latest information is flashed onto the screen. This is only possible when the news items are fairly short or are references where to find the detailed news. Alternatives are full-fledged printed newsletters. Short, on-site meetings are another possibility. Teaching update material can be combined with teaching advanced material. The logistics (single site or multiple sites, size of software, complexity of software and its use, physical distance of maintenance to user, centralized or decentralized organizational structure, etc.) often favor one option over another.

▶ It increases the visibility of the software. Software dies if it is not used. A productive software therefore needs a user base. As individuals who had been using the software leave, get promoted, or are assigned other responsibilities, the original user base thins naturally. Well taught and publicized training can act as a powerful marketing tool. In instances where we have an iterative development of related products, such as a family of software development tools or a toolset for performance analysis and capacity planning, training in one of the software products provides the chance to introduce sister products.

While user training and reference manuals are important, system and installation manuals are no less critical for continued user satisfaction. In order to write the system manual, we can start with the design summary and the system test specifications. The first tells us what the internals of the system look like, the latter what was tested, why, and what the expected answers were. If it was worth testing, it probably is worth describing to the operations staff and the maintenance people. Similarly, we can deduce the installation manual from the installation test specifications. User and operator training manuals are completed prior to system testing (but after the test plan is complete) and are tested during that stage. At the same time, operating staff is trained so that by the time the system is ready for turnover, there are enough knowledgeable people to operate and use it.

Problems and Questions

1. Your job is to write a user training manual for TAP. Which documents from the development phases will you use? What information do they contain that you wish to use?

Organize this material into a detailed keyword outline. Show how learning progresses in whole work units. Which type of organization have you chosen? Why?

Look through the specification-based test cases for TAP. Which of these qualify as examples? Which of the keywords in the detailed outline can be used for an instant index? How would you organize it?

2.   Based on the specifications for PAS, develop a user reference manual. Because it is an experimental system with few users who are experienced in its development, try to be as concise as you can.

3.   Develop a standard index and an instant index for the user reference manual for PAS.

4.   Assume that PAS is used at one installation. Which types of user feedback would you suggest to

▶   determine the need for further training of current users,

▶   identify new users and train them, and

▶   identify and "broadcast" answers to common questions.

Investigate how these mechanisms that you chose could be implemented on your computer system.

11.4.   User Feedback and Maintenance Procedures

This section discusses how to organize maintenance. Change procedures and release procedures must be fixed prior to the installation of a system. The cornerstone is a well-defined change procedure that is responsive to the needs of the user and the technical and economical feasibility of a change. The first order of business then is to discuss ways of effective user feedback and evaluation.

The preceding section discussed ways to identify and meet training demands through targeting inadequate user knowledge. This is an important maintenance problem because it causes early software obsolescence through loss of user productivity. This leads to decreased user acceptance and loss of use. To deal with these problems, we must be able to distinguish between training problems (which we can solve with the techniques suggested earlier) and problems innate in the software product itself. If the real problem is not so much lack of training but awkward user interface features, weak functionality, or counterproductive command or menu sequences, maintenance may have to start. If product requirements are violated, it will be corrective. If the situation is due to a slowly expanding scope for the software or an increase in (unforeseen) types of usages, maintenance is perfective. If, due to changes in the environment, previously smooth usage has become cumbersome, maintenance is adaptive. This can happen when data or files for the system change but the system still insists on old formats. There is also a gray area between training problems and software shortcomings: commands or instruction patterns that are hard to remember. That may be a design flaw, in which case improvements are possible, or it may be that some usages of the system are hard to remember because of the complexity of the software, in which case it is unavoidable. The goal of successful maintenance is to identify and remove obstacles to user productivity. Therefore we must design user feedback mechanisms that clearly identify these obstacles.

User feedback can be passive or active. Passive feedback does not require maintainers to actively seek out information. It is provided either by the users who submit requests or by monitoring the usage of the system.

Table 11.1 Feedback options.

Passive	Active
User request forms 1. Paper	User interviews
2. Electronic mail	User questionnaires
Software usage pattern monitor	Installation management plan

Let us discuss the formal written user request first. According to [Mccl81] it should contain the following information:

▶ **Name.** This identifies who the user is. We might want to add the type of user if there are several (ask for log-in ID to identify department; information should be short and easily provided). We need enough information to respond to the person requesting a change.

▶ **Date.** This helps to determine how long it took to respond to the request. As deadlines are set for processing user requests, we should know exactly when the response must be out. No requests should get "buried."

▶ **Software identification.** It is important to know which system, program, or feature is meant by the request. The more detailed the description of the software, the easier it will be to target maintenance. A user might for instance have a request concerning a particular statistical routine in SAS or IMSL. Another may report problems with paging in an operating system or with a particular statement in a compiler. A third may request adaptation of a program to deal with indexed files in addition to sequential ones.

▶ **Issue identification.**   Here users describe in more detail what the problem is and how they want the software to change. The user should not be required to translate needs into technical terms but state the issue as it relates to productivity needs at the user level.

▶ **Type of maintenance.**   A check whether it should be classified as corrective (a functional or quality error), adaptive, or perfective maintenance. In either case, we need the following three types of information to determine how the request should be dealt with:

1. *Severity.* The problem that led to the request could potentially be classified into one of any number of categories. Because the kind of decision making that we will have to do here need not be complicated by many levels of severity, we only define three:

   ▶ *Circumventable.*   A problem is circumventable if there are other means of using the software that achieve the same use, do not run into the problem, and provide equivalent functionality. If the substitute function of an editor does not operate correctly all the time, we can circumvent that problem by using the delete and insert functions instead. Note that this example indicates that circumventing the problem may not always be as efficient.

   ▶ *Minor.*   A problem is minor if standard operation of the software does not run into any difficulties. A minor problem could be a typing error in a printout, wrong indentation in a printed table, or fragmentation of a file on a disk (as long as there is not enough I/O contention to make it into a major performance problem). Classification of requests can change when the environment (hardware, software, workload) changes. Performance problems mentioned in requests often change in severity over time (usually they worsen, unless something is done about it).

   ▶ *Halt.*   User requests are the most pressing when the underlying problem virtually eliminates any user productivity. System conversions, if delayed, can render the software inoperable, because the software cannot be operated any more and user productivity has come to a halt. Some errors, severe performance problems, or security loopholes do this. A user once desperately tried to "crash" a system when he found out that somehow the password protection mechanism had broken down and all information and programs were open for anyone to see and use. Luckily he succeeded. The system was down. Severity classification is also "halt" if the request is about a violation of the service agreement.

2. *Deadline.* A deadline can be given in either of two ways: a date or a classification. If a date is given, then the situation is clear for the user but needs to be translated into one of several action possibilities for maintenance planning:

▶ *Immediate action.* Those are the maintenance activities that cannot afford any delay. Violation of service agreements or a "crashing" system for important types of usages usually necessitate immediate action. Such maintenance activities often try to remedy newly discovered critical faults, but if the deadline is close, they may be sparked by new government regulations or the conversion to new hardware or software. These nonerror situations more often fall into the next category of urgency, however.

▶ *Batchable, soon.* This deadline classification applies for maintenance activities that, while not requiring immediate action, should be undertaken in a timely fashion. (Note the legal term "timely fashion"—you may often find that the maintenance agreement describes certain work to be done in just that: a "timely fashion"). In this category, we group all modification that we are required to include in our next planned maintenance activity. Because multisite and multiversion software does not take kindly to isolated changes in various copies of the program and because we do not wish to provide the user with a daily changing product, most modifications are batched. This means that a series of modifications is done in one maintenance effort.

▶ *Next release.* Updates on software and accompanying manuals tend to make software, documents, manuals, and multiple copies of the software "drift apart." To counteract this and "start fresh," new releases of the product are scheduled. Besides establishing a new "baseline" for the product and all its customers, we usually find new or adapted features and (hopefully improved) quality characteristics such as better performance. Changes that can wait until the next release are often of the perfective or adaptive kind.

▶ *Can wait.* These types of changes are, while nice (users would not have asked for them otherwise), strictly optional. Such change requests may or may not be complied with.

3. *Requirement(s) affected by change.* Changes that users request may either enforce compliance of the software with its requirements (in case of error), or entail modifications of the existing requirements (adaptive or perfective maintenance). In either case, the requirements affected by the change should be stated. They can fall into any of the categories of requirements that were discussed in Chapter 3 and

4: functional requirements, performance, reliability, security, etc. The reason why we would like to know about the affected requirements is to have a starting point for the activity and its planning. Furthermore, some of the qualitative requirements necessitate a specialist (e.g., performance or security) and thus need special planning if no such specialist is part of the maintenance person or team assigned to the software.

Whether we deal with errors, adaptations, adding new features or improving existing ones, we have the same needs for information. Derived information that will help us to make a maintenance plan for the proposed changes include answers for the following: the deliverable(s) of which development phase are affected by the change? To what extent are they affected? This has a big impact on the cost of each change. Figure 11.8 shows a sample user request form.

When it is impractical, impossible, or unpopular to mandate user change request forms, we can determine whether it is feasible to implement a software monitor that records usage patterns and errors made by the users automatically. After such data is recorded, we add a data reduction step in which we can determine which errors are made most frequently, whether usage patterns are awkward and could be improved, and the like. This requires more analysis and interpretation by the maintainers, because they receive their information indirectly. It can lead to improving user productivity through enhancements and targeted instruction. Sometimes changes in manuals will help significantly. The interaction between user and maintainer has become indirect, and the user does not get the feeling of being directly involved in the change process. Misunderstandings can lead to actually undesirable changes.

Active user-maintenance feedback requires that the maintenance staff instigate the collection of knowledge about desirable and necessary modification to the software. An installation management plan may indicate what new hardware or software will be coming in by what date and thus indicate necessary maintenance activities (of the adaptive variety). User interviews can reveal problems with the current product, but the users who are interviewed should be representative. Otherwise the maintenance effort can end up being misguided. User questionnaires may be sent out, asking users about the degree of satisfaction of the system, what they would most like to see changed, which features they want to have added, etc. User interviews and questionnaires can work well if designed parsimoniously. Nobody wants to spend valuable work time filling out long, overly detailed questionnaires.

Whichever feedback mechanism we choose, it is important to make the users feel that they are important, that it is *their* productivity that counts and directs maintenance efforts. Because of this we should do the following:

▶ Report to the user what happened to his user request, what the effect of analyzing software monitor data was, and what conclusions were drawn from user inter-

Name: _____ Date: _____ Software identification: _____

Issue:

_____

_____

_____

Type of maintenance (check):   Requirements affected:

1. Corrective   ☐   _____

2. adaptive   ☐   _____

3. perfective   ☐   _____

Severity of Problem (check one):   Why:

1. circumventable   ☐   _____

2. minor   ☐   _____

3. halt   ☐   _____

Deadline:give date _____

        or classification (check one):

              1. immediate action   ☐

              2. soon   ☐

              3. next release   ☐

              4. can wait/optional   ☐

Figure 11.8 User Request.

views or questionnaires. Feedback on a user request and what happened to it should occur within a fixed time (about one week). This way the maintenance team shows that requests do not land in a "circular file."

▶ Announce changes resulting from a series of requests as part of a newsletter. A newsletter is also a good forum to explain how to prevent often made mistakes.

▶ Fulfill any service agreement. A service agreement can consist of the functional and qualitative requirements and specific deadlines by when corrective maintenance has to have been completed when errors come up. Quality maintenance will respond to user requests as described in the service agreement. Sometimes there is no formal service agreement. Then general maintenance guidelines take over. It is a good idea to have them, because they help to prioritize and evaluate possible maintenance activities.

This leads us to the next step: evaluating user requests. It helps greatly if such requests are written and formal. Even if there are no formal user requests, we should design a form similar to the one of Figure 11.8 to be submitted by the staff who analyzes user needs for the various feedback methods. So, for a uniform discussion of change evaluation, let us assume that a written, formal change request exists. First, we need evaluation priorities. An example would be a rank ordering such as "deadline is more important than severity of error." Then a request with the characteristics

deadline is as soon as possible (ASAP), severity is circumventable

would have to be dealt with before a request indicating

deadline is soon, severity is halt.

If we number deadline and severity levels as in Table 11.3 the above ranking can be described as (1,3) before (2,1).

Such a lexicographic ordering is not always practicable, nor desirable. We can develop a priority matrix for possible combinations of deadline urgencies and severity classes. Table 11.2 shows an example—the lower the number, the higher the priority.

Table 11.2 Priority trade-offs for request evaluation.

Error severity deadline	Circumventable	Minor	Halt
ASAP	9	2	1
Soon	10	3	4
Next release	11	6	5
Optional	12	8	7

Ordering requests through such derived priorities will facilitate request evaluation and suggest a possible sequencing of maintenance activities. Not all types of maintenance are treated the same, because not all software has the same needs. Therefore we find different rank orderings or trade-off tables. If there is more than one category of information to be considered, we may also display values within each category (deadline, severity, complexity, etc.) graphically and make our trade-offs by comparing graphs. Standard maintenance graphs for various types of software can tell us how to justify which type of maintenance. They represent desired maintenance profiles. Figure 11.9 shows an example. We assume three levels of complexity: low (1), medium (2) and high (3).

Anything under the desired maintenance profile would be done before the requests that cross it or are above it. We can even use the graphs to see how maintenance requests

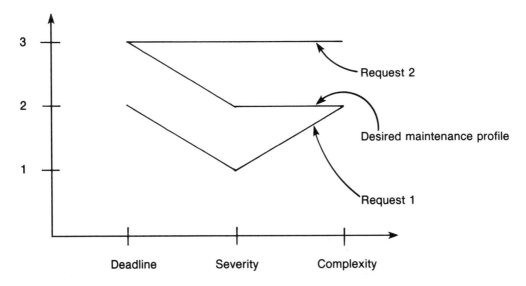

Figure 11.9 Maintenance Graphs.

change over time, and we can use the information indicating the urgency of requests as an indicator of how alive the software is and how well it has been maintained. If many requests lie beyond the desired maintenance profile, it indicates problems with maintenance, maintainers, users, or all three and should be investigated.

With some experience we can figure out which maintenance requests (as a function of their composite values in all categories) will be hard or problematic and which will be straightforward and easy.

While these methods of establishing priorities indicate what should be done first, second, third, etc. from the user's point of view and according to general evaluation guidelines, the resulting order of requests is only a first cut. In which order maintenance is actually carried out is determined not only by this first evaluation step, but also by technical priorities. They are as follows:

▶ Simplest changes first (less complexity costs less). In the simplest form, we can rank complexity as we did above : low (1), medium (2), and high (3). A refinement is to distinguish complexity of the change request by phase. If a change affects more than one development phase deliverable, the complexities in each phase may well differ. It is not uncommon for a change in requirements to be easy, while it is quite difficult to design and implement the change. An even more detailed complexity assessment uses weights to represent the number of sections of each document that are affected by the changes and the number of modules of code involved. We could also use the number of functional areas as a further indicator of change complexity. A more detailed approach to estimate complexity not only helps to indicate the complexity of the changes for each development phase deliverable, but it also pinpoints the cumulative effect of changes.

▶ Batch changes that affect the same system part should be done together. This may actually make it possible for us to include some low priority changes, simply because they can be made at negligible extra effort with those at high priority. When a change request has high evaluation priority in the first cut, it drives the maintenance plan. Other changes that fit into that plan can be included, even if they rank lower on the totem pole.

▶ A request that has been ranked lower can end up much higher if work on it needs to start immediately in order for it to be done by the deadline indicated. Thus the user-specified deadline needs to be restated in terms of necessary starting date so that the change will be completed on time. This is something the user cannot do and therefore, we cannot ask about it in the user request form. Changes that have the same characteristics, except for their latest starting date (LSD), can be ranked by that date. Thus the request with the earliest LSD is the most important if meeting deadlines has first priority.

▶ Maintenance needs and cost-effectiveness are different for software that differs in projected lifespan. The same is true when we look at the longevity of the changes themselves. A program with a long expected lifespan is worth more expensive changes. We can expect to recoup the cost of maintenance in the future. Maintenance work is mandatory if the software is supposed to live long. The longer software lives, the more likely the need for changes becomes and the more changes will likely have been made. For these three reasons, software with a long projected lifespan will likely have more adaptive and perfective maintenance. If the projected lifespan is short, we may not be willing to invest in extensive maintenance. At least we should analyze whether a substantial request is really worth it.

Software for performance analysis, for example, may work with sufficient accuracy to model systems with device utilizations of up to 80% but show significant approximation errors for utilization values that exceed that threshold. Before we develop further modules that can deal with high utilization situations, we should first look at the expected use of the software. If it is rarely used for modeling such situations or if they represent obvious problems and solutions, it is usually not necessary to extend its modeling capabilities. Neither do we have a strong case for perfective maintenance if alternate software covers these scenarios. We also would not do involved maintenance if there were plans to replace the software in the near future. It is simply not worth it to put a lot of money into changes. Longevity of the software also affects how we react to problems, whether an all-out effort is made to keep the product viable and to increase its usefulness or whether we choose the "minimum maintenance option," i.e., the one that costs the least but not necessarily helps the most.

Longevity of changes also affects what maintenance is to be done and when to do it. The tax program (TAP) requires adaptation to the current year's schedules every year. Unless tax rules change drastically, the changes to existing schedules and forms will probably be substantial but not extensive enough to require a major rewrite of TAP. There is some time to adjust to new forms. When errors occur during the preparation of taxes, they must be fixed fast: very few people do their tax return months ahead of time, so deadlines for error correction are tight. We probably would not want to spend much effort in improving or modifying TAP during tax season, but we would batch all changes for the next year's version.

Long-lived changes usually go hand in hand with higher expected return on investment (i.e., even more expensive changes are worth it). Short-lived changes need to have a higher pay-back per unit time in order to make them worthwhile. We also would not select change options that make further change more difficult or impossible.

▶ If some of the requested changes are similar to changes already planned for the next revision, so much the better. We've already planned for them. What can change is the timing and the extent of the changes. This happens when the new urgency or severity of the current change request ranks higher than what was previously considered. Some low-ranking changes may fit easily into the current list of maintenance activities and could be accomplished with negligible effort, because related work is already to be performed. If we had planned to revise the print modules for TAP or PAS to a different format, we might easily be able to include a change request that asks us to print out some internally available data that does not occur on the reports at this time. An example for TAP is to print running totals of all categories of tax data. We may be able to deal with some more change requests along the way. Sometimes new change requests cause the current batch of planned changes to be revised. This happens when a more critical, higher priority change has come up.

All these reasons can cause a rearrangement of user requests due to technical priorities. When we have established an order of change requests, we should regroup them by

▶ parts affected by the change,

▶ functional areas, i.e., which functional area(s) will be the target of which proposed maintenance activities, and

▶ qualitative areas, i.e., which qualitative aspect of the software is affected, such as performance, reliability, security, etc.

This exercise is helpful to streamline maintenance activities, assess the necessary maintenance effort, and reduce the cost of individual change by grouping them together as they are related in any of the above areas. If the resulting schedule for dealing with user requests violates user deadlines or set service levels, we should try to negotiate with the user liaison or user representative (if there is someone like that). In the absence of this option, we can still try to do a trade-off between user and technical priorities. Where possible, we should lean towards the side of the user. Table 11.3 gives a short synopsis of the user request evaluation. It helps to have a formal maintenance coordinator. This facilitates uniformity and consistency in the maintenance process. The role of the maintenance coordinator is to match user priorities with the business objectives of the maintenance function. If user request evaluation is the task of one or few individu-

Table 11.3 User request evaluation.

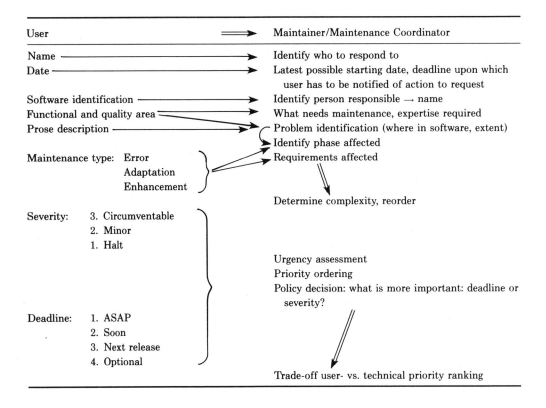

als, there is less chance of shifting priorities. The same study also reports that a maintenance coordinator also reduces the amount of user support required and asserts that there is more control over the maintenance process when we remove as many peripheral tasks from the maintenance programmer as possible.

The result of this analysis is a maintenance project with a set objective, a cost estimate, and a deadline. The maintenance project encompasses all changes that have been grouped into the current batch. The objectives are given through the user request forms. Cost estimates are based on the estimation methods described in Chapter 14. The inputs to these estimations are complexity of the change in terms of function or quality, the number of modules and documentation sections affected by it, and the quality of the baseline code (how well it is structured, its readability, etc.). In summary, the maintenance coordinator assigns priorities to batches of changes, identifies phases and parts affected (what, not how), and does a preliminary complexity assessment so that time and cost estimates can be made.

Next, we seek a detailed plan to implement the changes. We need an impact assessment for all possible change options. This is conceptually similar to the option analysis performed during requirements analysis and also during design when design alternatives were evaluated.

Problems and Questions

1. Consider the following change requests for TAP and evaluate and describe them as in Table 11.3. State your assumptions if you have to make any because the user failed to make them. Explain the maintainer's reasoning, and state the underlying product objectives that guide your evaluation. What is the user ranking of the change requests as opposed to the maintainer's ranking?:

   a) Deductions are not transposed properly between forms (error, minor, soon).

   b) Some types of deductions are excluded from the computation (error, major, ASAP).

   c) A user may have a need for carrying over of previous tax credits into the current year (enhance, circumvent, optional).

   d) One user needs to fill out one line of Schedule D, because his investment fund had capital gains distributions last year (enhance, minor, optional).

   e) Someone wishes to buy TAP, but only if he can use it for multiple returns for several people (enhance, circumventable, ASAP). Assume that an increased market for your product is of medium importance. It is more important to satisfy current customers.

534 Operation and Maintenance

Before you decide on a ranking, determine alternatives as you would have during feasibility study and state whether, if at all, your evaluation changes.

2. Consider the following change requests for PAS and evaluate and describe them as in Table 11.3. State your assumptions if you have to make any because the user failed to make them. Explain the maintainer's reasoning, and state the underlying product objectives that guide your evaluation. What is the user ranking of the change requests as opposed to the maintainer's ranking?:

a) PAS does not merge results from more than two files (error, circumventable, ASAP).

b) PAS crashes when the wrong type of results file is specified for STATISTICS or COMPARISON. All accumulator contents are lost (error, minor, soon).

c) PAS ignores pointer variables for analysis (error, halt, ASAP).

d) Another instructor wants to use PAS, but his programs are in FORTRAN (enhancement, halt, optional).

d) A research project using programs wants to collect PAS measurements to compare coding styles but needs analysis information tabulated differently and needs counts on subsets of data that are definable by the user (enhancement, minor, next release).

e) PAS doesn't compute $f(x)/f(m)$ properly for some large data—it is unclear where the error is (error, halt, ASAP).

11.5. Maintenance Techniques

The actual maintenance work means carrying out the changes that have been grouped into the current maintenance activity. Each maintenance activity can be carried out using one of these three approaches:

▶ top-down or full-range maintenance,

▶ bottom-up maintenance, and

▶ sandwich maintenance.

Top-down or full-range maintenance gets its name from the fact that it proceeds along all phases of the software development life cycle, starting "at the top" with modifying requirements to the bottom, i.e., retesting code modifications. First, we identify the functions, features, and quality requirements that need to be changed or added if the maintenance is perfective in nature. Then we state the change in requirements terms. The modification needs to be made to the requirements document, and those parts that are affected by the change need to be revalidated using the techniques described in Chapter 3. Additions also need to be phase tested.

Then we identify the parts of the specifications and the specification document that are affected by the changes. These might be functional changes, state changes, modifications of transitions between states, different ranges for input or output values, or conditions for processing. We should use cross-phase identification for determining the degree of regression testing of these changes. This means that we determine from the requirements which parts of the specification document correspond to the requirements we just changed. It also means that we identify at this point which tests of the specification document have to be redone. Those tests that were also used during the testing of the code we can earmark for regression testing. New test cases that need to be developed also are candidates to be reused for testing code changes.

From the modified and regression-tested specifications, we proceed to identify the design parts that are affected by the changes. This includes major software component(s) and their individual module parts. Then we state which changes in the design are necessary. These can include adding one or more new modules (representing a more extensive solution or new features or functionalities) or substituting new modules for old ones (such as implementing a different searching or sorting algorithm, a different optimization procedure, and the like). In determining interfaces and modules for the modified design, we should evaluate the cohesiveness and the strength of modules just as we did originally during the design. When a module now seems to do more than one function and falls below the desired quality level for module strength, we may have to perform functional extraction just as we would have for such a module during the design phase of the first development cycle. This also applies for the case when functionally identical parts are contained in several modules. Functional abstraction is often necessary when previously rudimentary features are expanded in subsequent maintenance activities.

Lastly, the modified or new modules need to be interfaced properly with their environment. This can involve developing new interfaces when new modules are designed or when they derive, through functional extraction, from existing ones. More often, existing interfaces need to be modified. When such changes are made, *all* modules affected by the change need to be modified to reflect the new interface. The list of such modules is determined through the old interface test plan for the design and the program or system structure (architecture) design. It is essential for continued quality of the design document that all changes be well documented. Otherwise the design document will drift away from the software itself and become useless quite rapidly. As phase documents become inaccurate, the maintainer inevitably has to discard them as a maintenance support document and is forced to work from code alone. This is a much more time-consuming, error-prone, and painful maintenance situation.

Before design modifications are decided upon, we should check their compliance with the major design approach. It is vital that the original design approach and subsequent maintenance design activities be consistent. Mixing object-oriented design with control-oriented techniques and misusing design objects and algorithms for means not intended usually backfire; there will be sets of usages for which they will not work. A vivid, if depressing example of a maintenance disaster that is based on violations of this rule is described in [Spie76] (cf. [Pari83], p. 269-275). As with most other problems, this particular maintenance disaster is brought about not by one single bad decision, but by a series of seemingly small "redesign" activities. The cumulative effect of these misunderstandings of the original design approach for the compiler in the story killed the software. Its former functioning was irretrievably lost. Nor could anyone determine anymore what it should have been (except the author of the sad story). This also suggests that in cases where potentially dangerous modifications are made, we should be able to "roll back" to a safe previous version of the software. Unfortunately, this can be and usually is very expensive and not considered cost-effective. It involves saving a complete copy of all phase deliverables of every phase for a specific software version to which we can return when a later one proves to be nonmaintainable or exhibits problems that can no longer be fixed or isolated any more. Keeping modifications to a design consistent with its original approach and major design decisions does much to prevent such problems in the first place.

If there are alternatives, we should go for the smallest, least intrusive change. This holds for design and code. Because every change disturbs the status quo, it has a potential of error, which becomes even more likely as changes accumulate.

We perform a regression phase test for the parts of the design that are affected by the modifications (interfaces between modules, modules themselves) using applicable test cases from the previous design phase test—this ensures that those parts of the design that should still work the same way they did before still do. For new features or functional modifications, we develop new test cases. When we make design changes to improve qualitative aspects (performance, reliability), the algorithms still have to produce the same results and need to be regression tested using the old test cases.

When the phase test of the design additions and modifications is complete, we need to identify the code changes for implementing the modified design accurately. First we identify the program, program parts, or software components that are affected by the change. Next we identify the code modules that are to be changed and determine where the newly designed modules are to be added or substituted. Interfaces that belong to the sphere of the change are tagged and an impact assessment of the change is made so that all parts of the code that can possibly be affected by the change are explicitly identified. This is called ripple effect analysis [Mccl81].

Then the code changes are made. Because there will usually be a series of changes, we need to determine which changes to make first. The simplest changes are made first. When more than one change is to be made in a module, we batch them together and make them all at once. This can rearrange the sequencing of changes.

Regression tests for these modules need to be run to ascertain that what worked before the change will still work and that the new or modified code also works. We classify regression test into either unit tests or integration tests. Unit tests first need to identify the unit test paths affected by the changes. We need path identification and a test case depository from which we can select applicable old test cases for the paths to be retested. Paths that need to be regression tested are identified using the information gained during the previous step when code changes were identified and the impact of changes was assessed. Structure-based tools, which can determine paths based on control flow and data flow analysis, also help to plan and execute regression tests. Regression testing is similar to putting two path patterns on two overhead transparencies on top of each other to see where they differ. In the comparison we need to determine the following:

▶ Which statements have been changed? Paths that fall into this category need to be regression tested.

▶ Which variables are affected by the change, either directly or indirectly? (Paths and interfaces that refer to these variables need to be regression tested.) When a local variable is changed, we must check where in the module itself that has an impact. This means at least partial regression test of the unit. We also must check indirect effects of the change: can variable values of the changed variable influence flow of control, execution conditions, or other possibly global variable values? Then more than a unit test is necessary, because the change permeates outside the module.

▶ Which conditions are affected by the changes? (Paths containing those decisions need to be regression tested. So do any new paths when previously impossible transfers of control become possible due to such changes.)

Planning for these tests is not done after the changes have been made, but before, when the impact of the changes is assessed. In fact, determination of what will have to be regression tested is equivalent to impact assessment or ripple analysis.

While the existing unit test cases may have been developed as structure or specification-based test cases, the selection of existing test cases for regression testing has been based on structural changes. This does not mean that the test cases selected for regression testing must be structure based; they may well have been developed using specifications. We may also develop new, specification-based test cases by using specification test cases newly developed in the current maintenance activity. Because a single maintenance activity can have very few, this may actually be a fast and straightforward way of developing regression tests for unit or integration testing.

Integration testing during top-down or full-range maintenance requires an interface assessment between the changed or newly developed modules, its callers, and the modules that are called by them. For this we need a (modified) calling hierarchy that has, we hope, been annotated by interfaces between modules in the hierarchy. Which modules call or use the modified module? What is the effect of the change on them? Maybe the ranges of variable values that are accepted by the modified module are smaller or larger than before. Timing considerations may have changed, which is important for distributed and real-time software. Possible error states may now be different. Does the calling module make any assumptions regarding these characteristics? Which? Are they still fulfilled? If not, can that lead to problems? We should carefully investigate any defensive coding (cf. mutual suspicion as in [Myer76]) to see whether it still applies or has to be changed to reflect the modified circumstances. For example, if an optimization routine was changed to accept positive and negative variable values when before it only handled positive ones, we need to change the range checks in the beginning to reflect that. Otherwise, the module will still refuse to deal with negative values.

Global or shared variables are also part of the interface. If they have been changed, a reference list of affected modules needs to be established. All variables in the interface of modified modules need to be retested if they are directly or indirectly affected by a change. We may have to retest the interfaces using variables that pass data (value parameters), pass the variable itself or a pointer to it, or control execution of a module. Looking at the degree of coupling between a changed module and its environment is extremely helpful to determine the degree of interface testing necessary. We can see both what the complete interface is and, using the knowledge about changes within the module, which part of the interface needs to be retested.

Planning for regression testing of code proceeds in three steps. We identify those test cases from earlier phases that tested program or system parts before that still have to work the same way now but have been affected by changes. New test cases are added for testing newly developed code. Old test cases that used to test no longer existing code should be purged; otherwise someone might try to rerun them during the code testing phase in the next evolutionary cycle or maintenance activity and misinterpret results. We also purge old test cases when a newly developed test case contains the old one.

When errors are discovered during the regression test of code, the same debugging rules apply as during the testing phase of the original development. There is one marked difference in dealing with them: we may find that some errors were introduced not during software development but during an earlier maintenance activity. Then we should determine what the root of the problem is (misunderstanding the functioning of the code, interfaces between parts, design decisions, or the extent of a solution are frequent errors during maintenance) and correct the error in *all* implicated phase deliverables. In case of a major problem we may need to reestimate the effort and resources necessary to correct it, be forced to do a major rewrite, or roll back to a previous version of the software while the problem is being worked on.

Table 11.4 shows a synopsis of top-down or full-range maintenance. Most perfective and some adaptive maintenance is done through a series of top-down maintenance activities, each of which proceeds through all phases of the original development life cycle.

Table 11.4 Top-down or full-range maintenance.

---

1. Identify function, feature, quality requirement.
    State change in requirements terms.
2. Identify specifications affected by changes:
    - ▶ user interface,
    - ▶ functional changes,
    - ▶ states/transitions,
    - ▶ I/O ranges.
3. Identify design parts affected by changes:
    - ▶ major components,
    - ▶ parts thereof.
    State change in design necessary:
    - ▶ new module,
    - ▶ functional extraction from old module,
    - ▶ interfacing module to new or existing, but changed ones.
    Check compliance with major design approach.
4. Identify code changes:
    - ▶ program or software components,
    - ▶ modules new/modified.
    Impact assessment:
    - ▶ interfaces,
    - ▶ ripple effect.
5. Make changes:
    - ▶ simplest first,
    - ▶ batch all changes in one module.
6. Regression test:
    - ▶ unit test paths affected (statements, variables, conditions),
    - ▶ integration test—interface assessment,
    - ▶ test cases: old, new, purge.

This is at the heart of evolutionary development. Table 11.5 lists the major objectives of analyzing phase deliverables during maintenance.

Table 11.5 Rationale for maintenance activities of Table 11.4.

---

1. Understand intent and framework.
2. Understand effects on user.
3. Understand design approach and intent.
4. Understand manifestation of design and impact of changes on code.
5. Quality implementation of changes.

Top-down or full-range maintenance not only applies when major changes have to be made due to different user needs or necessary adaptations, but this type of maintenance can also be called for when an error is found that clearly indicates a requirements violation and is therefore best dealt with at the requirements level. An example of such an error would be a missing functionality:

▶ A tax form in TAP has not been implemented, "forgotten," or has been implemented so badly that it has to be redeveloped and we cannot use the original approach (i.e., design).

▶ Tax rules changed. This means that the functional requirements about how to implement tax preparation have changed and the software must be adapted to this. Because it is a functional requirement, we have to modify the functional requirements diagram and make appropriate changes in the specifications, the design, and the code, and we retest and update all documents. Consider that in this case we probably should keep a copy of the old tax system around because we will not be able to redo example tax returns of previous years with the newly adapted system. We have a limit of three years on this, just as for the returns themselves. This thankfully limits the number of versions we have to maintain in operational or mothballed status. Retaining previous years' versions is not necessary if the maintenance involved adding an implementation of a new form or schedule, such as Schedule D for capital gains and losses, because the augmented tax system will have to be able to do returns with or without Schedule D.

▶ Some language features of the source language for PAS are not recognized or PAS does not provide any usable treatment of those features; we must go back to an early phase for dealing with this error.

▶ The user interface requires a major redevelopment because it has been very inefficient to use and the users complain about it a lot.

▶ Alternate languages, such as C or FORTRAN, are to be analyzed with PAS. These are major enhancements, but because this is a foreseeable enhancement, we had to modularize the lexical analyzer so that it becomes independent of the command interpreter and the routines that gather the statistics. This way we just add code to select the appropriate language analyzer; the rest of the system can stay the same. What does need to be changed are the requirements (new functionality scope), the specifications (what are operators and operands in the new language), the design (how do we recognize those operators and operands), and some of the support routines (e.g., the one recognizing an invalid source file extension).

In any of these situations, work begins with early phase deliverables and proceeds to those of later development phases. This is not always the case. Many errors and some perfective and adaptive maintenance analyzes and modifies deliverables bottom up. In this case, we start with the code itself, where the error occured or where a change has become necessary. Then we take the change back up to earlier phase deliverables as far as necessary to make them consistent with the modified code. This approach is taken, for example, when we do a performance analysis of a piece of software to identify in which parts of the software most of the resources are spent. Assuming that we selected the best possible algorithm, we do not start from the design, working down to the code (top down), but we analyze the code, modify it, and then see which changes need to be made to the design to make it consistent with the modified code.

While many errors can be rectified by looking at the code first, this may not be the best approach. It really depends on where the error was made. An error made in an early phase and dragged through to software completion should be fixed using a top-down approach, while one made later in the development life cycle is better handled with a bottom-up approach. Working backwards from the code is also necessary when documents of earlier development phases are inadequate, inconsistent, not up-to-date, or missing and when it is unclear where to start (design? requirements? or what?). In the case of updating inadequate early phase documents, design decisions and many of the original requirements need to be reconstructed working backwards from the code. [Heni80] describes such a method and derives many of the rules for writing requirements and specifications, which we encountered in Chapters 3 to 5. Note that we can also conceptualize debugging as a bottom-up maintenance activity: we have a problem reported, it needs to be fixed, and we are trying to understand where in the code it is caused, so that we can go and remove the error. Sometimes bottom-up maintenance becomes necessary when new errors are introduced through maintenance or evolutionary development cycles.

When TAP does not deal with deductions correctly, we can first try to find out what actually happens. Is it that the rules are not implemented correctly? Is it that some types of deductions are skipped (maybe because they are not covered in the rules and

TAP does not know what to do with them? Is it that TAP miscalculates deductions? Maybe the running total that we designed for the deduction list is erroneously "reinitialized" so that it in essence ignores part of the deduction data in the list? We can look for the places in the code where these computations happen and see whether we find the error. Then we would back up to the previous phase and see whether the error existed there already, and so forth.

When PAS seems to compute the similarity quotient $f(x)/f(m)$ erroneously for large amounts of data, the situation is a little different. We can't just recompute the figures by hand, walking through the code in a manual simulation. It would take too long. We need to isolate the error otherwise. Because the computation of the similarity quotient was tested during development, we might try to find out how the current input data are different from the test data. Maybe they have different value ranges. Maybe they are merged result data from different analysis files. Maybe the usage pattern of PAS is different (sequence of commands). We need to investigate possibilities, and as soon as we narrow the alternatives, we look at the code and work it from there.

Lastly, we may need to perform a maintenance task in a sandwich manner. A problem may involve either identifying a requirement that is violated or needs to be added or modified. At the same time, it is not possible to proceed through a straightforward identification of the corresponding specification aspect to an adaptation or modification of the next phase documents. Rather, we must pinpoint the sections of code involved. Then we proceed to analyze the change request and its proper implementation starting from both ends of the development cycle documents.

Regardless how we proceed in the maintenance task, it is very important to update all documents, should they stay useful and alive for the future life of the software. We need to apply much of the strict update regulations that govern newsletters, such as periodic law reports used by attorneys for law research. The sheer volume of new cases would create a total mess unless strict methods and change control where applied.

As we did during the development phases, all documents that have been changed need to be validated again: the changes themselves, whether they fit properly with the rest of the material (interfaces), whether the changes are consistently carried through all phases, and whether all implications of the changes have been investigated for correctness.

Sometimes changes are very trivial or very urgent and there is not time for a lengthy document update. Then we may approve shortcuts to the full validation procedure for all documents involved. The following restrictions apply:

▶ only for small changes, i.e., small errors and omissions,

▶ only for ASAP deadlines, or

▶ only if the document update follows *guaranteed.*

We must *not* allow shortcuts

▶ for multiple versions of a system, unless there is a way to keep track of which change was made to which system and the volume of not fully documented changes is so small that all updates can be made and reviewed in no more than one man week, and

▶ for multiple sites. The same regulations for shortcuts apply as in the multiple version case.

The reason for restrictions to documentation shortcuts is that the danger of getting into a maintenance mess is too great: the software and its various phase documents tend to drift apart even faster, especially when there is no strict control of "small," "innocent" changes. Even when the urgent changes are small, we should still discourage releasing them when documentation has not been updated and only maintainer notes on the change exist. When a shortcut is allowed, a strict deadline should be set and enforced for documentation update.

Version control is especially important for software that has been distributed to several sites [Zelk79]. If we allow undisciplined changes at each site, we will soon have as many versions of the system as we have sites. The same problems are discovered and solved (maybe, but often not the same way) at various sites. We soon end up with numerous different software systems. Having central control of changes ensures that the "same" version of a software system at different sites will stay the same. Note that we may have to twist arms a little when a site is understandably reluctant to "fix something that isn't broken" for fear of creating a new problem where none existed. As we mentioned before, we need to establish a new "base" to provide consistency and continuity.

A new release to all sites ensures that. If maintenance is to support more than one successive version or release of a system, we not only need a full set of all development documents for each version, but we must be able to determine how versions differ from each other. This means we have to keep a description of what has changed between successive releases and the major effects of these changes and references. This information is collected and can be recorded during impact assessment.

Ideally we would like to collect all versions of a system and then distribute a single new one. The fact is, however, that changes, especially when urgent, are often made when and where required. This creates two needs:

▶ We need to compile individual changes into a master version that can slowly evolve to the next release level. This also helps to avoid "rediscovering" the same problem over and over at different sites. If we make the change and test it on a copy of the site or master version, we also have the added benefit of not disturbing site operation.

▶ We must keep track of which site has which change implemented. Having a formal change request helps greatly, because it identifies the site where the change was made and the action items that describe the nature of the changes as a reaction to the change request. In addition, keeping a copy of the current site version lets us reproduce the user reported error without having to access the site version.

When there are many sites, the potential proliferation of site systems, their copies for maintenance purposes, plus the master version quickly limits the amount of site specific change we can and should allow. Hence the rules of batching change.

Problems and Questions

1. Assume that all change requests of exercises 1 and 2 of Section 11.4. came from different sites. Which would you batch? How?

2. Do a detailed assessment for any of the changes that you would make in order to implement the change requests in exercises 1 and 2 of Section 11.4. Include a plan for regression test.

11.6. Software Obsolescence and Death

Even with the best of care, a software system will not live forever. How do we then recognize and deal with slowly dying or comatose software? Consider first what the aging process does to operational software.

After software development is complete, the software product is released to the customer(s) or user(s). [Dema82] reports that most software experiences a series of failures during its early operational life until it stabilizes after about six months. Then there is a period of productive stable operation until changes become necessary to keep the product productive (serving the users' needs). These changes, even in the best of environments tend to leave behind newly introduced errors, which are then found and corrected. Continuing change, the addition of features, and modification of interfaces to the software product's operating environment, result in increasing complexity of the software and its associated documentation. This reflects increasing functionality but often slowly deteriorating structure, unless steps are taken to prevent or retard this aging process. Increasing complexity makes any new changes more expensive and hence less cost-effective. There will be a point when software will have to be replaced. Slow decay is usually also accompanied by a slow drifting apart of the development and operational documents from the code and an increased difficulty to understand what the code does. This then leads to the following:

▶ Coding assumptions, since they are unknown, are violated, introducing new complexities and errors.

▶ It becomes increasingly impossible to make substantial changes, because their impact is not understood. Therefore even changes for errors only touch the surface and rarely address the underlying cause. This further obscures and deteriorates the software.

▶ Because the product is no longer well understood, proper document update is either not done at all or done poorly, thus widening the rift between code and documentation.

Because we cannot adapt confusing software, it becomes impossible for it to grow with change. The software becomes less useful, and its user base dwindles. It dies. If maintenance tries to make changes in spite of poor understanding of the software and its changes, the software will also eventually cease to function and die—unless we can roll back to a previous version that still has enough operational capability to serve the users' needs. This may also enable us to get out of a dead end into which some earlier maintenance decisions have led. Roll back recovery is not cheap, however. The costs are twofold: those of keeping old versions in a reinstatable state, mothballing them so-to-speak, and the cost of redeveloping changes from there.

Mothballing software has its own risks. Maybe the software's operating environment has changed—hardware, operating system, interfacing software. It is easy to lose or otherwise compromise data, programs, and documentation. Lastly, users may be unwilling to "roll back."

How can we reduce the code-documentation drift and keep software alive and maintainable longer? First we use development techniques that promote maintainability, because they increase understandability, consistency of parts, and modularity: a design and implementation with high module independence and clean, simple interfaces helps to keep software understandable and to make changes easy. So does information hiding and the use of abstract data types and levels of abstraction. Standards and machine independent code also promote a long software life. So do well tested products. We should keep test cases and phase test rigorously in order to take out errors early (they are less costly then).

When changes are made, it is vital to stick to the basic development method and to the major design strategies that were at the heart of the original development. Understanding the design rationale is important if we want to fit changes naturally into the existing software. When code is changed, we have to revise all documentation and phase deliverables so that they reflect the current product. Part of the testing phase during maintenance is to check for consistency between them.

As software structure deteriorates, we can plan for a major overhaul: code is restructured according to the rules described in Chapter 9. All documents are revised, not just where the change occured, and they are checked for correctness and consistency. We make an effort to identify and purge all old features that are no longer necessary and all references and connections to these purged features. A major overhaul can be expensive. Because of this, it must be cost-effective. If it is cheaper to buy a new product, we certainly would consider that strongly. Another option is to develop a new system from scratch. In this case, we cancel the necessary overhaul but do not phase out the software immediately. We can content ourselves with superficial fixes and corrective maintenance until the new system becomes available. In this case it is very important that we plan for the future, so that we have a replacement when the current software will no longer do. Whether to give software a facelift or not should be decided through goals. These include cost limits for a software's operational life or requirement on a return on investment.

They must be coupled with "drift" indicators or software sickness measures. When a dangerous level is reached, the maintenance methods described in earlier sections of this chapter should be used. We must stop and either disallow changes for a while until the problem is under control or give up the software as a "hopeless" case. Indicators of trouble are as follows:

▶ Do the same categories of changes become increasingly expensive to do? Record and plot the cost per change in each category. When it rises appreciably, yet no major changes have been made in the recent past, the software is now so complex that it costs significantly more to maintain. Costs approaching projected limits signify ill health.

▶ Has the number of reported problems that require corrective maintenance increased? Record user problem requests normalized by operational time. This situation can be modeled very extensively as in [Musa87]. We can also record the proportion of error requests. It is higher than it used to be, but no major work on the software has been done to account for higher problem rates during the stabilization period? Both indicate deteriorating reliability. Further changes will make the software even more prone to error. Stop adaptive and perfective maintenance and concentrate on bringing perfective maintenance under control [Musa87].

▶ Is the urgency of changes higher? Higher urgency indicates that the software is increasingly not meeting the needs of the user in a very vital area of their work.

▶ Has the user base decreased? Software without users is practically dead. If the user base is steadily decreasing, find out why. The software may be obsolete or has never met the users' needs and its use was forced on them by decree, i.e., the software was never accepted. Low use may indicate that the potential user base has decreased, reducing the market, but not necessarily the proportion of users in the market. This gives information on whether the software is not working well enough, has been replaced by other software or manual procedures, or is doing fine, but not making as much money. In the last case, we may be able to enhance it to appeal to more users.

▶ Are cost estimates of changes overrun by increasing amounts? This indicates a decreasing quality of cost-estimation for maintenance activities. If it used to be better in the past, it may indicate that software has become increasingly complex and revisions in the evaluation of the maintenance effort predictions are necessary. Look at the budget (are such increased costs justifiable) and at the service agreement or the requirements (are longer times to modify the software acceptable).

▶ Has the complexity of the code and the documentation increased beyond a planned threshold? This can indicate that it is time to restructure, prepare a major overhaul, or throw the software away and replace it.

▶ Lastly, look at the proportion of unchanged to changed code to see what the preserved originality of the software is. This can be used as an easily measurable, indirect indicator of the state of a software product. Past experience shows that lack of originality is associated with seriously ailing software. This fraction is different for different development quality. A lower quality software product will not be able to stand as much change as a well developed one. If change incorporated rewriting modules or substituting new modules for old, with simple interfaces, the number of changed lines of code may be large, but the effect on maintainability is small. Therefore we should not use this as a sole indicator.

Besides gradual software death, there is also a more immediate end to software life: obsolescence and replacement. If a better or more economical way is found to do the job with different software or no software at all, the old software will no longer be used. We may keep it for contingency situations, but most often we throw it away or put it in "permanent storage" (with the same result). Many programs become obsolete because they will not run on a new machine or because the software cannot be ported or adapted to a new environment. For all these reasons, we may have to discard a product. This does not mean that it was a bad piece of workmanship or that maintenance did a bad job. It simply outlived its usefulness.

11.7. Summary

This chapter discussed major issues during operation and maintenance. This phase can include merely corrective maintenance or a series of development cycles, depending on the process model for the software development life cycle. Subsequent development cycles may require the need for a budget, for scheduling, and for planning. The degree of formalism varies. This chapter explained maintenance activities that go on during change cycles and between changes.

Consistency between documents and code is a major factor that influences the continued viability of software and the effort that goes into understanding the software and its changes. This includes training manuals. This chapter emphasized writing and updating manuals so as to avoid document drift. It also provided outlines for training and reference manuals. We discussed ways to structure information in a manual, the role of definitions, cross-referencing, and two important types of indices, the standard and the instant index.

Next we discussed active and passive feedback options: user request forms, software usage pattern monitors, user interviews, user questionnaires, and the installation management plan. A sample user request form detailed the information necessary for an evaluation of a user request.

We used maintenance graphs to prioritize the importance of change requests. Table 11.3 provided a structured framework for user request evaluation. This evaluation takes a user request form, analyzes it, determines the complexity of a change, and assesses the urgency and user-defined priorities. These are mapped with the technical impact, such as effort required and the maintenance plan for the software product. The resulting ranking forms the basis for maintenance decisions.

Section 11.5. discussed full-range maintenance, bottom-up maintenance, and sandwich maintenance. Table 11.4 provided a detailed list of activities that comprise full-range maintenance. We also discussed the rationale behind these activities.

Not all changes are equal. Therefore, procedures may differ for trivial changes, very urgent changes, or complex changes that require formal planning and significant commitment of resources. We discussed ways to relax some of the formal procedures while preserving consistency between documents and control over the maintenance process. We also explained version control and how to deal with new releases.

Lastly, we discussed ways in which software can become obsolete or die and what can be done about it. Section 11.6. provided a list of questions to identify "sick software."

Maintenance often swallows in excess of half the effort of a software organization. One single chapter cannot hope to provide all the solutions. Rather, we hoped to convey a working understanding of important issues and techniques. Literature on maintenance is still sparse, as are the tools that facilitate making *changes*. Most of the tools that help with making changes are file comparators or tools that support version control and configuration management [Tich82]. The interested reader is referred to [Cash80], [Lien78], [Lien80], [Lien81], [Pari83], [Pari84], [Mccl81], the proceedings of the International Conferences on Software Maintenance, and a special issue of the *IEEE Software Magazine* in May 1986.

► Part II ◄
Management

▶ 12
Management by Metrics

12.1. Overview

The first part of this book presented techniques and methods for all phases of the software development life cycle. Included were examples of procedures that guided the reader through development of a software system from the time it has been accepted as a project to its operational state.

Why does the material on software project management start with a chapter on metrics and measurement? The reason is simple; a big part of the management effort involves evaluating the development process (or its plan), assessing the status and quality of the deliverables of various phases, and making decisions on feasibility and implementations options. All of them not only require measurement but also are part of planning and/or controlling software development, which are management responsibilities. It is very difficult to evaluate the status or quality of a software development project and to make objective decisions without accurate, reliable measurement. This is at the heart of reliable planning, performance and productivity appraisal, control, and product evaluation. As deMarco [Dema82] says, "You cannot control what you cannot measure." Because of the overriding importance of measurement and evaluation of software development, we begin Part II with a chapter on measurement. Measurement is done using appropriate units. Such units of measurement are called *metrics*.

The approach taken could be described as MBM or "*Management by Metrics.*" Metrics rarely make sense without a reference level (standard or objective) against which to compare a measured item. So one could regard this as an extension of "Management by Objective." Metrics have been added to quantify objectives and measure their attainment. This approach is hardly new. While many texts do not explicitly mention metrics, they advocate quantification of how well goals and objectives have been reached ([Park80], [Dema82]). The specific term for objectives or goals may differ (e.g., KRA or *key result area* in [Park80]), as do terms for their quantification (e.g., MOE or *measure of effectiveness* in [Park80]). Yet essentially all these quantitative approaches use metrics to determine goal achievement. This book does the same, but calls a metric a metric, software or otherwise.

Measurement would be ineffective if it were based on metrics that do not possess validity (they measure the right thing) or reliability (they measure it the right way). Unfortunately, many contemporary metrics have been accused of lacking one or the other. This in itself does not preclude basing management on quantitative methods. Rather, it means that before any metric is included in a metric portfolio of a development environment, it needs to be examined for quality. New metrics need to be designed and validated so that they pass quality standards. This may mean that one starts out with a few quality metrics (cf. [Cont86] for a thorough evaluation of many existing metrics), and new ones are added over time as they become available or when they have proven their usefulness during an experimental stage.

The dire need for development of high quality metrics prompted this chapter—it provides an overview of methods for developing and evaluating metrics. Software management should have some familiarity with this, because it improves objective evaluation, strengthens estimating power, and sharpens decision making. Knowing what it takes to develop metrics and models also helps in estimating the effort necessary for the development of new metrics. Although few managers will do their own data collection and analysis during metrics development, it is advantageous to be familiar with the issues involved. This is why Section 12.3. gives a survey of how metrics and models are developed, while at the same time avoids formulas and details on specific techniques. The interested reader is directed to appropriate literature to find information on how to actually apply the techniques mentioned.

Some companies leave the development and collection of metrics to specialists; sometimes they are grouped as part of a development organization and sometimes they are part of a software quality assurance group whose charter is to assess the quality of the software development process and its resulting products.

While it is apparent that much work is still needed to make software development more measurable, many companies have begun to institute the use of metrics (cf.

[Grad87] for a program to do that). Quantitative approaches have long been advocated ([Park80], Dema82]).

This chapter begins with definitions and examples of various types of metrics. After explaining methods for developing metrics (12.3.) an example section (12.4.) presents a variety of metrics that can be used by managers during software development. Then a formal framework for evaluation and decision making (12.5.) is introduced. The next chapters will look at the management activities associated with all phases of software development and refer to the metrics as needed.

After reading this chapter, the reader will know what types of metrics exist and how they are used. He will be familiar with metrics and model development procedures. He will be familiar with specific examples of process and product metrics and with software quality evaluation. He will also know a family of methods for formal evaluation and decision making.

12.2. Software Metrics

12.2.1. Types of Metrics

Product and Process Metrics

We have encountered a variety of metrics throughout this book for measuring aspects of software under development. Most often, measurements were taken at the end of a phase test as a means to compare the quality of the deliverable to an objective or standard, to measure the magnitude of the remaining effort, or to measure the complexity of the phase deliverable or the product. Measurement was important for status assessment at any given phase: whether the development plan with its schedules and its budget was still on target or whether size or complexity, and hence the required effort, was overestimated, underestimated, or stable during a given phase.

In all cases, the indicators aimed at clarifying—and quantifying—some quality of either a phase deliverable or the development process itself. The first type of metric is called a *product metric*, because it is used to measure an aspect of product quality (phase deliverable or software).

A *process metric* on the other hand quantifies attributes of the development process and its environment [Cont86]. Process metrics measure resources required or expended, the effect of development techniques, support tools, and management on output variables, such as effort, time, and schedule. Process metrics are used to estimate time, cost, and resource requirements, but they also help to clarify the status of the project and its compliance with the development plan (effort, cost, time). Because a well conceived development process (good techniques, management, schedule, etc.) supports and influences quality software development, the two types of metrics are not independent. It is at times difficult to tell whether a specific metric is a process or a product metric. It may qualify as both.

Indirect Metrics and Models

Product metrics usually quantify some aspect of quality related to the software qualities of Table 4.1. Hence these metrics measure software reliability, maintainability, adaptability, performance, and the like. They are high level factors of software quality. It is not always possible to measure them directly, especially when the metric is *predictive*; i.e., the software is not developed yet and the metric is used to predict its operational quality. Then subfactors and attributes of phase deliverables are measured that correlate with the levels of quality of the higher level factor we wish to predict. This is an *indirect metric*. A functional relationship between such factors and the outcome we wish to predict is called a *model*.

When measuring an aspect of software quality *a posteriori*, i.e., looking at the finished product, it still may be necessary to use indirect metrics.

Example: Performance Attributes

Performance has at least three attributes:

▶ execution time or, alternately, response time, turnaround time, throughput;

▶ storage needs, primary and secondary; and

▶ data transmission capacity.

Even those may be broken down further. If a software or hardware monitor is used to measure software performance in any of these three areas while executing a benchmark, a metric is used *a posteriori*. Models can be built that use information about the software (e.g., module execution times or frequency of module execution) to predict performance. Such models represent predictive metrics. Hence, metrics can model quality aspects of software.

Often it is impossible to directly measure a quality factor of software or intermediate deliverables during the life cycle. Then only the most important contributing factor is measured instead. This makes it still an indirect metric.

Example: Indirect Metric for Similarity

Program analysis as introduced in Chapter 2 measures the degree of similarity between programs. Similarity is determined by writing style and content, and both are evidenced through use of variables and operations. In the style metrics, the characteristic quadruple (number of unique operators n_1, number of unique operands n_2, total number of operators N_1, total number of operands N_2) was determined to be the most important determinant of writing style, and hence, of similarity. We assume that programs that perform the same function are compared. The characteristic quadruple is an indirect metric for this quality. Similarity was then based on these measures, building a statistical model. Figure 12.1 shows this indirect modeling approach to determining similarity between programs.

Example: Predictive Planning Model

Metrics related to the characteristic quadruple are vocabulary and implementation length. Both measure size, an important factor in predicting effort and cost.

Section 2.4.2.2. gave vocabulary n and implementation length N as

$$n = n_1 + n_2$$
$$N = N_1 + N_2 = \sum_{j=1}^{n_1} f_{1j} + \sum_{j=1}^{n_2} f_{2j}$$

It is intuitively obvious that larger programs tend to be more complex and cost more to develop and maintain. Larger programs also tend to have a bigger vocabulary and use more operators and operands. They also have more lines of code (LOC). Figure 12.2 gives a pictorial view of the relationship between metrics and model development for planning variables.

The "?" in the formula indicates that factors other than size may be influencing the output parameters of the model. These model formulas will only work if size has a crucial influence on time, cost, and resource requirements for a project and if the relationship between size and complexity is strong. If this is not the case, the model may work for some projects but not for others. When size is not the only significant contributor to the planning variable, the models to predict them are multidimensional and more complex.

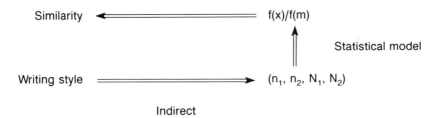

Figure 12.1 Indirect Metric.

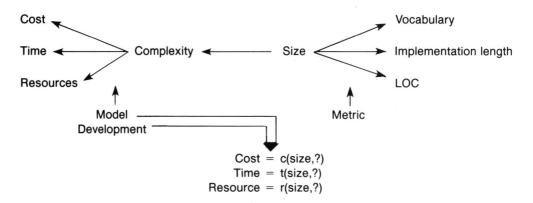

Figure 12.2 Possible Metrics for a Predictive Model.

A *model* is a relationship of the form $y = f(x_1, x_2, \ldots, x_m)$. Y is the variable we wish to predict. It is called the *dependent variable*. The x_i are the *independent variables* on which the prediction of y depends. There are two ways to establish this functional relationship:

▶ The first is through statistical analysis of case data. This is an *empirical model*. Many cost estimation models are of this type. They are as representative as the data upon which they are based and the quality of the statistical inference methods that are used.

▶ The second is established through analytic reasoning and proofs that establish the relationship between independent and dependent variables. Analytic queueing models used for performance analysis are of this type. Some *analytic models* posit a family of functions with situational constants. Those have to be either measured separately or estimated through statistical methods—the model is *calibrated* to its application environment.

In either case, simplifying assumptions may be necessary to keep the model practically usable and analytically solvable. In statistically derived modules the number of independent variables is often reduced, especially when some of them have been shown to be highly correlated. Eliminating independent variables may make the model environment dependent ("setting one variable element of the environment to a constant"). Then the modeling function must be readjusted to different environments (i.e., *recalibration*).

Analytic models tend to simplify their environment and independent variable behavior. Otherwise they might not be able to solve the modeling problem mathematically. For example, many analytic models are based on solutions for stochastic processes. Assumptions about the probability distributions underlying these processes make closed form solutions possible. Popular distributional assumptions are Poisson, negative exponential, Erlang, Weibull, uniform, and normal distributions [Triv82]. When the real world violates those simplifying assumptions, the accuracy of the models may be compromised. Knowing the range of applicability for each model avoids poor results.

As with other indirect metrics or predictive models based on historic or experimental data, statistic inference methods determine the *confidence, validity*, and *reliability* of the model. Confidence is defined as the % of predicted values that fall within a given range of true values. A good model has most values fall within a small interval. Validity measures how close the estimates are when the model is run on the data used to create it. Validity determines whether the model predicts what it should. Reliability refers to the degree of correlation of modeling results. When applied to similar situations, the results the model provides should be close.

Table 12.1 summarizes the metrics types defined in this section.

Table 12.1 Metrics types.

Metrics types	Discriminating factor (What is measured)
Product vs. process	Result of development activity vs. how things are done.
Direct vs. indirect	Quality characteristic itself is measured vs. contributing factors, which are measured and then related to quality or target characteristic.
Predictive vs. a posteriori	Before vs. after quality characteristic (first is model, second is metric that may be combined with model).

Problems and Questions

1. Go through the chapters of this book and determine which metrics or models are used to measure which product or process of software development. Classify them according to Table 12.1.

2. What is the difference between a metric and a model?

3. What are metrics used for? Why do we measure? Why is measurement an important management support activity during software development?

12.2.2. Scales and Their Levels of Measurement

The range of values of a metric is called a *scale* or a *measurement scale*. Metrics are used to measure levels of characteristic features, or *attributes*, of interesting and important items. This is then used to compare alternatives against each other, against an objective, or against a standard. The right choice of a scale is important: measuring the distance between two cars can be done in inches or feet, but the distance between two cities is better measured in miles.

Scale Development

Some attributes are easily quantified. For example, response time can be measured in seconds and number of lines of code may be used as a metric for size. Many important characteristics are harder to measure, however, because they are not easily quantified. Such qualitative attributes require explicit *scale development* in order to make them measurable.

First, one must precisely define the attribute. The definition must be easy to understand, unambiguous, and singly dimensioned. Anyone with the ability and education to understand the term should know exactly what it means, because the vaguer the definition, the harder it will be to have two experts agree on the same meaning, much less come to the same evaluation.

If an attribute has more than one dimension, then more than one dimension has to be measured. That really implies that the "attribute" is a factor (defined as a higher level characteristic) and needs to be broken down further. Sometimes, however, an attribute with multiple dimensions need not be refined further, which is the case when one dimension has overriding importance or the others are irrelevant to the evaluation at hand.

Attribute scales can be language-based or numerical. Examples of language-based scales are "Good, Fair, Poor," or "Blue, Red, Yellow," while a numerically based scale could be a rating from 1 to 5 or from 27 to 391. Usually numerical scales are chosen when the scores will be used within formulas of any sort. In this case, the scale should exhibit certain properties in order to make it fit for such use.

Scale development begins with defining *anchor points*. These are often the extreme values of the scale. After defining the extreme points, one may proceed to a point in the middle of the scale and so forth (method of bisection). The objective is to define precisely what a point on the scale means so that any person who is qualified to do the measurement (the *rating* as it is called for qualitative attributes) will arrive at about the same rating as someone else for a given attribute level.

After a scale has been defined, it must be evaluated for quality. Two very important qualities are *validity* and *reliability*. A validity check ascertains that the scale measures what it should, while a reliability test is concerned about whether the scale will produce the same result when used more than once. Measurements need to be predictable: an inch does not change no matter who measures the item.

Example: Quality of Documentation for Software

How could this attribute be defined? First, one questions what quality of documentation could or should be. Quality of documentation covers several issues. Three of the more important ones are as follows:

1. Does the documentation contain the information needed?

2. How long does it take to find the information (alternatively, how well is it organized?)

3. How understandable is the information? (alternatively, how well is it presented?)

Assuming that these are all the important aspects of the quality of documentation, the term "quality of documentation" has three dimensions that need to be measured separately. A possible scale for the first dimension might be "always, usually, often, rarely, never." The scale for the time it takes to find the useful information could be "a few minutes, hours, days, weeks, never." Assuming the information can be found, how should its effectiveness be measured? This third scale could range from clearly to incomprehensibly. The first two examples have rather precise gradations of quality, while the last just labels the extremes, showing that a lot more work is required to make this into a usable scale. A possible "middle point" would be "average." This is good enough provided one can precisely determine what "average" means.

Levels of Measurement

The granularity of a scale depends on how it is to be used. It must be fine enough to distinguish different alternatives but not finer than needed. Measurements are often analyzed through statistical methods, and not all statistical techniques work with any level of measurement. There are four characteristics for measurements:

1. **Distinctiveness.** All one can say about a scale that has this characteristic is that there are different values such as "Left" and "Right" or "A" and "B." There is no relationship between them. One cannot say that A is smaller than B or that Left ranks higher than Right. These relationships are simply not defined. An example during software development would be different types of development techniques: top-down design, iterative enhancement, bottom-up design, mixed design. Any design falls into one or the other of these categories, but the scale does not indicate which is better. It only discriminates between them.

2. **Ordering in Magnitude.** If a scale has this property, a ranking is possible, such as Left > Right or A < B. Relationships between the points on the scale are defined. Nothing is said, however, about how much the difference between two values is or what it means.

For example, consider the first dimension of quality of documentation. It evaluates whether the documentation contains the information needed. There is an implied ranking from "always" to "never." It is unclear, however, what the difference between the values means or how much it is.

3. **Equal Intervals.**   Scales with equal intervals between their values define what the distance between points is and how much it is. A scale from 20 to 100 with equal intervals means that the difference between 100 and 98 is the same as between 25 and 23.

4. **Absolute Zero.**   Having an absolute zero on the scale means that a measurement value exists that measures the absence of the property in question.

Table 12.2 [Alle79] shows which levels of measurement exhibit which characteristics. The levels of measurement are *nominal, ordinal, interval*, and *ratio*. Arithmetic manipulations of measurements made on a nominal level are not meaningful, even if the distinct points on the scale are defined as numbers. Because there is no definition of a relationship between them it is not clear what adding or multiplying them means. Statistical techniques must be appropriate for the level of measurement (cf. Section 12.3).

Table 12.2   Levels of measurement and their characteristics.

Characteristic	Level of Measurement			
	Nominal	Ordinal	Interval	Ratio
Distinctiveness	yes	yes	yes	yes
Ordering in magnitude	no	yes	yes	yes
Equal intervals	no	no	yes	yes
Absolute zero	no	no	no	yes

12.2.3.   Metrics in the Software Development Lifecycle

12.2.3.1.   Quality Metrics for Requirements and Specifications

Requirements collection and analysis attempted to state requirements in quantifiable terms, so that the finished product could be measured and compared to its requirements. Metrics for requirements state unmistakably what desired software quality is and whether the finished product reaches those quality levels. Depending on the specific quality aspect, quality could be absolute (a quality is there or it isn't) or relative (where several levels of quality are possible).

Relative Quality Metrics

Measuring levels of a quality attribute and comparing it to the product objectives provides a relative indication of quality.

Using the degree of attainment of an objective as a metric requires an interval scale of measurement. The section on evaluation and decision making will show how to combine aspects of the software development process into an overall indicator of quality.

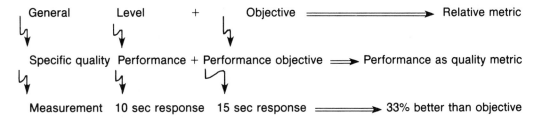

Figure 12.3   Metrics and Objectives.

Example: Metrics for Requirements Checklist of Table 4.1

Let us now suggest a few metrics for some of the quality areas:

▶ **Human factors.**   This dimension of quality relates to the productivity of the end user and how a software product enhances or hinders it. End user productivity is affected by aspects, such as the time it takes novices to learn how to use the software or how fast experienced users can get their work done. Lastly, it is affected by the rate of errors that users make in using the software. Training time and the time dealing with errors are "overhead" that takes away from getting work done. This time may not always be significant enough to be included in an evaluation.

▶ **Portability.**   A very straightforward measure can be created by normalizing the effort needed to port software between target systems by the size of the software.

▶ **Maintainability.**   This could be measured as the effort to keep software operational. The effort can be categorized whether it was spent fixing errors or making adaptations to the software.

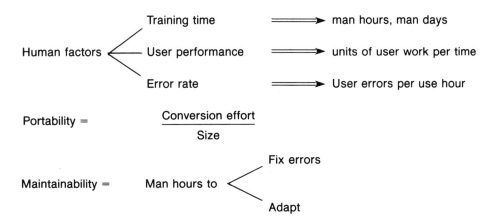

Figure 12.4   Some Example Quality Metrics.

Metrics for Constraints and Benefits of Table 4.1

It is much easier to measure what *is* than to predict accurately what *will be*. One can, for example, measure the skill levels of personnel, divide by a count of all personnel available, and arrive at an average skill level. To use these measures for estimating schedules is much harder. Likewise, process metrics can be defined for schedule compliance, resource usage, cost, etc., but predictive use is more difficult. We usually try to identify process metrics for the current phase. These are then used to parameterize models to predict future levels of factors that measure the software development process. Figure 12.5 gives the factors contributing to personnel resources and to the process model.

Going back once again to Section 4.4., there is still another important decision variable for the software product that should be measured: tangible benefits.

Example: Evaluation of Tangible Benefits for TAP

For the tax preparation system, tangible benefits were measured in dollars. The following attributes of tangible benefits could be measured:

▶ tax consequences of errors avoided in tax preparation which are caught by TAP,

▶ penalties avoided through the use of TAP, and

▶ increased income through tax reduction.

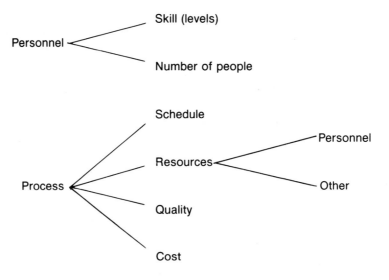

Figure 12.5 Estimation and Prediction.

Metrics similar to the requirements metrics can be developed for the specifications. They are based on the multiplicity and size of input and output classes, complexity of the associated processing requirements or functions, and the nature of states and transitions between states. These are the main dimensions of work for the specification phase.

12.2.3.2. Quality Assessment During Design

During the design phase, a two-dimensional metric of structural quality was introduced (cf. 8.3.): module strength and module coupling. Both are measured on a scale from 1 to 7, with high scores indicating a good design. The quality metric and a set of objectives determine a relative quality metric as suggested in Figure 12.3.

It is not obvious what measurement levels should be set as an objective for a project nor what appropriate standards are. Past projects are measured *a posteriori*, and data for ongoing projects is collected. Statistical analysis of the data helps

▶ to determine which attributes contribute significantly (in a statistical sense) to the output variables that are to be measured, and

▶ to establish functional relationships between the attributes and the output variables.

These two steps are at the heart of metrics validation and model development.

Example: Error Collection during Walk-Throughs

Section 8.6.2. discussed a quality evaluation process based on error collection during walk-throughs. These errors relate to the quality of the design. The parts of the design with a high concentration of errors are weak. Quality measurement through error collection provides a focusing tool: modules that exceed the standard for error counts (as defined through the above process) need special attention (rework, quality improvement efforts, refusal to accept design, etc.).

12.2.3.3. Quality Assessment for Code

Under the premise that the quality of a piece of code can be measured by its adherence to coding standards, one can define the number of infractions normalized by size as an indicator of "negative" quality. When this number exceeds a threshold, improvement becomes necessary. This can happen during development or during the operational life of the software. Thus a metric can be used to

▶ evaluate current quality,

- ▶ gauge quality changes over time, and

- ▶ make decisions whether to improve quality.

This also applies to particular quality areas such as performance.

12.2.3.4. *Phase-tests and Residual Errors*

Using the set of test cases that is used during phase test or any of the code testing phases is not necessarily a good benchmark for predicting quality, especially for phases before the system test. The simple reason is that the earlier we find an error, the less we have left for later. We need to distinguish between the errors found during a phase test and the residual errors that have not been detected. This we do in subsequent phases or during operation. One can only determine the quality of work in any given phase if the error can be identified and classified appropriately as originating in a given phase. Thus this method for quality measurement hinges on the ability and quality of error counting.

The best approach is then to evaluate products of the requirements phase "as is." We use the residual error count to predict residual errors in later phases (i.e., design, coding, testing, operation). As residual error counts of later phases become available, these estimates can be refined. If at any point in the development the residual error count becomes too high, we can stop further development and raise the quality of the completed phase deliverables. Acceptable quality depends on the objectives and priorities for development and on the representativeness of the benchmarks and on how the deliverables of earlier phases are used. Counting errors during development as an indicator of (lack of) quality has to be approached with a great deal of care; otherwise it may just lead to less testing because then we will find fewer errors.

12.2.4. Quality Metrics

While an evaluation method may be obvious and show high face validity, its underlying component metrics may not be. Measurement and any lower level predictive metrics or models must be accurate, valid, and reliable. Often there are more than two levels of measurement, metrics and models. If errors are incurred at every level, chances are they will build up, and values for the output variables of the highest level model will be wrong and unusable.

It may not be clear how many parameters need to be included in determining a metric or a model of software behavior with respect to some desired quality.

Example: Reliability of Code

Most code, if executed long enough and thoroughly enough, will encounter failures. They can be measured and then used to compute reliability. However, this is often too late for quality estimation; we want to know the quality beforehand, not after problems occur, so that something can be done about it on time. Reliability of code has often been linked to its complexity, which correlates with such characteristics as

▶ loops,

▶ size,

▶ variedness and quantity of input and output variables and classes,

▶ whether all variables have been declared and initialized or not,

▶ whether all functional boundaries have been explicitly defined and are checked in the code, and

▶ accuracy requirements.

These input variables correlate with the number of errors in a piece of software. The list is not exhaustive. A predictive model of code reliability will not be efficient if it has to consider all possible factors that contribute to reliability.

It is necessary to simplify. This is at the heart of many predictive metrics or quality models. It also means that it is impossible to discriminate between situations that differ in parameter values not included in the metric or model. Thus the range of use of a metric must be clearly defined.

To summarize, it is easy to define metrics; the plethora of metrics testifies to that ([Boeh76B], [Cont86], [Coop79], [Gilb77], [Hals77], [Mcca77], [Mcca80], [Moha79], [Perl81]). We must show that they reliably measure what they claim to measure. They must be open to changes in the environment and to changes of factors and attributes that they do not take into account. Measurements must not contradict each other. Because indirect measures or metrics-based models often rely on constants that are specific for a given development environment, such indirect metrics or models need to be recalibrated (the constants need to be determined again or adjusted) when they are used in a different environment. Validation can be difficult when it is based on limited experimental or historical data.

The following section discusses common methods of developing a metric or a model. They usually start out with an objective, i.e., what we wish to measure, and then proceed through identification of factors that contribute to higher or lower quality levels to model definition and validation.

Problems and Questions

1.   What limits the applicability of models?

12.3. Metrics and Model Development

This section serves as a management overview of the issues involved and of the major techniques used to develop metrics and models. It is not meant to teach working knowledge of model development. Rather, it intends to provide the reader with the proper framework for model development and with a list of useful techniques. The references can be consulted to provide the missing detail.

To illustrate the development of metrics and models, let us assume that we wish to determine a metric for an aspect of software quality, but that it is not clear which of the factors contributing to that quality is the most decisive. Factor identification determines the major contributing factor (or a small set of them) for the software quality aspect in question. This can be done by measuring the individual factors in a series of experiments and then analyzing how they relate to the desired quality.

Example: Factor Identification for Reliability Metric

One may wish to determine whether the number of decision statements in a program influences its reliability (number of failures found). First, one determines how strongly these two quantities correlate. One probably would also measure size, because it might have an effect on these variables. In this case the dependent variable is reliability. The independent variables are decision statements and size.

Often there are many more potential independent variables. An example of such a situation are models that try to predict the overall cost, effort, or development time of a software project. Even the reduced number of independent variables that influence the dependent ones (cost, effort, and time) can easily exceed a dozen (e.g., [Wals77]—29 variables, [Jens84]—13 variables, and [Boeh81]—15 variables). This does not mean that they are all apparent in the modeling function. Sometimes they are captured in an "environmental constant" whose value changes with changing development environments. Because many of the development environments can be quite stable across projects, this provides a means of reducing the number of independent variables, sometimes to two or three.

12.3.1. Preliminary Steps

There are three preliminary steps to model and metric development for derived metrics that depend on a set of lower level contributing factors:

▶ Identify the dependent variable and determine a direct metric for it. Use the rules on how to develop a measurement scale.

▶ Identify all independent variables that need to be considered and determine a direct metric for them. Independent variables are sometimes called *factors*. One can think of factors as parameters that appreciably influence the outcome of an evaluation or the level of a dependent variable in a model. One can also think of factors as an identifiable component of overall need (as specified in software requirements).

In order to avoid bias and pseudo-objective evaluation, *quality factors* need to be identified. Their characteristics are as follows:

a. **Relevant.** The factor stands for an important component of overall need, not something that makes very little difference.

b. **Comprehensive.** While one should not bother with unimportant factors, one should also not go overboard and neglect to consider relevant factors. Neglecting relevant factors biases model results.

c. **Nonoverlapping.** When factors overlap there is the danger that some qualities are taken into account twice. This can bias an evaluation. In a model it means using more factors than necessary.

d. **Operational.** Factors should be conducive to metrics. If given a choice of two different factor definitions, it is preferable to choose the one for which a metric is more easily defined.

Factors are either quantitative or qualitative. *Quantitative factors* lend themselves more easily to measurement such as profit in dollars, development time in man months, lines of noncomment code for size, execution time as a performance index, reliability as the fraction of errors found over time, etc.

Qualitative factors are not as easily measured. Often it is difficult to measure them at all. Frequently they refer to perceived, human qualities. Examples include some items often associated with (nonquantifiable) benefits, such as increased employee morale, but they also might be factors like quality of the documentation, quality of user training, or user friendliness of the man-machine interface. One should not measure quality of documentation by volume or by frequency of update alone. Likewise the quality of user training is not only dependent on the number of training courses but on the teacher's knowledge, on the ability of the teacher to communicate, his availability, etc.

To measure the qualitative attributes of a factor, they must be broken down into contributing subfactors on subsequently lower levels. This may be done by asking, "What does it mean to have quality x? What things does quality x imply?" until the level is low enough to allow measurement.

Factors are often not directly measurable; rather, what is measured is an *attribute*. An attribute is a particular quality, characteristic feature, or performance variable closely related to the factor. One can think of attributes as the lowest level factors to be measured directly.

▶ Measure dependent and independent variables. The measuring sample must be large enough to allow meaningful statistical evaluation. The more independent the variables, the bigger the sample needs to be. If we had, for example, four points to fit a cubic function, we can do so exactly. But if the measurements contain any errors, they cannot be identified—there are just enough points to fit the curve but not enough to determine any error estimates for the curve fitting. Statistical techniques exist that determine the required sample size for measurement experiments ([Koba78], [Triv82]).

12.3.2. Factor Identification

Statistically significant relationships between independent and dependent variables are identified. This step of model and metric development has two objectives:

▶ Reduce the independent variables to the smallest number. This keeps the model or metric simple. We must be able to determine which of the independent variables are equivalent.

▶ Establish a relationship between the (reduced) set of independent variables and the dependent one.

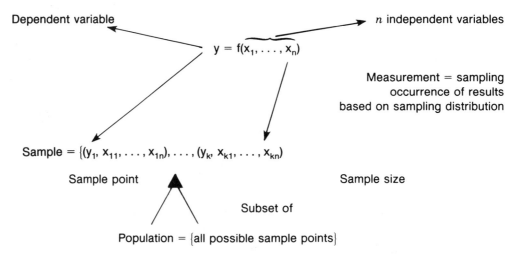

Dependent variable

n independent variables

$$y = f(x_1, \ldots, x_n)$$

Measurement = sampling occurrence of results based on sampling distribution

Sample $= \{(y_1, x_{11}, \ldots, x_{1n}), \ldots, (y_k, x_{k1}, \ldots, x_{kn})\}$

Sample point

Sample size

Subset of

Population $= \{$all possible sample points$\}$

Figure 12.6 Measurement.

There are four major methods to identify factors: *correlations*, a *scatter plot, factor analysis*, and *analysis of variance*. They require different statistical techniques. Factor identification is a statistical technique to cluster factors (i.e., independent variables) into groups whose effect, statistically speaking, is comparable. Then only one factor in each group needs to be considered, because the other factors behave almost identically.

Example: Human Factors

We want to determine which of the human factors of Figure 12.4 needs to be measured and made part of a quality model. If the three components of human factors, i.e., training time, user performance, and error rate, all end up in the same factor class, only one of them needs to be measured. This will simplify a model tremendously.

Model development is different from decision making. Decision making bases the selection of quality factors on objectives; i.e., we know which ones to select and how important they are to the project. During the first phase of model development we may not know which independent variables explain and determine the behavior of the dependent one, so relationships between them need to be quantified.

Many quality factors can be arranged hierarchically where a higher level factor is determined by a set of lower level ones. For software, such an arrangement is called a *quality tree*. It can become very big. Therefore, it is advantageous if the measurement of higher level factors can be simplified to the measurement of only one or a few lower level ones. Factor analysis can help to identify which ones.

Relationships between variables of different phases also must be identified. This is a prerequisite for establishing measures and models for certain types of quality across phases. Usually the metrics and model parameters change from one phase to the next, but the dependent variable (e.g., reliability, effort remaining) will not. Quality levels that represent the same type of quality at various phases need to be correlated. A model is developed for predicting quality levels for later phases from earlier ones based on measurement data. Figure 12.7 gives a summary of all major techniques for factor identification.

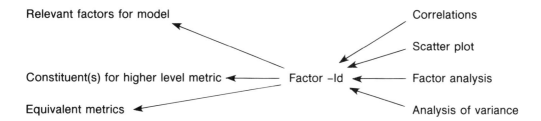

Figure 12.7 Factor Identification.

Not all statistical techniques for factor identification are equally applicable. Some require higher levels of measurement than others. The parametric methods make assumptions about the probability distribution underlying the measurements and the relationship between the independent variables. Parametric assumptions usually require that measurements are taken independently of each other from a normally distributed population, that the populations have about the same variance, and that the measurement is at least at the interval level.

Table 12.3 summarizes important techniques to perform such statistical analyses. All of them can be performed with statistical tools, and we should not expect to have to compute the individual measures by hand or write our own programs to do it. Therefore the precise formulas are not given. For further information see [Cont86], [Triv82], [Alle79], [Koba78], or any of the references mentioned with specific techniques. We will explain the range of applicability for each technique. Common tools that support statistical analysis are SAS, IMSL, and SPSS.

Scatter Plot

The simplest way to determine whether two variables are related is the scatter plot. The x axis usually shows the independent variable, the y axis the dependent one. This is a first approach to establish the possible relationship between variables. Based on whether the points form somewhat of a line, some other discernible curve, or are all over the graph, we can decide to check with one of the statistical packages. The scatter plot is by definition two-dimensional and therefore cannot show more complex relationships between several variables. Often a pair-wise comparison between independent variables is sufficient to show whether they are related.

Correlation Coefficients

The next step in statistical analysis is to compute correlation coefficients. The choice of methods depends on the characteristics of the metric for each variable and on the statistical properties that are assumed to hold for the population as a whole. The Pearson Product Moment correlation coefficient ([Alle79], [Cont86], [Kend61]) and the Spearman Rank correlation coefficient are probably among the most commonly used. They both compute the degree of relationship between two variables, but they make different assumptions.

The *Pearson Product Moment* is a parametric statistic. It assumes a linear relationship between the two variables, and it requires an interval or ratio level of measurement of both variables. They must be continuous or multistep, and multistep variables should have a large range of possible values. While there is often no problem ([Alle79]), one should be very careful when using the Pearson Product Moment with ordinal measurements.

Table 12.3 Statistical techniques.

Name	Applicability
Scatter diagram	*Between measures of two sets of variables
	*Visually establish type of curve
	*Only two-dimensional
	*Follow with statistics using SAS, IMSL, SPSS
Correlations	
Pearson Product Moment	*Parametric
	*Linear relationship between two variables
	*Needs interval or ratio scale
	*Continuous or multistep variables
	*Beware when using with ordinal scale
Spearman Rank	*Nonparametric
	*Between pairs of variables
	*Needs ordinal measurement scale
	*Continuous, multistep variables
	*May be overly conservative when many ties in rank
Kendall's Tau	*Alternative to Spearman Rank
	*More tedious than Spearman Rank
Chi-square test	*Nominal measurement level
	*Multivariate
Phi	*Two dichotomous variables
	*Special case of Pearson PM, with reduced range
Tetrachoric correlation	*Pair of artificially dichotomized vars
	*Both bivariate normal
	*Not simple formula
Point-biserial correlation	*One dichotomous, other continuous or multistep variable
	*Reduces Pearson PM to simpler formula
Biserial correlation	*One artificially dichotomous, other continuous or multistep variable
	*Normally distributed
Factor analysis	*Determine minimal number of factors
	*Multivariate
	*Linear relationship between related, orthogonal between unrelated factors
	*Determines amount of variance of dependent variable explained by each independent one
Coefficient of determination	*Square of correlation
	*Same restrictions as correlations
	*Explain percentage of variance in one variable accounted for by the other

The *Spearman Rank* correlation coefficient on the other hand does not make parametric assumptions and only assumes at least an ordinal level of measurement. It requires, however, that both variables be continuous or multistep. *Kendall's Tau* is an alternative to the Spearman Rank correlation coefficient, but it is more tedious to compute ([Alle79], [Hays73]).

The *Chi-square* test ([Triv82], [Cont86]) can be used when some of the variables can only be measured at the nominal level, such as when the effect of the presence or absence of a development technique is measured.

The *Phi* coefficient and *tetrachoric correlation* establish the degree of relationship between two dichotomous (i.e., 0 and 1 as values) variables ([Alle79]). The latter assumes bivariate normal distributions for both variables, which must have been artificially dichotomized ([Lord68]). Such variables could have been originally of the multistep variety, but values were "lumped together" to indicate qualities such as achieving a development deadline or not or reaching performance goals or not.

Matters become more complex when one of the two variables is dichotomous, but the other one is continuous or multistep. Depending on whether one of the variables is dichotomous or artificially dichotomous, we compute either the *point-biserial* or the *biserial* correlation coefficient ([Alle79]). The latter reduces the Pearson Product Moment to a simpler formula and thus makes the same parametric assumptions.

Factor Analysis

Factor analysis groups sets of factors into classes. All factors in the same class have the same effect on the dependent variable. One selection from a class is sufficient to describe the inputs to a model. Factor analysis, however, assumes that nonrelated factors are orthogonal and that any relationship between factors is linear. This can produce less than satisfactory results when they are not related linearly.

Coefficient of Determination

The last set of statistical indicators states the amount of variance in a factor that can be accounted for by another. In the case of two factors, the correlation coefficient is squared to obtain the coefficient of determination. For situations with more than two variables, an analysis of variance (ANOVA) becomes necessary [Triv82]. ANOVA also assumes a linear relationship between factors.

Even when it is clear that variables are not related linearly, it may be possible to transform them into linear data by taking logarithms or by inverting the function. This, however, presupposes knowledge about the type of function. A scatter diagram may have provided such information.

12.3.3. Fit Model

Once related factors have been identified, this information is used to fit a model. Models range from hand calculations to sophisticated formulas, such as the ones for queueing network models that are used to analyze or predict performance. They can be analytic (such as performance indicators based on stochastic modeling and some reliability models) or experimental. To remain mathematically tractable, analytic models may simplify reality considerably.

Experimental models have been developed through statistical inference techniques, not through reasoning from assumptions about the environment to an analytic conclusion. Experimentally developed models derive their accuracy from the quality of the measurements and experiments on which their statistical derivation is based.

Either type needs to be validated to make sure that the model does what it set out to do, but they will only be as good as the sampling data upon which they are based. Because models often contain constants as summary descriptors for specific environments (development methods, programming language, development tools, application area, organization), environmental constants may have to be adjusted.

Regression

Based on the results of factor identification, one of three types of regression is performed: linear (or multilinear in case of a multivariate model), nonlinear with a polynomial of fixed degree, or regression where the general type of function is known and the best fitting constants for the sampling data need to be determined.

The Pearson Product Moment and factor analysis give an indication of the variables that are linearly related. In this case, linear regression determines the model. The modeling function has the form

$$y = a_0 + a_1 x_1 + a_2 x_2 + \ldots + a_n x_n$$

The Pearson Product Moment and linear regression are related. There is a simple formula to determine an estimate for y through the independent variable x which uses the Pearson Product Moment. The coefficients for the regression line constitute a least squares fit. This means that the constants in the modeling function are determined so that the sum of the squares of the differences between the actually measured values of the dependent variable y and the estimates using the modeling function will be the smallest possible for any choice of constants a_i ($i = 0,...,n$). It is not necessary to fit the curve using a least squares fit. Another option is to determine the constants by minimizing the mean relative error and maximizing the predictability. There will be more on this later when model evaluation is discussed.

If the relationship between variables is not linear and if the function cannot be transformed into a linear one, nonlinear regression techniques become necessary. Since they are somewhat complicated, it is best to use one of the available packages. Many will fit a polynomial of some fixed degree that the user specifies. The family of modeling functions looks like

$$y = a_0 + a_1 x^{b_1} + a_2 x^{b_2} + \ldots + a_m x^{b_m}$$

where m is the degree of the polynomial, and a_i and b_i are its determining constants. Note that this only specifies a regression function for two variables. One would have a sum of polynomial expressions for a multivariate nonlinear model. Another nonlinear regression function is a sum of powers:

$$y = a_0 + a_1 x_1^{b_1} + \ldots + a_n x_n^{b_n}.$$

Since there are many more constants than in a linear regression function, there is more flexibility to find constants so that the errors are small. But in order to have predictive quality one also needs a bigger sample. The data must exceed the minimum number of measurements to achieve a unique determination of the constants. These "extras" determine the quality of the fit. If there are not enough "extras," it is impossible to say whether a particular function will work well beyond the sample.

In general, it is preferable to find a function with few constants to fit. First, it is an easier problem. Second, the sample upon which the curve fit is based can be smaller. Many modeling attempts make use of this by positing a function such as

$$y = a\, x_1 + b\, x_2^c + d^{x_3}.$$

Well known effort and cost models, such as the Rayleigh-Putnam Model and Halstead's effort model, are based on that. Statistical packages fit the curve and evaluate the fit. It may be advantageous to determine a least squares fit or some other appropriate measure analytically if the error measure is easy to determine and to differentiate. To discuss feasibility and optimality of various solution methods goes well beyond the scope of this book. Please refer to [Triv82] for details.

Limitations of Regression

Regression packages are very powerful. However, one should be aware of some potential problems before using a model derived through regression:

▶   Brute force regression will not always produce desirable or understandable results. [Motl77] shows, in a study on relating program characteristics (independent variables) to the number of defects in a program (dependent variable), that while the quality of the fit to the data was excellent (as evidenced by a very high coefficient of determination), the predictive quality and the meaning of some of its constants is questionable ([Cont86]). One of the problems was that many independent variables in the function were related. This led to negative coefficients which prevented adding the combined influence of a variable twice. This did not always make sense. For example, the amount of comments in the code correlated positively with the number of defects.

▶ Because of the shortcomings of brute force regression, even with sufficiently large and carefully collected databases, it is important to use some expert judgement to fine-tune the regression function. This may mean to assume specific types of functions. Then a regression curve-fit can determine its constants. The cost model COCOMO [Boeh81] derives much of its success from combining expert judgment with judicious regression. Every relationship between variables expressed through specific, regression-derived constants should have a sensible explanation.

▶ Be aware of the limits of the type of regression analysis used. For example, in the study cited above [Motl77], program size was, unexpectedly, *not* the independent variable explaining most of the dependent variable's variance (number of defects), even though it had been linked to the number of defects before and even though it is intuitively appealing. Such a result does not necessarily mean that defects are not dependent on size. It may mean that they are not *linearly* related (which is the type of correlation that was used in the analysis). Or it may be that many of the other "independent" variables in the study are related to size (nonlinearly), and thus they obscured the results. Apparent small influences of an independent variable on a dependent one may be due to improper regression assumptions.

12.3.4.   Model Evaluation

Finding the regression constants determines the model. Now we need to evaluate the quality of its estimates. Figure 12.8 shows the relationship between model determination and model evaluation.

A model should always be evaluated on the sample data upon which the derivation of its constants is based. It should at least perform well for those, but it also must be evaluated against new data. These new data should be representative of the model's use, and the model should perform equally well. When using a model, it is important to keep in mind that it cannot be expected to work in situations for which it was not developed. For example, if measurement data from small programs is used to develop a model on program behavior, it cannot be expected to work on big programs and vice versa. Model use usually involves interpolation, not extrapolation.

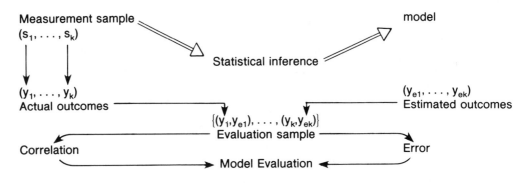

Figure 12.8 Model Development and Evaluation.

There are two types of evaluation criteria: first, the errors should be small when the estimated values (y_e) for the dependent variables from measured independent x_i are compared to the actually observed y values. But for a model with good predictive quality, the estimated values y_e must correlate highly to the actually measured values y. This means that, statistically speaking, they constitute samples drawn from the same population. This measure by itself, however, is not good enough. A cost model that consistently underestimates might show good values for the correlation between y and y_e values, but the model is only useful if one can gauge by how much it tends to underestimate or if it is used merely to rank projects by estimated cost. In such a situation it is more important that the ranks be accurate than that the estimates themselves be totally correct. The need for accurate predictions also requires that the differences between estimated and actual values be small. Both evaluation criteria are used for the model evaluation procedure. Table 12.4 gives a synopsis of the statistial methods used for model evaluation.

The two correlation measures are the coefficient of multiple determination and the prediction quality indicator. The *coefficient of multiple determination* measures linear correlation of pairs of variables. During model evaluation it is the pair of actual value and predicted value for the same set of independent variable values. The *prediction quality indicator* states which fraction of the measurement sample shows a mean relative error of no more than a given percentage d. [Cont86] suggests that 75% of the sample should show no more than a 25% mean relative error.

The measures of error magnitude for the model are mean relative error, mean magnitude of relative error, and mean squared error. The last measure was one of the model determination criteria in the previous step. *Mean relative error* is computed as follows: compute the differences between estimated and actual y values, normalize them by the actual value, add them all up, and divide by the sample size. Unfortunately, negative errors can be masked by positive ones. To avoid this, one can use the magnitude of each difference instead and compute the *mean magnitude of the relative error*. [Cont86] chose,

Table 12.4 Model evaluation methods.

Correlation	Errors
1. Coefficient of multiple determination	1. Mean relative error
	2. Mean magnitude of relative error
2. Prediction fraction at level d	3. Mean squared error

as the measure for model error, the quality cutoff point of 25% for the mean relative error.

A model that obtains good values under one measure does not necessarily get good values under another. A set of evaluation measures must give both a measure of the prediction quality and a measure of the errors the model is making, because these two aspects of model quality do not substitute for each other.

Problems and Questions

1. What can happen if we develop a model linking size to the number of decision variables, and we use

  ▶ individual program modules only, or

  ▶ programs that exceed a thousand lines of uncommented source code only?

Will we be able to use one model for predicting values in the other set of data? Why or why not? Do you have an explanation why this might not work?

2. Go to your computer center and find out which statistial packages are available. For each package, establish a list of statistical methods that can be used for model development and evaluation. Describe the circumstances under which you would use each statistical method.

3. What would you have to change in PAS to make it help you to develop a model that predicts the characteristic quadruple from the number of lines of code? Evaluate the model once you have made the changes. Why does the model not work well for all four indicators yet work well for some?

12.4. Example Metrics

12.4.1. Process Metrics

Phase evaluation is a generally useful approach for evaluating how well a development phase was carried out. A checklist of items (actions to carry out or objectives to achieve) must be developed. Afterwards the quality of the development process for the phase is scored by counting the degree of compliance with the stated items. A basis for determining degree of compliance is either 100% (i.e., dividing the score by the maximum possible score for each item) or any preset compliance standard (i.e., dividing the achieved score by the score which corresponds to the compliance standard for it).

An example of such phase evaluation using a derived metric is to measure the testing process as described in Chapter 10. Table 10.1 listed approaches for unit testing that can be used to derive tested items, the type of testing (e.g., structure-based testing), and how to evaluate the testing progress. Test criteria state the objectives on which to base the degree of testing (the metric). It can be defined as the fraction of tested to untested code (or decision transfers). Minimally thorough testing would require that all decision transfers be executed at least once, resulting in a 100% compliance standard. This compliance is measurable.

Similarly, the specification test matrix of Table 10.2 also gives test items and testing objectives. These are used to measure compliance with testing procedures (a process metric for the testing phase) and to evaluate testing progress. One can define standards and compliance with standards through scoring and normalization.

The bebugging or fault injection method also provides a model for assessing progress and estimating residual errors and testing confidence. The metric is the number of errors found. The model is driven by this independent variable. A testing strategy using a combination of testing methods should state the actual items on the checklist, normalize the checklist into a metric and use this combined testing metric to evaluate the testing phase.

Another example of normalizing a checklist into a metric is in Chapter 16, which lists a series of guidelines for software development. Scoring scales for each guideline measure compliance with the guidelines. This degree of compliance measures the quality of the software development process.

12.4.2.   Product Metrics

In the case of direct factor prediction (e.g. functional correctness, cost, schedule), the model is driven by program attributes. Examples of such important program attributes are complexity and size.

12.4.2.1. Size

Size is one of the most important program characteristics, because it is related to the cost and effort of development, the number of errors in a program, and the productivity of the software developers, to name just a few. The early phases need to estimate the size of the program in order to predict from this estimate the cost and effort for program development. As can be imagined, this is not the only reason for size metrics. Size metrics and models emphasize different size-related aspects of software.

Lines of Code (LOC)

The most direct size metric is to measure lines of code (LOC) or thousands of lines of code (KLOC). This metric, while the most direct, is also a problematic one. At the very least, we have to define what a line of code is. Does it include comments? Declarations? Which languages? The latter is important because a program in assembly language has more statements (with equivalent functionality) than a program in a high level language. We need to adjust for that. Another difficulty occurs for languages, like PASCAL, that allow one statement to be spread over several lines or allow several statements on one line. Is spreading one statement over five lines equivalent to five LOC, and are five statements on one line one LOC? This can lead to a metric that is not very reliable, especially when styles vary and when programs are short, because then such differences become relatively more pronounced. On the other hand, when coding standards and a stable set of techniques for software development exist, such individual differences tend to decrease when measuring or predicting size for larger programs. Like it or not, the LOC metric is still one of the most widely used today.

The LOC metric is a measure of overall program size, function, and data. Other size metrics either specialize in measuring what they consider most relevant for size or try to avoid the problems with the LOC metric by measuring size-related aspects of a program that are less subject to misinterpretation. The token count $N = N_1 + N_2$ is an example of the latter. The total number of operators and operands used is related to program size. Splitting statements across lines is no longer an issue. Halstead's software science also offers an estimated length equation that is based on the number of unique operators and operands needed to develop the program. Neither measure, however, has done well in practice.

Other Size Metrics

Other measures focus attention either on the functions/actions or the data. Table 12.4 gives a summary of size metrics, whether they are action or data oriented and during which phase they are first directly measurable.

One can develop models that predict size of future phase deliverables based on currently measured size. These models either predict size for the next phase or estimate program size when the software is fully developed. Figure 12.9 shows the steps in prediction and the modeling functions needed. Function point estimations have done well as overall effort predictors. One can use either the number of activity boxes or the number of identifiable functions at specification time as the basis for a function point model. This gives an early effort prediction model. The chapter on estimation (14) provides more details on these and other predictive models for effort, cost, staffing, and schedule.

All size measures of actual code are language dependent. More statements are needed to express the same function in a lower level language than in a higher level one. The size

Table 12.5 Size metrics during software development.

Phase	Type	Metric
RA	A	Number of activity boxes in the requirements diagram
RA	D	Number of data dictionary items
SP	A	Number of identifiable functions in specifications (function points)
SP	D	Number of inputs/outputs that need to be defined (in terms of elementary data)
DS	A	Number of modules
C	AD	LOC/KLOC
C	AD	Token count $N = N_1 + N_2$
C	AD	Estimated length equation $EL = n_1\log_2 n_1 + n_2\log_2 n_2$
C	D	Number of variables declared/used

Note: RA - requirements analysis; SP - specifications; DS - design; C - code; A - action/function oriented; D - data oriented; AD - considers both data and function.

of the code also depends on qualitative objectives for the software. For instance, performance constraints often require shorter programs, while security constraints may require adding specific checks that make the program longer. The same can happen for reliability constraints. This means that in predicting size, adjustments will be necessary based on the types of qualitative requirements that apply. Software size is also dependent on its inherent quality. Sometimes structured programs are shorter than unstructured ones. For all these reasons, estimating size is not an easy task, but it is important for predictive models that support software project management. When considering one specific software quality (size), the assumption is that other aspects that influence the dependent variable remain stable. In particular, the development environment must be stable. Accurate model prediction with empirical models must be based on sufficient historical data which has been measured *consistently*.

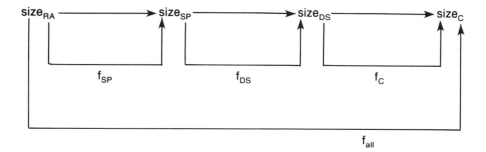

Figure 12.9 Phase-Based Size Models.

12.4.2.2. *Complexity*

Besides size, complexity and its resulting code also influences what a programming project will cost to develop and maintain. Once the software exists, complexity is a major determinant of maintainability, testability, and reliability. Complexity metrics are even more plentiful than size metrics ([Bela79], [Bela81], [Beny79], [Chap79], [Curt79], [Curt81], [Harr82], [Mcca76], [Stor79]). Before choosing one of them, one should first ask "complexity of what?" The major types of complexity metrics measure the following:

▶ **Functional complexity.** This measures control flow complexity via characteristics of paths in the code, nesting levels of statements, and the density of decisions.

▶ **Data complexity.** Here we measure the complexity of data that are local to a module, but also the complexity of the interfaces ([Basi75], [Chap79]). The simplest such measure would be to count local and shared data in a module.

▶ **Overall complexity.** Composite metrics include [Ovie80] and Halstead's Software Science difficulty measure ([Hals77]). It is given by

$$D = (n_1/2)(N_2/n_2)$$

Whether one uses a measure of functional or data complexity or a composite depends on the intended use of the metric and whether the software to be measured is data or function oriented. If it is not clearly more function or more data oriented, a combination metric should be used. However, the combination metrics are either more complex to apply, or, in the case of Halstead's difficulty D, researchers have "little confidence in the application of this portion of software science to longer, more complicated programs" [Cont86].

Let us discuss some of the function-oriented complexity metrics. The simplest is probably to count the decision frequency as

$$DF = \frac{number\ of\ decisions}{size}$$

Another functional complexity metric that has been very popular because it is simple and easily automatable is McCabe's cyclomatic complexity ([Mcca76]). It represents a module as a directed graph, similar to the structure-based unit testing strategies. Cyclomatic complexity is then defined as

$$v = edges - nodes + 2.$$

An alternate definition is

$$v = number\ of\ predicates\ +\ 1.$$

While cyclomatic complexity was originally defined for measuring the complexity of code, it can be used for measuring complexity of earlier phase deliverables, provided one can represent them as a directed graph. Specifically, the connectedness of the requirements diagram and the state transition diagram of the specification phase could be evaluated in an analogous fashion (using the definition based on edges and nodes). A measure for design complexity specifically related to the degree of modularization is the combined measure of functional cohesiveness and interface complexity (cf. design chapter).

Most complexity metrics only measure one aspect of complexity. The specification complexity measure in Table 12.6, for example, addresses the complexity of the state transitions but not the input or output. Complexity measures for module interface complexity at the code level such as Basili's segment/global usage pair or Chapin's Q measure ([Chap79]) are relatively complicated, which may have contributed to their limited use.

Table 12.6 Complexity metrics.

Phase	Metric
RA	Connectedness of requirements diagram
SP	Cyclomatic number for state transition diagram
DS	Functional cohesiveness and interface complexity
C	Cyclomatic number
C	DF
C	Difficulty D
C	Segment/global use pair [Basi75]

The degree of coupling (listed as a design complexity metric in Table 12.6) has been shown to correlate with the number of errors in a program [Troy81]. The complexity metrics that use path characteristics or control flow as indicators for the inherent complexity of a program also correlate with reliability, specifically with the number of errors found and the time to find errors. A last complexity metric that uses the graph representation of a program to measure its complexity is the knot count [Wood79]. This metric counts the number of edges that cross each other in a planar representation of the program graph.

12.4.2.3. Summary

There is a wealth of size and complexity metrics. Both are important contributors to other software qualities and to process metrics. We can use size and complexity metrics to

▶ measure software size and complexity as independent variables and use them to assess other dependent qualities, such as reliability, maintainability, or design quality; and

▶ estimate size and complexity and use the estimates to predict cost, time, schedule, or the size and complexity of later phase deliverables.

Size and complexity are lowest level software attributes and are often used as independent variables for a model. They are measurable directly on a work-product, be it requirements diagram, specifications, design, or code. They do not require the execution of code, only a static analysis. They are usable in an early phase to predict size, and other quantities of interest for later phases.

Problems and Questions

1. Run the acceptance test for PAS (TAP). Determine software quality by measuring whether all quality requirements are met. Normalize the count of errors by the size of PAS (TAP). What is the measured failure intensity (i.e., errors per unit of size)? Use several size measures. Do they give the same ranking of quality for two pieces of software? Which size measure do you prefer? Why?

2. What is the testing coverage for the acceptance test of PAS and TAP?

3. Determine the complexity of at least four programs of your choice using different complexity metrics. Rank the programs in order of decreasing complexity for each metric. Does this ranking stay the same when different measures are used? How about rankings according to size? Which of the metrics seem most meaningful when the programs are not written in the same language? Why?

4. What would you have to change in PAS to be able to determine some of the size and complexity metrics for programs that are given in Tables 12.4 and 12.5? Rank the implementation difficulty for the various size and complexity metrics. Which do you consider most useful? Why?

5. Use a statistical technique to determine correlation between the similarity index of PAS and the following complexity metrics:

▶ DF,

▶ difficulty, and

▶ cyclomatic number.

Given that the similarity index uses metrics of both function (operators) and data (operands), which do you expect to do better? Why? Which statistical technique should you use? Are any of the complexity metrics related enough to similarity to warrant replacing the characteristic quadruple and the similarity index by a complexity measure and comparisons between them? Do you think that such a "simplification" is realistic? Why or why not?

6.   Set up a procedure whereby you count development size at each phase of the software development life cycle for a series of development projects. Then determine a model that lets you estimate the size of any deliverable of a subsequent phase based on previous size as in Figure 12.9. Which of the model classes (linear, power function, exponential) work best? How does that relate to the metrics suggested in Chapter 4 to evaluate complexity of development?

12.5. Evaluation and Decision Making

12.5.1. Formal Framework

This section presents a formal framework for evaluation and decision making. It explains how to use metrics for the quantification of objectives and achievement levels. This method may also be used to develop standards. Chapter 16 will apply this formal framework to establish quantifiable guidelines for software development and show how to use them to track progress.

The framework itself is very general. It is applicable when a situation needs to be evaluated, when objectives need to be traded off against each other, and when decisions are to be made. These decisions may involve a variety of alternatives and objectives. One may look for a feasible alternative, an optimal alternative, or one based on a required level of cost-effectiveness. Two areas that use this framework successfully are computer service evaluation and computer service selection ([Witt83], [Vonm82], [Vonm83]).

Any situation with enough criteria to make an evaluation nonobvious and complex is a candidate for formal evaluation. Human beings have been shown to be able to handle only a very limited number of evaluation criteria at a time. If this number is much higher than about five to nine, the human mind automatically simplifies by ignoring some of the criteria, and an evaluation based upon limited criteria will inevitably be biased.

A formal approach helps to control the complexity of the problem when there are many alternatives, many evaluation criteria, or no obvious choice. It will be easier to defend a decision. It will be more objective and more transparent and the impact of changes can be assessed better. The evaluation itself is conducive to improve communication between the people involved in the evaluation. People must formalize goals, assumptions, and preferences underlying the evaluation. An objective method based on valid and reliable metrics is also more likely to gain the support of others.

The following are component activities of evaluation and decision making:

1. **State the problem.** The goal of the evaluation is specified. This may be deciding which of a variety of possible software development projects to choose or which of a set of possible solutions to implement.

2. **Determine feasible alternatives.** Sometimes the alternatives are already given, but the issue of whether there are any other possible alternatives should be resolved. This could be the case when a set of potential software development projects is to be evaluated to choose the project that will further company goals the most. Another scenario might be that long-range objectives have been stated and a set of software development projects must be identified to further those objectives.

3. **Refine selection criteria.** The selection of alternatives was based on a match of project characteristics to objectives or selection criteria. For further evaluation and selection, those selection criteria need to be refined so that they better discriminate between the different alternatives. For example, one of the criteria may have been "increase in productivity." A crude measure of this criterion would be yes/no, and a fine one would answer "how much" or at least enable a ranking of the alternatives.

4. **Develop measures for them.** More precise evaluation and selection criteria require more precise metrics. This is a step that is crucial to the objectivity and ultimate success of the entire procedure. There may not be a ready-made applicable metric at hand. Some criteria are inherently qualitative and may require a new metric. Human factors are notoriously complicated to evaluate and measure. In order to find quality metrics, one may have to adapt methods from areas outside of computer science, e.g., management science and psychometrics. Computer science itself provides metrics in the areas of performance measurement and software metrics.

5. **Definition of measurements is only one step towards the measured result.** Measurement tools are also needed. This is similar to the difference between defining a distance metric "inches" and a measurement tool "ruler." One has to consider how measurement will be taken. Measurement experiments need to be designed. How often should be measured? When? How long? How much data is needed? What is to be done with them?

6. **Preference assessment defines the relative importance of the evaluation criteria with respect to each other.** It should be performed before any measure-

ment data are available so as not to bias the evaluation. Establishing preferences is necessary for trade-off analyses.

7. **Specify the decision rules.**   Every evaluation has an objective. Examples include the selection of the most promising project, the selection of the best design for a software system, or establishing medium range goals for a DP department. Based on what needs to be decided there are a variety of decision-making rules which can be used to come to a decision ([Vonm82], [John77]). Usually, the type of decision making will influence which rule should be chosen and even how preference assessment and measurement should be performed.

8. **Make a decision.**   This step applies the rule to the data and performs a series of what if questions to explore how stable or volatile the decision is, what the impact of changes and errors in measurement data or preferences would be, etc.

From Evaluation Criteria to Factors

Evaluation criteria can mean anything from long-term objective to maintainability of the finished software product, such as return on investment or percentage of market share. Factors such as projected profitability and productivity of potential projects will appreciably influence related objectives. The steering committee identifies DP objectives for the department. For a software development effort, the user needs are identified during requirements analysis.

Levels of factors correspond to the levels in the organizational hierarchy and to the complexity of the development effort. There can be many factors. This complicates goal setting and progress tracking. Unless quality factors are chosen, an objective evaluation will not be possible because factors may be either unmeasurable or lead to biases.

Factors come in various categories. They may be mandatory or desirable. Mandatory means that unless a characteristic is present (sometimes to a specific degree), the alternative is infeasible and must be discarded. Desirable factors are those quality characteristics that one would like but is willing to trade-off. Those are actually the ones whose measurement will help to distinguish between alternatives.

Finally, factors fall into the following three categories. They can be cost or benefit related—all the factors dealing with cost and return in revenues. They can be functional. These factors relate to which functions need to be performed or are involved to achieve a set of objectives. The last category, performance, relates to the time frame within which the objective can be achieved.

Factors, since they are components of an overall need, are often not directly measurable. Rather, what is measured is an *attribute*. Metrics for attributes will come in a variety of units of measurement. Some are in dollars, others in time (such as response time), and others in the form of points on a scale or as percentages (availability of services). If these measures are to be combined into an overall measure of quality so that alternatives can be compared in their entirety, we must transform them into commensurable units.

All attribute levels are related to the value of an alternative. A function that relates attribute levels to their usefulness is called a *utility function*. Utility functions for individual attributes are called *local* utility functions, while those for overall factors are called *global*.

Utility levels for various attribute levels can be combined according to a *decision rule*. Decision rules fall into different categories according to their construction (formal or informal), according to the procedure they follow (one-step, multistep, with or without feedback), and according to the purpose of decision making (selecting a feasible, optimal, or suboptimal solution). The type of decision rule influences requirements for the input data, i.e., what type of measurement needs to be taken. It also influences the complexity of the entire evaluation and decision-making procedure, the degree of expertise required, as well as any computational requirements. The nature of the results, their reliability, and their flexibility all depend on the type of decision rule.

This detailed approach is not always necessary or desirable. When the evaluation and selection problem is simple enough or the risk of an incorrect decision is small, the less expensive route is preferable. Many correct decisions are made by intuition. Following a formal approach when it is beneficial does not mean that one's intuition is to be avoided. Rather, without a systematic procedure one is set up for a series of possible problems.

There are several problems with informal methods. The first is poor factor selection. This can mean not measuring the right thing, measuring it the wrong way, or not measuring something significant at all. Too often the factors that are hard to measure, like human factors, are ignored. This results in an overemphasis on cost and performance and other "technical" factors. Naturally, such results are biased and produce a very subjective and limited evaluation. Further compounding the problem are incommensurate data and inadequate levels of measurement. Another problem lies in using weak decision rules that are subjective and *ad hoc* and don't consider many factors realistically. Finally, sensitivities in the environment, in the factors themselves, and in the preferences are often not considered.

If any one of those problems can pose a significant risk to the objectives of the DP department or the company as a whole, then it is certainly worthwhile to follow a systematic approach.

There are, of course, situations when a quantitative evaluation is indicated, but upper management seems to disregard this, seemingly dictating "arbitrary" answers and overriding carefully developed quantitative suggestions. It is possible that the quantitative evaluation was only directed at one piece in the puzzle. The ultimate decision was made using outside information. This additional information may have been more important but was unavailable to the authors of the evaluation.

The problem may also be political. More discussion on such issues can be found in Section 13.5. For now, it is assumed that an objective evaluation of facts is a desirable goal.

The key to successful evaluation is to identify a set of good quality factors and to quantify as much as possible so as to minimize and localize subjectivity. Objective decision rules, tailored to the specific situation, should be used. And, to support storage and processing of data one might want to use a computerized tool. Such a tool is also helpful to ask quick what if questions and can hold historical data in a database so that an empirical knowledge base about the quality of evaluations and decision making can be built. This in itself will improve the process over time. Figure 12.10 illustrates the evaluation and decision making process.

12.5.2.   Example: Software Quality Evaluation

12.5.2.1.   Requirements

We will base software quality evaluation on functional and quality requirements. The evaluation is structured hierarchically according to Table 4.1. Figure 12.11 shows the quality tree that has been adapted from this requirements checklist. Other well-known software quality trees are [Boeh76B], [Mcca77], [Mcca79], [Mcca80].

Requirements provide important information for software quality evaluation:

▶ Which qualitites are important for the current evaluation effort? This information is used to prune the tree of those quality factors or attributes that are irrelevant to the evaluation. If, for example, security is not an issue, one would delete that part of the tree. If there are several lower level attributes to a higher level quality factor, but only some of them apply (as in the case of lifetime expectations), one should also remove those that are not currently important. Most often the evaluation tree is much smaller than the one of Figure 12.11.

▶ For each quality factor, there should be a measurable statement of quality expectations. For example, if response time has to be under 20 seconds, that constitutes the standard against which to measure. In this particular instance, assume that a response time of 25 seconds was measured. It is compared to the desired standard of 20 seconds as follows:

$$(25\text{-}20)/20 = 25\% \text{ off.}$$

This is a 75% compliance. However, things do not always work out this easily, nor need it be clear just how useful a 75% compliance record is. It can at least be stated whether or not requirements have been fulfilled. Sometimes, as in the response time example, one can even determine the degree of compliance.

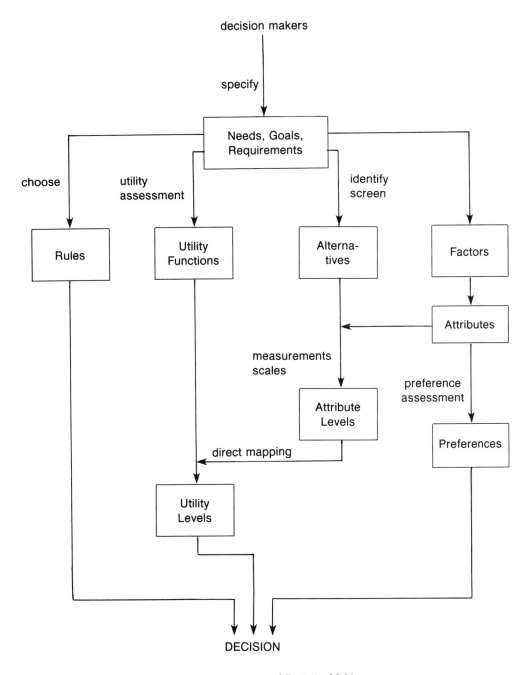

Figure 12.10 Evaluation and Decision Making.

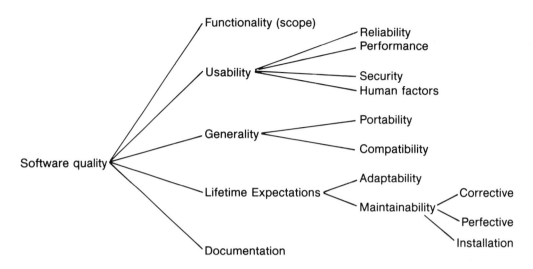

Figure 12.11 Software Quality Dimensions.

▶ There should be an indication of which requirements are more important than others to establish preferences. Requirements are used to analyze project feasibility and therefore have to indicate possible trade-off areas. It may, for example, be more important for a real-time system to restrict development to a set of core functions, rather than have a wider range of functionality and not meet performance requirements. For software quality evaluation, the corresponding problem is to qualify the comparative worth of a quality factor as it contributes to overall software quality. It may be more important to meet reliability requirements than to satisfy performance requirements.

▶ An indication of how much each quality level is worth should exist. Percentage of compliance is an indication of the relative worth of a quality dimension. An example would be making the performance requirement 80% of the time. Achieving 80% of the best possible value translates into 100% compliance. How much does that actually contribute to overall software quality? Worth or contribution to quality in an area may not be the same as degree of compliance. A degree of compliance of 20% or less may actually represent zero value to the user. On the other end of the spectrum anything higher than the standard may just be "icing on the cake"—in this case exceeding requirements does not further increase the quality value of the software.

▶ An indication of how to perform trade-offs between different quality dimensions makes it possible to compare measures in different quality areas. One might have to make a decision whether it is better to have faster response time or a higher level of security or more security versus a higher level of functionality. Decision rules (which should be based on statements in the requirements) should help to make such decisions. Another application of decision rules concerns the combined worth of different quality areas. Is there a willingness to trade off measurements in different quality areas at all? Completely? Only partially? If quality values for one quality area are low, will that appreciably depress overall quality, no matter how good the software evaluates in other areas? Or can higher quality levels in other areas compensate for a low score? When comparing software products, one needs to know how to assess differences in quality.

12.5.2.2. *Failures as a Negative Measure of Quality*

One way to assess overall software quality is to count requirements violations for the software. The fewer violations of requirements (errors), the higher the quality of the software. This approach requires experimenting with the software by executing a representative set of test cases or a benchmark. Test cases represent the most probable use of the software (operational profile).

A failure occurs when the software violates any requirement. Failures are normalized by execution time. This reflects the attitude that if a program is used three times per month and fails twice, it is less reliable than one that is used 100 times per month and fails twice. Quality is proportional to how long software runs without failure.

With a systematic approach to developing requirements, one can specify failures by functional and qualitative requirements categories. Failure counts are grouped by category. Total failure count measures overall software quality. Based on values for each area of quality, one can establish a quality profile using actual quality levels versus objectives and plot software measures for each quality dimension to indicate graphically in which area any given software is strong or weak.

There are several assumptions and problems with this failure-based approach to software quality evaluation:

▶ We need precise requirements (as described in Chapters 3 and 4) to count errors reliably.

▶ While the number of errors is a specific undisputable metric, using it to evaluate overall software quality really just pushes the measurement problem backwards. The real issue becomes specifying in each quality dimension what an error is.

▶ An error measure tends to be better with large systems than with small programs because of the averaging effect.

▶ Counting errors is a negative quality measure, indicating the degree of lack of quality, instead of a positive one indicating the presence of quality. Because of this we cannot compare the quality of two programs that have an equal number of errors, even though one might be of higher quality than the other.

▶ How many errors are found during a benchmark and whether that is a valid indicator of software quality during its use depends on how the software is used. If different people use software differently, quality may differ for the same piece of software. Thus one cannot readily depend on having the same quality for two different customers, especially when different user types are possible.

▶ Counting errors does not include a measure of cost.

▶ Some errors may affect user-perceived quality more than others. It depends on which dimensions and levels of quality they consider more important. Thus we should perform a preference assessment.

▶ For maintenance purposes we may need to know how errors are distributed over all quality dimensions, e.g., whether most failures are functional or performance related or whether they mostly tend to be concentrated in particular functional areas or spread "all over."

When the number of errors found during a benchmark is a measure of quality, errors should be measured separately for each requirement category.

12.5.2.3. Factors and Metrics

We have seen that software quality evaluation usually requires more than counting errors. One must consider the relative importance of functional and quality areas and what the levels mean for overall software quality.

The first step is to define a measurement scale (metric) for each. We show metrics for each quality area. This is then used with preference assessment, value assignment, and a method for combining individual indicators of value to achieve a measure of overall worth. Quality metrics are refined to the factor level, and we will discuss each factor in turn. Scales are developed for each of the factors in the software quality tree of Figure 12.11.

Functionality

A failure-based measure of functionality encounters failures in three different categories:

▶ a function was not implemented at all (such as missing Schedule A for TAP or computing the similarity index in PAS);

Table 12.7 Functionality.

Factor	Attribute	Measure
Functionality	Missing	Number of failures
	Wrong	Number of failures
	Incomplete (scope)	Number of failures

▶ a function, when executed, produces the wrong result (TAP computes the wrong gross income, PAS fails to count certain types of operands); and

▶ a function is incomplete (PAS recognizes only a specific subset of PASCAL, not all of standard PASCAL; TAP fills in all required schedules but does not compute taxes itself and needs the user to look up the appropriate tax in the table).

Not all of these errors reduce the functionality of software equally. Therefore relative importance and preferences for errors in these areas will be established. This will be done against objectives in the requirements. The occurrence of failures depends very much on the set of benchmarks used to evaluate functionality. Some of the errors in the software may not be uncovered at all.

Reliability

Reliability requirements address the effect of system, software, and user failure or errors. The attributes contributing to reliability are system reliability, software reliability, and the effect of user errors. A three item ranking scale for failures in these three areas are minor failures, serious failures, and those that bring the system to a halt. In order to make this into a proper measurement scale, one needs to define minor, serious, and halt type errors in each reliability category. They can be defined either through the productivity delay they incur (in man-hours) or via the cost (in $). Another option is to use delay or cost directly and disregard the three types of errors completely. This provides a finer grain of measurement but is not always needed.

Table 12.8 Reliability—effect of failure.

Factor	Attribute	Measure
Reliability	System	(Minor, serious, halt)
	Software	Delay
	User	Cost

Whether to choose a three point ranking scale or a ratio scale via cost or delay due to failure, depends on the accuracy of measuring (how precisely can we measure or estimate delay and cost?) and how the measurements will be used. The choice of scale also depends on what is more important, delay or cost. One might have a two-dimensional attribute that requires containment of cost and delay simultaneously, in which case both need to be measured. The requirement may read, "In case of system or software failure, delay may not exceed one day, cost must be less than $100."

Similarly, minor, serious, and halt failures may be defined by giving ranges of values for delay and cost. While classifications into the three scale values may suffer from inaccurate measurements at the boundaries between minor, serious, and halt, if such situations are rare, one can expect rather reliable measurements.

A failure-based approach evaluates (lack of) quality by defining a measure to compare software against a standard. If the standard (set by requirements), is met, no loss of quality has occurred. If the standard is not reached, a failure has occurred and is counted. At the crux of this method lies the possibility of reliably determining the occurrence of a failure. This is done by measuring the quality level of an attribute directly, then deducing the occurrence of a failure by comparing the quality level to the associated standard. Since the last step repeats itself, we will henceforth only present the measures for quality levels of attributes.

Performance

Table 12.9 Performance.

Factor	Attribute	Measure
Performance	Response time	Seconds
	Turnaround time	Minutes
	Storage primary	Kbytes
	Storage secondary	Kbytes
	Data transmission	Bits per second (bps)

Not all the attributes listed for performance may apply. Therefore only the relevant ones should be selected. Some of the attributes that support quality performance present classic trade-off situations: faster execution time often requires more storage and vice versa. It is important to clearly state the relative importance of each performance attribute.

Portability

Portability can be measured via the effort it takes to port software from one machine to another. The actual metric would be to measure the amount of time it takes to do so (i.e.,

Table 12.10 Portability.

Factor	Attribute	Measure
Portability	Effort to port	Man month Amount of machine dependent code 1—fraction of modules affected

man-months). This, however, is only available after the software has been ported, and most often one would like to know how hard it will be to port the software beforehand. A metric needs to be found that will predict the desired measure, i.e., effort to port. One such indicator is the amount of machine-dependent code in LOC or KLOC. As long as it is measured consistently, it should be a pretty good indicator of portability. Note, however, that it is a "lumpy" one. No distinction is made of the number of places code may have to be changed in order to port the software. The more machine-dependent code is distributed throughout the system, the harder porting tends to be. One could use the number of interfaces between machine and higher software levels as another measure. Lastly, the higher the proportion of modules unaffected by porting software is, the more localized necessary changes will be. This simplifies porting. A measure of localization of porting effort is

$$1 - \frac{number\ of\ modules\ requiring\ portability\ work}{total\ number\ of\ modules}$$

Given sufficient data for a statistical analysis, both code-based metrics can be used to develop a model to predict porting effort. Care needs to be taken, however, when the software environment changes, even if it is only with regard to the experience of the staff. Then one may have to adjust for any changes.

Compatibility

Table 12.11 Compatibility.

Factor	Attribute	Measure
Compatibility	As is Effort to make it so	Fraction functionality new vs. old Man-hours Number of interfaces that need to be rewritten (size, complexity)

Software may be compatible with another piece of software, a whole collection of software, or with previous versions of the same software. This must be defined. It may be necessary to assess the degree of compatibility as the software is now, in which case a benchmark is run to see how well it does with that task, whether it has all the functionality required (it can be measured as in Table 12.7). Estimating the effort required to make it compatible is more involved. Ultimately, an effort measure (man-months) is needed. Similar to the portability model and the measures derived to drive it, one can develop a compatibility effort model as a function of the size and the complexity of the interfaces between the different software products or their usages. The number of interfaces, which indicate boundaries of compatibility, should be kept small during software development. This will make it easier to control that they in fact provide compatibility. And as the post facto evaluation measure shows, such software will also have good scores.

Adaptability

Adaptability is influenced by modularity and by the degree of data and function independence. During design, the design quality measures can serve as an indication of adaptability. During operation, the fraction of modules not requiring change when the software is adapted serves as a situation dependent measure of adaptability. Using this for software quality evaluation, a "benchmark" describes a set of potential adaptions and determines how the software behaves for them. On a requirements level, one could even set a standard against which the adaptability index will be measured.

Table 12.12 Adaptability.

Factor	Attribute	Measure
Adaptability	Modularity Data independence Function independence	cf. design measures
	Need to adapt	Fraction of modules not needing change

Instead of the need to adapt, one also could try to estimate the adaptation effort as a function of the measures in Table 12.12. As all these measures and their multiplicity show, finding measures for quality attributes is not difficult, but it may become difficult to keep the process under control. This was one of the reasons to prune the quality tree to the essentials and is why we must carefully examine all potential metrics to see whether they are actually indicative of the quality that is to be measured. They all, with no exception, represent a simplified view of actual quality—but there would be no need to refine to lower level attributes if it were possible to measure the higher ones directly.

Maintainability

Maintainability is influenced by many factors (cf. Chapter 11). We selected four attributes that influence the maintainability of a program. The first is a measure of cohesiveness of modules and coupling between modules. The second is a measure of characteristics within modules. The third uses the stability of the software in the past as an indicator of how hard it will be to keep the software operational. The last addresses the fact that as software and its documentation drift apart, maintenance becomes increasingly complicated.

Documentation quality in turn is not easily measured directly, as a previous attempt at defining a scale showed. The table lists three further attributes that contribute to documentation quality and for which measurement scales need to be defined. For all but the first attribute of documentation quality in Table 12.13, one could have used the previously suggested scale. But it did not include a measure of consistency. If that is not an issue (because it has been thoroughly checked and recently approved and there have been no changes), one can do without this dimension. In most maintenance situations, however, it is an important attribute to measure.

Table 12.13 Maintainability.

Factor	Attribute	Measure/next lower level
Maintainability	Modularity	cf. design measures
	Complexity	DF, cyclomatic number
	Error history	Failure/time
	Documentation quality	Consistency with code
		Completeness
		Readability

A comparison of the attributes for adaptability and maintainability shows clearly that some of them are related. In this case, one should determine whether and for which factor an attribute is the primary contributor and only measure it for that factor. In almost all instances, one important ingredient to quality is the complexity of the code. This is attested to by the fact that in some of the earlier studies, complexity correlated with number of errors and time to find errors.

12.5.2.4. Summary

The failure-based ranking method related the measured quality to the required quality level and counted a failure if the software was unable to reach it. As pointed out previously, this is a negative quality measure. All but the first quality measure (cf. Table 12.6) measure positive quality (what works instead of what does not). Which approach to choose depends on the situation. A failure-based quality measure has better discriminating power for evaluating lack of quality in software, while the other ones compare levels of positive quality beyond fulfilling requirements.

A structured method for evaluation is not just possible during the operational phase when the code actually exists. From the validation techniques described for the end of every phase, one can deduce similar quality trees and determine measures for them. Whether evaluation happens at the end of a development phase or during operation, three areas of evaluation emerge: quality, effort, and phase testing. Quality evaluation assesses the deliverable as is against its requirements. Characteristics of the deliverable (specifications, design, code) that are quantifiable by metrics can be used to develop and drive effort estimators. Phase models only predict quality and effort for the next phase, while life-cycle models predict operational software quality and total development cost. Lastly, guidelines and metrics were used to indicate the degree of testing and to measure when testing was completed.

Unfortunately, very few of the metrics used to measure quality on the user level are either directly measurable or easily predictable from metrics of earlier phase data. This requires the development of measurement scales and their statistical validation.

Measurement scales were determined for comparative evaluation and during development to assess quality and status and to predict the future. The first required using a benchmark of hypothetical software uses and proposed changes to determine quality in all important areas. Evaluation is after the fact. The second aims to predict what will happen in the future. One may or may not choose between alternative implementation options based on these predictions.

12.5.3. Measurement and Analysis

After scales have been developed or adapted for all attributes, a series of representative measurement experiments is designed, performed, and analyzed. That implies the definition of a set of representative situations that are to be measured, i.e., the benchmarks. For quality of documentation this requires defining the types of uses for the documentation and the kinds of questions typically being asked. Exhaustive measurement is often impractical due to the volume of data that would have to be measured. All collected measurement data needs to be analyzed. Sometimes means and variances or even distributions and confidence intervals need to be established. Since not all possible situations may have been actually measured, methods for estimating and forecasting are used to model unmeasured behavior. Such models are often constructed using measured data as a starting point. In simpler situations where the evaluation of a small set of situations is all that is required, no elaborate statistical analysis of data may be necessary.

Measurement and analysis can incur various kinds of errors that will perturb and falsify the results. The first source of errors lies in inadequate measurement tools. If they measure too crudely, they lack the necessary ability to discriminate between differing alternatives. If they cannot filter out the effect of noise in the environment, measurement data is inaccurate.

The second possible error is statistical. Statements about mean values and variances and the like require certain sample sizes to obtain desirable degrees of confidence. Measurement is often an expensive activity. "How little can I measure yet still get results that are statistically meaningful?" Extrapolation based on measured data assumes that the future behavior will follow the same pattern that the measured data shows. If the behavior of the attribute does not follow that assumption, the estimated measures will be wrong.

The third possible error is due to changes in the environment that affect the measurement of an attribute. This is often the case when the metric is too distant, i.e., when the values can be influenced by changes other than changes in the attribute. An example would be to measure customer satisfaction by the number of retained accounts. This metric can be very misleading because it is influenced by economy, technical innovation, and a host of things other than whether the customer is satisfied with a software product.

The last source of error occurs when attributes that need measuring or the assumptions upon which metrics are based change. Any evaluation carries some risk. For more volatile situations, or when a significant amount of money is at stake, a risk analysis is necessary. A very superior, but highly risky project is sometimes shelved in favor of a software development project with less value and less risk. Depending on the amount of risk involved, contingency plans are formulated for various risk levels of alternatives. The overall value of an alternative thus often includes a risk assessment and an evaluation of the cost of a contingency plan. The next chapter will discuss these issues.

12.5.4. Utility Assessment

Measuring and analyzing all attributes for all alternatives results in a series of scores in various units of measurement. The next step will be to transform them into one standard unit of measurement, which will be the value of an attribute, service, or factor. Utility functions for a factor relate attribute levels to their corresponding values. There are two types of methods to estimate a utility curve, the *category method* and the *direct method*.

Category Method

The category method is used for qualitative attributes with a fixed number of attribute levels. By asking "How much is this particular attribute level worth?" or "What attribute level does it take to give you 90% of the maximum value?" a utility curve is estimated.

The first dimension of quality of documentation dealt with whether the document contains the information needed. The rating scale was "always, usually, often, sometimes, never." Assume that the utility scale is from 0 (not useful at all) to 1 (maximum usefulness). Table 12.14 shows two different utility functions that could be derived for this attribute.

Table 12.14 Category method.

| Language Scale | Quality of documentation/accessability, 0-1 utility scale | |
	Utility 1	Utility 2
Always	1.00	1.00
Usually	.75	.50
Often	.50	.25
Sometimes	.25	.12
Never	0.00	0.00

The second utility curve represents a much higher need for accessibility of information and consequently shows a much faster decline in value for lower levels of the attribute than the first. The first utility function is more gradual in its designation of values for the attribute levels. That can signify that the users of the documentation are more willing to search longer and still feel that the documentation is basically adequate.

Direct Method

Quantitative variables use the direct method for utility curve estimation. First, we define the value of *anchor points*, extreme values at the spectrum of attribute levels (the highest and the lowest attribute level, for example). After that, attribute levels in between are assigned their utility values. This happens in one of two ways. The *variable interval* method takes utility levels and assigns attribute levels to them. The *fixed interval* method takes attribute levels and finds corresponding utility levels. If the interval between points for which an attribute-utility relationship has been defined is halved at every step, *bisection* is used. It works for variable or fixed interval method.

Assume that a utility function for the factor "Functionality" needs to be developed. The attribute metric will be f, the number of failures in the benchmark that consists of r runs. The anchor points are $f = 0$ and $f = r$. No failures receive a utility of 1 ($u(0) = 1$). Failures in every run are assigned a utility of 0 ($u(r) = 0$). The fixed interval method determines the relationship between attribute levels and corresponding utility. If it is linear, then

$$u(f) = 1 - (f/r)$$

is an appropriate utility function. If the software does not have any worthwhile func-tionality once the failures exceed a value r_{min}, but utility is still proportional to f, the util-ity function shows a sharper decline and becomes zero for values of f exceeding this threshold. Its utility function is given by

$$u(f) = \begin{cases} 1 - (f/r_{min}), & f < r_{min} \\ 0 & \text{otherwise.} \end{cases}$$

In general, if there is a higher emphasis on low number of failures, there will be a sharper decline in utility as the number of failures grows. It may not decline to zero as in the second utility function, but reach a low, slowly decreasing value when the threshold is crossed. This could be modeled by an exponential utility function

$$u(f) = e^{-f}.$$

This function assumes a very large number of runs and models an exponential decline in value. Even with larger numbers of failures, there will still be some, albeit negligible, value left. Scaling factors can adjust for desired slope.

The *variable interval method* can be used when the attribute is a measure of compli-ance with objectives or standards. Assume a utility function for reliability is to be devel-oped (cf. Table 12.8). Many scoring methods in fact assume that there is a one-to-one relationship between compliance and utility. Then the degree of compliance *is* the util-ity function. This assumes a linear relationship between compliance and utility. But that is not always realistic.

Then the nature of the function may be determined through a user interview:

Q: If I want full value ($u(c) = 1$), what degree of compliance do I require at minimum?

A: At least 95%.

$\Rightarrow u(c) = 1$ for $c \geq .95$

Q: When is there no appreciable reliability left?

A: When more than 60% of the time reliability objectives are violated.

$\Rightarrow u(c) = 0$ for $c < .4$

Q: What do you consider a decent system in terms of how it reacts to failures?

A: When it complies with my reliability objectives at least two thirds of the time.

$\Rightarrow u(c) = .5$ for $c = .67$

Q: How about below? Is compliance about proportional to the value you attach to it?

A: Yes.

$\Rightarrow u(c) = (15/32)c - (3/16)$

Q: How about above the halfway mark?

A: It is a slow growth at first, and towards the latter part it increases very quickly.

$\Rightarrow$ we will use an exponential function for this part of the utility function.

The answers may not be as easily given as the ones here. The interviewers may have to do some explaining and paraphrase the user situation in user terms. Other potential interviewer questions are "What happens, if the first five test runs fail? How representative are they of actual software usage?"

The more often such types of runs would occur in practice, the more adversely it affects utility. It is usually a good strategy to present questions with the type and frequency of different system usages in mind. In this way one can establish the utility curve of Figure 12.12.

Other Types of Utility Assessment

The quality of the utility curve depends entirely on the quality of information given by the user on what certain attribute levels are worth. If this relationship between attribute levels and their value cannot be established, evaluators and decision makers tend to use the degree of compliance with standards or the fraction of achieved score versus maximum possible score as the utility function. This implies a linear relationship between attribute level and its value to the user and does not take into account the possibility of accelerated decrease in worth. Consequently computations using such linear utility functions may be way off the mark. Even if the assumption of linearity simplifies the problem, one should at least consider the possibility of nonlinear utilities before adding normalized scores (degree of compliance is a normalized score).

The examples demonstrated that utility curves come in a variety of shapes. They can be linear, concave, convex, S-shaped, bounded, or totally unique. They represent the specific values that the evaluator assigns to a particular attribute.

Linear curves signify that there is a steadily increasing value for an increasing attribute level. For an attribute such as productivity, this would mean that every additional

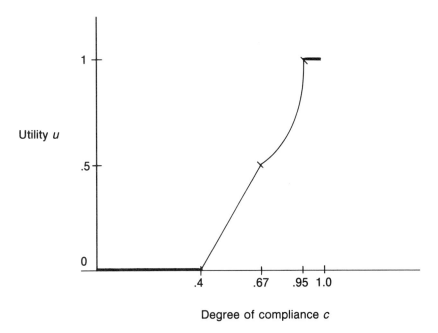

Figure 12.12 Utility Curve for Reliability.

line of code per time frame adds the same increment of value, whether it is the 100th or 1000th line of code per time frame. It is easy to see that not all attributes will have a constant incremental utility.

There are situations that can best be described by "the more I get, the more I want." A proper utility curve for such a situation would have an increasing incremental utility. Convex curves have this property.

Other situations may see utility rise very sharply for the smaller attribute levels, but after a target level is reached, higher attribute levels are not worth more. Many performance objectives (e.g., response time) tend to fall into this category. This calls for concave functions.

Still other situations require attribute levels to be within a given range to be useful, and if they are, they are at their maximum utility. These utility functions are block-shaped. An example would be evaluating the desirability of different paging rates in a virtual memory system. Utilization objectives suggest a minimum paging rate, while response time objectives will limit paging rates to an upper useful bound.

Block-shaped utility curves are rarely found when evaluating software. More frequent are those that represent a step from no value at all ($u = 0$) to full value ($u = 1$) from a given threshold onwards. S-shaped utility curves are generalizations of these threshold functions. They model situations where the value of an attribute is low and improves very gradually up to a point where utility rises sharply. After a while it reaches a plateau and utility increases level off again.

Another "generalized threshold" curve can be deduced through priority rankings for degrees of quality and functionality during the requirements stage. Anything below "absolutely necessary" would have a utility of 0, "important" would rise gradually to a utility level of 1, and adding optional features will not increase utility any further. Figure 12.13 shows these various utility curves. They are general utility curves, and actual utility functions would have to be tailored to the particular demands and objectives of the situation.

12.5.5. Preference Assessment

At this point all measurements have been transformed into commensurable units of value. Before combining all values we consider the relative importance of factors. This is done through *preference assessment*. Although methods of preference assessment are

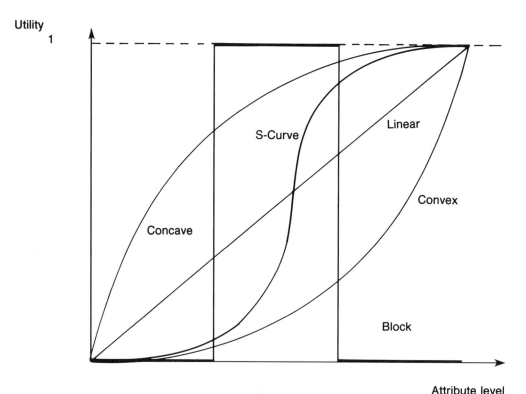

Figure 12.13 Sample Utility Curves.

explained after measurement techniques, preference assessment should be performed before or independently of them so as not to be biased by measurement results. The type of preference assessment done will influence what kinds of decision rules can be used for the final comparison between alternatives.

No Preference Assessment

While scoring models may not say so, they often are based on no preference assessment at all. No preference assessment implicitly assumes that all factors are of equal importance. Although it simplifies the evaluation procedure it can be very unrealistic.

Partial Preference Assessment

Partial preference assessment defines a rank ordering of the factors. It is used with an ordinal level of measurement. Scores or utility values cannot be combined with each other in any way. This limits the applicable decision making methods.

One could decide that for a given software, the quality factors functionality, compatibility, reliability, and maintainability are ranked as follows

$$functionality > reliability > maintainability > compatibility.$$

Full Preference Assessment

Full preference assessment assigns weights to all factors, which represent the relative importance of a factor. Full preference assessment is only possible with at least an interval level of measurement.

One could refine the ranking in the partial preference assessment to read, "functionality is twice as important as any of the others. The other quality factors have equal importance."

This translates into the following weights:

$$
\begin{aligned}
w_f &= 2/5 && \text{(functionality)} \\
w_r &= 1/5 && \text{(reliability)} \\
w_m &= 1/5 && \text{(maintainability)} \\
w_c &= 1/5 && \text{(compatibility)}
\end{aligned}
$$

In a full preference assessment, weights can be assigned in two different ways, client explicated or observer derived.

In the *client explicated* method, weights are assigned to each hierarchy element (because of the stepwise refinement approach to attribute definition there will be a hierarchy of factors. The leaves of the tree are the attributes). These weights are then normalized. One could also call this the "parts approach." The method works in several steps. To focus the evaluators' attention on the most important factors or attributes, they must be ranked. The highest ranking attribute receives a score of 100. All others are assigned values relative to the most important. The next step is to compare attribute weights on a pair-wise basis to make sure the weights are assigned in a plausible manner. As [Witt83] points out, such a pair-wise comparison can be very cumbersome unless the factors are organized into a hierarchy. Then only those factors that are on the same level in the same subtree need to be compared. That reduces the number of comparisons drastically. The last step is to normalize all the weights.

The other approach to preference assessment is the *observer derived* method. It is based upon multiple regression or analysis of variance. Attribute preferences are derived indirectly. The latter is preferable when the preferences of past decisions are supposed to be guiding future ones or when the preferences of a significant number of people (a large user base, for example) should go into determining preference weights.

Figure 12.11 gives a hierarchy of software quality factors. Weights are assigned according to the method suggested in [Witt83]. The first step is to determine relative preference for the highest level factors. The relevant factors and their weights are assumed to be the same as in the previous example. How are weights on the next lower level developed? This depends on the definition of the attributes for these factors and on their number. Assuming the attribute definitions of Tables 12.6 to 12.12, we quantify relative importance for each attribute.

One may decide, for example, that for functionality, it is three times as important that present functions perform correctly than to have no missing functions (for details on these three dimensions of functionality see Table 12.7). Incomplete and missing functions carry the same weight. This gives the following weights:

Relative	Absolute (Scale out of 100, adjusted by $w_f = 2/5$)
1. Wrong 3	$(3/5)(2/5) = 24/100$
2. Missing 1	$(1/5)(2/5) = 8/100$
3. Incomplete 1	$(1/5)(2/5) = 8/100$

In order to define the actual weights, we need to know the node weight for functionality. w_f was 2/5. It is used to normalize the weights.

Similarly, one may decide that the reliability of the software is the only important aspect to consider for the reliability factor. Then $w_{r_2} = 20/100$, $w_{r_1} = w_{r_3} = 0$.

Assume that the maintainability attributes complexity and documentation quality relate 3:1, and compatibility's only important aspect is "as is" compatibility. Figure 12.14 gives the software quality evaluation tree for all relevant factors, annotated by preference weights.

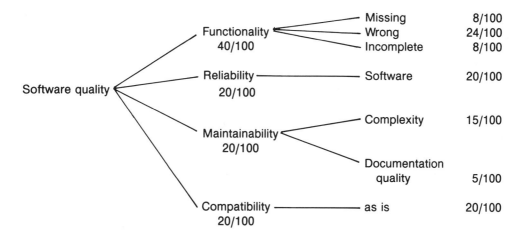

Figure 12.14 Full Preference Assessment.

Weights at the leaves are normalized. This preference assessment assumes that lack of complexity of the modules is three times more important than documentation quality. Modularity and error history are not considered important for maintainability in this particular scenario. This can happen when there are few modules and no available error history because the software is new. The user is only interested in "as is" compatibility, not in making the software compatible.

12.5.6. Decision Rules

The last major step in the evaluation is to apply one of many possible decision rules. The choice of rule depends on the qualifications of the decision maker, the requirements of the situation, the type of preference assessment, and the level of measurement. For example, *ad hoc* decisions work fine when the situation is simple and rather obvious, when the decisionmaker is an expert, and when no formal justification for the decision is needed or wanted.

12.5.6.1 Lexicographic Ordering

Screening methods rely on partial preference assessment. Often they compare alternatives to a standard or a reference point. Anything that is worse than the reference point is rejected. Alternatives that are worse in all areas (dominance comparison) are also rejected. Alternatives that do not fulfill mandatory requirements are rejected. Factors are ranked according to their priorities, and this ranking is used to develop a lexicographic ordering of all alternatives. The highest alternative is chosen.

Assume that a set of proposed software development projects needs to be evaluated. The factors to be considered are given in Table 12.15 in order of importance with corresponding factor levels for the alternatives. Lexicographic ordering would eliminate A2 and A3 first, because the expected profit is not as high as for A1 and A4. In the next step, A1 would be rejected because it has the higher risk of the two remaining alternatives. One ends up with an alternative with low usability and longevity, compared to an alternative that would make 10% less profit but has much higher ratings in all other areas (A3).

Table 12.15   Lexicographic ordering.

Factors	A1	A2	A3	A4
1. Profitability	1Mio	.5Mio	.9Mio	1Mio
2. Risk	High	Low	Low	Med
3. Longevity	Low	High	High	Low
4. Usability	Med	High	High	Low

Lexicographic ordering is rather insensitive to trade-off situations. A more suitable method is needed if trade-offs need to be made. Most often one of a variety of scoring methods will be used.

12.5.6.2.   Scoring Methods

Scoring methods multiply scores (in this case utilities) with preference weights and combine them in various ways to an overall score for every alternative. The form of the scoring function simulates which trade-off one is willing to make.

Additive Scoring Model

In an *additive scoring* model, the preference weights are multiplied by their corresponding utilities and summed up and divided (normalized) by the sum of all the preference weights. Such a function allows a complete trade-off between its factors, especially when weights are close to equal. Obviously such a complete trade-off of qualities against each other is not always possible or desirable.

Table 12.16 shows three alternatives with an identical overall score. Two of them have low scores in one area, which they balance with a high score in another, while the third alternative is more even in its quality aspects. The scoring model gives all three the same score. One might say it is somewhat shortsighted. Additive scoring models are very popular, though.

Table 12.16 Additive scoring model.

Factor	Preference weight	Utilities A1	A2	A3
Portability	.3	.1	1.0	.5
Maintainability	.2	.8	1.0	1.0
Size	.1	.5	1.0	.9
Performance	.4	1.0	.1	.5
Total		.64	.64	.64

It has been suggested in [Cont86] to evaluate software quality based on Boehm et al.'s [Boeh76] software quality hierarchy. This hierarchy with its high level software characteristics and primitive attributes as leaves of the tree is larger than the one proposed in Chapter 4. It also suffers from the fact that a great many of the quality attributes are hard to quantify and that many of them are dependent. [Cont86] suggests determining measurement scales for every attribute. Each score is then normalized by its maximum attainable value. The result is a score between 0 and 1. It represents a utility. As pointed out before, such a utility assessment implies a linear relationship between attribute level (score) and utility. The slope is determined by the reciprocal of the maximum attainable score

$$u(score) = (1/max)\ score$$

for all attributes at leaf level.

The overall quality indicator is computed as

$$SQ = \sum_{i=1}^{n} w_i u_i(score_i) \quad with \quad \sum_{i=1}^{n} w_i = 1, \quad w_i \geq 0$$

where n is the number of leaves in the tree.

This chapter approached software quality evaluation differently:

▶ It introduced the concept of utility, which makes evaluation more flexible, user-oriented, and accurate than a normalized score can.

▶ It emphasized the fact that the tree can be pruned early so that not all aspects need to be evaluated, even if they aren't important. This corresponds to assigning a zero weight to a subtree, and thus effectively deleting it from the general tree. Pruning trees also had the advantage of reducing potentially dependent factors.

▶ It emphasized the importance of factor independence. A software quality evaluation is made less prone to bias by

   ▶ using a metric that applies to more than one attribute only once (for the most preferred, but with properly adjusted weights) and

   ▶ determing overlap statistically through correlation (cf. section 12.2) and subtracting the overlap effect from the score.

   While both are more work, they also provide higher accuracy.

▶ It emphasized the fact that utility in different factor areas *cannot* always be traded off against each other completely, because the situation may be such that quality scores are needed in several factor areas simultaneously, if software quality is to be high.

Additive scoring models, such as the one mentioned in [Cont86], will not provide this flexibility of individual factors or overall value. This is not to say that additive scoring models are not valuable. They are merely specialized tools for situations with specific assumptions about factor and attribute utilities and about how to combine them into a measure of overall quality.

Another additive scoring model is Parikh's productivity metric ([Pari84B], [Pari82]). Starting with the assumption that productivity is a function of functionality, quality, and effort, he proceeds to suggest stating each in clear, explicit, reasonable objectives. This corresponds to the characteristics that were deemed necessary for requirements (cf. Chapter 4). Productivity factors in this model are quantity of production, number of errors uncovered during development and during the early part of software operational life, the quality of documentation, the number of compilations necessary (because of errors), performance characteristics (such as memory requirements and processing speed), resource constraints (schedule, budget), and the degree to which requirements have been met.

In the productivity model these factors are not arranged in a hierarchy. Therefore, all weights that are assigned during client explicated preference assessment need to be compared pair-wise. The lack of a hierarchy does not allow Witte's ([Witt83]) more parsimonious method. One could, however, rearrange some of the factors using the software quality tree of Figure 12.11 and the requirements checklist of Table 4.1 as a model. Some of the metrics of Tables 12.7 to 12.13 can also be accomodated.

When these factors are arranged in a hierarchy, one obtains Figure 12.15 for the productivity evaluation model. This will simplify the development of weights.

Some factors are missing or are at best lumpy. The missing ones are those mentioned in the software quality tree of Figure 12.11, but missing in Figure 12.15. The factor "Functionality" may be lumpy if we assume that it subsumes those factors (security, re-

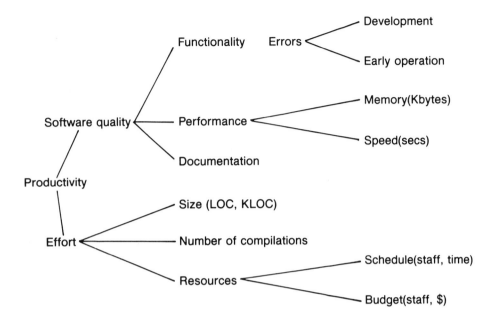

Figure 12.15 Hierarchy for Productivity Metrics.

liability, maintainability, and the like). The issue of errors comes up again, just as it did
in the error-based approach to modeling software quality.

This productivity evaluation technique, once again, needs clear instructions on how
to identify errors. They are characterized by unmet requirements. Performance and
documentation requirements are handled separately. This implies a sliding measurement scale for their quality as opposed to the binary error/no error measurement that
counting errors implies. All evaluations for factors are done in factor specific metrics.
The evaluation is done *post facto*, against a quantified statement of project goals. Each
attribute or factor is annotated with a "best possible" score. These best scores are used
to normalize attained scores for all attributes and factors. This way, the degree of
achievement is computed as a quantity between 0 and 1. Thus, once more, degree of
achievement in terms of normalized scores represents a linear utility function. Normalized scores are combined with their respective weights additively for the overall measure of productivity. The goal is to get the overall productivity measure as close to 1 as
possible.

The advantages of this additive scoring model of productivity evaluation are that

▶ it is requirements driven,

▶ it states clear goals and evaluation criteria,

▶ it provides an easy computation of the productivity index, and

▶ includes quality as an important contributing factor to effective lifetime productivity, in addition to the size of the developed software and the effort expended to develop it. This is important since the traditional productivity measure of

$$P = \frac{volume\ produced}{time}$$

is too lumpy. Volume produced should really read "volume produced at acceptable quality level." For software development it is nonobvious how quality (or the lack thereof) affects volume of code produced. Therefore it makes sense to separate these factors as Parikh does.

The disadvantages of Parikh's productivity model are as follows:

▶ no definition of what an error is makes this a very lumpy and potentially inaccurate measure;

▶ linear utility functions based on degree of goal achievement do not always reflect reality;

▶ complete trade-off between factors is not always an accurate evaluation strategy; and

▶ the linearized factor approach (all factors at same level) makes full preference assessment hard, because it requires pair-wise comparison of all weights. The 9 factors in the model require 36 such comparisons. The hierarchical approach only needs 10.

With the techniques presented in this chapter, the model can be modified to deal with every one of these potential disadvantages. This involves

▶ arranging factors in a hierarchy,

▶ testing the assumption of linearity of the utility functions,

▶ taking advantage of more parsimonious preference assessment, and

▶ testing the assumption of complete trade-off between factors.

Based on the demands of a specific development situation, the original model may or may not be immediately applicable. Where it isn't, it can be modified to suit.

Multiplicative Scoring Model

There are evaluation and decision making problems when some factors cannot be traded off against each other or when a set of factors is required to have a certain level of value; otherwise the alternative as a whole decreases in value. This type of situation calls for a *multiplicative scoring model*. When combining individual factor and attribute worth and preferences, utilities now show their preference weights as exponents and the weighted utilities are multiplied with each other. The resulting product is normalized using the inverse sum of the preference weights as exponent for the entire expression.

$$U = \left(\prod_{i=1}^{n} u_i^{w_i} \right)^{1/\left(\sum_{i=1}^{n} w_i \right)}$$

In case of normalized preference weights, the sum is 1, which simplifies computation. This type of formula is very sensitive to changes in individual utilities. A single low utility can decrease the value for the entire alternative.

Table 12.17 shows the results for the multiplicative scoring model using the same data as the additive scoring model in Table 12.15.

Table 12.17 Multiplicative scoring model.

Factor	Preference weight	Utilities		
		A1	A2	A3
Portability	.3	.1	1.0	.5
Maintainability	.2	.8	1.0	1.0
Size	.1	.5	1.0	.9
Performance	.4	1.0	.1	.5
Total		.45	.40	.61

The multiplicative model penalizes the low scores of alternatives A1 and A2 much more than the previous additive one. It gives preference to alternative A3 by a rather wide margin, because A3 does not have any single low score.

In general, multiplicative scoring models work very well when it is possible to point out alternatives where an extremely low score somewhere renders the alternative significantly less desirable. This ability to make such low scores visible diminishes as the utilities increase. That means, in essence, that if no extremely low scores are to be expected, an additive model might work just as well and would be faster because of the simpler operations involved.

In a situation where objectives are such that any decrease in a factor will appreciably decrease overall software quality, no matter how high the utility of other factors is, one should use a multiplicative model. It says in essence, "I'm not very willing to compromise on any quality area by trading it off against another. I want *all* factors to be of high quality. Otherwise I don't consider the software as high quality." With n leaves in the software quality tree, one substitutes

$$SQ = \prod_{i=1}^{n} u_i^{w_i} \qquad \text{(multiplicative model)}$$

for

$$SQ = \sum_{i=1}^{n} w_i u_i \qquad \text{(additive model)}.$$

The normalization factor $\Sigma \, w_i$ was eliminated, since it will be equal to 1 for normalized weights anyway.

The effect of rapid decline for multiplicative models when individual utility levels decline becomes more pronounced as the number of factors increases. A multiplicative model has higher discriminating power between several uneven alternatives and when individual utility levels are not very high but some are close.

Multilinear Scoring Models

There are situations where some of the factors can be traded off against each other and others cannot. Then we should use a *multilinear* approach that reflects the factor dependencies in its multiplicative part and complete trade-off in its additive part. Usually the multiplicative part consists of a sum of utility pairs that are multiplied with each other and with a combined preference weight for the pair-wise occurrence of the factors. This requires establishing pair-wise preference weights. It is more common with observer derived preferences, since they are based on statistical analyses and can determine such dependencies numerically. Independent factors are simply multiplied by their preference weights. Such a rule is also called *hybrid* because it combines multiplicative and additive models.

12.5.6.3.   *Summary of Models*

Table 12.18 shows example formulas for all three types of scoring models.

The advantage to using one of the scoring models is that it becomes very easy to ask a whole series of "what if" questions, especially when using a programmable pocket calcu-

Table 12.18 Scoring rules.

Type	Scoring formula
Additive	$\left(\sum\limits_{k=1}^{n} P_k U_k\right) \Big/ \left(\sum\limits_{k=1}^{n} P_k\right)$
Multiplicative	$\left(\prod\limits_{k=1}^{n} U_k{}^{P_k}\right)^{1/\left(\sum\limits_{k=1}^{n} P_k\right)}$
Multilinear	$\sum\limits_{k} P_k U_K + \sum\limits_{jk} P_{jk} U_j U_k$

lator or a computer to do the computations. One can examine the effect of preference changes, of perceived value changes (i.e. utilities), and of sensitivities of the solution to changing attribute levels; one can examine the robustness of a decision with respect to all kinds of changes. A scoring rule for decision making is most advantageous when there is a multitude of alternatives and factors and a set of people involved in an evaluation exercise.

12.5.7. Value Profile

The biggest problem with scoring methods is one inherent to all methods that result in a final score: what does it mean? What do the differences between scores mean? A score is a summary statement about the value of an alternative. It can and should reflect adherence to a company standard for reaching a long range goal or describing software quality. In cases where not only the final score, but the individual utility levels or even factor levels are important, such as during software development, it should be augmented by an attribute or utility profile. This can be compared to the standard or target profile for the software development process or whatever else is to be analyzed. Profiles then should follow the basic shape of the standard. If they are generally higher, the standards have been exceeded; if they are lower, compliance is not quite achieved, but the distribution of effort is about right. A profile that looks vastly different, even though it complies with standards in individual areas, represents ill-directed efforts and should be a case for concern and redistribution of effort along the lines of the standard.

Figure 12.16 shows an example for a standard, and it shows profiles for several alternatives. Curve S is the standard, curves A1 and A2 represent efforts with proper distribution along the mandates of the standard, and A3 shows a situation that does not distribute its efforts optimally with respect to the standard. This is a type of pattern matching: one tries to keep the shape of the curve similar to the shape of the standard or objectives. Deviations are allowed as long as they follow the standard.

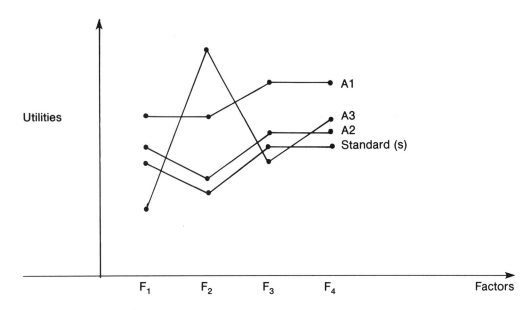

Figure 12.16 Value Profiles with Standard.

12.6. Summary

This chapter emphasized the importance and the feasibility of a formal approach to measurement and evaluation. Good management is impossible without enough quantitative information to make decisions, to plan, and to monitor that the plan is carried out. Metrics and measurement provide this quantitative information. This chapter discussed existing metrics and the development of new ones. Metric development cannot be complete without metric validation. Statistical techniques for assessing the quality of a metric were given. All sections showed how to apply the concepts to various aspects of software development. We placed particular importance on measuring software quality and the achievement of objectives.

The concepts presented in this chapter have been used in a variety of contexts, and in fact they can be used in any situation that is complex and nonobvious enough to warrant a formal approach to measurement and decision making. [Witt83] suggests formal decision-making procedures for computer service evaluation, and [Klei80] uses them for evaluation of computer systems. Rules for metric development apply not just for software metrics but also in an area of psychology called psychometrics [Alle79].

The choice of actual measurement methods is directed by the objective, rather than by one of the many known metrics. Thus, goal-oriented metrics are developed top down.

In this way, measures will be in tune with the user scenario, with its particular evaluation criteria, and with the way preferences can be assessed.

The evaluation and decision-making models all have their specific advantages and disadvantages. This essentially means that there is no one best method to use; rather, one must select the best option available for a given situation. A systematic approach to data collection, preference assessment, and decision making is often crucial to success. Lastly, some of the methods in this chapter lend themselves nicely to automation. This is particularly true for decision making methods. Automation has the following advantages:

▶ Sensitivity analysis is greatly simplified. The computer can reevaluate rather quickly whatever changes in attribute levels, utility functions, set of factors, evaluation, or decision rules one cares to make.

▶ Historical data can be kept to compare the accuracy of evaluations based on estimates (for example in project selection, feasibility studies, project planning) with *post facto* data. This enables an evaluation of the estimation process itself, provides feedback on its quality, and can be used for learning. Estimates that were way off the mark should be examined very carefully to find out what the wrong assumption was and which factors may not have been taken into account or not given proper emphasis. In this way the quality of estimation will increase over time.

▶ It is conceivable that a tool with a historical database can be used for teaching. This however goes beyond the scope of this book and would probably require adding expert system capability to represent a changing knowledge base and levels of sophistication.

The objective of this chapter was to provide enough knowledge about metrics, models, and their development to assist the reader in basic applications. An excellent book on software metrics and models is [Cont86]. [Alle79] contains useful information on scale development and evaluation. [Grad87] discusses how to set up a metrics department in an organization. [Hube74], [John77], [Klei80], [Vonm83], and [Witt83] describe a variety of evaluation and decision-making methods that include utility functions, the technique chosen in this chapter.

Problems and Questions

1. What software qualities do you know that are qualitative? Try to develop a measurement scale for at least two of them. Where do they fit into the software quality hierarchy of Figure 12.11?

2. Develop a program that allows you to investigate how overall quality indices change when additive or multiplicative models are used. You should be able to vary and compare what happens when you change

  a) the number of factors,

  b) value of utility levels,

  c) preference weights,

  d) number of alternatives, or

  e) decision-making rules (dominance, lexicographic ordering, additive, multiplicative)

3. What can additive and multiplicative scoring models do that lexicographic ordering cannot do?

4. Why and when should we apply formal evaluation and decision-making methods? Do you see any limitations to these methods? Can you give examples when such a formal approach is unnecessary or would not be able to provide us with reliable, correct answers?

▶ 13
Feasibility and Early Planning

13.1. Overview

This chapter guides the reader from long-term objectives, project selection, and feasibility study to a top-level project plan via successive steps of interpretation and refinement. It starts out (13.2) with issues relevant to project selection. The major premise is that project selection should be guided by the objectives that a company has set for itself, and projects should support achieving these objectives. This means that objectives have to be interpreted relevant to project selection. Section 13.2.2. gives an example of how to do that.

Management by metrics requires measurable goals to be set for all objectives. Section 13.2.3. discusses metrics for goal achievement at the corporate, department, and project level. Two case studies (13.2.4. and 13.2.5.) show how to select projects and how to define objectives and metrics for them. The first case study discusses the situation of a firm that develops software for PCs. The second case study deals with an in-house software development department that serves other parts of the company.

Once projects have been selected as supportive of company or department objectives, their feasibility is evaluated. Section 13.3. discusses all phases of a feasibility study. Section 13.3.1. defines the goals and major questions of the feasibility study. Section 13.3.2. discusses how to plan a feasibility study. Part of a feasibility study is to perform a requirements analysis. The management and decision-making aspects are discussed in Section 13.3.3. (detail on technical aspects is in Part I, Chapters 3 and 4).

The results of a requirements analysis may consist of several alternatives on how to proceed with a project. These have to be investigated further so that they can be ranked in the recommendation that the feasibility study team submits. This usually requires refinement of alternatives (13.3.4.).

Often information that could guide evaluations of feasibility and achievement of objectives is spotty or unavailable. When there are risks for a project due to incomplete information about how things could turn out, it is very important to assess them and to determine whether the degree of risk justifies embarking on a project. Section 13.4. discusses two types of risk: risk due to project factors (13.4.1.) and risk due to bias when evaluations are based on expert judgment (13.4.2.).

Scoring methods for risk assessment that help to reduce the amount of subjective bias and provide a quantitative, objective risk assessment procedure are suggested (13.4.3.). They can be paired with a statement of desirable or allowable risk. Since a company usually has a set of projects that are active or in the planning stage, this concept is extended to set goals for and to measure aggregate risk for all projects in the portfolio.

The risk assessment methods so far require some degree of knowledge about risk factors and their probable impact. Usually they also involve knowledge of the probabilities that certain desirable or undesirable events happen. If such information is unavailable, methods that evaluate desirability of projects under complete uncertainty need to be employed (13.4.4.).

When risk factors can be identified, steps may be taken to reduce risk. Section 13.4.5. discusses these steps and uses an example to illustrate risk reduction.

Not all risks and obstacles to feasibility are project factors. A very important issue that can jeopardize project success is resistance by others and the resulting political moves or game playing. A feasibility study should evaluate this aspect as well. Section 13.5. discusses reasons for resistance to projects and gives strategies to cope with it before, during, and after a project. Emphasis is given to negotiating commitment that makes a project feasible.

A feasibility study usually requires assessing the feasibility of possible approaches, which often means determining a top-level project plan. Section 13.6.1. discusses options for different degrees of phase overlap and the complexity and the risk involved in these options. It is followed by a checklist of planning activities for a project (13.6.2.). Section 13.6.3. describes a phased plan for a single release with phase overlap and optional prototyping activities. Considerations for planning multiple releases are discussed in Section 13.6.4.

The activities described in this chapter are geared towards illustrating work that happens early in a project's life, which often, in fact, determines whether there is to be a project at all. These activities need to ascertain technical feasibility, manageability, and political feasibility. Their assessment results in a preliminary plan (top-level project plan) that is refined before a project gets under way.

Managers should be familiar with the concepts in this chapter, since they should be able to recognize "winners" from "losers" and avoid committing resources to projects that do not stand a chance of supporting company or department objectives. Achieving such objectives defines success.

13.2. Project Selection

13.2.1. Long-term Objectives

Corporate goals and higher level management decisions direct project selection and priorities within a project portfolio. This software project portfolio reflects the medium and long range plans of an organization. Exactly what time frame is considered long-range depends on the dynamics and the stability of an organization. Long-range planning goes beyond any particular project or application; a five year planning cycle is considered typical. Usually it is related to what is called *critical success factors* [Rock82] or *key result areas* [Park80]. They affect the success of an organization as a whole. These areas or factors are often not stated in a way that directly mandates certain software development efforts. They reflect what is most important and critical for an organization; i.e., if it does well in these areas, the benefits to the organization will increase significantly, and, on the other hand, poor performance in an area recognized as critical is also damaging. Examples of key result areas are productivity, profitability, innovation, and market position.

Target achievement levels for the critical success factors state *long-term objectives*. From these long-term objectives, organizational policies are derived to further their achievement. Every part of an organization will have to align its policies with them. The data processing department and any department that does software development must select projects that fit with overall policies for the organization. This top-down approach in which goals are translated from the top down and refined and tailored to individual departments down to the employee level is called *management by objective*.

The implementation of such goals does not always proceed smoothly. There may be misunderstandings, new government regulations, a changed public perception, or counterimplementation [Keen81] from within the organization. Any of these forces of entropy can deflect objectives and modify or thwart their realization. This may take the form of games, played to preserve the status quo.

DP policies and the software development projects they generate may impact a variety of other departments. The support and reaction of those departments is often critical to the selection of successful projects. A supportive development staff will also contribute significantly to furthering the success of a project. For these two reasons the DP manager or department head will want to include in the goal setting team

▶ subordinate managers and

▶ representatives of any group affected by a decision.

The team interprets higher level goals for the DP department and sets specific goals for it. Often there is a variety of possible interpretations for a declared objective.

Where appropriate, the DP objectives also need to be analyzed for the impact they will have on the industry and environment and whether the goals can be expected to be achieved within a realistic time frame. Besides an assessment of the goals' impacts, it is critical that everyone knows the objectives. An explicit, official definition is important.

Multiple objectives tend to conflict with each other. There may be areas for trade-off. With constraints on resources, only the most important objectives may be realizable. Therefore objectives must be prioritized as to their relative importance (preference assessment). Usually we rank objectives.

We must measure not just whether objectives have been achieved, but the degree of quality of achievement as well. Metrics for the objectives must be defined. When objectives can be quantified with a sufficient degree of accuracy, it becomes possible to precisely specify success criteria in terms of target levels. Sometimes such targets are specified as ranges as opposed to a single value, or a target may be met when it reaches a specific quality level. This includes dates (by when does the objective have to be met), cost (what is the overall budget for the realization of the goals), and quantity or quality of achievement. It may be an event that has either occurred or not.

It is often possible to choose between a variety of possible metrics. Productivity for example can be measured as the complex measure discussed in Chapter 12, as released lines of code per employee, as machine utilization, or, in production environments, as added value per capita. Profitability, market position, and innovation, cited earlier as potential objectives, also lend themselves to a variety of potential metrics. The metric that will reflect the degree of target achievement the best should be selected, i.e., the most representative yet accurate metric.

The situation in the industry can change quickly, especially in the data processing field. Major long-term goals and objectives should be checked and revised every year. When drastic changes in the marketplace occur, one may have to plan proactively and be prepared to change course even more quickly.

13.2.2. Example: Productivity

This section uses a case study to explain how to interpret a productivity objective and how to define targets and metrics for it. The objective is to increase productivity by at least 20% for the next five years.

The key result area is productivity. The target is 20%. The realization time frame (deadline) is five years. The implications of this objective depend on the type of DP department. There are three possible interpretations.

1. **Service department.**   If it is a service department, as it often is, this can be a mandate to automate some manual procedures or to improve existing software systems to make other departments more productive. Such projects might be electronic mail, computerized wordprocessing, or an integrated accounting and financial system. These projects affect a number of user departments that have their current practices of doing business and often their own (partial) software support. Depending on the current state of operations, the change due to introducing new software may be drastic. To ensure cooperation and a successful new system, it is important to enter into a dialogue with all departments affected by the change and to win their approval, if not their active cooperation. If they will not accept the software product, its development will have been a waste of effort.

2. **DP department productivity.**   Increasing productivity may also mean increasing the DP department's own productivity. This can involve investigating modifications in software production methods and maintenance procedures. It can involve capacity planning and tuning activities, improving the performance characteristics of production software, building software development support tools, etc. All of these are projects or ongoing activities, which, once instituted, will change the way the DP department does business. Therefore, DP staff should be involved in deciding on and planning for those changes.

3. **Software development productivity.**   In an organization whose main line of business is the development (and maintenance) of software, increasing productivity can mean

▶ developing more products for sale in the same amount of time or

▶ reducing costs of development and maintenance of software.

Which of these two is chosen depends on the definition of productivity.

High Level Definition of Productivity

If productivity has been defined as

$$productivity = \frac{product\ revenue}{production\ cost},$$

then we can try either of the above approaches to increase productivity, provided that the products that we develop are actually capable of producing revenue. Note that "production cost" may include maintenance costs to keep products viable and customers satisfied.

This productivity metric is very high level. It is affected not only by the efficiency of the software developers but also by marketing and sales. A very good product with lousy promotion may score low with this metric. Often, this productivity measure is applied separately to marketing and sales (i.e., product revenue $) and to software production (i.e., production cost $). Since the performance of both parts of the organization contribute to its overall productivity, it makes sense to include them in a high level productivity indicator.

For the software development and maintenance group we must refine the productivity indicator to reflect the level of productivity by

▶ measuring aspects they can control and are responsible for, and

▶ considering aspects of productivity that relate directly to the higher level productivity measures.

Productivity Definition for Software Development

For software development and maintenance, productivity is often defined as

$$productivity = \frac{size \ of \ products}{time \ to \ develop \ them}.$$

Cost has become immaterial, and so have quality, marketability, and maintenance effort. This can become a liability.

Problems with Productivity Metrics

The "size over time" productivity metric is easily rigged and then loses its power for objective evaluation:

▶ The first problem is artificial extension of product size by abusing a size metric. A count of source lines of code can be enlarged by

    ▶ splitting statements across lines,

    ▶ selecting a longer version of an algorithm for implementation, and

    ▶ splitting a program into more modules because more procedure and function prologues and epilogues will be needed, thus enlarging total program size.

▶ The second is artificial reduction of development time. This is usually done by spending less time on a development activity or by measuring time improperly:

   ▶ While less time testing is very common, it will increase maintenance effort. It merely shifts effort from an activity for which time is measured, and thus controlled, to one where it isn't. Productivity is artificially inflated. Symptoms are an increasing percentage of maintenance effort and a decreasing (existing product) or never increasing (new product) customer base.

   ▶ Less time documenting has the same effect as above.

   ▶ QUAD implementation also promises more productivity and it delivers less of a product in the long run.

▶ Resources (money) are poured into a project to complete it in less time.
   While there is some trade-off between cost and time, it is limited. In some large-scale projects, the major cost factor is labor related. Failure to consider this fact promises very high costs with little savings in time.
   More experienced people do a better (and often faster and therefore more highly productive) job. They are also more expensive. We should not expect to be able to cut costs by using less experienced people—often it will not only take longer but cost more as well [Broo75].

This is not an inclusive list. The first two items shift effort (and thus time) from development to maintenance. Note that reusing code in more than one product (partial product duplication) is not considered a falsification of the size metric, since it is indeed a means to increase programmer productivity.

In addition to being vulnerable to artificial increase, productivity can also artificially *not* increase, due to inadequate time measurements. Let us assume that an organization introduced new software development techniques and tools to increase productivity. In order to quantify the hoped for increase in productivity they keep measuring staff working hours. Much to everybody's surprise, there is no decrease in time charged to the various software development project accounts. The new methods lose credibility and are no longer supported by management. What actually happened was that the software development staff, being considered professionals, had been working unpaid overtime. Therefore overtime hours had not been measured. Any increases in productivity that reflect a decrease in overtime hours will not show up in the time measurement. Thus development techniques that increased productivity by decreasing overtime got an undeserved bad evaluation.

Proper Use of Productivity Metrics

Does this mean that we cannot or should not use productivity measures, nor measure any other key result area because it can be abused? No. We need to provide standards and rules for measuring product and time objectively. We must require quality standards for the product at every major development milestone and time measurement standards for the time component of the productivity metric.

Align Projects with Higher Level Productivity Goals

Every interpretation of higher level goals for a specific project needs to be assessed for how it affects the organization and how much the project will contribute to those objectives.

Taking the two productivity metrics into account, the following questions must be answered for a project under consideration.

▶ Does it have a potential of high revenue? This is determined by product quality, timeliness, and promotion and sales. Marketing must estimate how marketable the software will be, what can be charged for it, and project sales volume. One must consider timeliness, whether the product will be long-lived or have a short span of profitability, whether there is enough sales support to meet demands, and what the impact of the competition will be. Software developers, on the other hand, must determine whether it is feasible to develop the product within constraints set by the market window and at a quality and cost that makes the software sellable.

▶ Will it cost too much? Every part of the production and distribution chain contributes their own cost figure. For software developers it is mainly the cost to develop the software and, if maintenance is to be provided, the cost to keep it operational. If we are providing software maintenance but do *not* include its cost in overall product cost, we rob ourselves of any way to quantify software maintenance cost and its effect on productivity. Considering that often 50% of the effort is spent in maintenance, this is a *very* sizable cost factor. Ignoring maintenance cost in the profitability calculations opens the door to shifting effort from development into maintenance, because its cost can no longer be controlled.

▶ Can the software be developed with a reasonable productivity ratio (size over time)? This ratio would vary as a function of problem complexity, support documents, training, application language, and the like. We can set objectives for different project classes and evaluate a project based on this type of information. Ideally, lower productivity indices should have higher revenue to make the effort worthwhile. Sometimes, however, competition and longer term goals lead us to develop a "loss leader," which does not give the return on investment that we set as an objective.

13.2.3. Medium-Range Planning

Action Plans

Once objectives, metrics, and targets have been defined, action plans for achieving them need to be developed. This will generate project ideas for software development. This is *medium-range planning*. Actual project ideas are identified, selected, and prioritized as to whether and when they are to be started during the planning period (usually three to five years). This requires quantification of costs and benefits. Besides generating ideas for new software development endeavors and choosing the feasible and most beneficial ones (aligned with company objectives), they need to be sequenced. Budget constraints are also considered in selection and sequencing. The result is a portfolio of projects that further the declared objectives of the DP department.

Project Selection

Project selection is done on several levels. Major project areas are identified by a long-range steering committee that can solicit specific project ideas from DP management, present or future users, and any departments affected by such a product or project. These project families are then analyzed to select the most reasonable ones and to establish budget targets for them. Promising ideas are then authorized for a feasibility analysis. The steering committee bases its selection on a variety of factors. These include how well the project is aligned with established DP policies and how much seems reasonable to spend on it (budget); this is related to expected benefits that may be realized as a return on investment or as achieving one of the key objectives with their associated metrics and target levels. The time span within which results must be realized is also important.

A critical issue is how manageable the project is. An unmanageable project poses a considerable risk because there is no assurance that the project can or will be successful. Important aspects contributing to manageability are as follows [Park80]:

▶ management know how (are there managers who know how to manage such a project),

▶ department morale (is the staff in the department willing to buy into this project),

▶ labor relations,

▶ involvement of sponsor (the more another organization is involved and has influence over a project, the less manageable it becomes),

- ► organizational structure, and

- ► technical expertise.

This list is not prioritized and very likely cannot be. No matter how favorable other manageability factors are, without adequate expertise software development is not likely to succeed. The manageability factors influence project risk. The steering committee may make estimates for all these factors, but because of the lack of detailed information, they very likely are more like "guess-timates." They often represent targets that allow the project to be accepted into the project portfolio until further information is obtained.

Feasibility Study

To find out more about how right or wrong those first estimates were, a *feasibility study* is commissioned. Since a feasibility study is a project in itself, it needs to be planned and must have clearly defined (measurable) objectives. People have specific responsibilities. They need all relevant background information and may require briefings and preparation. A schedule and criteria for the nature and quality of the deliverables must be established. The objective of a feasibility study is to affirm and document with greater accuracy the estimates that the steering team made, which led to the acceptance of the project into the project portfolio.

Let us now consider some examples how to set, measure, and evaluate long-term and medium-range objectives.

13.2.4. Case Study: PC Software Firm

A software firm caters to users of personal computers but specializes in a very narrow application area (such as tax preparation, accounting, stock market analysis, insurance underwriting, etc.). The company is relatively new, yet expanding. Due to the general software market situation, competition is likely to increase unless the company can continue to dominate the market. Key result areas are in order of priority:

1. **Return on assets (ROA).**   This is the highest priority because the company's income derives from its current software products. It must maintain market dominance to survive until it can develop and establish further software products. The measure of return on assets is $. One can use the current ROA as a base figure. More likely, it needs an increase to finance new ventures. Targets for the future are set in terms of % increase over the base ROA. ROA is a high level measure. It must be translated into an objective that software developers and maintainers can understand and use.

Quality of the current software is a key contributor to keeping the market. The company must satisfy user needs to keep the market share or to expand it. Since user needs tend to change (all example products mentioned above are very vulnerable to new regulations, laws and changing requirements, and time constraints are such that software needs to adjust quickly), measures must be established to quantify how well users' needs are met. Metrics can be used that were developed around the software quality hierarchy in the previous chapter. This includes developing a user needs profile; pruning the quality tree to reflect relevant user needs; establishing proper metrics, preferences, and utility functions or quality profiles; and determining user-driven objectives for the profitability of the company. This specifically covers software quality.

The quality of user support must also be measured. This includes aspects such as

▶ effectiveness of problem reports and change requests (and actions resulting from them) and

▶ effectiveness of training.

User satisfaction of software and support determines quality. The firm should institute a user feedback system, as described in Chapter 11, to measure user satisfaction. One can set objectives and determine goal achievement with regard to this quantified user feedback system. The objective could be responsiveness measured in mean time to react to and to solve the users' problems. One can set quantitative goals using this metric and compare actual measurements against it.

Other efforts that keep or even increase market share relate to the quality of marketing, sales, and product delivery. Since they do not impact the software developers, they will not be discussed here. These areas define their own effectiveness metric and set their own objectives.

2. **Innovation.** Because the firm's application area is so narrow, and dominating the market is tenuous, the firm needs to develop new software products to diversify its product line and to replace old or obsolete products. If tax laws for personal tax returns are radically simplified, as law makers have repeatedly tried to do, none of the personal tax software will be of much use. At best, it will need major overhaul; at worst, the firm needs a new product.

How should one measure degree of innovation? One can set a goal of x new products on the market with a projected revenue of y \$, or the target might be to provide software support for z new types of application areas.

While it is risky to "put all eggs into one basket" (i.e., to stay within the same application area but provide a more comprehensive line of software products), it may be a smart move if no other competitor can provide a comprehensive set of integrated software products (tools) to tackle all relevant application problems in a given area of strength (e.g., taxes). This can also be the most efficient use of existing expertise.

On the other hand, branching into new application areas can provide more room for future growth. Thus innovation should consider goals in both directions. One might specify for example that 40% of the software development effort should be directed towards covering existing application areas better through integrating tool sets that support a range of related user activities. Accounting and tax preparation are related, and keeping investment accounts and stock market services also are related. The actual mix of effort in new versus existing application areas depends on projections of ROA and product viability for new developments.

Integrating software aimed at related applications is an objective that will direct the selection of software projects. One can measure goal achievement based on expenditures ($ or time) and estimate it based on schedule and cost estimates.

Innovation may also have time constraints, such as "we need at least one new product or new feature to an existing product every six months." This is a short-term measure of innovation that is visible to the user. It will influence software development: small projects (less than six months duration) can still be developed in one effort, while those that take longer must be developed through iterative enhancement. This makes it easier to comply with the six months release objective, but it will also enable us to solicit user feedback for a release, which can help us to provide a better accepted and more useful product in future releases. Thus iterative enhancement and sequencing of features into successive releases help to attain higher levels of user-perceived software quality over time.

Setting objectives for the hypothetical software firm influenced not only project selection but also how software is developed.

3. **Staff development.**   The firm needs staff to support company growth. It needs the manpower and expertise to support software development in new areas.

One can set objectives in various ways. The lumpiest is probably the number of software developers employed by the firm. This can be refined in terms of experience. The firm needs experience in the current application area, in software and hardware. To diversify, it also needs expertise in the new application area(s), possibly in new hardware and software. One can quantify existing experience by

- ▶ average level of formal training (in years),

- ▶ work experience (in years), and

- ▶ breadth of work experience (number of dissimilar projects worked on, number of application areas for which software was developed in the past and which are relevant to the company).

Work experience also includes a measure of familiarity with hardware and/or software relevant to hardware and software the company is or expects to be using. One can set targets, e. g., how many or what percentage of the people are supposed to have what degree of expertise in using business-relevant hardware and software. An example might be familiarity with a range of personal computers, such as the IBM PC line of products, Apple's line of personal computers, or AT&T's 3B20's. On the software side we may need expertise in MSDOS, CPM, UNIX™, and application packages such as LOTUS 1-2-3, DBASE, SUPERCALC, etc.

When defining these metrics, consider that quantification in this area is very difficult and can be misleading. Certainly, experience is valuable, but one programmer's three years of experience may be worth more than another's ten. While brilliance is what one would really wish for, how many people are brilliant? Assessing company staff experience by its very nature looks at the overall picture, not at individual evaluations. This is why relatively lumpy measures like the ones suggested above are used. They work on the average. Averages are measures of central tendency, and deviations and people ranked at extreme ends of the measurement spectrum are not considered strongly. Therefore, individual (expert) judgment is essential. Quantitative assessment should *support* thoughtful analysis and decision making, not automate or replace it.

A firm may have all the expertise necessary, but it will not do much good if the company experiences high staff turnover. Users want stability, and effective software development needs stability, too. Chapter 15 discusses specific issues connected with high and low turnover.

The software firm example derived some specific objectives, project selection and implementation, and staff development guidelines from a few major determinants of viability and success. In all cases, reasoning proceeded from the higher level objective to the lower level one. Higher level means closer to overall organizational goals and needs.

13.2.5. Case Study: Software Development Department

The next example is a software development department that has been providing software to support several functions for designing automobiles (e.g., finite element stress analysis, simulation of aerodynamic properties, graphics design support, etc). The current user population is captive, in-house, and generally satisfied with each software design tool, but, having been developed with no particular plan, the tools are too disjoint to provide high user productivity. Software developer productivity could be higher—they are too busy "putting out fires"—and software quality is not good enough. This puts a cap on new development. The department identified three key long-term objectives:

1. Improve quality of software products. This can be understood as a user perceived quality and requires decreasing failure rate as well as providing a higher degree of design tool integration.

2. Improve market share. The software tools are not necessarily restricted to the current user group. Some can be used to design other things. An opportunity exists to

capture a significant market share, because no one else seems to have tools that are nearly as powerful as the software products the department has developed—if their quality can be sufficiently improved.

3. Improve profitability. This is an objective at the corporate level and one of the reasons for objectives 1 and 2.

4. Develop internal project and maintenance standards. This is a consequence of items 1 and 2. Expanding customer base and streamlining maintenance requires standards.

How should these objectives be quantified and how should their achievement be evaluated?

1. **Quality.**   One can use the number of user change requests as an indicator of quality. As the user base expands, the department may experience an increase in requests, which may not accurately reflect a decrease in quality. The average number of user requests per user site, or a similar indicator, is probably more useful. One can set targets and monitor against them. If a target has not been reached within a predetermined range, it is time for corrective action (e.g., stopping new development and enhancements, rigorous retesting and debugging of the system, restructuring, revision of documents to stop document drift, or roll-back to an earlier version as a contingency measure).

More detailed measures are software quality profiles or a software quality index as suggested in Chapter 12. Both provide a ratio level of measurement.

2. **Market share.**   The target measure could be the percentage of increase in the number of customers or users: 25%, 50%, 100%, etc. Or it could be to try to determine the size of the total possible market, determine what part of it the current user occupies, and then decide how much to increase it. This success indicator depends on software quality and support but also on developing a viable marketing and sales force. The example firm does not have one yet—the software has been an in-house product.

3. **Profitability.**   Profit is usually sales income minus costs. If profits are to be improved, one needs to increase sales or cut costs or both. One can measure total profit, but it needs to be normalized by accounting time span. If the goal is to increase profitability by 30% next year, then one has to compare profits from last year to profits this year and determine whether they increased by 30% during this time. Applied to the software development group, increasing profitability means

▶ providing a high quality product that can achieve a good price and attract customers and

▶ reducing development and maintenance costs by streamlining operations.

The first can be measured as quality with a user-oriented quality measure (objective 1). The second relates to the last objective.

4. **Internal project and maintenance standards.**   We need two metrics. The first measures the success of putting standards in place by certain dates. The second quantifies their efficiency once they exist. The date itself is a firm target. Quality of the project and maintenance standards can be evaluated with the methods discussed in Chapter 12. An evaluation of the efficiency of the standards requires comparing productivity before and after instituting the standards. This is important because it quantitatively justifies them and thus contributes to their acceptance. It also may show that they are not helpful and shouldn't be used or that they must be modified. Consider the caveat about staff time measurement mentioned earlier.

Measuring the efficiency of standards with a productivity metric is questionable. There are many other factors that influence productivity and can bias the result. This makes it very difficult, if not impossible, to justify the introduction of standards directly, unless the major change was to introduce new standards. This, however, is rarely the case.

Objectives and quantification of key result areas will drive project selection. They also influence the selection of specific methodology, techniques, or standards.

Problems and Questions

1.   Take a project on which you worked. State what you, to the best of your knowledge, think the long-range objectives of the department were. Organize them. You may or may not end up with a hierarchy. Break them down to a level fine enough (attribute) so that you can define measurements for them. When you encounter qualitative attributes, develop a scale according to the method described in the previous chapter. What is the level of measurement?

2.   Let's assume you wish to use the productivity metric that measures size over time for a software development group. The organization's productivity metric is defined as product revenue per accounting period. Which constraints, rules, or standards do you need so that the software development group's productivity metric is not easily rigged and constitutes a proper refinement of the organization's? What precisely can the software development group contribute to overall organization productivity, because the software development group has control over the factor? Which aspect(s) does it not control? (How) do they depend on each other?

Discuss specifically the use of quality metrics, development time, and resources measurement to support additional objectives and targets for the software development group.

3.   Your company sells, leases, and maintains a series of small to medium size computers, complete with operating system and utilities. A series of compilers, database man-

agement systems, software development support programs, and mathematical software run on the operating system. It has been well accepted with a sound customer base. As far as you know your company's main business objective is to

▶ keep costs low and

▶ keep the market share

Recently you have heard that they plan to develop new hardware to make the machines faster and to provide more primary and secondary storage capacity. Your experience tells you that this will mean modifications to the operating system. In light of this situation, how do you interpret the company objectives for the operating system group? State the objectives so that they can be quantified, and suggest metrics and targets.

13.3. Feasibility Study

13.3.1. Set Evaluation Framework

Feasibility studies are commissioned for projects that looked promising during the project selection process. They were selected because they support objectives. For further assurance that the expected benefits or compliance with corporate directives are actually achieved, more detailed information and more precise estimates are needed. The objective of a feasibility study is to find out whether a project is justified and which implementation approach is best. One can, in a sense, consider a feasibility study as a quality assurance or validation phase where previous actions are validated (i.e., project selection and setting of constraints and goals). Figure 13.1 shows how the feasibility study affects goals and project specifications.

Determine Project Goals

The first step in a feasibility study refines the evaluation criteria. The input for this evaluation project are the reasons for the feasibility study. Some of those reasons may make the project mandatory and the feasibility study then becomes involved in investigating and comparing various ways of implementing the project. Examples of such mandates are corporate directives, government regulations, and auditing requirements, or it may be that there is no reasonable alternative to the computer.

The feasibility study team must know the purpose of the project, i.e., the long-range plans that caused the project to be of interest in the first place. The team also needs information on similar projects or previous feasibility study results about related or similar projects. Combined with a quantitative evaluation, this will serve as a basis for estimates for the new project. It will show where the other projects failed in their feasibility study or give clues as to why management chose not to go ahead before. Looking at similar projects helps to determine which of the evaluation categories and their meas-

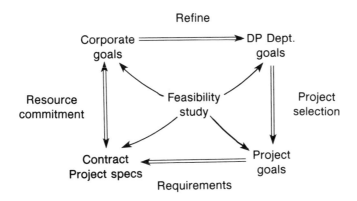

Figure 13.1 Feasibility Study as Quality Assurance.

urements provide relevant data for the current feasibility study. Of course, background information on the expected use of the software and its performance in all categories of goals needs to be known.

The goals are refined to the attribute level that reflects best and most objectively the performance of the software during its development and operation.

Let's take an example. The stated goal for a software development project is to complete it within a budget of $1.5 million dollars. The question for any alternative implementation is, "Can this alternative be implemented within this budget?" The refinement step is, "Which expenses contribute to overall development cost?"

One needs to know how project accounting is done, whether computer cost is part of the budget or a "free" service, and whether office supplies are included or considered fixed costs for the department and not part of the development budget. Other potentially fixed costs are secretarial services and library services. Then we decide on metrics and measurement methods for the attributes and the overall factor.

If profitability is a factor, it is necessary to find estimators for development cost, operations cost, and expected revenue. The questions are as follows:

▶ What are the costs we can incur during the software's lifetime?

▶ What influences these costs? and

▶ How do we measure and estimate them?

A variety of factors contribute to cost of operations: quality of the software, expected changes in user needs, etc. They relate to maintenance costs for corrective and perfective maintenance, which in turn, provides possible requirements for software reliability, modularity, portability, and possibly compatibility and size. Operations cost also includes the cost to run the software. This is influenced by its efficiency (performance indices such as CPU time, memory used, or whatever the charging algorithm on the target machines uses to compute charges).

Expected revenue depends on market share and the estimated number of clients. This is influenced by the quality of the software and relates to any of the functional and qualitative requirements discussed in Chapters 3 and 4. Examples include ease of use, response time and other performance requirements, reliability and accuracy of the computations, sophistication level of the functions, timeliness, perceived user need, etc.

One could try to measure (lack of) user satisfaction as percentage of users who cease leasing or buying the product. If the percentage rises, it may be for a variety of reasons that have nothing to do with the software itself: economy, stability of the company, quality of the salespeople, quality of the technical support staff, competition, pricing, etc. The measure is too distant.

The second problem are measures that do not distinguish between nonhomogeneous items. Measuring ease of use by the number of mistakes people make when using a piece of software does not distinguish the types of errors they make, nor the types of users (e.g. novice, intermediate, expert). Some users make errors on purpose to get the system to prompt them for parameters or command syntax they cannot remember. A system that invites the user to do that is user friendly in this particular area. All this is lumped together in the measure. While such a measure may be on target on the average, it can be way off for a particular project.

The degree of detail depends on the necessary accuracy of the estimates and the difficulty of forecasting factor levels. When higher level factors are refined, all possible refinements should be checked to see whether they are appropriate or necessary. Refinement is unnecessary when a factor can be measured directly. Sometimes one or two of the attributes or lower level factors suffice and the rest can be neglected, because they are not relevant.

Prioritize

Preference assessment is necessary because the final evaluation involves trade-off analyses. When compliance to project goals can be related to the compliance of higher level objectives, the project can be prioritized as to how much it will further them. The feasibility study team needs a precise description of the context and goals within which the software development effort is to be undertaken.

Derive Study Activities

Project goals drive the selection of study activities; these are primarily issues related to achieving these goals. The intent is to clarify open questions about whether the project can be developed within constraints and still achieve the goals stated.

Validate Evaluation Framework

This review checks whether the evaluation framework fits the goals and is detailed enough to permit planning. This is commonly done with an n + 1 − 1 review.

These steps establish the objectives of the study and determine the subjects to be covered. In measurement terminology, it determines what type of data is to be measured and how (for a summary of the phases within a feasibility study see Table 13.1).

Table 13.1 Phases of a feasibility study.

A. Evaluation Framework
1. DP Dept. goals => Project goals => Attributes — measurable
2. Prioritize — what/when/how/who
3. Derive study activities
4. Validate that evaluation framework fits with DP dept. goals and is detailed enough to enable planning — n + 1 − 1 review [Myer76]

B. Plan for Resources, Schedule of Feasibility Study
1. Schedule — Estimate time, delays, dependencies of activities.
2. Personnel requirements — Skills, preparation, #
3. Resources — Computer, library, travel, clerical support, etc.
4. Cost — Direct, indirect, shared
5. Constraints
6. Trade-off cost vs. usefulness — Value of information
(Approval by management)

C. Requirements Analysis
1. Functional/qualitative requirements — Present/projected (Chapter 3) performance, reliability, legal, etc. (Chapter 4)
2. Identification of alternatives — More than 1!
3. Development resources/schedule/cost — Per alternative
4. Operating resources/cost — Per alternative/present include maintenance
5. Risks/benefits/side effects — Per alternative/present
6. Evaluation and decision making according to stated measurable goals — Including measurement and ranking of alternatives

D. Refine Alternative(s)
1. Detail project activities and outline plan — Include conversion
2. Training and orientation of project personnel
3. Present results

13.3.2. Planning a Feasibility Study

A feasibility study is a project in itself. It is planned and controlled like any other project.

A project plan needs a schedule (*when*) and task assignments (*who*). To be able to answer when the feasibility study will be done and who will do it, the following information is necessary:

▶ skills and experience level required from the members of the feasibility study team,

▶ which activities can be done by whom,

▶ how long it will take them,

▶ what the dependencies between activities are, and

▶ how much flexibility exists for task assignment.

A feasibility study usually involves fact finding, research, and sometimes travel or additional learning. User interviews may be scheduled for proper requirements analysis, and cooperation must be negotiated. Results are condensed into a report or correlated with findings of other people on the team.

Major resources may be needed that range from access to facts (library, memos, user, reports with and without security restrictions, etc.) to building simulation or analytic models of aspects of the proposed solution. Sometimes "Quad" systems are implemented to assess how effective, reliable, user-friendly, etc. the proposed software is likely to be, or whether a key algorithm or novel approach will work. That can consume a considerable amount of resources (computer time, manpower). The user plays a significant role in the feasibility study. His help is needed to find out what the exact requirements are. We must consider the user and the activities he will be involved in when making a plan for the feasibility study.

A plan also needs a budget (*how much*). The budget includes cost of services needed, manpower, etc. based on identified activities and the time estimates for them. A good budget and realistic schedule depend on the accuracy of the work description. Therefore the mandate for the feasibility study should be as precise as possible. Specifically, it includes a description for the major research activities and the bounds of the study, i.e., what the feasibility study is about as well as what it is *not* about. For example, if the major question relates to the automation of accounting procedures in a medium size firm, the feasibility study does not necessarily extend to interface it with decision support for management. Or, if the performance of a family of algorithms is in question, data entry for software using these algorithms need not be. A precise definition of the bounds of the study simplifies planning because the problem is clearly defined. With vague boundaries, too much energy may be wasted investigating issues that are not important, and others may not receive the attention they deserve.

The feasibility study team must be made aware of any mandatory factors that pose absolute or tight relative constraints on the feasibility of an alternative. These constraints can be managerial, technical, or political. They encompass the impact of future plans as well as current or projected government regulations. A team investigating the feasibility of a student record-keeping system, for instance, may have to take into account regulations on draft for young men or requirements from the veteran's administration to monitor the progress of students they support. If some alternatives are risky or the project itself is high risk, the study team must know whether they must provide a contingency plan or an evaluation of possible fallback actions. It influences the amount of work of a feasibility study.

The feasibility study team may need access to privileged information. The degree of security clearance to be granted to members of the team can easily make the difference between a well-informed and an uninformed result. Are they to have access to certain physical areas of a plant? Of a piece of machinery? Of confidential designs or confidential policy information? Are they to keep certain information confidential? How is access to be granted? Most importantly, is time overhead involved? Can access be granted only at specific dates or times? If the team needs cooperation from other (user) departments, what kind of authority, if any, do they have? What kind of resources are available for the team? When and how long are they available? The term resources includes anything from office space, secretarial support, and transportation to computer time.

Lastly, the feasibility study plan must know about methods to be used during the study. This influences the needs for resources and time, and thus, both budget and schedule. Examples of such method guidance include

- ▶ inspecting similar systems,

- ▶ searching the literature,

- ▶ developing a simulator of a system to estimate performance and/or reliability, and

- ▶ modeling the proposed software to evaluate likely impact on current workload on the system and to determine whether there is enough capacity for additional work.

Some of the methods require more time and resources than others. They also yield different types of data with varying predictive accuracy. Method guidance implicitly states the desired accuracy of the study.

If it is not possible to come up with a good schedule or a good cost estimate for the feasibility study, it usually means that the mandate for it was too vague. Maybe department goals were not specific enough, or maybe the project goals were not sufficiently detailed to allow the definition of feasibility study activities.

If the activities remain too vague, the goals and objectives need to be clarified further. "Not knowing what to investigate" carries with it the danger of wrong conclusions and a useless feasibility report. In research projects it can be difficult to specify activities clearly enough to derive project plans. If this is the case, more time is needed to do enough research to assess feasibility of the project. How much time is often not clear, so [Park80] suggests to set a time frame arbitrarily. Actually it corresponds to the amount of money one is willing to spend on it. Due to the limited information and the feedback inherent in the study itself, the focus sometimes changes. Then budget and schedule need reevaluation. The resources planned for a feasibility study do not automatically stay the same when its focus changes. Any change requires formal approval.

The estimated cost of the feasibility study should be weighed against its usefulness and the reliability and accuracy of its predictions. A feasibility study tries to reduce the risk of failure by giving more information on the possibilities and assessing its cost. There is a trade-off between the value of the information provided by the feasibility study and its cost. On one end of the spectrum, one could try to implement the software system; then there is complete certainty how long it takes, how much it costs, what the functional and qualitative characteristics of the solution are, and whether project goals can be reached. On the other hand, management may not be willing to spend money on a feasibility study. Budget and other resources are provided with the mission to go ahead. The value of information of a feasibility study is zero.

In most successful projects the value attributed to a feasibility study falls somewhere in between. The more a company stands to lose if a project is not feasible and the less "free" information about potential feasibility is available, the more money will be spent. It is ultimately cheaper to spend $20,000 to find out that a project is not feasible than to end up with a $2,000,000 failure.

13.3.3. Requirements Analysis

Once the plan for the feasibility study is approved, the study team begins a requirements analysis. The level of detail corresponds to the objectives of the feasibility study. This involves the user or user classes—that is why the user's role and his involvement had to be clarified in the plan for the feasibility study—or at least a "fictitious user," e.g., marketing department, potential user, etc. The study team may perform a complete requirements analysis as described in Chapter 3 and 4.

At this point the study team has a pretty good understanding of what is needed. It should communicate this understanding to the user, or to whoever represents him, by letting him review the requirements.

Next, possible alternatives for solutions are identified. Solutions fall into several categories. First there are the straightforwardly different ones. They distinguish themselves by *fundamentally different approaches* to solving the problem, e.g., a centralized versus a decentralized database or a centralized versus a distributed software system.

Second, there are *variations to a basic solution* when different gradations of features are possible. One may have more or fewer features or different sophistication levels. These types of alternatives occur in scenarios with high flexibility for a feasible solution and high possibility for trade-off between project goals. Typical questions in such a situation are, "What is the basic solution core which is the same for all variations?" or "What are the possible variations?"

The variations could entail a more or less sophisticated user interface or adding a variety of more sophisticated functions to the basic ones. Some of them usually are more useful than others.

A solution core could be a basic word processing system. Added features are superscript and subscript capability, full mathematical notation capability, diagramming features, footnoting, indexing, and cross-referencing—the possible range of alternatives is wide and obviously constrained by project goals such as cost target, timeliness, etc.

Other alternative solutions differ in the *approach to achieve full functionality*. Implementation may be a one step development effort, after which the software in its entirety is operational, or it may involve a phased approach, where basic functionality is developed, put into operation, and given more, or more sophisticated, functions over time. The advantages and disadvantages depend on project goals.

In the word processing example the basic word processing system can be installed as a phase 1 effort; rudimentary math notation may be added next, cross referencing third, etc. All of these variations on the basic theme constitute different alternatives that need to be evaluated and compared. In some cases there will be a big number of alternatives with many avenues for trade-offs. Then a formal approach to evaluation as described in Chapter 12 is very helpful, if not crucial, to success.

All major alternative approaches are candidates for further investigation. Then those alternatives that are obviously worse than others are rejected. The study team can use any of the screening methods, such as dominance or lexicographic ordering.

For each remaining alternative the study team has to investigate resource requirements, schedules and development costs.

Costs are based on time estimates for activities and on quantity and quality of the resources. These include hardware and software for development and conversion from the old system (manual or automated) to the new one. Costs associated with this resource are due to acquisition of new equipment, its installation, or due to loss of capacity of the existing equipment, because part of it is used for production during development. Software to support development may have to be bought, leased, or developed. Test harnesses, simulation software, and design tools are examples of such support software.

How much of the expense is charged to the project and at what instances in time actually depends on the use by other development teams and on how the resource is depreciated (which depends on its projected lifetime, cost, and the depreciation method). Some of the money for new or upgraded resources may not come out of the project budget. Even so, the cost still constitutes a side effect for whatever account will ultimately pay for it.

Resources are considered in schedules. It is important to know how long it will take until the resource is available and when it will be available versus when it is needed. This will have an impact on the schedule. For example, when a machine upgrade or modification, such as adding another disk drive or more main memory or adding a laser printer, has a delivery times x weeks beyond when the project ideally needs it, the project will be delayed by x weeks, unless other parallel activities can be scheduled or the delay is buffered through lag time in some other activity.

Another example deals with sole access to a shared resource, such as exclusive use of a machine for testing a new operating system on a computer that is used for production. How much time will/can the machine be available exclusively for the developers? Is that feasible for the development needs? When a software system is run in parallel operation, i.e., both old and new system at the same time, does that influence the productivity of the user department(s) that use the same computer, because of performance degradation?

The second category of resources revolves around personnel requirements (skills, training, consultants, secretaries, anybody from other departments, etc.). More experienced people work more efficiently but are more expensive. What level of expertise is required for feasibility? What are the alternatives for staffing? Is there enough expertise available in-house or are outside consultants needed? How much will that cost? When will they be available? Cooperation from outside departments is considered a risk factor. It is important to assess the feasibility of such cooperation, when it is to take place, how long, and what amount of work it will require, and then to contrast that to possible or known commitment by the outside department.

When development involves new techniques or a new application area, at least part of the development team will need training. Whether that training can be accomplished, how much it will cost, and how long it will take, are questions to be answered. Another area of training relates to paths of professional growth for team members. This training also takes time and effort, whether it be time off for courses and workshops or on-the-job training. On-the-job training is time consuming, although not as visibly. When less experienced people are assigned to a task, it takes longer and they need more supervision. Professional growth relates to DP department goals (personnel improvement, work satisfaction, productivity), and its feasibility for a project and possible implementations of such training often must be considered.

People need office space and supplies for their work. If the development staff has already been hired, they have offices and it is not an issue. This issue must be considered when new or temporary staff is to be hired or when people are moved. For example, can they be located sufficiently close to each other for easy communication? What if the project gets people "on loan"? Do they need a second office or desk space? Is it available? Will it cost something? If the development team is scattered across sites, what are the means of communication? Are they sufficient? Effective? How will the arrangement affect schedule? Cost (e.g., telephone bills, travel, communication overhead)?

Access to information and degree of cooperation from other departments are further categories of resources. Information, especially privileged information, is a major resource. It is not always made available or only at a high cost. If it is available, it may be scattered, and it must be collected and analyzed. That in itself can be a sizable project requiring manpower and time. Access to information (a source of power) can prevent departments from cooperating with development. The feasibility study team has to assess what type of information they need, what it will cost, and how long it will take to obtain it.

For all resources, costs are estimated. Costs include salaries and overhead costs for project personnel and their training, cost for equipment (amortization and business cost can be considered), any cost sharing between departments, conversion cost for everybody affected by the conversion as well as for the group doing it, cost for development and publication of new policies to reflect usage of the new system, and cost for the development of new job descriptions and of new operation manuals. Some of these costs are due to side effects, since they are not directly incurred by the development group. Rather, they are costs for the department(s) that will use or are affected by the new system. Conversion cost when the old and the new system operate in parallel is one example. There are installation costs due to personnel time and equipment resources used by the development group. There are also costs for the user who may see a loss of productivity due to the conversion while people adapt to the change. Time estimates depend on a variety of factors, among them the nature of the activities, the resources available, and on interdependencies between activities and people or organizations.

Operating costs and operating resources of the alternatives are analyzed. This includes both hardware and software requirements, as before. It often requires a formal capacity planning activity where the effects of the new workload due to the new system and its development are assessed. The types of effects to consider include that of new software on current workloads running on the current hardware system, the performance of the new software system on the current hardware, and, if a hardware upgrade is planned, the resulting impact on the performance of current and new workloads. For techniques to do such capacity planning studies see [Ferr78], [Ferr83], and [Stra80]. Alternately, the new software system may require new equipment altogether, such as data entry devices, printers, forms, etc. Some of the costs associated with new equipment are start-up costs and day-to-day operating expenses. Operating costs include expenses for operating and maintenance personnel, overhead, supplies, training of new people, etc. One aspect of operations cost is the cost of software maintenance. Maintenance cost often surpasses development cost, and this can be a substantial amount of effort and money.

The study team now investigates the risks and benefits for all alternatives. Since risk analysis is a major effort, it is discussed in the next section in more detail. There are two types of risks, those due to the quality of the feasibility study and those due to the problem itself. Examples of the first type are changing or ill-defined requirements, poor planning, wrong estimates of projected results, lack of cooperation during the feasibility study from other departments (they may be future users or indirectly affected by the proposed software system once it is implemented), and, finally, potential change in scope for the project that changes or even nullifies the evaluation of the feasibility study. All of these increase the risk of a wrong prediction and thus are potential risk factors.

Project characteristics that affect the degree of risk are related to the complexity of the project and the availability of technology and methods to deal with it. Example risk factors relate to the degree of innovation (i.e., technology; techniques and algorithms that are unfamiliar to the user; very tight constraints, such as high reliability, high visibility, and impact on customer relations; and the variability, flexibility and generality desired such as a diversity of functions—possibly for a variety of different departments—and the resulting multiple human interfaces). The number of locations where the new software system is to be run, the amount of distribution, and the volatility of the current situation are further risk factors. Other potential risks relate to the availability of the right people for development and to the capacity of hardware or software to support the application; i.e., they relate to the availability and quality of the resources.

Besides risks there are also benefits to consider. For every alternative the expected benefits need to be specified and analyzed. Benefits can be tangible or intangible. Tangible benefits are quantifiable in monetary terms such as cost reduction or profit improvement. Which benefits are to be considered depends on the project goals, because they enumerate and classify what benefits the project should realize. Intangible benefits are items such as improved employee morale, legibility of reports, and improved decision making. They are hard to quantify.

At times benefits are expressed in probabilistic terms, such as an improvement in response time as a probability distribution. Whether the full distribution is considered in a computation of benefits, or just mean and variance, depends on project goals.

The last step in the requirements analysis (Phase C of Table 13.1) is to compare all alternatives along factor areas (functional, qualitative, cost, risk, benefit, side effects) and to make a recommendation. Since the evaluation framework was based on a quantitative, metric-oriented approach, measured results can be compared to targeted attribute levels. Alternatives that do not perform well are eliminated. For the rest, a decision-making rule is used that is appropriate to choose the most promising remaining alternative.

A quantitative approach makes it possible to state how close an alternative is to stated goals. Sometimes alternatives are close to each other and the uncertainty inherent in a feasibility study may not allow us to distinguish between them reliably and thus to decide between them at all. Then there are multiple choices.

13.3.4. Refine Alternatives

For all remaining alternatives, further project planning refines project activities to a degree of detail that allows the development of a project plan. This outline plan is the basis for further project management. The plan provides for all development activities including conversion and all training associated with it.

This phase (Phase D of Table 13.1) also implies informing the affected staff (i.e. the development team) of the results of the feasibility study. Reinventing the wheel by having the development team rediscover the results of the feasibility study team is a waste of time. Communication between the feasibility study team and the development group ensures continuity in development and increases the understanding of the rationale underlying a particular development strategy. Buy-in on the part of the development team increases morale and improves effectiveness.

The results of the feasibility study are also presented to management (or sponsors). This should be in a form that makes it easy for them to decide whether to go ahead with the recommended alternative and indicates why and where some alternatives fell short. It is important to realize that a feasibility study is more than recommending *the* solution and ditching the others. It is a document that helps management and project sponsors to assess strengths and weaknesses of alternatives, to understand their side effects, and to assess confidence in the results of the study and the feasibility of the project. With enough information, management or sponsors may decide to increase the budget and to select a more expensive alternative with a larger scope or more flexible functionality. Or they may decide that the simplest solution is still good enough and slash the budget accordingly.

Still another possibility is to take measures of eliminating risk. An example would be to negotiate commitment from a "risky" department. Another would be to take steps to eliminate or reduce possible side effects. Budget negotiations between departments to share development costs as well as projected benefits are another possibility. The managers' success in following these options rests on the quality of the feasibility study report that gives them the data they need to negotiate effectively. A well prepared feasibility study report not only enables management to assess project quality but also establishes the credibility of the feasibility study team and the results it produced.

In addition to the full report, a short management summary (about one to five pages) with major objectives, conclusions, and key reasons is recommended [Frie79]. A presentation of the major findings to the managers and/or sponsors is also useful for larger projects [Park80]. Besides providing a forum for presenting the results in more detail than a written summary can provide, it also increases the visibility of the feasibility study team and its members and provides a forum for recognition. The developers' representatives also profit from such a presentation.

The organization of the written report best follows the outline of the phases of the study (minus Phase B, which is a planning phase for the feasibility study). All methods and findings are mentioned and discussed in the body of the report, and details on methods and results belong in the appendices. Since "pictures speak a thousand words," diagrams are highly recommended, especially those that show comparative evaluation for important objective areas. Diagrams are useful for both the report and a presentation. They also are a terrific means of summarizing or of illustrating mechanisms and technical results to the nonexpert.

Problems and Questions

1.   One side effect of a proposed project alternative is considered to increase the profitability of department XY by 10%. The same alternative, however, will likely overrun the target budget by 10%. It looks like a toss-up. Is it? Explain. Make an example. (Hint: All other things being equal, how do the higher level goals and their prioritization affect the evaluation? Consider goals from which objectives for the DP department and department XY were derived).

2.   Company Softax has a product line for preparing individual tax returns. They expect the following to happen

▶ fierce competition for the market;

▶ possibility for drastic changes in the individual tax laws, where returns will be simplified to the point that the company's tax software for individual returns will be obsolete and unsalvageable; and

▶ more regulations and laws for corporate tax payers, business accounting, pension and benefit plans.

The key result areas were identified (in order of priority) as

▶ innovation,

▶ profitability, and

▶ productivity.

The proposed project portfolio includes the following:

▶ Use existing tax expertise to get into the corporate and pension/benefits market, i.e., develop support software for that;

▶ Produce an inexpensive, high-sales volume, simple financial record-keeping and tax preparation system for the least expensive line of personal computers that will be attractive even when tax laws change, because it can do simple financial record keeping as well; and

▶ Branch out into new business, develop a software tool that can evaluate cost of employee benefits plans (health plans, worker's compensation insurance, pension funds, etc.) for companies as a computerized decision support tool that helps them to find the most advantageous plan options within government regulations.

If development cost and development time do not matter, which of these projects would you choose? If cost layout matters, which should come first? If market window matters, what should the ranking be? Explain your choices. Does profitability enter into any of your decisions? Why or why not?

3.   Review the feasibility study of Chapters 3 and 4. Assume you are an entrepreneur and are considering implementing the tax system (TAP) from the preceding chapters. Also assume that the tax laws will not be drastically simplified. Complete the feasibility study from the managerial viewpoint of Chapter 13. Would you embark on the project if you had six months and all computer resources, a business associate who will do the marketing, help with sales, and one firm corporate client, such as an accounting firm that does a lot of tax preparation? Explain your decisions. Do not forget maintenance. Tell us how you would go about doing this project.

13.4. Risk and Uncertainty

13.4.1. Project Risk

Risk is related to uncertainty and incompleteness of information—if one knew exactly what would happen, there wouldn't be any risk. The more effort is put into obtaining information that is complete and accurate, the less risk is involved because undesirable outcomes can be avoided. During the feasibility study, information is the least detailed and the most incomplete. The biggest number of things can still "go wrong." As tasks get done and phases complete, more and more is known about how the project is faring. It is obvious whether completed activities were successful or not. This information can increase or decrease the chances of failure and success and thus increase or decrease the risk of failure. The number of alternative actions also decreases as the project gets further underway.

Example: Risk due to Hardware Order

A project has one major risk factor, namely whether or not a piece of hardware arrives on time. All other factors affecting success or failure of the project are lumped together. Table 13.2 shows the joint probabilities of project success (or failure) and timely arrival of the new hardware (or its late arrival). The marginal probabilities of project success (failure) are computed in the bottom row by summing up the quantities in each column. The rightmost column shows the marginal probabilities of timely or untimely arrival as the sums of each row.

Table 13.2 Project risk factor analysis.

| | Project | | |
Hardware arrives	Success	Failure	P(arrival)
On time	.54	.06	.60
Not on time	.02	.38	.40
P(project outcome)	.56	.44	1.00

The table shows that it is almost as likely for the project to succeed as to fail. The event "project success and hardware on time" contributes most to the success probability. The chance of having the project succeed when the hardware doesn't arrive on time is very slim. At the point where this assessment takes place, the probability that the hardware will arrive on time is 60%.

Later into software development there will be a point when it is clear whether or not the hardware has come on time. How will that change the probabilities of success and failure? Conditional probabilities show the probability of success given that the hardware has arrived (or not). Assume that "on time" denotes the event "hardware arrives on time" and that "success" means "project success." This yields:

$$P \text{ (success} \mid \text{on time)} = P(\text{success, on time})/P(\text{on time}) = .54/.60 = .90$$
$$P(\text{success} \mid \text{not on time)} = P(\text{success, not on time})/P(\text{not on time}) = .05$$

The risk of failure decreased significantly when the information that hardware arrived on time became available. There is a very low probability of success after the machine arrives late.

To reduce the risk of failure, the machine could be ordered well ahead of time, even to the point of delaying the start of the project until the new hardware had arrived (implications of such a decision need to be assessed; this may not always be desirable or feasible). Another way to reduce the risk is to shift the effects of failure to the firm that contracts to absorb all negative effects of failure should they deliver the hardware late.

The method used in this example is based on the following relationship from probability theory. Assume there are two events that can happen, E_1 and E_2. Then the probability that event E_1 happens if E_2 is known to have happened $(P(E_1 \mid E_2))$ is given as the fraction of the probability that both E_1 and E_2 happen $(P(E_1, E_2))$ and the probability that event E_2 happens $(P(E_2))$:

$$P(E_1 \mid E_2) = \frac{P(E_1, E_2)}{P(E_2)}$$

$P(E_2)$ has to be greater than zero.

13.4.2. Risk of Bias

Judgment under uncertainty uses heuristics to approximate unknown information. Inherent in such judgment is the risk of bias, even for experts. The risk of bias is the more pronounced the less standardized the evaluation procedures are and the less one can rely on proven quantitative methods and techniques. This is one more reason to use a quantitative approach to evaluation and decision making as discussed earlier. Tversky and Kahneman [Tver74] describe some of the common heuristics and biases that people exhibit when they make decisions under uncertainty.

One of the more important types of biases during feasibility studies deals with a heuristic [Tver74] called "adjustment from an anchor." It is used in numerical prediction, such as estimation and risk assessment, when relevant data are available. In the evaluation of complex conjunctive or disjunctive events, risks are often underestimated.

When planning for the development of a new software system, the probability of success can become very low when the number of possible outcomes is large (outcome is used in the probabilistic sense, meaning one combination of phenomena that can happen as the result of development activities). This can lead to unwarranted optimism.

Example: Conjunctive Events

Assume the very simplistic case that each end of a development phase can produce three levels of quality for their deliverables (low, medium, high). There are six phases, i.e., problem analysis (PA), requirements analysis (RA), specifications (SP), design (D), testing (T), and maintenance (M). There are a total number of

$$card\ (\{low,\ medium,\ high\})\ ^{card\ (\{PA,\ RA,\ SP,\ D,\ T,\ M\})} = 3^6$$

or 729 possible outcomes. For each one, the probability of occurring has to be assessed for how it relates to project success or failure.

Example: Disjunctive Events

Risk assessment is often faced with a disjunctive set of events where the project will fail if any of a number of aspects fail. Without proper quantification this can lead to an underestimation of the probability of project failure.

Assume that budget compliance, schedule met, and adequate software quality are different events. They occur with probabilities P(B), P(S), and P(Q) respectively. Then the probability of project success is

$$P(success) = P(B)P(S)P(Q)$$
$$P(failure) = 1 - P(B)P(S)P(Q)$$

Table 13.3 shows how fast the probability of project failure increases even when the probabilities of success for the three critical factors only decrease slightly.

Table 13.3 Project success as a function of 3 factors.

P(B)	P(S)	P(Q)	P(success)	P(failure)
.90	.90	.90	.729	.271
.80	.90	.90	.648	.352
.80	.80	.90	.576	.424
.80	.80	.80	.512	.488
.70	.90	.90	.567	.433
.70	.70	.90	.441	.559
.70	.70	.70	.343	.657

Even an almost 50-50 chance of project success (not very good) requires rather high levels of success probabilities in the three success factors (all 80%). If even one of them drops to 70%, the chances are only slightly more than even that the project will succeed. With more factors to consider, this behavior becomes even more pronounced.

Subjective Probabilities

Another problem is the bias inherent in subjective probabilities. For some factors the feasibility study estimates subjective probabilities for success or failure. This is an inexpensive, very useful practice if bias can be limited or eliminated. One very common way to deal with this is the Delphi technique. It is based on group consensus. An independent coordinator combines anonymous estimates from several experts into a single estimate and makes this mean or median estimate available to the experts for feedback. Extreme estimates are often removed. Whether all or only some estimates are made available depends on the situation and the number of estimates. Since members of a feasibility study team are experts in different aspects of the study, their estimates will reflect different emphases and, so it is hoped, cancel out biases because they would be based on different viewpoints. A group meeting or iterations of the anonymous procedure establish a consensus on the final estimate.

Group meetings are usually faster and less cumbersome, but they require a democratic attitude. As soon as some group members dominate others (better speaker, more assertive, playing politics, through authority), the estimate reflects that bias. Then an anonymous consensus is preferable. This is done by iterating the anonymous estimation process until a consensus is reached. While this method preserves the anonymity of the estimators, it does not provide the open discussion about estimates and issues connected with the problem. Still another way of varying the Delphi method is to preserve the anonymity of the estimates at each iteration, yet still have a group meeting to discuss the current round of estimates before the next set of estimates is submitted. Which of the variations of the Delphi method is appropriate depends on which factors are likely to cause bias. There is no need for the more involved anonymous method if bias due to politics or strong personalities is unlikely.

Bias [Tver74] mostly represents misconceptions and violations of the laws of probability and statistics. While biases cannot be avoided entirely, a formal framework based on sound statistical principles and ongoing evaluation of the results will likely reduce or eliminate subjective bias (for example see [Hube74]). That was one of the reasons to suggest measurement and structured decision-making methods. Bayesian statistics [Morr77] are another method to quantify subjective probabilities. In either case, enough expert opinions are needed to be statistically valid; otherwise the evaluation may fall prey to the "law of small numbers," attaching too much significance to too small a sample.

13.4.3. Scoring Methods

Risk in itself is not something to be avoided at all costs. Risks can be taken as long as the aggregate risk to the DP department, when all its projects are considered, stays within acceptable limits. McFarlan [Mcfa81] suggests the concept of a portfolio of projects, some of which have higher risk levels than others. When choosing new projects, individual project risk and aggregate risk of currently active projects is considered. A proper risk structure depends on the company and its environment. Very competitive market situations usually ask for some higher risk projects that utilize forefront technology (increasing project risk) to gain a leading edge in the market. Other reasons for higher risk projects (in terms of probability of failure, not necessarily in terms of money cost for failure) are to keep development staff interested and to educate them in the use of new techniques and technology. A high risk, low budget project can familiarize development staff with a new machine and reduce the risk to a larger budget, follow-up project.

The types of risk parallel the types of resources and projects goals. Metrics for risk in all these areas measure the degree of uncertainty of whether the resources are available and what impact possible levels of availability will have on project success. Goals are usually stated in terms of benefits, budget, development time, resulting software quality, and acceptance criteria for the product. There are many questions to be answered. Will benefits be realized? What happens if they are not? What are the consequences of budget and schedule overruns or of less than required software quality? Which factors influence these types of risk? [Mcfa81] cites three major risk dimensions:

▶ project size (complexity),

▶ experience in technology, and

▶ project structure (management planning and control).

The larger and more complex a project, the higher the resulting risk score. Risk is compounded by little experience in technology and low project structure. Within the three dimensions of risk, factors are identified and constituent attributes developed that are similar to the hierarchical method of measurement of Chapter 12. Weights measure the relative importance of attribute and factor areas to each other. McFarlan uses an additive scoring model to compute an overall score for every project. Since factors relevant to major risk dimensions change with organizations and over time, a structured tree of risk factors and their attributes must be developed individually and modified over time to reflect changes in an organization and its software development policies, expertise, and focus.

Example: Microcomputer Firm

A small microcomputer firm develops and maintains software packages for personal computers. Its risk assessment tree is given in Figure 13.2.

This risk assessment tree considers McFarlan's three risk dimensions: size, structure, and technology. The software firm established that total development time, the number of people involved in development, and the number of user departments or types of users for which a product is developed are the major complexity factors contributing to risk. In the structure area, they identified three subfactors: the environment, general stability, and management structure. A reliable user representative and a well organized market analysis that is favorable for the product will reduce risk. Lesser quality in these areas will increase it. A lack of stability will also increase the risk of failure. Personnel and project definition stability contribute to the degree of overall stability. Risk due to management structure falls into two areas: (1) management structure, including role and task assignment within the team, and (2) the degree to which organizational struc-

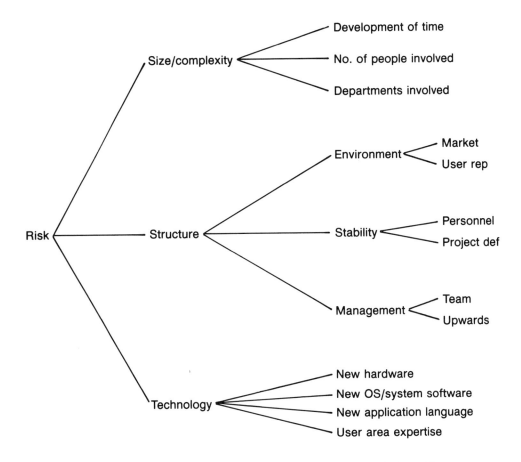

Figure 13.2 Risk Assessment Framework for Microcomputer Software Firm.

ture (upper management support) increases or decreases the risk of the project. Technology attributes risk to the degree new hardware, operating or system software, new application languages, and new user areas (with corresponding low degree of expertise) are involved.

The example about the microcomputer software firm was not intended to show a generally applicable risk assessment tree. In situations where user departments are involved in software development activities, the structure component of risk will contain areas relating to the level and organization of user cooperation (or the lack thereof) and the impact of change for the user (the more drastic the change, the higher the risk). Another possible way to establish a risk tree is to start with the list of items to be considered in the feasibility study (see Section 13.3).

A quantitative risk assessment procedure needs risk scales and corresponding scores for each leaf node. A full preference assessment establishes weights for all nodes at each level. The risk scales have commensurable units of measurement.

The microcomputer firm from the previous example measures risk on a very simple scale from 0 to 2, where 0 implies no measurable risk and 2 implies a high risk (scale 1 below). For size/complexity the following metrics are used (unnormalized weights in parentheses):

	Scale 1		Scale 2
1. Development time (1):			
Duration (months)	Risk score		
< 2	0		1
2–12	1		.5
> 12	2		0
2. Number of people involved (2):			
Number	Risk score		
< 5	0		1
5–10	1		.5
> 10	2		0
3. Departments or user classes (10):			
Number	Risk score		
1	0		1
2–3	1		.5
> 3	2		0

Compounding of Risk Factors

The relationship amongst factors at each factor level must be established. If risk is additively compounded, the additive scoring model with weights and normalization from Chapter 12 can be used. Low risk scores in one factor area trade off against higher risks in another.

These scores must reflect historical experience. The microcomputer software firm evaluated past experience and derived measures for the degree of risk from them. Which of the important factors influenced the three major success factors (budget, schedule, and quality) and by how much? For these relationships and the degree of risk inherent in not meeting levels of success in this project, quantitative relationships are quantified through preference assessment. These form the basis for selecting the metrics for the risk attributes in the above example. The weights (in parentheses) also derive from historical data.

Let's take an example of a lawyer's assistant. If scale 1 is used, a project of six month's duration with five people that will develop a lawyer's assistant for lawyers, paralegals, secretaries, and accountants would have a normalized score of

$$Risk(size) = (1 * 1 + 2 * 1 + 10 *2)/(1 + 2 + 10) = 23/13;$$

or close to 1.8. Assuming that the three risk dimensions are equally important and the other two have normalized values of

$$Risk(structure) = 1.6;$$

and

$$Risk(technology) = .4,;$$

the overall degree of risk is

$$Risk(project) = (1.8 + 1.6 + .4)/3;$$

or about 1.3. The scores must be normalized so they stay within the proper risk range.

In computing the overall project risk, an additive compounding of risk is assumed first. This is *not* always realistic and may reflect bias, with regard to disjunctive events [Tver74], that underestimates project risk. There are situations where, for project success, every risk area has to have a low risk score; otherwise risk increases on a multiplicative basis. But one cannot simply multiply risk scores because they reflect a disutility. Multiplying them would violate the rules of the utility schema proposed earlier. However, simple scaling can convert the risk scale into one having a range of zero and one. The absence of risk is 1 (complete utility), and the highest risk level is 0 (no utility). Then one can use the multiplicative model where utility declines multiplicatively with corresponding declines in factor utility.

Now assume the risk scores in scale 2 for the lawyer's assistant example. The weights for the risk attributes are the same as for scale 1. Assume further that *Risk(structure)* = .2 and *Risk(technology)* = .8. Then an additive compounding of risk on the highest level yields a project risk of

$$\begin{aligned} Risk(project) &= (Risk(size) + Risk(structure) + Risk(technology))/3 \\ &= ((1 * .5 + 2 * .5 + 0 * 1.0)/13 + .2 + .8)/3 \\ &= (.12 + .2 + .8)/3 = .37 \end{aligned}$$

This reflects a close to medium risk project. A multiplicative compounding of risk factors shows a very different picture:

$$\begin{aligned} Risk(project) &= Risk(size) * Risk(structure) * Risk(technology) \\ &= .12 * .2 * .8 = .02 \end{aligned}$$

The second evaluation indicates a very high risk project.

Setting Risk Targets for Project Portfolio

Risk scores for projects can also be used to compute a combined risk level for an entire portfolio and to compare it against portfolio objectives. Medium range planning sets these measurable objectives. They assure that the project portfolio contains the proper mix of high, medium, and low risk projects to meet productivity, service, and profit objectives. A company might have the following objectives:

1. No more than 20% high risk projects and

2. At least 5% high risk projects.

Percentage can be defined with respect to total portfolio budget. The company currently has ten possible projects in its portfolio. Two are low risk projects with a budget of $1 Mio each. Five are medium risk projects with budgets of $3 Mio each. Lastly, there are three high risk projects budgeted at $1 Mio each. The total portfolio value is $20 Mio. High risk projects are 3/20 or 15% of the total, well within the stated goal.

The risk score can be used to indicate the level of management approval needed to authorize projects. The higher the risk, the higher the level of approval needs to be.

13.4.4. Complete Uncertainty

Sometimes very little is known on which to base even subjective probabilities, and there certainly may not be enough information to derive objective probabilities from historical data. Therefore, the evaluation and decision-making rules of 13.4.1. and 13.4.3. do not apply. Even if the probability of project success or failure is not known, it may still be possible to determine what the cost of failure or the quantifiable benefits of success are. This information can guide the decision of whether the project should be undertaken. It can also help to decide which alternative is best. The decision is made with complete uncertainty about the likelihood of an outcome (i.e., project success), but it uses knowledge about the nature of the outcomes (i.e., potential payoffs or losses).

A very conservative decision rule minimizes losses. This is the *maximin* rule ([Lapi76], [Luce57]). The first step determines the minimum payoff (equivalent to maximum loss) for each alternative. Then the alternative that maximizes the minimum payoff is chosen.

The microcomputer software firm from previous examples is considering two alternatives for the implementation of an automated system to track project progress and analyze the status of a software development effort. Depending on the level of sophistication, this system has different degrees of benefit.

(a)   The system has a simple database and record-keeping system, with no advanced analysis features. It stores and retrieves simple facts about progress but does not analyze or interpret them.

(b)   The system uses advanced expert system technology to diagnose the project. It points out potential danger areas and suggests corrective action. It measures performance and quality automatically and correlates measurements with information in a project database.

The following financial benefits are expected, based on a market analysis:

	copies sold	* price/copy	= sales	dev. cost	maintenance cost	gross income
a	10K	$100	$1mio	$50K	$75K	875K
b	20K	$300	$6mio	$200K	$250K	5,550K

If the project fails, development cost is lost. That results in the following payoff matrix:

	success	failure
a	875;	−50
b	5,550;	−200

The minimum payoffs for alternatives a and b are −50 and −200 respectively. The maximum is −50 for alternative a. Therefore alternative a is chosen. This is a strategy to contain losses, but it is totally blind to the high payoff of alternative b.

If for instance the company could sustain a loss of $200K and was willing to gamble, it might go for the highest payoff and choose the alternative that maximizes the potential return. This is alternative b. Its maximum potential benefits are $5,550K. Choosing the maximum payoff for each alternative and then selecting the alternative that provides the biggest of those payoffs is called the *maximax* decision rule. For this example, because of the high potential payoff, it might be a reasonable strategy. Such an optimistic view can be very detrimental if potential losses are very high, since the rule is blind to losses.

For lack of information on the probabilities of success or failure one might assume that both outcomes are equally likely. Then one could determine the expected benefit (or loss, if it is negative) for each alternative and choose the one that has the biggest expected benefit.

For example, the expected benefit E(a) of alternative a is

$$E(a) = (875 - 50)/2 = 422.50.;$$

Similarly,

$$E(b) = (5,550 - 200)/2 = 5350/2 = 2675.$$

Alternative b is clearly preferable. This rule is called LaPlace or Equal Probability Rule [Boeh81].

If more is known about the likelihood of success, that should be considered, because that alternative may become more desirable. For example, assume that for alternative a *P(success)* = .9 and *P(failure)* = .1. For alternative b it is the other way around; i.e., *P(success)* = .1, P(failure) = .9. Then the expected benefits are

$$E(a) = .9*875 + .1*(-50) = 782.5$$
$$E(b) = .1*5550 + .9*(-200) = 375.$$

Since the probability of success for alternative b is so low, alternative a becomes preferable. More precise information about the likelihood of outcomes improves decision making.

There may be several possible events, not just success or failure. If the equal probability rule is to be used, it is important to define those events in such a way that they do not overlap. They should also occur with almost equal probability. Assuming that every possible outcome (or sample point) is equally likely, all events should have approximately the same number of sample points in them.

Project failure may be due to either inadequate quality or budget overrun. If the failure event is split into these two categories and the equal probability rule is used, the probability of success implicitly drops to ⅓ instead of ½, because there is one more event to consider. Nothing about the situation has changed, except that the assessment of success vs. failure is now 1:2 instead of 1:1.

If success and failure are still equally likely, and if for failure events it is as likely to be a budget overrun as inadequate software quality, then the situation is as in Table 13.4.

Table 13.4 Multifailure event probabilities.

	P
success	.5
failure budget	.25
quality	.25

This refinement step only makes sense if different consequences are to be expected, such as higher development cost when the budget is overrun. In the case of lower product quality, sales may be lower and maintenance will be more costly. Development and maintenance costs as well as sales figures need to be revised before reconsidering the situation.

The example assumes that failure to comply with the budget results in project failure and loss of development cost plus overrun ($-400K$). Inadequate software quality sells less copies and incurs increased maintenance costs but still lets the firm break even. Then the expected benefit for alternative b is

$$E(b) = .5*5,550 + .25*(-400) + .25*0 = 2,775$$

Alternative b is still very attractive.

13.4.5. Risk Reduction

The evaluator must compile enough information to make a reasonably good decision in accordance with project goals and software development objectives. If not enough information is available or the risk is too high, either more information must be gathered or risk must be reduced.

Risk reduction identifies the most risky aspects of a project first. Reducing their risk will reduce overall project risk the most. A table is compiled listing risk factors in descending order of their impact on overall project risk. This is shown in Table 13.5. There

Table 13.5 Risk reduction matrix.

Rank	Risk factor	% Overall Risk	Risk reduction activity
1	Staff expertise	40%	Training
2	Hardware on time	35%	Contract to off-load cost of failure
			Multiple orders at different vendors
			Don't start project until hardware available
			Reorganize project
3	Market window does not allow schedule overrun, schedule is tight (development time is risk)	25%	Incremental development
			Early identification of independent parts to allow maximum degree of parallelism to compress schedule
			Scale down effort to more manageable size
			Reduced functionality
			Stricter management control
			Reduced quality

are four columns. Column 1 identifies the risk by its rank (ties can be broken by rank-ordering risks that contribute equally to the overall project risk in an arbitrary fashion). Column 2 describes the risk in a short phrase. One can refer to a document for a further, detailed description of the risk. Column 3 states the degree to which any given risk contributes to overall project risk (as a percentage). Column 4 identifies all risk reduction activities that could be used to reduce the risk. One may include contingency plans because they reduce the effect of failure due to a risk factor. Or they may be considered as two different types of activities: risk reduction is proactive, while contingency plans are reactive (after things have gone wrong). Then there are two separate columns for them. For any given project, a balanced set of risk reduction activities and contingency plans should be in place. While it is better to avoid problems in the first place, it is also useful to have the additional "safety net" of a contingency plan.

At the beginning of the risk analysis part of the feasibility study, the risk reduction table serves as a tool for data collection and analysis. It is used again as a summary statement at the end. A comparison between the two shows the success of strategies to contain project risk. Very few projects are not risky at all. We must take active steps to contain the risk.

Problems and Questions

1.   Perform a risk analysis for the tax recording and preparation program (TAP). Assume that this program is to be developed by the small software firm that was described earlier in this chapter.

2.   Perform a risk analysis for the program analyzer project (PAS). Develop a risk reduction matrix. (Hint: Are there any other possible uses for the program analyzer, besides computing similarity indices?)

3.   The risk reduction matrix states the contribution of a risk factor to overall project risk. How can that help you to make decisions about overall risk reduction strategies for a project? (Hint: Will you always be able to do all possible risk reduction activities, or do you sometimes have to make trade-offs?) Give an example.

4.   What are advantages and disadvantages of quantifying risk? (Hint: Can you always be sure that the numbers you have are reliable?) Describe a strategy when you would use a quantitative approach to risk analysis and when you would not. When does it not make any sense to worry about risk at all?

13.5. Guarding against Failure

13.5.1. Resistance to Projects

This chapter has explained a variety of methods and formal procedures to avoid selecting the wrong project. Technical and managerial evaluation criteria guarantee good preparation for these aspects of the project. All too often projects that looked perfectly feasible from a technical standpoint fail and when members of the development team are asked why, they might respond "Oh, you know, it was all politics." At other times, the overriding importance of political factors in decision making and project proposal evaluation is used as an excuse to forego a well founded, structured feasibility study with formal methods, because "it does not count." If politics and the power of information have much to do with setting and achieving goals or thwarting them, we must deal with political issues during project selection and software development.

What causes political moves? Setting long-term DP objectives can imply drastic changes for an organization, how people do their work, and what information they control (which might be their source of power and not willingly given up). There is natural resistance to drastic change. As the complexity of the situation increases, the number of possible ways to counteract it do, too. With it the likelihood that those changes are successfully implemented diminishes. Even when the definition of objectives and specific projects does not imply drastic changes, there may be objections from managers, department heads, committee members on the steering team, etc. that cause problems. These problems may stem from the fact that the objectives threaten someone's turf (i.e., a low priority for a long-term objective that justifies the existence of a department or group, or a project that is done by one group but overlaps into the area of responsibility for another), increase the amount of work, or lessen someone's power and authority. People who try to make the project fail perceive the cost of change as being greater than the benefits they would receive. As a result, they will be more or less openly uncooperative. Or they will "misinterpret" a stated objective. They may select a project that is not aligned with company goals but less of a threat. They may even cause a project to flounder, because they fear it brings about undesirable changes. This is called Counterimplementation [Keen81].

Clear, specific, and measurable goals are less easy to "misinterpret." Simplicity of a project also helps, because the simpler the project the less room there is for playing games. Excellent environments for counterimplementation games are situations where goals are stated rather ambiguously and control mechanisms are lacking. The best defense is to enlist the support of a person with enough credibility, authority, and prestige to either win over potential adversaries or to deter them from counterimplementation.

Counterproductive forces have to be recognized before they can be dealt with. Good questions to uncover them are as follows:

▶ Who is likely to be affected by this goal/project?

▶ In which way?

▶ What is the reaction likely to be? Is it going to be favorable? Unfavorable?

▶ Is there a way to coopt people? If not, are they likely to play counterimplementation games?

▶ If support is very low, is there a possibility that the project really is a dumb idea and should be dropped?

One can also ask the same questions in a more affirmative way:

▶ Is there a reason to believe that all the departments affected by the goal or project have an honest interest in it and are willing to make a commitment?

▶ Is there reason to believe that after the new software is in place the users will actually use it? (e.g., when a software development tool is installed, there is plenty of room to make the best tool a failure if it is not accepted and not used by the people who are supposed to be its users.)

▶ Is it possible to negotiate the goal or the project with all parties that are affected by it so a consensus can be reached that still constitutes a viable and beneficial project?

Other issues that will have a great deal of influence over possible opposition to a project's implementation have to do with administration.

▶ Who are the people whose cooperation is critical for the success of the project?

▶ Which other elements are critical? This often has to do with organizational structure and the channels one has to go through in order to get approval or have a support service performed that may well be critical.

▶ Are the people one has to deal with in these matters likely to be uncooperative? Will they react with delay tactics or give mere tokens of cooperation without actually cooperating?

▶ Is there any way to work around them or to break their resistance?

13.5.2. Games

People who do not want to cooperate, but feel pushed to do so, often respond with games. Part of the preparation for a successful project is to assess which games are most likely and how to counteract or to prevent them. That can involve actually redesigning the project plan to avoid obstacles, i.e., making the project more independent from people who are likely to oppose it.

Games come in three flavors [Bard77]:

1. **Divert resources:** Project resources such as time, equipment, money, personnel, are used for other purposes. It results in inadequate resources and can make the project

fail. For example, there is an agreement that department A is to lend part of an employee's time to department B. But the supervisor does not reduce that person's work responsibilities for department A, maybe even sets explicit priorities that work for department A is to come first. The person ends up not having enough time to devote to his task assignment for department B, even though an "assignment" has been made. There is no control by department B over that employee. No corrective action can be taken to ensure proper sharing of the employee's time.

2. **Deflect goals:**   Projects have explicit goals to accomplish. If they are not written down or are worded ambiguously, it is easy to change the scope of the project, making it too small to be useful or too big to be realistic. This game can also take the form of perpetual negotiation about goals with other departments, resulting in constant changes of plans where nothing ever gets done. The project then eventually collapses when people get tired of talking about it.

3. **Dissipate energies:**   This game exploits lack of control mechanisms. It is especially easy to play when the project spans several spheres of control. One game strategy is refusing to take responsibility for an assignment ("we will help as much as we can, but this of course will depend on the staffing level and the other work we have to do"). No effective management control is possible. Another strategy is to shift responsibilities from person to person so that even if performance is bad no one is "responsible" (one can always blame the person who worked on it earlier). Another way to dissipate energies is to make the project highly visible because it is something "perfect" and will result in the "best" system of the kind ever implemented—in other words an unrealistic setup. The player gets out before it is too late so that he does not have to take the blame for its failure.

Games are not only played during the very early phases. They happen just as much during later phases of the software development life cycle. They follow the same principles, even though they may manifest themselves in different variants. A good (and entertaining) book explaining some of the more common games people play to achieve their goals is [Bern64]. Berne's concept of games is based on *transactional analysis*. Games are characterized as a set of transactions that are often repetitive and superficially plausible, but with a hidden meaning, aiming at a well-defined, predictable outcome. Each game has at least two game players and most of the games that endanger project success or create political trouble fall into the category of destructive games. A source that more specifically deals with games played during software development—games that can endanger software quality control procedures—is found in [Your79]. Yourdon identifies 8 out of Berne's 35 games as games frequently played during software development:

1. **The Alcoholic.**   This is a very hard "game" to beat, because the primary player is addicted to destructive behavior (always blowing deadlines, shoddy work, noncooperation). This game is played against a persecutor (usually the manager) and a rescuer (coworker). Sometimes other players inadvertantly or openly help the alcoholic to continue destructive behavior. Refusing to play the game is the only effective way to end this game, because pressure and more rules only provide a better backdrop for this game.

2. **Now I've got you, you SOB.**   In this game one person overreacts to the mistakes of another and blows them all out of proportion. There may be two hidden agendas. The person may be very angry to begin with, and the mistake is used to justify the rage. The second underlying reason may be that the player can, through concentrating on his anger, avoid recognition of his own deficiencies. In a walk-through or at a planning meeting, this game can be very disruptive and destroy the goodwill of needed allies, and it will make negotiations much harder. Avoid having such a person in a setting where he can do harm. If that is not possible, it may be feasible to alert the rest of the group to the game.

3. **See what you made me do.**   This game player uses interruptions, suggestions, and criticisms as reasons why he "had" to make a mistake. Thus he avoids taking responsibility or vents anger about being criticized. Avoiding this game player or isolating him and making sure that one does not have to take over his responsibilities is the best tactic. We can see this game played when people do not agree with decisions and want to make them fail.

4. **Harried.**   This game player is unable to say no and, although overworked, takes on any new assignment. He falls further and further behind and makes more and more mistakes. Clear work assignments and control of responsibilities will counteract this game.

5. **If it weren't for you.**   This game is often played by the DP Manager against his programmers. It consists of blaming another person for a mistake that caused some unrealistic dream of the blamer to be unfulfilled; e.g., "If the accounting department would cooperate we could implement the most advanced financial system there ever was, our firm would become famous, and I would be promoted to vice president." Refusing to play this game is the only way to counteract it.

6. **Look how hard I tried.**   This is also called the martyr game and is usually played by a programmer against a manager or by the manager of another department who must cooperate but really doesn't want to. Showing signs of hard work, like mounds of memos, overtime, etc. is geared to solicit sympathy and to show that one isn't to blame for the failure. Staying away from the player is the most successful strategy.

7. **Schlemiel.**   This game consists of a player who continues to make stupid mistakes and a victim who continues to forgive but builds up rage in the process until he blows up

and gives the schlemiel a reason for resentment. Openness and direct actions for change geared towards protecting the victim from the schlemiel are most successful.

8. **Yes-But.**   In this game every suggestion to solve a problem is met with opposition pointing out the shortcomings of the proposed solution. While critical assessment of the quality of a proposed solution is important and constructive, this game derives satisfaction from shooting down any and all solutions, none is good enough. It can be very effective in counterimplementation, because nobody wants to embark on a risky or questionable project. This game is stopped by turning the table around to the player and asking him to resolve the problem and make a suggestion what to do. This works especially well when the basic feasibility is not in question and the only bone of contention is how perfect a solution is.

Yourdon suggests that one of the best ways to avoid those games is to avoid getting sucked into them in the first place. Where that is not possible, it is often feasible to undermine support for the game player by making the game apparent to all. Some games can be avoided or ended through clear, well planned task assignment with formal approval procedures, while others thrive on that because known responsibilities give the player the set-up to play his game (e.g., "Alcoholic").

13.5.3. Negotiating Commitment

Negotiating committed cooperation takes time. It is crucial to know how much time negotiation and approval from all involved parties will take and which resources are needed for negotiation. Likewise we must find out whether it is possible to work around people obstacles and if so, exactly what impact that will have on other resources and on the schedule. Is the project still feasible under those constraints? With a commitment from management or from an influential person who can facilitate the negotiation process, it is often possible to work around barriers or to delay or deter games so that they become nonthreatening to the success of the project.

The best attitude towards resistance to change and the resulting game playing is to look at it as one more area where feasibility needs to be established before a project can be considered worth pursuing. Just as one needs to make sure that resources like equipment and skill are adequate, one has to ascertain that the resource called "commitment" is available. Organizational goals caused the initiation of the project for which we are trying to establish feasibility. The negotiation process is an opportunity to convince all parties that the project furthers these goals and thus is in their own interests.

This positive attitude towards the negotiation process is likely to be more fruitful than going into negotiations with a mental framework of "how can I make them do what I want and prevent them from playing games on me." Games are essentially protective in nature. Someone on the defensive often does not see nor is he willing to accept alternative approaches, because he is too busy being defensive. That in itself can be counterproductive. The goal should be to decrease the need for defensive attitudes on both sides of the negotiating table.

We need to find out why protection is considered necessary and what is to be protected. Then it becomes possible to work on the underlying cause as opposed to trying to suppress symptoms (i.e., the game playing, the lack of cooperation). A positive attitude makes it easier to envision suggestions that work as incentives to cooperate.

When cooperation from everyone is not possible, we need at least a coalition powerful enough to ensure success in spite of remaining opposition. This depends on the resources such a coalition controls. With less cooperative forces, we must deflect their counterimplementation with what [Keen81] calls counter-counterimplementation. He summarizes tactical approaches of counterimplementers and of successful counter-counterimplementers in the following way:
Counterimplementers

1. lay low,

2. rely on inertia,

3. keep project complex, hard to coordinate, and vaguely defined, and

4. exploit lack of inside knowledge.

Counter-counterimplementers

1. make sure they have contract for change,

2. seek out resistance and respond,

3. rely on face-to-face contacts,

4. become an insider and work hard to build personal credibility, and

5. coopt users early

It is very important to be competent technically, to be specific about goals and responsibilities, to negotiate firm agreements, and to keep the project simple. A bigger project is broken into phases for tighter progress control. This leaves less room for a game player to maneuver, and opposition can be dealt with more effectively. A phased software development life cycle with well defined milestones and deliverables helps.

Resistance from people can be a major contributing factor for a project's failure. It can lead to false estimates for time and effort in the feasibility study report. Lack of management support is another compounding factor. There are other reasons why the results of a feasibility study can be deceptive: poor planning for implementation, which may cause wasted time and effort, and miscalculating anticipated results. This can happen when estimates of anticipated benefits have been wrong. While few people would complain about underestimating benefits, e.g., return on investment or increased productivity, it still indicates inaccurate estimates. Overestimation of benefits are more critical, because the project may never have gotten the go-ahead if it had been known that the benefits would be that low. If the scope of the project changes and the feasibility study has not considered them, the estimates on most any aspect of feasibility can change and consequently they do not mean much anymore. One may end up with a system that provides more capacity but also costs more.

Problems and Questions

1. (a) How can counterimplementation affect DP goals?

    (b) What can the manager of a project do to avoid counterimplementation on the part of his staff?

    (c) How can the selection of a project be affected by counterimplementation?

    (d) Give examples of counterimplementation and counter-counterimplementation when the following changes occur:

    ▶ introduction of new software developent techniques,

    ▶ change in management style, or

    ▶ new standards for software development, reflecting a change in priorities for software quality.

    (e) How would you plan for and counteract counterimplementation during

    ▶ feasibility analysis,

    ▶ risk assessment, and

    ▶ benefit analysis?

2. How would you build personal credibility as a manager with your staff, and your peers, and upper management? To answer these questions, use both company scenarios in Section 13.2. (How) does your answer differ for the two environments? Why does it or why does it not differ?

3. Assume that different groups are responsible for each phase of the software development life cycle. Sometimes there are problems between the groups. Implementation teams complain about "weird" designs and designers complain about infeasible require-

ments and that they often have to "do things over." In the process, methodology is "counterimplemented." Make some suggestions on how to counteract this. What is probably the most crucial action to take? Rank your suggestions in order of impact. Are there any risks inherent in your actions? Is there a way to reduce them?

13.6. Top-Level Project Plan

13.6.1. Planning Activities

Planning proceeds in the following steps:

▶ Define development activities, including the inputs they need and the outputs they generate.

▶ Determine dependencies between activities. This provides a graph similar to a requirements diagram, except that it is a network with no feedback cycles. An alternate representation of timing dependencies between activities is the Gantt chart (or bar chart). The length of every activity is denoted by the length of the bar representing it. Parallel activities are arranged vertically one above the other. Dependencies are indicated by vertical arrows between bars (activities). There will be examples of both types of charts later.

▶ Determine resources, staff, and time for each activity.

▶ Estimate cost and schedule based on network and resource allocation.

It helps to consider a checklist of activities when making a preliminary plan at the beginning of a software project. The major software development *planning* activities are as follows:

1. **Team creation.** This should be completed at the start of software development. The chapter on software development personnel describes this aspect in full detail.

2. **Architecture and design strategy.** This aspect of the project must be fully defined at the end of the feasibility study. It is one prerequisite to doing any sort of parallel or staggered development. It will drive all the other planning activities that follow.

3. **Number of releases and delivery strategy.** This also should be available at the end of the feasibility study, since it, too, drives the amount of parallelism in the software development process. In particular, it will influence the type of development facilities needed, the maintenance plan and the documentation plan.

4. **Acceptance test plan.**   A high level preliminary plan must be available at the end of the feasibility study; the detailed plan and generic test cases exist at the end of requirements analysis. Its formulation is based on a general quality assurance strategy.

5. **Customer support plan.**   It must be in place by the end of development of any (part) of the software system that is ready for release to a customer. The plan depends on maintenance procedures and support documents.

6. **The documentation plan.**   For the development, this plan has to be in place at the end of the feasibility study. The plan for providing documentation to the user needs to be available at the end of the specification phase.

7. **Quality assurance and testing plans.**   These kick in at several parts of the software development life cycle. Quality assurance plan and procedures (i.e., how to make sure that the software will possess the required quality) has to be known at the end of the feasibility study. One may not have to do much of anything if there is a methodology in place that can be incorporated by reference. The overall test plan should be known at the end of the feasibility study, but details are filled in all through the software development life cycle as discussed in Part I.

8. **Development facilities plan.**   Each phase needs its own facilities, even if it is only office space and computer time. During the testing phase, one may have to plan for extra hardware and software, a laboratory environment, a testbed, etc. Since some of it requires the acquisition or development of extra hardware or software, a plan should exist for this by the end of the feasibility study. The plan and the actions stemming from the plan will become more detailed as more detailed knowledge becomes available throughout the software development process. But that is due to its implementation. Planning for it must be done up front.

9. **Maintenance plan.**   The maintenance plan must be implemented by the time the software is turned over to the customer. Often it refers to an existing maintenance methodology (similar to the one described in the chapter on maintenance).

10. **Prototype.**   The prototype's objective is to clarify some of the concerns of the feasibility study and to help in decisions about what system should and can be developed and how to go about doing it. It needs to be available before the end of the feasibility study.

11. **Training plan.**   We need to know in which areas the development team is deficient. Training for the development team must be completed before the skills are needed. Customer training is planned in three areas: using the prototype (if it is to be used by the customers), evaluating the user interface at the end of the specification

phase, and using the completed system. Customer training is done during prototype development, during user interface development, and during system test. The last is also the time to train maintenance staff.

These plans must be evaluated, and then the project is sized and costs are estimated. There may be iterations in this planning process. Table 13.6 shows the activities, inputs, outputs, and dependencies between activities for the checklist of plans. The numbers in the table correspond to the activity numbers used above. Since the activity usually involves defining or developing whatever the output is (a plan), the table only lists the outputs. Inputs are defined in terms of the outputs of the preceding activities and thus can be deduced via the activity number under the column heading "preceding activity." Plans are evaluated in activity 12. Activity 13 is sizing and costing.

Figure 13.3 shows a box diagram for the planning activities. Figure 13.4 gives an event diagram of the planning process. The latter uses the activity numbers from Table 13.6. Only one iteration of the planning process is shown, but the planning process may iterate for several alternatives, because of cost and schedule constraints. Figures 13.3 and 13.4 show the prototyping activity with dashed arcs, since it does not always apply.

13.6.2. Phased Plan for Single Release

A plan for a single release follows the phases of software development:

1. **Requirements analysis**.   This phase produces a feasibility study, a requirements document, a project plan, and an acceptance test. The acceptance test is described as a detailed plan and a set of generic test cases that may not be in their proper syntactic form yet.

2. **Specifications**.   The deliverables of this phase are a functional specification document, a preliminary user manual, at least a high level design for the user interface, maybe a mock-up, a set of phase-test cases, and a subset of them that will be used during the testing phase of the code.

3. **Design phase**.   This phase produces a full design document, both structure and content, a programmer's handbook, unit test strategy, and integration test specification. The latter we need earlier if we have a lot of parallelism in the development plan.

4. **Coding phase**.   The end of the coding phase is marked by documented, compilable code, full unit test specifications, preliminary software documentation, and a full integration test plan.

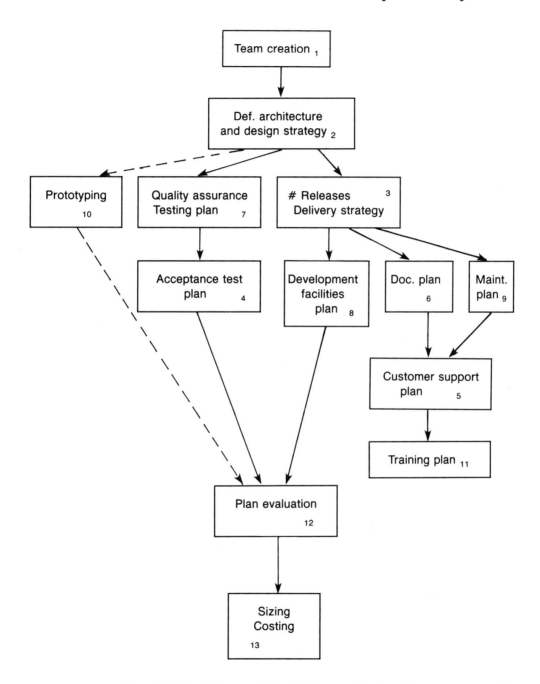

Figure 13.3 Block Diagram of Planning Process—One Iteration.

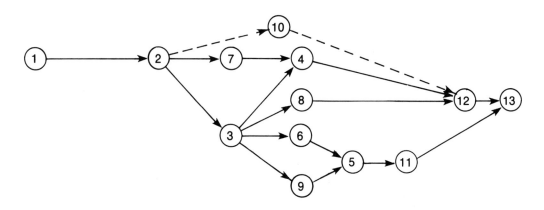

Figure 13.4 Event Diagram for Table 13.6.

Table 13.6 Activity list with precedences.

#	Activity/Output	Precedes Activity	Follows
1	Team creation/team	All	None
2	Architecture and design strategy	3	1
3	# releases, delivery strategy	8	2
4	Acceptance test plan	12	7,3
5	Customer support plan	11	9,6
6	Documentation plan	5	3
7	Quality assurance and testing plan	4	2
8	Development facilities plan	12	3
9	Maintenance plan	5	3
10	Prototype	12	2
11	Training plan	12	5,6
12	Plan evaluation	13	4,8,10,11
13	Sizing and costing	None	12

5. **Unit and integration test phase.** At the end of this phase, integrated code is available that was tested according to plan. A full system test plan exists. The system test is prepared and tests have been specified. The final acceptance test and site installation test have been fully specified. This is complemented by training manuals and the preliminary system and user reference manuals. System test change control procedures are in place.

6. **System test phase**.   At the end of system test, the system has been fully tested and is ready to be turned over to the customer for acceptance testing. Site and test procedures are prepared for the acceptance test. Revisions to code and documents from now on must be done according to system test change control procedures.

7. **Acceptance test**.   A signed acceptance agreement marks the end of the acceptance test. Customers and maintenance personnel (customer support) have been trained. Final versions of all documents and code (documented) have been put under change control. There is a fully specified set of maintenance procedures. Customer support personnel have been assigned responsibilities, and they are ready to do their work. Lastly, there is an operations plan for the software. This encompasses change control, quality assurance, conditions for future releases, feedback evaluation mechanisms, and further development plans.

Figure 13.5 shows a Gantt chart of a phased software development plan for a single release with some phase overlap. The wavy lines at the beginning of some of the activity boxes indicate that, at this point, planning and resource acquisition for the activity in the box are complete. This includes measurement support and staff training. In particular, staff must know the hardware before they make hardware related decisions. Training that involves software or implementation languages must be complete before the software is used or before interface decisions are made that relate to the software or language. There may be application programs and development tools, and training must be complete before they will be used. This depends on when software or language use starts. Programmers must know the implementation language before they start coding. An analyst must know the support tools before starting requirements analysis. These considerations determine training needs by phase and by tool or language. One must also specify *who* is responsible for using a tool, software, or implementation language and *when* they need to be able to do so. This may not always be as late as the start of a phase. If the project calls for prototyping during requirements analysis and feasibility study or for a mock-up during the specifications phase, skills may be needed earlier, at least for the people who are implementing the prototype or the mock-up.

Figure 13.5 shows a significant degree of overlap. This shortens the development schedule and utilizes people more efficiently. The starting point of the next phase must be carefully defined. There should *always* be a specific, identifiable partial deliverable and thus a reason why the next phase can be started. For example, the top two levels of the design hierarchy may have been defined and therefore one can be coded, while lower level modules still need to be fully designed.

Some of the bars show a PT (phase test) activity at the end. Part of the phase test can be done earlier during any given phase; i.e., there are small "slices" of the phase test

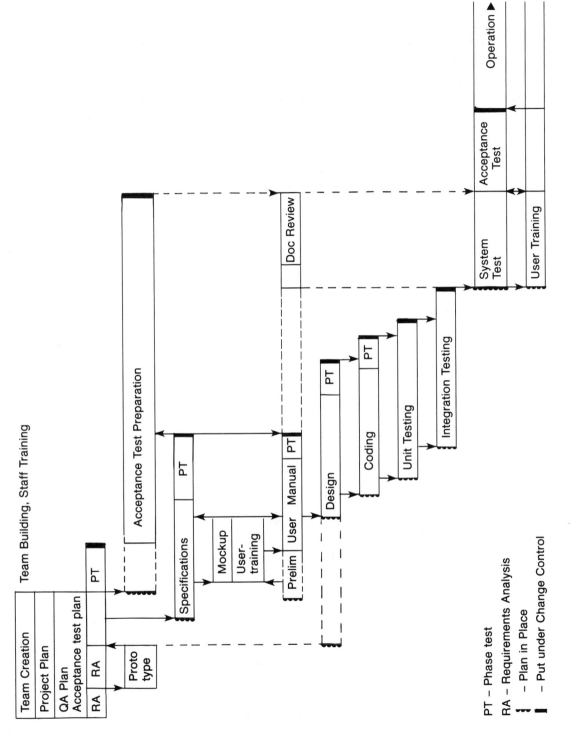

Figure 13.5 Phased Software Development Plan with Overlap for Single Release.

whenever cohesive parts of a phase deliverable become available. On a conceptual level, one could consider early phase-test slices of the design as tests of design "units" (modules) and then have the "design integration test" at the end of the design phase. For time estimation purposes, the phase-test slices were all collected at the end of a phase. The bold vertical line at the end of an activity bar indicates that the deliverable that results from the software development activity is put under change control (is baselined).

13.6.3. Multiple Releases

With more than one release, one needs to determine how to schedule them. There are principally two ways to attack this problem:

▶ Don't start working on the next release until a sufficient amount of user feedback has been received that makes it worthwhile to develop the next release. This approach is used for software that is developed all at once, then used for a while and not changed until there are compelling reasons to do so.

▶ Start working on the next release before the user feedback on the current release is in. This is more appropriate for versions of increasing functionality and a narrow market window and therefore considerable time pressures. Then customers who gave feedback in version k may not see their feedback implemented until version $k + 2$ or later (unless it required immediate corrective maintenance action). They will, however, receive a more powerful system at release $k + 1$, even though it may not address some of the customers' current concerns.

The more development overlaps, the more precise planning needs to be. Any "forgotten" activity can lead to immediate schedule overruns. It becomes more complex to avoid overutilization of resources (computer, human, etc.) and proper change control is much more critical and, if violated, potentially harmful. Now not only should documents be controlled between different development phases but also between subsequent versions/releases. This adds a whole new dimension of complexity. The novice in planning should limit and be very careful about version overlap, unless the software and its development environment are simple to plan for.

Consider a development plan with several versions or releases. For maximum parallelism one needs to define the starting points for the next development cycle (the next "release") by determining the minimum set of prerequisites.

Design for versions 1 and 2 can only be overlapped if all design of version 1 that is relevant to version 2 has been completed. Otherwise, the version 2 design bar in the Gantt chart must be added after the one indicating the design phase of version 1. Even more important, later phases will also need to be independent of each other. In particular, subsequent versions are not dependent on previously implemented code. Figure 13.6

a) Without V1-V2 dependencies:

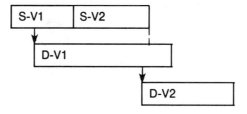

b) With V1-V2 dependencies:

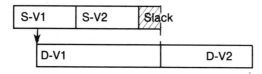

c) With code dependencies:

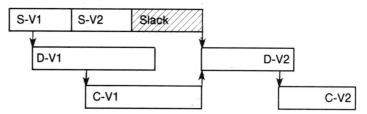

S—Specifications; D—Design; C—Code; V1—Version 1; V2—Version 2.

Figure 13.6 Specification-Design Overlap.

shows an example of specification-design overlap with and without various dependencies.

Figure 13.6a shows a situation where the design of version 2 only depends on the completion of its specifications but not on the completion of version 1's design. This allows the maximum parallelism. We assume that the specifications for version 2 depend on the completion of the specifications for version 1. Otherwise (e.g., relatively independent functions whose I/O interface can be defined after the top level specification decisions have been made), higher parallelism is possible.

Figure 13.6b assumes that the design of version 1 has to be complete before the design of version 2 can start. All other dependencies are the same as in Figure 13.6a. There is some slack time to complete the specifications for version 2.

Figure 13.6c assumes that design and code of the second version depend upon the code of the first version. This shows the most slack to complete the specifications for version 2. It results in the longest elapsed time.

Most cases allow one or the other type of overlap. When determining schedules, estimate elapsed times and end times for activities based on the degree of expected overlap. It depends on problem, methodology, and the availability of resources and staff. Cost estimation and scheduling uses the bars in the bar chart or the nodes in an event diagram and associates times and resource costs with them. This is discussed in Chapter 14.

Problems and Questions

1. What are the advantages and disadvantages of highly parallel development?

2. How do the planning needs change when you are developing software for your own needs with a life span of several years and modified versions about every half year? You also expect significant complexity in design and implementation.

3. You are asked to develop a syntax-oriented editor for the PASCAL dialect on your local PCs. It is to be a single version development, but you envision that as people use it and become more sophisticated, they will probably want support features for their programming project that have not been included. What planning activities will you need? What degree of parallelism can you expect? Use the graphical techniques in this chapter to explain your preliminary planning.

4. Which of the three degrees of parallelism of Figure 13.6 would you expect for PAS? Why? What is the safest option if you have no preset deadline that you need to fit but if it is important to meet the deadline once you have committed to it?

5. For each planning activity in Table 13.6, describe a situation where an activity plan is very simple or exists by default and a situation where the activity plan will be rather nonobvious and complex.

13.7. Summary

The activities described in this chapter illustrate work that happens early in a project's life, which, in fact, will determine whether there is to be a project at all. These activities need to ascertain technical feasibility, manageability, and political feasibility. Their assessment results in a preliminary plan (top-level project plan) in case a project is considered feasible. This top-level project plan is refined before a project gets underway.

Successful projects support long-term as well as short-term objectives. Such objectives differ with the type of department. We showed with the example objective "increase productivity" what that could mean for different aspects of a software organization (service, department operation, software development). Metrics for goal achievement help to select projects that then undergo a feasibility study. Two case studies (PC software firm, software development department) showed the top-down development of metrics for goal achievement that are detailed enough for project selection.

Section 13.3. discussed management aspects of a feasibility study and how it relates to the technical aspects of a feasibility analysis discussed in Chapter 4. We can consider the feasibility study as a quality assurance step that makes certain that goals at all levels will be supported by a project. We showed how to plan a feasibility study. It consists of four phases: setting the evaluation framework, planning for the feasibility study, analyzing requirements, and refining alternatives to the point of recommendations.

A major part of the feasibility study is to assess the risk of failure for a project and to make contingency plans. Section 13.4. discussed ways to analyze risk depending on the information available. Risk factors can be inherent in the project itself or due to evaluator bias. We discussed how to evaluate project risk and how to diminish risk due to evaluator bias. One major approach to reduce such bias is a structured evaluation method that is based on statistical principles.

A structured risk assessment procedure, which used the techniques for evaluation from Chapter 12, was introduced. It uses risk scales for individual risk factors and provides for additive and multiplicative compounding of risk. This method can also be used to set risk targets and to determine a proper risk portfolio. It is an extension of a method suggested in [Mcfa81].

When quantification of risk is impossible, these techniques are no longer applicable. We discussed several ways to make decisions under complete uncertainty. These include equal likelihood and maximax estimation. We also considered the effect of multiple events and duplicate outcomes. For a similar treatment of this topic see [Boeh81].

When risk is too big, either more information needs to be gathered to see whether it will be safe to embark on a project, or risk needs to be reduced. We discussed the concept of a risk reduction matrix to structure the formal assessment of risk reduction.

Some project risks are not technical, but human. We discussed how to recognize resistance and games, how to overcome resistance, and how to negotiate commitment to stop counterimplementation before it damages a project.

The outcome of the feasibility study is a requirements document and a top-level project plan. Section 13.6. discussed how to develop such a top-level project plan and the pros and cons of phase overlap from a management perspective. It explained all the planing activities for which management is responsible and how they are timed. We also developed a phased software development plan for a single release that allowed phase overlap. Modifications were suggested for multiple releases (evolutionary development), depending on which phases overlap. Overlap always makes planning more complicated, because there are more dependencies between activities. The impact of schedule changes for some development activities on overall schedule may be drastic.

This concludes top-level planning activities. Cost estimation and scheduling uses the activity bars in the bar chart or the nodes in the event diagram of the top-level plan and associates them with times and resource costs. This is the objective of several of the estimation techniques presented in the next chapter.

▶ 14
Models for
Managerial
Planning

14.1. Overview

After the initial planning and after the general project approach is fixed, we determine the time and cost for each activity in the plan. Cost and effort estimation is a project in its own right and needs a plan. This plan lists

▶ purpose and objectives of the estimation process,

▶ schedule and deliverables at the end of the estimation process,

▶ responsibilities for each aspect of the estimation project,

▶ how we will go about estimating (methods, tools),

▶ resources needed to do the job, and

▶ assumptions about the estimates and the estimation conditions that will impact the estimation process.

This chapter deals with models that are commonly needed to support managerial planning activities for software projects. The first type of models are also called network techniques because they represent the work activities of a software project as a network. The network is then analyzed. These models are used for scheduling to determine deadlines, start and end dates for project activities, and to identify time-critical parts of a software project. Section 14.2. describes two methods, CPM and PERT. The examples use the activity definitions for software project planning.

The second type of model provides support for cost and effort estimation, a very important planning activity. It also happens to be a part of software project management that has not been famous for accuracy [Thay82]. This is why Section 14.3. puts a great deal of emphasis on a systematic approach to cost and effort estimation, which includes selection of the methods. First, principles of cost estimation are discussed. Cost estimation is usually based on effort estimates. Algorithmic, experiential, and subjective effort estimation methods are described next. Each has its own range of applicability. Complementary techniques are suggested for improved accuracy in estimation. Examples highlight the models' uses and contrast how results can differ for the same estimation problem when various models are used.

Since all estimation techniques are based on being able to size a software development effort accurately, a section on software sizing (14.4.) explains various methods used for software sizing. Some are in widespread use, others are still experimental, but promising, and still others are in the research stage.

The summary (14.5.) points out existing limitations to estimation models and the manager's need for an overall perspective that goes beyond the project itself and includes organizational and human issues.

14.2. Network Models

It is possible to plan for a considerable amount of overlap during a software project. Planning for maximum overlap reduces total project time. It also increases risk, because there is no slack time or less than fully utilized resources that will be able to compensate when another development activity takes longer. If we build safety into each activity through conservative estimates, we can use network models, such as PERT or CPM, and Gantt charts to plan for maximum overlap of activities throughout the life cycle.

These techniques also determine

▶ the earliest and latest times that an activity can start,

▶ the most probable project duration, and

▶ all critical activities. An activity is considered critical when its late completion by
x days will also extend total project duration by x days. A critical path in an activity network consists of critical activities in chronological order.

Since we have already considered Gantt charts as a time planning tool, we will concentrate in this section on CPM and PERT networks. They can be very useful for scheduling software projects, but they have one drawback: we can only schedule a single iteration of a set of development activities. These networks do not allow cycling back to previous activities (phases). When this happens in a project, we have to revise the current scheduling network, reassign new durations to each activity, and then reevaluate the network. This requires computerized planning support. Another reason for a software tool is that normal evaluation of more than tiny networks quickly becomes unwieldy. With computerized support and guided reevaluation, these scheduling networks can be quite useful.

Let us explain CPM networks first. CPM is an abbreviation for *Critical Path Method*. A critical path is a sequence of activities (or software development phases) executed in sequence. Duration times of these activities determine overall project time, because there is no slack time for these activities (as opposed to some of the other, noncritical ones). Thus, if any of the activities that are part of the critical path take longer than projected, finishing the entire project is delayed by that same amount of time.

We assume that we have an activity list with precedences as in Table 14.1. We also need an estimate of the duration of each activity in the activity list. Table 14.1. gives those estimates for our example.

Table 14.1 Activity List for Software Project Planning.

#	Activity	Duration (days)	Next activity
1	Team creation	3	2
2	Architecture and design strategy development	7	3,7,10
3	Decide on number of releases, delivery strategy	2	4,6,8,9
4	Develop acceptance test plan	7	12
5	Develop customer support plan	4	11
6	Develop documentation plan	4	5
7	Develop quality assurance and testing plan	4	4
8	Plan for development facilities	3	12
9	Develop maintenance plan	4	5
10	Develop prototype	13	12
11	Develop training plan	4	12
12	Plan evaluation	3	12
13	Sizing and costing	3	—

CPM tries to answer common project planning questions:

1. What is the duration of the project? In the above example, the question would be how long will project planning take?

2. By how much (if at all) will the project be delayed if any one of the activities will take x days longer? For example, will planning take longer if the development of the acceptance test plan (activity 4) should take 10 instead of 7 days?

3. How long can certain activities be postponed without increasing total project duration? We could ask, for instance, what the latest starting time is for the development of the maintenance plan (activity number 9) without jeopardizing project duration.

CPM translates the activity list into a graph where the activities are arcs. The arcs are labelled with the activity number and the activity duration. For our example, Figure 14.1 shows the corresponding CPM graph to Table 14.1.

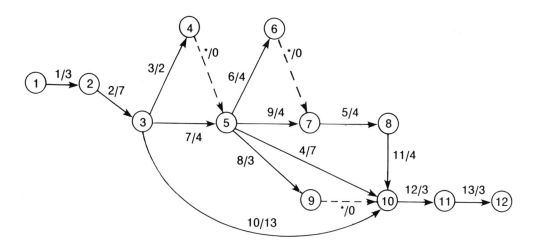

Figure 14.1 CPM Graph for Table 14.1

We introduced new "dummy" activities from vertices number 4, 6, and 9. They are drawn dashed. In this way we avoided multiple arcs between two adjacent nodes. CPM does not allow multiple arcs between neighboring nodes. Thus, the following situation,

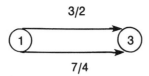

can be rectified by introducing a new node (numbered 2) and a dummy activity of zero duration between the new node (2) and the target node (3):

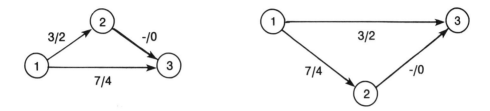

CPM does not allow feedback loops in the graph. In practice, this would indicate repeating the activities that are represented by the arcs in the loop or cycle for an unspecified number of times. This is not a good planning situation to be in. As soon as we know how many times we need to repeat the cycle, we can unroll it and the feedback loop is gone.

Let us look now at answers to the project planning question for our example from Table 14.1:

1. project duration is 32 working days;

2. even if development of the acceptance test should take 10 instead of 7 days, duration for the planning project will still be 32 days; and

3. the latest starting time for developing the maintenance plan (activity 9) is 14 days into the project. It also happens to be the earliest time that we can start this activity. This is because activity 9 is a critical activity.

Other critical activities are 1, 2, 7, 6, 5, 11, 12, and 13. These activities form two critical paths in the CPM network. In general, we have at least one such path in a CPM network. Here we have two because activities 6 and 9 happen to have the same duration. None of the critical activities may be postponed without a corresponding delay in total duration.

CPM can be used to determine deadlines for activities that affect other activities in a project. This is important for planning time and availability of resources (capacity planning), for identifying delays early, for cost planning, and for phase control in the software development process.

How should we identify activities for the CPM planning process? There are several rules of thumb that help in constructing your activity list:

1.   Use activities that are self-contained units of work with a clear deliverable. Don't chop activities into parts that do not have a meaning in themselves.

2.   Use comparable activity durations. Don't choose activity durations that are too different (such as 1 day versus 1000 days). You can always collapse several short activities into one or try to divide a long activity into several smaller ones.

3.   The smallest activity duration should be at least 3/1,000 of total project duration. This prevents excessively large graphs which represent an overplanned project. It only gives us a false sense of security and unnecessary detail.

4.   Use a computer to help set up and evaluate a CPM network.

These rules should help to define a proper activity list with its durations. The CPM network depicts dependencies between activities. Nodes between an activity arc in the graph represent the start and end events for that activity. There are some simple rules how to translate an activity list into a CPM graph.

1.   Activity A is characterized by a start event F and an end event G. Then we introduce an arc e_A from node v_F to node v_G

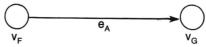

2.   Activities A_1 to A_k have to be finished before A_0 can start. There are no other activities in between. We draw this situation as shown:

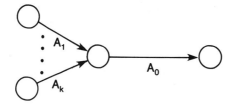

3. A_0 is the only required activity for A_1 to A_k to start:

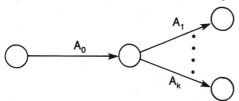

4. Multiple arcs between two adjacent nodes are not allowed. Insert "dummy" activities.

5. The network should not contain any circles.

6. If there is more than one activity that does not require completion of other activities, insert an artificial starting activity. This way the network will have a unique source (start event). Likewise, if there is more than one activity without any activity following it, insert an artificial ending activity. This way the network will have a unique sink (ending event).

7. If there is to be a delay of T time units between activities A_1 and A_2, insert a delay activity A_0 between them of duration T.

Now that we can draw a proper CPM network, we should investigate its properties. We have already heard of the critical path, which is a path of maximal length from the source node to the sink node. Its activities are critical activities, and its length is the shortest project duration.

Property 1: In every CPM network there is at least one critical path.

Before describing other properties we need some definitions.

▶ E_i = earliest possible time that event denoted by node v_i can happen.

▶ L_j = latest possible time that event denoted by node v_j can happen.

▶ d_{ij} = duration of activity denoted by arc from v_i to v_j.

▶ ES_{ij} = earliest possible start of activity denoted by arc from v_i to v_j.

▶ EE_{ij} = earliest possible end of activity denoted by arc from v_i to v_j.

▶ LS_{ij} = latest possible start of activity denoted by arc from v_i to v_j.

▶ LE_{ij} = latest possible end of activity denoted by arc from v_i to v_j.

Property 2: The earliest possible time that event denoted by node v_j can happen is given by

$$E_j = \max_i \left\{ E_i + d_{ij} \right\}$$

where i are indices of nodes having arcs to node j.

This property enables us to compute important timing characteristics for activities in the network. It is based on a topological sort of all nodes in the network. A topological sort uses the rank of nodes in a network as sorting criterion. Then nodes are numbered in order of increasing rank. The rank $r(v_i)$ of a node v_i is given as

$$r(v_i) = sup \text{ (all nodes having path ending in } v_i)$$

The renumbered nodes have the following property:

$$r(v_i) < r(v_j) \Rightarrow i < j$$

Ranks for the nodes in our example are given in Table 14.2. We renumbered nodes 7, 8, and 9 into 8, 9, and 7 because node 7 only had a rank of 5 compared to a rank of 6 and 7 for nodes 8 and 9.

Once the nodes are topologically sorted, we can determine earliest and latest start and end points of activities and the events associated with them. The formulas are as follows:

1. Determination of L_i ($i = n, n - 1, \ldots, 1$):

$$L_n = E_n$$
$$L_i = min \ (L_j - d_{ij}) \qquad\qquad for \ i = n - 1, \ldots, 1$$

The minimum is taken over all nodes j that have an arc originating at i and ending at j.

2. Determination of ES_{ij}, EE_{ij}, LS_{ij}, and LE_{ij}:

$$ES_{ij} = E_i$$
$$EE_{ij} = E_i + d_{ij}$$
$$LE_{ij} = L_j$$
$$LS_{ij} = L_j - d_{ij}$$

3. Determination of various buffer times:
   Total buffer time (TB_{ij})
   Free buffer time (FB_{ij})
   Independent buffer time (IB_{ij})

$$TB_{ij} = LS_{ij} - ES_{ij}$$
$$FB_{ij} = E_j - EE_{ij}$$
$$IB_{ij} = max \ (0, \ E_j - L_i - d_{ij})$$

Table 14.2 shows the results of computing node-related (i.e., event-related) scheduling information for the example graph of Figure 14.1. Table 14.3 lists the latest and earliest start and end times and buffer times for all activities. Note that *TB* values give the most optimistic buffer times (maximum slack built into the schedule) while *FB* and *IB* are more pessimistic.

Figure 14.2 shows a Gantt chart of the schedule analysis for our example. Each bar corresponds to an activity, and the length of the bar indicates activity duration. The

Table 14.2 Node-related CPM Analysis Information.

Node	Rank	New node no.	E	L
1	0	1	0	0
2	1	2	3	3
3	2	3	10	10
4	3	4	12	14
5	4	5	14	14
6	5	6	18	18
7	6	8	18	18
8	7	9	22	22
9	5	7	17	26
10	9	10	26	26
11	10	11	29	29
12	11	12	32	32

Table 14.3 Activity-related CPM Analysis Information.

Activity	Node-pair (new)	d	ES	EE	LE	LS	TB	FB	IB
1	(1,2)	3	0	3	3	0	0	0	0
2	(2,3)	7	3	10	10	3	0	0	0
3	(3,4)	2	10	12	14	12	2	0	0
4	(5,10)	7	14	21	26	19	5	5	0
5	(8,9)	4	18	22	22	18	0	0	0
6	(5,6)	4	14	18	18	14	0	0	0
7	(3,5)	4	10	14	14	10	0	0	0
8	(5,7)	3	14	17	26	23	9	0	0
9	(5,8)	4	14	18	18	14	0	0	0
10	(3,10)	13	10	23	26	13	3	3	3
11	(9,10)	4	22	26	26	22	0	0	0
12	(10,11)	3	26	29	29	26	0	0	0
13	(11,12)	3	29	32	32	29	0	0	0

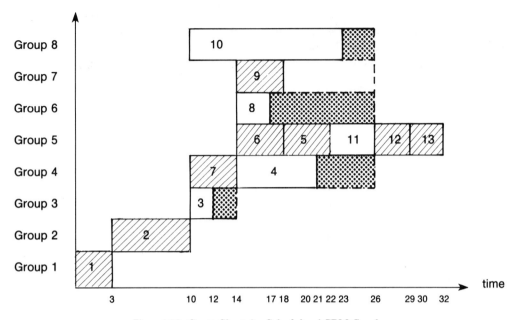

Figure 14.2 Gantt Chart for Schedule of CPM Graph.

start of the bar corresponds to ES_{ij}, its end to EE_{ij}. The dotted section of a bar indicates LE_{ij}, and bars with diagonal lines denote critical activities.

This scheduling information is used to assign responsibility and staff to an activity or sets of activities. A graphical method like the Gantt chart also makes it easier to spot over- or underutilization of resources and staff. Based on a list of staff and resource requirements by activity, we can determine what the distribution of resources and staff will be throughout the project. We can also identify possible inconsistencies, e.g., that two parallel activities require a common resource, but only one activity can use it at a given time. In that case, we can use buffer times for activities to shift activities. If, for example, activities 4 and 8 had to be done by the same person who could not do them at the same time, we could delay activity 8 until after activity 4 is finished—it would not increase project duration.

The y axis of the Gantt chart shows either names of people or groups whose responsibility is denoted by the activities in the row with their name. We can also define rows in terms of specific (scarce or critical) resources like computers, labs, special equipment, etc. Either will provide a schedule for the activities in the chart. Monitoring this schedule, we track actual time spent versus the time indicated in the chart. This indicates whether the project is on schedule or, if not, which activities could be delayed.

Sometimes the activity durations that we assumed to be fixed in the CPM network cannot be determined with that much accuracy. Then we analyze the activity network with probabilistic durations. Often we can determine some reasonable upper and lower bound on each activity duration as well as a most likely one. In this case, we can compute a weighted average duration for each activity. We use this average to analyze our network. PERT requires us to know an optimistic (O), a pessimistic (P), as well as a most likely (M) activity duration. The mean activity duration is then computed as

$$d_{PERT} = (O + 4M + P)/6.$$

The most likely duration has a weight of 4 compared to optimistic and pessimistic estimates. This corresponds to underlying probability distributions for activity durations with strong peaks. Parkin [Park80] suggests a different weighting scheme for flatter distributions:

$$d_{PARK} = (O + M + P)/3$$

This reflects a different likelihood of optimistic and pessimistic estimates. In this case we may not know which is the most likely (equal weights) or we may have a flat distribution. The corresponding variances for these average activity durations are

$$var_{PERT} = \{(O - P)/6\}^2$$
$$var_{PARK} = \{(O - P)/2\}^2$$

Critical paths variance is the sum of activity variances along the path when the activities are statistically independent. This is rarely the case. When they have dependencies, we must subtract covariances from the sum of variances (covariances can be negative or positive). They often are small when activity variances are. They are not likely to change the activities contained in a critical path when buffer times for noncritical activities tend to be large.

On the other hand, large variances and/or small buffer times can make another path into the critical one and lead to longer effective project time. We may want to determine CPM solutions for the optimistic and the pessimistic durations also. This way we can see what our best and worst schedules are and how the "mean" schedule will be affected by these potential fluctuations. For further details on these analyses see Parkin [Park80].

Problems and Questions

1. Assume the activity network of Figure 14.1. The following optimistic, most likely, and pessimistic estimates for activity durations are given:

	1	2	3	4	5	6	7	8	9	10	11	12	13
O	1	3	1	5	2	3	3	3	1	12	2	3	3
M	3	7	2	7	4	4	4	3	4	13	4	3	3
P	10	10	2	20	15	7	6	3	8	25	9	3	6

Compute average activity durations and variances with the PERT and the Parkin formulae. Then determine the critical path and shortest project duration for each. If the project proceeded optimally (activity durations marked "O"), what would the critical path and shortest project duration be? In the worst case (activity durations marked "P"), what are critical path and shortest project duration?

14.3. Cost and Effort Estimation

14.3.1. Cost Estimation

Cost estimation is based on planning information about the project as described in the previous chapter. Most information for initial cost estimation comes from the feasibility study and requirements analysis. When we estimate costs very early, there is less information upon which to base estimates and therefore this information is less detailed and the estimates may be less accurate. Software cost estimation is important for making good management decisions in a software project. It is also connected to determining how much effort and time a software project requires. Cost estimation has several uses:

- ► It establishes a firm, reliable budget for an in-house project.

- ► It facilitates competitive contract bids when a software house wants to get the contract for developing a specific software system. It is easier to make a close, competitive bid with accurate cost estimates. If they are too high, another competitor will outbid. If they are too low, money will be lost on the deal.

- ► It determines whether it is cheaper to develop software in-house, to contract for outside development, or to buy a software product off-the-shelf and customize it.

If we are able to determine cost and time estimates for each activity of a software project reliably, then we can determine overall project effort and cost. Often we use estimation to trade off development time, cost, and project scope (cf. Chapter 4). Software development can be a very complex set of tasks and if we hope to ever achieve reliable cost estimates and have projects that can stay within budget, we need to estimate systematically.

Software cost estimation faces many problems which, unfortunately, tend to perpetuate a rather poor state of the art. The development of a good predictive model (and cost estimation falls into this category) requires collecting historical data on time and cost requirements for projects. Without the time to collect accurate historical data and to develop and continually refine the resulting model, there is little chance of improving estimating performance. No manager can be an expert on cost estimation, if he has only done it a few times; he needs practice. Tracking project progress and increasing estimating skills are both reasons to reestimate periodically. As more about the project becomes known in successive phases, estimates become easier and more accurate. We can track the successive quality of estimates by comparing actual project cost to their estimates.

This also holds for time estimates. DeMarco [Dema82] even derives an estimation quality indicator. It is a function of the differences at each phase between projected and actual cost. The longer a project shows big differences between actual and estimated value, the poorer the quality indicator. We reestimate at least at the end of every phase. If a project is large and has been subdivided into subprojects, we may do the (re) estimation by phase completion of subprojects but possibly not for the entire project.

Since good cost estimation is a difficult task and needs objectivity, it has been suggested [Dema82] that it be done by an independent group. This has advantages and disadvantages. The advantage is that it will probably be more objective. The disadvantage is that if the independent estimators do not have good rapport with the people who provide them with the data for estimation, they may not stand a chance to obtain a realistic estimate for a project, because they may not get the "real" data. A separate estimation group is prone to counterimplementation and games.

It is very important to understand just what type of estimate is to be provided. It is a conservative one, i.e., an estimate that will take into account most contingencies and their cost? Is it an optimistic estimate, i.e., an estimate that only considers the best of circumstances when there are no unplanned delays or changes or unplanned turnover in the development group? Most often the required estimate will be some "most probable" estimate, one that is neither too conservative nor too optimistic.

At times management appears to not want reasonable estimates, because the figures do not fit into the constraints. It is ultimately cheaper, however, to face reality up front, and either cancel the project or provide sufficient resources for it, than to end up with a software system that was built in a slipshod manner because time and/or budget were running out.

Software cost and effort estimation techniques fall into three categories:

▶ with an algorithmic model,

▶ with an experiential, statistical model, and

▶ through subjective experience.

Within these categories, we can estimate either the whole effort in a top-down fashion or combine parts estimates from the bottom-up. We will explain each of these three categories in turn.

Cost and effort estimation are closely related, since effort is a prime cost driver. This is so because, despite new developments that try to make software development into a more capital intensive endeavor, software production is still primarily labor-intensive. Among recent efforts is the building of software components that can be reused. Reusability is a key issue in the capitalization of the software development effort, and it also applies to concepts and techniques. Application generators fall into this category as tools to make a software generating mechanism reusable. Knowledge engineering and the development of knowledge support environments also increase the reusability of the knowledge aspect of software development and its applications. These efforts require a major capital investment up front but create reusable goods, according to Wegner [Wegn84]. Once these have been developed, software production has the potential to yield much higher worker productivity, creating less human effort. When this technology is successfully transferred into the marketplace, cost estimation for software projects is likely to be different from today's.

Effort is often described in man-hours. This measures the number of hours the staff has worked on a project. Thus, if 10 people worked on a project for 2 weeks at a rate of 40 working hours per week, the cumulative man-hours spent on the project are

$$10 \ people * 40 * 2 \ hours = 800 \ man\text{-}hours.$$

Sometimes effort is measured in man-years or man-months. These units can be converted into each other using standard figures such as 40 hours per week, 50 weeks per year.

Effort itself is often considered a function of size or productivity. Most models measure size in LOC (lines of source code), sometimes called SLOC, or KLOC (thousands of lines of source code), also called KSLOC. As mentioned in the chapter on metrics, quality should be considered when counting size. More detail on sizing will be given in section 14.4. Productivity in most of these models is defined as amount of work (such as LOC) per unit of effort (in man-hours, man-months, or man-years). For other definitions of productivity see the chapter on metrics.

The formula that determines project cost as a function of effort often uses a loaded cost/man-hour or cost/man-month figure. This "loading" adds on overhead costs (on a per hour basis) that affect the labor portion of the budget (e.g., benefits and administrative and support services that are to be paid directly through the project budget). Many firms determine these unit costs per man-month by measuring cumulative labor costs per project and then dividing it by the number of man-months spent on the project. Thus, if a project has labor costs of $40,000 and it took half a month for 10 people, the cost per manmonth is

$$\$40,000 \ / \ (.5 * 10) = \$8,000.$$

Often costs that are directly attributable to effort constitute the most important part of cost estimation, or its only variable part. Then the key to quality cost estimation for the project is a reliable, accurate method to estimating effort and the unit cost multiplier.

Sometimes all other factors that are cost relevant are bundled into this unit cost per man-month. This does not mean that other costs do not exist. It merely assumes that there is a linear relationship between labor effort and other cost drivers that are not of the labor type; e.g., x manhours of testing will (on the average) consume about y hours of chargeable computer time. When such statements describe reality, cost estimation via effort prediction alone will be sufficiently accurate.

Some aspects of project cost constitute a fixed, basic up-front investment or start-up cost for a project. This can be estimated and dealt with separately (e.g., cost of hardware, software tools, etc.). It is added to the effort cost estimate. In the following sections we are mostly concerned with estimates that are related to the effort it will take to develop a software product and all its associated documents. In this situation the challenge in cost estimation is to determine

▶ a good estimate of effort for the project and

▶ a proper unit-cost figure that reflects the cost per man-month of effort.

The unit cost is determined using historical data, but this data has to be adjusted for fluctuations in market rate for salaries and for inflation at the very least. It may also be affected by a host of other variables that describe the particular environment within which a software product is developed (cf. the problems and questions of this section). It may also vary with the level of staff hired to do the job. Better people, while more expensive, can get the job done in less time [Broo75]. This means an increase in unit cost, accompanied by a decrease in effort.

While unit cost figures are often given for the project as a whole or "top-down," it is also possible to develop unit cost and effort estimators for only parts of a software project. The estimates are then combined for an overall project estimate (bottom-up estimation). This requires breaking down the software project work activities into what is called a work breakdown structure. This work breakdown can be done according to software development phases and activities within phases, but it also can be done according to the structure of the product that is being developed. When different unit cost estimators are used per phase or per activity, one also needs effort estimates for the same work units. One cost estimation method that uses a bottom-up approach is adapted from Fried [Frie79]

1.   Total cost is the sum of the costs for all different module types. Examples of module types are modules that

▶ provide a database interface utility,

- ▶ are edit modules,

- ▶ do updates,

- ▶ process,

- ▶ perform major or minor database extracts, and

- ▶ develop major or minor reports.

Fried lists 12 different types of modules. Thus

$$cost_{total} = cost_{type\_i}$$

2.   The cost for all modules of a type is the cost for one such module multiplied by the number of modules of a given type:

$$cost_{type\_i} = N_i * cost_{mod\_i},$$

where N_i is the number of modules of type i and $cost_{mod\_i}$ is the cost to implement one module of type i.

3.   Individual module cost is the sum of costs for three different activities associated with the development of the module: systems analysis/programming, data entry, and testing.

$$cost_{mod\_i} = cost_{anpr} + cost_{entry} + cost_{test}$$

4.   The cost for analysis and programming depends on the size of the module, a unit cost multiplier, and the productivity of the staff:

$$cost_{anpr} = (size*unit\_cost)/productivity,$$

where size is the size of one module and *unit_cost* is the charge per hour of systems analysis and programming. Fried [Frie79] assumes that each hour of programming requires 1.1 hours of systems analysis, so

$$unit\_cost = 1.1 \; charge_{analysis} \; per \; hour + $$
$$charge_{programming} \; per \; hour,$$

and productivity is measured in number of programming statements per hour.

5.   The cost of data entry follows the same basic formula. Fried assumes that productivity (i.e., the rate of data entry) is 125 COBOL statements per hour. This rate has to be adjusted for different languages.

6.   The cost of testing is the computer test hours per module per class multiplied by the hourly charge for test time.

This six step cost estimation technique assumes that a work breakdown structure exists in order for the modules to be programmed and that it would be available sometime during design at the latest. Earlier breakdown of modules may be available on a functional level based on a requirements diagram or the specifications. This makes the estimation of overall project cost, as well as costs by sets of modules or subsystems, possible. These costs are summed to an overall cost estimate.

This assumes that size per module can be accurately determined. When size is estimated through historical data, one must take the distribution of size into account. This can be done by adding a suitable number of standard deviations to the mean size per module.

In the above formulas, the effort estimate is described as size over productivity.

Problems and Questions

1. Which of the following variables influences effort, and which influences unit cost. Why and how?

- ▶ personnel (level, quantity),

- ▶ expertise,

- ▶ amount of overtime,

- ▶ high level languages,

- ▶ complexity of project,

- ▶ development approach,

- ▶ resource usage,

- ▶ computer leasing agreement, and

- ▶ degree of parallelism and schedule compression in work activities.

2. The chapter on metrics lists several productivity metrics. Which are usable in the cost estimation formulas above? Why? (How) does your answer depend on the metric used for size? Give examples.

14.3.2. Algorithmic Estimation Models

Examples of algorithmic models are Halstead's effort indicator [Hals77] and the Rayleigh-Putnam curve ([Putn78], [Putn84]).

The Rayleigh-Putnam Curve

The Rayleigh-Putnam effort model uses a negative exponential curve as an indicator of cumulative manpower distribution over time during a project. Manpower is measured in man-months. This does not exclude a potentially infinite project duration (on a more practical level we would be able to look at an "extremely long" project life). Project duration as a development deadline helps to determine total effort. It may be predetermined through market considerations or established deadlines. When there is some freedom in setting deadlines, we can compare the effect of deadline and hence project duration on effort needed.

Expected project effort for a given project duration is computed via the mean of the effort distribution curve $R(t)$. It quantifies how expenditure of effort is spread throughout the project's lifetime. Its density function is an indicator of a project's manpower utilization rate. This is the change in amount of man-hours that are used over time on a software project. The formulae are as follows:

1. The effort utilization rate is

$$\frac{dR}{dt} = 2Bate^{-at^2}$$

    This sharply increases during the first phases of a project, reaches a peak during coding and testing, and then levels off again during maintenance. This corresponds to the need for few people in the beginning of a project. During coding and testing, the number of people that work on a project increases and pushes up man-hour consumption accordingly. Fewer people are needed again during maintenance.

2. The cumulative effort up to time t is

$$R(t) = B\ (1 - e^{-at^2}),$$

    where
    B is the area under the curve (Zelkowitz et al. [Zelk79] interpret it as the total lifetime effort (development and maintenance) in man-months) and
    a determines the shape of the curve (how flat or peaked it is).

Project duration T and project time t are variables denoting elapsed time (in years or months) while R and B are effort variables (in manmonths).

[Cont86] assumes the following relationship between project duration T and the parameter a that determines shape of $R(t)$:

$$a = 1/(2T^2)$$

This may not hold for all projects. In fact, [Zelk79] assumes that $a = 1/T^2$. We can validate this relationship with finished projects that are similar to the project under estimation. We also evaluate the effort estimation of every finished project to see whether the assumptions were fulfilled. If the relationship between T and a is different, the following computations will change.

To determine the total project effort we substitute the formula for a into the effort formula R and compute $R(T)$:

$$E = R(T) = B(1 - e^{(-1/(2T^2))T^2}) = B(1 - e^{-\frac{1}{2}}) = .3945\ B.$$

The Rayleigh-Putnam model derives a difficulty metric as the fraction of the area under the curve and the square of project duration:

$$D = B/T^2$$

If we then assume that productivity is a power function of difficulty, the productivity formula has the following shape:

$$P = cD^f$$

Productivity is also defined as the volume of the product over man-hours expended (the effort):

$$P = size\ /\ R(T)$$

Equating the two productivity formulae we can then compute size as

$$size = P\ R(T) = cD^f\ R(T)$$

The Rayleigh-Putnam model determined the constant f in the productivity function as

$$f = -\tfrac{2}{3},$$

using nonlinear regression on historical data. Size is then computed as

$$size = cD^{-2/3}\ R(T) = c\ (B/T^2)^{-2/3} * (.3945\ B) =$$
$$.3945\ c\ B^{1/3}\ T^{4/3}$$

The first two factors can be combined into a single one, called the Technology Factor:

$$C = .3945 \ c$$

Then the size equation simplifies to

$$size = C \ B^{1/3} \ T^{4/3}$$

The Technology Factor combines the effect of using tools, languages, methodology, quality assurance procedures, standards, etc. In environments where this tends to change between projects and where this change affects the total effort, the quality of prediction can be affected by an inaccurate value for C. Determining C is based on historical data. We need project size, area under the effort curve, and project duration to compute C as

$$C = size \ / \ (B^{1/3} \ T^{4/3}).$$

In a similar manner, we can predict the area under the effort curve using historical projects. The effort indicator in this model combines a great variety of factors into few constants, in particular start-up efforts (which can amount to a significant part of overall project effort). Estimation accuracy is therefore not as good for small and medium-sized projects. Conte et al. [Cont86] report serious overestimation. [Zelk79] suggests to estimate only projects with an estimated effort of over 50 man-months with this method. [Cont86] also failed to confirm the relationship posited in the $R(t)$ function. Estimation accuracy is reasonably good for large projects. One way to overcome the inaccuracies due to start-up efforts is to decouple this effort from the rest of the project and to estimate the two parts separately.

One of the advantages of using the Rayleigh-Putnam curve is that we can investigate the effect of schedule compression on project effort. [Cont86] criticized this model, however, as seriously exaggerating this effect. Put more positively, this model is better suited to situations when schedule compression will significantly affect the project effort. This would apply to considerable compression and to projects with highly dependent parts. Consider possible phase overlap and the dependencies between phases and activities to determine whether the assumptions of the Rayleigh-Putnam model are fulfilled.

The main project aspects that the Rayleigh-Putnam model considers are size and project duration and how they affect overall effort. Other factors are either not considered or lumped into constants such as the technology factor and the relationship between a and T. Effort is very sensitive to the value of these factors. These characteristics restrict the practical usability of the Rayleigh-Putnam model. First, we cannot investigate with this model what it does not consider: we must not estimate projects that will show effort variations due to factors this model fails to include. We must ensure that the projects fulfill the assumptions underlying this model (in particular the shape of the curve that is posited, the difficulty metric used, and the relationship between a and T). [Zelk79] gives a derivation of the Rayleigh-Putnam equation from assumptions about the nature of problem solving in large software projects.

A variation of the Rayleigh-Putnam model is Jensen's model [Jens84]. It differs in the computation of the adjustment factor C, called an effective technology constant. C is a multiplier to the basic formula and is the product of a basic technology constant and 13 adjustment factors. They are similar to those used in COCOMO (cf. 14.3.3.). When Conte et al. [Cont86] tested the performance of Jensen's model against the Rayleigh-Putnam model, its performance was only slightly better. They consider the performance of both models relatively poor.

Halstead's Effort Model

Halstead's effort model is similar to the Rayleigh-Putnam model in that it stipulates a specific type of function to compute effort. It makes several assumptions about the estimating environment. There is a complete unambiguous specification of the code that is to be written. The effort includes the time required to study the specifications and to design, implement, and test the program. It is an effort estimator that assumes programmers are working alone and are knowledgeable about the implementation language. The effort estimator is based on the characteristic quadruple (cf. Chapter 2). It was defined as (n_1, n_2, N_1, N_2). Let n be the sum of unique operators and operands and N be the sum of total operators and operands. Then, assuming that definition and use of operators and operands is balanced, the resulting implementation effort is defined by Halstead as

$$E = .25 \; N^2 \; log_2 n.$$

This effort formula can be used to estimate effort, provided that we can find reliable predictors for N and n. Total usage of operators and operands is certainly language dependent. A language like Ada that allows the definition and usage of complex, composite data types and high level statement types will probably use less operands and operators as an equivalent Assembler program. Reviewing a big number of programs, we can also determine a relationship between the size of the resulting source code (in LOC or KLOC) and total operator and operand usage (N). Assuming a linear relationship, we have

$$N = L * size,$$

where L is a language dependent constant that varies between programming languages. [Cont86] then suggests to determine n via Halstead's equation

$$N = n \, log_2 \, (n/2) = L * size$$

or

$$size = (n \, log_2 \, (n/2))/ \, L.$$

Knowing n we can compute $log_2 n$. While we do not have a closed form solution of n, we can determine one numerically over any of a variety of methods able to solve this type of equation. Therefore, we have all information necessary to determine E as a function of size. [Cont86] approximates $log_2 n$ by N^a and gets Halstead's effort indicator as

$$E = .25 \, N^{2+a}.$$

The value for a ranges with the size of operator and operand usage. They report a ranging from .31 to .25 as N ranges from 320 to 9216 with a median value of $a = .28$. This gives an effort equation of

$$E = .25 \, (L*size)^{2.28} = cons * size^{2.28}$$

where

$$cons = .25 \, L^{2.28}.$$

This is a much larger coefficient than the one found in the Rayleigh-Putnam model (which also posits an exponential function). Thus we can expect that for large projects, the Halstead effort indicator will overestimate effort. It is meant to be applied to individual effort. We can, however, apply this technique to each module whose implementation effort needs to be estimated and then combine the estimation results bottom-up. Since effort is measured in "elementary mental discriminations," the numerical value must be converted into man-months. Based on 18 elementary mental discriminations per second, there are 1,000,000 per man-month, and E can be converted into man-months by dividing by a million.

Comparison

The assumptions of the Rayleigh-Putnam and that of Jensen's model are about the same, and those of the Rayleigh-Putnam and of the Halstead effort estimation models are fairly complementary. The scope of the Halstead model does not include support tasks such as preparing documents or user training. It estimates the concentrated, well-specified work of one programmer on one programming assignment. Another important difference is that the Rayleigh-Putnam model is probabilistic while Halstead's is not.

Example: Rayleigh-Putnam

1. Assume the technology constant to be C = 4,000. Size has been estimated at 200,000 LOC. Total lifetime effort is given by

    $$B = (1/T^4)*(200,000/4,000)^3 = (1/T^4)*(50)^3.$$

    Development effort E is given by

    $$E = .3945 \ B.$$

    If the target development period is two years, total lifetime effort B and development effort E become

    $$B = (1/16)(50)^3 = 7812.5 \ man\text{-}years$$
    $$E = .3945 \ B = 3,082 \ man\text{-}years.$$

    Productivity P is 64.0 LOC/man-year. Effort and productivity change as follows when development time varies between two and three years.

T	E	B	P
2	3082	7814	64.9
2.5	1262	3200	158.5
3	609	1543	328.4

    A higher C represents a more efficient development environment. Pressman considers $C = 2,000$ a poor software development environment. $C = 8,000$ describes a good environment with methodology, documentation and reviews and interactive execution mode. $C = 11,000$ is the technology constant for an excellent environment with automated techniques and tools ([Press87], p. 113). The effect of these various technology constants on the effort variables and on productivity is as follows:

2. $C = 8,000$
    $B = (1/T^4) * (25)^3$

T	E	B	P
2	385	977	519
2.5	158	400	1266
3	76	193	2632

3. $C = 11,000$
    $B = (1/T^4) * (18.18)^3$

T	E	B	P
2	148	376	1350
2.5	61	154	3295
3	29	74	6832

Example: Halstead

Assume that the language constant $k = 5$ (a language at a higher level than FORTRAN). The size of the finished program has been estimated at 200,000 LOC in about 125 modules. Average module size is therefore

$$size_m = 200,000/125 = 1600 \; LOC \; and$$
$$N_m = 1600*5 = 8000.$$

Based on [Cont86], the exponent a for the formula

$$E_m = .25*N^{2+a}$$

is $a = .25$. Therefore effort is given as

$$E = .25 * (8000)^{2.25} = 1.513*10^8 \; elementary \; mental \; discriminations$$

This corresponds to

$$E_m = 151.3 \; man\text{-}months.$$

Thus the software effort is estimated at

$$E = 125 * 151.3 \; man\text{-}months = 1576 \; man\text{-}years.$$

Had we estimated the software as a whole instead of by parts, the effort would have been

$$E_{whole} = 2.1147*10^5 \; man\text{-}months = 17,623 \; man\text{-}years.$$

While the first figure is in the same ballpark as the Rayleigh-Putnam estimate, the second certainly is not and points out clearly that the Halstead model should be used for modules in a bottom-up fashion.

Questions and Problems

1. Write a program that computes the manpower utilization rate and the expended effort using the Rayleigh-Putnam model. Use the program to answer the following questions:

    a) You are to vary the parameters B and T. How does the shape of the curve change? Plot the results.

    b) [Zelk79] assumes $a = 1/T^2$. Plot changes compared to the results in a.

    c) If B is total lifetime effort and T is development time, how will changes in T affect the shape of the cumulative project effort $R(t)$?

2. Assume you have a productivity objective $P = $ x for projects. With known technology factor and a known deadline on development time T, what other information do you need to estimate size and effort $R(T)$? How does your answer change if you know estimated project size? Use formulas to explain your answers.

3. Plot effort curves as a function of size using the Rayleigh-Putnam and the Halstead effort estimator. Indicate the amount of overestimation by cross-hatching the area between the two curves. Then assume that the software can be built in 20 modules each of size $S/20$ where S is the total project size. Compute effort for a module, multiply it by 20, and compare this result to the Rayleigh-Putnam model. How much better is it?

14.3.3. Experiential, Statistical Estimation Models

These models predict cost and/or effort for the entire project using a basic formula whose parameters are determined via a historic database and current project characteristics. Under this category we include Boehm's COCOMO model [Boeh81] and the Walston-Felix model [Wals77]. Also included is a very promising approach to effort estimation due to Bailey and Basili [Bail81]. These models are considered experiential or statistical, because they provide for adjustment factors that are computed via statistical methods using statistical data. A discussion of these models centers around COCOMO, since it is the most comprehensive empirical model for software cost and effort estimation published to date.

There is no model that performs well all the time. All validation studies of estimation models in [Cont86] clearly point out deficiencies in the estimating capabilities of all models. Nevertheless, all of them have their following among software professionals and all have their successes. The models' limitations point to the need for better or more flexible and adaptable models in general. Much work is necessary before software effort and cost estimation has accurate, valid, and reliable tools to do the job.

14.3.3.1. Top-Down Estimation Models

COCOMO Model

The COCOMO model is one of the most widely accepted and applied models for software effort and cost estimation. It uses statistical data fitting to a set of linear and nonlinear formulas. COCOMO is the most comprehensive of the models of this type. It considers a wide variety of factors that affect the software development effort. It includes estimation procedures for development time schedules, effort during development, and maintenance and effort breakdown by phase or activity. Development effort is modeled with a power function of the form

$$E = a * size^b * C,$$

where a and b are constants that change with the type of project estimate desired. There are three types of project estimation: the basic, the intermediate, and the detailed version. The size factor is the principal factor that influences effort, but there are a variety of other factors (15 of them) that together determine the adjustment factor C. Thus C is a function of 15 other factors that influence total project effort. These factors describe the impact of product attributes, hardware characteristics, personnel attributes, and project characteristics (Table 14.4).

Table 14.4 Cost Drivers for the COCOMO Model.

Product	Hardware
Software reliability	Performance requirements
Size of application database	Memory constraints
Complexity	Volatility of virtual machine
	Environment
	Turnaround time
Personnel	**Project**
Analyst capability	Use of software tools
Software engineering capability	Application of software engineering
Applications experience	methods
Virtual machine experience	Required development schedule
Programming language expertise	

Projects fall into three categories: organic, semidetached, and embedded. Organic projects are characterized by their relatively small size. They require little innovation, don't have a strict deadline, and are done in a stable development environment. Embed-

Table 14.5 Project Types.

| Type | Characteristics | | | |
	Size	Innovation	Deadline/Constraints	Dev.-Environment
Organic	Smallish	Little	Not tight	Stable
Embedded	Large	Greater	Tight	Complex hardware/customer interfaces
Semidetached	Medium	Medium	Medium	Medium

Table 14.6 Range of Constants in Effort Formula.

| | $E = a * size^b * C$ | | |
Type	a	b	c
Basic	2.4–3.6	1.05–1.2	1
Intermediate	3.2–2.8	1.05–1.2	Table lookup

ded type projects are on the other end of the spectrum. They are relatively large, have tight constraints and requirements, a greater degree of innovation, and more complex hardware and customer interface (use the risk profile of Chapter 13 to determine whether a project is organic or embedded). A project that falls between the two extremes is semidetached.

The parameter a ranges from 2.4 to 3.6 for the basic model from organic to embedded project. The corresponding b ranges from 1.05 to 1.2. In the intermediate model, a ranges from 3.2 to 2.8 and b from 1.05 to 1.2. The models differ in how the adjustment function is handled. The basic model assumes that there is no adjustment for any factor, $C = 1$. The intermediate model uses a series of values for the adjustment factors that can be looked up in a table. Cost factors come in four different categories. Each factor can be rated on its scale (from very low to extra high). Based on the complexity rating of each factor, a numerical adjustment value is assigned to the factor. These values are the result of curve fitting and thus based on historical data. Finally, all adjustment values are multiplied to create C.

From the estimate for total project effort, development time T is determined as a power function of effort. The constants vary with project type:

$$T = 2.5\ E^b,$$

where b ranges from .38 for organic mode to .32 for embedded mode projects. The shape of the curve is similar to the Rayleigh-Putnam model. The difference is that the COCOMO model explicitly takes into account the effect of a variety of influential environmental and project factors.

Validation results [Cont86] include a variety of projects over a time span of 15 years. Their budgets range from $2,000 to $1 million. The projects cover all types of applications in a variety of programming languages. Productivity figures range from 28 to 1250 lines of code per month. The basic model, being the most simplistic, performed least well when used against the database of projects that was used to determine the estimation parameters in its formulas. The intermediate model fares better. It performs excellently when the impact of requirements volatility is considered as an estimation parameter.

The biggest disadvantages of COCOMO are according to [Cont86] that COCOMO has too many parameters that need to be determined; they are often highly correlated and could be reduced. The estimation parameters that determine the constants in the formula are empirically derived, thus describing the effects of a specific environment. They may not do well elsewhere. Errors made in estimating size will overshadow all others. Conte et al. [Cont86] also suggest some improvements in the estimator for actual effort E that performs better than the original COCOMO formulas, but the authors consider "any expectation of significant improvement . . . unrealistic" [Cont86].

Other Top-Down Estimation Models

The Walston-Felix Study [Wals77] reported a single-variable model of the form

$$E = a * size^b,$$
$$where\ a\ =\ 5.2\ and\ b\ =\ .91.$$

These parameter values are specific for the projects that formed the statistical basis for the estimator. They cannot readily be applied generally. However, it is not difficult to develop one's own through a least squares fit of historical data. This data must be representative of the software projects to be undertaken in the future: it requires stability in personnel, requirements, hardware, and project characteristics. By its very nature, such a model cannot deal with variations in factors that may affect software development effort (other than size). This is not necessarily bad, it merely limits the model's applicability.

Models vary in the manner in which they take into account the effect of development attributes on effort. Bailey and Basili [Bail81] combine factors in three areas:

1. methodology (9 factors): MTH,

2. complexity (7 factors): CMP, and

3. experience (5 factors): EXP.

Within each category, scoring determines the value of the category as a whole and hence its impact on effort. Each individual factor is scored on a 0–5 scale. The adjustment factor is a weighted sum of these scores. The weights are determined using a multi-linear least squares regression with historical data on the following formula:

$$D = W_0 + W_1 * MTH + W_2 * CMP + W_3 * EXP$$

where

D difference between actual and estimated effort of historical projects normalized by estimated effort in case of underprediction ($D > 0$) or actual effort in case of overprediction ($D < 0$);

W_i ($i = 0, \ldots, 3$) are the weights to be determined;

MTH score of methodology factors (maximum 45, minimum 0);

CMP score of complexity factors (maximum 35, minimum 0);

EXP score of experience factors (maximum 25, minimum 0).

Once the weights W_i are determined, this weighted sum can be used to estimate that part of the effort of future projects that is due to environmental factors. This factor D is then used in two ways, depending on whether E_{old}, the old effort estimate, was too low or too high:

▶ underprediction: $E = (1 + D) E_{old}$

▶ overprediction: $E = (|1 + D|)^{-1} E_{old}$

The original estimator E_{old} was based on the following formula:

$$E_{old} = 3.5 + size^{1.16}.$$

Examples: COCOMO

Assume that the estimated size of the software is 200 KLOC. The basic model yields for the organic, semidetached and embedded modes the following effort estimates:

$$E_{org} = 2.4\ size^{1.05} = 2.4*(200)^{1.05} = 626\ man\text{-}months,$$
$$E_{sem} = 3.0\ size^{1.12} = 3.0*(200)^{1.12} = 1{,}133\ man\text{-}months,\ and$$
$$E_{emb} = 3.6\ size^{1.2} = 3.6*(200)^{1.1} = 2{,}077\ man\text{-}months.$$

The intermediate COCOMO model uses a table look-up to determine the adjustment factor C to the following formulas:

$$E_{org} = 3.2\ size^{1.05}$$
$$E_{sem} = 3.0\ size^{1.12}$$
$$E_{emb} = 2.8\ size^{1.2}$$

Assume the table look-up produced the following multipliers based on project characteristics:

Characteristic	Multiplier value
Low reliability	.88
High product complexity	1.15
Low application experience	1.13
High programming language experience	.95

All other factors are medium and have a rating of 1.00. Therefore the effort multiplier C is

$$C = .88 * 1.15 * 1.13 * .95 = 1.086.$$

This makes the three effort estimators

$$E_{org} = 906 \ man\text{-}months$$
$$E_{sem} = 1{,}231 \ man\text{-}months, \ and$$
$$E_{emb} = 1{,}755 \ man\text{-}months.$$

The development times for the three model types are given through the formulas

$$T_{org} = 2.5 \ E^{.38}$$
$$T_{sem} = 2.5 \ E^{.35}$$
$$T_{emb} = 2.5 \ E^{.32}$$

Thus development times for the basic and the intermediate model classes are (rounded to the nearest full month)

	Basic	Intermediate
Organic	29	33
Semidetached	29	30
Embedded	29	27

Example: Walston-Felix

Size is again assumed to be 200 KLOC. Then

$$E = 5.2 \ size^{.91} = 5.2*(200)^{.91} = 646 \ man\text{-}months = 54 \ man\text{-}years$$
$$P = 200{,}000 \ LOC/54 \ man\text{-}years = 3{,}700 \ LOC/year.$$

Procedure for Model Development

We now develop a procedure for establishing one's own estimation model. This procedure can use, at least as initial models, some of the models presented above. It then illustrates how to use them to evolve an estimation procedure that is tailored to specific environments. Table 14.7 summarizes these steps.

Table 14.7 Model Development Procedure.

---

1. Determine list of potential/most important effort and cost drivers.
2. Determine a scoring model for each effort and cost driver.
3. Select initial estimation model.
4. Measure and estimate projects and compare:
   a. Use Bailey and Basili's model to improve estimate.
   b. Use regression to determine correlation between drivers and reduce them.
   c. Use multiplicative model type (such as COCOMO) to determine driver values for adjustment tables and constants in estimation equation.
   d. Record project cost and man-months or man-hours to determine a unit cost figure.
5. Evaluate quality of estimation as part of project post-mortem.
6. Update and validate model at appropriate intervals.

According to the guidelines for model development in Chapter 11, the first task is to determine the independent and dependent variables for the model that is to be built. In this case we determine a list of factors that act as effort and cost drivers. There are many sources that can be consulted. One is a set of tables established by Walston and Felix [Wals77], from which the following example factors were gleaned:

▶ *Customer related factors*

customer interface complexity (how many types of customers and level of expertise of customers)
user participation in requirements and development
customer experience in application area

▶ *Personnel*

experience (hardware, software, application, methodology, tools)
qualification relative to job
degree of programmer involvement in early stages

▶ *Project*

degree to which hardware and software must be developed together
security constraints
complexity of code developed

        qualitative requirements/constraints
        amount of documentation per KLOC

▶ *Methodology and support environment*

        structured programming
        reviews, inspections, phase tests
        top-down development
        project organization
        tools

The factors that are considered important for a given environment or organization are selected for inclusion in the model. This goes beyond the characteristics of any particular project, because the aim is to describe the environment and all projects that are usually done at an organization.

The next step is to determine a scoring model for each factor that was identified as an effort or cost driver. A good example of such a scoring model can be found in [Boeh81].

The next step is to select an estimation model that is to be used initially. This can be one of the COCOMO models, the Walston-Felix equation, or Bailey and Basili's initial effort equation.

Since the goal is to develop a model that is based on statistical evaluation of historical data, the next step is to use the scoring and the estimation model on actual projects. This entails measuring the value of effort and cost drivers, estimating effort and cost, and comparing the estimated results to the actual project figures. Estimates can be improved using Bailey and Basili's model. A regression test determines correlation between factors in order to reduce them (the big number of factors is a serious obstacle to the statistical meaningfulness of models when not enough data points exist to have confidence into the results of curve fits). Then we can use one of the multiplicative model types to determine factor values for the tables that provide the adjustment multipliers and the constants in the estimation equation. We use curve fitting techniques on the data. Since part of the measurement objectives is to determine a unit cost figure, project cost must be recorded. It is also important to record actual effort expended (in man-months or man-hours). Both actual cost and effort figures are needed for model development.

At the end of each project, the quality of estimation is evaluated. Last, but not least, the estimation model is updated and validated. Even if no new regressions are run to modify the model, the data and an interpretation of what they mean for the quality of the estimation process must be recorded. We must define a threshold when a thorough model update is in order. This threshold can be given in terms of number of projects, trend in quality of estimation, or both.

14.3.3.2. Models Using Estimation by Parts

Some experiential, statistical models pursue a parts approach. This requires partitioning the project into chunks that can be evaluated and whose cost can be estimated. Since estimation is done for parts and then combined for an overall project estimate, it is also called bottom-up estimation. It usually requires a work breakdown structure that identifies the parts for which estimates are to be made. Work can be partitioned by phase or project activities or by function, subsystem, etc. of the product that is to be developed. The first type of partitioning results in a process-oriented work breakdown structure, the latter in a product-based work breakdown structure.

Phase Partitioning

Work is broken down by phase and within a phase by major activities. Then, based on the requirements for the parts, we determine overall project effort and cost. [Dema82] describes this method in detail and provides suggested initial estimation values for a series of small activities and their characteristics.

De Marco's Approach

He develops three predictors during three points in the software development life cycle to estimate effort for various development activities. They are

▶ **Bang.** This is a metric that measures the amount of functionality during early phases, i.e., system analysis. It is used to estimate design and conversion effort. Bang is estimated during problem analysis and measured during system analysis.

▶ **Design weight.** This metric measures the size and complexity of a design. It is used to estimate total effort, implementation effort, debugging effort, and machine time. Design weight is estimated during early design and measured at the end of the design phase.

▶ **Implementation weight.** This metric measures the size and complexity of code. It is used to estimate total effort, unit testing effort, integration effort, and machine time for testing. Implementation weight is estimated during early coding or detailed design and measured as data becomes available during the coding phase.

Two metrics, design weight and implementation weight, are used to estimate some of the same efforts but at different times during software development. This is the type of model discussed in Section 12.4.2. in the metrics chapter (cf. Table 12.5 and Figure 12.9). It provides feedback on quality of phase-specific metrics and their ability to predict accurately into the future. It also uses the latest data available to update and improve an estimate; it uses data based on design information. Later, when code is available, it uses data based on code to predict effort more accurately. It is an estimation and prediction model that is partitioned by phase as well as by activities within a phase.

At each estimation point, the actual measurement of the appropriate metric is taken or estimated according to the plan above. Measurements are used to predict various effort and cost indicators. These are then summed to arrive at an overall effort and cost estimate. The new estimates are compared against the old ones and adjusted.

Phase–Effort Model

The chapter on metrics (Chapter 12) also outlined a procedure for estimating time and cost by phase using a series of stepwise estimation functions across phases. They are based on size metrics that are phase specific. Figure 12.9 outlined the family of models necessary, while Table 12.5 provided examples of size metrics during software development. Each of these metrics can be used to build an effort and cost model.

The activities involved in estimation through the phase-effort model are by phase:

▶ **Requirements analysis**
at beginning:

  ▶ estimate size and effort of requirements. $size_{RA}$ could be estimated as number of activity boxes or number of data dictionary items; $effort_{RA}$ is estimated via a predictive model in man-hours, days, or months as a function of $size_{RA}$.

  ▶ estimate size of final code and total effort, e.g., $size_{code}$ in KLOC, $effort_{total}$ in man-months or man-years.

at end:

  ▶ measure $size_{RA}$ and $effort_{RA}$

  ▶ determine quality of estimation for the requirements analysis phase via D_size_{RA}, D_effort_{RA}. These can be defined analogous to D in the Bailey-Basili model.

  ▶ reestimate $size_{code}$ as a function of actual $size_{RA}$ and the adjustment factor D_size_{RA}.

  ▶ reestimate $effort_{total}$ as a function of the reestimated $size_{code}$, actual $effort_{RA}$, and the adjustment factor D_effort_{RA}.

  ▶ determine effort spent so far as $effort_{spent} = effort_{RA}$

▶ **Specifications**
at beginning:

- ▶ estimate size of the specifications (e.g., in number of identifiable functions, number of inputs and outputs that need to be defined) as a function of the actual size of the requirements: $size_{SP} = f_{RS}(size_{RA})$

- ▶ estimate effort of the specifications in man-hours, man-days, or man-months as a function of the size estimate for the specifications: $effort_{SP} = f_{SP} = f_{SP}(size_{SP})$

at end:

- ▶ measure actual $size_{SP}$ and $effort_{SP}$

- ▶ determine quality of estimation via D_size_{SP} and D_effort_{SP} (analogous to how it was done for the requirements phase).

- ▶ reestimate $size_{code}$ as a function of actual $size_{SP}$ and the adjustment factor D_size_{SP}.

- ▶ reestimate $effort_{total}$ as a function of the revised code estimate $size_{code}$, actual $effort_{SP}$, and the adjustment factor D_effort_{SP}.

- ▶ update $effort_{spent}$ by adding $effort_{SP}$ to it.

▶ **Design**
at beginning:

- ▶ estimate size of the design (e.g., in number of identifiable modules, number of major data structures per module) as a function of the actual size of the specifications: $size_{DE} = f_{SD}(size_{SP})$

- ▶ estimate effort of the design in man-hours, man-days, or man-months as a function of the size estimate for the design: $effort_{DE} = f_{DE}(size_{DE})$

at end:

- ▶ measure actual $size_{DE}$ and $effort_{DE}$.

- ▶ determine quality of estimation via D_size_{DE} and D_effort_{DE} (analogous to how it was done for the requirements phase).

- ▶ reestimate $size_{code}$ as a function of actual $size_{DE}$ and the adjustment factor D_size_{DE}.

- ▶ reestimate $effort_{total}$ as a function of $size_{code}$, actual $effort_{DE}$, and the adjustment factor D_effort_{DE}.

- ▶ update effort spent so far by adding $effort_{DE}$.

▶ **Coding and Testing**
at beginning:

- ▶ estimate effort of the coding and testing phase as a function of total effort estimate and effort spent so far: $effort_{CT} = effort_{total} - effort_{spent}$

at end:

- ▶ measure actual $size_{code}$, $effort_{CT}$, and $effort_{total}$.

- ▶ determine quality of estimation via D_size_{code}, D_effort_{CT}, and D_effort_{total} (analogous to how it was done for the requirements phase).

▶ **Post-project**
evaluate which formulas produced results that were

- ▶ +/− 20% accurate,

- ▶ +/− 50% accurate,

- ▶ +/− 80% accurate, and

- ▶ less than that.

analyze the reasons for deviations.
adjust for factors found (one must determine a suitable adjustment factor for every modeling function used).
put project data in database.
based on quality of estimation decide on redevelopment of any or all formulas.

Table 14.8. lists all models used and all measurements or direct computations for the phase-effort method.

Distribution of Effort Model

Even a rule of thumb as simple as the distribution of percentage of effort in each phase can establish estimates for a project, looking at cost and time of only the first phase. This method presupposes that we have been developing software using a phased development life cycle. As long as we stay with the same life-cycle definition, we can use historical data on effort, time, and cost distribution across phases. If the contents of the

Table 14.8 Models and Measurements for Phase-Effort Method.

Models	Measurements/Direct computations
Requirements analysis	
$size_{RA}$	$size_{RA}$
$effort_{RA}=f_{RA}(size_{RA})$	$effort_{RA}$
$size_{code}=f_{code}(size_{RA})$	D_size_{RA}, D_effort_{RA}
$effort_{total}=f_{total}(size_{code})$	$effort_{spent}:=effort_{RA}$
$size_{code}=f_{RA}(size_{RA}, D\_size_{RA})$	
$effort_{total}=f_R(size_{code}, effort_{RA}, D\_effort_{RA})$	
Specifications	
$size_{SP}=f_{RS}(size_{RA})$	$size_{SP}$
$effort_{SP}=f_{SP}(size_{SP})$	$effort_{SP}$
——————	D_size_{SP}, D_effort_{SP}
$size_{code}=f_{SP}(size_{SP}, D\_size_{SP})$	add $effort_{SP}$ to $effort_{spent}$
$effort_{total}=f_S(size_{code}, effort_{SP}, D\_effort_{SP})$	
Design	
$size_{DE}=f_{SD}(size_{SP})$	$size_{DE}$
$effort_{DE}=f_{DE}(size_{DE})$	$effort_{DE}$
——————	D_size_{DE}, D_effort_{DE}
$size_{code}=f_{DE}(size_{DE}, D\_size_{DE})$	add $effort_{DE}$ to $effort_{spent}$
$effort_{total}=f_D(size_{code}, effort_{DE}, D\_effort_{DE})$	
Coding and Testing	
$effort_{CT}=effort_{total}-effort_{spent}$	$size_{code}$
	$effort_{CT}$
	$effort_{total}$
	$D\_size_{code})$
	D_effort_{CT}
	D_effort_{total}

activities within a phase change significantly, we can no longer do that, unless we are able to map one life-cycle definition into another and assess the effect of dissimilarities.

Let us assume that we have the following effort distribution throughout the development phases of software projects (not including maintenance):

Requirements analysis	13%
Specifications	17%
Design	23%
Coding	13%
Testing	34%

If we have spent five man-months of effort on the requirements analysis and feasibility study, and if we decide that this new project falls into the same category of projects as the ones that are the basis for the average effort distribution above, we will spend the following effort on the other development phases (rounded to the closest integer):

Specifications	7 man-months
Design	9 man-months
Coding	5 man-months
Testing	13 man-months

This alone does not predict cost or elapsed time (schedule). For this, we can use other, but substantially similar, historical data.

How can we develop such an estimation table? For effort, we need to collect total man-hours spent. We can do the same for cost and elapsed time, but we need to assume an average type of resource cost that is proportional to effort and an average degree of parallelism in the work. This is reflected in the constant relationship between effort and elapsed time. The data collection sheet looks something like this:

	Man-hours(hrs)	Cost(K$)	Time (days or months)
Requirements analysis			
Specifications			
Design			
Coding			
Testing			
Total			

From this, average distribution of effort, cost, and elapsed time are determined. The type of planning and the development approach and the number of people all influence cost and elapsed time. This makes the %-rule of thumb often a crude estimation procedure. It should not be discounted, however, because there are situations when it applies; in stable environments and early in development, when more detailed and accurate data is scarce, this can be a very useful method.

Value of information versus risk was discussed in the previous chapter. Different levels of detail are associated with different value levels of information and estimation accuracy. This relates directly to risk. Thus distribution-of-effort estimators represent cheap information with higher risk potential. It is reduced by using different estimators for projects with varying project characteristics. The more the relevant project characteristics are identified and quantified, the closer this "refined" model will resemble some of the previous models.

Function Partitioning

This approach determines work breakdown structure according to the structure of the product and its functionality. One could use, for example, the structure of the requirements diagram (cf. example projects in Chapter 3). Effort and cost are associated with each element in the structure chart and then summed to obtain overall effort and cost.

Function partitioning was the basis for technical feasibility evaluation and requirements analysis in Chapters 4 and 13 (cf. complexity matrix to indicate the relative complexity of functions, and formal statement of functional and qualitative requirements as basis for trade-off analysis between options in functional and qualitative requirements). This information is function oriented. It can be used again to serve as independent variable for an estimation model that is function oriented. In particular, Figures 3.3 to 3.5 (for TAP) and Figure 3.6 (for PAS) provide possible work breakdown structures. Tables 4.5 and 4.6 contain information that can serve as input for effort and cost estimation models for these functions. They list relative complexity by product function and thus provide a basis for size, effort, and cost estimation.

A function-oriented work breakdown structure can also be used to evaluate the variations in effort and cost for all options that were considered during feasibility analysis. This simplifies trade-off analysis from the effort/cost perspective. Such trade-off analysis is much harder with other types of estimation models.

Once a system architecture exists, it too, can be used as a work breakdown structure. The implementation effort and cost for all major modules is estimated, and individual estimates are combined to an overall estimate. This estimate is compared to the earlier estimates and updated accordingly. If a formal method is used, adjustment factors can be computed as in the phase-effort method. Further reestimation occurs at the end of design for coding and implementation, again based on design functions and associated support tasks.

While the major partitioning approach is function oriented, it also has a phase partitioning component. Function partitioning and phase partitioning are often used side by side. It is felt that this improves the quality of the estimates, because both product and process are considered in the estimation process. Function partitioning must also consider a breakdown of support activities such as test planning, document preparation, user training, etc. (cf. Table 13.6 and Figures 13.3 and 13.5).

Problems and Questions

1. a) What is the range of the adjustment factor D in Bailey and Basili's model?

   b) What ranges can you derive for the weights w_i when you take into account the maximum and minimum scores for the three categories *MTH*, *CMP*, and *EXP*?

   c) Knowing that D is estimated using a linear, additive model, what can be said about possible trade-offs between scores in *MTH*, *CMP*, and *EXP*?

d)   What does it mean when w_0 is not equal to zero?

2.   What data need to be collected to develop a top-down experiential, statistical estimation model? How would you try to measure these data? Why did you select these data and not others?

3.   a)   What data need to be collected to develop the phase-effort model?

   b)   Discuss the usefulness of an adjustment factor similar to D (in Bailey and Basili's model) to improve the quality of estimation in the phase-effort model.

   c)   How could one use or develop models similar to COCOMO to predict effort at the beginning of each phase?

   d)   Which factors beside size ought to be included in this model development? Why?

14.3.4. Subjective Experience

Probably the most widespread subjective formal estimation methods in this category are Delphi and wide-band Delphi. A group of estimators submit their estimates to a moderator who compiles the results onto a master form, gives it back to each estimator, and lets them reevaluate these estimates individually and anonymously until they converge. We discussed this procedure earlier when we were trying to reduce the risk of bias.

If there is only one expert to develop an estimate, the Delphi method will not work. In this case, the expert will base his or her estimates on personal, past experience with similar projects he or she has done or seen before. Since both the Delphi method and individual expert judgment are subjective, they depend on

▶   the quality of the experts,

▶   their range of experience,

▶   whether they can accurately assess the similarity of projects, and

▶   whether they can adequately judge the dissimilarity of projects and how this dissimilarity will affect effort and cost compared to the other projects.

Subjective methods are only as good as the experts who are providing the estimates.

Estimates based on expert judgment may be top-down or bottom-up. Top-down estimates predict cost, effort, and time from the global properties of a software project. They rely on similarities and approach the estimation problem from a system level. Unfamiliar aspects of the project can be dealt with by using different estimation techniques for unfamiliar parts.

While expert judgment using project similarities in a top-down estimation approach gives an immediate perspective of the total cost, we then lack detailed information to justify these estimates. It is easy to overlook aspects of the project or of functionalities of the software that we are trying to build. Since we provide one overall estimate, top-down expert judgment cannot balance out individual estimation errors the way a bottom-up estimate can.

Overall cost estimation through expert judgment in a top-down fashion is indicated for early estimates (i.e., the detail for a bottom-up estimation is not yet available) and when we try to estimate the cost of buying and installing new software.

Later phases probably use a parts or bottom-up approach, since more detail on individual system components and their resource needs for development will be available.

14.3.5. Use of Estimation Methods

Reliable, quality cost and effort estimation for software development will use a combination of models and subjective estimation. For known projects and project parts we will use subjective expert judgment, since it is fast and under these circumstances, reliable. For large, lesser known projects, it is better to use either an algorithmic or an experiential model. If we approach cost estimation by parts, we may use expert judgment for some known parts. This way we can take advantage of both: the rigor of models and the speed of expert judgment. Since the advantages and disadvantages of each technique are complementary, using a combination of techniques will

- ▶ reduce the negative effect of any one technique,
- ▶ augment their individual strengths, and
- ▶ help to cross-check one method against another.

It is very important to continually reestimate effort and cost and to compare targets against actual expenditure at each major milestone. This keeps the status of the project visible and helps to identify necessary corrections to budget and schedule as soon as they occur. There will be no more surprises.

At every estimation and reestimation point, iteration is an important tool to improve estimation quality. The estimator can use several estimation techniques and check whether their estimates converge. Besides cross-checking the results, there are other advantages in such an approach:

- ▶ Different estimation methods may use different data. This results in better coverage of the knowledge base for the estimation process. It can help to identify cost and effort components that cannot be dealt with or were overlooked in one of the methods.

▶ Different viewpoints and biases can be taken into account and reconciled. A competitive contract bid, a high business priority to keep costs down, or a small market window with the resulting tight deadlines tends to have optimistic estimates. A production schedule established by the developers is usually more on the pessimistic side to avoid committing to a schedule and budget one cannot meet.

Even if only one or two techniques are used, one type of check is very important: comparing actual cost, time, and effort data to the estimates. This contributes to a measure of estimation quality. It will also provide the necessary feedback to improve the estimation quality in the future. One can use a metric for estimation quality similar to DeMarco's [Dema82] estimation quality index. It weights the amount of difference between the actual and estimated quantity with the proportion of project duration that it was in force. Thus the quality of an estimate that was two man-months off for half the project duration is

$$QE = .5 * 2 = 1.$$

This alone may not mean much, because it does not take into account the size of the project. It is better to normalize QE by total number of man-months (if effort is what we try to estimate). This provides an indicator for degree of inaccuracy. If our hypothetical project required 20 man-months, the degree of inaccuracy would be

$$DI = QE/20 = .05.$$

Such an estimation quality indicator can be used to do the following:

▶ Set standards.

▶ Identify estimation procedures that work well or don't work well.

▶ Target notoriously bad estimates for analysis. These may occur symptomatically in certain phases, indicating a need for revising the estimation procedure for a given phase. Or it may point to a trend that is due to slowly changing characteristics of projects (e.g., different applications, introduction of new methodology, and variations in languages, resources, personnel quality, or productivity).

▶ Provide an objective measure of evaluating estimation quality that can be used across projects, phases, people, and methodologies. We can use it to trace learning curves for individuals and to spot changed estimation environments (when the estimator starts to increase, indicating lower quality of estimation).

▶ Identify changes in software projects that require an update of estimated costs, effort, and time. Overall reevaluation can be conditioned on a threshold for DI for any phase: as soon as inaccuracy exceeds a target for the DI value, a reevaluation of estimates is triggered. The threshold may be set at 10% for some projects, at 25%, or down to 5% for others. The particular value depends on how tight budget and schedule constraints are and on the penalties associated with breaking the constraints.

▶ Identify a need for more accurate data collection for data that are inputs for the estimation process. Sometimes an analysis of poor estimates reveals that it wasn't the estimation procedure that was at fault, but the data that were used to derive estimates. If highly inaccurate data are used as input to the estimation process, it is not surprising that outputs (i.e., the estimates) are not accurate.

Another way to quantify the quality of estimation is via an adjustment factor of the type suggested in Bailey and Basili [Bail81]. It was discussed in Section 14.3.3.

It is also important to identify the goals of the estimation process, because it will influence the effort spent in estimating, its accuracy, and the methods used. The degree of accuracy and the purpose of the estimate need to be identified. This will vary between phases and across projects. Tight schedules with high risks require more accurate estimates than loosely defined projects with a relatively open-ended schedule. In most estimation tasks a base line for our estimation efforts is determined by the software life-cycle model that was chosen and by the methodology that is applied. If estimation does not cover all phases of the software development life cycle, it is necessary to identify those which are to be included. When making estimates, the estimator has to look at the quality of the data upon which estimates are based and at the various objectives, so that only as much estimation detail as is necessary and possible is provided. The more detailed knowledge is available about the project, the more accurate estimates can be.

Problems and Questions

1. Why is it advantageous to use two estimation methods instead of one? When would you use two estimation methods from the same category of methods, and when would you use estimation methods from different categories? Which categories?

2. Are there any reasons why one should use more than two estimation methods on the same project? Give the reasons or state why it is not necessary.

3.   In which phases would you use which types of estimation methods? Why?

4.   What project related factors will influence how you set the threshold for estimation quality?

5.   How can you set a threshold for estimation quality using an adjustment factor similar to the one in the Bailey-Basili model?

6.   Should you use estimation quality for performance appraisal? What is likely to happen if you do? What can you do to overcome the problem?

7.   If size and complexity of a project influence the choice of estimation methods, for which type of project would you choose any of the algorithmic estimation techniques?

14.4.   Software Sizing

Most of the software cost and effort estimation models rely on the projected software size as the major factor driving the estimation. This means that it is very important to have an accurate estimate of the projected size of a software product. At present, however, sizing is the weakest link in the estimation process. Progress in sizing of software is therefore the prerequisite for better estimates for the effort and cost involved in a software project.

In this section we will investigate the role of several size metrics in software cost estimation and discuss how to size a software project with these metrics. The first and most often used is lines of code (LOC), source lines of code (SLOC), or thousands of lines of code (KLOC). We have seen this metric used in all algorithmic and experiential effort and cost estimation models.

The second technique to size a software effort is to use function points [Albr79]. This technique can be used with an experiential or statistical model that relates the function point index to the effort involved in developing the software. It is not a technique that is ready for general use.

Related to the idea of function points is describing the functionality of each phase with indices describing the effort involved in translating it into the next phase (e.g., specifications into a design). If done for all phases, this would enable an estimation of overall effort in several steps, as well as provide an effort estimate by phase. A start in this direction was made by DeMarco [Dema82] and further suggestions have been made in the chapter on metrics. This would enable the development by phase of bottom-up estimation models that are connected to each other like pipes (cf. Section 12.4.2., Figure 12.9, and Table 12.5).

Sizing Using Lines of Code

LOC or more precisely SLOC is the most common metric for size today. It is easy to compute, has considerable tool support so that it can be measured automatically, and enjoys some reputation as being objective. Chapter 12 has already pointed out some of the problems with SLOC as an objective metric for measuring size and how easy it is to "doctor" an SLOC metric. Still, many experienced developers are able to guess the approximate number of SLOC using their experience and looking at the information available about the proposed software (such as specifications, requirements, design, etc.). It is easy to compare estimated SLOC to actual SLOC afterwards. This makes it useful for evaluating the quality of estimates and improving the estimation process.

When using SLOC as a size metric it is therefore imperative to

▶ define standard ways of measuring code;

▶ define estimators by programming language;

▶ set translation figures to reliably convert size estimates between programming languages;

▶ set standard scope of effort guidelines that specify which software activities are included in the estimate and which are not;

▶ attach quality characteristics so that only those lines are counted that fulfill minimum quality characteristics;

▶ describe standard development practices that are to be adhered to when developing the software, and define penalties when standards are not followed;

▶ not apply it to fourth generation languages, but instead redefine it in terms of number of queries or use function points;

▶ publish rules on how to measure SLOC so that all software developers know them;

▶ use a bottom-up estimate (by function) of software size as soon as functions have been identified during functional requirements analysis; and

▶ reestimate at the end of the specifications phase and the high-level and detailed design phases. Use these revised size estimates to reestimate effort and cost for the project.

With all the uncertainties that are contained in estimating size, it may be preferable to use a weighted size estimate combining optimistic, pessimistic and most probable size (similar to the activity durations used in the PERT scheduling technique discussed in Section 14.2.).

Phase-Specific Size Indicators

Effort and cost estimates need to be made early, but size estimates in SLOC are difficult to make during early phases. One way to overcome this difficulty is to use a different size metric that is closer to what is commonly described as a size relevant indicator. Function points are such a metric. So are Bang, design weight, and implementation weight [Dema82]. The size metrics of Table 12.5 also belong into this class of size indicators. They are used for estimation with the phase-effort model. Variations of this model include a method described in [Frie79] for estimating man-days for a single program. First the requirements are scored based on input, function, and output characteristics (e.g., data restructuring, data retrieval, input formats, output reports, etc.). Each characteristic is scored from simple to very complex. This is similar to the complexity evaluation matrix in Chapter 4. The overall score or project complexity factor is in fact the size estimator for the program. Fried points out that this approach is only to be used for programs for which detailed specifications are available. Since the estimated programming time is the project score multiplied by a factor that describes the level and knowledge of the programmer, programmer selection also must have been made. The score multiplied by the adjustment factor for expertise gives the estimated programming time. It in turn needs to be adjusted for loss and nonproject activities; 10% loss and 25% nonproject time are common.

Function points [Albr79] is a very similar size metric. It computes an unadjusted score based on external inputs, outputs, and queries or commands. Note that these entities can be identified through a requirements diagram or specifications. Each of these is scored according to complexity. Factors that determine the complexity score include the types of files and records that are accessed and the number of different data elements in a file. The total sum of these scores is the unadjusted number of function points. It is then adjusted by a so-called system complexity adjustment factor. This is similar to the adjustment factor of estimation methods (e.g., COCOMO, Jensen, Walston-Felix). Its precise form is

$$.65 + .01*(score\ of\ system\ complexity\ attributes)$$

Examples of system complexity attributes include technology factors, such as development tools, methodology used and hardware and software support, but they also include whether it is a telecommunications project or involves multiple sites. The adjusted function point can then be used as the independent variable in an effort or cost estimation model.

All of the methods explained here have some degree of similarity and show the same advantages and disadvantages. The biggest disadvantage is that they are prone to subjective misinterpretation without formal rules for scoring. The biggest advantage is that indicators of size are used in estimation models that are actually available at earlier phases in the software development life cycle and therefore can be measured directly.

Problems and Questions

1.   What makes a metric for size like function points or bang (programming) language independent? Is it independent of the notation used for requirements and specifications? Is it possible to switch between such notations and still compare projects based on function point index or bang value?

2.   Can or should phase-specific size indicators be used for top-down estimation methods like COCOMO? If yes, what adjustments need to be made?

3.   How would one go about developing a model that relates a phase-specific size indicator to a code metric like SLOC? Is such a model useful? For what?

14.5. Summary

This chapter discussed basic quantitative approaches to planning activities like scheduling, size, cost, and effort estimation. State of the art and promising new approaches were presented. Not all estimation methods are equally applicable. Therefore it was important to present each with their range of applicability. Almost all methods require data collection and analysis to make them practically useful for an organization. Sometimes this data collection has been done for the novice, and the appropriate adjustment factors or calibration constants can be found in the literature. While continuous measurement and evaluation of estimation quality is a prime contributor to improved project estimates, there are limits to possible improvement. They are due to a variety of issues:

▶   Technology changes rapidly in the software field and that influences estimation formulas.

▶   Estimation works within a feedback system. Estimates are used to set schedules, and they influence how work is done. This in turn is fed back to the estimation process in the form of data collection. This means that it is unrealistic to expect an estimation formula to, once developed, produce good estimates for an indefinite time.

▶ Rework due to low quality of deliverables might necessitate reestimation and rescheduling.

▶ Unforeseen turnover in project staff or management changes a situation, potentially making previous estimates obsolete.

▶ Simulation studies have shown that there is a tendency for underestimation to perpetuate itself even when adjustments to the estimation methods are made [Abde83]. This leads to serious deterioration in management effectiveness.

▶ Estimation methods predict how projects with given characteristics will most likely behave. Projects themselves are subject to statistical variations. Your project may be the one that falls near the tail end of the distribution and behaves differently. Then estimates will be off the mark.

Estimation and scheduling activities are part of a complex system with many factors that influence each other and are difficult to include in these models. Managerial planning can and should use these scheduling and estimation models to improve planning effectiveness, but it also should augment them with common sense and consider the particulars of a software project, its organization, and its people. This is why we turn to the subject of software project personnel next.

▶ 15
Project Personnel

15.1. Overview

The previous chapters looked at schedules, cost, goals, and feasibility. Providing an effective organization for the software development effort is another management issue. The goal is to organize both personnel and equipment resources so that they are used optimally. This chapter concentrates on the people who are a part of the software development effort.

Many techniques in previous chapters are most helpful when projects are quite sizable and complex. These techniques partition or structure projects into smaller parts, which can be controlled more easily. Examples of such structuring techniques are modularization, standard interfaces, structured programming, structured program design techniques, and languages such as PDL. These techniques also help to communicate ideas and solutions more easily to other members of the software development team. They structure a project so that parts can be assigned to a small number of people or, ideally, to one person without significant communication or work interdependence. The underlying premise is that a software development effort is more efficiently organized when the need for communication is reduced, because that uses time that could be spent on making progress with the project.

Formally structured programming teams with precise role definitions, combined with standards for structured software development, promise to improve the efficiency and effectiveness of software development teams. One of the first team concepts is the Chief Programmer Team or CPT ([Mill72], [Mill83]). Some report that they have always been successful using it [Mill85]. Others found high expectations shattered when its initial success could not be duplicated and the problems with software development did not go away. One reason for failures was the lack of technical expertise. Organization cannot compensate for lack of expertise. Another was that not everybody will function well in a team structure. Team concepts must be tuned to the people and the organization in which it exists. Their effectiveness is also influenced by the development environment, its standards, techniques, resources, and, of course, politics. It is not surprising that concepts must be adapted and tuned to provide the most efficient organizational form for a given development scenario. Other team concepts that will be discussed in this chapter are the Surgical Team or ST [Broo75], the Revised Chief Programmer Team or RCPT [Mccl81], and the Egoless Programming Team or EP [Wein71].

Structuring the human effort has the following advantages:

▶ It reduces complexity. Reducing complexity of the problem automatically reduces the complexity of the organization needed to solve it.

▶ It divides tasks into self-contained parts. Self-contained parts can be assigned to team members and carried out by them as their responsibility thus making them accountable for the work they do. This provides better control over the development effort.

▶ It makes it possible to assign parts to members of the software development team. These parts must be self-contained and defined so that the team member has all necessary skills to carry out the tasks.

▶ It reduces the communication overhead. When tasks are self-contained and the skill level is adequate, the team member can then carry them out with the least need for further clarification and communication with other team members. Highly interdependent tasks need more cooperation and communication.

▶ It uses the premise that specialization is more economical. Most people are not equally skilled in all tasks during the software development process. If we assign the most highly skilled person to a task, we get better quality and higher efficiency.

Some of the team concepts in this chapter try to employ the last concept, which is actually fairly old. Smith first advocated division of labor in 1776 [Smit76]. The concept was later taken up by C. Babbage in 1832 [Babb32]. He emphasized that learning smaller, more specialized skills decreases the learning time and at the same time increases skill due to repetition. Later, *The Principles of Scientific Management* [Tayl11] went even further in specialization, defining even smaller units of expertise and smaller tasks. This is the basis for assembly line work.

Programming also offers the possibility for considerable specialization and standardization. If taken to the extreme, this can lead to assembly line programming having all the pros and cons of assembly line work.

Ergonomics and psychology teach that different degrees of specialization require different types of motivation, skill levels, and values. For example, if a very strictly specified and standardized task is assigned to an individual with high creativity, growth, and responsibility needs, this person will very likely feel bored and dissatisfied; none of his needs are met. This should be considered when a team structure is defined for a development effort: personality traits or personality preferences can either facilitate or impede a set of task assignments within a chosen team structure.

This chapter will explain and apply organizational psychology and the concepts of task analysis and design as a framework to understand what does and does not motivate people (15.2.). It will then explain in detail the four team concepts mentioned above (15.3.–15.6.). Suggestions are made on how to recognize where these concepts must be tuned or modified and how to do that so that the development effort is organized optimally. It will take into account the concepts of organizational psychology, in particular task analysis and design and motivational theory.

Section 15.7. discusses how to select personnel to build a team for a software development effort. This includes formulating a needs statement, screening, job interviews, and a case study.

Leadership can be crucial for team success. Section 15.8. explains leadership styles, leadership functions, and factors that affect the effectiveness of leadership.

In a programming team, as in any other work group, conflicts may occur. Section 15.9. explains three categories of conflicts and offers techniques to resolve conflicts. Conflicts are defined as violations of expectations. Techniques for discipline and corrective feedback are illustrated that encourage positive changes. Case studies illustrate the concepts.

Section 15.10. discusses various organizational structures and how well they are suited to different software development efforts and team concepts. A productive match between organizational structure, project needs, and team structure is sought. Case studies illustrate all three organizational forms. The summary (15.11.) highlights the most important aspects of motivating and organizing people to avoid project problems and failure.

After reading this chapter, the reader will be familiar with how to motivate people, software developers in particular. He will know how to organize them into groups, how to build a team, and how to resolve conflict. The reader will be familiar with important leadership styles and how they affect projects and people. The reader will also know how to assess the effects of existing organizational structure on a software project.

Problems and Questions

1.   Why do we organize and structure software development teams? What are the goals of the structuring effort? How do they relate to structuring software development?

15.2.   Concepts in Organizational Psychology

15.2.1.   How Organizations View People

Types of Organizations

A team must fit into the overall organizational structure; otherwise there may be too much external friction or too little involvement with the rest of the organization, particularly its goals. How an organization, and therefore management, views the individual influences team organization and team management. Such views presuppose what motivates individuals and to what degree. Thus they indirectly define roles and set incentives. Let us look at three examples:

▶ the rational-economic view,

▶ the social view, and

▶ the self-actualization view.

1.   A rational-economic view of an individual assumes that people are primarily motivated by monetary compensation, and they calculate rationally what is best for them. Emotions and personal relationships interfere with this economic aim, and thus organizations need to neutralize and control emotions. These premises result in a very economically oriented organization with a high degree of control and little concern for people issues and human factors. Objectives are stated in quantifiable, nonhuman terms, and performance expectations often take the form of quotas. Managers must make all decisions and exercise tight control. Decisions that are best from a technical standpoint are most desirable. Incentives and rewards are tangible, mostly economic and for the individual. Penalties are emphasized to ensure compliance with standards. Everything is very organized and autocratic. There are regulations and standard operating procedures. The organizational structure tends to have many levels, each with a small span of control [Knud79].

2.   Other organizations view the individual as primarily motivated by social needs. Thus he or she is more responsive to the social forces of a peer group and derives satisfaction through having his social needs met. Work is not meaningful enough in itself. Such an organizational view has different objectives, management styles, structure, and reward systems. First, the organization is employee-oriented with a high concern for the welfare of its workers. This manifests itself in the benefit programs and in group participation in setting and implementing organizational goals. There is more informal communication than in the previous type of organization. Control is exercised primarily within groups through social pressure. It is important that decisions are accepted by a group, and leadership style is group-oriented and democratic. Incentives and rewards no longer are for the individual only. Rather, the organization works with group incentives. They are also no longer purely economic in nature. Nonfinancial and social rewards are emphasized. This type of organization is called social [Knud79].

3.   The social organization goes one step further, recognizing that an individual's highest level of needs, and therefore motivation, comes from self-actualization. Then an organization's objectives include the development of its employees to the point that the manager only frames the problem, and it is the individuals who make the plan and the decision as to how to solve it. Organizational structure merely serves as a facilitating tool, not as a control mechanism. Rewards are intrinsic to the work itself, such as added responsibility and control. This approach implies that individuals find their own rewards precisely because they are structuring the work on their own. The manager merely facilitates this by creating an environment which is amenable to doing that [Knud79].

Maslow's Need Theory and Types of Organizations

These three types of organizations parallel the stages of Maslow's Need Theory [Masl43]. It states that there is a hierarchy of needs for every individual, and the lowest unfulfilled need acts as the dominant motivator. As soon as the need is fulfilled, it loses its motivating power. Thus needs are dynamic and vary over time. Figure 15.1 shows the lowest needs as physiological. They include water, food, shelter, and sex. Next come safety from danger and deprivation. Third are social needs of belonging and acceptance through friendship and love. Next are ego needs which manifest themselves in status, recognition, prestige, and in wanting to feel adequate, strong, autonomous, and free. The highest level of need is self-actualization. It is reached when an individual has realized his or her potential for continued self-development and growth.

   The first organizational strategy works on the premise that safety is the prime motivator for work. To keep it as a motivator, it relies on fear of penalties. Depending on an individual's position in the organization ego needs may also be fulfilled, because higher positions in the hierarchy are vested with more status, autonomy, and power.

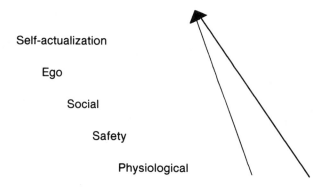

Figure 15.1   Maslow's Need Theory.

The second organization, on the other hand, emphasizes primarily fulfilling the social needs of an individual and partially tries to fulfill ego needs. Only the last form of organization deals with an individual's need for self-actualization.

Meeting Individuals' Work Needs

Does this mean that the latter organizational attitudes towards an individual are better than the first? Decidedly no. Needs vary over time. Furthermore, the intensity of need at a given level and what it takes to satisfy it is different for individuals. Some do not expect or want their social (or other higher level) needs fulfilled at work. They have family, hobbies, and clubs where they can attain their highest level of fulfillment. Further, needs change as a career develops from a period of experimentation, consolidation, wanting to make a mark, to maintaining one's position and recognition. Some people have more than one career and thus go through this development cycle more than once. For all these reasons organizational structure, leadership style, and reward structure should be flexible enough to accommodate the individual. Thus a judicious combination of the previous three organizational and management views of what motivates an individual should yield the best results.

Our objective is to develop a conceptual framework of how to determine goals, structure, management control, decision making and leadership styles, and reward systems for a software development team within an organization. We view this as a dynamic process that changes with the people involved in it. We must be able to recognize the current state. We are concerned about motivation because motivation, intrinsic to the job itself or extrinsic as a reward, leads to increased effort and job satisfaction. Negative motivation decreases performance and can lead to tardiness, absenteeism, and higher turnover. While extra pay is nice, one should not underestimate the positive effects of a work climate where everybody is treated courteously and where supervisors show respect for their subordinates and support their need for personal growth.

Problems and Questions

1.   How is Maslow's Need Theory related to the view an organization can have of its people? Which software firm would likely emphasize development standards, metrics, and norms more?

15.2.2.   Turnover and Job Satisfaction

Turnover has traditionally been a crucial problem for the software industry ([Cher81], [Labe80]), because the job market has been very favorable to the well-trained employee and it increases costs when an employee is replaced in an ongoing project. The fact that people are more inclined to leave has led to job hopping of astronomic proportions with a national turnover rate two to three times that of the average when we compare figures of [Coug80], [Bart83], and [Cher81] to [Hamn78]. The costs of replacing an employee vary with the phase of development and the individual's role in it, but it can easily exceed $10,000. New programmers have to be recruited and trained. This alone can be costly in today's labor market for DP professionals. The more highly specialized an application area, the longer it usually takes the new team member to master responsibilities or, alternatively, the more a specialist, who does not have to be trained, will cost. In any case, productivity will suffer. Projects may miss important deadlines and may even have to be scrapped when a crucial employee leaves. Because of sharp competition and because a lot of software is "protected" by trade secrets only, it can be very harmful to lose someone to a competitor. Even if no trade secrets are passed, knowledge and skill are.

The image of the department is also affected when turnover is high, because other departments, users, and other organizations conclude that there must be problems because they see a constant series of people with no continuity [Cher81]. As a result the DP department may be viewed as unreliable, "you never know who you will talk to the next time you need something; none of their guys is ever fully broken in, and you spend forever explaining the same old issue over and over again." When turnover is high, it may force an organization to hire extra people for a project to provide backup in case some of the team members leave. High turnover can also damage the image of the employer. Good, experienced people will avoid a company where turnover is high. They often assume that substandard management causes it. For many software developers it is as important therefore to maintain job satisfaction of their employees as it is to produce quality software.

Some companies pursue the reasons for turnover, mandating exit interviews or asking employees who leave to fill out a questionnaire. This is laudable, but to be effective in eliminating problems, an organization must do more:

▶ They should follow up on these stated reasons: the schedules are always too tight (I'm no longer willing to ruin my health), they deal with an impossible manager, or there is better career potential elsewhere. When dissatisfaction with the work, the supervision, or the reward system are discounted too easily, nothing will change for the better and the whole exercise becomes a waste of time.

▶ They should protect the leaving employee from the repercussions of being honest. It must not be possible for a manager (whose deficiencies are the reason for an employee's leaving) to damage the professional reputation of the employee through a bad reference.

▶ Without action, nothing will change. Without encouraging truthful statements, wrong reasons are given and the real problem remains unaffected.
Not all turnover is undesirable. It is a relief to see employees with unsatisfactory work performance leave. A group or organization also needs fresh blood, people with new perspectives on software development and its management. Thus we need to plan some turnover. What an organization does not want to see is unwanted turnover that hinders software development productivity.

Job Satisfaction

Job satisfaction is the single most reliable factor to predict low turnover, absenteeism, and tardiness ([Bart83], [Hamn78]). Therefore, increasing or maintaining job satisfaction is very important. Job satisfaction is correlated with organizational commitment, which measures the degree to which an individual accepts the goals and values of an organization, is willing to work for them, and wants to stay a member of the organization. It is also influenced by an individual's needs, goals, and motives, the work environment, age and job experience (older people tend to be more satisfied, partly because they have more realistic expectations [Hamn78]), and reward structure. If a DP organization wants to facilitate job satisfaction and reduce turnover, it must be aware of the following issues:

▶ They must know what people's needs, goals, and motives are. This makes it possible to respond to their needs and help them achieve their goals within the framework of the organization's.

▶ They should learn how to provide a work environment and task structure that are intrinsically rewarding because they fulfill people's needs.

▶ They should establish a fair reward system. According to Herzberg's Two Factor Theory [Herz59] there are few things more dismotivating and more undermining to job satisfaction than an inequitable reward system.

▶ They must provide growth paths for its employees, since self-actualization is the highest level need and therefore the highest level factor contributing to job satisfaction.

▶ They should figure out how to commit people to the organization's goals. Employees are much less likely to leave if they are committed to the organization.

The major costs of software development and maintenance are still labor costs for software professionals. Therefore, achieving high internal work motivation (and its resulting high quality work performance, job satisfaction, low absenteeism, and turnover) is a prime contributor to lower software costs.

Problems and Questions

1. Why is turnover such a critical problem in data processing? How can we soften the effects of turnover? How can it be reduced? What would have to happen to the DP industry for turnover not to happen any more? How is turnover related to productivity and job satisfaction?

15.2.3. Factors Affecting Project Organization

More specialized task definitions as part of a well-defined team specification promise that we no longer need the "renaissance man" (or woman) of programming who can do all jobs involved in software development equally well. Since people often have rather specialized skills and talents, this notion is rather unrealistic to begin with. Programming is a complex task. It involves a multiplicity of functions and at the same time requires high exactitude. Before selecting a specific team structure for a software development effort, we analyze the following areas:

1. **Manageability.** This refers to the degree of formalization that enables proper management control for quality, schedule, cost, etc. Goals and priorities play a major role because they determine and necessitate varying degrees of control in these areas.

2. **Team environment.** This is the "outside world." A software development team develops software for a user and thus has to relate to the user or its representative. The team is also part of the organization within which it is placed and has to interact with it.

3. **Product structure.** This refers to the final software product and the deliverables of intermediate stages. Examples are requirements, specifications, design, test plans,

etc. Product structure must facilitate division of labor. Activities required to produce a deliverable must be partitioned into tasks that are cohesive logical units of work with simple interfaces to other units.

4. **Needs.**   These include the needs of the individual team members and requirements that the individual team member has to meet. Here we include degrees of clarity of task assignment and the amount of communication needed between people. We also assess whether the task attributes are adequate for the individual's motivational needs. This process is called task analysis and design. The Job Characteristics Theory by Hackman and Oldham ([Hack76], [Hack80]) states that there are five different core job dimensions that influence three major psychological states. These three states are the primary determinants of motivation.

The five core job dimensions are

- ▶ **Skill variety.**   How many different skills does a job require?

- ▶ **Task identity.**   To which degree is a job done from beginning to end with a visible outcome?

- ▶ **Task significance.**   How does the job influence the environment?

- ▶ **Autonomy.**   What is the degree of freedom and independence to do the work? This refers to the freedom to set one's own schedule and to determine one's own procedures to get a task accomplished.

- ▶ **Feedback.**   How much information about the quality of work performance is given during the work?

The three major psychological states are

- ▶ experienced meaningfulness of the work,

- ▶ experienced responsibility for work outcomes, and

- ▶ knowledge of results.

Not everybody needs the same amount of task significance, autonomy, feedback, task identity, or skill variety to feel satisfied and comfortable with work assignments. How much an employee needs depends on individual growth need. People with high growth needs cannot keep doing the same old thing for a long period of time.

Some individuals require high scope tasks that have high levels in all core job dimensions. Others prefer to do one thing in one area, and they become overly stressed when a task requires too many skills, is too loosely defined (too much autonomy), or does not provide instant or frequent feedback. Because of this, we must look beyond job characteristics. First the skill level of a person is important. The more skills someone has, the less stressful a job is, but an overqualified worker can get bored. Kaiser's study [Kais84] reports that DP people like change, variety, growth, and learning. If they don't get it, they change jobs.

Case Study 1: Kim

Kim is an example of the effects of high growth needs. Her resume reads like a survey of the computing field. She has done just about everything that ever was challenging and new in this field over her 15 years of work experience. About two years ago, Kim was hired by a big bank as a performance analyst and capacity planner. When that happened she was ecstatic, even more so when they sent her to "modeling school," where she learned how to use sophisticated performance modeling packages to assess and predict system performance and capacity needs for the bank's computer system. She works hard, long hours, likes it, and within six months developed a methodology and software to manage performance of all systems. With everything in place, she is now sitting at her desk, twiddling her thumbs most of the day. There is nothing much to do, certainly nothing new. She starts reading every book on the theory of queueing models that she can find, but she is still bored and finds herself writing articles for conferences and trade publications. But all this isn't *work*. Relations with her boss are deteriorating. He doesn't seem to understand why she isn't glad that everything is running so smoothly and that she is getting big raises and more vacation time. Kim hardly ever takes vacations. He cannot promote her, because she is already at the highest level for her educational qualifications. After a year of frustration, Kim leaves the bank and joins a small microcomputer firm to help them develop a fast, new machine, even though she doesn't know much about that particular type of hardware. She is excited and can't wait to begin. Let's tackle a new area. Finally, she has something to do.

Reading this case, it is obvious that Kim has high growth needs and low tolerance for stagnation. She is willing and able to "find her own way" towards growth as her independent (and unrewarded) efforts for increased knowledge show. The new job offers a new challenge and professional growth, but one might ask: "For how long?"

Maybe she would have stayed with the bank if there had been a viable career path for her or at least a way to move (laterally) into a new specialist area of work. She had no possibilities for hierarchical advancement, because she did not have the "degree" required for it. Notwithstanding her formal education credentials, the path would have been blocked by her boss anyway. This lack of viable career paths aggravates unfulfilled growth needs. Often the model career path for DP is from entry level programmer to analyst to project leader to manager. This structure, however, does not provide a viable formal route for continued growth and challenge [Kais84]. This is why it is so vital that an organization establishes flexible career paths for its DP personnel. As it was, Kim wasn't even so much interested in becoming a manager but in doing something new and challenging. It is not enough to recognize the needs of members on a team. There must be instituted ways to fulfill them. This is why we need flexible career paths.

15.2.4. Motivation

Three basic work motives are important [Mccl61]:

- ▶ performing or becoming skilled in a task (we find strong goal orientation and a drive to compete with peers or against a standard);

- ▶ relationships (trust, interaction, openness, being part of the team); and

- ▶ influence and direction over people.

Motivation can be positive or negative and varies in intensity. Task-oriented motives are external stimuli. Internal motivators are personal preferences and needs.

It has been said that DP professionals have a very high motivating potential due to their high growth need ([Coug78], [Fitz78]). This is connected to the work motives, task, and influence (direction). Their social needs (the relationship area), however, are low. This is a motivational profile that is remarkably similar to that of engineers [Stev77]. It also implies that their skills in these areas are often not as well developed, because they are not motivated to develop them. Or it might mean that they experience more stress when faced with such tasks than people with higher relationship needs. Stevens and Krochmal [Stev77] profess that these personality traits result in the following turn-ons and turn-offs for the individual:
The turn-ons are

1. moving forward on project when he feels it is appropriate, and having and maintaining control over his progress;

2. being able to measure his own progress;

3. having to keep in touch only with project progress that affects him;

4. brief, to the point, pragmatic communication;

5. practical work; and

6. personal goals stated in specific project goals.

The turn-offs are

1. waiting for politics, etc. or things that he cannot control;

2. not knowing how he is doing or how work is progressing;

3. having to keep up with things that don't directly concern him such as administrative meetings;

4. policy statements, personnel forms, and regulations;

5. having to remember feelings, birthdays, and social events; and

6. group concerns and organizational goals.

These personal preferences shed considerable light on many problems in software project management, notably staffing and control [Thay82]. They also explain the preoccupation with tools and development methodologies over management procedures [Zoln82], but more technical gadgets cannot replace adequate management practices nor can new structured technique. Metrics only help if they can be tied to desired software quality, to means to achieve it, and to rewards for the individual and team for producing the expected output. The findings quoted for DP professionals represent averages. The motivators and demotivators are likely but not guaranteed to be present always or to a high degree.

One can also use this list to examine where and at what point in the software development life cycle a potential for turn-offs exist. Steps can be taken to reduce them and thus reduce or eliminate their demotivating effects. Consider item two, which states that not knowing how one is doing or how work is progressing is a turn-off. This can happen to analysts who are involved during the early phases of software development. The finished product depends on the quality of their work, but they might not know how good it turned out to be and how much of it was their doing until the product is finished (a year or more later).

What can be done about that? One possibility is to implement an objective requirements and specification evaluation method. Metrics are good, because they relate to a "turn-on." But they have to be reliable and valid predictors of quality. Then a feedback mechanism is needed to report back to the analysts whether there were any problems in their work and whether modifications were necessary (later stage feedback). An example of this happens when analysts are involved in $n - 1 + 1$ reviews. One can also inform them via electronic mail or hard copy. They should be in charge of executing necessary changes in documents that were their responsibility. They could also participate in a *post mortem* on the project. Another means of letting people know how work is progressing is to distribute progress reports on a regular basis and to make the schedule transparent. This has the added advantage that possible oversights are caught early, when the person whose part of the schedule turns out to be infeasible comes back and points it out. This also gives more task significance, identity, and autonomy.

Work motives are latent or dormant until there is a possibility that they can be fulfilled [Hamn78]. Beyond that, this list of motivators and demotivators provides a checklist for personal preferences and personal styles that needs to be considered and evaluated for every person when a new team is formed. A person's motivators will influence leadership style and group behavior.

The relationship-oriented manager is more likely to be influenced by the climate in his team. Thus he or she tends to avoid decisions about work that he or she knows will cause social or emotional conflict. Such managers are also more likely to fire someone not because of poor performance alone, but when it causes disruptions of group performance and leads to group conflict. Many managers are task oriented, however. They show many characteristics from the list of turn-ons described previously. They must have enough concern for relationships to keep the group together.

Before starting to evaluate existing team structures, let us explore the relationship between needs, goals, and motives (Figure 15.2).

Needs provide the basic energy and effort to pursue goals. Goals themselves are set subject to values [Hamn78]. Goals provide a focus and direct the available energy and effort towards achievement. Positive, reinforcing outcomes tend to increase or maintain motivation. For a software manager, this means that it is very helpful to know what a team member expects or values, what his or her goals are, and what rewards and incentives are perceived as positive and reinforcing. This knowledge enables the manager to properly direct the energy of a subordinate.

Case Study 2: Bill

Bill has recently graduated from college and is intent on establishing a stable financial basis for himself. His need is security. His declared goal is to make enough money to pay off his student loans and to start investing for the future. Monetary rewards will be very reinforcing because they help to achieve his goals. On the other hand, job uncertainty,

Needs	Energize
Goals	Direct and channel energy, effort, behavior
Motives	Maintain effort, modify needs (feedback)

Figure 15.2 Role of Needs, Goals, and Motives.

salary discrimination, or arbitrary management actions that make Bill feel that his job security might be threatened are demotivators. They would threaten his goals and thus create stress and decrease work satisfaction. Its possible effects include decreased productivity, a lower quality of work (more bugs in his software?), tardiness, and absenteeism, which ultimately may lead to Bill's leaving the company altogether.

Case Study 3: Jim

Jim has been a successful manager with a very reasonable salary. He owns a home, has turned over his investments to a firm, and appears content with his bachelor circle. The software group he is supervising likes him and respects him, but that does not seem to be all Jim wants. Recently he has become increasingly concerned about his position in the company and the fact that nobody seems to know or care how well received his software metrics are in the professional community. He wonders whether he will have a chance to get into a position with his company so that he can introduce his results into the development procedures. As it is, he has no influence in this matter whatsoever. Jim's needs are partly ego needs. His goal is focused on receiving recognition for his work and obtaining enough influence to have the results be used in his company. Therefore, Jim will probably feel a lot more motivated by a company award for his work or by being mentioned and acknowledged in the company newsletter. These are extrinsic motivators or outcome rewards. They happen after the work is done and are not part of the work itself. More freedom to pursue his software metrics work or assignment to a high visibility project because of his accomplishments are intrinsic motivators to keep Jim's efforts channeled and his motivation at a high level. Intrinsic motivators constitute rewards inherent in the task itself.

Problems and Questions

1.   Look at the list of turn-offs for DP people. For each item on that list, give an example when, during software development, a demotivating event might occur. Then suggest a means to reduce its occurrence and thus soften or eliminate its demotivating effects.

2.   How can we increase the motivating potential of the "turn-ons"? Take one "turn-on" at a time and suggest ways to organize a project so that it will occur or be facilitated. Can the software development methods from the previous chapters help? If so, how?

3.   Take the design for the program analyzer and assign parts of it to a team of five people for implementation. For each assignment assess

    a)   skill variety,

    b)   task identity,

c) task significance,

d) autonomy, and

e) feedback.

What type of person would you require for each assignment? Explain why. How can they in your opinion experience their assignment as meaningful, feel responsible for their work outcomes, and know about the result of their work?

15.2.5. Rewards

Rewards, in order to be effective as sustainers of motivation and performance, have to be directly related to job outcomes desired by the organization. This is why it is so important to tell people what is expected of them. A vague description of expected performance is easily misunderstood. An employee may concentrate on work or quality attributes for work that is either not high priority or downright undesirable.

Rewards should follow the task outcome soon enough so that the relationship between job performance and reward does not get blurred by time. When the reward or incentive comes too late, its reinforcing strength is diminished or lost. Because of this, we need spontaneity in a reward system. If we assume that high growth need people strive for quality in their work and take pride in it, simple acknowledgement on a personal level is often enough. Besides acknowledging the value of good work instantly, it also strengthens a feeling of belonging. The employee sees that someone cares that the work is good.

Rewards include money, promotions, or other benefits such as more vacation, group acceptance, and supervisor support. They aim at sustaining or increasing desired work outcomes. Desired work outcomes are usually specific levels of job performance (this includes speed of software development and quality of resulting software), productivity and low absenteeism and turnover. In order to maintain desirable job behavior, an individual has to perceive the rewards as equitable when compared to the rewards of peers. Social comparison theory [Hamn78] states that the ratio of rewards over effort expended to get it should be constant. If an individual's ratio is bigger than for the peer, he or she feels "overrewarded" and either feels compelled to put in more effort or rationalizes that the comparison person's effort is not as big as one's own after all. Either deliberation brings the ratio back in line. If the ratio of reward versus effort is smaller than the peer's, there is frustration and the feeling of being cheated, a perceived inequity.

Case Study 4: Anne

Anne has been with a software engineering consulting firm for six years. She is a senior consultant. Her colleague, Joe, has been with the firm for two years. A year ago, he was promoted to consultant. To attract better quality people, a new company policy was instituted that stated that new consultants would get an extra bonus of $3,000 their first year. Since there are no strings attached other than being new to the company, it is like getting a higher salary. In effect, Joe's salary with the bonus is now higher than Anne's. When she hears this in a casual conversation, she is furious. She complains to her boss, but he replies that it's the labor market that is doing that to her, that it does not reflect on her worth to the company. A short time later she applies for a leave of absence, threatening to quit even though she does not have another job lined up, mentioning job discrimination. Since the firm needs her expertise, they grant her the leave. A few weeks into the leave, she quits without having another job.

Anne's case illustrates the crucial role of monetary compensation in job satisfaction. Salary works less decisively as a reward than as a dissatisfier when it is perceived as inequitable and unfair. This is in line with Herzberg's Two Factor Theory [Herz59]. The same is true for decisions and rules that are perceived as arbitrary, illogical, or unfair. Badly planned reorganization and relocation are examples. They are considered arbitrary if employees consider them as happening too fast or when people feel they have no say in the matter, even though it influences their professional and private lives.

Equitable salaries are important in the software field because people's value can increase substantially very quickly to the point that company policy does not allow such raises because of a cap in salaries. People become dissatisfied and eventually leave when they start comparing themselves to their peers outside of the company. When they leave, the organization has to bring in new personnel at market rates. They may disgruntle their longtime employees with a salary differential that is perceived as unfair even within the company, because the new junior people earn more than the old senior ones.

Further turnover increases costs to the organization, because not only does it have to pay higher salaries to the new people than it would have to pay to the old ones who left, but productivity suffers due to the turnover. In the end, it would have been cheaper, more efficient, and less stressful to avoid such a rigid salary structure.

Sometimes unrealistic perceptions of the salaries of coworkers can lead to a wrong assessment of what is fair. The measure of comparison is usually the ratio of rewards vs. effort. For equal ranks this ratio should be equal. [Hamn78] suggests to publicize salaries and thus prevent dissatisfaction when employees wrongly think that a colleague earns more.

Problems and Questions

1. A programmer analyst is given the following choice of rewards after completing a critical software project on time and within budget:

   a)   increase in salary (permanent),

b) bigger bonus (one time payment),

c) extra vacation time,

d) choice of next project to work on,

e) promotion (technical level),

f) promotion (first line manager), and

g) free education.

Based on the choice of the programmer analyst, what might his unfulfilled needs be according to Maslow's Need Theory? Explain your answer.

2. Why is it so important to have a fair and flexible reward system?

15.2.6. Communication Networks

The advent of programming team structures was clearly motivated by the need for specialization and better management control through more explicit role definition. One improvement managers hoped to see was a decrease in the extra effort required to effectively communicate with every team member where interfaces in the work made that necessary. Let us look how existing organizational structure and the communication channels it provides (the communication network) influence team organization. Figure 15.3 shows some of the common forms of communication networks.

The lines indicate communication channels, the numbers positions in the network. The more connecting lines a position has, the more communication effort the position requires, and the more information it also acquires and controls. A position with several lines, therefore, spends a significant amount of effort communicating. This reduces the amount of time available for production work. The chain, the Y, and the wheel have crucial positions that not only have the most communication lines but also control the flow of information between positions. For the chain it is position 3 in the middle, for the Y it is position 5, and for the wheel it is position 3. Such positions are called central as opposed to peripheral positions, which only have one communication channel. Because of the higher inherent power in central positions, they give the location of leadership. Note that leadership positions are structurally defined and based on how crucial the position is with regard to the sharing and collecting of information. They will be leadership positions regardless of the communication skills of the person, his or her technical expertise or problem solving abilities, or whether the formal leader is someone else. The structure dictates the leadership. Because of this phenomenon, we should consider structure very carefully, especially when it involves eliminating communication lines (the declared goal of effective team organization). Formal leadership and structural leadership should coincide.

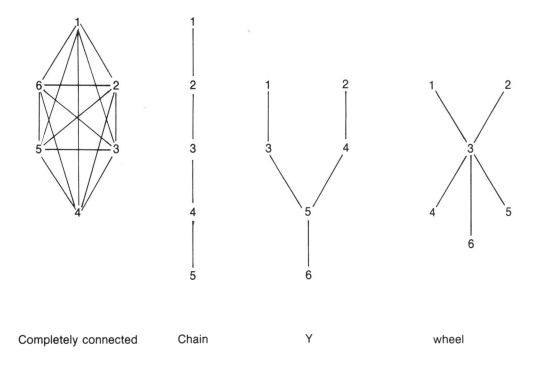

Completely connected   Chain   Y   wheel

Figure 15.3 Some Communication Networks.

Different positions in a network require different amounts of work. For a central position, this can lead to saturation when there is too much information to be processed and forwarded. Then the key position has an inordinate amount of work to do when compared with the peripheral positions in the network. Consequently, we need either a more skilled worker for this position, or we must face the fact that the central position is the bottleneck and that the peripheral positions are underutilized. Such a situation, underworked peripheral positions and the comparatively small amount of information they have, can lead to low satisfaction for group members [Knud79]. On the other hand, the communication effort is smaller than in the completely connected communication network, and thus the more centralized forms can be more efficient. Time critical project scheduling must consider this.

Whether centralized communication networks actually are more efficient depends on the software development task attributes. If it is a software development problem that is very interdependent and cannot easily or reasonably be partitioned into subproblems, then a more connected structure is better. This is also true when the problem is complex or when it is not clear just what the problem is (early phase of development or research problem) or what the solution looks like. Otherwise the software development effort is

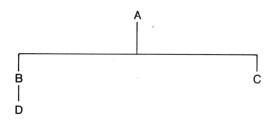

Figure 15.4 Example Design Structure.

amenable to partitioning, and a centralized structure with fewer communication lines and a central position can be chosen. The degree of saturation of the central position depends on the amount of information (interfaces!) and its complexity. Team structures may vary for different phases of software development: a completely connected one with few people would be best during the early phases, when problem and requirements definition are sought and the complexities of problem and solution are investigated. Later in the development life cycle, with sufficient decomposition, more centralized structures become efficient. Thus, task characteristics help to select a proper communication network.

Besides looking at communication channels *per se*, it is also useful to examine what information flows through them. It will give us a better understanding of how much work is involved in communicating.

Assume the following design:

Modules A, B, C, and D need to be assigned to Joe, Anne, and Jim for implementation. Figure 15.5 gives two possible ways of doing that and lists the interfaces between the three group members. Figure 15.6 shows the corresponding communication network.

	Alternative I		Alternative II	
Staff	Responsibility	Interfaces	Responsibility	Interfaces
Joe	A	A-B, A-C	A	A-B, A-C
Anne	B	A-B, B-D	B,D	A-B
Jim	C,D	A-C, B-D	C	A-C

Figure 15.5 Example Task Assignments.

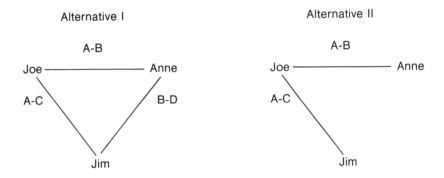

Figure 15.6 Annotated Communication Network.

Communication lines are annotated with the type of communication necessary, i.e., the interface that is common to both positions. We have only listed interfaces that require communication between people.

Alternative I results in a completely connected communication network. Alternative II is more centralized: Joe has the central position, Anne and Jim the peripheral ones. In deciding who should implement which module, we have to consider the amount of work involved in implementing each individual module and the communication overhead due to the interfaces. Lastly, it is important to know whether all team members would work well in particular communication networks. If we assume that Jim and Anne prefer to work on their own, if they have had trouble communicating in the past, or if they happen to work in different locations, alternative II would probably be better. If all three work in the same office, have done projects as a team with sufficient success before, and like talking about their work, alternative I is attractive. We should also consider how appropriate Joe's structural leadership role is for alternative II. Successful system integration will very much depend on him.

Problems and Questions

1. Look at the design of the tax record keeping and tax preparation system. Assume you have five people working on it. How would you distribute implementation responsibilities among the people? The constraints for selecting work assignments are

    a) all assignments should be approximately equal in implementation work,

    b) Person 1 and 2 do not like to work with each other,

    c) Person 3 is a very efficient communicator, and

    d) there should be as few interfaces between people as possible.

What is the resulting communication network? Which positions are central, and which are peripheral? Annotate the communication network with communication type (i.e., the module interfaces).

15.3.   The Chief Programmer Team (CPT)

The objectives of the *chief programmer team* or CPT are to provide a high degree of formalization within a strict organizational structure, clear leadership through the *chief programmer*, and the possibility for specialization through functional separation. The reporting structure is explicitly defined, as are the relationships between team members. Most job functions are explicitly defined. A rigid hierarchical structure facilitates management control, visibility of product and personnel, communication, and product structure. At least two team members, the chief programmer and the backup programmer are familiar with every aspect of the project. This provides continuity. The nucleus of the CPT involves the following individuals and their functional responsibilities:

1. **Chief programmer (CP).**   The CP is one of the technical experts. As the undisputed technical leader the CP

> ▶ is responsible for the team's success;
>
> ▶ develops all documents of the early phases, i.e., requirements, specifications, design;
>
> ▶ codes and tests the critical parts of the system; and
>
> ▶ (closely) guides and supervises the other team members.

These job responsibilities require considerable technical expertise and sound management experience.

2. **The backup programmer (BP).**   The backup programmer is the backup leader and peer to the chief programmer. He must be totally familiar with the project to be able to take over leadership when necessary and to participate in all important technical decisions. The backup programmer is responsible for the test plan and does research for the chief programmer. One could also call him the "vice president" of the team, because although he does not have the decision-making power of the chief programmer, he must have the chief's expertise and will take over this role when and if it becomes necessary. Because of this, the backup programmer has to possess the same high level skills as the chief programmer. None of the other job functions require both technical and managerial expertise to this degree.

3. **The clerical assistant or programming secretary (PS).**   The PS keeps all documents current and visible. The programming secretary also maintains the libraries, test data, test results, and all project documentation.

4. **The junior programmers (JP).**   These are junior personnel who implement the code according to the chief programmer's directives.

5. **Project administrator (PA).**   This is an optional role. The project administrator reports to the chief programmer, taking over some of the chief programmer's administrative tasks.

Communication Structure

The communication structure (Figure 15.7) is a wheel with the chief programmer (CP) at the center. The formal leadership coincides with the structural leadership. While it is possible that the peripheral positions of backup programmer (BP), project administrator (PA), programming secretary (PS), and junior programmer (JP) communicate with each other, it all has to be approved and therefore go through the CP.

   The major communication channels form a wheel. Possible minor ones are indicated with dashed lines. However, they can become a source of trouble if they "bypass" the CP. For this reason they should be controlled. The disadvantages of the wheel are

▶ possible saturation of the CP position, because it is central, and

▶ underutilization and dissatisfaction of the peripheral positions.

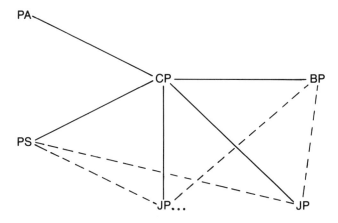

Figure 15.7 Communication Network of CPT.

Because of varying involvement of the members of a chief programmer team during the software development life cycle, the wheel structure is not stable. In the beginning, until design is completed to the point that work can be turned over to the junior programmers, the communication network will look like Figure 15.8.

From that point on, Figure 15.7 more appropriately describes the communication flow. If the CP lets the BP take over during the testing phase, since the BP is responsible for the test plan anyway and therefore might as well execute it, we could have a cross between a wheel and a Y structure. The BP occupies the central (i.e., structural) leadership position (Figure 15.9).

Because of the chief programmer's leadership and the clear role definitions for everybody, this team concept rates very high in the degree of formalization. When the chief programmer functions well, he provides the management control for quality, schedule, and cost. He sets the goals for the team members as he interprets them from higher level goals. No conflicts arise due to an ambiguous reporting structure or due to conflicting goals and directives set by several people. The team is relying solely on the chief programmer for interaction with its environment. The CP works with users and represents the team to the rest of the organization.

Requirements for Team Members

There are several classes of requirements. Highly qualified (both technically and managerially) individuals are needed for the positions of chief programmer and backup programmer. Individuals for these positions have to possess good people skills and be adequate communicators to relate well enough to the users or their representatives so that they can understand what the users want and need. They also must be managers who can plan and control the execution of a plan, set realistic goals and priorities, assign tasks, evaluate progress, and report on progress to the higher management level(s).

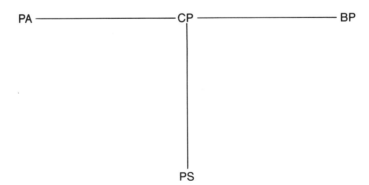

Figure 15.8 CPT Communication Network during Early Phases.

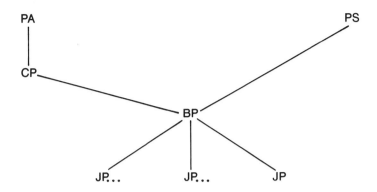

Figure 15.9 CPT Communication Network during Testing.

Third they must be technical experts in the field of application. They must be able to decide which aspects need to be investigated for a feasibility study, what the software's functions will be, and what the software solution will look like.

The junior programmers, on the other hand, need not be so universally gifted. Depending on the level of detail of the design specification they get from the chief programmer, they actually can have a very structured, specialized, narrow coding task with little control or room for creativity. Once the work is specified and assigned, there is little need for communication, and if so, only with the chief programmer. Due to the very specialized technical level at which the junior programmers work, they have little need for very outstanding communication skills, nor for the skills involved in requirements analysis and specification writing. They do not need management skills except for time management to structure their assigned tasks and to fit them into the schedule set by the chief programmer.

The programming secretary needs skills in word processing, technical writing, some programming experience and bookkeeping skills, and knowledge about file management and support tools for the project. Communication skills help to relate information about change control and document preparation.

When we rate these roles according to the core job dimensions, the CP has the highest ratings in all five, from skill variety to feedback. This can be very positive for an individual with high needs in all these areas. The CP must be fairly well balanced in his skills and work motivation in all three motivational areas: task, relationship, and influence/direction.

Potential Problems

An overemphasis on one area or a deficiency in another can lead to problems. This is clearly pointed out in a critique of the CPT concept [Mccl81], which mentions two major dangers. The first is to expect too much from the CP, the "Superprogrammer." The tasks during a project may just be too many for one human being to do. This situation is called role overload. Consequently, some areas of responsibility are neglected or deemphasized to the detriment of the software development effort. Usually those areas of work are neglected for which a person has the least motivation. If we want to avoid this problem, the size of the project should be limited.

Task redesign alleviates the problem of overload. Some of the CP's responsibilities are delegated. One way to split responsibilities is along major skill boundaries: managerial, administrative, and technical. Another option is to split the work according to development phases: requirements and specifications versus design and implementation. Since a considerable amount of communication is involved in either solution, it is not a very good idea to separate the functions strictly along one or the other of these dimensions. It leads to too much communication effort between different commands as responsibilities are shifted, unless very strict standards are imposed. Depending on the personalities involved, this may not provide enough autonomy to keep them satisfied.

The second danger is rooted in the amount of power and authority vested in the CP's role definition. If motivation in the area of power/influence is high, it may produce an authoritarian prima donna and leave other team members with a feeling of being subjugated and powerless. Whether or not this happens depends very much on the leadership style of the CP and the needs and expectations of the team members.

Leadership styles range from the directive (leader centered, autocratic) to the participative (group centered, democratic). The definition of the CPT mandates a directive leader. Whether this is appropriate or functional depends on the type of organization and the needs of its members. A social or self-actualizing organization runs contrary to the CP role definition. Then the CP's role must be modified to a more participative level.

The next factor influencing leadership style is group effectiveness. Leaders of a very effective team tend to be less directive, more concerned about their people, and more likely to give their team members some autonomy. If the skills of the team members are not sophisticated enough to allow them to make design decisions, or if time is pressing and prolonged negotiation over such issues as design options becomes a liability, a more directive leadership style results.

The needs and capabilities of the CP also influence leadership style. Does the CP value a directive style ("We need order and structure to be efficient") over a participative one ("This is not democracy, this is chaos and we will never get anything done"). Or does he value a participative style (cooperation) over a directive one (calling it despotic)? Confidence in the team member's abilities and willingness to work also influences how closely the CP guides them.

A participative leadership style in an organization that is basically directive can create a whole new set of stresses for the leader due to role conflict. There is pressure from above to be directive and expectations from team members to be participative. At times it is hard to comply with both. Role conflict can also occur when a person from within the team is promoted to chief programmer. The rest of the team may expect him to be "their" man, to play by team rules, and to protect them when they violate regulations and standards. For example, as a team member the leader may have complained about documentation standards just like everybody else and tried to undercut them. Now, as leader, he cannot expect much support in following them, just because he is the boss. On the contrary, the team may expect more leniency! Such role conflict can cause friction and conflict and is one of the reasons why some organizations do not promote someone to a leadership position for the group he or she has been working with.

If the preferred leadership style is too directive, the lack of checks for the CP's ego in the CPT's role definition can be dealt with through built-in, mandatory delegation of authority to make decisions. One can either rotate decision-making power through different phases or split it according to task areas: administrative, managerial, and technical. Although a person motivated by power will still pursue it, the additional checks soften the effect on team members. Team conflicts due to ego problems can be dealt with according to approaches suggested in [Dyer77]. We also discuss some of them in Section 15.8.

To whom are these responsibilities delegated? An obvious first solution is to the backup programmer who has all the qualifications of the CP but so far no guaranteed authority, unless voluntarily delegated from the CP. The CPT team concept can cause high levels of negative motivation due to a low ranking in the job dimension autonomy. When this situation occurs with a BP who has significant motivation levels in the area influence/direction, there is a danger of conflict: "Why am I working so hard when I do not make any difference anyway? I know as much as the CP, but nobody does what I think should be done. Why bother?" The result is lack of enthusiasm, lower performance, even absenteeism, or resignation from the job. None of these need occur if the relationship skills (and motivation) of the CP are well developed or if the autonomy needs of the BP are not very high. However, not everybody has the talents and personal preferences to be a good "vice president" whose role is to know it all but to stay in the background until called.

The BP may also suffer from a perceived role ambiguity, because "being a peer to the CP" does not clarify expectations by others very well, nor does it give any guidelines for how to fulfill expectations. This can create stress, especially when it is combined with pressure. Such role ambiguity is more likely to be a problem when the BP prefers a directive leader and the CP is a participative one.

The junior programmers may also lack enthusiasm when their work is overspecified for their skills and their needs. A JP may be very happy and content with a precise, low level design specification at first, but after developing some expertise the JP may resent the lack of involvement in design decisions. The work is not meaningful; an adequate picture of the whole product is missing. Reduced needs for communication with others, one of the declared objectives of the CPT, becomes a liability when a JP's relationship needs are not met.

Professional Growth

All these are potential dangers. They depend on the individuals and their personality preferences and how the CP deals with a given personnel situation. Where the CP realizes the growth needs of his staff and delegates part of the work to a JP who is ready for it, no problem need ever surface. Unfortunately, the CPT description does not give guidelines for how to realize and deal with such matters. The CPT provides a good learning environment for JPs when the CP and the BP are willing to pursue it. They would have to include sample task assignments for all levels of JPs, since a transition from JP to BP or even CP is only going to be successful if the JP has been trained in all areas the CP has to cover. This includes the high communication technical tasks such as developing user requirements and specifications. It spans all the technical, administrative, and managerial aspects of the entire software development life cycle. Unless a JP is trained in all of these, he may not be able to develop the talents as he needs or wants. We should remember that DP professionals are said to have high growth needs.

Suggested additional guidelines for training are

▶ evaluate growth need and motivations (what do they like to do?);

▶ evaluate major skill areas (what are they capable of or show promise in);

▶ involve the junior programmer in all of these areas (let JP do some of the work he can and wants to do);

▶ reevaluate additional needs and motivations (take stock and give feedback to JP); and

▶ add training and responsibilities in these areas to help the JP grow.

Training needs time and this must be built into the development schedule for the project. Training on the job takes time for both the teacher and student. Perhaps the idea of creating a good learning environment had been one of the goals of the CPT, but the definition of the roles was too static and did not adequately explain the progress of the JP and how to deal with it within the team structure. Additional responsibilities can be added in all areas, on the administrative, managerial, and technical level, with the objective to expose the JP over time to all the aspects of work of the CP. In our extended definition this also includes teaching. Some of the teaching responsibility can be delegated. It is also suggested that the JPs are familiarized with the skills of the programming secretary and the project administrator, if they are so motivated.

The needs of the individual team members influence leadership style as well. In particular, a participative leadership style is advisable when the team member has a high degree of independence, has the necessary knowledge and expertise to do an assignment or to solve a problem alone, shows that he is ready and interested to assume the responsibility for structuring his own work and making decisions, can tolerate the ambiguity that comes from *not* being told exactly what to do and how to do it, and has confidence in the group leader. In the absence of any of these, more participative leadership may either be unwanted, produce stress because the scope of work is too big, or reduce confidence in the CP (this is his job, not mine. Apparently he can't do it right, or why else would he come to *me* for help?). Any of these can decrease work motivation and job satisfaction.

Summary

The CPT is best suited for projects of limited scope. Projects have a hierarchical structure and can be partitioned into modules or units of work at the team members' skill and interest level. We need well rounded senior people, one with good leader qualities, the other with the qualities and inclinations to be a good "vice president," who cooperate well and are good communicators, are able to assess their JPs' motivational needs, and are willing to structure their work accordingly. We also need one team member with the skills required for a programming secretary.

Problems and Questions

1. Bob has been a JP with Bill for two years. He receives detailed design specifications for COBOL programs and codes and unit tests them. He respects his boss, likes his work, and produces reliable quality most of the time. When he is asked whether he would like to join the design group for a new payroll system, because he implemented significant parts of the last one, he declines, but offers to help to code and test it. How would you interpret his needs and goals?

2. Jane has been on the same team for a year. She has recently asked for permission to enroll in a company sponsored course on software development. Her work has been mostly in the testing of combinations of modules. She has shown good analytic skills, but when she has been left to write her own code, it has not been too good. She asks Bill whether she could get the job Bob has declined. Would you give it to her? Why or why not? If not, can you suggest means to qualify for it? How about alternate paths of growth? Are there any project constraints (or lack thereof) that would change your mind about your evaluation?

15.4. The Egoless Programming Team (EP)

The *egoless programming team* (EP) sits at the opposite end of the structure and formalism scale from the chief programmer team. The EP concept works on the basis of free cooperation with no specific roles or reporting structure within the team. Everybody is responsible for everything, and the team works toward a common goal in a totally democratic work environment. Leader and roles have been agreed upon by the majority of the team members. They are only assigned "until further notice" when a new agreement changes assignments. Thus team leadership may rotate. So may any other function. The idea behind this concept is to give full autonomy to the members of the team. There is no formalization of team structure that enables management control. It is thought to reinforce team spirit similar to the Volvo experiments ([Foyg76], [Gyll75]). This nonhostile, noncompetitive team environment is hoped to be an excellent learning environment, because everybody is involved in everything.

This team concept is also called *democratic team*. It combines the notion of egoless programming and a democratic work environment. Egoless programming is based on the premise that it is dangerous and unproductive to simply allow programmers to "sit on their code" and to regard it as an extension of their egos [Wein71]. This results in tunnel vision because of cognitive dissonance. The programmer is not able to find all the bugs, since that would hurt his perception of himself as a worthy and capable professional. Such an (unconscious) attitude that interprets the product of one's work as an extension of oneself is counterproductive in software development, because it slows the discovery of errors. When everybody shares all deliverables, this is no longer possible; code sharing becomes a matter of routine and better overall quality is the hoped for result. Also, since everybody is involved equally, the end product should be a better integrated system. Code exchange is mandated as an important part of the development with the hope of having a more visible, better readable, and more reliable system.

Code exchange, one of the major tenets of egoless programming, is possible even in nondemocratic teams. A chief programmer may for example institute this procedure for his or her junior programmers. However, the full benefit of the technique is reached better in less directive environments and therefore we have combined the idea of egoless programming and democracy in the concept of egoless programming team. The advantages of this kind of team are claimed to be

- ▶ increased team spirit,

- ▶ more work autonomy,

- ▶ more challenge and job variety for the individual team members,

▶ greater job satisfaction, and

▶ better software.

When we look at the requirements for the members of a team like this, all individuals must be able to

▶ function democratically;

▶ accept votes as binding (instead of sabotaging results one didn't vote for);

▶ handle lack of imposed structure;

▶ possess team building skills;

▶ accept cooperation and communication; and

▶ work on negotiation and conflict resolution.

An egoless programming team can be built according to a plan (e.g., [Dyer77]). The members are taught how to deal with the lack of imposed structure, which is sometimes perceived as chaos, especially in the early phases when plans, schedules, and important development decisions are to be made. The democratic process takes time, often too much, when conflicts arise and can't seem to be reconciled. Conflicts are to be expected in this kind of team, and the members must accept that and negotiate acceptable solutions without resorting to a (nonexistent) higher authority. Groups develop in the following stages:

▶ **Formation.**   This is when members of a team are selected.

▶ **Storming.**   This happens when positions of power are fought for.

▶ **Norming.**   During this phase the group gives itself rules.

▶ **Performing.**   The group works towards achieving a goal and is productive.

In an autocratic environment, the stages of team development are more or less predefined through team selection, through formal assignment of leadership power and sphere of influence, and through standards and norms for team members. Even in an EP, some supporting rules and guidelines (e.g., software development methodology and standards) can facilitate the normative process. The remainder of the stages are the work of the individuals on the team. How fast the group development stages prior to performance are passed depends a good deal on the maturity of the members and their personality traits. Norms are developed to simplify group influence processes. They are developed for matters of importance and usually evolve gradually. People with more status in a group may be able to get away with less norm compliance. Norms state what is acceptable behavior and what is not.

For example, a rule may state that no group meetings are to be held Friday afternoon but that everybody is expected to be available for meetings on Thursdays. Or after a while certain types of debugging problems are always given to Tom, because he knows best how to deal with them. This way, a group may develop into a team of specialists over time, not unlike the surgical team that we will discuss in the next section. The big difference for the surgical team is that roles are not predefined, the authority of the surgeon is not given *a priori* but is established in a democratic process.

Potential Problems

Until all team members know what is expected, they experience some role ambiguity. People who prefer a directive environment tend to have more trouble with this than those who do not expect or want to be told "what to do." When a team member slowly turns into a "sucker," i.e., he or she works harder than others and gets angry because other team members do not carry their weight (social loafing), it creates tension and conflict. The group leader (usually a group leader emerges) can experience role conflict, because he is to respond to management and to his or her group. Very cohesive groups (the EP has that as its goal) are not necessarily better performers. It depends on their perception of management. If management is seen as supportive, performance tends to be higher; if it is seen as threatening, performance can reach all time lows.

As mentioned before, the EP does not provide adequate management control. This democratic concept, also called "autonomous work groups," may have worked in auto production where tasks were well defined and repetitive, but software development often does not have these properties. It is significantly more complex and usually takes much longer than putting a car together. Some results indicate that probably morale is higher but the end product is no better. However, that could be of great benefit to a software production environment that has been plagued by high turnover.

There are other potential dangers for this team concept. The democratic approach often proves too loose for management control, not only because the performance of the individual cannot be evaluated easily but also because, since nobody has the decision-making power to settle disputes (over design decisions for example), the whole team can turn into a debating club where no work gets done. Decision making may be postponed "indefinitely." That leads to ill defined requirements and specifications. This is known to have disastrous effects for a software project [Boeh77].

Even if that is not the case, there is extra communication effort because of the completely connected communication network that the EP postulates. This effectively limits the size of the EP. It is said that the perfect group should have only as many members as needed to supply the necessary task and interaction skills. It should be odd-numbered, because it avoids pitting two factions against each other. An action taking group should not exceed seven people. In a group of two to seven people the demands on the leader are still low. The leader need not be directive. It is less likely that group work will be dominated by a few members or that group members are inhibited. Rules and procedures need not yet be formalized. There is less tendency for subgroups to form. Time requirements for communicating ideas and decisions are low [Hell76]. As the group grows, the effect of these factors grows and makes an efficient EP harder to build and to maintain.

During a crisis when leadership is needed, it is often hard to find somebody who is willing to assume it. Visibility of the team to the outside is another problem area. There is no one person to whom the user should talk to, there is no one person who is in charge of communicating with other teams or with management. This can be very confusing and frustrating.

Product structure, as in the case of the CPT, tends to parallel the (informal) team structure, which now depends on how team members relate to each other. The deliverables of early phases such as requirements and design specifications probably will not be quite as uniform. More people are involved and more different opinions must be reconciled and integrated. On the other hand, this can lead to a better thought out system. Studies have shown that more people, as long as they are sufficiently diverse and can get along with each other, are able to solve problems better. The limiting factor is the communication required. We are still talking about small groups (i.e., less than 15).

The individuals in the egoless programming team must like high skill variety or be able to negotiate a task commensurate with their talents and inclinations. This requires group skills from every team member. This is (according to [Coug78] and [Stev77]) not one of the fortes and motivational forces of the typical programmer. If they have not acquired these interpersonal skills, they may end up confused, experience a high degree of role ambiguity, and feel overstressed. The results can be motivational problems, frustration, anxiety, and escapist behavior like absenteeism, drinking, etc.

Since everybody works together very closely and since everybody is involved in every aspect of the software development process, task identity and task significance are high. Autonomy also is high to the point that team members who need more supervision to feel comfortable, start feeling confused or unmotivated. Nobody is "telling them what to do."

Feedback is built into the system through working so closely with each other. As a result, this team concept allows its members to experience the meaningfulness of their work and have knowledge of its results. It tends to have problems in how an individual perceives responsibility for work outcomes. A person with strong task motivation may be very happy in this environment but may also experience a lot of frustration when he feels that he knows best but others do not agree and he lacks the negotiation and relationship skills to deal with the situation. All members must have some relationship motivation. If there are too many people who have significant influence/direction motivation, they may all strive to be the informal group leader. Then severe conflicts may result. This concept seems to work best when

▶ the group is small, because there are fewer people to communicate with;

▶ the members acknowledge each other as equals; and

▶ they have enough expertise and are goal oriented enough to be able to set and achieve their own objectives.

Professional Growth

The claim that this team concept provides an excellent learning environment is only partially justified. A "new kid on the block" may initially pose more of a problem than be an asset. Often groups "isolate" unproductive members by giving them tasks that do not have significant impact on the group's success, thus pushing the junior member to the periphery. This avoids the extra teaching and communication effort and reduces the risk for the rest of the team. It also does not motivate the junior person a whole lot, because his task significance is then low. A better idea is to have a mentor for the trainee or to convince the group that besides developing software they also have the goal of educating the junior member. We make educating the junior team member as much a team objective as software development itself. As a reinforcement and additional motivator there must be a clear incentive (reward) for the team. An example might be instituting a mentor reward (competition between teams) or a monetary incentive for the group that is based on the relative learning achievement of the trainee. Teaching may be done by rotating mentorship. Everybody gets a chance to teach the newcomer.

Conclusion

The egoless programming team has some advantages over other teams in terms of autonomy for its members. Due to its poor management controls and high need for interaction and communication, it should be used only for very small teams where people relate well to each other. This limits the size of the project. It is a disastrous idea to use this concept with people who need close supervision or are not able to set realistic goals for themselves.

Problems and Questions

1. Tim just started his first job out of college. He got hired for a position that requires him to learn a new operating system. He is assigned to a group of three people who have

worked together as systems programmers for this operating system for several years and know each other well. They have the freedom to decide themselves what needs to be done and who will do it, and as long as service requirements are met, the group manager leaves them alone. After several weeks on the job, Tim feels frustrated because the others don't seem to take him seriously; the only work he has had so far was kiddie stuff as far as he is concerned (typing up memos about system changes to users, mailing them electronically, retrieving inactivated accounts, and getting doughnuts). The other three are working on a new system release. He feels left out. Even though there is so much expertise around him, no one seems to have the time to train him or even just answer some questions. After all, he does have a college degree. Why was he hired if he was not needed?

    a)   What do you think has happened?

    b)   As the group's manager, what would you do if Tim came to you complaining? Why? What are the pros and cons of what might happen as a result of your actions?

    c)   What would you do if you were Tim?

    d)   What would you do if you were one of the system programmers and Tim came to you with his frustration?

2.   An egoless programming team has been working very successfully for a while. Over time, the group increased and the informal leader of the group was formally promoted to first line manager. The group's members spend lots of time in the manager's office talking about technical issues, just like in old days. After a debacle in another group, the manager is assigned to supervise group 2 also. To offset the extra work, another supervisor is to be hired for group 1. She reports to him, and group 1 reports to her.

    a)   Why is this a problematic assignment for her?

    b)   What can go wrong? (Hint: Look at the communication network that has developed over time versus the newly created formal reporting structure.)

    c)   Can you suggest ways to rectify the situation?

    d)   Are there potential problems for group 2? What would you do?

3.   "A member-manager of an egoless programming team should not be promoted to the next level management position for that team, unless the new leader is from the original team."

    a)   Do you agree? Why or why not? Describe pros and cons by giving different scenarios.

b) What problems is the author of the statement trying to avoid?

4. Someone joins an egoless programming team that has been in existence for a while. The new team member gets very defensive when asked to share his code with the rest of the team during one of the code reading sessions. He has never done so and doesn't see any need for it. He shuns meetings, brings his work to them, and endlessly flips through print-outs. Assume you are the leader of the team and are expected to come up with a solution.

a) How would you motivate the new member to participate?

b) Why do you think it will work?

15.5. The Surgical Team (ST)

The structure of the *surgical team* (ST) is similar to that of the chief programmer team. Like the CPT, it is based on specialization, but it goes about it somewhat differently. The surgical team structure emphasizes task identity and task significance. This is achieved through defining roles in four areas of specialization: technical, administrative, editorial, and clerical. The team members have the following roles:

1. **Surgeon (SG).**   The surgeon is the technical head of the team. One significant difference between the ST and the CPT is that the Surgeon's role includes less administrative tasks. They are delegated to the administrator whose role is described below. The administrator reports to the surgeon. This narrows the skill variety for the Surgeon. Overly broad skill variety was one of the areas of concern in the earlier concept of chief programmer teams.

2. **Copilot (CP).**   The copilot has the same project responsibilities as the backup programmer. In addition, he is responsible for interactions with other teams. This added function enhances the role of the copilot, reduces the workload of the surgeon, and gives the copilot some visibility that increases his sense of influence and importance.

3. **Administrator (A).**   The administrator is responsible for personnel, budget, and procurement (including office space, computer time, technical tools), as well as relationships with management. This role requires limited technical expertise but sound administrative knowledge and experience and negotiating and planning skills.

4. **Editor (E).**   The editor generates all project documentation. The role requires good technical writing and communication skills and good relations with the rest of the team.

5. **Secretary (SE)**.   One or two may be needed to support the administrator and the editor. Typing and communication skills are required.

6. **Programming clerk (PC)**.   This role is the same as the programming secretary in the chief programmer team except for the functions assigned to the editor whose responsibilities were described above.

7. **Toolsmith (TO)**.   This function specializes in providing and keeping operational all necessary technical tools such as utilities, libraries, debuggers, and the like. Not all of this function was specified in the CPT and probably was assigned in part to a junior programmer and in part to the programming secretary. The role of toolsmith requires a good systems programmer as well as a communicator. Even though the editor is responsible for generation of the documentation, the toolsmith supplies what needs to be documented.

8. **Tester (TE)**.   This person implements the test plan provided by the surgeon and writes procedures for test data, test drivers, debugging and the like. He also should perform evaluation of tests and feedback to the group on its progress in implementation. The tester might be assigned data collection for cost and schedule estimates as well as quality predictions. More detail on this role is given in [Dema82]. The tester need not have the ability to implement a coded solution, but he does need the analytical talent to search for errors and enjoy finding them. A patient, perceptive, analytical, and detail-oriented mind is needed for this job. It is not enough to discover an error; the tester also has to find where and what it is. These talents are not the same as those found in a good designer or a reliable coder. While we can call the latter constructive, the tester's role is more "destructive" by comparison, in the sense that it emphasizes trying to take the software apart to find everything that could possibly be wrong with it.

9. **Language lawyer (LL)**.   This person is the team expert on programming language and knows the cost-efficient ways to implement the design specifications into structured code. This function is strictly defined in its skill aspects. It shows a high degree of specialization.

The surgical team structure is intended to provide a formal structure that will enable management control of quality, schedule, and cost within the limits of goals and priorities. The surgeon on this team, like the chief programmer on the other team, can exercise as much influence and direction as he/she desires.

The communications network of this team concept is given in Figure 15.10. The basic communication pattern is the wheel as in the CPT, but it has additional modifications. If the editor (E) is supposed to communicate directly with the team members, there is a second wheel structure with the editor as the central position, in contrast to the formal

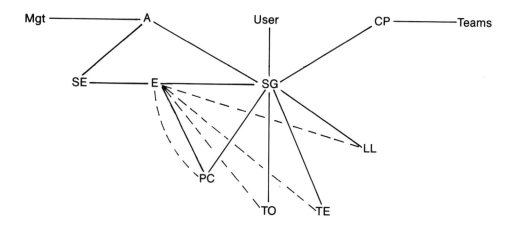

Figure 15.10 Communication Network of Surgical Team.

leadership role of the surgeon (SG). Figure 15.10 shows the second wheel in dashed lines. The peripheral positions of administrator (A) and copilot (CP) are enhanced. Communication is with management for A and with other teams for CP. The secretary (SE) has a potential role conflict built into the role, because he works with both the editor and the administrator. Who gives the secretary the work? Who has priority if the secretary is too busy to satisfy the both of them simultaneously? The reporting structure is a wheel, but communication is more or less completely connected. The topic of communication is rather specialized. In effect, we can annotate the communication lines to indicate which of the positions is in charge. Specializing roles and having them at the center of a wheel communication structure for every role structures communication and can improve efficiency.

Analysis

Compared to the chief programmer team, the role definitions for the surgical team are more explicit and narrow. Interactions of the team with its environment are considered in several roles: the administrator acts as a link with management; the copilot interfaces with other teams; the editor is in charge of project documentation and thus of intra team communication; and the surgeon works with the user group. A positive result of this division of "communication labor" is that communication in any of the areas listed above is the responsibility of only one person. This eliminates confusion and misunderstandings that can occur when one has to talk to ever changing team representatives. There is a potential problem, however, because the administrator lacks the negotiating authority of the surgeon and may have difficulties communicating with management.

Product structure will reflect the cooperation between the surgeon and the copilot in the early phases of software development. We can expect the same hierarchical software structure as in developments by the chief programmer team. Since project and product documents are written by one person, they should be uniform.

Let us look at the task dimension that describes needs and requirements for the individual. Skill variety is reduced for all team functions. This is a direct result of the higher degree of specialization, a goal of the surgical team concept. This greater degree of specialization can pose motivational difficulties, if the individual needs greater skill variety than the role allows. Task identity may suffer because the specialized skills of the functions may not be needed uniformly throughout the project. This reduces the sense of being involved in a job from beginning to end. On the other hand, more specialization means that tasks are completed faster. This provides more frequent feedback and more knowledge of the results.

Task significance is high because team members are given functions that identify them as experts. High task significance is considered to increase team morale and to improve individual recognition. This specialization provides much autonomy in each person's area of specialization with regard to procedures and methods, but each specialist's work is bound into the team's overall effort. Therefore, needs for communication and cooperation minimize the individual's control of his or her own schedule.

Some of the roles in the surgical team may be perceived as having insufficient autonomy due to the limited skill variety found in overspecialization. For example, the language lawyer may feel like a coding machine. The toolsmith may feel removed from the goals of the rest of the team, since tools are not necessarily bound to a particular project. However, feedback is generally good in this team structure and comparatively immediate, due to the need to use each other's work. Feedback is best organized using a phased approach to software development ([Zelk79], [Gilb83], [Metz81]), where a phase is not started until the previous phase has been completed successfully. Success is measured through a validation process through which all deliverables for a given phase must pass. This validation process provides feedback and continuity in communication across phases, especially when $n + 1 - 1$ reviews are used [Myer76] and people who were assigned to both the previous phase and the subsequent one participate in the validation.

Major potential difficulties with the Surgical Team structure stem from the limited skill varieties in some of the roles. People might not experience their work as meaningful enough. The roles of team members stress complementary skills that are reflected by complementary tasks. The surgeon and copilot share some of the core work equally, but the surgeon may still experience role overload and be stressed excessively by the number of skills the assignment requires. On the other hand, the copilot may have problems similar to the backup programmer in the chief programmer team, when high needs in the influence/direction area clash with lower autonomy of the role definition when compared to the surgeon.

The definition of the surgical team lacks any mention of a learning and training component. What are the potentials for growth and development in this team concept? Team members function only in their own areas of specialization. The concept of junior member is missing. This conflicts with DP professionals' high growth needs ([Coug78], [Fitz78]). One way to meet this need is to train team members for new and more complex tasks in their own specialities or, if a functional area during a project requires more than one person, to add a trainee who can learn under the supervision of the expert.

Another issue is how to train for the roles of surgeon or copilot. Since all the other roles are so specialized, any one alone cannot offer training in the many skills required of the surgeon. One remedy is to rotate a prospective copilot or surgeon through different functions on the team. For some functions, he may only have to serve as an apprentice, for others, he may have to acquire skills on the expert level. Thus we have defined a promotional path within a function (degrees of expertise) as well as beyond functions (various mixtures of expertise and sets of speciality areas). This additional personal development concept considers that adequate promotional paths are prime motivators for continued job satisfaction as they provide a pattern for fulfilling growth needs. The newly added concept of apprentice also serves to increase the sense of autonomy and of being in control for those roles that may be perceived as having little autonomy otherwise (for example the copilot or the language lawyer). A "Master" who teaches an "Apprentice" a skill is a position with control and autonomy.

Conclusion

The surgical team concept should work well with two well-rounded and highly qualified people who can adequately fulfill the roles of surgeon and copilot. We also must require that the other members of the team have specialized skills and interests and show task motivation in the areas defined by their functions. People with a need for high skill variety are not expected to function well in this type of structure in roles other than surgeon or copilot. If they show promise for these roles, they can be made apprentices for these positions. Or they can rotate through functions commensurate with their talents. This, however, requires a trade-off between loss of productivity due to less specialization and loss of productivity due to boredom with a given specialized task.

The surgical team considers very well that heterogeneous groups (groups composed of members with different skills and outlooks) combine greater amounts of knowledge. This results in a better chance for a good solution. They can be more efficient. Since it is a formally organized structure, sustained motivation should be higher, but the group will not be as flexible to adjust to frustration [Lamb73]. There may not be enough work for one or more experts. Sharing experts is not the ideal solution, however, because it can cause role conflict (if I only have so much time, which project is more important?). On the other hand, if done successfully, sharing an expert can help to integrate groups.

This can be desirable for larger projects. Experts can then serve as integrators, since it is known that technical expertise, not group leadership, are important for a person's integrating power.

Problems and Questions

1. Discuss the effects of turnover for the surgical team. Can and would you do anything to reduce the negative effects on the project and team when any one of the team members leaves the organization? Explain what you would or would not do and why.

2. Does the surgical team differ from an egoless programming team that has evolved into a team of specialists? If so, how? (Hint: Think about the software development life cycle and who is involved in which phase of it in the surgical team. Does leadership change in the egoless programming team over time?)

3. Mark is a language lawyer on a surgical team for a smallish project that is in the requirements stage. It is contemplated whether he should be assigned to another project to keep him busy. For the second project, he would be reporting to a different boss. What are the pros and cons of this second assignment? Under which conditions are you for it? (Hint: Look at quality of schedule, amount of work for Mark during different phases, potential role conflict. Does this mean that we should always discourage double assignments and prefer underutilizing people? State and explain your position. Under which circumstances would double assignment work out?)

4. Our language lawyer Mark from the previous question is assigned a trainee instead of working on a second project. Does that change your assessment of the issues in problem 3? Why or why not? Consider two cases:

    ▶ Mark likes teaching, or

    ▶ Mark doesn't like teaching, although he is moderately good at it.

15.6. The Revised Chief Programmer Team (RCPT)

This team concept by McClure [Mccl81] is a further development of the chief programmer team. It tries to remedy the following perceived shortcomings of the CPT:

▶ role overload of the chief programmer,

▶ inadequate level of autonomy for the backup programmer,

▶ team environment not sufficiently open and sharing,

▶ project depends too much on the quality of specific team members (e.g., the chief programmer),

▶ external visibility of the team members insufficient,

▶ inadequate formalization of individual responsibilities, and

▶ chief programmer given too much power.

McClure moves to overcome these shortcomings by redesigning the tasks and responsibilities given to the chief programmer and to the backup programmer. McClure renames the positions *project leader* and *coleader*. She reduces the project leader's responsibilities and power by creating two new positions:

1. The *administrator* will take over all administrative tasks of the chief programmer. The chief programmer reports to the administrator.

2. The *user liaison* is assigned another area of responsibilities that formerly belonged to the chief programmer. It deals with all direct contact with the user, represents the team to the outside, and coordinates project turnover with the maintenance group. The user liaison also is in charge of developing the test plan. The project leader merely reviews it.

These two additional roles reduce the project leader's responsibilities. On a small project, then, he may end up having too little work and responsibility. This can be overcome by putting him in charge of more than one project at a time. The revised chief programmer team concept clearly shows that some of the problems with the chief programmer team and the surgical team have been overcome. Work and recognition are more evenly shared, yet there is enough structure to enable adequate management control. As a matter of fact, the tasks of surgeon/chief programmer and copilot/backup programmer are more precisely defined than in the two other team concepts. There is more emphasis on interaction with the team's environment as evidenced by the two new positions of administrator and user liaison. The need for communication with other teams is explicitly stated. Preparing for maintenance is another issue not addressed directly in other team structures. In the RCPT it is explicitly assigned to the user liaison.

The revised chief programmer team concept should adapt to a wide variety of possible product structures because it is less strictly hierarchical. The primary involvement of three people—the administrator, the user liaison, and the project leader—should lead to a fairly unified product developed with a consistent design philosophy. The user liaison will ensure that the product meets the needs of the users.

Next, consider the requirements and needs of the individuals on such a team. The four nucleus positions—administrator, project leader, coleader, and user liaison—no longer require the same skill variety as in the other teams. These positions are created according to the concepts of division of labor and specialization. All technical tasks are the responsibility of the project leader and coleader. The administrator only handles managerial and administrative functions. The user liaison specializes in user/developer communication. All of these positions, however, will experience less skill variety than the chief programmer and backup programmer in the chief programmer team. The surgical team made a step in this same direction, but mostly for roles other than surgeon and copilot.

The surgical team and the revised chief programmer team differ markedly in the direction which specialization takes: The RCPT reduces skill variety for the positions most critical in the early phases of software development, whereas the surgical team specializes in the programmer positions but offers the other positions a much higher degree of skill variety. The RCPT mentions functions similar to those found in the surgical team but does not specify whether they should be done by a specialist or by several people jointly. The latter would result in a higher skill variety for everybody and increases the RCPT concept's potential for skill variety as well as task identity.

Task significance is higher in the RCPT concept than in the others unless the programmers are assigned specialist roles as in the surgical team. The RCPT gives the project leader considerably less autonomy in the administrative aspects of the project, but it still leaves freedom for creating schedules and procedures. Feedback among the four nucleus positions is expected to be fairly high, since they work together on a preliminary product (requirements and design) before the final product is ready for release. The amount of feedback for the programmers is uncertain and depends on work assignments and control mechanisms. The RCPT concept has good potential for structuring work in a meaningful fashion, for furthering a feeling of responsibility for work outcomes by all team members, and, possibly, for making the results of their efforts known to the team members. To ensure that this will actually happen, [Mccl81] suggested that someone from the development team be involved in product maintenance after the software has been delivered. Why that is supposed to give feedback to *all* members of the development team is unclear.

The nucleus of the RCPT requires people with different strengths and motivations. The administrator needs managerial skills, influence/direction activation as well as relationship motivation. The leader and coleader primarily need task motivation and some relationship motivation while the emphasis on these two areas of motivation are reversed for the user liaison. Programmers need to be task oriented.

The main skills required of the administrator are managerial and administrative. The project leader and coleader (Backup Programmer) need technical and communication skills, and the user liaison needs communication and negotiation skills and some technical knowledge. The programmers need technical skills. If people with these qualifications are available, the RCPT concept may be used successfully.

Again, the RCPT does not mention training and professional growth as part of the concept. We can apply the suggestions made for the previous team structures to include training and professional growth. Of all the team structures, the revised chief programmer team concept appears the most balanced and consequently is best suited for the most balanced set of people.

Problems and Questions

1.   How does the communication network of the RCPT differ from that of the CPT? Is there any difference for the peripheral positions in the network? Do the communication lines represent the same information as in the CPT? If not, what is different? Is the structural leadership position also the formal leadership position? If not, what is the effect? What are the chances for role conflict for the project leader? Explain.

2.   Should the project leader and the coleader make the same salary? Why or why not?

3.   Design a set of promotional paths for a new junior programmer that takes into account possible variations of interests and skills. Explain under which circumstances a particular path is appropriate.

15.7.   Personnel and Team Selection

The previous sections mentioned various dimensions of individual differences. Differences in how people regularly respond to situations define their type of personality. It is possible to measure, select and categorize many traits, e.g., with questionnaires or projective tests such as the Thematic Apperception Test or TAT [Mccl61]. While we might be tempted to use them to find a homogeneous match between applicant, team and organization, they should *not* be used for this purpose. There are a number of reasons for this. First, there is little to no evidence that links personality measures to good job performance. This is particularly true for managerial and administrative positions. Second, homogeneous teams, where members are similar to each other, are not necessarily better performers than heterogeneous teams, in which members are different from each other. Team research has shown ([Tria65], [Shaw71]) that groups with heterogeneous members are more likely to be efficient, because they cover a wider span of personalities, opinions, skills, and perspectives. There is considerable freedom to select people who complement each other so that the group as a whole has greater amounts of knowledge and is apt to try different approaches to solve a problem. Because different personalities approach tasks in different ways, a heterogeneous group is less likely to develop tunnelvision from "groupthink" [Jani72]. Groupthink is a phenomenon where cohesiveness of a group becomes dysfunctional. Unsettling information or difficulties are smoothed over and the group is not willing to examine difficulties properly. An example would be a design group when nobody speaks out about the potential effects of a major design decision on software performance. There is an attitude of "It'll work, this is not a problem" or "If no one mentions it, it must be okay" or simply nothing, because no one thinks about it at all. Later, when the software turns out to be too slow or to take too much memory, everybody is taken by surprise.

Problems of groupthink are less likely to occur with a more diverse group of people, when everybody has their "pet" issues they like to see considered, when a group of specialists is responsible to see that everything goes smoothly in their area (an example is the surgical team). Naturally, there is a trade-off—the negotiation phase, until everybody is satisfied that their points have been taken into account, may take longer. Last, but not least, selecting job applicants on the basis of personality may violate antidiscrimination legislation.

Rather than considering personality for selecting job applicants, we should combine the knowledge about an individual's preferences with the properties and possibilities an organization has to offer so as to facilitate job performance and work satisfaction.

The starting point to any recruiting effort is a clear statement of the needs of the organization or team and the resources available to fulfill that need. Pertinent questions are as follows:

▶ What are the specific technical, administrative and managerial skills required? Examples are user liaison work, designing a real-time system, coding in PASCAL, maintenance work for a payroll system in COBOL, knowledge of lexical analysis and parsing, budgeting for medium scale software projects, leading small teams of experienced people, etc.

▶ At what level should these skills be? One way of classifying them is junior, intermediate, senior. It is better to be more precise. This category also includes requirements about years of certain types of experience and educational qualifications.

▶ Are there preferences for these skills? How are they prioritized? Which are we willing to trade off against each other? Which or which skill levels are mandatory, which are desirable? Answers to these questions help to evaluate candidates on a comparative basis. We relate different strengths of different candidates to the overall hiring objectives.

Case Study: TAP

Assume we want to hire someone who could implement the tax system. After some deliberation, we come up with the following preferences:

Mandatory.   Familiarity with structured development techniques, basic knowledge of data structures and algorithms.

Priority 1.   Experience with IBM PC, DBASE, BASIC.

Priority 2.   Writing user manuals.

Priority 3.   Tax experience.

We are willing to accept minimal experience in any of the priority areas, but the more the better. Questions now must be asked to define the position:

► Are there any special rules and/or regulations that the applicant must comply with? Examples in this category include US citizenship or levels of security clearance as is often required for companies which do government or DOD contract work.

► If the applicant does not have all the necessary skills, who could teach new skills or upgrade existing skills? What will it cost?

► What are the work hours and where is the work to be performed? This describes requirements such as travel, regular overtime, shift work.

► What would the employee's assignment be after the current project is completed? Is it only a temporary position?

► Is there a promotional path for the applicant? What are the choices? How can these choices be ranked in terms of benefit for the organization? There may actually be several options that can be parameterized as to which type of applicant would fit into which career path. One company might have a good career path for people with administrative talents but not much for people with primarily technical interests. This should be pointed out to the applicant, because it can save much frustration and eventual turnover later. It also gives the organization an idea of how long the further developing skills of an employee might fit the organization's needs.

► To whom would the new employee report? Whom would the new employee supervise? Who would be his or her peers?

▶ At what level is the position? Junior, intermediate, or senior?

▶ What is the company prepared to pay for each level? This should illustrate salary with a minimum and maximum figure, benefits, vacation, and the ranges of nego- tiability. Some employees prefer less salary with more vacation, others have spe- cific benefit needs.

▶ Will the compensation level cause conflict with other employees who might com- pare their salaries to the newly hired one? What are we prepared to do about it? There might be a dichotomy between market rates for the new employee and what his or her peers are earning in the organization now. Higher salaries for the new- comer can cause friction and turnover amongst the present employees. Assessing the possible effects is important. So are actions to bring the rewards system back into a fair balance. One might give employees with higher seniority rewards other than salary (more vacation is a standard one, so are perks like a better office or other status symbols). Care must be taken not to discriminate. For example, if a male programmer analyst is hired at a salary higher than a female senior pro- grammer who has been with the organization for a while, the firm might not only lose their senior programmer analyst but might also face a lawsuit for job discrim- ination. Either one is a bad business deal. Unfortunately arguments like "we are only paying market rate" and "salary inversion is common in this business" usu- ally do not pacify the employees who are affected by what they perceive as unfair treatment.

▶ Which qualification levels are "barely acceptable" or risky so as to warrant a pro- bationary period?

This checklist includes more than what is required to write a job description for the following reasons:

1. It serves as a framework to determine the feasibility for fulfilling the perceived need and assessing the risks involved in hiring at various levels.

2. It can be used to look for appropriate personnel inside the company.

3. It can be used to screen the applicants by evaluating them according to items on this list. If we rank candidates according to the various dimensions of qualifications and cost to the company, we can translate the results into a table or graph for easier visual com- parison. We can treat actual measures as suggested in Chapter 12. Then we can apply an appropriate decision-making method based on quantified objectives.

4.   The framework provided by this checklist is wide enough to allow locating talent that might be used in another position (particularly when we look at the items experience, skills, levels, salary). We could combine several needs or open positions into one list. Then we add table entries for candidate evaluations, looking for the combination of people who best match the overall need. This way, we can hire a new team or part of a team.

During a screening or in depth interview make sure that each interviewer has the requisite technical knowledge. I will never forget the recruiter who answered my explanations that I was a performance analyst with experience in analytic modeling with "Oh, how interesting! Are you a fashion model or do you do ads on TV?" Such lack of technical expertise about basic terms of the trade do not make an employer attractive to a qualified applicant. Technically unqualified recruiters are also unable to screen out less qualified applicants reliably or rank them with sufficient precision. What they can do, however, is to prescreen for mandatory items such as schooling and quantifiable level of experience, special requirements such as security clearance, willingness to travel, working overtime, etc. This reduces work for the technical evaluation.

Tests must evaluate technical qualifications and knowledge only. They must measure items pertinent to the job requirements and approved by the EEOC. To avoid discrimination, they should be given to every applicant.

Who should conduct the interview? The goal of the interview is to find out how well the applicant is qualified and whether he will work productively within the position. For this reason, the following are good interviewers. The level of the position may make one or the other unnecessary.

- ▶ the person to whom the applicant will report,

- ▶ peers with whom the applicant will work,

- ▶ an independent person,

- ▶ personnel/benefits representative, and

- ▶ members of the search committee, if it exists.

The interview is a two way street. The applicant wants to know the environment in which he will be working as do the people who will have to work with him. While the prospective manager or superviser often knows best what he needs and can tell which of the applicants would fit best into the group, this can be a very subjective judgment and reflect personal bias. The same is true for coworkers. For this reason, an independent person sometimes is also chosen to evaluate the candidate. This independent person might come from another group or department. To keep this person truly objective and avoid a biased or uninterested evaluation, there should be rewards. For example, good perform- ance of the employee who was hired could be made the basis for a reward. The indepen- dent evaluator will also be more objective when the relations to the group for which the applicant is hired are not strained by competition or conflict. The personnel represent- ative can inform the applicant of benefits and general rules and rights in the organiza- tion and get information on specific needs of the applicant. For more senior positions there may be a search committee that evaluates all the candidates and then reports to the person who will ultimately hire the candidate. Usually several, often three, candi- dates are suggested with a ranking. A summary and detailed report accompany the suggestion.

The length of the interview depends on the level of the position. Some interviews take 30 minutes, others several days. A job interview should provide the applicant with infor- mation about the job, the organization, and its people. Job information must be detailed enough to show the specific duties and quality expectations of the position. For exam- ple, design and definition of interfaces, but no low level coding, participation in system integration tests, documentation, or specification and design reviews for system XYZ. Quality expectations can be expressed in terms of metrics, time constraints, and volume (see chapter on metrics). Sometimes there are company standards.

Problems and Questions

1.   Assume you are putting a group together to implement and maintain a tax record keeping and preparation system. Go through the checklist and develop a list of needs, a set of job descriptions, and evaluation criteria. Clearly state your assumptions where this is required to substantiate your assessments of needs and hiring constraints.

2.   When is it not worth it to spend a lot of effort on analyzing needs before hiring a programmer?

3.   Assume the following time requirements:

Duration	Activity
1 week	Prepare a job description
2 weeks	Clear job description with personnel
4 weeks	Advertising and interviewing
2 weeks	Decision time after job offer
2 months to 6 months	Integration of new employee (depends on level and role within team)

The project groups are organized as surgical teams. How are project deadlines affected when any one of the team members decides to leave? Assume that they statistically tend to leave towards the end of a phase. Schedule states that the project can be finished one month ahead of deadline. Will it help to pay the leaving employee a bonus if he or she gives notice six weeks ahead of time? Can you think of any other ways to reduce the risk of blowing deadlines because of turnover?

15.8. Leadership Strategies

Previous sections mentioned some of the activities and attitudes that can be called leadership. Sometimes leadership was directive such as in the case of the chief programmer team, elsewhere it was participative or democratic as in the egoless programming team. Leadership encompasses three major areas as shown in Figure 15.11.

From first level supervisor through middle management to top level management, issues shift from primarily technical to human to strategic planning. At the lowest level, enforcing software development standards, organizational norms of behavior, teaching subordinates the requisite skills, etc. is very important. In order to accomplish that effectively, we need, of course, an ability to deal with people. As a manager moves up, technical concerns decrease, but human issues and organizational planning concerns become more prevalent. This is in contrast to how DP professionals are often promoted and what their personal preferences are said to be. First, the technically most competent ones tend to be promoted. Second, their relationship motivation is low. For these two reasons, their overly technical emphasis as managers breeds some of the problems software development teams have. Human issues, although very important are often neglected.

1. Technical	Rules, norms, standards
	Teaching skills, knowledge
	Technical decisions
2. Human	Deal with people
	Adapt rules to situations and people
	Decision making
3. Planning	Long range
	Consider organization's environment
	Develop concept
	Planning decisions

Figure 15.11 Areas of Leadership.

Leadership Styles and Leadership Functions

Leadership styles vary the way in which leadership functions are performed. A list of such leadership functions is given in Figure 15.12. It is based on [Krec62]. The way in which a leader deals with these functions has a big impact on the satisfaction of his or her subordinates and on their performance, albeit not the only one. Technology, skills of the group members, quality and type of computing equipment, attitudes, expectations and motivations of the group members also play a role. Let us for the moment concentrate on leader behavior. Two major dimensions have been identified:

▶ A style that emphasizes consideration for the people is based on building an environment of mutual trust, a close group. When consideration is deemphasized, the leader is very impersonal. The amount of consideration a leader shows for his or her people is a very reliable predictor of subordinate satisfaction. How much consideration needs to be shown depends on the individual. A person with low relationship needs may not need nor want a very close relationship to their leader. The type of task and the maturity of the individual also make a difference. More structured tasks that are perceived as tedious or boring demand higher levels of consideration from the group leader for his or her people.

▶ Task concern, which manifests itself in the amount of structure which the leader gives to the group, is the second dimension of leader behavior. It relates to the degree to which the leader organizes work, defines who is to work with whom and on what, sets goals, enforces deadlines and gives directions. It is also called concern for production.

One can plot a leader's behavior in both dimensions on a graph, the Managerial Grid [Blak68]. From what we have learned earlier on what motivates people and the five core

Function	Do
1. Coordinate activities of team members	Scheduling, planning, task assignment.
2. Role model	Teach technical, human, managerial skills. Motivate to grow. Establish mutual trust, rapport and communication.
3. Formulate group goals	Project goals refined from higher level goals.
4. Represent group to outside	Responsibility for success or failure. Negotiate for resources, rewards.
5. Represent outside to group	Give rewards, feedback.

Figure 15.12 Leadership Functions.

job dimensions it is clear that scores in both dimensions of behavior need not necessarily be high. The amount of structure or supervision depends on a person's need for autonomy, for instance. Strictly defined tasks as we see in some implementation assignments and close supervision are both high in the task control dimension. Thus being supervised closely in a specialized, narrowly defined task can act as an added irritant. On the other hand, closer supervision can buffer the high scope of unstructured tasks, reduce the effects of ambiguity in work roles and the negative impact of crises on morale. Jobs with high intrinsic motivation may not require as much consideration on the part of the leader. Mature work groups may actually prefer a low profile style. What is most appropriate varies with the needs and skills of people and the specificity of the project.

Case Study: Research Project

The project tries to show the feasibility of a new technique to build distributed operating systems. The new technique is still somewhat vague and it is expected that the prototype kernel will provide some useful insights. The team has an experienced researcher as group leader, several mature systems programmers, and a couple of junior programmers who have never participated on a research project. The optimal degree of supervision will vary for the different types of programmers. The less experienced in the field will probably want guidance when faced with such an ambiguous project (not even our boss knows exactly what he is doing. How should we?) or feel "lost" if they don't get it; the more experienced might actually welcome the opportunity to pitch in their ideas and experience. The degree of discomfort at undefined or ambiguous work roles is very different for the two types of people. For the sake of simplicity we have concentrated on one factor, professional maturity. There are, of course, others to consider, which we have pointed out earlier.

The degree of concern for task and the concomitant amount of direction and supervision can range from very autocratic, where decisions are made centrally, to very democratic, where the entire group participates in the decision making. Leadership for any but the egoless programming team, which is by definition democratic, can range from totally directive to totally participative. In the directive environment, decisions are made unilaterally by the leader; there is no consultation with the group members, and no or very little input from group members in setting goals. The more the group members participate in decisions, are consulted, and have input in setting goals, the more participative the leadership style becomes. Figure 15.13 lists factors that favor autocratic or participative leadership.

Groups with a democratic leader tend to have higher work satisfaction, but performance is not always higher. It depends on the group's cohesiveness (groups in conflict or

Directive	Participative
Strong security needs	Higher order needs for self-fulfillment
Clear behavior expectations needed	More amenable to organization's goals
More respect in group leader	Group more committed to commonly set goals
Groups have difficulty finding consensus	Group more willing to achieve goals
Leader expected to take charge and responsibility	Can use knowledge and expertise of group to make better, more informed decisions

Figure 15.13 Factors Affecting the Effectiveness of Leadership Styles.

groups where people don't care about each other will not show many of the motivations that are listed in Figure 15.13). The nature of the work also makes a difference, since it determines intrinsic work motivation. So does the maturity of the team members. Time pressures usually call for a more directive leadership approach. In addition, all the democracy in the world will not help if the team members are not interested in the work or the decisions in which they are participating. What we can see in these factors affecting the satisfaction and productivity of the team is that it is not only the leader who influences the team, but the team influences its leader. In this sense we can use the theories of leadership behavior to engineer the job to fit the people. We may then find a chief programmer team with a participative leader, because both the leader and the team members prefer this style. Note that it is difficult for people to change their preferences about leadership style, which means we cannot change people radically to fit the job; we have to use task redesign to change the job to fit the people. This is why we have spent so much time explaining choices and modifications we can make to the job environment and the job itself. As deadlines approach or problems surface, it is likely that the amount of supervision increases and that it is not resented by the team members, because the chief programmer is in charge and taking responsibility. It makes it safer for them. As another example, a surgical team may have a surgeon who runs a very tight ship, because the schedule is very compressed, risk is high and stakes are, too. If the team members are aware of it and have bought into the group's goals, they again will be more tolerant or welcome more directive leadership, but on a standard, "easy" project, they might start a "palace revolution" if the surgeon were looking over their shoulders that much.

Several new theories of leadership behavior have emerged in the last years, but we have not included them here, because they would not provide substantially more insight or because there are doubts about the validity of the models. For more information, consult [Fied82], which explains in more detail how leadership effectiveness can be improved through a match between leader and group.

Problems and Questions

1.   Describe all situations when chief programmer and backup programmer have a good match of leadership style versus subordinate need. Specifically address the following factors as they can change:

▶ personal preferences,

▶ motivation (task, relationship, influence),

▶ relationship of CP vs. BP,

▶ maturity of BP,

▶ pressures, and

▶ nature of project.

Suggest in which areas of work and how much the chief programmer can and should exert supervision.

2.   How would you supervise a team of people who are developing requirements and performing feasibility studies for an advanced planning group? Assume that market pressure and visibility of the group are high as you would find in the micro software market. The team consists of mature software professionals and is very relationship oriented because a major part of their work is to translate between users (i.e., marketing) and designers. Which assumptions would you have to make for your answer and why?

15.9.   The Team in Conflict

In a programming team as in any other work group three types of conflicts may occur:

1. **Role conflicts**.   They exist when expectations of a team member are incompatible with reality. There is high potential for role conflict when a programmer works on two projects for two different managers, in general when a team member "belongs" to more than one group. When pressure mounts as deadlines approach, which role or project is going to have higher priority? Let's assume a programmer has two supervisors, one for each project he is assigned to part time. They each press him to do their work first. He cannot do both in time. Usually the side to which he feels the stronger affiliation will win out. But during such a situation, the programmer is likely to feel a great deal of stress. Similarly, a manager may experience role conflict to be "one of the team" and "one of the managers." Often technical issues and schedule or budget issues collide and are causes of such role conflict.

Role conflict can be very detrimental to performance when a great deal of energy needs to be expended to cope with it. Because of this, we should examine work assignments and team structure carefully for possible role conflict. If there is, the team structure or the work assignment can be revised to avoid problems. Where that is not feasible, additional rules can be negotiated. In the example about the programmer, negotiating priorities is one way to avoid role conflict. Or, while there are two assignments for the programmer, the supervisor could be the same person. Promoting a team member to manage the team he used to belong to, also carries with it potential role conflict of the type we have mentioned above. A sure way to avoid it is to promote the individual to be manager on a different team.

2. **Issue conflict.**   Members on a programming team might be at odds about the objectives for a software product they are trying to develop. They fight essentially over different types of software; e.g., is the goal to build a tax record keeping system or a system which keeps tax records and assists in preparing returns? Is the program analyzer for plagiarism detection only, or should it also be able to provide quality metrics? One may disagree about the facts, e.g., how much real storage is available or required, what the volume of transactions for the proposed hotel reservation system will be, etc. Discussions about proper methods for developing software and what design option to choose are other sources of conflict.

Different personal values can also cause conflict. They may relate to what a software developer thinks is a quality product. One team member may feel that quality was not considered as important as it should be, because testing was not done in full compliance to standards (his or the procedure manual's). At the same time, another member is more concerned with getting the product out the door as quickly as possible to keep the customer happy (at least a while).

Issue conflict cannot easily be avoided, but some of it shouldn't be. It is a healthy and natural part of problem solving and thus of software development. Only when it becomes dysfunctional and interferes with productivity should steps be taken to stop some of it. It is, of course, more economical to make basic procedural decisions such as development standards once for a longer time frame. Often they are made for the team. The same is true for facts, goals, and development methods. One might think that this eliminates the need for conflict. This is not quite true. Some team members may think that those decisions and rules were ill-advised, but since the decision has been made, their recourse is to work around the unacceptable, doing what one wants to do. Issue resolution "by decree" prevents open conflict resolution and can be more harmful than if it had been discussed and negotiated more democratically. What we are looking for is actual resolution of conflicting opinions on issues, not brushing them under the carpet. Note that not all decisions that need to be made entail conflict. That only occurs when it is important to people and they want and need to participate in the decision-making process.

Issue conflict also occurs when job performance is not what is expected (social loafing and piggy backing have been mentioned as sources of group conflict), when rules and procedures are not followed, and when norms are violated. They may be violated deliberately or because it hasn't been made clear enough how important it is to follow them. How does that apply to software development procedures that are crucial to successful software development? We can reduce conflicts that occur when software development procedures are violated or neglected if their importance and priorities are spelled out clearly. It has been well established experientially that programmers will build into the code what they perceive are the most important quality attributes; e.g., when they are told that "it has to be done on time," they will strive to meet the schedule (at the expense of reliability or functionality if need be). If they perceive performance as a very important objective, they will concentrate on that, possibly at the expense of clarity and maintainability. If no (clear) priorities exists, their own tend to be substituted, and we should not wonder that they conflict. Clear objectives, priorities, and procedures are very important to reduce the potential for unproductive conflict. It is usually more effective to discuss how to reach a known objective than to debate whether one was given the correct one.

3. **Interaction conflict.**   This is also called personality clash. There are people on a team who just cannot stand each other, cannot communicate, and cannot work together. This may evolve for a variety of reasons, far too many to list, but the effects on productivity can be disastrous. One way to avoid the worst clashes is to look at whether individuals would fit into a team and whether their personality, skills, and talents will fit the role on the team. A role mismatch can easily turn into an interaction conflict. For example, a backup programmer on a chief programmer team who wants more influence can grate very painfully against a directive chief programmer who doesn't give him or her the necessary "breathing space." Leadership styles as we have discussed them in the previous section can do a lot to prevent conflict or channel it into productive behavior.

Conflicts are not by definition bad. They can and do have many positive effects. They can stimulate interest in issues to which no one had paid attention before; e.g., a group becomes interested in software development methods or tools because they cannot agree on whether a particular method or tool should be used. Such interest results in better informed and more knowledgeable team members.

Conflict can bring issues out in the open that would not have been discussed otherwise; e.g., different opinions about the feasibility of a project draw attention to the risky issues. For instance, take timeliness and performance of a software product. While their feasibility is debated, people focus on them and in the conflict arguments for and against can be tested and a solution can emerge.

Personal and social change can occur as the result of conflict: a chief programmer may not have been aware just how abrasive her manner was perceived by several of her junior programmers. Now that she knows, she might decide to change her style. Or a junior programmer, who resents that his chief programmer is a woman who is, on top of that, younger than he is, may find that she is fair and capable and a very reasonable person to work with after all. Not all such conflict is positive. Some creates prejudice or decreases trust. Then people don't want to work any more with individuals who as they have "learned" have personal characteristics which they associate with trouble and conflict at work.

Conflict can lead to readjusting structure and organization. We can see this very clearly in the group forming phase for an egoless programming team when roles are fought for. Similar conflicts can occur when new members are added to a group or when a formal role change has to be assimilated into a group accepted one, and the like.

In the previous sections a lot of potential problems for various team structures have been discussed. We also mentioned ways to avoid some of those problems through reorganization, task redesign, and modification of roles in programming groups. Conflict often points to a need for such reorganization. Constructive conflict can lead to greater group unity and act as a stabilizing force, because a positive conflict resolution is bonding and reassuring.

What are the premises for positive conflict resolution? First, there must be enough openness to allow conflict to surface. Rules that allow this without hostility and destructive behavior are important. Pressure and threats are not conducive to that. Since conflict resolution almost always implies negotiation, it is important to provide a setting where conflict resolution is a winning proposition for all parties.

In software development various methods and techniques exist where issue conflict can be brought out into the open:

▶ In walkthroughs team members are *asked* to participate in the discussion of designs, specifications, etc.

▶ The egoless programming team is designed to encourage discussion of all aspects of software development for a given project. It provides a cooperative, open set-up to air and resolve issue conflicts.

▶ The leader-coleader concept in the surgical team, chief programmer team, and revised chief programmer team facilitates an open atmosphere on a smaller scale.

When conflict occurs, how should it be dealt with? How conflicts are resolved depends on the objectives of the people involved in the conflict. Let's assume there is a problem obtaining a shared common goal. Examples are reestablishing group unity in an egoless programming team or deciding on the design or on the feasibility of a project. Problem-solving techniques that are aimed at collecting and evaluating ideas will work in this set of circumstances. If more is involved in the conflict than solving a technical problem, persuasion can help. Persuasion refers to and emphasizes goals that are common to the parties in conflict, pointing out that it is in their common interest to (both) give in a little to advance the common goal. A mediator may actually do the persuading. For example, if two people on the design team are pitted against each other, defending their ideas, it can help to remind them that the common goal is software that fulfills requirements and specifications, and that the question whether design A or B should be chosen is only relevant with respect to that goal. The credibility of the mediator is crucial to success. If he or she seems biased towards one of the parties, the mediator usually does more harm than good.

What can we do about someone who does not share the common goal (e.g., quality software for this project), but insists on his or her own agenda (e.g., I want Joe out or I want to be right or I want my boss's job). Persuasion or problem solving hardly help here. Usually we find that the parties in conflict try to find allies to back them in the conflict. Politics are played out. This can be as straightforward as making sure before the design meeting that design A is backed by a majority of the team members. It can be a lot more involved as the following case shows.

Case Study: New Supervisor

As the result of a reorganization, a new supervisor was hired (Tom) to replace a well liked group leader (Jim) who was promoted and became the new supervisor's boss. Neither the group nor Jim liked it, but Jim's supervisor, Sam, had ordered it. There was resentment against Sam for breaking up the group. Without ever talking about it, Jim and his former group became allies in their fight against Sam and consequently against the new supervisor, Tom. They effectively isolated Tom by "going around him." Tom did not get enough support from Sam who was very busy and thus Tom didn't survive long. Tom resigned, Jim was "demoted" again, and while all this was going on, productivity was nil for three months.

Not all stories of political influence are negative. The one we just mentioned illustrates the conflict of interest and forming of factions.

Bargaining is another way to resolve conflict in situations where there is conflict of interest. The conflict is resolved, at least for a while, when the parties agree on a mutually acceptable course of action and outcome. Both usually have to pare down their expectations to find some middle ground with which they can both live.

For example, the chief programmer and her backup programmer both have needs for influence. They have a conflict of interest. So they have to bargain for a viable middle ground. The backup programmer may be put in charge of testing and user relations, and the Chief Programmer will control the rest. The bargaining process uses the position and influence of the bargaining parties. This is why the backup programmer may not get a full half share of responsibility. Negotiation skills can make up for some inferiority of position in a bargaining situation. A useful book about negotiation is [Cohe80]. It is based on the premise that for a lasting, productive working or business relationship, the parties need to work towards an outcome where both parties win. Negotiation is the process of finding out what constitutes a win and how little of a win is still acceptable. It may take some persuasion to convince the other that they are actually winning something desirable. Losing breeds resentment and therefore is not a good outcome for negotiations when one looks for a longer term business or work relationship. Then we would find games and counterproductive strategies (cf. 13.5).

Conflict as Violation of Expectations

There is another conflict theory that helps to understand the nature of conflict. It states that conflict is based on violation of expectations.

▶ Performance is not what is expected. The section on the egoless programming team mentioned social loafing or piggybacking. Other examples are absenteeism, continually blowing deadlines, inferior work quality (spaghetti bowl programs, badly unit tested code, incomplete requirements etc.).

▶ There is a violation of procedures and rules. Examples of norms that are sometimes violated are documentation standards, development guidelines, and testing requirements.

▶ Violation of trust occurs through intentionally destructive behavior: wiping out a set of files, pouring coffee all over a document, putting someone into a no-win situation; the list of such behavior is long. Section 13.5 mentioned some of it.

In some of these instances, brainstorming in order to find a solution to the problem won't help, nor will politics. Bargaining might. Often it is a matter of stopping undesirable behavior before it grows into a conflict or becomes routine. First of all, expectations and rules have to be laid out clearly and unmistakably. Often rules are broken, because "nobody made it clear that they were important." Many student teams that ressemble egoless programming teams and therefore experience many of its problems, run into severe conflicts and don't get much accomplished, precisely because they don't lay down rules in the beginning. The conflicts can be issue or relationship conflicts. People tend to substitute their own values and rules in the absence of given ones and that can cause conflict. Drawing up a "contract" of expectations helps tremendously.

Here are some of the guidelines one should observe when drawing up a cooperation agreement:

1. Specify a working communication mechanism. Since it is so important to talk to each other, there must be guaranteed ways to get in touch with team members. Electronic mail, phone numbers, setting up actual physical meetings are all ways to get in

touch with each other. The farther away some of the members are, the more important it becomes to make sure that everyone is reachable. Communication mechanisms may be graduated, reflecting the importance of the communication; it may be worth to drive an hour to a meeting when the quality of information and the urgency of the situation requires it, but at other times electronic mail or a conference call may suffice. We may distinguish between normal vs. crisis communication channels. How many student projects have been painful or unsuccessful because "I cannot get in touch with XYZ."

2.   Specify expectations for times of pressure or trouble. Specifically, how should the group deal with the situation when someone has to drop the project? (In industry we might substitute leaving the organization). Do we expect that person to tell us ahead of time? Who should get his or her work documents? People sometimes have crazy schedules for a while. Is the group willing to buffer such an individual for a while? How long? In student groups not everybody might be in favor of a group grade, where everyone on the project team gets the same grade. How will the group deal with social loafing or piggybacking?

3.   Divide up work early, precisely, and fairly. Share questions. Proof, test or evaluate each other's work in a truly egoless fashion. Establish a set of rules how to do that. Checking interfaces is especially important.

4.   Define how you intend to make decisions. Since a debating club never gets anything done, it is important to define a decision-making procedure with a deadline on making decisions. All decisions should be written down in a notebook. This prevents cop-outs and statements like, "Oh, I thought *you* would be responsible for this ... "

5.   When you have to interface with other groups, define, appoint, or elect one person to communicate with that other group. It is important to have consistency in representation, both personally and factually. The latter makes it very useful to write everything down. For clarity of issues and work outcomes, it is good to have the other group's representative countersign. This gives the process somewhat of a review character. It also ensures that everybody knows what the interfaces will look like and has agreed to them.

6.   When you have problems, don't let them drag out. One should talk to group members, the representatives of other groups, and, in the case of student groups, the teaching assistant or the instructor should get involved.

In a democratic group a conflict-resolution session can be organized to deal with the conflict. [Dyer77] posits the following conditions for such a session to be successful:

▶   all parties to the conflict are willing to work it out;

2

▶ everybody agrees that problems exists, what they are, and that everybody is responsible for working out a resolution;

▶ expectations are realistic: it is not important that after the session everyone "likes" each other, only that they understand each other and are able to work with each other; and

▶ the existence of differences and the need to negotiate a solution should be accepted. Don't focus on "fault."

This puts the group in conflict into a problem-solving frame of mind. During the conflict resolution session, every party to the conflict should list three types of things:

▶ what they would like to see the other party start doing,

▶ what they would like the other party to stop doing, and

▶ what they would like the other party to continue doing.

These lists are then shared and build the basis for negotiation. Items on each other's lists are traded off: "If you stop doing A, we will continue doing B." It may help to write down the agreement. The technique can be used for both individuals and groups in conflict. It is helpful to have a moderator or mediator, especially when there is a chance that negotiations might break down and a cool head is needed to prevent that.

Guidelines only set the stage; they do not prescribe one particular way of working in a (student) group. What they try to emphasize is that the most critical aspect of many (student) projects is interfacing people with each other and interfacing partitions of work. Group rules and expectations should keep that in mind and facilitate it.

Role of Discipline

The best contract or set of rules does not have any "bite," if it can't be enforced. What can we do to get team members in line? In an egoless programming team or a democratic environment, peer pressure often works. If that does not do the trick, isolation of the group member who violates the rules will follow. In effect, the individual is ostracized, "eliminated" from the group work. Where a manager with formal, disciplinary authority exists, the group may decide to elicit his or her help. Something like this happens when a student group—usually without the member who is perceived as "the problem"—comes to the professor and complains. When discipline or punishment is warranted, the leader or person with authority should consider the following guidelines for disciplining a group member who has not performed up to standards or otherwise has violated norms or procedures.

1.   Discipline works better before undesirable behavior is strong. That means criticizing a programmer's lack of proper documentation unmistakably and strongly the very first time it happens. Do not wait for the problem to go away. It won't.

If a person comes late to a group meeting, make it clear that this is *not* acceptable the first time around, not after the project is half over, when the behavior is ingrained and a "right" to it has been established. Then the latecomer may wonder "What is wrong with my boss all of a sudden? I've been coming late before. Is he taking out his own problems on me? Not with me, buddy!" It is much harder to reestablish rules once people have gotten used to ignoring them.

2.   A disciplining measure must be relatively intense and quickly follow the undesirable behavior. In this way it is clear what the punishment is for; e.g., when an important project failed because of inadequate management and a demotion is deemed appropriate, it should follow immediately after project cancellation, not half a year later when the manager's next review is up. Or when we want to make it stick that we mean business about structured code, a programmer could be required to work overtime to rewrite his program so that it conforms to programming standards. Again, action should happen the first time that he or she turns in unacceptable code.

3.   A reprimand should be task oriented and focus on what was done wrong. It should not be person oriented, nor should it focus on an impersonal, general behavior pattern. The latter is too easily interpreted as "he doesn't like me personally" and the issue, i.e., work behavior, is out of focus. When the problem is low productivity or lack of quality, it is much harder to personalize the problem into a people conflict such as "How can he do this to *me*?! He just doesn't like blacks" (or women, or blonds, or Irish—you name the convenient prejudice). The real problem with such diffusion is that it not only does not help to stop undesirable behavior, it may provide an excuse to continue or increase it, because *now* the superviser is seen as arbitrary and deserves what he gets. It also makes it possible for the person who doesn't perform up to standards to refuse to acknowledge that they did anything wrong or badly.

Staying focused on the task also provides a means to show not only what was wrong, but to contrast it with what was expected and how adequate performance can be reached. We can repeat what is expected of a person. Focusing on the task sometimes frees an individual to open up and say "I don't know how to do that. If I had, I would have done better." Now there is a chance to improve behavior through instruction. It is harder to get an admission of not knowing enough when the disciplining situation is perceived as personally threatening.

4.   Be fair and consistent. It is not consistent to threaten one programmer with firing him when they do not deliver their code on time when his colleague only gets a growl for the same problem.

5. Any disciplinary action of criticism must inform:

   ▶ what was done wrong and why,

   ▶ how to do better in the future, and

   ▶ consequences of continuous wrong behavior.

For example,

   ▶ **what/why**: the submitted modules were of inferior quality because during testing, standards were not followed.

   ▶ **how**: performance can be improved by following the testing standards.

   ▶ **consequences**: cannot approve vacation until the modules are finished at the required quality level.

6. Do not show remorse that you criticized. It weakens the effect and purpose of the criticism to the point of making it useless. Examples of such behavior are to apologize for the criticism or disciplining action or to grant time off or some other "reward" that comes right after the criticism but is not related to a rewardable outcome.

7. Do not discipline or criticize in front of others. It is embarrassing and makes a person lose face. It may lead the criticized employee to not improve job performance and to retaliate with subversive behavior. A complex software development project offers almost boundless opportunities for that. At the very least, the disciplined employee may avoid the manager. In a very cohesive group, the group may avoid him. Sides might be taken.

   The first six rules can be summarized as the "Hot Stove Rule" [Hamn78]. A hot stove burns immediately (rules 1,2) when it is touched, even the first time. It burns only when touched, regardless of who touches it (rules 3,4). It burns every time (rule 4). It is clear that the touch causes the burn and removing your hand from the stove will stop it (rule 5). A burn stays a burn (rule 6); the stove does not apologize.

Effectiveness of Discipline

How effective are criticism and discipline? Since they are negative, they will not be as effective in changing behavior as positive reactions (rewards) are. It is better to reinforce positive behavior (e.g., a somewhat well tested module) with a positive reinforcer or reward (e.g., pride in one's work), because it increases motivation. The emphasis should therefore be on rewards, not punishment. Rewards are more effective in sustaining high motivation when they are connected to the job itself. An enjoyable job is intrinsically motivating; the motivator is the job itself. Extrinsic motivation with higher salaries is not as effective for sustained high levels of motivation.

We should therefore build rewards into the job itself. To do that, we must know what a staff member likes and doesn't like about the job. We cannot reward all people the same, because they will not find it equally motivating. For one programmer it might be a reward to be put in charge of a project all by herself. A colleague, on the other hand, could very well feel overstretched by that prospect if he prefers less autonomy. For him, this would hardly be a reward.

It is important to be fair with rewards. An overrewarded individual feels guilty, and an underrewarded one feels angry. A typical complaint sounds like, "I busted my tail to analyze these requirements on time, had to sweettalk three departments into agreeing on a common database, and what do I get? A pat on the back and another lousy political assignment."

When a reward is promised, it should follow. Otherwise, people feel unfairly treated and angry. If they take a violation of their good faith very seriously, they might leave the organization. For example, a contract programmer was promised a bonus for signing a second contract, which would start three months after the first expired. When the second contract started earlier, the bonus was rescinded, because "he didn't need the extra money to tie him over." Small wonder that this programmer never wanted to have anything to do with the organization after that. They happened to lose a very knowledgeable, highly productive, and quality conscious programmer.

Realistically speaking, we cannot always give the individual what they would like as rewards, nor do organizational and business constraints (which can change literally overnight) allow perfect fairness. How can we avoid antagonizing good people when we have to disappoint their expectations? The number one issue is commitment to the organization and its goals, or at least to the department's or group's. If employees accept and stand behind these goals, they are more willing to compromise, to put up with a boring assignment for a while, to accept less than market rate salaries, and to pitch in for the common good. In such a case it is vital, however, that compromises be made fairly and across the board. Tolerance for "unfair" salaries, for example, will be very low in such a situation.

Problems and Questions

1. Karen and Anne have not liked each other from day one. They are both junior programmers in a chief programmer team that is run fairly democratically. They fight about every pointer and every If statement as if it were the absolute most crucial part of the project. Code reading sessions have become a pain to all participants. Everybody but the two fighting parties realize that Karen and Anne are using technical issues to camouflage their real ones. There are three other junior programmers besides Karen and

Anne. What options are available to deal with the conflict? State and explain a sequence of actions you would try in case the first actions do not have the desired effect.

2. How would you further (reward) positive, task oriented conflict on an egoless programming team, which while very cohesive, has become somewhat complacent? Primarily you wish to prevent groupthink's negative effects and make sure that the next project gets enough active attention.

3. How do you suggest we deal with the potential role conflicts inherent in the surgical team? Why do you think it works?

4. Why are punishment and criticism last and not first resorts?

5. Bob has been hired in his first job as a project leader. The software that is to be developed is in his area of specialty. After the first weeks he notices that some of his design decisions and implementation directives are quietly ignored by the most senior member of his team. Describe a "hot stove" approach to deal with the problem.

15.10. Organizational Structure and Software Development Teams

Section 15.2. explained different ways in which organizations view the individual and the team, and later, when we looked at the needs and motivations of individuals and teams, how such a view affects the organization of teams and task design. Both are also influenced by organizational structure. Organizational structure is the next higher structural entity into which software development teams fit. Software structure and team structure should be compatible. The same holds for organizational structure, since it will facilitate division of labor and managing the software development effort.

15.10.1. Software Development Phases and its Functions

People involved in the different phases perform different functions, e.g., requirements analysis, specification writing, design, implementation, testing, maintenance, and quality assurance efforts. These functions stay the same for all projects. We might even subdivide the functions further such as database development, user interface development, real-time software development, operating system development, communications, etc. The point is that for these functions, we can have experts who are highly specialized and therefore more effective. We can organize groups hierarchically, one group per functional area, with a manager or leader for each functional area and a project director to whom the managers of the functional areas report. The idea of specialists is essentially an extension of the surgical team concept, except that we now have more than one person being a specialist in a functional area, with a team leader who is responsible for managing this functional area for all projects for which the project director (his or her boss) is responsible.

The functional teams could be organized as democratic teams or as modifications of the other team forms that we have encountered. We have to say modifications, because some of the roles that were defined for them are not applicable when they fall outside of the functional boundary for the team. For example, a team of people who prepare requirements will not need a tester or a language lawyer. They might have to communicate with one from another functional group, but they would not have one within their functional area. The chief programmer team with appropriate modifications is a very good choice because it fits well into the strict hierarchical definition of the functional organization. We find relatively small spans of control built into this structure. The project director is the central controlling authority. The managers of functional areas control one functional specialty that ensures a uniform methodology across projects. In addition, it is hoped that software development is more effective, because we can exploit common aspects of projects by assigning them to a team of experts.

These advantages do not come without a price. First, we have to plan for a good deal of communication between groups to span functional boundaries. Formally defined documents throughout the life cycle and especially across functional boundaries become very important. They show how the work was done by a specific functional group, they can be reviewed before going on to the next functional activity, and they form a reliable communication vehicle (at least when they are good). In a functional organization it makes sense to have an intergroup liaison, similar to the user liaison role of the RCPT. To be successful, we have to require good communication skills and familiarity with the basics of the other functional areas with which this intergroup liaison has to communicate.

The second disadvantage is that decision making on project issues will be slower, since information has to travel all the way up the hierarchy to the project director. This has other side effects: the progress on projects becomes harder to control and the additional levels of hierarchy between the project director and the members of the functional teams make it more difficult to see what is actually happening. The team members, being specialists, will find it much harder to gain an overall perspective of the project, and their job satisfaction can be lower, because task identity is lost. To counteract this problem, the manager or project director should keep them informed about the project, even if they will not work on a particular phase.

Case Study: Functional Organization

Assume there are two major projects. Project one is to develop telephone switching software; project two is to provide telephone customer services. Management has decided to organize the department into functional groups, based on their definition of phases in the software development life cycle.

Functional area 1:   Requirements analysis and feasibility (Planning).

Functional area 2:   Specifications and high level design.

Functional area 3:   Implementation.

Functional area 4:   Operation and maintenance.

Figure 15.14 shows the functional organization for this set of projects.

This organization gives the functional area managers the possibility to reassign their staff according to market priorities. For example, there may be a great potential to capture the market if a certain customer service can be developed before the competition does so. If the projected market window is small, it may be more advantageous to shift more people from switching systems into customer services. This is done more easily in a functional organization. On the other hand, let's assume that requirements change. Area 1 has to analyze the change, communicate it to its area manager who then has to relate the updated document to the project director. After the project director approves it, it is sent down to the area managers for all the functional areas that are affected. They, in turn, communicate it to their groups. This does not just sound slow, it is. As a corrollary, if we do not expect such changes to be immediate, i.e., we have the time to go up and down the ladder, it is not a problem and the advantages of the functional organization will outweigh its disadvantages.

All functional areas may be subdivided further by project or project area when they become too big for one group. As we approach implementation (in our example one functional area), there is a structured software design. If the project is sizable, we have subsystems big enough to require a group each. Then we see more levels added for the implementation area. We may have a project manager, group leaders and staff. This adds two more levels of partitioning to the hierarchy.

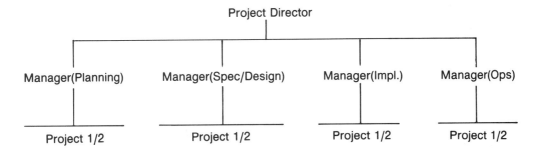

Figure 15.14 A Funtional Organization Example.

We will find a functional organization most helpful on a bigger project that needs a set of people, not just one specialist in a particular area. It is natural to organize them into a group. And this is the start of a functionally oriented organization. A functional organization is also advantageous when projects are somewhat different, but the ways to arrive at a solution are similar or have something in common. This could be hardware, or one project builds on another, but there is enough time overlap so that the group who is in charge of developing one piece of software cannot work on the other at the same time.

This is only one way to organize a set of projects within a hierarchial structure. As an alternative we could look at the software itself as the unit around which to structure the organization.

15.10.2. Software Project

An organization that structures its software development around individual projects is called project organization. As with most software, the structure is hierarchical. One group is assigned to each project. Every project has a manager. A project leader is in charge of a set of projects. This organization fits most naturally with the various team structures discussed in previous sections. Communication is reduced to intragroup communication; there is no need for intergroup communication as in the functional organization. Each group is in complete control of all aspects of its project. The project itself is visible and thus project control is facilitated. Within the group we see uniform methodology and structure, but not necessarily between groups. Decision making is much faster than in the functional organization. All technical and administrative decisions are made on the project level. Within the limits of the particular team structure chosen, we can expect motivation to be high, because identification with the project is easier than in the functional organization.

As projects grow in size and complexity, the limits of this type of organization become apparent. First, how many people can one manager reasonably expect to supervise effectively? Second, even if we can partition a project into subprojects, we will run into the communication barriers between (sub)project boundaries. Every project group has control over their own project. This can be a disadvantage when it is hard to establish and maintain a uniform methodology across project boundaries. When projects are not completely independent, we need a liaison person to communicate with other groups. This role we find in the revised chief programmer team, for example. We could also assign it to the backup programmer in the CPT or the copilot in the surgical team.

Another potential difficulty is the availability and sharing of expertise. A project-oriented organization must have all required skills within the group. If the entire group stays together throughout the entire software development life cycle, some roles may be underutilized or overworked. They tend to be underutilized when they are very special-ized and are only needed during some phases. Sharing specialists is difficult. It requires exact, reliable schedules when the specialist is to work on which project team. As soon as a project starts to have deadline problems, the others do, too, and the specialist the team "promised" at a certain time is still busy. It also can pose problems for the "migrant ex-pert" to be readily assimilated into the group. Every time a new member joins a group, it is a different group and will go through some of the group forming processes until it be-comes fully productive. This takes time. The time is shorter if the core group is stable and finds the same expert joining them time after time (looking at likely turnover and schedules of more than one year per project, this isn't very probable). The other alterna-tive is to have all specialist knowledge always reside in the group. This requires training or hiring sophisticated professionals, both of which is costly. For this reason, i.e., the lack of human and equipment resource sharing between projects, it is hard to achieve economies of scale.

Higher management, such as the project director, does not need to be involved very much in the project. This can have the effect that the project director loses track of its progress. This is why a project structure is prone to suffer from undetected false optimism.

When a project ends, team members need to be reassigned to a new project, or the team is split when the members get new but different assignments. At this time, a point of natural discontinuity, members tend to quit, resulting in a higher turnover than dur-ing the time they worked on the project. The functional organization does not suffer from this phenomenon, because not as many people experience the end of a functional task at the same time. This buffers the negative effects of turnover and spreads it over a longer time frame.

Which team structures fit into a project-oriented organization? Basically, they all do. The choice depends on the attitudes of the organization towards the individual, the availability of personnel, the leadership style of the project managers, and the needs of the team members.

Functional and project organization are complementary to each other. The strength of one is the weakness of the other. They are related to different structuring priorities of the software development effort. They also try to realize different types of goals. The project-oriented structure emphasizes reaching short term goals, namely project qual-ity and staying within budget and on schedule for a project. The functional organization on the other hand emphasizes long term goals, especially efficiency. This is illustrated by stressing and utilizing commonality among projects. Technology transfer and im-proving standards of operation throughout are facilitated. Critical skills and resources are shared and lead to economies of scale for software firms which do a lot of similar software development.

Both organizational forms have in common that every employee has one superior which reduces potential for role conflict, and the negative effects it can engender.

Case Study: Project Organization

Assume a firm specializes in microcomputer software. Currently there are two projects going, developing an overall database system and developing an advanced document preparation system. Figure 15.15 shows one project director, two project managers (one for each project) and two project groups.

This organization structures two projects with rather different emphasis. Therefore, there is less need to share special expertise, such as knowing about the microcomputer. We can assume that in such a small project, everyone knows about the machine and its system language anyway. The differences in the projects are bigger than the commonalities in problem skill. If the project director is very concerned about having uniform interfaces for all the firm's products, he or she may decide to have a functional separation into interface design and organize the remainder of the two projects in a project organization. The two project groups can be organized in any of the team structures or their modified forms that we have discussed earlier. When the projects are relatively limited in size as they are here, the groups will be small and an egoless programming team may actually be a very good choice. If the skills of the project man-

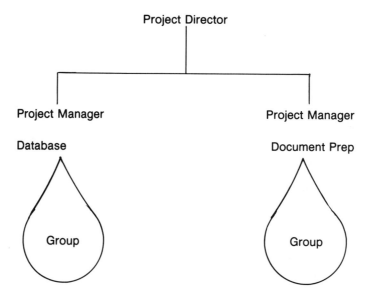

Figure 15.15 A Project Organization Example.

ager are much higher than most of his or her group, we may try a form of chief programmer team.

15.10.3. Using Phases, Functions, and Software Structure

Since functional and project organization complement each other in their advantages, it makes sense to try and combine them. This we find in the matrix organization where a project organization is superimposed on a functional one. The project manager is in charge of what is developed, and the functional manager controls how it is done in his or her functional area. We have lateral communication across functional boundaries in the project aspect when specialists are bound into a project. Vertical communication is also facilitated, because the extra level of management of the functional organization is missing. We have one manager for each functional area, one manager per project. The project managers report to the project director.

The main problem with this type of organization is that employees now can have two superiors. We have heard earlier that this can lead to role conflict, especially when one specialist is assigned to more than one project. Project priorities can become a problem. On the other hand, when it works, it can give the specialist an increased sense of autonomy to be able to balance his or her own load. Formal lateral and vertical communication lines make the structure more responsive to sharing of expertise, to project needs, and customer requirements. The latter is true, because the communication lines with the customer through the expert exist already. Decisions on project issues and functional procedures are made centrally by the respective managers. This reduces decision-making time. The major problem of this organization is vested in the double authority. When the functional and project managers have a good balance of power, they will negotiate continuously and provide each other with checks for time, cost, and performance, but if they cannot successfully do that, we have problems—what is progress, how are priority assignments handled, who evaluates performance—at the worst, the two can deadlock each other. This may be one of the reasons why a matrix organization is not very popular among some DP professionals. (Imagine two chiefs, one functional, one project. They both have strong needs for influence and power. Then add DP people's relatively low social need.)

There are many more managers. For small projects, the overhead is high. We should use a matrix organization only for projects with more than 10 people, and even that is low.

Case Study: Matrix Organization

Try to reorganize the previous functional organization into a matrix structure. We have a project director with functional area managers in planning, specifications and high level design, implementation, maintenance, and operation. Likewise, we have project managers for telephone switching and for customer services. The overall organization is given in Figure 15.16. It is only the major structural view. There can be several lower levels, especially when projects are big (hundreds of people). Planning could be subdivided into the two project areas and further into long-range planning, planning for specific types of customer services (every particular service is a project), hardware versus software groups, etc. The individual teams can be organized according to the needs and requirements of the task, the people, and the leaders. This organization offers a wide degree of freedom and we therefore see a lot of "mixed" structures in this form.

When designing a team structure within an organizational structure of any of the above forms, we must consider the particular advantages and disadvantages of these organizational structures. We must select the team organization to take advantage of the strengths of the organizational form and avoid its disadvantages. For some suggestions how to match team structures with organizational structure see [Shet84]. It requires careful reading, because some of the suggestions are questionable. More on organizational structures can be found in [Arth83], [Dale80], and [Karg80].

Problems and Questions

1.   Sam is a functional area manager for performance and systems in a large organization. He has recently started a project to develop some capacity planning software. Software development has provided a staff person for implementation. While she is supposedly working for him, she spends most of her time on another project. He is get-

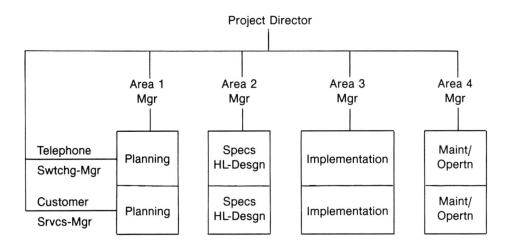

Figure 15.16   Matrix Organization Example.

ting frantic because his own deadline is approaching. What is the problem? What would you do? Why do you think it would solve the problem?

2.   Take the development of a modern operating system for three different machines. Show how you would organize it in all three organizational forms. Point out the strengths and weaknesses and how they would manifest themselves in the software. Are there any software development guidelines or procedures that could be made mandatory to counteract the risks somewhat? Which?

15.11. Summary

In this chapter, we explained the most widely advocated team concepts for software development projects, analyzed their characteristics, identified their strengths and weaknesses, and pointed out which work attributes and people characteristics are favorable and which are likely to pose problems within given team structures. These insights can and should be used to select an appropriate team structure for a given development effort and a given staff. While none of the team concepts by themselves can anticipate and deal with all the details and variations of human productivity, motivation, and interaction, they can be tailored to deal with the specific motivations and skills of the team at hand. We have shown that with some suggestions for tuning and adapting the various concepts we presented. Suggestions were made on how to integrate learning and professional growth into the team concepts. Some of the answers suggested throughout this chapter are based on methods for task design and redesign. For a good textbook on this topic see [Griff82].

Space limitations prohibited a full discussion of task and employee evaluation. However, job analysis questionnaires and core job dimension analysis tools are available (see [Griff82] and [Hack80]) as are methods for measuring motivation levels in the areas of task, relationship, and influence/direction. More general measurement instruments are available but require more effort to use than the more specialized evaluation instruments.

Teams and team building are not always feasible nor desirable. If it is not clear whether a team should be used, [Dyer77] explains how to evaluate such a situation. Team structure influences and is in turn influenced by organizational structure, and thus team design should go hand in hand with organizational design. We have provided a short introduction. Interested readers are referred to Knudson's [Knud79] and Hamner's [Hamn78] textbooks on management and organizational behavior.

At this time there are no experimental results that evaluate projects as a function of team structure and characteristics of team members, specifically for software development teams. Such data would provide a statistical basis for choosing one team concept over another. Together with concepts from task design and software development, such data could provide a valuable knowledge base for an expert system. It is hoped that a database like this can be developed through joint efforts between industry and academia in order to further broaden and deepen our understanding of software development as a team effort.

What we do have, however, is experiential case knowledge that tells us that the following four reasons are most often involved when a project fails:

1. **Incorrect staffing**.   Staff may not be suitable, because one must settle for the people available or the ones the organization can afford. They may not have the experience necessary to do the job properly, or the team may show a poor blend of personalities. We have tried to point out how to select personnel appropriately, how to organize teams to take advantage of people's characteristics, and how to deal with personality conflicts. These reduce the risk of failure due to incorrect staffing.

2. **Inappropriate reward system**.   Low or unfair salary or rewards that are not in line with performance (or inappropriate) cause great job dissatisfaction and turnover and can make a project fail. Previous sections have pointed out the relationship between performance and rewards, the appropriateness of rewards, and tailoring rewards to desired behavior.

3. **Poor management**.   If the leader is too directive and overbearing or not strong enough, it can cause failure. So can unrealistic expectations (too much work and not enough time) or lack of focus. Ineffective, ignorant leaders can make projects fail. We have pointed out important human factors that can help to improve management and use people resources effectively and efficiently. Time planning, scheduling, budgeting, and project tracking are discussed in other chapters.

4. **Counterproductive organizational structure**.   This can get in the way of work that needs to be done. In the previous sections we have given examples of how that can happen and how to soften the impact on the work in progress when it does occur. Often knowing the weaknesses of a structure and planning for controlling them is all that is needed.

In summary, this chapter tried to provide techniques and knowledge about how to recognize and deal with human issues in the software development life cycle so as to make projects succeed and take into account the needs of the people who work on them. There are questions whether the teams and team structures we have seen in the past will continue to exist. Application generators may do away with big teams. Sophisticated tools are geared to make the labor intensive software development industry into a more capital intensive one. More specialization is another hope to increase productivity and reduce labor costs. History has shown us, however, that as our tools, systems, and techniques became more sophisticated, so does the software. This suggests that some software development will actually be done with less, but more specialized, people, probably also with more user involvement during development. Many users have become more knowledgeable and are able and willing not only to participate in software development but to do some of it alone. But new problems and software applications will surely emerge and there will still be a need for sizable software development teams.

► 16 _____
Software
Development
Guidelines
_____

16.1. Overview

Development of quality software is a major effort, especially when software is developed for distribution and for a significant lifespan. Due to advances in programming and technology, new software developments are becoming bigger and bigger endeavors to solve larger and ever more complex problems. Examples include increasingly sophisticated expert systems for a variety of application areas (such as medicine, business, and military) and real-time systems for process control in manufacturing industries, in-space flight control, and SDI. These examples illustrate that increased sophistication and complexity of the solution trusted to a software system requires flexible and useful guidelines for its development.

This chapter concludes this text by tying together all the issues, techniques, and concerns. The approach to guidelines is, as throughout much of this book, one of measurement. This chapter provides a set of guidelines and suggests how to measure compliance.

The objective of having guidelines is to

▶ direct the effort where it is needed at a particular phase in the development life cycle,

▶ increase efficiency and effectiveness by steering towards the most efficient strategy available, not having to reinvent it all over again for successive projects,

▶ assess most situations that can occur during software development, and

▶ point out possible avenues of dealing with potential difficulties, be that preventing an inferior quality of requirements or late arrival of important hardware.

Besides steering development into the right direction and thus making it more efficient, guidelines can also be used to assess a given situation and to evaluate the quality of the solution. Not all guidelines have this property. Guidelines must be *operational*, i.e., measurable and objective, before, during, and after development. Guidelines that are helpful before software development starts can be used to help in *planning* the software development effort. This involves proper planning for personnel, equipment, and methodologies to be used during individual phases.

Managers must also be able to use them to *control the process* during development by

▶ enforcing and measuring how well the development plan is followed,

▶ revealing problems early through low scores in certain guidelines, and

▶ helping to control risks.

This can be done by proper assessment of the importance of (not) following some of the guidelines.

Finally, operational guidelines can be used for *evaluation of the project afterwards*:

▶ This involves an assessment of software quality,

▶ This provides feedback for the developers. This is known to be important for maintaining motivation but is often not available to developers when the software has been turned over and they are assigned to a new project.

▶ This helps the project team realize which parts of the development went smoothly, which parts didn't, and what impact that had on the development effort and the quality of the intermediate deliverables as well as the final product. Thus they can learn more from each project and carry the lessons over to the next one.

If guidelines are to help with all that, they have to exhibit the following characteristics:

▶ Compliance to the guidelines has to be measurable. Reliable, valid scoring rules measure how well the guideline is adhered to.

▶ Measurement interpretations explain what a specific score means for planning, development, and development evaluation.

▶ Guidelines also have to be comprehensive. They cover most development scenarios. If they don't, they are special purpose only, and not flexible enough for general use. Since software projects don't all have the same objectives or innate characteristics, some of the guidelines may not apply; others may apply, but their importance may vary. Because of this, a generally applicable set of software development guidelines should come with selection rules to tailor guidelines to specific development situations.

Guidelines fall into three major categories. They address technical concerns, product and quality control issues, and project control matters [Mccl81]. *Technical* guidelines cover questions of which methods and techniques to use, which support tools to employ, and how to deal with the hardware and software available. *Product control* addresses requirements, product planning, development, and maintenance. Quality control is concerned with validation and verification and with standards. *Project control* finally addresses developing and adhering to a project plan, approval standards, the project contract, the feasibility of the project and of the proposed solution, team organization, management, personnel, and user training.

The guidelines presented here are an extension of the ones in [Mccl81]. They are more comprehensive and have been reworked to make them applicable to all the objectives outlined above. In addition, it is shown how to use the guidelines for the purposes described above.

16.2. Guidelines and Their Interpretation

16.2.1. Technical Guidelines

a. Partition software development into stages.

This guideline reflects the "divide and conquer" philosophy that says that it is easier to solve several small problems than one big one. One of the more accepted ways to partition the development process into stages is the life-cycle model of requirements analysis, specifications, design, coding, testing, and maintenance. It is not the only possibility; other process models may be used as long as they provide clear, measurable boundaries between the phases with demonstrable deliverables.

Chapter 1 presented several life-cycle models and reasons for choosing one over another. Thus the measure of this guideline must consider not just whether or not one of the process models was chosen, but more importantly, it should be able to indicate the quality of such a choice. Sections 1.3. and 1.4. offer reasons for choosing a specific process model. These can form the basis for scoring.

b. Use appropriate design and specification techniques.

These techniques range from informal prose to formal procedures. Which is the proper one to use depends as much on the size and complexity of the project as on the background of the development team. In any event, they should address all dimensions of the problem and its solution.

Example: Real-time system dimensions.
Sequential aspects, concurrency, timing needs, interfaces, multiple levels of operation.

Example: Possible techniques.
Top-down design, bottom-up design, iterative enhancement, object-oriented design.

Not all of these techniques are equally applicable to every problem, and they all have best-case scenarios. It is not wise to prescribe one method without regard to the problem characteristics.

Chapter 5 states that for functional specifications at least input, processing, output, state transitions, and quality expectations need to be described. This is the minimum. Chapters 6–8 discuss all aspects of design using a variety of design techniques. Table 7.6. compares them and indicates which structuring technique is appropriate for which type of problem.

c. Select proper language.

Ideally one would like to prescribe higher level languages or special purpose languages, because they let the developer code more reliably and keep the developer closer to the problem level without encumbering machine details. This, however, is not always possible. Often, therefore, an additional step during the design phase is necessary to refine the design sufficiently so that coding in the low level language becomes easy and reliable. In this case, one should use a high level language (which may be of one's own manufacture, or an existing one such as ADA, ICON, MODULA-2) as an additional step. This helps to keep the development structured and produces naturally structured code. Whenever code needs to be read by someone after it has been written (practically always), it is a good idea to develop and use coding standards. When machine dependent features of a language are used, it should be clearly marked as such. This avoids maintenance problems.

d. Use structured programming.

Structure provides predictability and thus makes a program more understandable. If the software is to be programmed in a structured language, then the accepted standard set of structured statements can be used such as **IF-THEN-ELSE, DO-WHILE** and its variations, sequence, **CASE**, etc. If the language itself does not provide these constructs, their equivalents can be used as standard patterns. [Jens79] and Section 9.3. show how to simulate those higher level language constructs in "unstructured" languages. This is tantamount to establishing coding standards that provide additional structure. It is not restricted to commands only. Coding standards should also be applied to data objects, variables, and comments. Section 9.3. discusses coding standards.

e. Develop a test plan early, refining it as development proceeds.

This is important, because it enhances quality control, works as a checklist, and emphasizes the use of test methodologies, without which testing would still be reduced to a random bug search true to (a slight modification of) Murphy's Law: Testing fills the time available (which is usually very short). With a test plan for all phases of development there is no "forgetting about validation," because the steps are clearly outlined in the test document. For details on the test plan see Section 10.7. Also consult the last sections in Chapter 2 to 9 for phase-testing activities.

f. Do not reinvent the wheel.

Software developers should not try to show how well they can also implement a sorting routine (or any other algorithm) when there is a good one already around. It is simply a waste of time and money. Off-the-shelf software (and hardware) should be used *when it is well documented and supported.* These are important restrictions, because it may create more work to interface with the "ready" software than to write one's own. It also often happens that a software system has common modules in different subsystems. These should be identified and implemented early to avoid duplication of effort.

Reusability has become a major productivity enhancing characteristic (cf. [Bass87], [Bigg87], [Burt87], [Fisc87], [Garg87], [Kais87], [Lenz87], [Meye87], [Prie87], [Trac87], and [Wood87]). It is facilitated by developing data abstractions during design and by object-oriented programming. Design metrics that measure modularity can be used to evaluate the potential reusability of modules (cf. Section 8.3.). Reusability requires low degrees of coupling between modules and high degrees of functional cohesiveness within a module. Standard interfaces also help.

g. Provide state of the art development environment.

Just as no chemist would think about blowing his own test tubes, the software developer should also use the full support of the established operating system, the utilities, and special purpose packages. In addition, he should use automated software development tools where available. They were designed and built to support a variety of activities during all phases of software development, and their usefulness should not be underestimated.

Tool support exists for many development activities, such as testing, coding, design, version control, etc., and also for methodology support and many management activities, such as cost and effort estimation, scheduling, status reporting, and the like. Examples of tools that support coding and testing are checkout compilers, debuggers, static and dynamic analysis tools, test coverage analyzers, data flow analysis tools, test bed support tools, and all kinds of simulators, to name just a few. Much progress has been made in tool support for expert system development [Harm88]. For overviews of tools that support activities throughout the software development lifecycle see [Bars84], [Hend84], [Carl87], [Dart87], [Dows87], [Gogu87], [Harr87], [Reis87], [Reps87], [Tich87], and [Walk87]. As most of these references emphasize, the big boost to productivity of software development comes from an *integrated* environment where tools can be used as needed without worries about clumsy or nonexistent interfaces. Monolithic and isolated tools don't show much promise in increasing productivity.

h. Use people efficiently.

First, we should be aware of the trade-off between people and machine efficiency and let the machine and **CASE** tools do what they can do better and more efficiently than the human. Code optimizers are an example of taking advantage of machine efficiency. In general, with a few exceptions, simplicity and readability that enhance people efficiency are preferable to "efficient trick coding." It is too often unmaintainable. Where efficiency dictates changes, they can be done using "standard transformations" as suggested in Section 9.5.2.

It is important to consider the impact of a trade-off between people and machine during maintenance. Because a high part of software cost occurs during maintenance, it is advisable to strive for better quality, maintainable software. It is more people efficient. Chapter 15 discussed how to select, motivate, and organize people so that they can be as productive as their capabilities allow.

16.2.2.   Product Control Guidelines

a. Prepare detailed requirements statement with user involvement.

This is important and will ensure success, because knowing what is to be done is the first step of getting it done. A formal method or an agreed upon standard will make adherence to this rule more easily measurable. A detailed statement will also let everybody who is involved in the development process know what the problem solution requires. This includes the users or their representatives as well as the developers. When specified clearly, such a requirements statement can also serve as the basis for a contract. Chapters 3 and 4 discussed how to do that.

b. Prepare a product plan.

This should include the division of the overall software development effort into activities resulting in partial or preliminary products and deliverables. This way nothing gets forgotten and time dependencies between activities are clear (cf. Chapter 13). It should also include a test plan (cf. Section 10.7.). This test plan details validation and verification (V/V) for all phases of the software development life cycle, specifying testing standards as to what (specifications, design, code, etc.), how (methods, techniques, tools, equipment, documentation, evaluation), by whom (staff assignment), and when (time frame, schedule). The test plan should also specify acceptance criteria.

Milestones are another aspect of a quality product plan. They should be ordered in hierarchical fashion with major milestones corresponding to the completion of phases and minor milestones corresponding to activities within the phases. Each milestone should be associated with the end of an activity. Since most milestones are intermediate ones, the plan must specify which prerequisites for further activities should be or have been completed at this point. This becomes even more crucial when schedule compression and the resulting degree of parallelism is high.

c. Define interfaces in writing.

Special concern should be directed at interfaces, because a majority of the errors in software can be classified as interface errors. Interfaces should be defined clearly, explicitly, and completely in writing. Strict change control needs to be enforced (cf. Sections 10.6.3. and 11.4.).

d. Plan for complete product use, standard and nonstandard.

This means that besides "regular" features, one has to design, implement, and test for off-nominal inputs, off-nominal loads, and error recovery (cf. Section 10.3. to 10.5.). Chapter 5 stressed the importance of specifying the full range of input data, including boundary values. The design chapters (6–8) also discussed the importance of general algorithms and how to consider special cases.

e. Plan for maintenance early.

This can be done by keeping system documentation up to date, including cross references for fast access to development information, keeping test cases and error logs as well as corrective actions taken in a history file. Finally, it will greatly simplify maintenance if there is continuity of staffing. One of the implementors may continue to be involved in product maintenance, perhaps part-time, long enough to acquaint the maintenance staff with it. Details on maintenance activities can be found in Chapter 11.

f. Simplicity!

The product and documents should be easy to understand and test. This will have an impact on both corrective and adaptive maintenance. Section 11.3. describes how to write documents and manuals. It helps to work from a standard outline, because then documents are more predictable. Clearly designed and meticulously enforced strategies help, too (cf. Chapters 6–8).

g. Emphasize user involvement.

All too often the user is not involved enough at his or her level of understanding in the development effort and ends up with a product he neither wants nor knows how to use. This guideline emphasizes the use of reviews and documentation to keep the user informed. This is particularly important during requirements and specification phases. Chapters 3 and 4 emphasized user-driven requirements collection and analysis. Chapter 5 discussed the use of specifications to give feedback to the user about what he can expect the software product to be. This includes such techniques as mock-ups and the writing of a preliminary user manual. [Shne87] discusses the design of user interfaces that help to keep or make users productive. This cannot easily be achieved without user involvement during the defining stages of a product.

h. Produce and enforce standards.

There should be standards for every phase, for design, code, internal documentation, etc. to assure consistent product quality through the life cycle. These involve the use of standard outlines for documents, the use of techniques and tools, and standard ways of phase-testing and evaluation.

i. Have a quality assurance team.

A test team or quality assurance team can assist in continuous, objective validation/verification. Depending on the size of the group, department, or firm, the quality assurance "team" may vary in its composition:

▶ It may be a mutual support group, with changing quality assurance assignments for software developers who are assigned tasks that are independent of the deliverable they are helping to evaluate. Thus quality assurance assignments will vary over time. An example is "code swapping" to avoid tunnel vision. It is usually a good idea to assign quality assurance tasks to people who have a vested interest in the good quality of the product. On the other hand, such situations are also prone to counterimplementation (cf. Chapter 13).

▶ It may be accomplished in the form of $n - 1 + 1$ review assignments. There is a natural interest of the people involved in successive phases to start with a quality product.

▶ It may be a separate group or department that has no software development responsibilities. While such an arrangement is the most objective, it has also potential problems. In small organizations there may be insufficient work to keep the QA group busy. When that is not a problem, it may still have its disadvantages when people of the QA team are not insiders and fail to get the correct picture from the developers (cf. Chapter 13).

16.2.3. Project Control Guidelines

a. Work with a project plan and approval standards.

This necessitates the development of proper standards and their use. Plans were discussed in Chapter 13, and the development of standards-based metrics is discussed in Chapter 12.

b. Set, monitor, and control project goals and priorities.

Otherwise, they may be vague to begin with or prone to mis/reinterpretation and subversion. Alignment of project goals with departmental and organizational goals was explained in Chapter 12. Based on the risk analysis procedures of Section 13.4., the clarity and possible degree of control can be assessed. Risk reduction techniques help to keep potential problems under control.

c. Use historical data of similar projects.

Properly analyzed historical project data can highlight potential danger areas and point out where and why things went wrong before, so that wrong actions can be avoided in the future. Chapters 12 and 14 discussed measuring and the importance of proper metrics and the development of models based on historical data.

d. Keep corporate goals and the political climate in mind.

The most wonderful product on an abstract level may be a total failure in reality if it is not supported by company policy or if the political climate is adverse. Techniques that help to assess such situations and to steer clear of such problems were discussed in Chapters 12 and 13, in particular Sections 13.2. and 13.5.

e. Identify the user community.

After all, that is what the product is for. This starts when the problem is analyzed and a problem statement is prepared (cf. Chapter 2), proceeds through requirements collection and analysis (cf. Chapters 3 and 4), specifications (Chapter 5), and user training (Section 11.3.).

f. Use formal contracts or at least a letter of understanding.

It prevents disappointment, lawsuits, and needless hassle. In some cases the requirements document constitutes the detail information about contractual obligations. In any case, they specify the capabilities that the software will have and thus should be precise as well as understandable by the user. Chapters 3 and 4 discussed the development of a requirements document.

g. Choose a project team size and organization appropriate for the project and the experience of the team members.

Task assignment should be based on growth need, technical and interpersonal talent, and the preferences and expertise of the individuals [Vonm83B]. Each team member has to be made accountable for the work performed through project status reports, updates, approvals, and report distribution. Technical and management expertise should be taken into account when building a team. A concerted effort at developing and maintaining team spirit is also helpful for success.

Chapter 15 explains a variety of team structures that have been suggested and used in the literature. Their advantages and disadvantages are discussed, and guidelines point out how to make a team concept work for various software development scenarios. Chapter 12 also points out how to strengthen and maintain motivation of team members and how to build productive teams. The role of leadership and the importance of fitting a team into various possible organizational structures is also addressed. Teams will experience conflict. This why it is important that team members know how to deal with conflict. Chapter 15 describes how.

h. Enforce communication.

This includes communication both within the development team and with the outside, especially the users or their representative. The importance of communication with the users was stressed from the beginning of the software development life cycle: the role of user interviews (Chapter 2), user-derived requirements (Chapters 3 and 4), user feedback on the functional specifications (Chapter 5), and ongoing user feedback throughout the software's operational life (Section 11.4.).

Developers on a software team also need to exchange information with each other and with other teams. Some of the team concepts of Chapter 15 had specific roles assigned for liaison with other teams and with the user. How to analyze the communication network was discussed, along with the amount of effort that goes into communication.

Specific assignment for communication responsibilities is a safe way to ensure proper communication. Acting upon lax discharge of this responsibility is crucial; otherwise it becomes one more of the dreaded and avoided "overhead tasks."

i. Feasibility study.

Make sure that you can actually accomplish what you have set out to do. Knowing about the harder problems one will have to face is also advantageous, because once identified, they can be given more intensive attention. Chapters 3, 4, and 13 discussed methods that analyze and boost feasibility.

j. Have requirements analysis reviewed and approved.

Everybody should know what you are up to and agree to that. The activities and techniques that apply here were discussed under phase testing in Chapter 4. They promote not only accurate information but also its dissemination to all parties concerned. The early phases are often considered the most crucial to project success, and therefore, conscientious quality assurance is very important.

k. Determine the phases with highest emphasis and monitor them closely.

Since they have highest emphasis, they usually are critical to the success of the project. One cannot afford to let them slip. Risk analysis techniques of Chapter 13 and scheduling techniques of Chapter 14 support the identification, assessment, and risk reduction for critical activities in the software development process.

l. Plan for necessary training.

This should include technical and management knowledge in appropriate amounts for all target groups (users, maintenance staff, developers, and management). Section 11.3. discusses the importance of training. Section 13.6. includes the definition of a training plan that can span the entire development life cycle: developers have to be trained, users have to be trained to use the prototype, maintenance personnel have to be trained to support the product, operations staff needs to know how to service the software while it is operational, new and old users need to be trained, etc. In addition, training should be a built-in part of the job for high-growth need individuals. This last issue is discussed extensively in Chapter 15.

m. Use consultants when in-house experience is missing.

Following this guideline will ascertain that stock is taken of in-house competence. It will compare it with that from the outside so that the most cost-effective solution can be found without wasting time and resources trying to take on something too big. The techniques on personnel selection from Section 15.7. can be used to identify specific needs and to evaluate possible options.

n. Enhance motivation and job satisfaction through career paths, benefits, and a positive and effective environment.

Besides skill to do the job (or to learn how to do it), job motivation and job satisfaction are some of the prime contributors to the success of a software development effort. Chapter 15 emphasized this as one of the most important ingredients in highly productive development efforts. How to increase and maintain motivation is not merely a matter of some nebulous management technique that bears no kinship to software development. Instead, software development techniques and methodologies pose potentially severe restrictions on motivating potential through over-specialization and lack of task identity. This can seriously strangle productivity through turnover and job dissatisfaction. The case for judicious task design is obvious.

o. Use tools for project management.

These may be a combination of hardware and software that help to make, keep, and enforce better project plans and the timing of development activities. Tools are used to identify development activities and to schedule and control their progress (cf. Section 14.2.). Few people would, for example, evaluate the scheduling implications of a CPM or PERT network without the help of a computer program. Cost and effort estimation models can be supported through management support tools. Examples are COCOMO and SLIM ([Boeh81], [Lond87]). Software to keep track of task assignments and their progress are also available. Simple spreadsheet programs support financial and budget analysis. Decision support systems that support the decision methods presented in Sections 12.5. and 13.4.3. are also easily implemented. Configuration control also needs to be supported by software [Babi86].

p. Use work overlap to ensure continuity through development phases.

For example, if one of the people of the development team is also on the maintenance team, maintenance is usually greatly facilitated. Similar observations have been made for other phases. Significant degrees of parallelism in software development pose new challenges in this regard (cf. Section 13.6.).

q. Develop formal bug reports and change request procedures for the user.

This standardizes procedures for dealing with anomalies. Information essential for debugging and other maintenance activities is more easily reported. Additionally, this can be filed, and staff can go back later to see whether a phenomenon had occurred earlier and what was done about it. This can decrease the time needed for maintenance, make it more efficient, and keep the software more easily maintainable (cf. Sections 11.2., 11.4., and 11.5.).

r. Keep a development journal.

If some information doesn't seem to fit into the major documents, it may be because it is too temporary or because it is only relevant at a particular point in the development. Keeping a journal provides space for all the intermediate progress reports, formal and informal, of what development options were discussed and why decisions were made. After development is over, it can be used to evaluate the project, to learn from it, and to predict maintenance efforts. Some information may be included in formal documents (e.g., when Fagan's design rationalization is used, cf. Section 8.6.3.)

s. Develop and enforce a periodic review process.

This is a major instrument for quality control, for the project as well as for the project personnel. It prevents not knowing about less than adequate work and reveals problems right away as they occur rather than when it is too late to do anything about it. This is why the concept of phase testing was stressed throughout all chapters.

16.3. Tailoring the Guidelines

The set of guidelines is very general. There will be situations where some of them do not apply or have to be modified to be useful. On the other hand, even with a long list like this, there will be development scenarios where new guidelines must be added. Therefore, the guidelines should be tailored to the situation and to its particular needs and preferences. This can be done in a five step process:

Step 1. Analyze your development situation.   This should be done as part of the problem definition and requirements analysis anyway, with an emphasis on what it will take and what is available to do the job. In particular, the development situation should be analyzed with respect to resources, staff, time frame, and product requirements. The findings should be written down.

Step 2.   Go through the guidelines one by one and answer the following questions:

▶ What does this guideline mean in this particular situation?

▶ Does it apply?

▶ Which aspects of the guideline apply?

After examining the guidelines and analyzing them, the applicable guidelines should be written down *in their specific form* for a project. They then serve as a standard for this development effort.

Step 3.   Are there any guidelines to add? Add them. As mentioned before, a particular situation may call for additional guidelines. Those may pertain to any of the three areas. For example a big scale effort may lead to additional guidelines for communication between several project managers. Any additional guidelines must be as specific as possible, just as the original ones. We may need to split a guideline into two or more if it is too vague or contains too many elements.

Step 4.   Not all guidelines are equally important. Perform a preference assessment. It is important to make it clear that some guidelines are more important than others in what they stand for and try to accomplish. Unless preferences are indicated, they are all equally important (which is unrealistic in most cases), and the individuals on the development team will "deduce" preferences based on their own judgment and what they perceive management's preferences are. This may not be at all desirable, but it will influence the software development effort and the resulting product. We may, instead, perform a partial preference assessment (rank ordering) or a full preference assessment (weights for each guideline). Weights measure the relative importance of a guideline. The result of this step is a weighted set of guidelines.

Step 5.   Perform a sensitivity analysis when unsure about preferences to establish the impact of preference changes. It is usually rather informative to see how a situation changes when variables, in this case preferences, change. Preferences reflect the relative importance of various goals to be achieved simultaneously. It is not uncommon for goals to shift in emphasis during the development process. Therefore, it is a good idea to be able to assess just how much they can shift without changing the development strategy.

The result of tailoring is a set of guidelines for a particular development scenario.

16.4.   Using the Guidelines—the Scoring System

The guidelines can be used during and after software development to evaluate the project. The purpose of scoring in this context is to quantify the degree of compliance to each guideline. Scoring, however, requires measures for each guideline. This means that guideline compliance metrics have to be developed, and measurement methods have to be defined that state how to use the metrics. Finally, a method is needed for the evaluation of the development effort. If the current effort is to be compared to other ones, previous or parallel, a standard is required and metrics need to be normalized to make them comparable in situations where factors such as size of the development, level of skill of the staff, etc. vary.

First, consider the development of measures. When trying to develop measures for a guideline, existing metrics should be reviewed first, whether they are applicable (cf. Chapter 12). Guidelines should be scrutinized again and stated so that they are easy to understand, unambiguous, and singly dimensioned. It is much easier to develop valid and reliable scoring systems for guidelines with these characteristics. At times it may become necessary to rewrite the guideline, split it, or combine two guidelines to make them more amenable to scoring. In this case, part of the tailoring process has to be gone through again because the preferences need to be reassessed.

Scales for guidelines can be numerical or in symbols or in a language. Which one is used depends on the situation, the expected evaluators, and the use of the score (the level of measurement). The simplest would be a three point scale (not followed, somewhat followed, meticulously followed). Usually one starts out developing a scale by defining anchor points that are familiar to the user, measure a particular level (highest, lowest, etc.), are precisely defined, and are universally understood. Then other points on the scale are identified through interpolation. After a scale has been developed, its validity and reliability needs to be evaluated. A validity check tests whether the scale measures what it should, while a reliability test investigates whether it produces the same results when used more then once. There are standard techniques in psychometrics to do both kinds of tests [Alle79]. Another important point to consider when developing a scale is that it should provide sufficient precision to quantify the adherence to a guideline. For example a scale with a 0 for no compliance, a .5 for partial compliance, and a 1.0 for full compliance may be overly simplistic and not discriminating enough. In the beginning a significant amount of work is necessary to develop these metrics and to define how to measure the various guidelines. However, this is start up work, and once metrics are established, they don't need to be reinvented for every project all over again. With these metrics we can then score the project for every relevant guideline. Multiplying these scores with their guideline preference weights results in a project score at the time of evaluation, whereas the individual scores give a project profile. Both can be very useful in assessing the status of a development effort.

Often it is desirable to compare projects that are at the same point in their development life cycle or to compare different stages of the same project. In order to do this, we need to normalize scores to provide a basis for comparison. The vehicle for normalization may be a standard (i.e., a "perfect" project profile for each project) against which actual project profiles are compared. The ratio between the two relative successes is then a normalized quantity. Such an approach can also help to assess the relative probability of project success.

The development of standards is basically a learning process and is often retrospective. For this type of standard, successful projects of the same type are taken and scored in retrospect. The score (profile) is then the standard. This approach obviously is hampered by one major difficulty: the availability of the information needed to reconstruct the circumstances. To put it another way, if a retrospective standard is to be developed, evaluation data from past projects need to be collected and retained for new projects. Without such historical data this type of standard cannot be developed reliably, but over time with a sufficient database of past project evaluations, a set of company standards can be developed for a representative set of project types. This would include a set of standard preference weights based on project type, precise scoring rules, and evaluation criteria. Additionally, such evaluation should be a team effort because it smooths differences in judgment, increases awareness and motivation, and helps to develop a group consensus as opposed to an individual's opinion.

16.5. Improving the Score

One of the reasons for an ongoing evaluation of the software development effort was to spot budding problems before they become serious and while it is still possible to take corrective action without too much effort. The hypothesis behind using guidelines and scoring for compliance was that problems would show up in consistently low scores for associated guidelines. Thus monitoring of project scores would reveal problem areas, especially when scores are low at several checkpoints in a row. In order to make this concept work, guideline compliance needs to be scored at least at every major milestone, in critical situations and also at minor milestones. Both total and single guideline scores need to be examined. After measuring the current situation, the evaluator must determine whether the score(s) need improvement. That can be done by comparing them to the desired level as described earlier. At times not everything can be taken care of right away, but looking at which types of guidelines scored low will reveal which areas are weak; e.g., management scores for adequate planning may be too low. After assessing which areas are deficient, plans need to be made how to improve the deficient scores. Some will be more important than others; this is evident from the weights associated with guidelines. These weights reflect goals and preferences. One also should look at which action is the most cost-effective and consider the risk of changes (e.g., in management procedures to improve a low management score) compared to the impact it could have not doing anything.

Based on this analysis improvement methods are chosen for implementation, and projected improvement is estimated. This should be written down. At the end of the next cycle, when projected improvement is reevaluated against actual improvement, the usefulness of the actions needs to be determined. Actions with low pay-off will not likely be selected in the future, whereas successful ones will. This suggests that records should be kept for future reference that describe dos and don'ts for problem solution and prevention as an ongoing process. These could be considered "steering aids" to stay on target, i.e., to comply with a guideline. As such they can be considered another level of the guidelines, activated when the need arises. Obviously, keeping records on the usefulness of actions (or the lack of it) will improve knowledge about the software development process. It will improve the evaluation process itself and lead to empirically founded standards. All of these contribute to a smoother development process with less unpleasant surprises.

16.6. The Method in Summary

The previous five sections tried to explain a method that helps to develop and maintain guidelines that are quantitative and can be used to assess progress and suggest corrective action as software development progresses. The method consists of the following steps:

▶ identify the assessment team,

▶ tailor guidelines to project,

▶ score guidelines,

▶ improve score,

▶ normalize,

▶ make improvement decision, and

▶ evaluate decision.

These steps are iterative, especially the last five, and should be augmented by creating, maintaining, and improving a database of knowledge to arrive at a more controlled and better understood way of developing software. It should be realized that to cover the spectrum of different development situations, some of the discussions in this summary chapter had to be brief and general out of necessity. However, the aim was to present a method for developing and dealing with a quantitative evaluation of software development situations that is bound into the technical and management methods that this text has covered in its 16 chapters. Thus the objective of this last chapter was not to reiterate a lot of the material but rather to put it into perspective and to provide an assessment method for development scenarios.

Software development has often been said to defy control and preciseness, but as the approach of "management by metrics" showed, it need not be so. Moreover, using the techniques presented in this book can improve the development process through continued learning.

► Bibliography

[Abde83]
Abdel-Hamid, T. K. and Madnick, S. E., "The Dynamics of Software Project Scheduling," *CACM*, **26**, 5(May 1983), p. 340–346.

[Adam80]
Adam, A. and Laurent, J. P., "Laura, a System to Debug Student Programs," *Artificial Intelligence*, Nov. 1980, p. 75–122.

[Aho74]
Aho, A. V., Hopcroft, J. E., and Ullman, J. D., *The Design and Analysis of Computer Algorithms*, Addison-Wesley, Reading, MA, 1974.

[Akl83]
Akl, S. G., "Digital Signatures: A Tutorial Survey," *Computer* **16**, 2(February 1983), p. 15–26.

[Albr79]
Albrecht, A. J., "Measuring Application Development Productivity," *Proc. IBM Applications Development Symposium*, Monterey, CA, Oct. 1979, p. 83–92.

[Alle79]
Allen, M. J. and Yeh, W. M., *Introduction to Measurement Theory*, Brooks/Cole Publ., Monterey, CA, 1979.

[Ames83]
Ames, S. A., Gasser, M., and Schell, R. R., "Security Kernel Design and Implementation: An Introduction," *Computer*, **16**, 7(July 1983), p. 14–25.

[Amsc76]
Amschler, A., *Testdatenerzeugung innerhalb eines automatischen Testsystems fuer FORTRAN Programme*, Diplomarbeit, Univ. Karlsruhe, FRG, July 1976.

[Amsc78]
Amschler, A. K., *Proving Parallel Programs Correct*, MS Thesis, Duke University, Durham, NC, July, 1978.

[Ande74]
Anderson, R., *Proving Programs Correct*, Wiley and Sons, 1974.

[Arth83]
Arthur, L. J., *Programmer Productivity*, John Wiley & Sons, New York, NY, 1983.

[Ash70]
Ash, R. B., *Basic Probability Theory*, Wiley and Sons, New York, NY, 1970.

[Babb32]
Babbage, C., *On the Economy of Machinery and Manufactures*, Charles Knight, London, 1832.

[Babi86]
Babich, W. *Software Configuration Management*, Addison-Wesley, Reading, MA, 1986.

[Bail81]
Bailey, J. W. and Basili, V. R., "A Meta-model for Software Development Resource Expenditures," *Procs. 5th Intl. Conf. on Software Engineering*, 1981, p. 107–116.

[Bard77]
Bardach, E., *The Information Game: What Happens After a Bill Becomes a Law*, MIT Press, Cambridge, MA, 1977.

[Bars84]
Barstow, D. R., Shrobe, H. E., and Sandewall, E., *Interactive Programming Environments*, McGraw-Hill, 1984.

[Bart83]
Bartol, K. M., "Turnover Among DP Personnel—A Causal Analysis," *CACM*, Oct. 1983, p. 807–811.

[Basi75]
Basili, V. and Turner, D., "Iterative Enhancement: A Practical Technique for Software Engineering," *IEEE Transactions on Software Engineering*, Dec. 1975, p. 462–471.

[Basi87]
Basili, V. and Selby, R., "Comparing the Effectiveness of Software Testing Strategies," *IEEE TSE*, **SE-13**, 12(Dec. 1987), p. 1278–1296.

[Bass87]
Bassett, P., "Frame-Based Software Engineering," *IEEE Software*, July 1987, p. 9–16.

[Baue72]
Bauer, F. L., "Software Engineering," *Information Processing, 71*, North Holland Publishing Co., Amsterdam, 1972.

[Beiz83]
Beizer, B., *Software Testing Techniques*, Van Nostrand Reinhold, New York, NY, 1983.

[Bela79]
Belady, L. A., "On Software Complexity," *Procs, IEEE/NY Polytechnic Institute Workshop on Quantitative Software Models*, Oct. 79, p. 90–94.

[Bela81]
Belady, L. A., "Complexity of Large Systems," in [Perl81], p. 225–233.

[Bent82]
Bentley, J. L., *Writing Efficient Programs*, Prentice-Hall, Englewood Cliffs, NJ, 1982.

[Bent86]
Bentley, J. L., *Programming Pearls*, Addison-Wesley, Reading, MA, 1986.

[Beny79]
Benyon-Tinker, G., "Complexity Measures in Evolving Large Systems," *Procs. IEEE/NY Polytechnic Institute Workshop on Quantitative Software Models*, Oct. 79, p. 117–127.

[Bern64]
Berne, E., *Games People Play*, Grove Press, New York, NY, 1964.

[Best80]
BGS Systems: BEST/1 User's Guide, BE-80-20-3, Dec. 1980.

[Best82]
BGS Systems: BEST/1 User's Guide Supplement Release 7.0, TRN-BST-8202-0, 1982.

[Bgs83]
BGS Systems: CRYSTAL Modeling Package, Waltham, MA, 1983.

[Bigg87]
  Biggerstaff, T. and Richter, C., "Reusability Framework, Assessment, Directions," *IEEE Software, 4,*
  2(March 1987), p. 41–49.

[Blak68]
  Blake, R. R. and Mouton, J. S., *Corporate Excellence through Grid Organizational Development,* Gulf
  Publishing, Houston, 1968.

[Boeh76]
  Boehm, B. W., "Software Engineering," *IEEE Transactions on Computers,* C-25, no. 12, (Dec. 1976),
  p. 1226–41.

[Boeh76B]
  Boehm, B. W., Brown, J. R., and Lipow, M., "Quantitative Evaluation of Software Quality," *Procs. 2nd
  Intl. Conference on Software Engineering,* 1976, p. 592–605.

[Boeh77]
  Boehm, B., "The High Cost of Software," *Procs. COMPSAC 77—Program Testing Techniques,*
  Chicago, 1977.

[Boeh81]
  Boehm, B. W., *Software Engineering Economics,* Prentice-Hall, Englewood Cliffs, NJ, 1981.

[Boeh88]
  Boehm, B. W., "A Spiral Model of Software Development and Enhancement," *Computer, 21,* 5(May
  1988), p. 61–72.

[Booc83]
  Booch, G., *Software Engineering with ADA,* Benjamin Cummings, Menlo Park, CA, 1983.

[Bott85]
  Botting, P. J., "Prototypes vs. Mock-ups vs. Breadboards," *ACM SIGSOFT Software Engineering
  Notes, 10,* 1(Jan. 85), p. 18.

[Boye75]
  Boyer, R. S., Elspass, B., and Levitt, K. N., "SELECT—A Formal System for Testing and Debuggine
  Programs by Symbolic Execution," *ACM Sigplan Notices, 10,* 6(June 75), p. 234–245.

[Brad85]
  Bradley, J. H., "The Science and Art of Debugging," *Computerworld,* Aug. 19, 1985, p. 35–38.

[Broo75]
  Brooks, F., *The Mythical Man Month,* Addison-Wesley, Reading, MA, 1975.

[Brow73]
  Brown, A. and Sampson, W., *Program Debugging,* American Elsevier, New York, NY, 1973.

[Brow78]
  Brown, J. R., Kaspar, H., Lipow, M., MacLeod, G. J., and Merritt, M. J., *Characteristics of Software
  Quality,* North-Holland, New York, NY, 1978.

[Brow84A]
  Brown, D. B. and Herbanek, J. A., *Systems Analysis for Applications Software Design,* Holden Day,
  Oakland, CA, 1984.

[Brow84B]
  Browning, C., *Guide to Effective Software Technical Writing,* Prentice-Hall, Englewood Cliffs, NJ, 1984.

[Brow85]
  Brown, M. H. and Sedgewick, R., "Techniques for Algorithm Animation," *IEEE Software,* January
  1985, p. 28–39.

[Budd78]
  Budd, T. A., et al., "The Design of a Prototype Mutation System for Program Testing," *AFIPS Conf.
  Procs NCC 1978,* p. 623–627.

[Burt87]
Burton, B. A., Aragon, R. W., Bailey, S. A., Koehler, K. D., and Mayes, L. A., "The Reusable Software Library," *IEEE Software*, July 1987, p. 25–33.

[Cain75]
Caine, S. H. and Gordon, E. K., "PDL: A Tool for Software Design," *National Computer Conference, 44*, 1975, p. 271–276.

[Camp74]
Campbell, R., "The Specification of Process Synchronization by Path Expressions," *Lecture Notes in Computer Science, 16*, Springer Verlag, 1974.

[Carg83]
Cargill, T. A., "The Blit Debugger," *SIGPlan Notices*, August 1983, p. 190–200.

[Carl87]
Carle, A., et al., "A Practical Environment for Scientific Programming," *Computer*, Nov. 1987, p. 75–89.

[Cash80]
Cashmen, P. M. and Holt, A. W., "A Communication-Oriented Approach to Structuring the Software Maintenance Environment," *ACM SIGSOFT Software Engineering Notes, 5*, 1(Jan. 1980).

[Chan78]
Chandy, K. M. and Sauer, C. H., "Approximate Methods for Analyzing Queueing Network Models of Computer Systems," *ACM Computing Surveys, 10*, 3(Sept. 1978), p. 281–318.

[Chan81]
Chandrasekaran, S. and Radicchi, S., *Computer Program Testing*, North Holland Publ., New York, NY, 1981.

[Chap79]
Chapin, N., "A Measure of Software Complexity," *Procs. NCC*, 1979, p. 995–1002.

[Cher81]
Cherlin, M., "The Toll of Turnover," *Datamation*, April 1981, p. 209–212.

[Cohe80]
Cohen, H., *You Can Negotiate Anything*, Bantam Books, New York, NY, 1980.

[Cont86]
Conte, S. D., Dunsmore, H. E., and Shen, V. Y., *Software Engineering Metrics and Models*, Benjamin/Cummings Publishing Co., Menlo Park, CA, 1986.

[Coop79]
Cooper, J. D. and Fisher, M. J. (Eds.), *Software Quality Management*, Petrocelli, New York, NY, 1979.

[Coug78]
Cougher, J. D. and Zawacki, R. A., "What Motivates DP Professionals," *Datamation*, Sept. 1978, p. 116–123.

[Coug80]
Couger, J. D., *Motivating and Managing DP Personnel*, John Wiley and Sons, 1980.

[Coug84]
Couger, J. D., "Motivation of the Maintenance Programmer," Prentice-Hall, Englewood Cliffs, NJ, 1984.

[Curr86]
Currit, P. A., Dyer, M., and Mills, H. D., "Certifying the Reliability of Software," *IEEE TSE SE–12, 1*(Jan. 1986), p. 3–11.

[Curt79]
Curtis, B., "In Search of Software Complexity," *Procs. IEEE/NY Polytechnic Institute Workshop on Quantitative Software Models*, Oct. 1979, p. 95–106.

[Curt81]
Curtis, B., "The Measurement of Software Quality and Complexity," in [Perl81], p. 203–217.

[Dacs79]
Gloss-Soler, S. A., "The DACS Glossary—A Bibliography of Software Engineering Terms," Data & Analysis Center for Software, Griffis Air Force Base, Rome, NY, 1979.

[Dale80]
Daley, E. B., "Organizational Philosophies Used in Software Development," *Infotech State of the Art Review*, 1980, p. 45–66.

[Dart87]
Dart, S. A., Ellison, R. J., Feiler, P. H., and Habermann, A. N., "Software Development Environments," *Computer, 20*, 11(November 1987), p. 18–28.

[Davi77]
Davis, C. G., and Vick, C. R., "The Software Development System," *IEEE Transactions on Software Engineering SE-3,* 1 (Jan. 1977), p. 69–84.

[Deba75A]
de Balbine, G., "Design Criteria for the Structuring Engine," *Procs. 2nd USA-Japan Computer Conference*, Tokyo, August 1975, p. 422–466.

[Deba75B]
de Balbine, G., "Using the FORTRAN Structuring Engine," *Procs. Computer Science and Statistics: 8th Annual Symposium on the Interface*, UCLA, 1975, p. 297–305.

[Deba80]
DeBakker, J., *Mathematical Theory of Program Correctness*, Prentice-Hall, Englewood Cliffs, NJ, 1980.

[Dema79]
DeMarco, T., *Structured Analysis and System Specification*, Prentice Hall, Englewood Cliffs, NJ, 1979.

[Dema82]
DeMarco, T., *Controlling Software Projects: Management, Measurement and Evaluation*, Yourdon Press, 1982.

[Demi83]
DeMillo, R. and Merritt, M., "Protocols for Data Security," *Computer, 16*, 2(February 1983), p. 39–54.

[Demi85]
Deming, W. E., *Out of Crisis*, MIT Press, Cambridge, MA, 1985.

[Demi87]
DeMillo, R. A., McCracken, W. M., Martin, R. J., and Passafiume, J. F., *Software Testing and Evolution*, Benjamin-Cummings Publ., Menlo Park, CA, 1987.

[Denn83]
Denning, D. E., "Protecting Public Keys and Signature Keys," *Computer, 16*, 2(February 1983), p. 17–38.

[Dere76]
DeRemer, F. and Kron, H. H., "Programming-in-the-Large Versus Programming-in-the-Small," *IEEE Transactions on Software Engineering, SE–2*, 2(June 1976), p. 80–86.

[Deut82]
Deutsch, M. S., *Software Verification and Validation—Realistic Project Approaches*, Prentice-Hall, Englewood Cliffs, NJ, 1982.

[Dhes82]
Dhesi, R., "PET—Path Expression Translator and Design System," Project Documentation for Software Engineering Course with A. von Mayrhauser, Illinois Institute of Technology, Department of Computer Science, July 1982.

[Dijk68]
Dijkstra, E. W., "The Structure of the THE Multprogramming System," *CACM, 11*, 5(May 68), p. 341–346.

[Down85]

Down, T., "An Approach to the Modeling of Software Testing with some Applications," *IEEE TSE, SE–11*, 4(April 1985), p. 375–386.

[Dows87]

Dowson, M., "Integrated Project Support with IStar," *IEEE Software*, November 1987, p. 6–15.

[Dunn84]

Dunn, R. H., *Software Defect Removal*, McGraw-Hill, New York, NY, 1984.

[Duns85]

Dunsmore, H. E., "The Effect of Comments, Mnemonic Names and Modularity: Some University Experiment Results," *Procs. 2nd Symposium on Empirical Foundations of Information and Software Sciences.*

[Dyer77]

Dyer, W., *Teambuilding: Issues and Alternatives*, Addison-Wesley, Reading, MA, 1977.

[Fabr74]

Fabry, R. S., "Capability Based Addressing," *CACM, 17*, 7(July 1974), p. 403–411.

[Faga76]

Fagan, M. E., "Design and Code Inspections to Reduce Errors in Program Development," *IBM Systems Journal, 15*, 3(1976), p. 219–248.

[Fair78]

Fairley, R. E., "Tutorial: Static Analysis and Dynamic Testing of Computer Software," *Computer*, April 1978, p. 14–23.

[Fair85]

Fairley, R. E., *Software Engineering Concepts*, McGraw Hill, New York, NY, 1985.

[Feig83]

Feigenbaum, E. A. and McCorduck, P., *The Fifth Generation: Artificial Intelligence and Japan's Computer Challenge to the World*, Addison-Wesley, Reading, MA, 1983.

[Ferr78]

Ferrari, D., *Computer Systems Peformance Evaluation*, Prentice-Hall, Englewood Cliffs, NJ, 1978.

[Ferr83]

Ferrari, F., Serrazi, G., and Zeigner, A., *Measurement and Tuning of Computer Systems*, Prentice-Hall, Englewood Cliffs, NJ, 1983.

[Fied64]

Fiedler, F. E., "A Contingency Model of Leadership Effectiveness," in L. Berkowitz (Eds.), *Advances in Experimental Social Psychology*, Academic Press, New York, NY, 1964.

[Fisc87]

Fischer, G., "Cognitive View of Reuse and Redesign," *IEEE Software*, July 1987, p. 60–72.

[Fitz78]

Fitz-enz, J., "Who is the DP Professional?" *Datamation*, Sept. 1978, p. 125–128.

[Fjel79]

Fjelstad, R. K. and Hamlen, W. T., *Application Program Maintenance Study—Report to our Respondents*, IBM Corp. DP Marketing Group, reprinted in[Pari83], p. 13–28.

[Flon75]

Flon, L. and Haberman, A. N., "Towards the Construction of Verifiable Software Systems," *SIGPLAN Notices*, March 1975.

[Floy67]

Floyd, R. W., "Assigning Meanings to Programs," *Proc. Symposium in Applied Math., 10*, Am. Math. Soc., 1967, p. 19–32.

[Fox82]
   Fox, J. M., *Software and its Development*, Prentice-Hall, Englewood Cliffs, NJ, 1982.

[Foyg76]
   Foy, H. and Gadon, H., "Worker Participation: Contrasts in Three Countries," *Harvard Business Review*, May-June 1976, p. 71-83.

[Free75]
   Freeman, P., "Toward Improved Review of Software Designs," *Proc. NCC*, 1975, AFIPS. Reprinted in Freeman, P. and Wasserman, A. I., *Tutorial on Software Design Techniques*, Fourth Edition, IEEE Computer Society, Silver Springs, MD, 1983, p. 542-547.

[Free82]
   Freeman, D. P. and Weinberg, G. M., *Handbook of Walkthroughs, Inspections, and Technical Reviews*, Third Edition; Little, Brown & Co. Computer Systems Series, Boston, MA, 1982.

[Free83]
   Freeman, P., "Fundamentals of Design," in Freeman, P. and Wasserman, A. I., *Tutorial on Software Design Techniques*, Fourth Edition, IEEE Computer Society, Silver Springs, MD, 1983. p. 2-22.

[Frei72]
   Freiberger, W. (Ed.), *Statistical Computer Performance Evaluation*, Academic Press, New York, NY, 1972.

[Frie79]
   Fried, L., *Practical Data Processing Management*, Reston Publ., Reston, VA, 1979.

[Gane79]
   Gane, C. and Sarson, T., *Structured Systems Analysis: Tools and Techniques* , Prentice-Hall Englewood Cliffs, NJ, 1979.

[Garg87]
   Gargaro, A. and Pappas, T. L., "Reusability Issues and ADA," *IEEE Software*, July 1987, p. 43-51.

[Geha86]
   Gehani, N. and Gettrich, D. (Eds.), *Software Specification Techniques*, Addison-Wesley, Reading, MA, 1986.

[Gelp88]
   Gelperin, D. and Hetzel, B., "The Growth of Software Testing," *CACM*, **31**, 6(June 1988), p. 687-695.

[Gilb77]
   Gilb, T., *Software Metrics*, Winthrop, 1977.

[Gilb83]
   Gilbert, P., *Software Design and Development*, Science Research Associates, 1983.

[Gilb85]
   Gilb, T., "Evolutionary Delivery vs. the Waterfall Model," *ACM SIGSOFT Software Engineering Notes, 10*, 3(July 1985), p. 49-61.

[Gira73]
   Girard, E. and Rault, J.-C., "A Programming Technique for Software Reliability," *Procs. IEEE Symposium on Computer Software Reliability*, 1973, p. 44-50.

[Glad85]
   Gladden, G. R., "Letter on the Lifecycle," *ACM SIGSOFT Software Engineering Notes, 10*, 1(Jan. 1985), p. 14-15.

[Glas79]
   Glass, R. L., *Software Reliability Guidebook*, Prentice-Hall, Englewood Cliffs, NJ, 1979.

[Glas88]
   Glass, R., *Software Communication Skills*, Prentice-Hall, Englewood Cliffs, NJ, 1988.

[Gogu87]
Goguen, J. and Moriconi, M., "Formalization in Programming Environments," *Computer*, Nov. 1987, p. 55–64.

[Grad87]
Frady, R. B. and Caswell, D. L., "Software Metrics: Establishing a Company-wide Program," Prentice-Hall, Englewood Cliffs, NJ, 1987.

[Grif82]
Griffin, R. W., *Task Design—An Integrative Approach*, Scott Foresman, 1982.

[Gupt84]
Gupta, N. K. and Seviora, R. E., "An Expert System Approach to Real-Time System Debugging," *Proc. 1rst Conf. Artificial Intelligence Applications*, CS Press, Los Alamitos, CA, 1984, p. 336–343.

[Gyll77]
Gyllenhammar, P. G., *People at Work*, Addison-Wesley, Reading, MA, 1977.

[Habe75]
Haberman, A., *Path Expressions*, Technical Report, Carnegie-Mellon, Pittsburg, PA, 1975.

[Hack76]
Hackman, J. R. and Oldham, G. R, "Motivation through the Design of Work," *Organizational Behavior and Human Performance, 16*, 1976, p. 250–279.

[Hack80]
Hackman, J. R. and Oldham, G. R., *Work Redesign*, Addison-Wesley, Reading, MA, 1980.

[Hals77]
Halstead, M. H., *Elements of Software Science*, Elsevier, 1977.

[Hamn78]
Hamner, W. and Organ, D., *Organizational Behavior: An Applied Psychological Approach*, Business Publications, Inc., Dallas, TX, 1978.

[Harm88]
Harmon, P. and Maus, R., *Expert Systems—Tools and Applications*, Wiley and Sons, 1988.

[Harr82]
Harrison, W., Magel, K., Kluczny, R., and DeKock, A., "Applying Software Complexity Metrics to Program Maintenance," *IEEE Computer*, Sept. 1982.

[Harr87]
Harrison, W., "RPDE[3]: A Framework for Integrating Tool Fragments," *IEEE Software*, November 1987, p. 46–56.

[Haus84]
Hausen, H. L., (Ed.), *Software Validation: Inspection—Testing—Verification—Alternatives*, North Holland, New York, NY, 1984.

[Haye83]
Hayes-Roth, F., Waterman, D. A., and Lenat, D. B., "Building Expert Systems," Addison-Wesley, Reading, MA, 1983.

[Hays73]
Hays, W. L., *Statistics for the Social Sciences*, Holt, Rinehart & Winston, San Francisco, CA, 1973.

[Hein84]
Heintz, C., "Tax Planning vs. Tax Preparation Programs," *Interface Age*, Jan. 1984, p. 71, 76–80.

[Hell76]
Hellriegel, D. and Slocum, J. W., *Organizational Behavior: Contingency Views*, West Publishing, St. Paul, 1976.

[Hend84]
Henderson, P. (Ed.), "Proceedings of the ACM SIGSOFT/SIGPLAN Software Engineering Symposium on Practical Software Development Environments," *Software Engineering Notes*, **9**, 3(May 1984).

[Heni80]
Heninger, K. L., "Specifying Software Requirements fo Complex Systems: New Techniques and their Applications," *IEEE TSE*, *SE–6*, 1(Jan. 1980), p. 2-13.

[Herz59]
Herzberg, F., Mausner, B., and Snyderman, B., *The Motivation to Work*, John Wiley and Sons, New York, NY, 1959.

[Hetz84]
Hetzel, W., *The Complete Guide to Software Testing*, QED Information Systems, Inc., Wellesley, MA, 1984.

[Hoar69]
Hoare, C. A. R., "An Axiomatic Basis for Computer Programming," *CACM*, *12*, 10(Oct. 1969), p. 576-580.

[Hoar73]
Hoare, C. A. R., "An Axiomatic Definition of PASCAL," *Acta Informatica*, *2*, 3(1973), p. 335-355.

[Hoar74]
Hoare, C. A. R., "Monitors: An Operating System Structuring Concept," *CACM*, *17*, 10(October 1974), p. 549-557.

[Horn83]
Horn, R. and von Maryhauser, A., "A Primer on Software Quality Modeling," Project Report, Illinois Institute of Technology, May, 1983.

[Horo75]
Horowitz, E., *Practical Strategies for Developing Large Software Systems*, Addison Wesley, Reading, MA, 1975.

[Horo78]
Horowitz, E. and Sahni, S., *Fundamentals of Computer Algorithms*, Computer Science Press, Inc., Rockville, MD, 1978.

[Horo83]
Horowitz, E., *Fundamentals of Programming Languages*, Computer Science Press, Rockville, MD, 1983.

[Howa76]
Howard, J., "Proving Monitors," *CACM*, *19*, 5(May 1976), p. 273-279.

[Howd75]
Howden, W. E., "Methodology for the Generation of Program Test Data," *IEEE Transactions on Computers*, *C–24*, 5(May 1975), p. 554-559.

[Howd82]
Howden, W. E., "Contemporary Software Development Environments," *CACM*, *25*, 5(May 1982), p. 318-329.

[Howd85]
Howden, W. E., "The Theory and Practice of Functional Testing," *IEEE Software*, *2*, 9(Sept. 1985), p. 6-17.

[Howd87]
Howden, W. E., *Functional Program Testing and Analysis*, McGraw-Hill, New York, NY, 1987.

[Huan75]
Huang, J., "An Approach to Program Testing," *ACM Computing Surveys*, *7*, 3(Sept. 1975), p. 113-128.

[Hube74]
Huber, G. P., "Methods for Quantifying Subjective Probabilities and Multiattribute Utilities," *Decision Sciences*, *5*, 3(1974), p. 430-458.

[Huds84]

Hudson, D. H., "Comparing Commercial Tax Programs," *Interface Age*, Jan. 1984, p. 71–74.

[Ira83]

Information Research Associates, "Performance Analyst Workbench System (PAWS)," Austin, TX, 1983.

[Isod87]

Isoda, S., Shimomura, T., and Ono, Y., "VIPS—A Visual Debugger," *IEEE Software*, **4**, 3(May 1987), p. 8–19.

[Jack75]

Jackson, M. *Principles of Program Design*, Academic Press, New York, NY, 1975.

[Jack83]

Jackson, M. A., *System Development*, Prentice-Hall, Englewood Cliffs, NJ, 1983.

[Jani72]

Janis, I. L., *Victims of Groupthink*, Houghton Mifflin, Boston, MA, 1972.

[Jens75]

Jensen, K. and Wirth, N., *PASCAL User Manual and Report*, Springer Verlag, New York, NY, 1975.

[Jens79]

Jensen, R. W. and Tonies, C. C., *Software Engineering*, Prentice-Hall, Englewood Cliffs, NJ, 1979.

[Jens84]

Jensen, R. W., "A Comparison of the Jensen and COCOMO Schedule and Cost Estimation Models," *Procs. Intl. Society of Parametric Analysis*, 1986, p. 96–106.

[John77]

Johnson, E. M. and Huber, P. G., "The Technology of Utility Assessment," *IEEE Transactions on Systems, Man, and Cybernetics SMC*-7, 5(1977), p. 311–325.

[John85]

Johnson, W. L., "Proust: Knowledge-Based Program Understanding," *IEEE TSE*, March 1985, p. 267–275.

[Jone80]

Jones, C. B., *Software Development: A Rigorous Approach*, Prentice-Hall, Englewood Cliffs, NJ, 1980.

[Jone86]

Jones, C., *Programming Productivity*, McGraw-Hill, New York, NY, 1986.

[Kais84]

Kaiser, K. M., "DP Career Paths," *Datamation*, May 1984, p. 178–188.

[Kais87]

Kaiser, G. E. and Garlan, D., "Melding Software Systems from Reusable Building Blocks," *IEEE Software*, July 1987, p. 17–24.

[Karg80]

Karger, Murdick, *Management Engineering and Research* (3rd Ed.), Industrial Press Inc., New York, NY, 1980.

[Keen81]

Keen, P. G. W., "Information Systems and Organizational Change," *CACM*, **24**, 1(1981), p. 24–33.

[Kend61]

Kendall, M. G. and Stuart, A., *The Advanced Theory of Statistics, vol. 2, Inference and Relationship*, Hafner Publishing Co., New York, NY, 1961.

[Kern76]

Kernighan, B. W. and Plauger, P. J., *Software Tools*, Addison-Wesley, Reading, MA, 1976.

[Kern78]
Kernighan, B. W. and Plauger, P. J., *The Elements of Programming Style*, McGraw-Hill, New York, NY, 1978. (Second Edition)

[King75]
King, J., "A New Approach to Program Testing," *ACM Sigplan Notices*, *10*, (1975).

[King76]
King, J., "Symbolic Execution and Program Testing," *CACM*, *19*, 7(July 1976), p. 385–394.

[King84]
King, D., *Current Practices in Software Development*, Yourdon Press, New York, NY, 1984.

[Klei80]
Kleijnen, J. P. C., *Computers and Profits: Quantifying Financial Benefits of Information*, Addison-Wesley, Reading, MA, 1980.

[Knud79]
Knudson, H., Woodworth, R., and Bell, C., *Management—An Experiential Approach*, McGraw-Hill Series in Management, 1979.

[Knut68]
Knuth, D. E., *The Art of Computer Programming, Volume 1: Fundamental Algorithms*, Addison-Wesley, Reading, MA, 1968.

[Knut69]
Knuth, D. E., *The Art of Computer Programming, Volume 2: Seminumerical Algorithms*, Addison-Wesley, Reading, MA, 1969.

[Knut73]
Knuth, D. E., *The Art of Computer Programming: Volume 3: Sorting and Searching*, Addison-Wesley, Reading, MA, 1973.

[Koba78]
Kobayashi, H., *Modeling and Analysis: An Introduction to System Performance Evaluation Methodology*, Addison-Wesley, Reading, MA, 1978.

[Krau73]
Krause, K. W. and Smith, R. W., "Optimal Software Test Planning Through Automated Network Analysis," *Procs. IEEE Symposium on Computer Software Reliability*, 1973, p. 18–22.

[Krec62]
Krech, D., Crutchfield, R. S., and Ballachey, E. L., *Individual in Society*, McGraw-Hill, New York, NY, 1962.

[Labe80]
LaBelle, C. D., Shaw, K., and Helenack, L. J., "Solving the Turnover Problem," *Datamation*, April 1980, p. 144–152.

[Lamb73]
Lambert, W. W. and Lambert, W. E., *Social Psychology*, Prentice-Hall, Englewood Cliffs, NJ, 1973.

[Land81]
Landwehr, C. E., "Formal Models of Computer Security," *ACM Computing Surveys* **13**, 3(Sept. 1981), p. 247–278.

[Land83]
Landwehr, C. E., "The Best Available Technologies for Computer Security," *Computer* **16**, 7(July 1983), p. 86–100.

[Lapi76]
Lapin, L., *Quantitative Methods for Business Decisions*, Harcourt Brace Jovanovich Inc., New York, NY, 1976.

[Laue75]
Lauer, P. and Campbell, R., "Formal Semantics of a Class of High Level Primitives for Coordinating Concurrent Processes," *Acta Informatica*, Springer Verlag, **5**, 1975, p. 297–332.

[Laue78]
Lauer, H. C. and Needham, R. M., "On the Duality of Operating Systems," *Proc. 2nd Intl. Symposium on Operating Systems*, IRIA, Oct. 1978, reprinted in *Operating Systems Review 13*, 2(April 1979), p. 3–19.

[Leat83]
Leathrum, J. F., *Foundations of Software Design*, Reston Publ., Reston, VA, 1983.

[Lenz87]
Lenz, M., Schmid, H. A., and Wolf, P. E., "Software Reuse through Building Blocks," *IEEE Software*, July 1987, p. 34–42.

[Leve77]
Leverett, B., "Performance Evaluation of High-Level Language Systems," Technical Report, Carnegie-Mellon, 1977.

[Lewi82]
Lewis, T. G., *Software Engineering: Analysis and Verification*, Reston Publ., Reston, VA, 1982.

[Lien78]
Lientz, B. P., Swanson, E. B., and Tompkins, G. E., "Characteristics of Applications Software Maintenance," *CACM 21*, 6(June 1978).

[Lien80]
Lientz, B. P. and Swanson, E. B., *Software Maintenance Management*, Addison-Wesley, Reading, MA, 1980.

[Lien81]
Lientz, B. P. and Swanson, E. B., "Problems in Applications Software Maintenance," *CACM 24*, 11(Nov. 1981).

[Lipt75]
Lipton, R. J., "Reduction: A Method of Proving Properties of Parallel Programs," *CACM 18*, 12(Dec. 1975). p. 717–721.

[Lisk73]
Liskov, B. H., "The Design of the VENUS Operating System," *CACM 15*, 3(March 1973), p. 144–149.

[Lond87]
Londeix, B., *Cost Estimation for Software Development*, International Computer Series, Addison-Wesley, Reading, MA, 1987.

[Lord68]
Lord, F. M. and Novick, M. R., *Statistical Theories of Mental Test Scores*, Addison-Wesley, Reading, MA 1968.

[Luce57]
Luce, R. D., "Games and Decisions," Wiley, New York, NY, 1957.

[Luke80]
Lukey, F. J., "Understanding and Debugging Programs," *International Journal Man-Machine Studies*, February 1980, p. 189–202.

[Mart85]
Martin, J. and McClure, C., *Diagramming Techniques for Analysts and Programmers*, Prentice-Hall, Englewood Cliffs, NJ, 1985.

[Masl43]
Maslow, A. H., "A Theory of Human Motivation," *Psychological Review*, July 1943, p. 370–396.

[Mcca76]
McCabe, T. J., "A Complexity Measure," *IEEE TSE SE–8*, 4(Dec. 1976), p. 308–320.

[Mcca77]
    McCall, J. A., Richards, P., and Walters, G., *Factors in Software Quality*, 3 volumes, RADC-TR-77-369, Rome Air Development Center, Griffis Air Force Base, Rome, NY, Nov. 1977.

[Mcca79]
    McCall, J. A., "An Introduction to Software Quality Metrics," in *Software Quality Management*, Cooper, J. D. and Fisher, M. J. (Eds.), Petrocelli Books, Inc., 1979, p. 127–142.

[Mcca80]
    McCall, J. A. and Matsumoto, M. T., *Software Quality Metric Enhancements*, 2 volumes, RADC-TR-80-109, Rome Air Development Center, Griffis Air Force Base, Rome, NY, April 1980.

[Mccl61]
    McClelland, D. C., *The Achieving Society*, Van Nostrand Reinhold, Princeton, NJ, 1961.

[Mccl81]
    McClure, C., *Management of Software Development and Maintenance*, Van Nostrand Reinhold, New York, NY, 1981.

[Mcfa81]
    McFarlan, F. W., "Portfolio Approach to Information Systems," *Harvard Business Review* **59**, 5(1981), p. 142–150.

[Melt75]
    Melton, R. A., "Automatically Translating FORTRAN to IFTRAN," Procs. of Computer Science and Statistics: 8th Annual Symposium on the Interface, UCLA, 1975, p. 291–296.

[Metz81]
    Metzger, P. W., *Managing a Programming Project*, Prentice-Hall, Englewood Cliffs, 1981.

[Meye85]
    Meyer, B., "On Formalism in Specifications," *IEEE Software* **2** *(1)*, Jan. 1985, p. 6–26.

[Meye87]
    Meyer, B., "Reusability: The Case for Object-Oriented Design," *IEEE Software* **4**, 2(March 1987), p. 50–64.

[Mill72]
    Mills, H. and Baker, F., "Chief Programmer Teams," *IBM Systems Journal* **11**, 1(1972), 1(1972), p. 56–73.

[Mill74]
    Miller, Jr., E. F., Paige, M. R., Benson, J. P., and Wisehart, W. R., "Structural Techniques for Program Validation," *COMPCON* **74**, p. 161–164.

[Mill75]
    Miller, Jr., E. F., "RXVP: An Automated Verification System for FORTRAN," *Procs. of Computer Science and Statistics: 8th Annual Symposium on the Interface*, UCLA, 1975.

[Mill81]
    Miller, E. and Howden, W. E. (Eds.), *Tutorial: Software Testing and Validation Techniques*, Computer Society Press, New York, NY, 1981.

[Mill83]
    Mills, H., *Software Productivity*, Little, Brown & Co., 1983.

[Mill85]
    Mills, H. Private communication, 1985.

[Mime75]
    Miller, E. and Melton, R., "Automated Generation of Testcase Datasets," *ACM Sigplan Notices* **10**, 6(1975), p. 51–58.

[Moha79]
    Mohanty, S. N., "Models and Measurements for Quality Assessment of Software," *ACM Computing Surveys* **2**, 3(Sept. 79).

[Morr77]
Morris, P. A., "Combining Expert Judgements: a Bayesian Approach," *Management Science 23*, 7(1977), p. 679-693.

[Morr85]
Morris, J., "Software Engineering and AI," *ACM SIGART Newsletter 92*, p. 2.

[Motl77]
Motley, R. W. and Brooks, W. D., "Statistical Prediction of Programming Errors," RADC-TR-77-175, Rome Air Development Center, Griffis Air Force Base, NY, May 1977.

[Moze82]
Mozeico, H., "A Human/Computer Interface to Accomodate Learning Stages," *CACM 25*, 2(Feb. 1982), p. 100-104.

[Murr85]
Murray, W. R., "Heuristic and Formal Methods in Automatic Program Debugging," *Proc. 9th Intl. Joint Conference Artificial Intelligence*, Morgan Kaufman Publishers, Palo Alto, CA, 1985, p. 15-19.

[Musa87]
Musa, J. D., Iannino, A., and Okumoto, K., *Software Reliability: Measurement, Prediction, Application*, McGraw-Hill, 1987.

[Myer75]
Myers, G. J., *Reliable Software Through Composite Design*, Petrocelli, New York, NY, 1975.

[Myer76]
Myers, G. J., *Software Reliability: Principles and Practices*, Wiley Interscience, New York, NY, 1976.

[Myer79]
Myers, G. J., *The Art of Software Testing*, Wiley and Sons, 1979.

[Myer83]
Myers, B. A., "Incense: A System for Displaying Data Structures," *Computer Graphics*, July, 1983, p. 115-125.

[Nass73]
Nassi, I. and Shneiderman, B., "Flowchart Techniques for Structured Programming," *SIGPLAN Notices ACM 8*, 8(August 1973), p. 12-26.

[Naur63]
Naur, P. (Ed.), "Revised Report on the Algorithmic Language ALGOL 60," *CACM 6*, 1(1963), p. 1-17.

[Orr77]
Orr, K., *Structured Systems Development*, Yourdon Press, New York, NY, 1977.

[Ostr88]
Ostrand, T. J. and Balcer, M. J., "The Category-Partition Method for Specifying and Generating Functional Tests," *CACM 31*, 6(June 1988), p. 676-686.

[Otte76]
Ottenstein, K. J., "An Algorithmic Approach to the Detection and Prevention of Plagiarism," *Technical Report, Purdue University*, IN, 1976.

[Ovie80]
Oviedo, E. I., "Control Flow, Data Flow, and Program Complexity," *Procs. IEEE COMPSAC*, Nov. 1980, p. 146-152.

[Owic75]
Owicki, S., *Axiomatic Proof Techniques for Parallel Programs*, Ph.D. Thesis TR75-251, Dept. of Comp. Science, Cornell University, Ithaca, NY, 1975.

[Owic76A]
Owicki, S. and Gries, D., "Verifying Properties of Parallel Programs: An Axiomatic Approach," *CACM 19*, 5(May 1976), p. 279-385.

[Owic76B]
Owicki, S. and Gries, D., "An Axiomatic Proof Technique for Parallel Programs I," *Acta Information 6*, Springer Verlag, 1976, p. 319–340.

[Owic76C]
Owicki, S., "A Consistent and Complete Deductive System for the Verification of Parallel Programs," TR76-278, Dept. of Comp. Science, Cornell University, Ithaca, NY, May 1976.

[Owic77]
Owicki, S., "Specifications and Proofs for Abstract Data Types in Concurrent Programs," TR133, Digital Systems Lab., Stanford Electronics Labs., Stanford University, April 1977.

[Pari82]
Parikh, G., *How to Measure Programmer Productivity*, published by G. Parikh, Chicago, IL, 1982.

[Pari83]
Parikh, G. and Zvegintzov, N., *Tutorial on Software Maintenance*, IEEE Computer Society Press, Silver Spring, MD, 1983.

[Pari84]
Parikh, G., "Contributions on Software Maintenance," *ACM SIGSOFT Software Engineering Notes 9*, 2(April 84), p. 114–115.

[Pari84B]
Parikh, G., *Programmer Productivity*, Reston, Publishing Co., Reston, VA, 1984.

[Park80]
Parkin, A., *Data Processing Management*, Winthrop, Cambridge, MA, 1980.

[Parn72]
Parnas, D., "On the Criteria to Be Used in Decomposing a System into Modules," *CACM 15*, 12(Dec. 1972), p. 1053–1058.

[Parn79]
Parnas, D., "Designing Software for Ease of Extension and Contraction," *IEEE Transactions on Software Engineering 5*, 2(March 1979), p. 128–138.

[Perl81]
Perlis, A., Sayward, F., and Shaw, M., *Software Metrics: An Analysis and Evaluation*, MIT Press, Cambridge, MA, 1981.

[Perr83]
Perry, W. E., *A Structural Approach to Systems Testing*, QED Information Sciences, Wellesley, MA, 1983.

[Pfle87]
Pfleeger, S. L., *Software Engineering—the Production of Quality Software*, MacMillan, New York, NY, 1987.

[Prat83]
Pratt, T., *Programming Languages: Design and Implementation*, Prentice-Hall, Englewood Cliffs, NJ, 1983.

[Pres87]
Pressman, R. S., *Software Engineering—A Practitioner's Approach*, second edition, McGraw-Hill, New York, NY, 1987.

[Prie87]
Prieto-Diaz, R. and Greeman, P., "Classifying Software for Reusability," *IEEE Software 4*, 1(January 1987), p. 6–16.

[Putn78]
Putnam, L. H., "A General Empirical Solution to the Macro Software Sizing and Estimating Problem," *IEEE Transactions on Software Engineering 4*, July 1978, p. 345–361.

[Putn84]
Putnam, L. H., Putnam, D. T., and Thayer, L. P., "A Tool for Planning Software Projects," *Journal of Systems and Software*, **5**(Jan. 1984), p. 147–154.

[Quir85]
Quirk, W. J. (Ed), *Verification and Validation of Real-Time Software*, Springer Verlag, Berlin, 1985.

[Rapp85]
Rapps, S. and Weyuker, E., "Selecting Software Test Data Using Dataflow Information," *IEEE TSE* **11**, 4(April 1985), p. 367–375.

[Reis84]
Reiss, S. P., "Pecan: A Program Development System that Supports Multiple Views," *Proc. 7th ICSE*, IEEE Computer Society, Los Alamos, CA, 1984, p. 324–333.

[Reis87]
Reiss, S. P., "Working in the Garden Environment for Conceptual Programming," *IEEE Software*, November 1987, p. 16–27.

[Reps87]
Reps, T. and Teitelbaum, T. "Language Processing in Program Editors," *Computer*, Nov. 1987, p. 29–40.

[Reyn81]
Reynolds, J. C., *The Craft of Programming*, Prentice-Hall, Englewood Cliffs, 1981.

[Rock82]
Rockart, J. F., "The Changing Role of the Information Systems Executive: A Critical Success Factors Perspective," *Journal of Capacity Management* **1**, 2(1982), p. 110–124.

[Ross77]
Ross, D. T. and Schoman, K. E., "Structured Analysis and Requirements Definition," *IEEE Transactions on Software Engineering* **3**, 1(Jan. 1977), p. 6–15.

[Royc70]
Royce, W. W., "Managing the Development of Large Software Systems: Concepts and Techniques," *Proc. WESCON*, (Aug. 1970).

[Sche83]
Scheel, R. R., "A Security Kernel for a Multiprocessor Microcomputer," *Computer* **16**, 7(July 1983), p. 47–54.

[Sedl83]
Sedlmeyer, R., and Thompson, W., "Knowledge Based Fault Localization in Debugging," *Proc. ACM SIGSOFT/SIGPLAN Software Engineering Symp. on High Level Debugging*, (March 1983), p. 25–30.

[Sevi87]
Seviora, R. E., "Knowledge-Based Program Debugging Systems," *IEEE Software* **4**, 3(May 1987), p. 20–32.

[Shaw71]
Shaw, M. E., "Group Dynamics," McGraw Hill, New York, NY, 1971.

[Shaw79]
Shaw, M., "A Formal System for Specifying and Verifying Program Performance," Technical Report, Carnegie-Mellon, 1979.

[Shet84]
Sheth, D., *Software Projects, Personnel and Teams—A Managerial View*, MS Thesis, Illinois Institute of Technology, Chicago, IL, Dec. 1984.

[Shne77]
Shneiderman, B., Mayer, R., McKay, D., and Heller, P., "Experimental Investigations of the Utility of Detailed Flowcharts in Programming," *CACM* **20**, 6(June 1977), p. 373–381.

[Shne80]
Shneiderman, B., *Software Psychology—Human Factors in Computer and Information Systems*, Winthrop Publishers, Cambridge, MA, 1980.

[Shne82A]
Shneiderman, B., Keynote Address, ICCM 1982, New Orleans, LA, April 1982.

[Shne82B]
Shneiderman, B., "Designing Computer System Messages," *CACM 25*, 9(Sept. 1982), p. 610–611.

[Shne87]
Shneiderman, B., *Designing the User Interface*, Addison-Wesley, Reading, MA, 1987.

[Shul79]
Shulman, S., *A Survey of Software Tools for Software Development*, MS Thesis, Illinois Institute of Technology, Chicago, IL, 1979.

[Sinc84]
Sincovec, R., and Wiener, R., *Software Engineering with Modula-2 and ADA*, Wiley, New York, NY, 1984.

[Sloa72]
Sloane, N. J. A., "On Finding the Paths through a Network," *Bell System Technical Journal*, 1972, p. 371–390.

[Smit76]
Smith, A., *An Inquiry Into the Nature and Causes of the Wealth of Nations*, Modern Library, New York, NY, 1936 (originally published in 1776).

[Smit81]
Smith, C. U., "Software Performance Engineering," *Proc. Computer Measurement Group Conference XII*, Dec. 1981, p. 5-14.

[Somm82]
Sommerville, I., *Software Engineering*, Addison-Wesley, Reading, MA, 1982.

[Spie76]
Spier, M. J., "Software Malpractice—A Distasteful Experience," *Software—Practice and Experience*, 6 (1976), p. 293–299.

[Spir77]
Spirn, J. R., *Program Behavior: Models and Measurement*, Elsevier, New York, NY, 1977.

[Stan80]
Standish, T. A., *Data Structure Techniques*, Addison-Wesley, Reading, MA, 1980.

[Stan82]
Stankovic, J. A., "Software Communication Mechanisms: Procedure Calls Versus Messages," *Computer*, April 1982, p. 19-25.

[Stev77]
Stevens, H. P. and Krochmal, J. J., "Engineering Motivators and Demotivators," *IEEE 1977 National Aerospace and Electronic Conference*, p. 162–168.

[Stor79]
Storm, I., "An Index of Complexity for Structured Programs," *Procs. IEEE/NY Polytechnic Institute Workshop on Quantative Software Models*, Oct. 79, p. 130–133.

[Stra80]
Strauss, M. J., *Computer Capacity—A Production Control Approach*, Van Nostrand Reinhold, New York, NY, 1972.

[Stuc73]
Stucki, L. G., "Automated Generation of Self-Metric Software," *Procs. IEEE Sysposium on Computer Software Reliability*, 1973, p. 90.

[Swed72]
  Sweda, R. A., *Information Processing Management*, Van Nostrand Reinhold, New York, NY, 1972.
[Taus77]
  Tausworthe, R., *Standardized Development of Computer Software, Part 1: Methods*, Prentice-Hall, 1977.
[Taus79]
  Tausworthe, R., *Standardized Development of Computer Software, Part 2: Standards*, Prentice-Hall, 1979.
[Tayl11]
  Taylor, F. W., *The Principles of Scientific Management*, Harper and Row, 1911.
[Teic72]
  Teichroew, D., "A Survey of Languages for Stating Requirements for Computer Based Information Systems," *Procs. 1972 FJCC*, AFIPS Press, 1972, p. 1203-1224.
[Teic77]
  Teichroew, D., and Hershey, E. A., "PSL/PSA: A Computer Aided Technique for Structured Documentation and Analysis of Information Processing Systems," *IEEE Transactions on Software Engineering 3*, 1 (Jan. 1977), p. 41-48.
[Thay82]
  Thayer, R. H., Pyster, A., and Wood, R. C., "Validating Solutions to Major Problems in Software Engineering Project Management," *Computer*, August 1982, p. 65-77.
[Tich82]
  Tichy, W. F., "Design, Implementation, and Evaluation of a Revision Control System," *Procs. 6th Intl. Conf. Software Engineering*, IEEE, Tokyo, Sept. 1982, p. 58-67.
[Tich87]
  Tichy, W. R. "What Can Software Engineers Learn from Artificial Intelligence?," *Computer*, Nov. 1987, p. 43-54.
[Trac87]
  Tracz, W., "Reusability Comes of Age," *IEEE Software*, July 1987, p. 6-8.
[Tria65]
  Trianotsis, H. C., Hall, E. R., and Ewen, R. B., "Member Heterogeneity and Dyadic Creativity," *Human Relations 18*, 1965, p. 33-55.
[Triv82]
  Trivedi, K. S., *Probability and Statistics with Reliability, Queueing and Computer Science Applications*, Prentice-Hall, Englewood Cliffs, NJ, 1982.
[Troy81]
  Troy, D. A. and Zweben, S. H., "Measuring the Quality of Structured Designs," *Journal of Systems and Software*, 2 (June 1981), p. 113-120.
[Tver74]
  Tversky, A. and Kahnemen, D., "Judgement under Uncertainty: Heuristics and Biases," *Science 165*, Sept. 27, 1974, p. 1124-1131.
[Vand80]
  Vandendorpe, J., *A Crash Tolerant B-tree Data Structure for a Database Retrieval System*, Ph.D. Dissertation, Illinois Institute of Technology, Chicago, IL, August 1980.
[Vant78]
  Van Tassel, D., *Programming Style, Design, Efficiency, Debugging, and Testing*, Second Edition, Prentice-Hall, Englewood Cliffs, NJ, 1982.
[Voge80]
  Voges, U., Gmeiner, L., and von Mayrhauser, A., "SADAT—An Automated Testing Tool," *IEEE Transactions on Software Engineering 6*, 3 (May 1980), p. 286-290.

[Vonm81]
von Mayrhauser, A. K., "Cost/Performance Comparisons for Structural Analysis Software on Mini- and Mainframe Computers," *Proc. CPEUG 81*, Nov. 17-19, 1981, San Antonio, TX.

[Vonm82]
von Mayrhauser, A. K. and Witte, D. E., "Evaluation and Decision-Making Procedures in Computer Service Selection," *Journal of Capacity Management 1*, 2 (1982), p. 145-159.

[Vonm83]
von Mayrhauser, A. K. and Witte, D. E., "Formal Approaches to Computer Service Selection," *Procs. ECOMA 11*, Oct. 1983, Copenhagen, p. 50-56.

[Vonm83B]
von Mayrhauser, A. K., "Characteristics of Software Development Team Structures and Their Impact on Software Development," *Procs. CPEUG*, Oct. 1983, San Francisco, CA, p. 150-160.

[Vonm84]
von Mayrhauser, A. K., "Software Development Guidelines: A Measurement Approach," Procs. CMG XV, San Francisco, CA, Dec. 1984, p. 15-19.

[Walk87]
Walker, J. H., Moon, D. A., Weinreb, D. L., and McMahon, M., "The Symbolics Genera Programming Environment," *IEEE Software*, November 1987, p. 36-45.

[Wals77]
Walston, C. E. and Felix, C. P., "A Method of Programming Measurement and Estimation," *IBM Systems Journal 16*, 1(1977), p. 54-73.

[Wegn84]
Wegner, P., "Capital Intensive Software Technology," *IEEE Software 1*, 3 (July 1984), p. 7-45.

[Wein71]
Weinberg, G. M., *The Psychology of Computer Programming*, Van Nostrand Reinhold, 1971.

[Wein82]
Weinberg, G. M., *Understanding the Professional Programmer*, Little Brown Publishers, Boston, MA, 1982.

[Wels79]
Welsh, J. and McKeag, M., *Structured System Programming*, Prentice-Hall, Englewood Cliffs, NJ, 1979.

[Weyu88]
Weyuker, E. J., "The Evaluation of Program-Based Software Test Adequacy Criteria," *CACM 31*, 6 (June 1988), p. 668-675.

[Wirt71]
Wirth, N., "Program Development by Stepwise Refinement," *CACM 14*, 4 (April 1971), p. 221-227.

[Wirt83]
Wirth, N., *"Programming in MODULA-2*, Second Corrected Edition, Springer-Verlag, 1983.

[Witt83]
Witte, D. E., *A Methodology for Computer Service Selection*, PhD Thesis, Illinois Institute of technology, Chicago, IL, May 1983.

[Wood79]
Woodward, M. R., Hennell, M. A., and Hedley, D., "A Measure of Control Flow Complexity in Program Test," *IEEE TSE SE-5*, 1 (Jan. 1979), p. 45-50.

[Wood80]
Woodward, M. R., "Experience with Path Analysis and Testing of Programs," *IEEE TSE SE-6*, 3 (May 1980).

[Wood81]
Woodfield, S. N., Dunsmore, H. E., and Shen, V. Y., "The Effect of Modularization and Comments on Program Comprehension," *Procs. 5th Intl. Conf. on Software Engineering*, March 1981, p. 215-223.

[Wood87]
Woodfield, S. N., Embley, D. W., and Scott, D. T., "Can Programmers Reuse Software?" *IEEE Software*, July 1987, p. 52-59.

[Wulf74]
Wulf, W. A., Levin, R. and Harbison, S., "HYDRA: The Kernel of a Multiprocessor Operating System," *CACM 17*, 6 (June 1974), p. 337-345.

[Wulf81]
Wulf, W. A., Levin, R. and Harbison, S., *HYDRA/C.mmp: An Experimental Computer System*, McGraw-Hill, 1981.

[Your79]
Yourdon, E., *Structured Walkthroughs*, Prentice-Hall, Englewood Cliffs, NJ, 1979.

[Your79B]
Yourdon, E. and Constantine, L. L., *Structured Design*, Prentice-Hall, Englewood Cliffs, NJ, 1979.

[Zelk78]
Zelkowitz, M. V., "Perspectives on Software Engineering," *ACM Computing Surveys 10*, 2 (1978), p. 197-216.

[Zelk79]
Zelkowitz, M. V., Shaw, A. C., and Gannon, J. D., *Principles of Software Engineering and Design*, Prentice-Hall, Englewood Cliffs, NJ, 1979.

[Zieg83]
Ziegler, C. A., *Programming System Methodologies*, Prentice-Hall, Englewood Cliffs, NJ, 1983.

[Zoln82]
Zolnowski, J. C. and Ting, P. D., "An Insider's Survey on Software Development," *6th Intl. Conf. Software Engineering*, Tokyo, Japan, Sept. 14-16, 1982.

Author Index

Subject Index

KLOC, 581, 696, 703, 711–712, 726
Knot count, 584
Knowledge engineering, 696
KRA, 554

Language lawyer, 767, 769
Layer, 256, 258–259, 268, 295
Layout, 193
Leader, 748, 773
    behavior, 781, 783
Leadership, 733, 748, 816
    areas, 780
    factors, 733
    functions, 733, 781
    strategies, 780–784
    structural, 751
    style, 734–736, 744, 756–757, 759, 781–783
Lease, 98
Least squares, 575
Legislature, 230
Level
    of abstraction, 210
    of measurement, 559–562, 571
    see also Layer
Lexicographic ordering, 609–610
Lifecycle
    embedded phased, 20–21
    eternal development, 17–18
    evolutionary, 16–17, 98, 123, 504
    expert system, 18–20
    metrics, 562–566
    non-sequential, 3, 16–22
    sequential, 3, 12–15
    waterfall, 3, 12, 15, 504
Lifetime expectations, 84, 96–97, 121
Load
    balancing, 230
    test, 190
LOC, 581, 696, 703, 706, 726–727
Loops, 404–405, 416–417, 426–427

Macro, 146
Mailbox, 260
Mailing system, 264
Maintainability, 83–84, 96–97, 119, 204, 249,
        254–258, 295, 341, 380, 482, 505, 546–547
    measurement, 556
Maintenance, 101, 144, 340, 501–549
    activities, 503, 507, 540
    adaptive, 11, 97, 503
    corrective, 11, 84, 97, 503
    organization, 97, 522

perfective, 11, 84, 503
personnel, 502
plan, 671–672, 813
procedures, 671, 675
Man
    hours, 696, 700–701, 713, 728
    months, 696–697, 700, 713, 724
    power distribution, 700
    power utilization rate, 700
    years, 696
Manageability, 629–630, 679, 739
Management, 553–824
    by metrics, 553–621, 823
    by objective, 554, 623
    scientific, 733
Manager, 741–744, 754
Managerial grid, 781–782
Manual, 9, 13, 344, 814
    drift, 535, 543–545
    installation, 520
    reference, 514–517
    simulation, 196
    system, 520
    training, 97, 512–514
    user, 9, 97, 151, 153, 170, 189, 814
Market
    analysis, 104
    window, 82, 724
    position, 624, 631, 633–634
Maslow's need theory, 735–737
Master/slave, 263
Maximax rule, 659, 680
Maximin rule, 658–659
MBM, 553–621, 823
MBO, 554, 623
Measure
    of effectiveness, 554
    of structural quality, 325–329
    unit of, 281
Measurement, 553–556, 559–562, 570, 587,
        600–601
    a posteriori, 556
    characteristics, 561–562
    cost and effort, 714–716
    level of, 559–562, 571
Mentor, 764
Menu-driven, 144, 146–148
Menus, 146–147, 178–182
Message
    error, 94, 142, 189
    interprocess, 260–265
    terminal, 142